Third Edition

A GUIDE TO
Health
Insurance
Billing

MARIE A. MOISIO, MA, RHIA

Consultant

MARQUETTE, MICHIGAN

DELMAR
CENGAGE Learning™

Australia • Brazil • Japan • Korea • Mexico • Singapore • Spain • United Kingdom • United States

A Guide to Health Insurance Billing, Third Edition
Marie A. Moisio

Vice President, Career and Professional Editorial: Dave Garza

Director of Learning Solutions: Matthew Kane

Senior Acquisitions Editor: Rhonda Dearborn

Managing Editor: Marah Bellegarde

Product Manager: Jadin Babin-Kavanaugh

Editorial Assistant: Lauren Whalen

Vice President, Career and Professional Marketing: Jennifer Baker

Marketing Director: Wendy Mapstone

Senior Marketing Manager: Nancy Bradshaw

Marketing Coordinator: Erica Ropitzky

Production Director: Carolyn Miller

Production Manager: Andrew Crouth

Senior Content Project Manager: Kenneth McGrath

Senior Art Director: Jack Pendleton

Technology Product Manager: Mary Colleen Liburdi

Technology Project Manager: Brian Davis

For product information and technology assistance, contact us at
Cengage Learning Customer & Sales Support, 1-800-354-9706

For permission to use material from this text or product, submit all requests online at **www.cengage.com/permissions.** Further permissions questions can be e-mailed to **permissionrequest@cengage.com**

Current Procedural Terminology (CPT) © 2009 American Medical Association. All Rights Reserved.

Library of Congress Control Number: 2010929462

ISBN-13: 978-1-4354-9298-1

ISBN-10: 1-4354-9298-6

Delmar
5 Maxwell Drive
Clifton Park, NY 12065-2919
USA

Cengage Learning is a leading provider of customized learning solutions with office locations around the globe, including Singapore, the United Kingdom, Australia, Mexico, Brazil, and Japan. Locate your local office at: **international.cengage.com/region**

Cengage Learning products are represented in Canada by Nelson Education, Ltd.

To learn more about Delmar, visit **www.cengage.com/delmar**

Purchase any of our products at your local college store or at our preferred online store **www.cengagebrain.com**

Notice to the Reader

Publisher does not warrant or guarantee any of the products described herein or perform any independent analysis in connection with any of the product information contained herein. Publisher does not assume, and expressly disclaims, any obligation to obtain and include information other than that provided to it by the manufacturer. The reader is expressly warned to consider and adopt all safety precautions that might be indicated by the activities described herein and to avoid all potential hazards. By following the instructions contained herein, the reader willingly assumes all risks in connection with such instructions. The publisher makes no representations or warranties of any kind, including but not limited to, the warranties of fitness for particular purpose or merchantability, nor are any such representations implied with respect to the material set forth herein, and the publisher takes no responsibility with respect to such material. The publisher shall not be liable for any special, consequential, or exemplary damages resulting, in whole or part, from the readers' use of, or reliance upon, this material.

Printed in the United States of America
1 2 3 4 5 6 7 12 11 10

Table of Contents

CHAPTER 4: **International Classification of Diseases, Ninth Revision, Clinical Modification (ICD-9-CM)** 83

Preface

INTRODUCTION

Insurance billing is an excellent career choice in the health care industry. Employment opportunities are available in physicians' offices, rural hospitals, regional medical centers, ambulatory surgery centers, specialty clinics, and other health-related agencies. *A Guide to Health Insurance Billing* covers introductory information, examples, and application exercises that develop a foundation for becoming an insurance billing specialist.

OBJECTIVES

The primary objective of *A Guide to Health Insurance Billing* is to expose students to health insurance billing topics. The text is intended to provide students with opportunities to become familiar with health insurance terminology; understand the legal implications of insurance billing; develop a basic understanding of medical coding systems; and accurately complete health insurance claims.

FEATURES OF THE TEXT

The features and benefits of this text are designed to encourage student success. They are as follows:

- Learning objectives and key terms, abbreviations, and phrases help identify essential information in each chapter.
- Diagnosis and procedure coding exercises include several degrees of difficulty—from simple to complex.
- Reinforcement exercises allow students to check their progress throughout each chapter.
- Practical examples provide clarification of health insurance terms, procedures, and regulations associated with health insurance billing.
- Separate chapters cover details on Electronic Data Interchange (EDI) and insurance payers.
- Separate chapters cover coding concepts, with Coding Challenge exercises that include Procedure Reports, and a chapter on ICD-10-CM.
- End-of-chapter reviews and challenge exercises include objective and subjective measures of student comprehension.
- The Superiorland Clinic Practice Manual (Appendix A) is an extensive application exercise that features 20 case studies that provide practice completing CMS-1500 claims, encounter forms, coding from office notes, and UB-04 claim forms.
- Internet links in each chapter provide resources for locating the most current information about key topics.

NEW TO THE THIRD EDITION

- Fully updated to the most current guidelines, billing forms, and code sets
- Features a new and improved SimClaim student practice software paired with 20 case studies in Appendix A
- 59-day trial of EncoderPro.com Expert

SUPPLEMENTS

The following supplements accompany the text:

Instructor's Manual

The *Instructor's Manual* provides sample course syllabi, additional chapter quizzes and exams, complete answer keys for all exercises and activities, and blank forms that can be used to create additional billing exercises.

ISBN-10: 1-4354-9296-X   ISBN-13: 978-1-4354-9296-7

Instructor Resources

The Instructor Resources are available on CD-ROM and online. The Instructor Resources provide many aids to help the instructor plan and implement a course for health insurance specialists.

The Instructor Resources include the following:

- **Computerized Test Bank in ExamView** makes generating tests and quizzes a snap. With over 900 questions and different styles to choose from, you can create customized assessments for your students with the click of a button. Add your own unique questions and print rationales for easy class preparation.
- Customizable instructor support **slide presentations in PowerPoint** format focus on key points for each chapter.
- The *Instructor's Manual* contains various resources and answers for each textbook chapter.

ISBN-10: 1-4354-9295-1   ISBN-13: 978-1-4354-9295-0

Online Companion Site at CengageBrain

Additional textbook resources can be found online at www.cengagebrain.com.

Items listed as Instructor Resources are password-protected. For access to protected content, see the *Instructor's Manual*. To access the Student Companion site from CengageBrain, follow these instructions:

- Go to http://www.cengagebrain.com, type author, title or ISBN in the **Search** window.
- Locate the desired product and click on the title.
- When you arrive at the Product Page, click on the **Free Stuff** tab Use the **"Click Here"** link to be brought to the Companion site.
- Click on the Student Resources link in the left navigation pane to access the resources.

Student Resources

- Blank forms
- SimClaim claims completion software (available as both online and downloadable versions)
- Code updates as they become available

Instructor Resources

- All the Instructor Resources are provided including the *Instructor's Manual*, computerized test bank, and chapter presentations in PowerPoint.

About the Author

Marie A. Moisio, MA, RHIA

Marie Moisio has over 25 years of experience in health information management. She was an Associate Professor at Northern Michigan University (retired in 2003). Ms. Moisio has 15 years of teaching experience in medical billing, medical coding, and health information processing. Her resume shows that she was also the director of a health information department at a 400-bed regional medical center and a 450-bed regional psychiatric treatment facility. She was a consultant for several long-term care facilities and physician offices. Her knowledge and experience include health information management, compliance, coding practices, and auditing insurance claims and documentation. She has offered several workshops about the legal aspects of health information management and documentation. Ms. Moisio has written other books for Delmar, Cengage Learning, including *Medical Terminology for Insurance and Coding, Medical Terminology: A Student Centered Approach,* and *Understanding Laboratory and Diagnostic Tests.*

REVIEWERS AND CONTRIBUTORS

The publisher and the author would like to extend a special thank-you to the reviewers and contributors who gave recommendations and suggestions throughout the development of this textbook. Their experience and knowledge were valuable resources for the author.

Technical Reviewer and Contributor

Judith E. Fields, CCS, CCS-P, CPC, CPC-H
Southeast Kentucky Community & Technical College
Coding Program Instructor
Harlan, Kentucky

Reviewers

Laurie Dennis, CBCS
HIBC Instructor
Florida Career College
Clearwater, Florida

Rashmi Gaonkar, BS, MS
Senior Instructor
ASA Institute
Brooklyn, New York

Annette Jackson, MBA, CMRS
Subject Area Coordinator
Medical Administrative Assistant (Billing Emphasis) Program
Bryant & Stratton College
Eastlake, Ohio

Joshua Maywalt, MBA, NCICS, NCMOA
Office Administrator, Medical Billing and Coding Instructor
Central Florida Institute
Orlando, Florida

Lynne Padilla, CPC, CHI
Medical Curriculum Developer, Medical Editor
Allied Business Schools
Laguna Hills, CA

Barb Parent
Insurance Billing Specialist
Marquette Internal Medicine and Pediatric
Associates
Marquette, Michigan

Agnes Pucillo, LPN, RHCE, AHI, CMBCS
Medical Billing and Coding Instructor
Prism Career Institute
Cherry Hill, New Jersey

Tonia A. Seay-Josephina, CPAR, RMC,
RMM, CPC
Medical Billing and Coding Instructor
Advanced Career Training
Atlanta, Georgia

Sharon Skonieczki, BS MA, CMA (AAMA)
Academic Dean, Medical Program Director
Elmira Business Institute
Elmira and Vestal, New York

Ruth Thibault
Business Manager
Marquette County Medical Care Facility
Ishpeming, Michigan

Marta E. Urdaneta, PhD
Program Director, Health Science
Program Coordinator, Health Service
Administration
Keiser University
Ft. Lauderdale, Florida

Joshua J. VanDusen
Medical Assisting Instructor
Miller Motte Technical College
Chattanooga, Tennessee

Acknowledgments

Two very special individuals provided me with outstanding support throughout the revision process. Jadin Babin-Kavanaugh, Product Manager, was faultless in her guidance, advice, and moral support. Jadin is a first-class professional, and I sincerely hope that I will work with her again! Elmer Moisio, my husband of 38 years, willingly assumed many, many domestic responsibilities so that I had the time to work on this revision.

How to Use this Text

CHAPTER 4

International Classification of Diseases, Ninth Revision, Clinical Modification (ICD-9-CM)

LEARNING OBJECTIVES

Upon successfully completing this chapter, the reader should have the knowledge to:

1. Identify the four Cooperating Parties responsible for maintaining and updating ICD-9-CM.
2. Describe the value of the American Hospital Association (AHA) publication *Coding Clinic for ICD-9-CM.*
3. Follow the ICD-9-CM coding conventions for assigning diagnostic and procedure codes.
4. Explain the features of the three ICD-9-CM volumes.
5. Define all cross-reference and coding instruction terms.
6. List diagnostic and procedure coding steps in the order of performance.
7. Explain the difference between a primary diagnosis and a principal diagnosis.
8. Discuss the significance of a principal procedure.
9. Accurately code diagnoses and procedures presented in this chapter.

KEY TERMS

American Health Information Management Association (AHIMA)
American Hospital Association (AHA)
Carryover line
Category
Centers for Medicare and Medicaid Services (CMS)
Closed biopsy
Code first [the] underlying condition
Coding conventions
Concurrent condition
Congenital
Connecting words
Cooperating Parties
Current Procedural Terminology (CPT)
Due to
E codes
Encoders
Etiology
Exclusion note
Failed procedure
General note
Histological
Hypertension Table
Inclusion note
International Classification of Diseases, Ninth Revision, Clinical Modification (ICD-9-CM)
International Classification of Diseases, Tenth Revision (ICD-10)
Late effect
Main term
More specific subterms
National Center for Health Statistics (NCHS)
Nonessential modifier

83

Objectives and Key Terms

The Objectives lists the expected learning outcomes for the chapter. Review the objectives before and after studying the chapter. Key Terms give an overview of the new vocabulary in each chapter. Each term is highlighted in the chapter and defined on first usage. A complete definition of each term appears in the glossary at the back of the book.

Overview

Each chapter begins with an Overview that provides a brief synopsis of the topics covered in the chapter. The Objectives and Overview together provide a framework for studying the chapter content.

OVERVIEW

As mentioned in Chapter 1, the two main coding systems associated with health insurance claims processing are the *International Classification of Diseases, Ninth Revision, Clinical Modification* (ICD-9-CM) for medical diagnoses and procedures and *Current Procedural Terminology* (CPT) for physician and other provider services and procedures. This chapter covers ICD-9-CM, which remains in effect until the *International Classification of Diseases, Tenth Revision* (ICD-10) is adopted. Chapter 5 presents an introduction to ICD-10.

Accurate coding is crucial to reimbursement and the avoidance of fraud and abuse charges. Insurance billing specialists need at least a basic understanding of medical coding. The purpose of this chapter is to provide the student with a foundation for ICD-9-CM coding. Topics presented include the following:

- Unique characteristics of *Volumes 1, 2,* and *3*
- Coding conventions, such as special instructional notes and the meaning of punctuation marks
- Sections of each volume that apply to physician office coding
- Coding guidelines from Sections II and IV of the ICD-9-CM Official Guidelines for Coding and Reporting

To gain the most from this chapter, have ICD-9-CM *Volumes 1, 2,* and *3* readily available as references. Some exercises provide opportunities to practice using the code books. This chapter also includes several figures and tables adapted from the 2010 official version of ICD-9-CM. The figures and tables allow the student to complete some of the review exercises if the code books are not available.

EXAMPLE

Jenny, a 16-year-old high school sophomore, just received the results of her kidney scan. The physician tells Jenny that she has polycystic kidneys and explains that she was "born with" this condition. Even though Jenny is 16, the diagnosis of polycystic kidneys is coded as a congenital anomaly.

Chapter 15: Certain Conditions Originating in the Perinatal Period

Chapter 15 codes classify conditions specific to a newborn. The condition must be associated with the **perinatal period**, which begins before birth and lasts through the 28th day of life. Most perinatal conditions are resolved by time, treatment, or death. However, some conditions manifest themselves later in life.

EXAMPLE

Rachel is being treated for vaginal cancer. Rachel's health history reveals that her mother took the antinausea medication DES (diethylstilbestrol) during her pregnancy with Rachel. The physician explains to Rachel that her current condition could be a result of intrauterine exposure to DES.

In this case, the vaginal cancer is assigned the appropriate malignant neoplasm code. Intrauterine DES exposure is a significant factor in the development of vaginal cancer. Therefore, the code for vaginal cancer is selected, and the code for diethylstilbestrol (DES) from Chapter 15 is also assigned.

Examples

Examples appear throughout the text and serve to provide further explanation of key concepts.

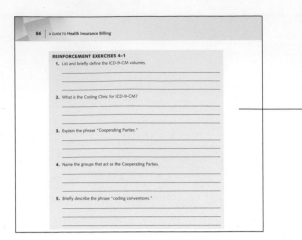

Reinforcement Exercises

Reinforcement Exercises appear throughout the chapters and allow for immediate practice with concepts.

Summary

The Summary at the end of each chapter recaps key concepts and can serve as a review aid when preparing for tests.

SUMMARY

This chapter provided an introduction to ICD-10-CM, the *International Classification of Diseases, Tenth Revision, Clinical Modification*, and ICD-10-PCS, the *International Classification of Diseases, Tenth Revision, Procedure Coding System*. These classification and coding systems are scheduled for implementation on October 1, 2013.

Both ICD-10-CM and ICD-10-PCS are substantially different from ICD-9-CM. The new coding systems are expanded for increased specificity, and codes consist of alphanumeric characters. Once implemented, ICD-10-CM will be used by all health care agencies for coding and reporting. ICD-10-PCS is intended to be used by hospitals and other inpatient health care agencies for coding and reporting procedures. Because of the specific nature of both systems, documentation in the patient's medical record will be subjected to an increasing level of scrutiny.

REVIEW

156 | A GUIDE TO Health Insurance Billing

REVIEW EXERCISES

Write a short answer for each statement.

1. A temporary or permanent medical problem or condition resulting from an illness or injury.

2. Residual condition that remains after the illness or injury has been resolved.

3. Used to calculate the extent of a burn injury.

4. Short name for ICD-9-CM Volume 1.

5. Short name for ICD-9-CM Volume 2.

6. Diseases, conditions, or injuries printed in bold and flush left in the *Alphabetic Index*.

7. Precedes subterms and is placed immediately after the main term.

8. Codes in the Neoplasm Table are arranged by

9. Direct the billing specialist or medical coder to look elsewhere.

10. Lists of conditions that are coded to the same ICD-9-CM code.

11. Lists of conditions not covered by a specific ICD-9-CM code.

12. Placing diagnostic codes in the correct order.

13. Supplementary classifications or codes that are frequently assigned in a clinic, office, and outpatient setting.

14. Directions and guidelines that assist in accurate code assignment.

CODING CHALLENGE

Read the following medical reports and write the diagnoses and procedures in the space provided. Assign the correct ICD-9-CM diagnosis and procedure codes. Sequence the codes according to principal diagnosis and principal procedure guidelines. These cases relate to inpatient episodes of care.

1. DISCHARGE SUMMARY

PATIENT: Walker, Lamar
ADMISSION DATE: November 16, 20xx
DISCHARGE DATE: November 18, 20xx
ADMITTING DIAGNOSES: 1. Urinary retention secondary to benign prostatic hypertrophy. 2. Chronic obstructive pulmonary disease.
DISCHARGE DIAGNOSES: 1. Benign prostatic hypertrophy, secondary urinary retention. 2. Chronic obstructive pulmonary disease.

continued on the next page

Review Exercises and Coding Challenges

At the end of each chapter, there are Review Exercises to test your understanding of content and critical thinking ability.

The coding chapters feature Coding Challenge exercises that provide practice coding from medical reports.

How to Use the SimClaim Student Practice Software

SimClaim is an educational tool designed to familiarize you with the basics of claim form completion. Because in the real world there are many rules that can vary by payer, facility, and state, every effort has been made to make SimClaim generically correct in order to provide you with the broadest understanding of claim form completion.

How to Access SimClaim

To access the SimClaim software program, refer to the information on the printed access card bound into this textbook. SimClaim for *A Guide to Health Insurance Billing,* Third Edition, is designed for use with the case studies found in Appendix A, the "Superiorland Practice Manual." The case studies and forms printed in Appendix A are also provided in the SimClaim software.

Main Menu

From the Main Menu, you can access the SimClaim program three different ways: Study Mode, Test Mode, and Blank Form Mode.

- Click on **Study Mode** if you want feedback as you fill out claim forms for the Appendix A case studies.
- Click on **Test Mode** to fill out claim forms for the Appendix A case studies if you are ready to test yourself. There is no feedback in this mode, and your completed claim form(s) is graded and can be printed and e-mailed to your instructor.
- Use **Blank Form Mode** if you wish to use the SimClaim program to fill out a blank CMS or UB-04 form with another case study provided by your instructor.

Please note that while a blank, editable, printable UB-04 form is provided in SimClaim, there is no grading provided for the UB-04. You will need to complete it, print it to PDF, and then submit it to your instructor for grading.

SimClaim Support

You may also access SimClaim support documentation from the Main Menu. Support includes Block Help videos, a glossary, and a list of common abbreviations. While using SimClaim in any mode, if you need help entering information in a particular block, simply click on Block Help for instructions.

General Instructions and Hints for Completing CMS-1500 Claim Forms in SimClaim

Please read through the following general guidelines before beginning work in the SimClaim program:

- **Turn on Caps Lock:** All data entered into SimClaim must be in ALL CAPS.
- **Do not abbreviate:** Spell out words like street, drive, avenue, signature on file, Blue Cross Blue Shield, etc. No abbreviations (other than state abbreviations) will be accepted by the program.
- **Do not use "Same As" or "None" in any block:** If patient information is the same as insured information, you must enter that information again on the claim.
- **There may be more than one Diagnosis Pointer in Block 24E:** For SimClaim case studies, there may be more than one diagnosis pointer required in Block 24E.
- **Amount Paid:** If there is no amount paid indicated on the case study, you must enter "0 00" in Block 29.
- Follow accepted form guidelines on punctuation use in the form. The NUCC CMS-1500 claim form instruction manual may be downloaded from www.nucc.org.
- For additional help, refer to the Block Help documentation within the SimClaim program.

How to Access the EncoderPro.Com— Expert 59-Day Trial

With the purchase of this textbook, you receive a free 59-day trial to EncoderPro.com Expert, the powerful online medical coding solution from Ingenix. With EncoderPro.com, you can simultaneously search across all three code sets.

How to Access the Free Trial

Information on how to access your 59-day trial of EncoderPro.com Expert is included on the printed tear-out card bound into this textbook. Your unique user access code is also printed on the card. Be sure to check with your instructor before beginning your free trial because it will expire 59 days after your initial login.

Features and Benefits of EncoderPro.com

EncoderPro.com is the essential code-lookup software for CPT, ICD-9-CM, and HCPCS code sets from Ingenix. It gives users fast searching capabilities across all code sets. EncoderPro.com can greatly reduce the time it takes to build or review a claim and helps improve overall coding accuracy.

During your free trial period of EncoderPro.com Expert, the following tools are available to you:

- **Powerful Ingenix CodeLogic search engine.** Search all three code sets simultaneously by using lay terms, acronyms, abbreviations, and even misspelled words.

- **Lay descriptions for thousands of CPT codes.** Enhance your understanding of procedures with easy-to-understand descriptions.
- **Color-coded edits.** Understand whether a code carries an age or sex edit, is covered by Medicare, or contains bundled procedures.
- **ICD-10 Mapping Tool.** Crosswalk from ICD-9-CM codes to the appropriate ICD-10 code quickly and easily.
- **Great value.** Get the content from over 20 code and reference books in one powerful solution.

For more on EncoderPro.com or to become a subscriber beyond the free trial, email us at **esales@ cengage.com**.

CHAPTER 1

The Insurance Billing Specialist

LEARNING OBJECTIVES

Upon successful completion of this chapter, the reader should have the knowledge to:

1. Describe at least 10 responsibilities of an insurance billing specialist.
2. Identify at least five personal qualifications and five technical qualifications associated with insurance billing specialist positions.
3. Provide three examples that illustrate the importance of medical terminology to insurance billing activities.
4. Describe five different job opportunities related to the insurance billing process.

KEY TERMS

American Academy of Professional Coders (AAPC)

American Health Information Management Association (AHIMA)

American Medical Billing Association (AMBA)

Certification

Certified coding assistant (CCA)

Certified coding specialist (CCS)

Certified coding specialist—physician-based (CCS-P)

Certified healthcare reimbursement specialist (CHRS)

Certified medical billing specialist (CMBS)

Certified medical billing specialist–hospital (CMBS-H)

Certified medical reimbursement specialist (CMRS)

Certified professional coder (CPC)

Certified professional coder–hospital (CPC-H)

Certified professional coder–payer (CPC-P)

Claims assistance professional (CAP)

Insurance billing specialist

Insurance collection specialist

Insurance counselor

Medical Association of Billers (MAB)

Medical coder

Medical coding

Medical terminology

National Electronic Billers Alliance (NEBA)

Patient account representative

Personal qualifications

Technical qualifications

OVERVIEW

The health care industry offers employment opportunities in many different specialities. Most people know about clinical career choices, such as medicine, nursing, physical therapy, medical assisting, physician's assistant, and other patient-contact jobs. Although these professions are highly visible, the health care industry relies on a large nonclinical workforce, which is collectively known as support staff.

As the name implies, the support staff assists not only the clinical staff but also the health care industry as a whole. The health care industry is somewhat like an iceberg: Clinical jobs represent the tip of the iceberg, and support staff jobs represent the rest of the iceberg. Figure 1–1 illustrates some job titles for support staff employees. The position of each title does not reflect the importance or value of the profession.

This book focuses on the roles and responsibilities of the insurance billing specialist, and this chapter serves as an introduction to the insurance billing specialist.

INSURANCE BILLING SPECIALIST

An **insurance billing specialist** is as an individual who processes health insurance claims in accordance with legal, professional, and insurance company guidelines and regulations. As part of the health care industry, insurance billing specialists work closely with the financial and managerial areas of a health care agency. The insurance billing specialist is a key player in the financial operations of an agency or medical office.

Tasks assigned to an insurance billing specialist can range from collecting patient insurance information to resolving billing problems between the office, patient, and insurance company. Regardless of the responsibilities associated with insurance billing, anyone who works in this dynamic field must possess certain personal and technical qualifications. Both types of qualifications are important, and the degree of emphasis placed on each depends on the individual employer.

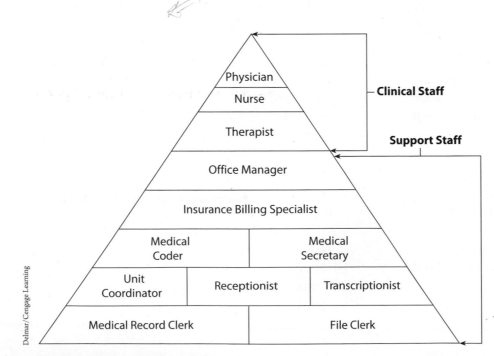

FIGURE 1–1 Support Staff Job Titles

Personal Qualifications

Personal qualifications are those behaviors that define the character or personality of an individual. Personal qualifications include terms such as *aggressive, aloof, assertive, cooperative, ethical, hardworking, reliable,* and *self-motivated.* These qualifications are difficult to measure and are often based on an observer's interpretation. Qualities you identify as assertive and hardworking could be considered by others as aggressive.

Employers try to quantify personal qualifications by describing behaviors that exemplify the qualification. For example, *cooperative* describes the ability to work with others; *assertive* relates to the ability to communicate with others; *reliable* measures one's attendance and ability to complete tasks; *ethical* characterizes one's ability to maintain confidential information and adhere to rules and regulations. These types of descriptions are part of (or should be part of) the job description.

Personality inventory tests can identify personal qualifications. A personality inventory is exactly what the name implies: a series of questions designed to identify aspects of an individual's personality or personal characteristics. Personality inventory tests have become a routine part of the employment application process.

The highest-rated personal qualifications—as identified by office managers and personnel directors—include assertiveness/confidence, honesty, and reliability. For insurance billing specialist positions, employers seek individuals who are ethical, self-motivated, detail-oriented, able to maintain confidential information, and capable of adapting to change. Table 1–1 lists key personal qualifications and examples of behaviors that demonstrate each qualification.

TABLE 1–1

Personal Qualifications	
Personal Qualification	**Behavioral Examples**
Adaptable	Accepts shift and holiday rotation schedule; willing to learn new software features; interested in cross-training
Assertive; confident	Speaks clearly with eye contact; asks questions; describes goals; answers questions directly
Cooperative	Works or has worked on group projects; interested in learning overall office workflow
Detail-oriented	Accurately alphabetizes a list of names; accurately organizes a list of numbers; accurately completes health insurance billing forms
Ethical	Adheres to insurance billing guidelines; refrains from negative comments about current and previous coworkers and employers
Honest	Leaves office supplies at the office; uses sick time according to agency policy
Maintains confidentiality	Maintains professional confidences (i.e., patient information); does not contribute to rumors or gossip
Reliable	Is ready to work at the beginning of the shift; completes tasks within assigned deadlines
Self-motivated	Initiates work assignments; organizes work area

Most people believe they are honest, reliable, ethical, and able to maintain confidentiality. Assessing your ability to adapt to change and your attention to detail is more difficult. Professional, legal, and insurance company regulations that govern health insurance billing practices are continually revised. A simple clerical or data entry oversight might delay or deny payments for services provided. Success as an insurance billing specialist depends on the ability to accurately complete and submit insurance claims.

REINFORCEMENT EXERCISES 1–1

Write the name of the personal qualification described in each statement.

1. Olivia is at her desk and ready to tackle her assignments when the workday begins.

   dependable

2. Linda refuses to answer her fiancé's questions about his boss, a recent patient at Linda's office.

   confidentiality

3. Brian tells his supervisor that he used the wrong insurance code on the claims he sent out yesterday.

   Ethical/live

4. Tawanda calls Dr. Shaski and asks for clarification concerning the diagnosis for Mrs. Gervais.

   Detail oriented

5. Hank reviews the new instructions for electronic claims submission before submitting Medicare insurance claims.

   Self motivated

6. Monroe reviews Mrs. Mattson's insurance form and discovers that "vasectomy follow-up" was noted as the reason for the office visit. He flags the insurance form for determination of the correct reason for Mrs. Mattson's office visit.

   _____

Technical Qualifications

Technical qualifications are measurable abilities and skills that one can learn through education and experience. Basic skills include the ability to keyboard (data entry), read, complete simple math functions, use correct grammar in written and oral communications, accurately record telephone or voice mail messages, and follow directions. Table 1–2 lists these basic skills and application examples.

In addition to basic skills, the insurance billing specialist must have a working knowledge of medical terminology and be familiar with medical coding protocols. Virtually all financial aspects of a medical practice depend on thorough documentation of the patient's condition and accurate medical coding of diagnostic and treatment terms.

Medical terminology is the language of the health care industry. A working knowledge of medical terminology is more than memorizing lists of words. The insurance billing specialist must be able to:

- Read and understand medical reports.
- Recognize the relationship between diagnostic statements and treatments provided.
- Identify discrepancies in medical documentation.

Example A illustrates the ability to recognize the relationship between diagnostic statements and the treatments provided. Example B illustrates the ability to identify discrepancies in medical documentation.

EXAMPLE A

The diagnosis and subsequent treatment of strep throat should be supported by a throat culture test result that identified the streptococcus bacteria.

EXAMPLE B

The diagnosis prostatitis (inflammation of the prostate gland) should not appear in the medical record of a female patient.

TABLE 1–2

Technical Qualifications	
Technical Qualification	**Application Examples**
Data entry (keyboarding)	Updates computerized patient records and financial and insurance records
Documenting messages	Retrieves voice mail messages; accurately takes and routes telephone messages
Math skills	Updates patient accounts; calculates charges for billing; reconciles amount paid with amount owed
Oral communication skills	Answers questions and telephone inquiries by using complete sentences and correct grammar
Ability to follow directions	Reviews and implements new procedures related to insurance billing tasks
Written communication skills	Formats memos; composes letters, fax, and e-mail messages; uses correct grammar, punctuation, and spelling

Medical coding is the process of documenting medical information as numeric codes. Two major coding systems apply to medical information: the International Classification of Diseases (ICD) and Current Procedural Terminology (CPT). Chapters 4 and 5, respectively, discuss these two coding systems.

Both coding systems are revised annually. The insurance billing specialist must keep current with coding practices. This is accomplished by attending workshops, seminars, and other continuing education (CE) events. Insurance billing specialists and medical coders who are certified by a professional association are often required to attain a specific number of CE credits within a given time frame. Failure to fulfill CE requirements may lead to the revocation of credentials and the loss of employment.

REINFORCEMENT EXERCISES 1–2

Write the name of the technical qualification described in each statement.

1. Martha entered patient insurance files into the financial database.

   Data entry

2. Roger completed several letters of inquiry and sent them to different insurance companies.

   Written Communication

3. Lisa's first job every morning is to scan the office voice mail system for priority messages.

   Documenting message

4. Per office policy, Rosa updates her insurance billing manual as soon as she receives new guidelines.

   Ability to follow direction

5. Lucy provided Mrs. Washington with an estimate of her out-of-pocket expenses for her scheduled mammography.

   Math skill

EMPLOYMENT OPPORTUNITIES

Employment opportunities in the medical insurance billing field range from hourly entry-level billing clerk positions to five-figure management positions. Jobs are available in medical offices, hospitals, clinics, insurance companies, government agencies, medical suppliers, and consulting firms. An insurance billing specialist with extensive experience can own and operate a successful insurance claim processing business. Figure 1–2 is a generic job description for an insurance billing specialist.

JOB DESCRIPTION

POSITION TITLE: Insurance Billing Specialist

SUMMARY: Accurately completes and submits health insurance claims following legal, professional, and insurance company guidelines. The work is detail-oriented, repetitive, and involves extensive communication with others.

RESPONSIBILITIES: The listed responsibilities are intended to be representative rather than all-inclusive.

1. Abstracts identification, health insurance plan, and diagnoses and treatment information from the patient record.
2. Uses abstracted information to accurately complete health insurance claim form(s).
3. Follows applicable coding conventions to accurately assign numeric codes to each diagnosis and treatment statement.
4. Reviews policy and guideline bulletins (updates) from health insurance companies and organizations.
5. Applies updated regulations and guidelines to all insurance claim completion activities.
6. Monitors denied or rejected claims to identify the clerical mistakes or clinical omission that generated the rejection.
7. Notifies clinical and support staff of changes in insurance regulations and guidelines that affect documentation of patient information and insurance billing procedures.
8. Assists clinical and support staff in resolving documentation problems related to insurance claims.
9. Posts insurance payments and adjustments to patients' financial records.
10. Keeps patient information confidential.
11. Adheres to office policy and procedures related to work attendance, breaks, vacation, and sick leave.

MINIMUM QUALIFICATIONS
1. High-school diploma, or equivalent, and one year experience as an insurance billing specialist OR graduate of an insurance billing specialist education program.
2. Demonstrated knowledge of medical terminology, including names of diseases, clinical procedures, basic anatomy, and physiology.
3. Keyboarding skills, including data entry, updating databases, word processing, and other related skills.
4. Familiarity with at least one major word-processing software program, such as Microsoft Word or WordPerfect.
5. Ability to work cooperatively and independently as necessary.

DESIRABLE QUALIFICATIONS
1. Demonstrated knowledge of current procedural and diagnostic coding conventions.
2. Certified Medical Billing Specialist (CMBS) or Certified Medical Reimbursement Specialist (CMRS) credentials.

FIGURE 1–2 Insurance Billing Specialist Job Description

⚹ Job titles such as billing clerk, medical biller, insurance claims processor, and reimbursement specialist are sometimes used in place of insurance billing specialist. Larger group practices and hospital billing departments often employ individuals who specialize in specific types of health insurance billing.

EXAMPLE

Segway Physicians, Inc., a 15-physician group practice, has a large insurance billing department. The department includes a Medicare billing specialist, a Medicaid billing specialist, and a Blue Cross/Blue Shield billing specialist. These specialists develop insurance billing expertise in their assigned areas.

Other job opportunities related to the insurance billing process include:

- **Claims assistance professional (CAP):** He or she assists patients in completing the paperwork necessary to obtain insurance payments. Claims assistance professionals can work for health care agencies or operate their own businesses.
- **Insurance collection specialist:** He or she works with insurance companies to resolve billing and payment problems.
- **Patient account representative:** He or she helps the patient identify the amount that health insurance pays for a given service and how much the patient must pay. A patient account representative is also called an **insurance counselor**.
- **Medical coder:** He or she assigns numeric codes to diagnostic, procedure, and treatment information.

Health insurance billing positions have a common group of responsibilities and tasks in addition to the specific duties associated with the individual position. Common tasks and responsibilities for all positions include the ability to:

- Abstract information from patient records.
- Communicate via fax, e-mail, telephone, letters, and memos.
- Demonstrate an understanding of insurance billing legal and ethical issues.
- Follow office policies and procedures.
- Maintain a positive working relationship with patients, staff, and visitors.
- Operate word-processing equipment.
- Participate in continuing education activities.

Specific duties related to each health insurance billing position depend on the job and employer preference. Table 1–3 lists each position and gives examples of additional responsibilities for that position.

In addition to the specific duties listed in Table 1–3, each health insurance billing position is associated with a particular employment setting. Claims assistance professionals usually work directly for the client or patient and are often self-employed. Insurance collection specialists usually work for medium-to-large health care agencies, such as physician group practices or hospitals. These specialists represent the interest of the health care agency when any problems with insurance payments occur. Patient account representatives, who are employed by large multispecialty clinics or hospitals, work to establish payment options before services are provided.

TABLE 1–3

Insurance Billing Position Responsibilities	
Position	**Responsibilities**
Claims assistance professional	• Helps individuals, clients, or patients submit medical bills to insurance companies • Explains the content of insurance company documents to the client, individual, or patient • Communicates with medical office and insurance company staff on behalf of the client
Insurance collection specialist	• Works with patients, insurance companies, and employer health benefits representatives to resolve insurance billing and/or payment problems • Reviews insurance forms to identify patterns of errors that result in unpaid or rejected claims • Monitors medical coding accuracy • Provides insurance form completion training to medical office staff • Maintains knowledge of regulations related to insurance collection practices
Patient account representative	• Discusses insurance coverage with the patient • Contacts the insurance company to verify the patient's eligibility and the amount to be paid by insurance • Helps establish a payment plan for the patient

REINFORCEMENT EXERCISES 1–3

1. List three job titles that are synonymous with *insurance billing specialist.*

Billing Clerk,

medical biller

reimbursement Specialist

2. The _____ helps clients complete the paperwork necessary to obtain insurance payments for medical bills.

Claims assistance professional

3. Melinda met with the _____ in order to find out the amount insurance would pay for her impending surgery.

Insurance Collection Specialist

continued on the next page

continued from the previous page

4. List three minimum qualifications that are often listed on an insurance billing specialist job description.

Ability to comunicat cleary

oprate basic office machi, Fllow office poliy

Undastaun of billing guide and rules

5. Identify five common tasks associated with insurance billing positions.

Recored Patient information, answer phone

Commmicate with coder, Fill the pDorm

Follow the guide lisme and rules

EDUCATIONAL, CERTIFICATION, AND CAREER OPPORTUNITIES

Medical insurance billing has become increasingly complex, and most employers now require successful completion of some kind of formal education. Insurance billing specialist programs include courses such as medical terminology, anatomy and physiology, medical insurance processing, medical coding, word processing, and English. These programs are usually between one and two years long. A one-year program is known as a certificate or diploma program, and a two-year program usually results in an associate degree. These programs allow you the opportunity to acquire the technical qualifications discussed earlier in this chapter.

Certification is a process that involves successful completion of a professionally recognized exam. Employers know that education and/or experience are needed to pass national or professional exams. Professional credential exams are viewed as objective measures of an individual's expertise in a given field. Several professional associations offer certification or credentialing exams related to medical billing and medical coding. Table 1–4 lists the name and website of medical billing professional associations, the exams offered by the association, the requirements to take the exam, and the title associated with successful completion of the exam. The exams include questions related to insurance billing, medical terminology, and medical coding.

Certification specifically related to medical coding significantly increases career opportunities for an insurance specialist. Table 1–5 lists the name and website of professional associations that offer medical coding certification exams, the requirements to take the exam, and the title associated with successful completion of the exam.

Each professional association's website has the most current information about credentials, certification exams, and member services.

Career opportunities differ from employment opportunities in that the word *career* brings to mind professional growth and development. A career ladder or career path indicates that the individual is moving toward a higher goal. Advancement along a career path is accompanied by an increase in status, responsibility, and pay. Career advancement is accomplished through acquiring additional education and experience. Once career goals are met, the individual must stay current in all aspects of his or her chosen field.

TABLE 1–4

Medical Billing Certification Exams	
Professional Association	**Certification Exams**
American Medical Billing Association (AMBA): www.ambanet.net	• **Certified Medical Reimbursement Specialist (CMRS):** Individuals with medical billing experience in various health care settings
Medical Association of Billers (MAB): www.physicianswebsites.com	• **Certified Medical Billing Specialist (CMBS):** Individuals currently working in a medical office, a health insurance company, or an insurance billing agency; an entry-level billing and coding exam • **Certified Medical Billing Specialist-Chiropractic Assistant (CMBS-CA):** Individuals working in a chiropractic agency; an intermediate level exam • **Certified Medical Billing Specialist-Hospital (CMBS-H):** Individuals working in a hospital; an intermediate-level exam covering the differences between inpatient and outpatient billing
National Electronic Billiers Alliance (NEBA): www.nebazone.com	• **Certified Healthcare Reimbursement Specialist (CHRS):** Individuals with experience in all areas of the medical billing profession

TABLE 1–5

Medical Coding Certification Exams	
Professional Association	**Certification Exams**
American Academy of Professional Coders (AAPC): www.aapc.com	• **Certified Professional Coder (CPC):** Current experience working in home health, ambulatory surgery centers, physician office or group practice; associated degree recommended • **Certified Professional Coder-Hospital (CPC-H):** Current experience working in hospital-based outpatient departments or ambulatory surgery centers; associate degree recommended • **Certified Professional Coder-Payer (CPC-P):** Current experience working for insurance companies or insurance billing services; associate degree recommended • **Speciality Certifications:** Various medical coding certifications related to specific medical specialities; associate degree recommended
American Health Information Management Association (AHIMA): www.ahima.org	• **Certified Coding Associate (CCA):** An entry-level exam; six months of medical coding experience or completions of a medical coding training program • **Certified Coding Specialist (CCS):** Three or more years of current experience in a hospital (inpatient) setting and demonstrated knowledge of anatomy, physiology, pathophysiology, and pharmacology • **Certified Coding Specialist–Physician-Based (CCS-P):** Three or more years of current experience in physician office settings and demonstrated knowledge of anatomy, physiology, pathophysiology, and pharmacology

Beginning your career path as an insurance billing specialist can provide opportunities for advancement. Experience, education, and certification can lead to positions such as claims or billing department supervisor, medical office manager, collections manager, and medical practice manager. Insurance billing specialists with extensive insurance claims processing experience can establish a successful medical billing service. Table 1–6 provides information about these positions.

TABLE 1–6

Career Positions
Billing Department Supervisor • Two or more years of current experience in all areas of health insurance billing • Medical billing certification highly recommended • Supervises insurance billing specialist • Communicates with physicians, patients, and insurance companies to resolve insurance processing problems
Collection Manager • Two or more years of current experience in all areas of health insurance billing, including resolving problems related to collecting payment for services • Medical billing certification highly recommended • Communicates with patients, insurance companies, and collection agencies to secure payment for overdue or past due accounts
Medical Office Manager • Two years of current experience in a medical office • Medical office manager certification highly recommended • Associate's degree in office management or business administration recommended • Establishes procedures for overall office functions • Performs duties associated with staffing the office • Communicates with physicians, office supervisors and staff, patients, and sales representatives
Medical Practice Manager • Associate's degree in accounting, business, or management required • Bachelor's degree highly recommended • Three or more years of accounting or business management experience in health care • Communicates with physicians, hospital administrators, vendors, regulatory agencies, and other external agencies in matters related to the business and financial functions of the medical practice • Responsible for all financial and business functions of the medical practice • Establishes and implements policies that comply with state and federal laws and regulatory agency requirements
Owner, Medical Billing Service • Five or more years current experience in all areas of health insurance billing • Two years of supervisory or management experience

continued on the next page

continued from the previous page

- Associate's degree in business, management, accounting, or health care administration
- Communicates with physicians, medical office managers, medical practice managers, insurance companies, and sales representatives
- Establishes medical billing (insurance claims submission) contracts with health care providers
- Establishes and implements policies and procedures that comply with state and federal laws and regulatory agency requirements

REINFORCEMENT EXERCISES 1–4

1. List three courses that are essential to an insurance billing specialist education program.

CMRS

CMBS

CMBS-H

CHRS,

2. Spell out each abbreviation and then name the professional association that offers each credential.

CMBS

Certified medical Billing sphs

CMBS-H

certified medical Billing Spen - Hospal

CMRS

certified medical Reimbured Spist

3. Briefly describe the differences between the three medical coding certification exams offered by AHIMA.

CCS + ...

CCA - Entry level - 6 to ed ...

4. Spell out and briefly describe CPC and CPC-H. Name the professional association that offers these credentials.

Certified profnal Coder work thru office ...

... womy own Past Horid ...

ABBREVIATIONS

Abbreviations are a fact of life in the health care industry. Table 1–7 lists the abbreviations presented in this chapter.

TABLE 1–7

Abbreviations and Meanings	
Abbreviation	Meaning
AAPC	American Academy of Professional Coders
AHIMA	American Health Information Management Association
AMBA	American Medical Billing Association
CAP	claims assistant professional
CCA	certified coding assistant
CCS	certified coding specialist
CCS-P	certified coding specialist–physician-based
CE	continuing education
CHRS	certified healthcare reimbursement specialist
CMBS	certified medical billing specialist
CMBS-CA	certified medical billing specialist–chiropractic
CMBS-H	certified medical billing specialist–hospital
CMRS	certified medical reimbursement specialist
CPC	certified professional coder
CPC-H	certified professional coder–hospital
CPC-P	certified professional coder–payer
CPT	Current Procedural Terminology
ICD	International Classification of Diseases
MAB	Medical Association of Billers
NEBA	National Electronic Billers Alliance

SUMMARY

An insurance billing specialist is a key player in the financial operation of health care agencies. This individual processes health insurance claims in accordance with legal, professional, and insurance company guidelines and regulations. By observing an individual's behavior and by using personality inventory tests, one can identify personal qualifications. Technical qualifications are measurable skills that one can learn through education and experience. Employment and career opportunities for insurance billing specialists are readily available.

REVIEW EXERCISES

Short Answer

1. Describe the different types of jobs that represent clinical and nonclinical career choices.

page 2

_____

_____

_____

2. Briefly define *insurance billing specialist.*

page 2

_____

_____

_____

3. List the office staff who work closely with the insurance billing specialist.

_____

_____

_____

Definition of Terms

Fill in the blank beneath each definition with the appropriate term from the following list: certification, certified coding specialist, certified professional coder, claims assistance professional, insurance billing specialist, insurance collection specialist, insurance counselor, medical coding, medical terminology, patient account representative, personal qualifications, technical qualifications.

1. Credential offered by the American Health Information Management Association.

    C e S

2. Individual who processes health insurance claims in accordance with legal and professional guidelines and regulations.

    Insurance billing specialist

3. Behaviors that identify the character or personality of an individual.

    _____

4. Documenting medical information as numeric codes.

    medical coding

5. An individual who helps clients complete health insurance paperwork.

    Claims assistan professional

6. Language of the health care industry.

   medical Temenuy

7. Measurable abilities and skills.

   persal qualitia, temica

8. Helps resolve billing and payment problems between the medical office and the insurance company.

   Billie asoneisplusr

9. Establishes payment options before services are provided.

   Patien account repernahive

10. Successful completion of a professionally recognized exam.

    Imra colver

11. Credential offered by the American Academy of Professional Coders.

    CPC

Matching

Match each term in Column A with the appropriate item in Column B.

Column A	Column B	
a. self-motivated	1. interested in cross-training	_h_
b. reliable	2. works well with others	_f_
c. ethical	3. adheres to attendance policies	_h_
d. detail-oriented	4. initiates work assignments	_a_
e. data entry	5. maintains confidentiality	_c_
f. cooperative	6. updates financial records	
g. communication skills	7. verifies diagnosis codes	_8_
h. adaptable	8. uses correct grammar and spelling	_9_

COMPREHENSION EXERCISES

1. Why does the insurance billing specialist need a working knowledge of medical terminology?

2. Select the three personal qualifications that you believe are most important. Write a brief report explaining why you chose each of them.

_____

_____

_____

_____

_____

_____

CRITICAL THINKING EXERCISES

1. Review the personal and technical qualifications listed in Tables 1–1 and 1–2. Compare the qualifications with the information in the Insurance Billing Specialist Job Description (Figure 1–2). Are the qualifications addressed in the job description? Match the qualification(s) with the corresponding statement(s).
2. Access the Medical Association of Billers website to review the sample certification exam questions.

WEBSITES

American Academy of Professional Coders (AAPC): www.aapc.com
American Health Information Management Association (AHIMA): www.ahima.org
American Medical Billing Association (AMBA): www.ambanet.net
Medical Association of Billers (MAB): www.physicianswebsites.com
National Electronic Billiers Alliance (NEBA): www.nebazone.com

CHAPTER 2

Legal Aspects of Insurance Billing

LEARNING OBJECTIVES

Upon successful completion of this chapter, the reader should have the knowledge to:

1. Briefly define all general medical-legal terms presented in the chapter.
2. Identify six key components of an authorization to release information form.
3. Discuss the advantages and disadvantages of the electronic release of information.
4. Provide ten examples of fraudulent activities and eight examples of abuse activities.
5. Explain abbreviations for the six government agencies associated with fraud and abuse prevention.
6. Describe six steps associated with fraud protection and prevention.
7. Discuss the Privacy Rule and the Security Rule enacted under the Health Insurance Portability and Accountability Act of 1996.

KEY TERMS

Abuse
Center for Medicare and Medicaid Services (CMS)
Confidential information
Confidentiality
Covered entities
Department of Health and Human Services (HHS)
Department of Justice (DOJ)
Durable power of attorney
Electronic protected health information (EPHI)
Emancipated minor
Embezzlement
Employer liability

Federal Bureau of Investigation (FBI)
Fraud
Guardian
Guardianship
Guardianship of the estate
Guardianship of the person
Health care fraud
Health Insurance Portability and Accountability Act of 1996 (HIPAA)
HIPAA Privacy Rule
HIPAA Security Rule
Malfeasance
Malpractice
Minimum necessary
Misfeasance

Negligence
Nonfeasance
Office of Civil Rights (OCR)
Office of the Inspector General (OIG)
Power of attorney
Privacy officer
Protected health information (PHI)
Release of information (ROI)
Respondeat superior
Statute of limitations
Subpoena
Subpoena duces tecum
Workforce members

OVERVIEW

Health care is a heavily regulated industry. Clinical staff must be licensed or certified as required by state law. Health care organizations must follow strict local, state, and federal regulations that govern everything from building size to the types of services offered. In addition to governmental regulations, the health care industry is affected by the code of ethics associated with clinical and support staff occupations. The combination of governmental regulations and occupational codes of ethics contributes to the legal aspects of the health care industry.

Health insurance organizations and practices are not exempt from the legal requirements of the health care industry. Legal issues range from the obvious confidentiality of patient information to the more obscure areas of billing fraud and abuse regulations. Physicians, nurses, business managers, and accountants have always been subject to and concerned about the legal and ethical implications of their work. However, legal and ethical issues apply to every individual who works in a health care job.

Many governmental regulations and occupational codes of ethics directly affect the insurance billing specialist. The insurance billing specialist has access to confidential and sensitive information. Patient medical and financial information, business and billing practice information, physician and clinical staff documentation patterns, and information related to payments received from government-sponsored insurance programs are essential for insurance billing activities.

This chapter provides an overview of the basic legal issues associated with the health care industry. Issues such as confidentiality, the release of information, and guardianship are covered. Legal issues directly related to insurance billing practices, such as fraud and abuse, are also presented. The insurance billing specialist should know that just like the clinical and administrative staff, the insurance specialist is accountable for his or her own actions in regard to these legal issues.

ORIGIN OF LEGAL ISSUES

Legal regulations originate from three primary sources: local, state, and federal government organizations and agencies. Each governmental unit has a restricted scope of influence. Township building codes may vary within a county but may not contradict state and federal laws. In some areas, the federal government has left regulation to the states, as in clinical staff licensure and certification. Some federal laws, such as civil rights laws, cannot be overturned by any governmental unit. Health care agencies must comply with regulations from all levels of government. These regulations cover everything from building codes to the licensing of health care providers. The following example illustrates county, state, and federal laws or regulations associated with the health care industry.

EXAMPLE
County building codes may require that the clinic or hospital have a certain number of ramped entrances. The county, however, cannot pass laws governing clinical licensing.

State licensing laws for clinical staff ensure that individuals involved in direct patient care meet certain practice standards. However, state governments cannot pass laws that change Medicare regulations.

The federal government establishes regulations related to receiving payment from the Medicare health insurance program.

GENERAL LEGAL TERMS

Several general legal terms and concepts apply to the business practices of the health care industry. Laws that address the emancipated minor, embezzlement, employer liability, guardianship, malpractice, negligence, statute of limitations, and subpoena of records affect the clinical and administrative functions of physicians' practices. The insurance billing specialist may be directly or indirectly affected by these general legal principles. Table 2–1 lists and summarizes the general legal terms. A discussion of each term or phrase follows Table 2–1.

TABLE 2–1

General Legal Terms and Definitions	
Term	**Definition**
Durable power of attorney	Power of attorney that remains in effect after the individual who grants the power of attorney dies or is declared incompetent
Emancipated minor	An individual who has not reached the age of majority, usually 18, who lives independently
Embezzlement	Stealing money
Employer liability	Employer's responsibility for employee job-related actions; known as *respondeat* (reh-SPON-dee-at) *superior,* which literally means "let the master respond"
Guardian	Individual legally designated to act on behalf of a minor or an incompetent adult
Guardianship	Legal authority to act on behalf of a minor or an incompetent adult
Guardianship of estate	Legal authority over financial resources and other assets
Guardianship of person	Legal authority over personal and medical decisions
Malpractice	Any professional behavior of one individual that results in damages to another individual; bad practice
Negligence	Failure to exercise the appropriate standard of care, resulting in injury
Power of attorney	Voluntary transfer of decision-making authority from one competent individual to another competent individual
Statute of limitations	Period of time associated with legal liability
Subpoena	A legal document requesting an individual to appear in court; literally means "under penalty"
Subpoena duces tecum	A legal document requesting an individual to bring records to court

Emancipated Minor

An **emancipated minor** is an individual who has not reached the age of majority as established by state law but who lives independently, is self-supporting, and has decision-making rights. An emancipated minor is usually younger than 18 years old. Emancipation is usually accomplished by petitioning the appropriate court and providing documentation or other evidence of self-sufficiency, by entering into a legal marriage, or by joining the armed forces. An emancipated minor makes all decisions without parental or guardian approval and is responsible for his or her own debts. Keep in mind that not all states recognize emancipated minors.

Many states allow individuals who are younger than 18 and who have not been emancipated to agree to certain types of medical care. The types of care allowed range from birth control counseling to receiving emergency treatment for a sports injury. Although the insurance billing specialist is not involved in treatment decisions, determining who is responsible for paying for the treatment can raise questions.

> **EXAMPLE**
> Is the emancipated minor covered by the parent's health insurance?
> Can the parents or guardian be held responsible for a bill that results from providing services to a person under age 18 who has not been emancipated?

If the physician or provider treats emancipated minors or individuals under age 18 without parental consent, responsibility for payment must be clearly identified.

Embezzlement

Embezzlement is briefly defined as stealing money that an individual has access to but does not have any legal claim to take, keep, or spend. Common examples of embezzlement are found in accounting practices and trust fund management. The insurance billing specialist does not routinely have access to or responsibility for the actual money associated with a specific medical practice. However, if your job description includes posting payments and depositing funds, you should take steps to protect yourself from accusations of embezzlement.

Employer Liability

Employer liability means that the employer is responsible for the actions of employees that are within the context of employment. The Latin phrase **respondeat superior** ("let the master answer") is a legal description of employer liability. Although it may be comforting to believe that the employer is accountable for the employees' behavior, in reality, accountability rests with each individual.

The insurance billing specialist is accountable for the results of his or her actions related to health insurance claims submission. In fact, the Medicare definition of fraud states that the "violator may be an employee of any provider, billing service . . . or any person in a position to file a claim for Medicare benefits." Insurance billing specialists cannot excuse employment-related actions by saying, "I was only doing what I was taught (or told) to do." As individuals in support staff positions achieve both professional and financial recognition, they assume more responsibility for their actions.

Guardianship and Power of Attorney

A **guardian** is as an individual who is legally designated to act on behalf of a minor or an incompetent adult. **Guardianship** is the legal authority to act as an individual's guardian. For example, a child may have a court-appointed guardian because the parents are absent or deceased. The guardian can be given different types of authority, such as guardianship of the child's financial resources—known as **guardianship of the estate**—or guardianship of the child's personal and medical decisions—known as **guardianship of the person**.

Each type of guardianship can involve specific or limited areas of control or can be fairly broad in scope. The guardian may have the authority to give consent for medical treatment but may not have authority to use the individual's assets to pay the medical bill. On the other hand, a guardian with control of financial decisions may not have authority for medical treatment.

In divorce situations, issues of custodial rights and decision-making rights are similar to guardianship issues. Although one parent may have custody, the divorce decree may allow joint decision-making. Without joint decision-making rights, the noncustodial parent has few if any rights to deny or authorize treatment. Either the custodial or the noncustodial parent may be responsible for the medical bills. Divorce decrees often address this responsibility by naming which parent has medical financial responsibility for the minor. The courts usually assign medical financial responsibility to the parent, custodial or not, who has health insurance.

Guardianship and custodianship can be problematic issues for both clinical and support staff. Clinical staff must be certain that the person authorizing treatment has the authority to do so. The insurance billing specialist must make a good-faith effort to have accurate information regarding medical financial responsibility when submitting insurance claims.

Power of attorney is the voluntary transfer of decision-making authority from one competent individual to another competent individual. The individual who has granted the power of attorney can revoke the power of attorney at any time. The power of attorney automatically ends when the person granting the power of attorney dies or is declared incompetent. A **durable power of attorney** is identical to a standard power of attorney—with one important exception: A durable power of attorney remains in effect even after the individual granting the power of attorney dies or is unable to make decisions. A good example of a health-related durable power of attorney is the document used to designate a specific person to make medical decisions if the competent individual is unable to communicate on his or her own behalf.

> **EXAMPLE**
> Mrs. Smith is scheduled for triple coronary bypass surgery. Her risk factor is very high. Mrs. Smith asks her son John to complete the durable power of attorney form that the surgeon gave her. When properly executed, this document gives John the power to authorize or refuse medical treatment in accordance with his mother's wishes if she is unable to do so herself.

A patient does not have to grant the durable power of attorney to a blood relative; he or she can select any competent individual as the designee. The individual selected as designee must agree to accept the power of attorney, cannot benefit from the death of the patient, and cannot be associated with the health agency providing care to the patient.

Malpractice

Malpractice is defined as any professional behavior of one individual that results in damages to another individual. Malpractice simply means "bad practice" and is usually applied to the conduct of the physician. Malpractice has three categories: (1) **malfeasance**, which means that the wrong action was taken; (2) **misfeasance**, which means that the correct action was done incorrectly; and (3) **nonfeasance**, which means that no action was taken when action was necessary.

> **EXAMPLE**
>
> Removing a healthy uterus because a patient has uncomfortable menstrual periods is an example of malfeasance. Incomplete removal of a malignant uterus is an example of misfeasance. Failure to remove a malignant uterus is an example of nonfeasance.

Insurance billing specialists are seldom accused of professional malpractice. Unless they are intentional, insurance processing errors fall under insurance abuse laws. Insurance abuse is discussed in the fraud and abuse section of this chapter.

Negligence

Negligence is the failure to exercise the standard of care that a reasonable person would exercise in similar circumstances. Negligence occurs when failure to exercise the standard of care results in injury. Physicians and other health care providers are the usual targets of malpractice lawsuits based on negligence. Examples of negligence include: failure to notify the patient of an abnormal test result; failure to provide coverage for patients when the physician is on vacation (abandonment); and failure to explain the side effects of a medication.

Statute of Limitations

Statute of limitations is the period of time during which an agency, business, or individual is vulnerable to civil or criminal proceedings. Statutes of limitations vary from state to state. Clinical and support staff should have a working knowledge of the statute of limitations related to their professional conduct. Statutes of limitations are often described in state laws that govern business practices, health or medical treatments, and corporate or individual liability.

Insurance billing specialists are affected by statutes of limitations that govern the business practices of the medical office. For example, a medical practice has a limited time period in which to initiate legal action against an insurance company for payment delays, against an individual for nonpayment, and for resubmitting rejected claims. Because the billing specialist knows about these time frames, legal actions can be taken as necessary. The insurance billing specialist must also know the time limits associated with claims submission.

> **EXAMPLE**
>
> The insurance billing specialist at Northern Clinic fails to submit an insurance claim in a timely manner. The insurance company denies payment because the claim was not received within the prescribed time frame. The billing specialist informs the patient that legal action is necessary to obtain payment from the insurance company.

Subpoena of Records

A **subpoena** is a legal document signed by a judge or an attorney that requires an individual to appear in court as a witness. The word *subpoena* is Latin for "under penalty." **Subpoena duces tecum** means that the individual should appear and "bring records with you." A subpoena is served to a specific individual, and the individual can only bring records within the scope of his or her responsibility.

In a medical office, a subpoena is usually served to the physician, the business manager, or the medical record professional. Most medical offices designate one employee as the keeper of the medical records. Only that employee can legally accept a subpoena duces tecum related to patient records. Because the billing specialist is not the usual keeper of medical records, the specialist cannot accept such a subpoena.

In order to be enforceable, a subpoena must be properly served by being handed directly to the prospective witness. Once a subpoena is delivered, the individual is obligated, under penalty of law, to appear at the proceedings as directed. Deliberate disregard for a subpoena is considered contempt of court and is punishable by a fine, imprisonment, or both.

REINFORCEMENT EXERCISES 2–1

Write the correct legal term for each description.

1. Stealing money from an employer.

Embezzlement

2. Designated to act on behalf of a minor or an incompetent adult.

Guardian

3. Legal authority to act on behalf of an individual.

Guardianship

4. Authority to authorize medical treatment.

C. Person

5. Failure to provide appropriate services at the appropriate time.

Negligence

6. Under penalty of law, bring the records with you.

Subpoena

7. A minor who lives independently, is self-supporting, or is a part of a legal marriage.

Emancipated minor

8. Let the master answer.

Employer law

9. Employer responsibility for employee actions within the scope of employment.

Job related responda

10. Authority over financial resources.

Leadership of estate

continued on the next page

continued from the previous page

11. Failure to act as expected.

12. Bad practice that results in damage or injury.

13. Authority to act on behalf of a competent individual.

CONFIDENTIAL INFORMATION

Confidential information is information that is not open to public inspection. The principle of **confidentiality** presumes that certain information is not shared with others. State and federal laws affirm that an individual's medical, financial, and educational information is confidential. Confidentiality belongs to the individual and not to the information itself. For example, health care statistics are the end product of information taken from patient medical records. The information is gathered and analyzed without including patients' names, so confidentiality is maintained.

Topics related to confidentiality include the Health Insurance Portability and Accountability Act of 1996; release of information guidelines; special considerations related to positive human immunodeficiency virus (HIV) test results; acquired immunodeficiency syndrome (AIDS), alcohol, and substance abuse records; requests for information by telephone; and guidelines for facsimile (fax), e-mail, and Internet transmissions.

Insurance billing specialists are directly involved in releasing patient diagnosis and treatment information by mail and electronic means. The billing specialist also responds to telephone inquiries concerning the status of insurance claims. Calls come from insurance company representatives, employer benefits representatives, and patients.

As a general rule, it is poor practice to release any patient information on the telephone, via fax, or by e-mail. It is difficult to verify the identity of the caller, to know who retrieves fax reports, and to ensure the security of e-mail messages. However, electronic communication is a fact of life, and it is legal to use these tools. Policies and procedures that govern the release of confidential information should describe confidentiality safeguards related to telephone, fax, and Internet activities.

Health Insurance Portability and Accountability Act of 1996 (HIPAA)

In 1996, U.S. Congress enacted the **Health Insurance Portability and Accountability Act**, commonly known as **HIPAA** (HIP-ah). This law established a set of national standards for the protection of certain health information. Under HIPAA, the U.S. **Department of Health and Human Services (HHS)** issued the Standards for Privacy of Individually Identifiable Health Information, commonly known as the **Privacy Rule**. The **Office of Civil Rights (OCR)**, which is part of HHS, is responsible for implementing and enforcing the Privacy Rule. The HIPAA Privacy Rule has been in effect since 2003 and has had a profound effect on the confidentiality and release of information policies and procedures for the entire health care industry. Simply put, the HIPAA Privacy Rule gives individuals a federally protected right to control the use and release of their health information.

Table 2–2

HIPAA Privacy Rule Covered Entities		
Entity	**Definition**	**Example**
Health Plans	Individual or group that pays for medical services	Health, dental, vision, and prescription medication insurers; HMOs; employer-sponsored group health plans; government and church-sponsored health plans; multi-employer health plans
Health Care Providers	Institutions or individuals that provide health care services; any other person or organization that furnishes, bills, or is paid for health care services	Hospitals; long-term care facilities; medical offices; ambulatory health offices/facilities; physicians; dentists; nurses; allied health professionals
Health Care Clearinghouses	Organizations that process information for health plans	Billing services; community health management information systems

The information in this chapter is a very brief summary of the Privacy Rule and is based on the *Office of Civil Rights Privacy Rule Summary*. Because the Privacy Rule has been and continues to be modified, the most current information is available on the OCR website at www.hhs.gov/ocr/privacy. In addition, professional associations, such as the American Health Information Management Association (AHIMA), are excellent resources for information about complying with the Privacy Rule.

The HIPAA Privacy Rule applies to **covered entities**—that is, health plans, health care clearinghouses, and any health care providers who transmit health information in electronic form. Table 2–2 gives a brief definition and some examples of covered entities.

The HIPAA Privacy Rule defines and limits the circumstances under which an individual's **protected health information (PHI)** is used or disclosed. Protected health information is individually identifiable health information that relates to: a person's past, present, or future physical or mental health condition; the health care services provided to the person; or the past, present, or future payment for health care services provided to the person. In general, protected health information can be released only with the written authorization or consent of the individual. A parent or legal guardian may give consent on behalf of a minor child or an incompetent adult. The Privacy Rule allows the release of protected health information without written consent when:

- The information is subpoenaed.
- The information is needed to defend the health care provider or agency in a lawsuit.
- The information is necessary for life-saving emergency treatment.
- The patient is covered by Medicaid or workers' compensation health insurance programs.
- The information is needed to comply with another law—for example, to report suspected child abuse.

The Privacy Rule limits the use of, disclosure of, and request for protected health information to the **minimum necessary**. Minimum necessary is only that amount of information needed to accomplish the intended use, disclosure, or request. For example, the billing specialist may release only the information necessary to obtain payment for services provided; nursing students may access only the records of patients assigned to them; and maintenance staff may not access any protected health information.

In order to comply with the provisions of the Privacy Rule, the covered entity must:

- Develop and implement written privacy policies and procedures for the use of, release or distribution of, and request for protected health information.
- Designate an individual, often called a **privacy officer**, who is responsible for enforcing the policies and procedures.
- Develop and implement policies and procedures that limit access to and use of protected health information based on the specific roles of **workforce members**, defined as employees, volunteers, trainees, and other persons under direct control of the agency.
- Train all workforce members in its privacy policies and procedures.
- Apply appropriate sanctions against workforce members who violate privacy policies and procedures.
- Maintain reasonable and appropriate safeguards to prevent violations of privacy policies and procedures—for example, securing medical records with lock and key or pass code.
- Provide a written notice of the agency's privacy practices related to the use and disclosure of protected health information to individuals who receive services from the agency.
- Develop procedures that tell an individual how to submit a complaint related to violations or suspected violations of privacy policies and procedures.
- Identify the contact person or office that is responsible for receiving the complaints.
- Develop policies and procedures that tell an individual how to review, obtain a copy of, and amend his or her protected health information.

Billing specialists work with protected health information and are responsible for maintaining the privacy of PHI according to the written policies and procedures of their employers. Self-employed billing specialists must establish and maintain business practices that comply with the Privacy Rule. Failure to comply with a Privacy Rule requirement is a civil offense and may result in monetary penalties of $100 per failure, not to exceed $25,000 per year for multiple violations of the same Privacy Rule requirement in a calendar year.

HIPAA Security Rule

Ensuring the security of patient information is not a new concept. Patient information must be protected against damage, loss, theft, and unauthorized access. Paper, microfilm, or microfiche patient information can be stored in locked cabinets and file areas equipped with a sprinkler system. Access can be controlled by assigning to the file area staff members who are responsible for retrieving patient records and by providing keys to a limited number of individuals for times when the file area is not staffed. In today's environment, patient information is often stored electronically, which presents unique challenges for security.

In February 2003, HHS adopted standards for the security of **electronic protected health information (EPHI)**. EPHI is protected health information maintained or transmitted in electronic form. These standards are commonly called the **HIPAA Security Rule**. The Security Rule, which is part of HIPAA, describes federally mandated patient information security regulations. The Security Rule became effective in April 2003. All covered entities—which include health plans, health care clearinghouses, and any health care provider—were required to comply with the requirements of the Security Rule by April 21, 2006. The **Center for Medicare and Medicaid Services (CMS)**, a division of HHS, is responsible for administering the Security Rule.

The information presented here is a very brief summary of the Security Rule and is based on the final rule published in *Health Insurance Reform: Security Standards* by Fed. Reg. (February 20, 2003). The most current information related to the Security Rule is available on the CMS website at www.cms.hhs.gov/SecurityStandard. In addition, professional associations are excellent resources for information about complying with the Security Rule.

While the HIPAA Privacy Rule covers all protected health information, the Security Rule only applies to protected health information that is electronically stored and transmitted. Electronic storage includes but may not be limited to computer hard drives, digital memory cards, magnetic tapes or disks, optical disks, and servers. Electronic media transmission includes but may not be limited to the Internet, leased lines, private computer networks, dial-up lines, and the physical movement of removable/transportable electronic storage media (e.g., disks, CDs, and magnetic tapes). The Security Rule did not include paper-to-paper fax and telephone transmissions in the definition of electronic media transmission.

The HIPAA Security Rule standards are grouped into five categories: administrative safeguards, physical safeguards, technical safeguards, organizational requirements, and policies and procedures and documentation requirements. Although it is beyond the scope of this text to include a detailed review of all standards, Table 2–3 briefly summarizes the standards for each of the five categories.

TABLE 2–3

Summary of HIPAA Security Rule Standards
Administrative Safeguards
• Analyze risks to security.
• Implement policies/procedures to prevent, detect, and correct security violations.
• Provide security awareness training for all employees.
• Identify a security official/officer.
• Limit access to EPHI as appropriate to a specific position, job, or function.
• Develop procedures to create and maintain retrievable exact copies of EPHI and/or restore any lost data.
• Apply appropriate sanctions against employees who fail to comply with security policies and procedures.
Physical Safeguards
• Implement policies and procedures to limit physical access to electronic information systems.
• Provide physical protection against unauthorized users for all workstations that access EPHI
• Implement procedures to protect the physical safety of hardware and electronic media that is moved into, out of, and within the facility.
• Implement procedures to remove EPHI from electronic media before the media are made available for reuse.
• Implement procedures regarding the final disposition (destruction, archiving, retention) of EPHI and/or the hardware or electronic media on which it is stored.

continued on the next page

continued from the previous page

Summary of HIPAA Security Rule Standards
Technical Safeguards
• Assign a unique identifier for all authorized users.
• Establish procedures for obtaining EPHI during an emergency.
• Implement policies and procedures to protect EPHI from improper destruction or alteration.
• Implement security measures that protect EPHI against unauthorized access during transmission via an electronic communications network.
Organizational Requirements
• Contracts with business associates (individuals or agencies that provide contractual services to the covered entity—e.g., billing services) must include provisions that direct the business associate to implement administrative, physical, and technical safeguards that protect EPHI and comply with the HIPAA Security Rule.
• Group health plans must implement administrative, physical, and technical safeguards that protect EPHI and comply with the HIPAA Security Rule.
Policies and Procedures and Documentation Requirements
• Implement reasonable and appropriate policies and procedures necessary to comply with the HIPAA Security Rule.
• Maintain policies and procedures in written (including electronic) form.
• Retain policies and procedures for six years from the date created or last in effect, whichever is later.
• Review and update policies and procedures as needed.

Billing specialists are involved in the electronic transmission of electronic protected health information and are responsible for maintaining the security of EPHI according to the written policies and procedures of their employers. Self-employed billing specialists must establish and maintain business practices that comply with the Security Rule. Failure to comply with a Security Rule requirement is a civil offense and may result in monetary penalties of $100 per failure, not to exceed $25,000 per year for multiple violations of the same requirement in a calendar year.

Release of Information (ROI)

Because confidentiality belongs to the individual, the individual has the right to authorize the release or distribution of his or her confidential information. Authorization is accomplished with a **release of information (ROI)** form. In nearly all circumstances, confidential information can be released only with the written authorization or consent of the individual. A parent or legal guardian may give consent on behalf of a minor or an incompetent adult.

The release of information authorization form must contain the items listed in Table 2–4. All items should be filled in before the patient is asked to sign the form. Figure 2–1 is an example of a properly completed release of information form. Note that conditions related to HIV status, AIDS, and alcohol and drug abuse have separate statements authorizing release of that information.

```
                    MOISIO MEDICAL GROUP
                     714 HENNEPIN ROAD
                   MARQUETTE, MICHIGAN 49855

              AUTHORIZATION FOR RELEASE OF INFORMATION


     Moisio Medical Group is authorized to release the following
        (Name of Agency)
     information from the health record of Erik William Mattson,
                                            (Patient name)
     06/30/1972      , for the period covering March 199x
     (Date of Birth)                              (Beginning date)
     to April 20xx  .
        (Ending date)
     The information is to be released to Maria Gervais, MD,

     999 West College Road, Marquette Michigan 49855, for the
     (Name and Address)
     purpose of continued patient care                    .

     Information to be released includes (check all that apply, cross out non-
     applicable items):

       ✔  Complete health record    ✔  History and Physical Exam

       ✔  Procedure Report          ✔  Laboratory Test Results

       ✔  Progress/Office Notes     ✔  Other test results

     Other Reports:          N/A



     I authorize the release of health records related to:

      NO   HIV status

      NO   Acquired Immunodeficiency Syndrome (AIDS) and/or AIDS

           related complex (ARC)

      NO   Alcohol and substance abuse treatment records.

     This authorization expires on      6/12/20xx    .
                                        (Expiration Date)
      Erik Mattson                      3/12/20xx
     (Patient/Legal Representative)       (Date Signed)
```

FIGURE 2–1 Authorization for Release of Information

Under the HIPAA Privacy Rule, patient information can be released without written authorization when:

- The patient record is subpoenaed.
- The information is needed to defend the physician in a lawsuit.
- There is a question of child abuse and, in some states, elder abuse.
- The patient is covered by Medicaid or workers' compensation health insurance programs.

In emergency situations, which is defined in most states as life-threatening, information may be released without authorization. When these circumstances exist, only enough information to satisfy the need for emergency treatment can be released.

Table 2–4

Release of Information Items	
Item	**Description**
Identification	Physician or agency name(s) and patient name, address, and date of birth
Time frame	Date of service, office visit, or hospital admission and discharge dates
Information to be released	Checklist of reports and special authorization statements
Purpose of disclosure	Self-explanatory
Date(s)	Date signed and expiration date
Signature(s)	Patient or legal representative

Release of Information for HIV, AIDS, or Alcohol and Drug Abuse

Information related to AIDS, positive HIV test results, and alcohol and drug or substance abuse can be highly prejudicial. Federal and state laws exist to provide an individual with additional safeguards concerning the release of such information. The patient must provide written authorization before the release of AIDS, HIV status, or alcohol or drug abuse information. Even the diagnostic and treatment codes for these conditions cannot be released unless the patient gives written consent.

The ROI authorization form in Figure 2–1 includes a section that gives the patient the opportunity to authorize the release of sensitive information. Before submitting claims that contain HIV, AIDS, or substance abuse information, the insurance billing specialist must be certain that the patient has signed a valid authorization.

Telephone Release of Information

The billing specialist receives phone calls related to the status of insurance claims. Telephone inquiries can come from the insurance company, the patient, or someone acting on behalf of the patient. Before releasing any information over the phone, the billing specialist tries to identify the caller.

Caller identification is a telephone service available in most locations. There is often a fee for this service. The insurance billing specialist must have a phone with a display console that automatically shows the name and number of the caller. The caller can block the transmission of the identification information, and the telephone console then displays the message *blocked* or *caller unknown*.

If the office does not use caller identification or if the caller's identification is blocked, reasonable steps must be taken to verify the identity of the caller. Ask the caller to identify the date of service, the type of service, and the nature of the problem. When the caller is not the patient or insurance company representative, ask for a written request. Another option is to take the caller's name and phone number. Return the call *only* when you are certain that the caller has a right to the information.

Any information given over the phone must be documented and kept in the patient's record. Include the date and time of the call, a summary of the information given, the name of the caller, and the name or initials of the insurance billing specialist.

When the caller is an attorney, *never* reveal any patient information via the telephone. Inform the attorney that he or she must submit the request in writing and accompany it with a valid release of information authorization signed by the patient or the patient's legal representative. Electronic requests submitted by or in the name of an attorney should be handled like a telephone request. Always respond to an attorney's request in writing with a copy of the communication filed in the patient's record.

Facsimile Release of Information

Facsimile (fax) machines are an efficient and effective way to move information from one location to another. Fax transmissions are particularly useful in a health care setting when a need arises to immediately communicate with other health care providers.

EXAMPLE

For a patient scheduled to see several physicians in a large group practice whose offices are in different locations, each physician can fax his or her findings as the patient moves from one appointment to the next.

The billing specialist can fax information to the insurance carrier in order to resolve reimbursement problems. Using fax transmissions, insurance carriers can quickly notify billing specialists about changes in coverage or claims-processing procedures.

Fax transmissions present unique confidentiality challenges. Questions such as who actually receives the fax, where the fax machine is located, and who has access to fax messages must be considered. Before faxing patient information, the insurance billing specialist should find answers to those questions. Figure 2–2 is a sample procedure for faxing patient information.

1. Before sending patient information via fax:

   - You must have a written authorization from the patient.

   - Call/ask the person who is requesting the information these questions:

     a. Do you have direct access to the fax messages?

     b. Where is the fax machine located?

     c. Is the fax machine location open to all employees, passers by, or others?

     d. How often are fax messages retrieved?

     e. Who distributes fax messages?

2. If you are satisfied with the security of the fax message, continue with Step 3. If you are not satisfied, call/ask the individual requesting the information to send a request in writing.

3. Complete the fax transmittal cover sheet.

   - In the Remarks section note the information sent.

   - Recheck all fax numbers before transmittal.

4. Enter the fax number and documents and wait until transmission is complete.

5. Retrieve the fax cover sheet when it is returned with the completed statement of receipt.

6. File the returned fax cover sheet in the patient's record.

Delmar/Cengage Learning

FIGURE 2–2 Procedure for Faxing Patient Information

```
                        NORTHERN CLINIC, INC.
                          714 Hennepin Road
                    Marquette, Rhode Island 55555
                      Telephone: (505)555-5555
                        FAX NO. 055—005-5555


    TO: _____     DATE: _____
         (Receiver's Name)

                                         TIME: _____
         _____         (AM or PM)
         (Receiver's Address)

    FAX NUMBER: _____

    FROM: _____
          (Your Name and Department)

    REMARKS: _____

             _____


    TO THE RECIPIENT: PLEASE FAX THIS COMPLETED STATEMENT TO
    THE SENDER. FAX NUMBER: 055-005-5555. THANK YOU.


    I, _____, received _____
                                    (pages with cover sheet)

    from_____ on _____ at _____.
                                    (date)      (time) AM/PM


    IF YOU HAVE RECEIVED THIS TRANSMITTAL IN ERROR, PLEASE
    NOTIFY THE SENDER IMMEDIATELY. PHONE: (505) 555-5555.

    RETURN THE INFORMATION BY FAX: 055-005-5555.

    THE INFORMATION IN THIS TRANSMISSION IS CONFIDENTIAL AND
    LEGALLY PRIVILEGED. THIS INFORMATION IS INTENDED ONLY FOR
    THE USE OF THE INDIVIDUAL OR ENTITY NAMED ABOVE.

    IF YOU ARE NOT THE INTENDED RECIPIENT, ANY DISCLOSURE,
    COPYING, DISTRIBUTION, OR ACTION TAKEN ON THE BASIS OF
    THIS INFORMATION IS STRICTLY PROHIBITED.
```

FIGURE 2–3 Fax Transmittal Cover Sheet

The fax cover sheet for all health care agencies must include a confidentiality statement. Figure 2–3 is a sample cover sheet that addresses the challenges of faxing patient information.

The American Health Information Management Association (AHIMA) has developed a practice brief that covers faxing patient information. This document is an excellent resource for billing specialists and other health professionals who transmit information via fax. To access the practice brief, go to the AHIMA website (www.ahima.org) and then search for the practice brief titled *Facsimile Transmission of Health Information*.

Internet and Electronic Release of Information

Electronic release of patient information includes Internet and e-mail communications. The HIPAA Privacy Rule and Security Rule *do not* expressly prohibit the use of either of these

Legal Aspects of Insurance Billing | 35

TABLE 2–5

Internet Security Measures	
Security Measure	**Description**
Access report(s)	Maintains an ongoing record of Internet communication of patient billing/medical information
Encryption	Transforms information into a form that is unreadable by unauthorized users
Firewalls	Hardware and software applications that control incoming and outgoing Internet transactions; they prevent unauthorized Internet access to the office's computer files while allowing office staff to use the Internet
User authentication	Assigning a unique identifier to individuals who communicate via the Internet
Written policies	Implementing and enforcing policies and procedures that address Internet transmissions of patient billing and medical information

methods. Both rules do require that health care agencies implement policies and procedures that protect against any tampering with and unauthorized disclosure of (or access to) protected health information.

The benefits of processing insurance claims via the Internet and other electronic methods are evident. The billing specialist can submit claims directly to insurance company data files. Billing software can be equipped with validation capabilities that flag an insurance claim when information is missing or inconsistent. In order to use the Internet for any patient-related applications, security safeguards must be in place. Table 2–5 identifies and describes Internet security measures. These precautions allow the insurance billing specialist to take advantage of this communication tool.

Billing specialists who send and receive patient information by e-mail must take the following actions to ensure that e-mails are secure:

- Protect his or her password.
- Never leave a message onscreen when the terminal is unattended.
- Double-check and/or verify the e-mail address of the intended recipient.
- Limit the content of the e-mail to the minimum information needed to achieve the purpose of the communication.
- Obtain automatic confirmation that the recipient received the e-mail.

Billing specialists must stay current with the standards, regulations, and laws that cover access to and the use and disclosure of patient information. The professional associations noted in Chapter 1 are excellent resources. In addition, HHS websites, including those for the Center of Medicare and Medicaid Services and the Office of Civil Rights, provide a wealth of information about the privacy and security of protected health information.

REINFORCEMENT EXERCISES 2–2

Provide a short answer for each statement or question.

1. List three general categories of confidential information.

   _____

   _____

   _____

2. Briefly describe the HIPAA Privacy Rule.

   _____

   _____

   _____

3. What is the meaning of the Privacy Rule phrase "minimum necessary"?

   _____

   _____

   _____

4. Discuss the difference(s) between the Privacy Rule and the Security Rule.

   _____

   _____

   _____

5. What do the initials ROI mean in the context of medical billing?

   _____

   _____

   _____

6. Which types of patient medical information require special consideration prior to release?

   HIV, AIDS, alcohol and
   substance records abuse

   _____

continued on the next page

continued from the previous page

7. What steps can be taken to verify caller identity prior to releasing information over the telephone?

Identify date of service, the type of service and name of problem, they not patient are written resp

8. When is it permissible to release patient information to an attorney?

Patient must sign

9. Identify confidentiality challenges associated with fax transmissions.

Who is actual received, where the fax located who is fax machen acced to coredard

10. Briefly describe encryption, firewalls, and user authentication as Internet security measures.

useedbie form by unauthred user Hadward safter control incomy outgary messay assign uniquidetifar to inducing who commcau via internr

INSURANCE FRAUD AND ABUSE LAWS

HIPAA made health care insurance billing fraud a federal offense. Federal law enforcement agencies are available to seek, find, prosecute, and punish any individual involved in insurance fraud and/or abuse. HIPAA also established a Fraud and Abuse Control Program. Under this program, three major federal agencies have active roles in investigating fraud and abuse. These federal agencies are the **Office of the Inspector General (OIG)**, which is part of **HHS**; the **Federal Bureau of Investigation (FBI)**; and the **Department of Justice (DOJ)**.

The OIG is responsible for cases associated with Medicare, Medicaid, workers' compensation, and other federal health care insurance programs. The OIG can levy fines on and exclude violators from receiving payment from federal programs. The FBI investigates fraud cases that involve either federal or private health insurance programs but does not take disciplinary action. The OIG and FBI refer fraud and abuse cases that fall under federal criminal law to the DOJ.

In order to help all sectors of the health care industry comply with HIPAA antifraud provisions, the OIG has issued compliance program guidelines. A billing compliance program

Delmar/Cengage Learning

FIGURE 2–4 Abbreviations Spoken Here!

allows physician offices to monitor the entire health insurance billing process. The purpose of a compliance program is to eliminate billing and coding errors. As an essential player in the billing process, the insurance billing specialist has a definite stake in eliminating errors and participating in the compliance program. Figure 2–4 shows an insurance billing specialist with visions of legal abbreviations dancing in her head.

Fraud

Although fraud and abuse are often used in the same context, they have different meanings and carry different penalties. The difference between fraud and abuse is the person's intent. Fraud is deliberate, and the person knows his or her actions are deceptive. Abuse presumes that there was no intent to be deceptive and that the errors are unplanned.

Medicare defines **fraud** as "the intentional deception or misrepresentation that an individual knows to be false or does not believe to be true and makes, knowing that the deception could result in some unauthorized benefit to himself/herself or some other person." HIPAA defines **health care fraud** as "knowingly and willfully [executing], or [attempting] to execute, a scheme or artifice—(1) to defraud any health care benefit program; or (2) to obtain, by means of false or fraudulent pretenses, representations, or promises, any of the money or property owned by, or under the custody or control of, a health care benefit program." Simply stated, fraud is an attempt to obtain something you are not entitled to have. Keep in mind that the attempt itself is fraud, regardless of whether any gain or benefit is realized.

Health insurance billing fraud usually means that someone is illegally attempting to collect insurance payments from government health insurance programs. Most health insurance billing fraud is targeted at the Medicare program. The Center for Medicare and Medicaid Services (CMS) is part of HHS. The CMS is responsible for managing Medicare. According to CMS guidelines, the person attempting fraud may be "a physician or other practitioner, a hospital or other institutional

TABLE 2–6

Fraudulent Activities
Fraudulent Diagnoses • Falsifying the diagnosis • Misrepresenting the diagnosis • Selecting a diagnosis based on reimbursement
Billing for Services Not Rendered • Equipment such as crutches and dressing changes • Hospital visits • Laboratory or other diagnostic tests • Cancelled or missed appointments • Phantom billing and billing for services rendered to patients who do not exist or who are deceased
Medical Coding Errors • Upcoding: selecting a diagnostic code based on reimbursement • Leveling: using the same code for all office visits • Unbundling: assigning individual medical or office visit codes to services or diagnoses that are covered by a single code

provider, a clinical laboratory or other supplier, an employee of any provider, a billing service, a beneficiary (patient), Medicare carrier employee (insurance company employee), or any person in a position to file a claim for Medicare benefits." The insurance billing specialist certainly qualifies as "any person in a position to file a claim for Medicare benefits."

Health insurance fraud activities fall under three main categories: fraudulent diagnoses, billing for services not rendered, and medical coding errors. Table 2–6 presents examples of fraudulent practices within each category.

The insurance billing specialist is responsible for submitting information about services provided, diagnoses, and medical codes to the appropriate insurance program. The billing specialist has a legal and ethical obligation to verify the accuracy of that information. The following scenarios illustrate this obligation.

EXAMPLE

Services Provided

Mrs. Yoha's bill lists charges for an office visit, six lab tests, and an EKG. "Sore throat" is the reason for the office visit. Because there appear to be more tests than needed for a sore throat complaint, the billing specialist discusses the claim with the supervisor, who checks the record for supporting documentation. There is none. Either the supervisor or the billing specialist talks to the physician. The physician insists that the tests were done, but the paperwork has been misplaced. The billing specialist does not submit an insurance claim for services until the documentation is available.

Accurate Diagnosis

The physician writes ulcerative colitis as the diagnosis for a new patient. The only test done was a complete blood count (CBC). Diarrhea is listed as the reason for the office visit. Because ulcerative colitis cannot be diagnosed with a CBC and a complaint of diarrhea, the billing specialist reviews the patient record for additional documentation that verifies the diagnosis. If no other supporting information is available, the physician either provides the information or changes the diagnostic statement. The billing specialist does not submit an insurance claim with a questionable diagnosis.

Medical Coding

The physician has circled cholecystitis (inflamed gallbladder) as the patient's diagnosis. The office manager has provided the insurance billing specialist with a list of physician-approved, frequently used medical codes. Cholecystitis with obstruction (574.91) is the only listed cholecystitis code. Because there is a significant difference in the payment for treating an inflamed gallbladder with obstruction versus one without obstruction, the insurance billing specialist reviews the patient record or asks the physician for clarification. The billing specialist does not submit an insurance claim unless the selected medical code is supported by the documentation in the patient record.

Fraud Prevention and Reporting Incentives

Insurance billing specialists can actively participate in fraud prevention as well as protect themselves from being drawn into any fraudulent behavior. Table 2–7 summarizes fraud prevention and protection strategies.

An employee of the insurance company, a health care agency, or the patient can report fraudulent activities. Under federal law, insurance companies and billing services are expected to report fraudulent billing practices. The federal government provides monetary incentives and rewards to help reduce or eliminate fraudulent practices.

TABLE 2–7

Fraud Prevention Strategies
Six Steps to Fraud Protection and Prevention
1. *Never* alter information in a patient medical record.
2. *Never* add a diagnosis to an insurance claim form that is not documented in the patient medical record.
3. *Never* add a procedure to an insurance claim form that is not documented in the patient medical record.
4. *Always* follow current billing and coding practices.
5. *Always* complete insurance claim forms fully and accurately.
6. *Always* ask for clarification when the documentation does not support the diagnosis or procedure.

The Federal False Claims Act provides financial incentives when suspected fraudulent activities are proven true. Any individual who reports the fraud may receive 15%–25% of any judgment.

EXAMPLE

In an actual case, a provider paid $500,000 in fines for submitting fraudulent claims to Medicare. The individual who reported the fraudulent claims scheme received between 15% and 25% of that $500,000 fine.

HHS has implemented a program that rewards anyone who alerts Medicare to possible acts of fraud and abuse. Individuals who report fraud and abuse in the Medicare program are eligible for rewards of up to $1,000. The reward is paid when the information is not already a part of an ongoing investigation and when the information helps recover Medicare funds.

Billing practices are now being monitored at every level— from the individual patient to government-sponsored fraud and abuse investigation agencies.

Penalties for Fraud

The civil, criminal, and administrative penalties associated with fraud are intended to punish and prevent fraud. These penalties range from requiring an office to implement an insurance billing compliance program to extensive fines and, in the worst cases, imprisonment. Health care providers, insurance companies, and billing services can also be excluded from all federally funded health care programs. Table 2–8 summarizes the civil, criminal, and administrative penalties connected with fraud.

TABLE 2–8

Penalties for Fraud
Administrative Penalties • Coding and billing educational activities • Exclusion from participation in Medicare and Medicaid programs
Civil Penalties • Monetary penalties, without imprisonment • $2,000 to $10,000 for each item or service of a fraudulent claim • Fine of three times the amount of a fraudulent claim
Criminal Penalties • Monetary penalties and/or imprisonment • No limits for monetary fines • Up to ten years in prison for knowingly and willingly carrying out or attempting to carry out a fraudulent scheme • Twenty years in prison if the fraudulent scheme results in serious bodily harm to a patient • Life in prison if the fraudulent scheme results in the death of a patient

REINFORCEMENT EXERCISES 2–3

Provide a short answer for each statement.

1. Briefly define fraud.

_____

_____

_____

2. Give two examples of health insurance fraud.

_____

_____

_____

3. List and describe the three types of information the insurance billing specialist should review for accuracy.

_____

_____

_____

Spell out these abbreviations.

1. HIPAA

Health insurance Portability and accountability act

2. OIG

Office of the inspector General

3. HHS

Department of Heath and human service

4. FBI

Federal Beeru of investigation

5. DOJ

Department of Juitud

6. CMS

center of mediaid and medica server

Abuse

The Medicare definition of **abuse** states, "Abuse involves actions that are inconsistent with accepted, sound medical, business, or fiscal practices . . . that directly or indirectly result in unnecessary costs to the [Medicare] program through improper payments." The difference between fraud and abuse is the person's intent. However, both fraud and abuse have the same result: They take money from the Medicare insurance program. Fraud is an intentional act; abuse is not.

> **EXAMPLE**
> A physician who orders an EKG on every Medicare patient solely to increase his or her income could be found guilty of fraud. A physician who consistently bills for the highest level of office visit because he or she spends a lot of time with patients can be found guilty of abuse.

In the first example, the physician is engaged in a deliberate attempt to make more money from Medicare. In the second example, the physician believes the time spent with the patient justifies billing the highest level of office visit. Unfortunately, he or she is using the wrong criteria. Office visits are paid based on the nature of the problem, not solely on the time spent with the patient.

Health insurance abuse activities fall under three main categories: inadvertent billing and coding errors; excessive charges for services, equipment, or supplies; and billing for services that are not medically necessary. Table 2–9 presents examples of abusive insurance practices for each category.

The insurance billing specialist is at higher risk for abuse than for fraud. Unintentional coding and billing errors that result in overpayment by Medicare or any insurance company may qualify as abuse.

TABLE 2–9

Health Insurance Abuse Activities
Billing and Coding Errors
• Billing errors that result in overpayment
• Billing Medicare for services covered by another insurance program
• Medical coding errors that result in overpayment
• Submitting claims for medically unnecessary services
• Using outdated criteria for selecting medical codes
Excessive Charges
• Billing for prescription refills
• Billing for telephone conversations with the patient
• Charging Medicare patients more than other patients
Unnecessary Services
• Excessive referrals to other health care practitioners
• Performing more tests than necessary to reach a diagnosis
• Scheduling follow-up visits that may not be necessary

Abuse Prevention and Reporting Incentives

The insurance billing specialist can protect him or herself from charges of insurance abuse by following current billing and coding guidelines. Outdated insurance billing and coding references increase the risk of abuse. The insurance billing specialist is well-advised to keep current on the yearly changes in ICD and CPT codes.

Insurance companies provide bulletins that describe acceptable and up-to-date insurance billing practices. Professional associations offer workshops and seminars that address changes in medical coding procedures. Government insurance programs routinely alert physicians' offices about changes that affect the insurance billing process. This information should be made available to the insurance billing specialist. If the employer does not routinely share these bulletins and updates, the insurance billing specialist must take the initiative and ask for the information.

The insurance billing specialist is in a unique position to help administrators and physicians identify potentially abusive practices. The following example illustrates this point.

> **EXAMPLE**
>
> The insurance billing specialist alerts the office manager that Medicare patients have more laboratory tests done than other patients. The office manager reviews the patients' records to identify reasons for the difference. The reasons could include the following:
>
> - Medicare patients' problems are more complex.
> - Tests are necessary to rule out various diagnoses.
> - Physicians are ordering all tests covered by Medicare.
>
> If the documentation in the patients' medical records supports the medical necessity of all lab tests, there is no cause for concern. However, if it appears that the tests are done because Medicare pays for them, the office manager discusses the situation with the physicians. The physicians must either provide documentation that supports the medical necessity of the lab tests or reduce the number of tests. In either event, the potential problem is resolved internally before it draws the attention of external reviewers.

The financial incentives for reporting abuse are more limited than the incentives for reporting fraud. Individuals who report suspected abusive practices are eligible for rewards of up to $1,000. The reward is paid when the information is not already a part of an ongoing investigation and when the information helps recover Medicare funds. Because the Federal False Claims Act addresses fraudulent activities, the reporting rewards identified in that act do not apply to abuse.

Penalties for Abuse

The penalties associated with abuse are intended to educate rather than punish. Administrative remedies are used to correct abusive practices. The usual penalties include educational sessions, recovering insurance overpayments, and withholding further insurance payments.

Educational sessions may focus on insurance billing practices, medical coding activities, and Medicare guidelines. Recovering insurance overpayments simply means that the organization must return all money received as a result of the abusive practice. Insurance payments can also be withheld or delayed until the abusive practice is discontinued.

REINFORCEMENT EXERCISES 2–4

Provide a short answer for each statement or question.

1. Briefly define abuse.

_____

_____

_____

2. What are the three main health insurance abuse categories?

_____

_____

_____

3. Name the usual penalties associated with abuse.

_____

_____

_____

4. What is the key difference between fraud and abuse?

_____

_____

_____

ABBREVIATIONS

Table 2–10 lists the abbreviations presented in this chapter.

TABLE 2–10

Abbreviations and Meanings	
Abbreviation	Meaning
CMS	Centers for Medicare and Medicaid Services
DOJ	Department of Justice
EPHI	electronic protected health Information
FBI	Federal Bureau of Investigation

continued on the next page

continued from the previous page

Abbreviations and Meanings	
Abbreviation	Meaning
HHS	Department of Health and Human Services
HIPAA	Health Insurance Portability and Accountability Act of 1996
OCR	Office of Civil Rights
OIG	Office of *the* Inspector General
PHI	protected health information
ROI	release of information

SUMMARY

The insurance billing specialist must be familiar with general medical-legal terms, ranging from confidentiality to fraud and abuse. Confidentiality is a principle that presumes that certain types of information are not shared with the public. The patient has control over the release of his or her confidential information. Release of information usually requires the patient's written authorization. The authorization form must clearly describe the information to be released. It is necessary to obtain the patient's written authorization in order to release alcohol and substance abuse, HIV, and AIDS information.

HIPAA established a set of national standards for the protection of certain health information. The HIPAA Privacy Rule gives individuals a federally protected right to control the use and release of their health information. The HIPAA Security Rule applies only to protected health information that is electronically stored and transmitted.

Insurance fraud is intentional; abuse is not. HIPAA makes health care insurance billing fraud a federal offense. Three main categories of health insurance fraud are:

- Submission of fraudulent diagnoses
- Billing for services not rendered
- Medical coding errors

Fraudulent billing and coding practices can result in serious civil and criminal penalties, ranging from monetary fines to imprisonment. There are financial incentives for reporting health insurance fraud.

Abuse includes actions that directly or indirectly result in financial gain. Health insurance abuse falls into three categories:

- Inadvertent billing and coding errors
- Excessive charges for services, equipment, or supplies
- Billing for services that are not medically necessary

The insurance billing specialist is at a higher risk for abuse than fraud and is in a unique position to help identify potentially abusive billing practices.

REVIEW EXERCISES

Definitions of Terms

Briefly define these legal terms and phrases.

1. Emancipated minor

   _____

   _____

   _____

2. Embezzlement

   _____

   _____

   _____

3. Subpoena

   _____

   _____

   _____

4. Subpoena duces tecum

   _____

   _____

   _____

5. Respondeat superior

   _____

   _____

   _____

6. Malpractice

   _____

   _____

   _____

7. Covered entities

   _____

   _____

   _____

8. Protected health information

_____

_____

_____

9. Workforce members

_____

_____

_____

10. Electronic protected health information

_____

_____

_____

Short Answer

1. List four examples of situations where patient information can be released without written authorization.

_____ Life _____

_____

_____

2. Describe the differences and similarities between health insurance fraud and abuse.

_____

_____

_____

3. Give an example of or briefly describe how the insurance billing specialist can verify the accuracy of the services provided, diagnoses, and medical codes.

_____

_____

_____

4. What is individually identifiable health information, as described in the HIPAA Privacy Rule?

_____

_____

_____

5. Give three examples of physical safeguards and three examples of technical safeguards, as described in the HIPAA Security Rule standards.

_____

_____

_____

Abbreviations Review

Spell out these abbreviations.

1. FBI _Fedral Beary of investigquin_

2. CMS _Center of medreud and midcare serve_

3. HIPAA _Health Insuren Portabilimy Accoutabiy Act_

4. OIG _office of the einspector gereal_

5. ROI _Realse of information_

Matching

Match each term in Column A with the appropriate item in Column B.

Column A	Column B	
a. civil penalty	1. billing fraud; federal offense	b
b. HIPAA	2. manages the Medicare program	e
c. criminal penalty	3. using medical codes to increase payments	d
d. upcoding	4. fines; exclusion from programs	a
e. CMS	5. fines; imprisonment	c

Comprehension Exercises

Identify each statement as an example of fraud or abuse.

1. Excessive charges for services, equipment or supplies. _abuse_

2. Billing for services never provided. _Fraudal_

3. Unbundling charges for laboratory tests. _Fraual_

4. Scheduling frequent follow-up visits that may not be necessary. _abuse_

5. Changing the date of service. _Fraudll_

6. Using outdated criteria for selecting medical codes. _abuse_

7. Upcoding. _fraudd_

8. Billing individual components of a treatment over several days when all treatment was provided in one visit. _Fraud_

9. Billing for calling in prescription refills. _abuse_

True or False

Mark each statement as true or false.

1. Incentives for reporting abuse are the same as incentives for reporting fraud.   ___f___

2. The Federal False Claims Act addresses fraudulent activities.   _____

3. Insurance payments can be withheld until an abusive practice is discontinued.   ___T___

4. Abuse is intended to take money from Medicare.   _____

5. Criminal penalties are used to punish those who engage in abusive practices.   _____

6. The insurance billing specialist may notice potentially abusive practices before the physician.   _____

INTERNET EXERCISE

Locate the Office of Civil Rights (OCR) privacy page at www.hhs.gov/ocr/privacy and then click How to File a Complaint.

1. List the languages available under the heading How to File a Health Information Privacy Complaint in Multiple Languages.
2. Click the Health Information Privacy Complaint Form Package and then find the address for the OCR's regional office in your state.

CRITICAL THINKING EXERCISES

1. Develop a confidentiality in-service training session for new employees.
2. Write a procedure that covers nursing and allied health students' access to protected health information.

WEBSITES

American Health Information Management Association: www.ahima.org
Centers for Medicare and Medicaid Services: www.cms.hhs.gov
Office of Civil Rights: www.hhs.gov/ocr
Office of the Inspector General (OIG): www.oig.hhs.gov

Introduction to Health Insurance

LEARNING OBJECTIVES

Upon successful completion of this chapter, the reader should have the knowledge to:

1. Describe and define health insurance and the health insurance industry.
2. Briefly explain all health insurance policy and health care provider terms and phrases presented in the chapter.
3. Differentiate between direct pay, indirect pay, and third-party reimbursement methods.
4. List and discuss the three third-party reimbursement methods presented in the chapter.
5. Differentiate between employer-sponsored health insurance plans, government-sponsored health care programs, and individual health insurance policies.
6. Describe the four government-sponsored health care programs presented in this chapter.
7. Identify similarities and differences among managed care organizations.

KEY TERMS

Accept assignment
Admitting physician
Assignment of benefits
Attending physician
Birthday rule
Capitation
Coordination of benefits (COB)
Co-payment (co-pay)
Coverage
Dependent
Direct pay
Employer-sponsored health insurance plan

Episode-of-care reimbursement
Exclusion
Exclusive provider organization (EPO)
Fee-for-service
Government-sponsored health care program
Group model
Health care provider
Health insurance
Health maintenance organization (HMO)

Independent practice association (IPA)
Indirect payer
Individual policy
Insurance policy
Integrated delivery system (IDS)
Managed care
Managed care organization (MCO)
Maximum allowable fee
Network model
Per capita
Policyholder

Preferred provider organization (PPO)	Pre-existing condition	Staff model
Preauthorization	Premium	Third-party payer
Precertification	Prepaid health	Third-party
Predetermination	plan	reimbursement
	Service provider	Waiver

OVERVIEW

This chapter provides a basic review of the health insurance industry and the historical factors that influenced the growth of the industry. This chapter answers questions such as these:

- What is health insurance?
- How does someone get health insurance?
- Who pays for health insurance?
- What do all those health insurance terms mean?

The information covered in this chapter is the foundation for subsequent chapters. The concepts, terms, and definitions presented here are used repeatedly throughout the text.

DEFINING HEALTH INSURANCE

Throughout our lives, we are exposed to all types of insurance: life insurance, which provides identified survivors with money in the event of our death; car insurance, which provides money to pay bills that arise from a car accident; and liability insurance, which provides money for bills that arise from our professional or personal actions. An **insurance policy** is the document that describes the situations covered by a particular type of insurance. An insurance policy is a legal contract between the individual and the company that provides the insurance. The policy sets forth the conditions of the contract and the cost of the contract. The cost of the contract, called a **premium**, is a fee paid at regular intervals by the policyholder.

In many ways, health insurance is no different. Health insurance provides money to pay bills generated by receiving health care related services. Situations covered by health insurance are described in the health insurance policy, the policy is a legal contract, and the cost of the contract is called the premium. **Health insurance**, therefore, is defined as a contract that provides money to cover all or a portion of the cost of medically necessary care.

Health insurance differs from other types of insurance in one important area: While the individual is almost always responsible for providing life, car, and liability insurance, health insurance is often provided to the individual as an employment benefit. In addition, the state and federal government are also involved in providing health insurance for certain populations: people over 65 years old, individuals receiving public assistance (welfare), and individuals with certain conditions, such as blindness and end-stage renal disease.

Health Insurance: Then and Now

Prior to the 1940s, most Americans paid their own medical bills. People were treated and cared for in their homes and were expected to pay for that care and treatment. This type of payment is called **direct pay**, which means that the patient or individual pays the physician or health care practitioner for provided services. Figure 3–1 illustrates the direct pay concept.

FIGURE 3–1 Direct Pay

Individuals who could not afford to pay were given essential treatment at no charge. It was during this time that various religious and fraternal groups provided health care services to the poor.

It is important to remember that prior to the 1940s, only the most serious illnesses were called to the physician's attention. Babies were born at home, with or without a midwife in attendance; everyday scrapes, bruises, and uncomplicated broken limbs were treated with home remedies; and hospitals were viewed as the place to go when you were sick enough to die. The family doctor routinely made house calls and would care for the citizens of a given community from birth to death.

Between the late 1920s and early 1940s, individuals began banding together to find ways to improve health care in local communities. As a result, contracts between a specific group of individuals and local hospitals and physicians were developed. Each member of the group paid a premium in order to be included in the contract. The contracts outlined the medical services available to group members and the fees that the physician or hospital would receive for providing the services. These contracts were known as **prepaid health plans**, the forerunners of current health maintenance organizations (HMOs). Prepaid health plans, including HMOs, are discussed in the "Managed Care" section of this chapter.

Beginning in the 1950s, rapid advances in medical care, technology, and medications set the stage for a more complex and costly health care environment. Hospitals became centers for disease treatment and surgical procedures as well as places to recover from illnesses. Physicians believed they could use their time more efficiently and treat more patients if the patients came to the physician rather than the physician going to the patients. As medical care became more centralized and costs increased, memberships in prepaid health insurance plans expanded.

Another factor influencing the growth of health insurance plans was the practice of employers offering health insurance coverage as a benefit of employment. This practice gave rise to **employer-sponsored health insurance plans**. With an employer-sponsored health insurance plan, the employer pays all or part of the premium to purchase health insurance for employees and their dependents. The increase in employer-sponsored health insurance plans can be traced to World War II. Because many employers had to comply with government-enforced pay scales, paid health insurance plans were used to recruit and retain good employees. As a result of these and other factors, the responsibility of paying for health insurance shifted from the individual to the employer.

Between 1965 and 1966, federal and state governments entered the health insurance industry by establishing **government-sponsored health care programs**. These programs—the Civilian Health and Medical Program of the Department of Veterans Affairs (CHAMPVA), Medicare, Medicaid, and TRICARE—were designed to provide health insurance to specific populations. Table 3–1 describes the original intent of these programs. Each program is discussed in detail in subsequent chapters.

Under employer- and government-sponsored health insurance plans, the employer or government agency negotiates a contract with an insurance company and pays all or part of the premium needed to maintain the contract. The insurance contract describes the individuals

TABLE 3–1

Government-Sponsored Health Care Programs	
Term	**Definition**
CHAMPVA	Federal health insurance program for spouses and dependents of veterans with service-connected disabilities or of veterans who died because of such disabilities
Medicaid	Combined federal/state health insurance program that covers people who meet specific financial need requirements; also called Medical Assistance Program
Medicare	Federal health insurance program for people aged 65 or older and retired on Social Security, railroad retirees, federal government retirees, individuals legally disabled for 24 months, and persons with end-stage renal disease (kidney failure)
TRICARE (CHAMPUS)	Civilian Health and Medical Program of the Uniformed Services; federal health insurance program for spouses and dependents of active-duty uniformed personnel and personnel who have died while on active duty and for retired personnel, including their spouses and dependents
Workers' Compensation	Health insurance program that requires employers to cover medical expenses and loss of wages for workers who develop job-related health problems; mandated by federal and state governments

FIGURE 3–2 Indirect Pay

included in the contract, the medical services covered by the contract, and the amount of money that the physician or hospital receives for providing the services. When an individual receives a covered service, the insurance company reimburses the physician or hospital. This is known as **indirect** or **third-party payer**.

Payment for medical services is often negotiated between the employer or government agency, the insurance company, and the physician or health care provider with the patient in the role of bystander. Figure 3–2 illustrates this point.

Employer- and government-sponsored health insurance plans remove the individual from the direct responsibility of either purchasing an **individual policy** or paying the full cost for health care services.

REINFORCEMENT EXERCISES 3–1

Provide a short answer for each statement.

1. List the similarities between health insurance and other types of insurance.

_____

_____

_____

continued on the next page

continued from the previous page

Provide the correct term for each insurance-related definition.

1. Fee paid to maintain the insurance contract _____

2. Document that describes the conditions of the insurance contract _____

3. Provides money to cover all or a portion of the cost of health care services _____

Write the correct term after each definition:

direct pay, indirect pay, individual policy, prepaid health plan

1. Forerunners of current health maintenance organizations.

   Prepaid Health plan

2. Patient pays for care.

   direct pay

3. Self-provided health insurance.

   Individual Policy

4. Another term for third-party payer.

   Indirect pay

Briefly describe each phrase.

1. Employer-sponsored health insurance plan

   Employer paid all or part of the premiums of
   insurance policy by employee

2. Government-sponsored health care program

   medicare, medicaid CHAMPVA, pror

MANAGED CARE

Managed care is broadly defined as any method of organizing health care providers that gives people access to high-quality, cost-effective health care. Managed care can be traced to the early 1900s, when large industries—such as railroad, lumber, and mining—established prepaid medical plans to serve employee health care needs.

One of the first nonindustrial prepaid programs was the rural farmers' cooperative health plan established in 1929 by Michael Shadid. He sold shares for $50 each to build a new hospital, and each shareholder was entitled to receive discounted medical care. In addition, each member of family paid annual dues to cover the cost of medical care, surgery, and house calls. The health plan grew, and in 1934, the cooperative's medical staff was partially supported by 600 family memberships.

In the 1930s and 1940s, a number of prepaid group plans were formed that served a broader population and were supported by the local business community. The plans prospered, even though they often faced opposition from the majority of physicians. These predecessors of today's health maintenance organization (HMO) models included:

- Group Health Association in Washington, D.C. (1937)
- Kaiser Permanente Medical Care Program in California (1942)
- Group Health Cooperative of Puget Sound (1947)
- Health Insurance Plan of Greater New York (1947)
- Group Health Plan of Minneapolis (1957)

In these early prepaid group plans, physicians shared the risk of financing health care. Physicians took the chance that they could treat their patients within budgeted costs. If a patient's treatment exceeded the budget, the physician absorbed the extra costs.

Early prepaid group plans also reduced the incentive to hospitalize patients. Because a single premium covered inpatient and outpatient care, physicians treated patients on an outpatient basis when appropriate and avoided unnecessary and expensive hospitalizations.

During the 1970s, **health maintenance organizations (HMOs)** were the predominant type of managed care plan. An HMO is a prepaid group practice that can be sponsored and operated by the government, insurance companies, consumer groups, employers, labor unions, physicians, and hospitals. An HMO provides a specific range of inpatient and ambulatory health care services to its members. In 1973, President Richard Nixon signed the HMO Act, which made it easier to set up and operate an HMO. The HMO Act of 1973 attempted to support the development of HMOs and to ensure some degree of quality care.

During the 1980s, managed care programs were a small segment of the health insurance industry. In the 1990s, managed care became a dominant player, and today, industry estimates indicate that managed care programs handle approximately 90% of all medical bills.

The primary objective of managed health care programs is to control health care costs. Managed care programs try to achieve this goal by:

- Obtaining reduced fees for services provided to members of the managed care program
- Controlling patient access to specialized care
- Eliminating unnecessary services
- Integrating health care delivery and payment systems through prepaid fees
- Establishing fixed rates for provider (and hospital) services

Employers and patients usually benefit most from managed health care. Employers benefit because employee health insurance costs are less with managed care plans than with fee-for-service plans. Patients benefit because insurance co-payments are generally lower for managed care plans than for traditional health insurance plans. In addition, most managed care plans promote health education and preventive health care practices, such as well-child visits, regular physical exams, smoking cessation programs, and diabetes management classes. The education and prevention approach is intended to increase quality of life and lessen the demand for more expensive health-related services.

The disadvantages of managed care lie primarily in the area of choice. Choice is controlled by financial considerations because most managed care plans will only pay for services rendered by providers who are part of or contract with the plan. In addition to financial constraints, most managed care plans do not allow self-referral to specialists. If an individual wants to see a specialist, the family physician or internist must generate a referral. Because of these limitations, some patients believe they have little control over their treatment options. It is important to note that an individual does have the option of seeing any provider, as long as the individual is able and willing to pay for the services.

In today's health care environment, all prepaid health plans are called **managed care organizations (MCOs)** or managed care systems. This text uses *managed care organization* as the generic term for prepaid health plans.

MANAGED CARE ORGANIZATIONS

Three general models of managed care organizations exist: health maintenance organizations (HMOs), preferred provider organizations (PPOs), and integrated delivery systems. In the past, distinguishing one type of managed care organization from another was fairly easy. HMOs, PPOs, and traditional fee-for-service plans were distinct and mutually exclusive. Although these distinctions have become somewhat blurred, with each type of organization attempting to incorporate the best features of the others, differences do exist.

Providers who participate or who are part of an MCO are reimbursed for services rendered to members of the manage care plan. There are four basic types of provider reimbursement: salaried, capitation, fee-for-service, and negotiated or discounted fee. Table 3–2 describes these reimbursement methods.

In all types of MCO models, the member pays a premium to the MCO and in return is eligible to receive services from providers who participate in the program. The premium may be paid by the individual, an employer, or a government agency.

Health Maintenance Organization Models

There are four general types of HMO model: the staff model, the independent practice association (IPA), the group model, and the network model.

Staff Model

In a **staff model HMO**, the HMO operates and staffs the facility or facilities where members receive treatment. All premiums and other revenues accrue to the HMO. Physicians and other providers receive a salary and other incentives, which may include profit sharing. In addition to comprehensive medical coverage, staff model HMOs frequently offer preventive care and patient

TABLE 3–2

Provider Reimbursement Methods	
Method	Description
Salaried	Providers, including physicians, are employed by the MCO; benefits include malpractice insurance, life insurance, a retirement plan, and incentives for increased productivity
Capitation	Applies primarily to physician providers, who receive a set fee per month per enrolled member, regardless of the number of patient visits or frequency of services provided
Fee-for-service	Providers are reimbursed for each individual service
Negotiated or discounted fee	Similar to fee-for-service, except that providers agree to treat members (enrollees) of a managed care plan for a reduced fee

education programs to their members. Staff model HMOs usually have more overhead costs than other models because they maintain their own facilities.

Independent Practice Association (IPA)

An **independent practice association (IPA)** is an HMO that contracts directly with physicians who continue to practice in their private offices. IPA physicians are compensated by various reimbursement methods, including capitation, fee-for-service, and discounted fee-for-service. Refer to Table 3–2 for a description of these reimbursement methods.

IPA HMOs usually have a large network of physicians who agree to treat IPA members. The IPA also contracts with other providers, such as hospitals and laboratories, and pays them on a fee-for-service basis.

Unlike staff model HMOs, independent practice associations do not have the costs associated with maintaining a facility. Because IPAs usually have a large physician network, they have less control over physicians' practice patterns. However, IPA members have a greater choice of primary care physicians.

Group Model

A **group model HMO** establishes contracts with physicians who are organized as a partnership, professional corporation, or other association. The group model HMO compensates the medical group for contracted services at a negotiated rate. The medical group is responsible for compensating its physician members and contracting with hospitals for patient care.

Network Model

A **network model HMO** contracts with more than one physician group, and it may contract with single- and multi-specialty groups. Any number of group practices, IPAs, and staff models can be joined together by a management HMO to form a network model HMO. The different groups are coordinated to allow patients to use any physician within the network. Each physician works out of his or her own office and may provide care for individuals who are not part of the HMO.

Preferred Provider Organization (PPO)

A **preferred provider organization (PPO)** is an MCO that contracts with a group of providers, who are called preferred providers, to offer services to the MCO's members. The preferred providers are paid a **maximum allowable fee**, which is the most a PPO will pay the physician or other health care provider for a given service; a discounted fee-for-service; or a capitation fee. Providers are willing to accept a reduced payment in return for a high patient volume.

The PPO encourages members to seek services from the preferred providers by eliminating or reducing the member's co-payment. If a member elects to receive services from a nonparticipating provider, the member must pay a higher co-payment. PPOs have grown in popularity because they provide the benefits of HMOs in reducing health care costs, and they preserve the ability of the individual to choose a provider.

Exclusive Provider Organization (EPO)

An **exclusive provider organization (EPO)** is similar to a PPO in that the MCO contracts with health care providers to obtain services for members. However, EPOs restrict members to the participating providers for all health care services. If an EPO member receives services from a non-EPO provider, the member is responsible for paying the bill. Employers whose primary objective is to reduce health care benefit costs usually select an EPO managed care system.

Employees are more likely to accept the restrictions of an EPO because the employer is paying for the health care benefit at little or no cost to the employee.

Integrated Delivery System

An **integrated delivery system (IDS)** is an MCO that brings together physicians, physician groups, hospitals, HMOs, PPOs, insurance companies, management services, and employers to integrate all aspects of patient care into one comprehensive system. In addition to basic health care services, the system may include physician services, hospitalization, dental care, vision care, prescription drugs, billing services, and workers' compensation.

REINFORCEMENT EXERCISES 3–2

Fill in the blank.

1. The primary objective of _managed Health care program_ is to control health care costs.

2. A(n) _Hmo_ is a prepaid group practice.

3. _MCOs_ is a generic term for prepaid health plans.

4. The _____ attempted to support the development of HMOs and ensure quality care.

5. The main disadvantage of managed care is in the area of _____.

6. Most managed care plans do not allow _Self refferal_ to specialists.

Briefly describe or define the listed HMOs.

1. group model

   _____

2. independent practice association

   _____

3. network model

   _____

4. staff model

   _____

HEALTH INSURANCE TERMINOLOGY

Like any other specialized industry, the health insurance industry has a unique vocabulary. Establishing a basic understanding of the more commonly used health insurance and billing terms and phrases is essential for developing a successful career in this dynamic field. Commonly used terms and phrases are categorized as health insurance policy terms and health care provider terms.

Health Insurance Policy Terms

A **health insurance policy** is a legal contract between an individual or a group of individuals and a company or government program that describes how the medical bills of the individual or group will be paid. As a legal document, a health insurance policy contains terms that are unique to this type of document. The health insurance policy affects the individual or group who purchases the policy, the company or governmental agency that sells or provides health insurance policies, and physicians and other providers who receive insurance payments.

Health insurance policy terms are organized and described as they apply to insurance policy purchasers, insurance companies, payment, and the insurance policy itself. Physician- and provider-related terms are discussed later in this chapter.

Terms for Insurance Policy Purchasers and Insurance Companies

In the retail/wholesale industry, individuals or groups who purchase something may be called buyers, customers, owners, or clients. The health care industry also has a variety of terms associated with those who purchase health insurance policies. These terms include designations for the actual purchaser of the health insurance policy—the **policyholder**—and designations for individuals who are allowed to use the insurance policy, such as **dependents**. Table 3–3 lists the health insurance policy terms associated with the purchase, ownership, and use of the policy.

The insurance company or government program that sells or provides health insurance policies is also described by a variety of terms. The terms are listed and defined in Table 3–4. Note that the first three terms are used interchangeably.

TABLE 3–3

Terms Associated with the Purchase, Ownership, and Use of a Health Insurance Policy	
Term	Definition
Applicant	Individual applying for health insurance
Dependent	Person(s) financially supported by the insured (i.e., spouse, children, and others as described in the policy)
Group contract	Health insurance policy purchased by an organization or corporation that covers a defined group of individuals and eligible dependents (e.g., the employees of an organization/corporation or members of a union or professional association)
Individual contract	Health insurance purchased by an individual; usually includes dependents
Insured	Person or organization that purchases the health insurance and is protected against financial loss caused by illness
Member, policyholder, recipient, subscriber	Other terms for *insured*
Personal contract	Another name for *individual contract*

TABLE 3–4

Health Insurance Company Terms	
Term	Definition
Insurance carrier	Insurance company that sells the health insurance policy and administers the terms of the policy
Insurance company	Organization that sells health insurance policies; also known as *insurance carrier* or *insurer*
Insurer	Another term for *insurance carrier*
Private insurance carrier	Nongovernmental insurance company (e.g., Aetna Insurance, Metropolitan Insurance, and Wausau Insurance); also known as a *commercial insurance carrier*
Third-party payer	Individual or corporation that pays all or part of a patient's medical bills; the insurance company/carrier

REINFORCEMENT EXERCISES 3–3

Provide a short answer for each statement or question..

1. Briefly describe the term "insured."

_____

_____

_____

2. List three additional terms for "insured."

_____

_____

_____

3. What is a dependent?

_____

_____

_____

4. Briefly describe the term "insurance carrier."

_____

_____

_____

continued on the next page

continued from the previous page

5. List two additional terms for insurance carrier.

_____

_____

_____

6. Aetna Insurance is an example of what type of insurance carrier?

_____

_____

_____

Terms Related to the Policy

Health insurance policy terms include general terms such as **premium** (the fee paid to the insurance company for the health insurance policy) and terms related to **coverage**, which identifies the medical conditions that may or may not be included in the insurance policy. Coverage terms range from straightforward **exclusions**—conditions not covered by the policy—to **pre-existing conditions**, which are vaguely identified as problems the individual had before the insurance policy was in effect.

While every insurance policy has unique clauses and conditions defined in the policy, some terms are commonly used in most insurance policy documents. General health insurance policy terms are described in Table 3–5. Terms related to coverage are listed in Table 3–6.

TABLE 3–5

Health Insurance Policy General Terms	
Term	**Definition**
Premium	Fee paid to the insurance company to keep the health insurance policy active; paid monthly, quarterly, or annually by the insured (individual) or group
Grace period	Number of days allowed between the premium due date and cancellation of health insurance coverage; usually 10 to 30 days
Guaranteed renewable	Insurance company must renew the health insurance policy as long as the premiums are paid; renewal may be limited by age or may be for life
Conditionally renewable	Insurance company may refuse to renew the health insurance policy at the end of a payment period; reasons stated in the policy often include age or employment status
Optionally renewable policy	Insurance company may or may not renew the health insurance policy on a specified date; may increase rates and decrease coverage
Cancelable policy	Insurance company may cancel the health insurance policy at any time for any reason
Noncancelable policy	Insurance company must renew the health insurance policy; the policy may have age-related limitations

TABLE 3–6

Health Insurance Coverage Terms	
Term	**Definition**
Benefit	Amount paid by the insurance company for covered medical expenses; either a percentage of the charge or a specific dollar amount; may be paid to the insured or to the health care provider
Hospital benefit	Amount paid by the insurance company for hospital expenses; either a percentage of the charge or a specific dollar amount; may be paid to the insured or to the hospital
Surgical benefit	Amount paid by the insurance company for expenses related to a surgical procedure; either a percentage of the charge or a specific dollar amount; may be paid to the insured or to the health care provider
Major medical benefit	A fixed amount of money available for the lifetime of the insured and any dependent; pays for unusually large medical expenses resulting from continued illness or serious injury
Extended care benefit	Amount paid by the insurance company for nursing facility or long-term care expenses
Exclusions	Situations that are not covered by a health insurance policy; examples may include self-inflicted injury, work-related injury, and injuries suffered during military service; expenses arising from exclusions are not paid by the insurance company
Pre-existing conditions	Health conditions that were treated or existed before the individual was covered by the health insurance policy; expenses arising from pre-existing conditions are not usually paid by the insurance company
Waiting period	Period of time before specified illnesses or accidents are covered by the insurance policy; expenses arising from illnesses or accidents during the waiting period are not paid by the insurance company until the waiting period has expired; also known as an *elimination period*
Waiver	An attachment to the insurance policy that excludes conditions that would otherwise be covered by the insurance policy; expenses arising from conditions identified in a waiver are not paid by the insurance company

Exclusion, pre-existing condition, and *waiver* describe conditions not covered by the insurance policy. Each term applies to specific circumstances.

Exclusions are part of most health insurance policies and address conditions that are often covered by other types of insurance. Because work-related injuries are covered by workers' compensation insurance and military-service-related injuries are often covered by veterans' health insurance, most insurance companies exclude those injuries from coverage.

Pre-existing conditions are specific to the insured and are not usually listed in the insurance policy. The policy contains general language that indicates noncoverage of pre-existing conditions.

> **EXAMPLE**
>
> MaryAnn is a new employee of Erika Electric Company and is eligible for health insurance. Before (and since) joining the company, she has been treated for bleeding ulcers. Erika Electric's health insurance carrier may, under the pre-existing condition clause, deny coverage for treatment MaryAnn receives for her bleeding ulcer. Some insurance policies allow the pre-existing condition to be covered if the condition does not recur for a certain amount of time, such as one year.

A **waiver** (sometimes called a rider) is a specific attachment or addition to the health insurance policy that excludes covered conditions. The waiver may apply to a specific individual or specific group that is part of the insurance plan. Waivers are often used to protect the insurance company from paying out large claims.

> **EXAMPLE**
>
> Rodney is purchasing health insurance, and he has a strong family history of colon cancer. His current rectal exams are normal. The insurance agent tells Rodney that a waiver excluding coverage for colon cancer treatment lowers the monthly premiums.

REINFORCEMENT EXERCISES 3–4

Provide a short answer for each item.

1. The fee paid to keep the health insurance policy active.

   _____

   _____

   _____

2. The amount paid by the insurance company for a covered medical expense.

   _____

   _____

   _____

3. An attachment to the insurance policy that excludes conditions otherwise covered by the policy.

   _____

   _____

   _____

continued on the next page

continued from the previous page

4. Conditions not covered by the insurance policy.

_____

_____

_____

5. Briefly describe the difference between grace period and waiting period.

_____

_____

_____

6. Define the phrase "major medical benefit."

_____

_____

_____

Terms Related to Payment

Health insurance policy terms associated with paying the medical bills are listed and defined in Table 3–7.

TABLE 3–7

Health Insurance Payment Terms	
Term	**Definition**
Assignment of benefits	Permission granted by the insured that allows the insurance company to send payments directly to the physician, health care provider, hospital, or nursing facility
Claim	Request for payment of a covered medical expense; sent to the insurance company; may be submitted by the insured or by the health care provider
Time limit	Number of days allowed to submit a claim
Deductible	Specified amount of money that the insured must pay for covered medical expenses before the insurance policy begins to pay; usually an annual amount per individual or family
Coordination of benefits	Health insurance policy clause that applies to an individual covered by more than one medical insurance policy; requires that the combined benefits paid by the policies do not exceed 100% of the medical expenses

continued on the next page

continued from the previous page

Primary payer	Term used to describe which health insurance policy will pay first when an individual is covered by more than one health insurance policy
Secondary payer	Term used to describe which health insurance policy will pay second when an individual is covered by more than one health insurance policy
Preauthorization	Determination of whether a specific service or treatment is medically necessary and covered by the insurance policy; required by many insurance companies
Precertification	Determination of whether a specific treatment or service is covered by the insurance policy; required by many insurance companies
Predetermination	Determination of the potential dollar amount the insurance company will pay for a specific treatment or service
Reimbursement	Receiving payment for services rendered

The phrase **accept assignment** is used to identify physicians and providers who accept the benefit paid by the insurance company as payment in full for a specific service. If there is a difference between the insurance company's benefit and the provider's charge, the patient does not have to pay that difference.

> **EXAMPLE**
> Medical Health Insurance, Inc., pays $45 for brief office visits for services such as follow-up care for a non-life-threatening condition (e.g., psoriasis). Sara has health insurance through this company, and her dermatologist charges $50 for a brief office visit. The dermatologist accepts the insurance company's benefit for brief office visits. As long as Sara assigns the insurance benefit to the dermatologist, the $45 is accepted as payment in full.

The phrase **assignment of benefits** is used to identify who actually receives the insurance payment.

> **EXAMPLE**
> Juanita's physician's office submits insurance claims for the patients. The insurance clerk asks Juanita to sign an assignment of benefits authorization form. The clerk explains that by signing the authorization, Juanita's insurance company will send the insurance payment directly to the physician's office.

It is important to remember that Juanita does not have to assign the insurance benefit to the physician. The insurance company will send the payment to Juanita unless she has assigned the benefit to the physician.

Whether benefits are assigned to the provider or retained by the patient, the patient or his or her legal representative is responsible for ensuring that the medical bill is paid. Exceptions include prepaid health plans, such as those provided by HMOs, and capitation reimbursement, whereby the insurance company automatically sends the insurance payment directly to the provider.

The **birthday rule** determines the primary payer when the patient is a child living with both parents and each parent carries health insurance. Under the birthday rule, the primary payer is the parent whose birth month and date comes earlier in a calendar year. Only the month and date are considered under the birthday rule. Therefore, a parent with a February birth month would take precedence over a parent with a December birth month. If both birthdays fall in the same month, the birth date is used to determine which insurance company is the primary payer. Therefore, a February 1st birth date takes precedence over a February 5th birth date. If both birthdays fall on exactly the same month and date, the policy that has been in effect the longest is considered primary.

Demographics show that most husbands are older than their wives. Therefore, the birth year is disregarded in order to prevent a disproportionate number of primary payer designations being assigned to men's insurance policies.

Coordination of benefits (COB) applies when the individual is covered by more than one insurance policy. Billing decisions are made so the total amount of money paid by all insurance companies does not exceed the total bill. Figure 3–3 illustrates coordination of benefits.

EXAMPLE

Lisa has health insurance with her employer and is also covered by her husband's health plan. Both policies pay 80% of the bill. Lisa currently has a medical bill for $100. Submission of claims must be coordinated between Lisa's policy and her husband's policy so that only one company pays the 80%. If Lisa submitted the same bill to both companies and received 80% from each one, she would receive more money than the total bill.

Co-payment, also called **co-pay**, is defined as the dollar or percentage amount that the patient must pay the provider for each visit. The majority of insurance policies, including most issued by government-sponsored programs and HMOs, require some type of patient co-payment. If possible, it is good practice to collect the co-payment at the time of service.

WITH COORDINATION OF BENEFITS	WITHOUT COORDINATION OF BENEFITS
STATEMENT	STATEMENT
Balance Due.................$100.00	Balance Due.................$100.00
Lisa's Insurance	Lisa's Insurance
80% of $100.............$ 80.00	80% of $100.............$ 80.00
Balance Due.............$ 20.00	
Husband's Insurance	Husband's Insurance
100% of balance.........$ 20.00	80% of $100.............$ 80.00
TOTAL RECEIVED.........$100.00	TOTAL RECEIVED.........$160.00

FIGURE 3–3 Coordination of Benefits

A fixed dollar amount co-payment is exactly that: The patient must pay a fixed amount for each episode of service or office visit.

EXAMPLE

Victoria's private insurance company requires a $20 co-payment for every office visit. Her last appointment included four separate lab tests, and the total bill was $200. The insurance billing specialist collected the $20 co-payment from Victoria and then billed the remaining $180 to the insurance company.

With percentage co-payments, the patient pays a fixed percentage of the total bill.

EXAMPLE

Louis has health insurance with 80/20 coverage: The insurance company pays 80% of the bill, and Louis is responsible for the other 20%. Louis completes his annual visit, which costs $100. He stops at the insurance billing desk and assigns the benefit to the physician. The insurance billing specialist tells Louis that the insurance company pays $80 for the visit, and Louis is responsible for the remaining $20.

Other common percentage co-payments include 90/10—which means that the insurance company pays 90% and the patient pays 10%—and 50/50, with the insurance company and the patient paying an equal share of the medical bill.

Preauthorization, precertification, and predetermination are activities that help determine if the insurance company will pay the bill. **Preauthorization** determines the medical necessity of the treatment.

EXAMPLE

Ling's mother and sister died from ovarian cancer. She wants to have an oophorectomy (removal of the ovaries) as a preventive measure for ovarian cancer. Ling does not know if her health insurance covers oophorectomy as a preventive procedure. Ling or the billing specialist contacts the insurance company representative to find out if the procedure qualifies as an authorized medical necessity.

Precertification identifies whether a treatment is covered by an insurance policy.

EXAMPLE

Helen wants to have the bags under her eyes removed. She believes that this problem makes her look older and prevents career advancement. Helen meets with a surgeon who assures her that surgery will correct the problem. Helen or the billing specialist contacts the insurance company to verify whether the surgery is covered.

Many insurance companies require preauthorization or precertification. The term "preauthorization" is sometimes used to include the determination of medical necessity and insurance coverage for a specified treatment.

Predetermination, a function of the billing department, provides an estimated insurance payment for a given treatment. The insured is responsible for paying the balance.

EXAMPLE

Terrell is scheduled for a total hip replacement that costs about $1,000. Prior to surgery, the billing specialist contacts the insurance company and learns that Terrell's insurance covers 90% ($900) of the bill. Terrell is informed that he is responsible for the $100 balance.

REINFORCEMENT EXERCISES 3–5

Provide short answer for each statement or question.

1. A request for payment of a covered expense is a(n) _____.

2. Determination of medical necessity and insurance coverage of a particular treatment is known as _____.

3. Determination of insurance policy coverage is called _____.

4. Determination of the potential dollar amount that will be paid for a particular treatment is known as _____.

5. Receiving payment for services rendered is called _____.

6. What is the difference between assignment of benefits and accepting assignment?

   _____

   _____

   _____

7. What is the difference between coordination of benefits and co-payment?

   _____

   _____

   _____

8. What is the birthday rule? Give an example.

   _____

   _____

   _____

Health Care Provider Terms

At one time, the physician was the primary (if not sole) provider of medical care to individuals, who were always called patients. Today, other professionals provide many health services to individuals, who are called patients, clients, residents, or recipients. Nurse practitioners, nurse midwives, physician assistants, dietitians, physical therapists, medical assistants, and pharmacists are just a few examples of other health care professionals now providing care or services.

The phrase **health care provider** is the generic term for anyone who provides health or medical services to persons who need such services.

The health insurance industry uses a variety of titles and terms that refer to the health care provider. These terms range from the obvious "physician" and "surgeon" to the vague phrase **service provider**, which can be interpreted as anyone from an occupational therapist to a nursing facility aide. Health insurance may pay for services rendered by other health care professionals. Table 3–8 describes insurance policy terms that refer to health care providers. Terms and phrases that require additional explanation and examples are discussed after the table presentation.

TABLE 3–8

Health Insurance Provider Terms	
Term	Definition
Admitting physician	Physician who arranges the patient's hospital admission; may not be responsible for patient's care during the hospital stay
Attending physician	Physician responsible for the patient's care during the hospital stay
Case manager	Health care professional who coordinates the care of patients with long-term problems
Group practice	Three or more health care providers who share equipment, supplies, and personnel; usually refers to a physician group practice
Health care specialist	Health care provider other than the primary care physician; may refer to physician specialist or others such as an optometrist, a podiatrist, or a chiropractor
In-network provider	A health care professional who provides services to individuals covered by a particular health insurance policy and who accepts the insurance company's approved fee for each service; also known as a participating provider
Limited license practitioner	Nonphysician health care professional licensed to perform specific services; examples include clinical social workers, clinical psychologists, and psychologists
Nonparticipating provider	A health care professional who does not contract with insurance companies and does not accept an insurance company's approved fee for services; also known as an out-of-network provider
Out-of-network provider	Another term for nonparticipating provider
Participating provider	Another term for in-network provider
Physician	Health care professional licensed to practice as a medical doctor (MD) or an osteopathic doctor (DO)
Physician specialist	Physician who provides health care services related to a specialty or subspecialty, such as cardiology, oncology/hematology, endocrinology, or gastroenterology

continued on the next page

continued from the previous page

Health Insurance Provider Terms	
Term	**Definition**
Physician extender	Nonphysician health care professional licensed by the state to perform specific health related activities; includes physician assistants, nurse anesthetists, nurse practitioners, and nurse midwives
Primary care manager	TRICARE term for primary care physician
Primary care physician	Physician responsible for providing all routine health care and determining the need for referrals to physician specialists; usually includes family practice, internal medicine, and pediatric physicians
Referring physician	Physician who arranges for the patient to see another physician or health care provider

The insurance billing specialist must give careful attention to the terms "admitting physician" and "attending physician." The **admitting physician** arranges for the patient's admission to the hospital. The admitting physician is entitled to receive reimbursement for the services provided to the patient as part of the admission process. When the admitting physician *does not* treat the patient throughout the hospital stay, the admitting physician is not entitled to additional reimbursement.

The **attending physician** is the physician responsible for the patient's care during the hospital stay. If the attending physician *did not* provide services during the admission process, the attending physician should not bill for admission services.

REINFORCEMENT EXERCISES 3–6

Briefly define each term.

1. Case manager

_____

_____

_____

2. Health care specialist

_____

_____

_____

continued on the next page

continued from the previous page

3. Primary care manager

_____

_____

_____

4. Primary care physician

_____

_____

_____

5. Admitting physician

_____

_____

_____

6. Attending physician

_____

_____

_____

7. Describe the difference between a participating provider and a nonparticipating provider.

_____

_____

_____

PAYING THE BILL WITH HEALTH INSURANCE

As previously defined, a health insurance policy is a contract that provides money to cover all or a portion of the cost of medically necessary care. The contract may be between the employer and the insurance company, the government program and the insurance company, or the individual and the insurance company. In order for a medical bill to be paid, someone must notify the insurance company that services have been rendered.

During the early days of health insurance, physicians and hospitals submitted the claims to the insurance company. Health care providers viewed this as a service to the patient and as a way to ensure that the medical bill would be paid. The patient would sign the appropriate document that allowed the insurance company to pay the provider. As previously defined, this is called assignment of benefits.

As more insurance companies entered the health insurance market and insurance policies became more complex, many health care providers stopped submitting claims for the patient. Physicians saw this as a way to reduce administrative costs. As a result, the number of unpaid medical bills increased. Patients could pay all or part of the medical bill at the time of service, submit the claim, receive payment from the insurance company, and keep the money.

In the late 1980s, in order to ensure reimbursement for services rendered, physicians and other health care providers resumed submitting claims to health insurance companies. Also, federal regulations mandated that providers must file claims for Medicare recipients. Receiving payment from someone other than the patient—that is, the insurance company—is called **third-party reimbursement** or third-party payment. Third-party reimbursement methods include fee-for-service, episode of care, and capitation.

Fee-for-Service

Fee-for-service, charging a price or fee for each individual service, is the traditional reimbursement method. Under this method, every service is itemized and charged to the patient's account (Figure 3–4).

> **EXAMPLE**
>
> During an annual physical examination, the physician also completes a Pap smear, removes the sutures from a laceration, and removes a wart from the patient's hand. The patient is charged for each individual service, even though the services were completed during one office visit.

FIGURE 3–4 Illustration of Fee-for-Service Reimbursement Method

FIGURE 3–5 Episode of Care

Episode-of-Care Reimbursement

Episode-of-care reimbursement is charging a lump sum for all services associated with a particular problem, illness, condition, or procedure. Surgical care is often associated with the episode-of-care reimbursement method. A surgical episode-of-care fee would include preoperative visits, the actual surgery, and routine postoperative care. Obstetrical services are another example of this type of reimbursement method. An obstetrical episode-of-care fee would cover routine prenatal visits, physician attendance at the delivery, and routine postnatal care of the mother. Figure 3–5 illustrates episode-of-care reimbursement.

Services covered by an episode-of-care fee must be clearly identified to the patient. Additional or unexpected services or services related to complications are usually billed on a fee-for-service basis.

Capitation

Fee-for-service and episode-of-care reimbursement methods depend on the number of services, individual or grouped, provided to the patient. **Capitation** is a reimbursement method that depends on the number of individuals covered by the health insurance contract.

Under capitation, the health care provider receives a fixed amount, or fee, on a **per capita** (per person) basis. The fee is paid at predetermined intervals, such as monthly, quarterly, semiannually, or annually. The number of services provided does not affect the fee. A simple instance of capitation reimbursement is described in the following example.

EXAMPLE

Erika Electric Company has 100 employees, and each employee has two dependents. The company provides health insurance for all 300 employees and dependents. Family Practice, Inc., a respected medical practice, has a reputation for providing thorough annual physicals to all age groups. Erika Electric provides full coverage for annual physical examinations as part of the company's wellness program. In order to manage the cost of this benefit, the company is interested in paying for the annual physical examinations on a per-person basis.

Representatives of Erika Electric Company or the company's insurance carrier and Family Practice, Inc., meet and establish a formal agreement. The agreement states that Family Practice, Inc., will provide annual physical examinations for the 300 employees and dependents of Erika Electric. Erika Electric will reimburse Family Practice, Inc., at the rate of $100 per employee and dependent for a total of $30,000, to be paid in semiannual installments.

Under the capitation reimbursement method, health care providers are reimbursed for the number of individuals in the contract rather than by the number of services provided. Therefore, if only 150 Erika Electric employees and dependents actually have an annual physical examination, Family Practice, Inc., still receives the full $30,000.

Capitation is commonly associated with prepaid health insurance plans, such as those offered by health maintenance organizations. However, any organization that provides health insurance can negotiate a capitation reimbursement method. This type of reimbursement may be used to cover selected services, as described in the example, or it may be expanded so that health care providers receive a fixed fee for providing comprehensive services.

REINFORCEMENT EXERCISES 3–7

Provide a short answer for each item.

1. What is third-party reimbursement?

_____

_____

_____

2. Describe the traditional reimbursement method.

_____

_____

_____

3. Briefly define and provide one example of episode-of-care reimbursement.

_____

_____

_____

4. Describe capitation as a reimbursement method.

_____

_____

_____

ABBREVIATIONS

Table 3–9 lists the abbreviations presented in this chapter.

TABLE 3–9

Abbreviations and Meanings	
Abbreviation	**Meaning**
COB	coordination of benefits
EPO	exclusive provider organization
HMO	health maintenance organization
IDS	integrated delivery system
IPA	independent practice association
MCO	managed care organization
PPO	preferred provider organization

SUMMARY

This chapter provided a brief overview of the health insurance industry and some historical factors that influenced its growth. Terms associated with health insurance were presented and organized as health insurance policy terms and health care provider terms. Direct pay, indirect pay, and third-party reimbursement methods were defined and discussed.

Managed care organizations include all managed health care models and can be found in every state. The primary goal of all managed care organizations (MCOs) is to provide quality health care services while containing health care costs. Managed care affects all segments of the health care industry. Providers are under considerable pressure to offer services for reduced or negotiated fees, and consumers are encouraged to choose providers who participate in managed care plans.

REVIEW EXERCISES

Matching

Match the terms in Column A with the definitions in Column B.

Column A	Column B	
a. benefit	1. noncovered situation	_____
b. claim	2. payment for services	_____
c. coverage	3. policyholder	_____
d. dependent	4. amount paid by insurance company	_____
e. direct pay	5. request for payment	_____
f. exclusion	6. an attachment to the policy	_____

Column A	Column B	
g. insured	7. cost of insurance policy	_____
h. premium	8. person supported by the insured	_____
i. reimbursement	9. patient pays the bill	_____
j. waiver	10. included and excluded conditions	_____

Fill in the Blank

Write the correct insurance term or phrase for each statement.

1. An HMO that contracts with physicians who continue to practice in their private offices is called a(n) _____.

2. A(n) _____ encourages members to receive services from participating providers by reducing the members' co-payment amount.

3. The most restrictive type of **an MCO** is a(n) _____.

4. An HMO that owns, operates, and hires personnel for its health care facilities is called a(n) _____.

5. The fee established by a PPO is called the _____.

6. Another term for indirect pay is _____.

7. The _____ is the number of days allowed between the premium due date and cancellation of the health insurance policy.

8. A _____ is the time that must pass before certain illnesses or accidents are covered by the health insurance policy.

9. The number of days allowed for submitting a claim is called the _____.

10. The _____ is responsible for providing all routine health care and determining the need for referrals to physician specialists.

Definitions

Briefly define the listed health insurance terms.

1. Accepts assignment

_____

_____

_____

2. Assignment of benefits

_____

_____

_____

3. Deductible

_____

_____

_____

4. Pre-existing condition

_____

_____

_____

5. Case manager

_____

_____

_____

6. Physician extender

_____

_____

_____

7. Group practice

_____

_____

_____

8. Co-payment

_____

_____

_____

9. Insurance carrier

_____

_____

_____

10. Birthday rule

_____

_____

_____

Identification

Identify the correct government-sponsored health care program associated with each statement: TRICARE, CHAMPVA, Medicaid, Medicare, workers' compensation.

1. Based on financial need _____

2. Job-related health problems _____

3. Covers people aged 65 and older _____

4. Uniformed personnel and dependents _____

5. Employers must provide this insurance _____

6. Uniformed services–related disabilities _____

7. Covers end-stage renal disease _____

8. Also called Medical Assistance Program _____

9. Active-duty and retired military personnel _____

10. Covers railroad retirees _____

Short Answer

1. Describe what is meant by the terms "preauthorization," "precertification," and "predetermination." How are these activities related?

_____

_____

_____

2. What is the difference between a primary payer and a secondary payer?

_____

_____

_____

3. Explain the terms "participating provider" and "nonparticipating provider." Include any alternate terms for each.

_____

_____

_____

Abbreviation Review

Write out and give a brief definition for each abbreviation.

1. IPA

_____

2. PPO

_____

3. EPO

_____

4. COB

_____

CRITICAL THINKING EXERCISES

Read each case summary and then answer the questions that follow.

Case Summary A

Towanda has health insurance through her employer. She recently visited her family physician. As she reviews her bill, she notices that each service has a separate fee. At the billing desk, Towanda signs a form that lets the insurance company pay the physician directly. She leaves the office feeling confident that the bill will be paid.

a. What type of insurance does Towanda have?

_____

_____

_____

b. Name the reimbursement method described in the case.

_____

_____

_____

c. Why can the insurance company pay the physician directly?

_____

_____

_____

Case Summary B

Roberto has just learned that his prostate must be removed. He is concerned about the cost, and his physician refers him to the billing specialist. Roberto is relieved when he learns that the pre-operative office visit, surgery, and normal postoperative care are included in one fee. The billing specialist calls the insurance representative and finds out about how much the insurance company will pay for Roberto's treatment. In addition, the billing specialist informs Roberto that his supplemental insurance can be billed for the remaining balance. Roberto is relieved that finances will not be a problem.

1. What type of reimbursement method is described in this case?

_____

_____

_____

2. Did the billing specialist do a predetermination for Roberto's treatment? How can you support your answer?

_____

_____

_____

3. Why does the billing specialist not submit the full claim to both of Roberto's insurance companies?

_____

_____

_____

Case Summary C

Elmer has been to his physician at least six times this year. At every visit, at least four blood tests are done, and he often has one other problem taken care of. Elmer's health insurance plan uses a reimbursement method that depends on the number of individuals covered by the insurance contract.

1. What type of reimbursement method is described in this case?

_____

_____

_____

2. Does the number of services affect the reimbursement amount?

_____

_____

_____

3. Could Elmer belong to a health maintenance organization?

_____

_____

_____

WEBSITE

Centers for Medicare and Medicaid Services (CMS): www.cms.hhs.gov

International Classification of Diseases, Ninth Revision, Clinical Modification (ICD-9-CM)

LEARNING OBJECTIVES

Upon successfully completing this chapter, the reader should have the knowledge to:

1. Identify the four Cooperating Parties responsible for maintaining and updating ICD-9-CM.
2. Describe the value of the American Hospital Association (AHA) publication *Coding Clinic for ICD-9-CM*.
3. Follow the ICD-9-CM coding conventions for assigning diagnostic and procedure codes.
4. Explain the features of the three ICD-9-CM volumes.
5. Define all cross-reference and coding instruction terms.
6. List diagnostic and procedure coding steps in the order of performance.
7. Explain the difference between a primary diagnosis and a principal diagnosis.
8. Discuss the significance of a principal procedure.
9. Accurately code diagnoses and procedures presented in this chapter.

KEY TERMS

American Health Information Management Association (AHIMA)
American Hospital Association (AHA)
Carryover line
Category
Centers for Medicare and Medicaid Services (CMS)
Closed biopsy
Code first [the] underlying condition
Coding conventions
Concurrent condition
Congenital
Connecting words
Cooperating Parties
Current Procedural Terminology (CPT)
Due to
E codes
Encoders
Etiology
Exclusion note
Failed procedure
General note
Histological
Hypertension Table
Inclusion note
International Classification of Diseases, Ninth Revision, Clinical Modification (ICD-9-CM)
International Classification of Diseases, Tenth Revision (ICD-10)
Late effect
Main term
More specific subterms
National Center for Health Statistics (NCHS)
Nonessential modifier

Not elsewhere classified (NEC)

Not otherwise specified (NOS)

Open biopsy

Open procedure

Perinatal period

Primary diagnosis

Principal diagnosis

Principal procedure

Puerperium

Residual

Secondary condition

Section

See

See also

See category

See condition

Sequencing

Significant procedure

Subcategory

Subclassification

Subterm

Use additional code, if desired

V codes

OVERVIEW

As mentioned in Chapter 1, the two main coding systems associated with health insurance claims processing are the *International Classification of Diseases, Ninth Revision, Clinical Modification* (**ICD-9-CM**) for medical diagnoses and procedures and *Current Procedural Terminology* (**CPT**) for physician and other provider services and procedures. This chapter covers ICD-9-CM, which remains in effect until the *International Classification of Diseases, Tenth Revision* (**ICD-10**) is adopted. Chapter 5 presents an introduction to ICD-10.

Accurate coding is crucial to reimbursement and the avoidance of fraud and abuse charges. Insurance billing specialists need at least a basic understanding of medical coding. The purpose of this chapter is to provide the student with a foundation for ICD-9-CM coding. Topics presented include the following:

- Unique characteristics of *Volumes 1, 2,* and *3*
- Coding conventions, such as special instructional notes and the meaning of punctuation marks
- Sections of each volume that apply to physician office coding
- Coding guidelines from Sections II and IV of the ICD-9-CM Official Guidelines for Coding and Reporting

To gain the most from this chapter, have ICD-9-CM *Volumes 1, 2,* and *3* readily available as references. Some exercises provide opportunities to practice using the code books. This chapter also includes several figures and tables adapted from the 2010 official version of ICD-9-CM. The figures and tables allow the student to complete some of the review exercises if the code books are not available.

INTERNATIONAL CLASSIFICATION OF DISEASES, NINTH REVISION, CLINICAL MODIFICATION (ICD-9-CM)

The *International Classification of Diseases, Ninth Revision, Clinical Modification* (ICD-9-CM) is the medical coding and classification system used in the United States to gather information about diseases and injuries. ICD-9-CM is an adaptation of the *International Classification of Diseases, Ninth Revision* (ICD-9), which the World Health Organization (WHO) of the United Nations developed.

ICD-9-CM is a classification system that provides numeric codes for diagnoses, injuries, and procedures. The codes are contained in three volumes:

- *Volume 1* is a numeric tabular list of disease and injury codes.
- *Volume 2* is an alphabetic index of diseases and injuries.
- *Volume 3* is a combined tabular list and alphabetic index of procedure codes.

Volume 3 is used to code inpatient hospital procedures, whereas *Current Procedural Terminology* (CPT) is used to code physician office, ambulatory center, and hospital outpatient department procedures. CPT is published by the American Medical Association and is covered in Chapter 6 of this book. The official version of ICD-9-CM is available only on CD-ROM from the U.S. Government Printing Office in Washington, D.C. ICD-9-CM coding products are also available from commercial publishers. Electronic versions of the code books, called **encoders**, are also available from commercial sources. Although each publisher may offer special editorial features, the codes are the same as those published in the official version. The official version of ICD-9-CM is the reference of choice for this book.

The ICD-9-CM is updated every year, and changes are effective October 1 of that year. The **Cooperating Parties**, which consist of two professional associations and two governmental agencies, are responsible for maintaining and updating ICD-9-CM.

The Cooperating Parties are:

- **American Hospital Association (AHA)**
- **American Health Information Management Association (AHIMA)**
- **Centers for Medicare and Medicaid Services (CMS)**
- **National Center for Health Statistics (NCHS)**

Table 4–1 describes the responsibilities of each party.

The ICD-9-CM Coordination Committee, which is composed of several federal ICD-9-CM users, is an advisory committee to the Cooperating Parties.

As shown in Table 4–1, the AHA publishes the *Coding Clinic for ICD-9-CM*. This valuable resource is released quarterly and is considered the official publication for ICD-9-CM coding guidelines. The information provided in the *Coding Clinic* is regarded as advice from the four Cooperating Parties. Billing specialists and medical coders in all settings, including physicians' offices, clinics, and hospitals, can rely on the *Coding Clinic* for up-to-date coding advice.

The *ICD-9-CM Official Guidelines for Coding and Reporting,* which became effective October 1, 2003, is published by the Department of Health and Human Services (HHS). These guidelines, which are updated annually, provide additional information for assigning ICD-9-CM codes.

The ICD-9-CM contains specific guidelines called **coding conventions**. Coding conventions include instructional notes, abbreviations, cross-reference notes, punctuation marks, and specific usage of the words "and," "with," and "due to." The conventions are a standard method for organizing ICD-9-CM entries and also provide mandatory rules for assigning medical codes.

TABLE 4–1

Responsibilities of the Cooperating Parties for ICD-9-CM	
NCHS	Maintains and updates the diagnosis portion of ICD-9-CM
CMS	Maintains and updates the procedure portion (*Volume 3*)
AHA	Maintains the Central Office on ICD-9-CM to answer questions from coders; publishes the *Coding Clinic for ICD-9-CM,* the official guidelines for ICD-9-CM usage
AHIMA	Provides training and certification for coding professionals

REINFORCEMENT EXERCISES 4–1

1. List and briefly define the ICD-9-CM volumes.

_____

_____

_____

2. What is the Coding Clinic for ICD-9-CM?

_____

_____

_____

3. Explain the phrase "Cooperating Parties."

_____

_____

_____

4. Name the groups that act as the Cooperating Parties.

_____

_____

_____

_____

5. Briefly describe the phrase "coding conventions."

_____

_____

_____

ICD-9-CM COMPONENTS

As stated previously, ICD-9-CM has three volumes: the Tabular List of Diseases and Injuries (Volume 1), the Alphabetic Index of Diseases and Injuries (Volume 2), and the Tabular List and Alphabetic Index of Procedures (Volume 3). Historically, the volumes were published as three separate books. Publishers now offer a variety of options, such as a combination of Volumes 1 and 2, with the alphabetic index placed before the tabular list.

Volume 1: Tabular List of Diseases and Injuries

Volume 1, the Tabular List of Diseases and Injuries, includes the following sections:

- Seventeen main chapters—listed in Table 4–2—that classify diseases and injuries by body system or **etiology** (cause).

TABLE 4–2

Tabular List Main Chapters	
Chapter Title	**Code Categories**
1. Infectious and Parasitic Diseases	001–139
2. Neoplasms	140–239
3. Endocrine, Nutritional, and Metabolic Diseases and Immunity Disorders	240–279
4. Diseases of Blood and Blood-Forming Organs	280–289
5. Mental Disorders	290–319
6. Diseases of the Nervous System and Sense Organs	320–389
7. Diseases of the Circulatory System	390–459
8. Diseases of the Respiratory System	460–519
9. Diseases of the Digestive System	520–579
10. Diseases of the Genitourinary System	580–629
11. Complications of Pregnancy, Childbirth, and the Puerperium	630–679
12. Diseases of Skin and Subcutaneous Tissue	680–709
13. Diseases of the Musculoskeletal System and Connective Tissue	710–739
14. Congenital Anomalies	740–759
15. Certain Conditions Originating in the Perinatal Period	760–779
16. Symptoms, Signs, and Ill-Defined Conditions	780–799
17. Injury and Poisoning	800–999

- Two supplementary classifications called "Classification of Factors Influencing Health Status and Contact with Health Services," commonly known as **V codes**, and "Classification of External Causes of Injury and Poisoning," commonly known as **E codes**.
- Four appendices that include codes for information about specific diseases and accidents.

Although most of the chapters in the *Tabular List* have self-explanatory titles, Chapters 11, 14, 15, 16, and 17 need a brief explanation.

Chapter 11: Complications of Pregnancy, Childbirth, and the Puerperium

Chapter 11 codes classify conditions that affect the management of pregnancy, childbirth, and the **puerperium**. The puerperium is the period of time that begins at the end of the third stage of labor and continues for six weeks. Codes from Chapter 11 are assigned only to conditions affecting the mother, not the newborn.

Chapter 14: Congenital Anomalies

Chapter 14 codes classify abnormal conditions that are **congenital**, which means "present at or since the time of birth." Although a congenital anomaly is present at birth, the condition may not manifest itself until later. Therefore, Chapter 14 codes may be assigned to patients of any age.

> **EXAMPLE**
> Jenny, a 16-year-old high school sophomore, just received the results of her kidney scan. The physician tells Jenny that she has polycystic kidneys and explains that she was "born with" this condition. Even though Jenny is 16, the diagnosis of polycystic kidneys is coded as a congenital anomaly.

Chapter 15: Certain Conditions Originating in the Perinatal Period

Chapter 15 codes classify conditions specific to a newborn. The condition must be associated with the **perinatal period,** which begins before birth and lasts through the 28th day of life. Most perinatal conditions are resolved by time, treatment, or death. However, some conditions manifest themselves later in life.

> **EXAMPLE**
> Rachel is being treated for vaginal cancer. Rachel's health history reveals that her mother took the antinausea medication DES (diethylstilbestrol) during her pregnancy with Rachel. The physician explains to Rachel that her current condition could be a result of intrauterine exposure to DES.

In this case, the vaginal cancer is assigned the appropriate malignant neoplasm code. Intrauterine DES exposure is a significant factor in the development of vaginal cancer. Therefore, the code for vaginal cancer is selected, and the code for diethylstilbestrol (DES) from Chapter 15 is also assigned.

Chapter 16: Symptoms, Signs, and Ill-Defined Conditions

Chapter 16 includes medical codes for signs, symptoms, abnormal test results, and ill-defined conditions that are not associated with a diagnosis that can be classified or coded in another ICD-9-CM chapter. Simply put, Chapter 16 codes classify conditions that are of questionable or unknown etiology. These codes should never be used when a more definitive diagnostic code is available. Signs and symptoms related to conditions associated with a specific body system are assigned codes from the appropriate ICD-9-CM chapter. Signs and symptoms associated with more than one disease or body system are coded to Chapter 16.

Chapter 17: Injury and Poisoning

Of all the chapters in ICD-9-CM, Chapter 17 has the least descriptive title. This chapter includes codes not only for injuries and poisoning but also for burns, adverse effects caused by external factors, complications of trauma, and complications of surgical and medical care or treatment. Chapter 17 can classify a simple fracture caused by falling off a skateboard as well as a complex injury, such as being stabbed in the eye with a wooden stick. Table 4–3 lists the sections in Chapter 17.

Tabular List Format

Each chapter in *Volume 1* is a numeric list of diseases and injuries organized by sections, categories, subcategories, and fifth-digit subclassifications. A **section** is a group of three-digit categories that represent a single disease or a group of closely related conditions.

TABLE 4–3

Sections of ICD-9-CM Chapter 17 Injury and Poisoning	
Section	Range of Codes
Fractures	800–829
Dislocation	830–839
Sprains and strains	840–848
Intracranial injury, excluding those with skull fracture	850–854
Internal injury of the thorax, abdomen, and pelvis	860–869
Open wound of head, neck, and trunk	870–879
Open wound of upper limb	880–887
Open wound of lower limb	890–897
Injury to blood vessels	900–904
Late effects of injuries, poisonings, toxic effects, and other external causes	905–909
Superficial injuries	910–919
Contusions with intact skin surface	920–924
Crushing injuries	925–929
Effects of foreign body entering through an orifice	930–939
Burns	940–949
Injury to nerves and spinal cord	950–957
Certain traumatic complications and unspecified injuries	958–959
Poisoning by drugs, medicinal and biological substances	960–979
Toxic effects of substances chiefly nonmedical as to source	980–989
Other and unspecified effects of external causes	990–995
Complications of surgical and medical care not elsewhere classified	996–999

EXAMPLE

"Diseases of Esophagus, Stomach, and Duodenum" (530–537)

A **category** is a three-digit code that represents a single disease or a group of closely related conditions.

EXAMPLE

531, Gastric ulcer

Subcategories consist of four digits and provide more information about the disease, such as the site, cause, or other characteristics. A period or decimal point precedes the fourth digit.

EXAMPLE

531.0 represents an acute gastric ulcer with hemorrhage (.0), 531.1 is an acute gastric ulcer with perforation (.1), and 531.2 is an acute gastric ulcer with hemorrhage and perforation (.2). The fourth digit clearly includes important information about the gastric ulcer.

Subclassifications are represented by a fifth digit and allow for even more specific information about the disease. Fifth-digit lists are found at the beginning of a chapter, section, category code, and subcategory level. Fifth digits include as many numeric selections as necessary to complete the description of the disease.

EXAMPLE

The three-digit category code 531, gastric ulcer, has two fifth-digit choices: 0, which means without mention of obstruction, and 1, which means with obstruction. Therefore, code 531.00 represents an acute gastric ulcer (531), with hemorrhage (.0), without mention of obstruction (0). Code 531.01 represents an acute gastric ulcer with hemorrhage and with obstruction.

Figure 4–1 is an example of fifth-digit subclassifications at the chapter, category, and subcategory level.

Billing specialists and medical coders must pay close attention to fourth-digit subcategories and fifth-digit subclassifications. If the fourth and fifth digits are available, they *must* be included on the claim. Insurance carriers will deny payment for any claim that does not have the appropriate fourth or fifth digit.

LOCATION	DESCRIPTION
Chapter	Chapter 13. "Diseases of the Musculoskeletal System and Connective Tissue" (710–739) The following fifth-digit subclassification is used with categories 711–712, 715–716, 718–719, and 730: 0 unspecified site; 1 shoulder region; 2 upper arm; 3 forearm; 4 hand; 5 pelvic region and thigh; 6 lower leg; 7 ankle and foot; 8 other specified sites; 9 multiple sites
Category	434 Occlusion of cerebral arteries The following fifth-digit subclassification is used with category 434: 0 without mention of cerebral infarction; 1 with cerebral infarction
Subcategory	550.0 Inguinal hernia, with gangrene The following fifth-digit subclassifications apply to this subcategory: 0 unilateral or unspecified (not specified as recurrent); 1 unilateral or unspecified, recurrent; 2 bilateral (not specified as recurrent); 3 bilateral, recurrent

Delmar/Cengage Learning

FIGURE 4–1 Examples of Fifth-Digit Subclassifications

Supplementary Classifications

The *Tabular List* has two supplementary classifications:

- "Supplementary Classification of Factors Influencing Health Status and Contact with Health Services" (V01–V82)—also called V codes.
- "Supplementary Classification of External Causes of Injury and Poisoning" (E800–E999)— also called E codes.

V codes provide a mechanism to classify interactions with health care providers when the individual is not sick. V codes also provide additional information about the individual's medical condition. As the name implies, the letter *V* precedes these codes. Figure 4–2 shows examples of V codes.

V codes

**PERSONS WITHOUT REPORTED DIAGNOSIS ENCOUNTERED
DURING EXAMINATION AND INVESTIGATION OF
INDIVIDUALS AND POPULATIONS (V70-V82)**

Note: Nonspecific abnormal findings disclosed at the time of these
examinations are classifiable to categories 790-796.

V70   General medical examinations
Use additional code(s) to identify any special screening
examination(s) performed (V73.0-V82.9)

V70.0 Routine general medical examination at a health care facility
Health checkup

> **EXCLUDES** *health checkup of infant or child over 28 days
> old (V20.2)
> health supervision of newborn 8 to 28 days old
> (V20.32)
> health supervision of newborn under 8 days old
> (V20.31)
> pre-procedural general physical examination
> (V72.83)*

V70.1 General psychiatric examination, requested by the authority

V70.2 General psychiatric examination, other and unspecified

V70.3 Other medical examination for administrative purposes
General medical examination for:
    admission to old age home
    adoption
    camp
    driving license
    immigration and naturalization
    insurance certification
    marriage
    prison
    school admission
    sports competition

> **EXCLUDES** *attendance for issue of medical certificates
> (V68.0)
> pre-employment screening (V70.5)*

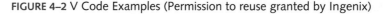

FIGURE 4–2 V Code Examples (Permission to reuse granted by Ingenix)

E codes

DRUGS, MEDICINAL AND BIOLOGICAL SUBSTANCES CAUSING ADVERSE EFFECTS IN THERAPEUTIC USE (E930–E949)

Includes: correct drug properly administered in therapeutic or prophylactic dosage, as the cause of any adverse effect including allergic or hypersensitivity reactions

Excludes: *accidental overdose of drug and wrong drug given or taken in error (E850.0–E858.9)*
accidents in the technique or administration of drug or biological substance such as accidental puncture during injection, or contamination of drug (E870.0–E876.9)
administration with suicidal or homicidal intent or intent to harm, or in circumstances classifiable to E980–E989 (E950.0–E950.5, E962.0, E980.0–E980.5)

See Alphabetic Index for more complete list of specific drugs to be classified under the fourth-digit subdivisions. The American Hospital Formulary numbers can be used to classify new drugs listed by the American Hospital Formulary Service (AHFS). See Appendix C.

E930   Antibiotics

Excludes: *that used as eye, ear, nose, and throat [ENT], and local anti-infectives (E946.0–E946.9)*

E930.0   Penicillin

Natural   Semisynthetic, such as:
Synthetic   ampicillin
                               cloxacillin
                               nafcillin
                               oxacillin

E930.1   Antifungal antibiotics

Amphotericin B   Hachimycin [trichomycin]
Griseofulvin   Nystatin

E930.2   Chloramphenicol group

Chloramphenicol   Thiamphenicol

FIGURE 4–3 E Codes (Permission to reuse granted by Ingenix)

E codes describe the external cause of injury and poisoning, and they are often assigned with Chapter 17 codes. As the name implies, the letter E precedes these codes. Figure 4–3 shows examples of E codes.

Following this chapter's coverage of ICD-9-CM coding conventions, both V and E codes are discussed in depth.

Appendices

Historically, the *Tabular List* (*Volume 1*) included five appendices:

- Appendix A: "Morphology of Neoplasms"
- Appendix B: "Glossary of Mental Disorders"
- Appendix C: "Classification of Drugs by the American Hospital Formulary Service (AHFS) List

- Appendix D: "Classification of Industrial Accidents According to Agency"
- Appendix E: "List of Three-Digit Categories"

Effective with the October 1, 2004, update, Appendix B, "Glossary of Mental Disorders," was removed from the official government version of ICD-9-CM. The four remaining appendices provide additional information for coding and classification purposes.

When this text was published, the appendices retained the original letter designations. Some commercial publishers may renumber the appendices.

Appendix A, "Morphology of Neoplasms," provides a list of optional codes for the **histological** (tissue) type and behavior of neoplasms. This appendix is also known as the M codes. The codes consist of five digits preceded by the letter M. The first four digits identify the type of tissue, and the fifth digit describes the behavior of the neoplasm. Table 4–4 lists examples of the four-digit tissue codes.

The behavioral fifth digit of each M code is delineated by a slash followed by the number 1, 2, 3, 6, or 9. Fifth digits retain their meaning regardless of the histology code. Table 4–5 lists the M code fifth digits and their meanings. M codes are used primarily by cancer registries and are always accompanied by the appropriate neoplasm code from Chapter 2 of the main classification section.

EXAMPLE
Code M8010/0 describes a benign epithelial tumor.

TABLE 4–4

Sample Four-Digit Tissue Codes	
Tissue Code	**Type of Neoplasm**
M8010–M8043	Epithelial neoplasms
M8090–M8110	Basal cell neoplasms
M8140–M8381	Adenomas; adenocarcinomas
M9180–M9200	Osteomas; osteosarcomas
M9820–M9825	Lymphoid leukemias

TABLE 4–5

M Code Fifth Digits and Meanings	
Fifth Digit	**Meaning**
/0	Benign (noncancerous)
/1	Uncertain whether benign or malignant; borderline malignant
/2	Carcinoma in situ; intraepithelial, noninfiltrating, noninvasive
/3	Malignant (cancerous), primary site
/6	Malignant, metastatic site, secondary site
/9	Malignant, uncertain whether primary or metastatic site

Appendix C, "Classification of Drugs by American Hospital Formulary Service (AHFS) List," includes a listing of the AHFS drug categories and the appropriate ICD-9-CM codes. The *American Hospital Formulary Service* is a publication that categorizes drugs into related groups. Each category or group has a specific ICD-9-CM code.

EXAMPLE

Penicillins (AHFS classification 8:12.16) are coded to 960.0, anticoagulants (AHFS classification 20:12.04) to 964.2, and insulins (AHFS classification 68:20.08) to 962.3.

Appendix D, "Classification of Industrial Accidents According to Agency," classifies industrial accidents according to agency. In this appendix, agency means the active force or substance that caused the accident, such as equipment, material, or the working environment. This classification, which was adopted on October 12, 1962, by the Tenth International Conference of Labor Statisticians, is used infrequently.

Appendix E, "List of Three-Digit Categories," is organized by ICD-9-CM chapter and lists the three-digit categories with titles in each chapter.

Appendices A through E are part of the official version of ICD-9-CM published by the U.S. Government Printing Office. Commercial ICD-9-CM coding references may include these appendices and also others.

REINFORCEMENT EXERCISES 4–2

1. Identify the two methods used to classify diseases and diagnoses listed in Chapters 1–17 of the *Tabular List*.

   _____

   _____

   _____

2. What is the difference between the puerperium and the perinatal period?

   _____

   _____

   _____

3. List four additional categories of diseases or injuries found in Chapter 17, "Injury and Poisoning."

   _____

   _____

   _____

continued on the next page

continued from the previous page

4. Provide a brief explanation of each term.

a. Section

_____

_____

_____

b. Category

_____

_____

_____

c. Subcategory

_____

_____

_____

d. Subclassification

_____

_____

_____

Volume 2: Alphabetic Index of Diseases and Injuries

Volume 2, the *Alphabetic Index of Diseases and Injuries,* is referred to as the *Alphabetic Index* or simply the *Index.* As the name implies, this volume is organized alphabetically by disease or condition and is the key to finding codes in the *Tabular List* (*Volume 1*). Codes selected from the *Alphabetic Index must* be verified by reviewing the description of the code in the *Tabular List.*

The *Alphabetic Index* contains these sections:

- "Alphabetic Index to Diseases and Injuries"
- "Table of Drugs and Chemicals"
- "Alphabetic Index to External Causes of Injury and Poisoning" (E codes)

In addition to these sections, the *Alphabetic Index* has neoplasm and hypertension subterms arranged in tables. The table features of the *Alphabetic Index* are discussed later in this chapter.

The *Alphabetic Index* follows a unique format that includes indentation patterns and alphabetization rules.

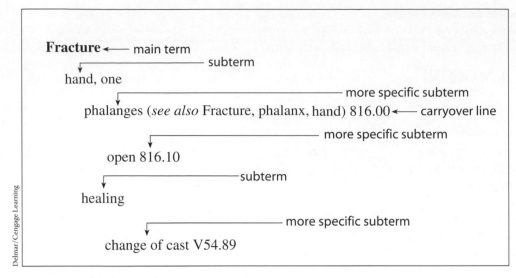

FIGURE 4–4 *Alphabetic Index* Organizational Pattern

Indentation Patterns

Diseases and conditions are generally classified as main terms, subterms, more specific subterms, and carryover lines. Each of these phrases has a specific and consistent indentation pattern.

Main terms are diseases, conditions, or injuries, such as appendicitis or a fracture. Main terms are set flush with the left margin, begin with a capital letter, and are printed in bold.

Subterms identify the site, type, or etiology for diseases, conditions, or injuries. Subterms are indented under a main term by one standard indentation, which is about two spaces. They begin with a lowercase letter and are printed in regular type.

More specific subterms are indented under a subterm by one standard indentation, farther to the right as needed. More specific subterms are listed in alphabetical order, provide additional information related to subterms, and are printed in regular type.

Carryover lines are used when a complete entry does not fit on one line. Carryover lines are indented two standard indentations to avoid being confused with subterms and more specific subterms. Figure 4–4 is an example of this organizational pattern.

The *Alphabetic Index* is carefully organized to conserve space. The structure of the *Index* is at times confusing and frustrating. However, billing specialists and coders must carefully follow the indentations to arrive at the correct code. When faced with literally pages of subterms, as with pneumonia codes, always begin with the main term and follow the subterms and more specific subterms until the correct description is located.

Although most conditions can be located by the name of the disease, condition, or injury as the main term, there are exceptions. Table 4–6 lists and provides examples of additional main terms.

Alphabetization Rules

The *Alphabetic Index* follows a letter-by-letter alphabetization format, with the following exceptions:

- Ignore single spaces between words.
- Ignore single hyphens within words.

TABLE 4–6

Additional Main Terms	
Main Term	**Description/Examples**
Anomaly	Congenital conditions, which are present at the time of birth, are listed alphabetically by anatomic site under the main term "Anomaly."
Delivery	Conditions identified as "delivery complicated by" are listed alphabetically under the main term "Delivery."
Labor	Conditions that complicate or affect the progress of labor are listed alphabetically under the main term "Labor."
Pregnancy	Conditions identified as "pregnancy complicated by" are listed alphabetically under the main term "Pregnancy."
Puerperal	Conditions originating in the puerperium—the time period between the end of third-stage labor and six weeks—are listed alphabetically under the main term "Puerperal."
Complications	Conditions originating as a complication of medical or surgical care are listed alphabetically under the main term "Complications."
Late, effect of	Conditions that originate as a result of treatment for an illness or injury are listed alphabetically under the main term "Late, effect of."

- Ignore the final "s" in possessive forms.
- Subterms for numerical characters and words indicating numbers are listed in *numerical order*.
- Subterms preceded by "with" or "without" are placed immediately after the main term.

Examples of these exceptions are provided in Figure 4–5.

In addition to "with" and "without," the *Alphabetic Index* makes special use of the words "due to" and "in." These words express a relationship between main terms and subterms as well as between subterms and more specific subterms. "Due to" and "in" are listed alphabetically in the *Index*. The main term "fracture" is a good example of a "due to" entry.

EXAMPLE

Fracture . . .
   with
   internal injuries in same region . . .
   acetabulum . . .
   acromion (process) (closed) . . .
   cuneiform . . .

due to
   birth injury . . .
   gunshot . . .
   neoplasm . . .

In this example, the "due to" entries describe a causal relationship—i.e., fracture due to a birth injury, gunshot, or neoplasm.

EXCEPTION	EXAMPLE
Ignore:	
S in the possessive form	**Addison's** anemia
Single hyphens within words	**Addison-Biermer** anemia
Single spaces between words	**Addison-Gull** disease
	Addisonian crisis
Numerical Order:	

Numerical characters and words indicating numbers	**Paralysis, paralytic**
	    nerve…
	        Third or oculomotor
	        Fourth or trochlear
	        Sixth or abducens

	Accessory (congenital)
	    Chromosome(s) NEC 758.5
	        13–15…
	        16–18…
	        21 or 22…

With or **Without:**	

Immediately after the main term or related subterm	**Appendicitis** 541
	    with
	        perforation…540.0
	            with peritoneal abscess 540.1
	        peritoneal abscess 540.1
	
	    acute…
	    amebic…

Delmar/Cengage Learning

FIGURE 4–5 Exceptions to Alphabetization Rules

REINFORCEMENT EXERCISES 4–3

Provide the correct term in each blank.

1. Diseases and conditions set flush left and printed in bold are called _____.

2. _____ identify the site, type, or etiology for diseases, conditions, or injuries.

3. When a complete entry does not fit on one line, a _____ is indented two standard indentations from the subterm.

4. Congenital conditions are usually located under the main term _____.

5. _____ is the main term when the condition is the result of a surgical or medical complication.

6. How are numerical characters and words indicating numbers listed in the *Alphabetic Index*?

_____

continued on the next page

continued from the previous page

7. Where would you look to find the subterm "with"?

_____

8. What are the main terms for conditions that complicate pregnancy, childbirth, or puerperium?

_____

Locate the main entry "Anomaly, anomalous (congenital) (unspecified type)" and give an example of an entry for each of the following anatomical sites. include the ICD-9-CM code.

1. Brain

_____

2. Heart

_____

3. Hip joint

_____

4. Spinal cord

_____

5. Ear

_____

Tables

The *Alphabetical Index* has three tables that provide a systematic arrangement of codes for hypertension, neoplasms, and drugs and chemicals with associated E codes. Proper use of these tables gives the billing specialist access to more-complex combinations of subterms and E codes. The format and alphabetization rules for these tables are consistent with the rest of the *Alphabetic Index*. Figures 4–6 through 4–8 are examples of these tables. Refer to these figures as you read about the features of each table.

Hypertension Table

The **Hypertension Table** has three main column headings, as shown in Figure 4–6. These headings are as follows:

- **Malignant:** A severe form of hypertension with vascular damage and a diastolic pressure of 130 mmHg or greater; the hypertension is out of control or there was a rapid change from a benign state.
- **Benign:** Hypertension is mild and in control.
- **Unspecified:** No documentation of benign or malignant status is stated in the diagnosis or patient's record.

	Malignant	Benign	Unspecified
Hypertension, hypertensive (arterial) (arteriolar) (crisis) (degeneration) (disease) (essential) (fluctuating) (idiopathic) (intermittent) (labile) (low renin) (orthostatic) (paroxysmall) (primary) (systemic) (uncontrolled) (vascular)...	401.0	401.1	401.9
with			
chronic kidney disease			
stage I through stage IV, or unspecified...	403.00	403.10	403.90
stage V or end stage renal disease...	403.01	403.11	403.91
heart involvement (conditions classifiable to 429.0–429.3, 429.8, 429.9 due to hypertension) (*see also* Hypertension, heart)...	402.00	402.10	402.90
with kidney involvement—*see* Hypertension, cardiorenal			
renal involvement (only conditions classifiable to 585, 586, 587) (excludes conditions classifiable to 584) (*see also* Hypertension, kidney)...	403.00	403.10	403.90
with heart involvement—*see* Hypertension, cardiorenal			
failure (and sclerosis) (*see also* Hypertension, kidney)...	403.01	403.11	403.91
sclerosis without failure (*see also* Hypertension, kidney)...	403.00	403.10	403.90
accelerated (*see also* Hypertension, by type, malignant)...	401.0	—	—
antepartum—*see* Hypertension, complicating pregnancy, childbirth, or the puerperium			
cardiorenal (disease)...	404.00	404.10	404.90
with			
chronic kidney disease			
stage I through stage IV, or unspecified...	404.00	404.10	404.90
and heart failure...	404.01	404.11	404.91
stage V or end stage renal disease...	404.02	404.12	404.92
and heart failure...	404.03▲	404.13▲	404.93 ▲
heart failure...	404.01▲	404.11▲	404.91 ▲
and chronic kidney disease...	404.01	404.11	404.91
stage I through stage IV or unspecified...	404.01	404.11	404.91
stave V or end stage renal disease...	404.03	404.13	404.93
cardiovascular disease (arteriosclerotic) (sclerotic)...	402.00	402.10	402.90
with			
heart failure...	402.01	402.11	402.91
renal involvement (conditions classifiable to 403) (*see also* Hypertension, cardiorenal)...	404.00	404.10	404.90
cardiovascular renal (disease) (sclerosis) (*see also* Hypertension, cardiorenal)...	404.00	404.10	404.90

FIGURE 4–6 Hypertension Table (Permission to reuse granted by Ingenix)

Correct utilization of the Hypertension Table depends on careful observance of indentations and checking the *Tabular List* as directed.

After the main entry "Hypertension, hypertensive," several terms appear in parentheses. These terms are **nonessential modifiers**, which means they do not affect code selection. If no other diagnostic information is given, the billing specialist selects the code 401.9 from the Unspecified column. If the diagnostic statement specifies malignant or benign hypertension, the code comes from one of those columns. The billing specialist must verify the codes by reviewing the description in the *Tabular List.*

The indentation "with" indicates that another condition exists *with* the hypertension, but the relationship is not necessarily causal. The first indentation under "with" is "chronic kidney disease." Under chronic kidney disease, the first indentation is "stage I through stage IV or unspecified." The codes for this condition are 403.00, 403.10, and 403.90. To select one of these codes for hypertension with chronic kidney disease stage I through stage IV or unspecified, the diagnosis must include information about chronic kidney disease.

The second indentation under "chronic kidney disease" is "stage V or end-stage renal disease." To select a code from this entry, the diagnosis must identify the chronic kidney disease as stage V or as end-stage renal disease.

The second indentation under "with" is "heart involvement (conditions classifiable to 429.0–429.3, 429.8, 429.9 due to hypertension) (*see also* Hypertension, heart)." To select codes 402.00, 402.10, or 402.90, the diagnosis must include a heart condition that falls into one of the codes listed with this indentation. The instructional note "(*see also* Hypertension, heart)" gives the coder another subterm that may be helpful in selecting the correct code.

The first indentation under "heart involvement" is "with kidney involvement (*see* Hypertension, cardiorenal)." The coder must go to the subterm "cardiorenal" to continue coding. The entry "Hypertension, hypertensive, cardiorenal (disease)" lists codes for hypertension with both heart and kidney involvement.

Neoplasm Table

The Neoplasm Table is an extensive *Alphabetic Index* entry that is used to code neoplasms according to the behavior of the tumor. The term "neoplasm" literally means "new growth," and not all neoplasms are malignant. A malignant neoplasm code can be assigned only when the pathology report confirms the presence of a malignancy. Never assign a malignant neoplasm code on the basis of a suspected or rule out diagnosis.

Correct utilization of the Neoplasm Table depends on careful attention to the diagnostic statement, reading and following all instructional notes, and careful use of the *Alphabetic Index.* Figure 4–7 is a sample of the Neoplasm Table. Refer to the figure as you read the explanation.

The Neoplasm Table provides codes for malignant, benign, uncertain behavior, and unspecified neoplasm. The table is arranged alphabetically by anatomical site. The codes listed with each site describe the behavior of the neoplasm.

Malignant neoplasms are cancerous and are coded as follows:

- **Primary:** The site where the neoplasm originated.
- **Secondary:** The site to which the neoplasm has spread.
- **In situ:** The malignant cells have not spread.

Benign neoplasms are not cancerous and do not spread or invade other sites. "Uncertain Behavior" describes a neoplasm that cannot be identified as benign or malignant. In these cases,

| | Malignant | | | | Uncertain | Unspecified |
	Primary	Secondary	Ca in situ	Benign	Behavior	Nature
Neoplasm, neoplastic..............................	199.1	199.1	234.9	229.9	238.9	239.9

> *Notes— 1. The list below gives the code numbers for neoplasms by anatomical site. For each site there are six possible code numbers according to whether the neoplasm in question is malignant, benign, in situ, of uncertain behavior, or of unspecified nature. The description of the neoplasm will often indicate which of the six columns is appropriate; e.g., malignant melanoma of skin, benign fibroadenoma of breast, carcinoma in situ of cervix uteri.*
>
> *Where such descriptors are not present, the remainder of the Index should be consulted where guidance is given to the appropriate column for each morphological (histological) variety listed; e.g., Mesonephroma — see Neoplasm, malignant; Embryoma — see also Neoplasm, uncertain behavior; Disease, Bowen's — see neoplasm, skin, in situ. However, the guidance in the Index can be overridden if one of the descriptors mentioned above is present; e.g., malignant adenoma of colon is coded to 153.9 and not to 211.3 as the adjective "malignant" overrides the Index entry "Adenoma — see also Neoplasm, benign."*
>
> *2. Sites marked with the sign * (e.g., face NEC*) should be classified to malignant neoplasm of skin of these sites if the variety of neoplasm is a squamous cell carcinoma or an epidermal carcinoma; and to benign neoplasm of skin of these sites if the variety of neoplasm is a papilloma (any type).*

	Primary	Secondary	Ca in situ	Benign	Uncertain Behavior	Unspecified Nature
abdomen, abdominal	195.2	198.89	234.8	229.8	238.8	239.9
cavity	195.2	198.89	234.8	229.8	238.8	239.9
organ..	195.2	198.89	234.8	229.8	238.8	239.9
viscera	195.2	198.89	234.8	229.8	238.8	239.9
wall	173.5	198.2	232.5	216.5	238.2	239.2
connective tissue	171.5	198.89	–	215.5	238.1	239.2
abdominopelvic	195.8	198.89	234.8	229.8	238.8	239.9
accessory sinus — *see* Neoplasm, sinus...						
acoustic nerve	192.0	198.4	–	225.1	237.9	239.7
acromion (process)	170.4	198.5	–	213.4	238.0	239.2

FIGURE 4–7 Neoplasm Table (Permission to reuse granted by Ingenix)

the pathology or lab report is inconclusive and the pathologist is unable to make a definitive diagnosis. "Unspecified" is used when the documentation does not support a more specific code.

Although the Neoplasm Table is organized by anatomic site, neoplasm diagnoses are not. The diagnosis must first be located in the *Alphabetic Index*, which then directs the billing specialist to the Neoplasm Table.

EXAMPLE

To code the diagnosis cervical carcinoma, in situ, the billing specialist locates the main entry Carcinoma in the *Alphabetic Index*. The direction at the entry is "see also Neoplasm, by site, malignant." Under *Neoplasm, neoplastic, cervix (cervical) (uteri) (uterus),* the billing specialist selects the code from the Malignant, Ca in situ column. He or she must verify the code by reviewing the description in the *Tabular List*.

Table of Drugs and Chemicals

The Table of Drugs and Chemicals is located after the last entry in the *Alphabetic Index*. Drugs and chemicals are listed in alphabetical order and include everything from antibiotics to zinc. This

Substance	Poisoning	External Cause (E-Code)				
		Accident	Therapeutic Use	Suicide Attempt	Assault	Un-determined
1-propanol	980.3	E860.4	—	E950.9	E962.1	E980.9
2-propanol	980.2	E860.3	—	E950.9	E962.1	E980.9
2, 4-D (dichlorophenoxyacetic acid)	989.4	E863.5	—	E950.6	E962.1	E980.7
2, 4-toluene diisocyanate	983.0	E864.0	—	E950.7	E962.1	E980.6
2, 4, 5-T (trichlorophenoxyacetic acid)	989.2	E863.5	—	E950.6	E962.1	E980.7
14-hydroxydihydromorphinone	965.09	E850.2	E935.2	E950.0	E962.0	E980.0
A						
ABOB	961.7	E857	E931.7	E950.4	E962.0	E980.4
Abrus (seed)	988.2	E865.3	—	E950.9	E962.1	E980.9
Absinthe	980.0	E860.0	—	E950.9	E962.1	E980.9
beverage	980.0	E860.0	E934.2	E950.4	E962.0	E980.4
Acenocoumarin, acenocoumarol	964.2	E858.2	E934.2	E950.4	E962.0	E980.3
Acepromazine	969.1	E853.0	E939.1	E950.3	E962.0	E980.3
Acetal	982.8	E862.4	—	E950.9	E962.1	E980.9
Acetaldehyde (vapor)	987.8	E869.8	—	E952.8	E962.2	E982.8
liquid	989.89	E866.8	—	E950.9	E962.1	E980.9
Acetaminophen	965.4	E850.4	E935.4	E950.0	E962.0	E980.0
Acetaminosalol	965.1	E850.3	E935.3	E950.0	E962.0	E980.0
Acetanilid(e)	965.4	E850.4	E935.4	E950.0	E962.0	E980.0
Acetarsol, acetarsone	961.1	E857	E931.1	E950.4	E962.0	E980.4
Acetazolamide	974.2	E858.5	E944.2	E950.4	E962.0	E980.4
Acetic						
acid	983.1	E864.1	—	E950.7	E962.1	E980.6
with sodium acetate (ointment)	976.3	E858.7	E946.3	E950.4	E962.0	E980.4
irrigating solution	974.5	E858.5	E944.5	E950.4	E962.0	E980.4
lotion	976.2	E858.7	E946.2	E950.4	E962.0	E980.4
anhydride	983.1	E864.1	—	E950.7	E962.1	E980.6

IGURE 4–8 Table of Drugs and Chemicals (Permission to reuse granted by Ingenix)

table enables the coder to select the appropriate poisoning code and associated E code. Figure 4–8 is a sample of the Table of Drugs and Chemicals. Refer to this figure as you read the explanation.

Poisoning is a condition caused by drugs, medicines, and biological substances when taken improperly or not in accordance with physician orders. Examples of poisoning are taking or receiving the wrong medication in error, taking or receiving the wrong dose of the right medication in error, overdose, prescription drugs taken with alcohol, and mixing prescription drugs and over-the-counter medications without physician advice or consent.

The Table of Drugs and Chemicals lists the names of the substances, the poisoning code for each substance, and five columns of E codes. The E code columns are labeled Accident, Therapeutic Use, Suicide Attempt, Assault, and Undetermined. Unless the patient record clearly states otherwise, the E code is selected from the Accident column. A poisoning code is never used in conjunction with an E code from the Therapeutic Use column. Diagnostic statements can include other problems caused by the poisoning.

EXAMPLE
A child is treated for hives caused by ingesting her brother's psoriasis medication, triamcinolone. The billing specialist codes the hives as the reason for the visit and may also code the wrongful ingestion of triamcinolone as an accidental poisoning.

REINFORCEMENT EXERCISES 4–4

1. List the names of the three tables located in the *Alphabetic Index*.

_____

_____

_____

2. Write a brief definition for the following Hypertension Table main column headings.

a. Malignant

_____

_____

_____

b. Benign

_____

_____

_____

c. Unspecified

_____

_____

_____

3. What is the purpose of the Neoplasm Table?

_____

_____

_____

4. Write a brief definition for each of the general categories listed in the Neoplasm Table.

a. Malignant

_____

_____

_____

continued on the next page

continued from the previous page

b. Benign

_____

_____

_____

c. Uncertain Behavior

_____

_____

_____

d. Unspecified

_____

_____

_____

ICD-9-CM Coding Conventions

A thorough understanding of ICD-9-CM coding conventions is necessary to accurately assign diagnostic codes. Coding conventions fall into five categories:

- Cross-references
- Instructional notes
- Connecting words
- Abbreviations
- Punctuation

Cross-References

ICD-9-CM cross-references, which are usually found in the *Alphabetic Index,* include "see," "see also," "see category," and "see condition." The cross-references direct the billing specialist to look elsewhere in the code book(s) before assigning a code.

The **see** cross-reference is a mandatory direction, and the billing specialist or coder must refer to the term identified after the word "see."

> **EXAMPLE**
> Under the entry Labor, with complications, the cross-reference note states "see Delivery, complicated." To ensure accurate coding, locate the Index entry Delivery, complicated, and continue from that entry.

See also directs the coder to another entry in the *Alphabetic Index* when the entry under consideration does not provide the needed code. Basically, "see also" means "if you cannot find the code you need here, check at this other location."

EXAMPLE

Pneumonia, caseous code 011.6 is cross-referenced by "see also Tuberculosis." If code 011.6 does not accurately reflect the diagnosis in the patient's record, the billing specialist refers to the Tuberculosis entry for the correct code.

See category directs the coder to a three-digit category code in the *Tabular List*. As with the "see" reference, the direction "see category" is mandatory.

EXAMPLE

Under the Index entry Paralysis, paralytic, several entries follow the subterm brain. Brain, hemiplegia, due to previous vascular lesion is followed by the instruction "see category 438." The billing specialist must review category 438 in the Tabular List for information about this condition.

See condition identifies times when an adjective describing the disease or condition was used as a main term.

EXAMPLE

The diagnosis is written as lobar pneumonia. The insurance biller uses lobar as a main term and finds the entry Lobe, lobar in the Alphabetic Index. The cross-reference states "see condition." In this case, pneumonia is the condition. The insurance biller locates Pneumonia, lobar in the Alphabetic Index in order to find the correct code.

Instructional Notes

Instructional notes provide additional guidance for accurate code selection. The types of instructional notes are:

- General notes
- Inclusion notes
- Exclusion notes
- Use additional code, if desired
- Code first [the] underlying condition (disease)
- Code, if applicable, any causal condition first

General notes are found in all three ICD-9-CM volumes. In the *Alphabetic Index,* general notes are usually printed in italics and boxed. The most common application of general notes is to identify fifth-digit subclassifications in the *Tabular List* and *Alphabetic Index.* General notes are also used to clarify unique coding situations.

EXAMPLE

The main entry Fracture has general notes that (1) describe open vs. closed fractures, (2) provide direction for coding multiple fracture sites, and (3) identify fifth digits for certain categories of codes.

Inclusion notes are lists of conditions that are similar enough to be coded or classified by the same medical code. Inclusion notes are found at the beginning of a chapter and immediately following category, subcategory, and subclassification codes.

EXAMPLE

Atherosclerosis, the narrowing of an arterial wall caused by deposits of fat and cholesterol, is coded to category 440. The inclusion note for the category lists several diagnoses, such as arteriosclerosis, arteriosclerotic vascular disease, and atheroma, which are covered by category 440.

Exclusion notes are easy to identify because the word "Excludes" is italicized and printed in a box. Exclusion notes are found immediately below the code to which the exclusion applies. A condition listed under the exclusion note cannot be coded or classified by the medical code that has the exclusion note. A code or range of codes for the excluded condition is part of the exclusion note.

EXAMPLE

The 440.9 atherosclerosis code has an exclusion note that reads "Excludes: atherosclerosis of bypass graft of the extremities (440.30–440.32)." The coder knows that 440.9 is not the right code for the excluded condition and is directed to look at codes 440.30–440.32 for the appropriate code.

Use additional code, if desired means that more than one code may be necessary to provide a complete picture of the patient's problem.

EXAMPLE

The diagnosis of vaginitis, inflammation of the vagina, is supported by a lab test that reveals the presence of E. coli (Escherichia coli). The code for vaginitis directs the coder to "use additional code, if desired, to identify the organism." The billing specialist must be certain that the test results confirm a causative organism before assigning an additional code. If the condition mentioned in the Use additional code instruction is documented in the patient's record, the additional code should be included.

The instruction **Code first [the] underlying condition** indicates that the patient's condition is a manifestation of an underlying disease. The code for the underlying disease must be listed before the manifestation. This instruction applies to inpatient coding. In the physician office setting, the first code listed is the code that applies to the reason for the office visit.

EXAMPLE

The diagnosis diabetic retinitis requires two codes: one for the diabetes and one for the retinitis. If the patient is treated in the hospital, the diabetes code must be listed before the retinitis code. The diabetes is the underlying condition that causes the retinitis. In other words, retinitis is a manifestation of the patient's diabetes. If the patient is treated for retinitis in a physician's office, retinitis is the reason for the office visit. The code for retinitis is listed first, and the code for diabetes is included on the claim form as a concurrent condition.

Code, if applicable, any causal condition first means that the code with this instructional note may be sequenced or listed first as the principal diagnosis when the causal condition is unknown or not applicable. If the causal condition is known, then the code for the causal condition must be sequenced or listed first as the principal diagnosis.

EXAMPLE

In the Tabular List, Chapter 16, "Symptoms, Signs, and Ill-defined Conditions," code 788.3 urinary incontinence includes the instructional note "Code, if applicable, any causal condition first, such as: congenital ureterocele (753.23); genital prolapsed (618.00–618.9); and hyperplasia of prostate (600.00–600.9 with fifth-digit 1)." If the diagnosis includes any of the listed conditions as the cause of the urinary incontinence, then the code for the condition must be sequenced before the code or urinary incontinence.

REINFORCEMENT EXERCISES 4–5

Identify the coding convention described by each statement.

1. Lists the conditions or diagnoses covered by a particular code.

   _____

2. Lists the conditions or diagnoses not covered by a particular code.

   _____

3. Identifies the patient's condition as a manifestation of another disease or problem.

   _____

4. More than one code is used to describe the patient's condition.

   _____

5. Adjective was used as a main term.

   _____

6. Mandatory cross-reference to a three-digit code.

   _____

7. Look further if necessary.

   _____

8. Mandatory cross-reference.

   _____

Connecting Words

Connecting words, which are subterms listed primarily in the *Alphabetic Index,* indicate a relationship between the main term and associated conditions or causes of disease. Commonly used connecting words include "associated with," "complicated (by)," "due to," "during," "following," "in," "of," "secondary to," "with," "with mention of," and "without." Except for "with" and "without," the connecting words are listed in alphabetic order under the main term. Figure 4–9 illustrates the use of connecting words "due to," "in," and "with." Narrative examples for each of these connecting words follow Figure 4–9.

```
Pneumonia...
        with influenza, flu, or grippe 487.0
        adenoviral 480.0...
        bacterial 482.9...
        due to
            adenovirus 480.0...
            Chlamydia, chlamydial 483.1...
        in
            actinomycosis 039.1
            anthrax 022.1 [484.5]...
```

FIGURE 4–9 Connecting Words

The phrase "**due to**" indicates a causal relationship between two conditions.

EXAMPLE

The diagnosis pneumonia **due to** adenovirus means that the pneumonia is caused by an adenovirus organism. Because there is a cause-and-effect relationship between the virus and the pneumonia, the correct code is 480.0.

The connecting words "with," "associated with," and "in" identify codes that require two elements in the diagnostic statement.

EXAMPLE

The category for influenza is 487. A diagnosis of pneumonial influenza or influenza **with** pneumonia results in code 487.0, Influenza with pneumonia. Both conditions must be documented in order to use code 487.0.

The diagnosis pneumonia **in** actinomycosis means that the patient has actinomycosis (a chronic systemic disease that often involves the lungs) and has developed pneumonia because of the disease. The correct code for pneumonia in actinomycosis is 039.1, Actinomycotic infections, pulmonary. Both the actinomycosis and the pneumonia must be documented in order to use code 039.1.

The word "and" means "and/or" when it appears in the title of a code.

EXAMPLE

Code 616.10, Vaginitis **and** *Vulvovaginitis*, unspecified, indicates that the code can be assigned to either condition.

Abbreviations

The abbreviations **NEC (not elsewhere classified)** and **NOS (not otherwise specified)** have the same meaning in all ICD-9-CM volumes. NEC and NOS are associated with the codes that include the fourth or fifth digits 8 and 9. These codes are known as residual subcategories.

NEC means that the diagnosis or condition, no matter how specific, does not have a separate code.

EXAMPLE

The diagnosis lumbar hernia, the protrusion of an abdominal organ into the loin, is specific but does not have a separate code. Lumbar hernia is one of several hernia diagnoses coded as 553.8, Hernia of other specified sites. The usual fourth or fifth digit for NEC conditions is the number 8.

NOS means the same thing as "unspecified." This abbreviation is found only in the *Tabular List.* NOS codes should be used only when the diagnosis or the patient's medical record does not provide enough information for a more specific code.

EXAMPLE

Regional enteritis, an inflammatory disease of the intestine, can affect the small intestine, large intestine, or both segments of the intestine. If the diagnosis is stated simply as regional enteritis and no additional information is available, the correct code is 555.9, Regional enteritis, unspecified site. However, if the diagnosis is stated as regional ileitis, the correct code is 555.0, Regional enteritis, small intestine. The ileum is part of the small intestine, and therefore the term ileitis identifies the small intestine as the specific site of the regional enteritis. The fourth or fifth digit for NOS codes is the number 9.

Punctuation

Punctuation marks such as parentheses ( ), slanted square brackets [ ], square brackets [ ], colons:, section marks §, braces }, and double braces { } are used to provide additional information for accurate coding. Some commercial ICD-9-CM publications do not use all punctuation marks.

Parentheses ( ) are used to enclose words that do *not* affect code selection and to enclose cross-references such as *see also.* Terms within the parentheses are called nonessential modifiers, which means they may or may not be included in the diagnostic statement.

EXAMPLE

Category 440, Atherosclerosis, includes the diagnosis arteriosclerosis (obliterans) (senile). Obliterans and senile are enclosed by parentheses. They are nonessential modifiers, need not be present in the diagnostic statement, and have no effect on code selection. The correct code for senile arteriosclerosis is 440.9, Generalized and unspecified atherosclerosis.

Square brackets [ ] are used to enclose synonyms, alternate wordings, abbreviations, and phrases related to a section, category, subcategory, or subclassification. Information in square brackets is not required as part of the diagnostic statement.

EXAMPLE

Arteriosclerotic heart disease [ASHD] is included in the code 414.00, Coronary atherosclerosis, narrowing of the arteries of the heart. The abbreviation ASHD is included in square brackets because ASHD is synonymous with arteriosclerotic heart disease.

Square brackets are also used to note fifth digits associated with a specific code.

EXAMPLE

The diagnosis Osteoarthrosis, generalized, is coded as 715.0, and the fifth digits 0, 4, and 9 are located under the code in square brackets [0,4,9]. An accurate code for Osteoarthrosis, generalized must include one of the three acceptable fifth digits. The 0 means site unspecified, 4 is the hand, and 9 is used when multiple sites are stated in the diagnosis.

Slanted square brackets [ ], found only in the *Alphabetic Index,* enclose the manifestation code associated with an underlying condition.

EXAMPLE

The alphabetic entry Anthrax, with pneumonia 022.1 [484.5], identifies the code for anthrax infection first and then the pneumonia code in slanted brackets. The pneumonia is a manifestation of the anthrax infection.

The underlying condition must be listed first, with the manifestation code listed second. For physician office coding, the reason for the office visit is listed first on the insurance claim form.

Colons : are used with inclusion and exclusion notes and are placed after the included or excluded condition. Additional descriptions are indented and listed beneath the included or excluded condition. The diagnosis must contain at least one of the descriptions in order to apply the inclusion or exclusion note.

EXAMPLE

The subcategory 528.0, "Stomatitis, inflammation of the mucosal membranes of the mouth," lists stomatitis with five indented descriptions as the exclusion note. One of the five indented descriptions is herpetic (054.2). With this information, the billing specialist knows that herpetic stomatitis is excluded from the 528.0, "Stomatitis" subcategory.

Braces and double braces—{ and { }—serve the same purpose as colons. They connect a list or series of descriptions or diagnostic terms with a common stem or with a main term. Braces are used in the *Tabular List* to reduce repetitive wording by connecting a series of terms on the left with a statement on the right. Some ICD-9-CM coding references drop the use of braces and rely on colons to connect terms and statements or repeat the main statement with a series of terms:

461 Acute Sinusitis
Includes:
Abscess, acute, of sinus
Empyema, acute, of sinus
Infection, acute, of sinus…

Section marks § are used in the official Government Printing Office version of the ICD-9-CM. The section mark is placed at the left of any three- or four-digit code that requires a fifth digit. Other publishers use a variety of unique signals or marks, such as small flags or color-coded keys, to identify the fifth-digit requirement. Table 4–7 summarizes ICD-9-CM punctuation marks.

TABLE 4–7

ICD-9-CM Punctuation Marks	
Punctuation Mark	**Example**
Parentheses ( )	Enclose words that do not affect code assignment: Arteriosclerosis (obliterans) (senile)
Square brackets [ ]	Enclose information that does not affect code assignment: Arteriosclerotic heart disease [ASHD]
	Identify fifth digits associated with a specific code: 715.0 Osteoarthrosis, generalized [0,4,9]
Slanted square *[ ]* brackets	Enclose the manifestation code associated with an underlying condition:
	Anthrax, with pneumonia 022.1 *[484.5]*
	Pneumonia is the manifestation of the anthrax infection.
Colons :	Identify required descriptions for exclusion and inclusion notes:
	528.0 Stomatitis *Excludes: stomatitis:* *acute necrotizing ulcerative (101)* *aphthous (528.2)* *gangrenous (528.1)* *herpetic (054.2)* *Vincent's (101)*
Section mark(s) §	§662 Long Labor
	662.0 Prolonged First Stage
	[0,1,3]
Braces {	Serve the same purpose as colons
Double braces { }	Serve the same purpose as colons

REINFORCEMENT EXERCISES 4–6

Identify the coding convention described in each statement.

1. Indicates that a specific diagnosis does not have a separate code.

   _____

2. Means the same as "unspecified."

   _____

3. Used to enclose or highlight fifth digits associated with a specific code.

   _____

continued on the next page

continued from the previous page

4. Causal relationship between two or more conditions.

_____

5. Identifies codes that require documentation of two conditions.

_____

6. Connect a list of descriptions with a main term.

_____

7. Encloses nonessential modifiers and cross-reference terms.

_____

8. Enclose manifestation codes.

_____

9. Identifies the need for a fifth digit.

_____

Coding convention practice

1. Locate the main entry "Pneumonia." Review this multicolumn entry and find an example for NEC, NOS, "due to," "with," "see also," and "see."

_____

_____

_____

2. Locate the main entry "Diabetes mellitus." Where is the word "mellitus" located? Is there a boxed instructional note? If yes, what is included? Write out the full entry for the first NEC code.

_____

_____

_____

3. Locate the entry "Diabetic cataract." What is the first code? Is another code listed? If yes, what is the significance of the code? Write out the code. Find both codes in the *Tabular List*.

_____

_____

_____

ICD-9-CM OFFICIAL GUIDELINES FOR CODING AND REPORTING

The Centers for Medicare and Medicaid Services (CMS) and the National Center for Health Statistics (NCHS) develop and update guidelines for coding and reporting *by* using ICD-9-CM. The guidelines provide instructions in situations where ICD-9-CM does not provide instructions. The ICD-9-CM coding conventions take precedence over the guidelines. The Cooperating Parties—CMS, AHA, AHIMA, and NCHS—approve the guidelines. The guidelines are included in the official government version of the ICD-9-CM, *in* the Coding Clinic for ICD-9-CM published by the American Hospital Association *and in commercial ICD-9-CM publications.*

It is beyond the scope of this text to review the entire contents of the guidelines, which are available on the CMS *web*site at www.cms.gov. Section IV, "Diagnostic Coding and Reporting Guidelines for Outpatient Services," and Section II, "Selection of Principal Diagnosis," are included in this chapter.

Section IV. Diagnostic Coding and Reporting Guidelines for Outpatient Services

The guidelines in Section IV of the ICD-9-CM Official Guidelines for Coding and Reporting are approved for hospital and provider-based outpatient services and office visits. This includes outpatient or ambulatory surgery, admission for observation, and physician office visits. Under the Guidelines, the terms **encounter** and **visit** are used interchangeably to describe outpatient service contacts. The reason for the encounter or visit is called the **first-listed diagnosis,** although some providers also use the term "**primary diagnosis.**" A summary of the guidelines is presented here and illustrated with examples as needed.

Guideline IV.A. Selection of first-listed condition (diagnosis)

In determining the first-listed diagnosis, ICD-9-CM coding conventions as well as the general and disease-specific guidelines take precedence over the outpatient guidelines. Always begin the search for the correct code assignment through the *Alphabetic Index.* Never begin the initial search in the *Tabular List.*

1. Outpatient surgery: When a patient presents for outpatient surgery, code the reason for the surgery as the first-listed diagnosis *(reason for the encounter),* even if the surgery is not performed due to a contraindication.
2. Observation stay: When a patient is admitted for observation for a medical condition, assign a code for the medical condition as the first-listed diagnosis. When a patient presents for outpatient surgery and develops complications requiring admission for observation, code the reason for the surgery as the first-listed diagnosis, followed by codes for the complications as secondary diagnoses.

Guideline IV.B. Codes from 001.0 through V89

Appropriate ICD-9-CM codes, from 001.0 through V89, must be used to identify diagnoses, symptoms, problems, complaints, or other reasons for the encounter/visit.

Guideline IV.C. Accurate reporting of ICD-9-CM diagnosis codes

For accurate reporting of ICD-9-CM diagnosis codes, the documentation should describe the patient's condition by using terminology that includes specific diagnoses as well as symptoms, problems, or reasons for the encounter. There are ICD-9-CM codes to describe all of these.

Guideline IV.D. Selection of codes 001.0 through 999.9

Codes 001.0 through 999.9 are frequently used to describe the reason for the encounter. These codes are from the section of ICD-9-CM for the classification of diseases and injuries.

Guideline IV.E. Codes that describe symptoms and signs

Codes that describe symptoms and signs, as opposed to diagnoses, are acceptable for reporting purposes when a diagnosis has not been established (confirmed) by the provider. *ICD-9-CM Volume 1*, Chapter 16, "Symptoms, Signs, and Ill-Defined Conditions," *(780.0-799.9)* contains many but not all codes for symptoms.

Guideline IV.F. Encounters for circumstances other than disease or injury

ICD-9-CM V codes are used to report encounters for reasons other than disease or injury.

Guideline IV.G. Level of detail in coding

ICD-9-CM diagnosis codes are composed of 3, 4, or 5 digits that provide greater specificity. Use the full number of digits required for a code. A three-digit code is assigned only when further subdivisions (4th or 5th digits) are not available. A code is invalid if it is not assigned to the highest level of specificity. The assigned code must be supported by the documentation in the patient's record.

> **EXAMPLE**
> Pansy is seen with a diagnosis of conductive hearing loss. The four-digit subcategory 389.0 Conductive hearing loss has 8 fifth-digit codes: 389.00 Conductive hearing loss, unspecified; 389.01 Conductive hearing loss, external ear; 389.02 Conductive hearing loss, tympanic membrane; 389.03 Conductive hearing loss, middle ear; 389.04 Conductive hearing loss, inner ear; 389.05 Conductive hearing loss, unilateral; 389.06 Conductive hearing loss, bilateral; and 389.08 Conductive hearing loss of combined types. In this case, the four-digit code 389.0 Conductive hearing loss is incorrect. Because fifth-digit codes are available, code 389.00 Conductive hearing loss, unspecified is correct.

Guideline IV.H. ICD-9-CM code for the diagnosis, condition, problem, or other reason for encounter/visit

List first the ICD-9-CM code for the diagnosis, condition, problem, or other reason for the encounter or visit shown in the medical record to be chiefly responsible for the services provided. List additional codes that describe any coexisting conditions. In some cases, the first-listed diagnosis may be a symptom when a diagnosis has not been established (confirmed) by the physician.

> Mark is seen in the physician's office for heart palpitations. He also has diabetes mellitus, type II, that is under control. The first-listed diagnosis is palpitations, code 785.1. Diabetes mellitus, type II, controlled, code 250.00 is listed as an additional code for a coexisting condition.

Guideline IV.I. Uncertain diagnosis

Do not code diagnoses documented as "probable," "suspected," "questionable," "rule out," "working diagnosis," or other similar terms indicating uncertainty. *Do* code the condition(s) to the highest degree of certainty for that encounter/visit, such as symptoms, signs, abnormal test results, or other reasons for the visit.

This differs from the coding practices that apply to short term, acute care, and psychiatric hospitals as well as long-term care facilities.

> **EXAMPLE**
>
> Selina was seen in the physician's office with complaints of vertigo, nausea, and a headache. Rule out inner ear infection. In this case, if the inner ear infection is not confirmed, code the vertigo, nausea, and headache. The physician should indicate which symptom is primary.

Guideline IV.J. Chronic diseases

Chronic diseases treated on an ongoing basis may be coded and reported as many times as the patient receives treatment and care for the condition(s).

Guideline IV.K. Code all documented conditions that coexist

Code all documented conditions that coexist at the time of the encounter/visit and require patient care or affect treatment and management. *Do not* code conditions that were previously treated and no longer exist. However, history codes (V10–V19) may be used as secondary codes if the historical condition or family history has an impact on current care or influences treatment.

Guideline IV.L. Patients receiving diagnostic services only

When a patient receives only diagnostic services during an encounter/visit, sequence first the diagnosis, condition, problem, or other reason for the encounter/visit shown in the medical record to be chiefly responsible for the outpatient services provided during the encounter/visit. Codes for other diagnoses (e.g., chronic conditions) may be sequenced as additional diagnoses.

For encounters for routine laboratory/radiology testing in the absence of any signs, symptoms, or associated diagnoses, assign V72.5 and a code from subcategory V72.6. If routine testing is performed during the same encounter as a test to evaluate a sign, symptom, or diagnosis, it is appropriate to assign both the V code and the code describing the reason for the nonroutine test.

For outpatient encounters for diagnostic tests that have been interpreted by a physician and the final report available at the time of coding, code any confirmed or definitive diagnosis(es) documented in the interpretation. Do not code related signs and symptoms as additional diagnoses.

> **EXAMPLE**
>
> Joel is seen for a colonoscopy because of frequent rectal bleeding, with a probable diagnosis of ulcerative colitis. In this case, the insurance billing specialist has two options:
>
> A. Submit the insurance claim before the results of the colonoscopy are available. The first-listed diagnosis in this option is rectal bleeding. Rectal bleeding is coded and sequenced first because that is the reason the colonoscopy was performed. The endoscopy is coded to the appropriate CPT category.
>
> B. Wait until the results of the colonoscopy are available and then submit the insurance claim. The diagnosis listed in the colonoscopy report is selected as the first-listed diagnosis, and coded and sequenced first. The endoscopy is coded to the appropriate CPT category.
>
> Because the results of the colonoscopy should provide a more specific diagnosis than rectal bleeding, option B is the best choice.

Guideline IV.M. Patients receiving therapeutic services only

For patients receiving only therapeutic services during the encounter/visit, sequence first the diagnosis, condition, problem, or other reason that is chiefly responsible for the encounter/visit. Codes for other conditions may be sequenced as additional diagnoses.

An exception to this guideline applies when the encounter is related to chemotherapy, radiation therapy, or rehabilitation. In these cases, the V code that identifies the treatment is listed first. The diagnosis or reason for the treatment is coded and listed after the V code.

Guideline IV.N. Patients receiving preoperative evaluations only

For patients receiving preoperative evaluations only, a code from category V72.8 "Other specified examinations" that describes the preoperative consultation is listed first. The reason for the surgery is coded and listed as an additional diagnosis. Also, code any findings related to the preoperative evaluation.

> **EXAMPLE**
>
> LaMar, whose medical treatment for an enlarged prostate has been unsuccessful, is seen for a preoperative evaluation prior to his scheduled TURP (transurethral resection of the prostate). The physician's note indicates that LaMar is diabetic and has hypertension.
>
> In this case, the insurance billing specialist selects the V code that describes a preoperative evaluation. The V code is listed first, the code for enlarged prostate is second, and the codes for diabetes and hypertension are listed as additional diagnoses.

Guideline IV.O. Ambulatory surgery

For ambulatory surgery, code the diagnosis for which the surgery was performed. If the postoperative diagnosis is known to be different from the preoperative diagnosis at the time the diagnosis was confirmed, code the postoperative diagnosis since it is the most definitive.

> **EXAMPLE**
>
> Because of the presence of several polyps, Maureen underwent a polypectomy of the descending colon. Familial polyposis was the preoperative diagnosis. The physician's postoperative note states that five polyps were removed—four benign and one malignant. Colorectal cancer is the postoperative diagnosis.
>
> In this case, the postoperative diagnosis, colorectal cancer, is more definitive than familial polyposis. Colorectal cancer is coded and listed first. Do not code familial polyposis. The procedure is coded to the appropriate CPT category.

Guideline IV.P. Routine outpatient prenatal visits

For routine outpatient prenatal visits when no complications are present, code V22.0, "Supervision of normal first pregnancy," and V22.1, "Supervision of other normal pregnancy," are the first-listed diagnosis codes. These codes should not be used in conjunction with codes from Chapter 11, "Complications of Pregnancy, Childbirth, and the Purperium."

Section II. Selection of Principal Diagnosis

The guidelines in Section II, "Selection of Principal Diagnosis," apply to services rendered in non-outpatient settings, such as hospitals, rehabilitation facilities, and nursing homes. In these settings, the principal diagnosis is the condition established after study to be chiefly responsible for the patient's admission for care. The code for the principal diagnosis is sequenced first on the insurance claim. A summary of guidelines A through J, with examples as needed, is included here. Additional information about inpatient coding and reporting is presented in Chapter 9, "Common UB-04 (CMS-1450) Completion Guidelines."

Keep in mind that Section II guidelines for selecting the principal diagnosis(es) apply to inpatient care, and ICD-9-CM coding conventions take precedence over Section II guidelines.

Guideline II.A. Codes for symptoms, signs, and ill-defined conditions

Codes for symptoms, signs, and ill-defined conditions from *ICD-9-CM* Chapter 16 are not to be used as a principal diagnosis when a related definitive diagnosis has been established.

> **EXAMPLE**
>
> Lekeitia is admitted to the hospital for severe nausea, vomiting, headache, and a stiff neck. The laboratory workup confirms the diagnosis of bacterial meningitis. Lekeitia is hospitalized for six days and is treated with intravenous antibiotics.
>
> In this example, bacterial meningitis is selected and coded as the principal diagnosis.

Guideline II.B. Two or more interrelated conditions, each potentially meeting the definition for principal diagnosis

When two or more interrelated conditions potentially meet the definition of principal diagnosis, either condition may be sequenced first, unless the circumstances of the admission, the therapy provided, the Tabular List, or the Alphabetic Index indicate otherwise.

> **EXAMPLE**
>
> Following a car accident, Ramone was admitted with the diagnoses of closed fractures of the humerus and shaft of the ulna and radius. Both fractures were reduced without internal fixation.
>
> In this example, either fracture may be selected as the principal diagnosis.

Guideline II.C. Two or more diagnoses that equally meet the definition for principal diagnosis

In the unusual instance when two or more diagnoses equally meet the criteria for principal diagnosis as determined by the circumstance of admission, diagnostic workup, and/or therapy provided, and the Tabular List, Alphabetic Index, or other coding guidelines do not provide sequencing instructions, any one of the diagnoses may be sequenced first.

> **EXAMPLE**
>
> Wanda was admitted for elective surgery. A cystocele was repaired, and she also underwent a hemorrhoidectomy for prolapsed internal hemorrhoids.
>
> In this example, either the cystocele or prolapsed internal hemorrhoids may be selected as the principal diagnosis.

Guideline II.D. Two or more comparative or contrasting conditions

In the rare instance when two or more contrasting or comparative diagnoses are documented as "either/or" (or similar terminology), the diagnoses are coded as if confirmed and sequenced according to the circumstances of the admission. If no further determination can be made as to which diagnosis is principal, either diagnosis may be sequenced first.

> **EXAMPLE**
>
> Irritable bowel syndrome either/or spastic colitis.
>
> Because neither irritable bowel syndrome nor spastic colitis is confirmed, either one of these diagnoses may be selected as the principal diagnosis and sequenced first.

Guideline II.E. A symptom(s) followed by contrasting/comparative diagnoses

When a symptom(s) is followed by contrasting/comparative diagnoses, the symptom(s) code is sequenced first. All contrasting/comparative diagnoses should be coded as additional diagnoses.

> **EXAMPLE**
>
> Chen was admitted with symptoms of periodic vomiting with blood present in the vomitus, indigestion, and a low-grade fever over the past two weeks. Following workup, Dr. Samuelson dictated the following diagnostic statement: "Vomiting with frank blood due to either bleeding gastric ulcer or bleeding esophageal ulcer."
>
> In this example, the symptom "vomiting with frank blood" is selected as the principal diagnosis and sequenced first. "Bleeding gastric ulcer" and "bleeding esophageal ulcer" are coded as secondary diagnoses.

Guideline II.F. Original treatment plan not carried out

Sequence as the principal diagnosis the condition that after study occasioned the admission to the hospital, even if treatment was not carried out because of unforeseen circumstances.

> **EXAMPLE**
>
> Travis was admitted for gastric bypass surgery. His diagnoses are morbid obesity and poorly controlled non–insulin-dependent diabetes mellitus, type 2. Prior to the beginning of surgery, he exhibited an episode of hypotension and the surgery was cancelled.
>
> In this example, morbid obesity is the principal diagnosis because it was the reason for the admission. Morbid obesity is coded and sequenced first. Non–insulin-dependent diabetes mellitus, type 2, poorly controlled, is coded as a secondary or complicating diagnosis.

Guideline II.G. Complications of surgery and other medical care

When the admission is for treatment of a complication resulting from surgery or other medical care, the complication code is sequenced as the principal diagnosis. If the complication is classified to categories 996 through 999 and the code lacks the necessary specificity in describing the complication, an additional code for the specific complication should be assigned.

> **EXAMPLE**
>
> Oksana was treated for peritonitis following recent gastrointestinal surgery. The peritonitis was caused by the presence of nonabsorbable suture material accidentally left in her abdominal cavity.

In this example, the complication code for a foreign body accidentally left during a procedure is coded as the principal diagnosis. An additional code for peritonitis is also be assigned.

Guideline II.H: Uncertain diagnosis

If the diagnosis documented at the time of discharge is qualified as "probable," "suspected," "likely," "questionable," "possible," "still to be ruled out," or other similar terms indicating uncertainty, code the condition as if it existed or was established. The bases for these guidelines are the diagnostic workup, arrangements for further workup or observation, and initial therapeutic approach that correspond most closely with the established diagnosis. This guideline applies only to inpatient admissions to short-term care, acute long-term care, and psychiatric hospitals.

EXAMPLE

Carla was admitted for acute onset of several episodes of explosive diarrhea and severe cramping within the past 24 hours. Patient described the stool as dark brown, "slimy," and foul-smelling. She was placed on a clear liquid diet and treated with intravenous hydrocortisone. Stool samples were taken for laboratory analysis. Colonoscopy was deferred pending resolution of acute symptoms. After three days, she was discharged on Prednisone. She is scheduled for a colonoscopy as an outpatient on Monday. Final diagnosis: probable ulcerative colitis.

Because the patient was admitted and treated for symptoms consistent with ulcerative colitis and an additional diagnostic procedure is scheduled, ulcerative colitis is the principal diagnosis and coded as if the condition existed.

Guideline II.I. Admission from observation unit

1. Admission following medical observation: When a patient is admitted to an observation unit for a medical condition, which either worsens or does not improve, and is subsequently admitted as an inpatient of the same hospital for the same medical condition, the principal diagnosis is the medical condition that led to the hospital admission.
2. Admission following postoperative observation: When a patient is admitted to an observation unit to monitor a condition (or complication) that develops following outpatient surgery and then is subsequently admitted as an inpatient of the same hospital, the principal diagnosis is the condition established after study to be chiefly responsible for the inpatient admission.

EXAMPLE

Elmer underwent a transurethral resection of the prostate (TURP) as an outpatient procedure. Following the procedure, he exhibited a fever and hematuria (blood in the urine). He was admitted to an observation unit, and his condition did not improve. Elmer was then admitted as an inpatient for further treatment for fever and hematuria.

In this case, the principal diagnosis is hematuria because it is the reason for the inpatient admission. Fever may also be coded as an additional problem.

Guideline II.J. Admission from outpatient surgery

When a patient receives surgery in the hospital's outpatient surgery department and is subsequently admitted for continuing inpatient care at the same hospital, the following guidelines should be followed in selecting the principal diagnosis for the inpatient admission:

- If the reason for the inpatient admission is a complication, assign the complication as the principal diagnosis.
- If no complication or other condition is documented as the reason for the inpatient admission, assign the reason for the outpatient surgery as the principal diagnosis.
- If the reason for the inpatient admission is another condition unrelated to the surgery, assign the unrelated condition as the principal diagnosis.

Diagnostic coding can be a challenge for any insurance billing specialist. There are several ICD-9-CM coding conventions to follow, and the coding guidelines described here are equally important. One final coding rule actually supersedes all others: Code only the conditions, problems, diagnoses, and procedures that are clearly documented in the patient's medical record.

REINFORCEMENT EXERCISES 4–7

Read each statement and mark It as True or False. Make the change(s) necessary to make the False statements true.

1. CMS and NCHS develop and update the Official Guidelines for Coding and Reporting.

2. The terms "encounter" and "visit" describe *hospital* inpatient services.

3. The first-listed diagnosis is the condition or disease responsible for the hospital admission.

4. History codes may be used as secondary codes.

5. Routine outpatient prenatal visits are coded to *ICD-9-CM* Chapter 11, "Complications of Pregnancy, Childbirth, and the Purperium."

6. Symptoms, signs, and ill-defined conditions should not be used as a principal diagnosis.

7. A confirmed postoperative diagnosis is the first-listed diagnosis.

8. ICD-9-CM codes must be assigned to the highest level of specificity.

continued on the next page

continued from the previous page

9. In a hospital setting, "probable" or "suspected" diagnoses may be coded as if the condition existed.

10. ICD-9-CM coding conventions take precedence over the Official Guidelines for Coding and Reporting.

ASSIGNING ICD-9-CM DIAGNOSTIC CODES

Accurate code assignment depends on three activities:

- Selecting diagnostic codes
- Sequencing diagnostic codes
- Following the official coding guidelines and all ICD-9-CM coding conventions

Only those diagnoses that are clearly documented in the patient's medical record are coded and submitted with the insurance claim.

Selecting the Diagnostic Codes

As with any task, there is a standard procedure for selecting ICD-9-CM diagnostic codes. The steps for code selection are enumerated and discussed here, and examples are provided.

1. Identify the main term(s) in the diagnostic statement. (In this example, the main term is in bold.)

   EXAMPLE
   Urinary tract **infection** due to E. coli.

2. Find the main term(s) in the *Alphabetic Index.*

   EXAMPLE
   Locate "Infection" in the Index.

3. Review the diagnostic statement for additional information concerning the main term.

   EXAMPLE
   "Urinary tract" identifies the anatomic location of the **infection.**

4. Review the subterms listed under the main term to determine if an entry matches the additional information in the diagnostic statement.

   EXAMPLE
   "Urinary (tract)" is a subterm listed under *"Infection."* There is no mention of *"due to E. coli."*

5. Follow any cross-reference instructions such as "see" or "see also." If there are no cross-reference instructions, note the code listed with the subterm entry.

> **EXAMPLE**
>
> The code for *"Infection, urinary (tract) NEC"* is 599.0.

6. **Check the code listed in the *Alphabetic Index* with the description in the *Tabular List*.**

> **EXAMPLE**
>
> Code 599.0 in the Tabular List is described as "Urinary tract infection, site not specified." Two synonymous terms, "bacteriuria" and "pyuria," are listed. The exclusion note identifies "candidiasis of urinary tract (112.2)." The coder is directed to use an additional code to identify the organism, such as "Escherichia coli [E. coli]" (041.4).

7. Read and follow all inclusion, exclusion, and other instructional notes.

> **EXAMPLE**
>
> Code 041.4 identifies the organism E. coli.

8. Assign the code(s) to the highest level of specificity:

   - Select a three-digit code only when no four-digit code is available.
   - Select a four-digit code only when no five-digit code is available.
   - Select a five-digit code when a fifth-digit subclassification is available.

> **EXAMPLE**
>
> Code 599.0 is the highest level of specificity for urinary tract **infection** due to E. coli. There is no fifth-digit subclassification.

9. Select and assign all codes that complete the diagnostic statement.

> **EXAMPLE**
>
> Urinary tract infection due to E. coli is coded 599.0, 041.4.

Step 6 is bolded for a very important reason. Because the *Tabular List* provides a complete description of conditions included and excluded under a particular code, a competent insurance billing specialist *never* codes directly from the *Alphabetic Index*.

Sequencing Diagnostic Codes

To ensure that the health care agency receives appropriate reimbursement for services, diagnostic codes must be accurately listed on the insurance claim (CMS-1500). Placing diagnostic codes in the correct order is called **sequencing**. Sequencing depends on the type of health care agency and on the definition of first-listed diagnosis and principal diagnosis.

The **first-listed diagnosis** is the condition noted as the reason for a specific encounter or visit. First-listed diagnosis criteria apply to outpatient settings, such as a physician's office.

> **EXAMPLE**
>
> A patient is seen in the office for strep throat. During the exam, the physician also reviews the current status of the patient's diabetes. The first-listed diagnosis in this case is strep throat (the reason for the visit) and is sequenced first on the insurance claim. Diabetes can be listed as a concurrent or secondary condition.

A **concurrent condition** is a problem that co-exists with the first-listed diagnosis and complicates the treatment of the first-listed diagnosis. A **secondary condition** is a condition that co-exists with the first-listed diagnosis but does not directly affect the outcome or treatment of the first-listed diagnosis.

The **principal diagnosis** is the diagnosis determined after study to be the reason for the patient's admission to a hospital. Principal diagnosis criteria apply to hospital or inpatient coding.

EXAMPLE

A patient is admitted to the hospital for rectal bleeding. After the appropriate tests, colorectal cancer is identified as the diagnosis. The principal diagnosis in this case is colorectal cancer, even though the initial reason for hospitalization was rectal bleeding.

Improper sequencing of diagnostic codes can lead to inadequate reimbursement for services rendered; denied or delayed reimbursement for services rendered; and, in a worst-case scenario, charges of fraud or abuse. Strict adherence to ICD-9-CM coding conventions, sequencing guidelines, and the *Official Guidelines for Coding and Reporting* prevents reimbursement problems.

REINFORCEMENT EXERCISES 4–8

Provide a short answer for each statement or question.

1. List three activities that lead to successful coding.

_____

_____

_____

2. What is the difference between the first-listed diagnosis and the principal diagnosis?

_____

_____

_____

Rank each statement from 1 to 9. Place a 1 in front of the first step for selecting an ICD-9-CM diagnostic code and a 9 in front of the last step.

_____ Assign the code(s) to the highest level of specificity.

_____ Identify the main term(s) in the diagnostic statement.

_____ Follow any cross-reference instructions.

_____ Check the code listed in the *Alphabetic Index* with the description in the *Tabular List*.

continued on the next page

continued from the previous page

_____ Find the main term(s) in the *Alphabetic Index*.

_____ Select and assign all codes that complete the diagnostic statement.

_____ Review the subterms listed under the main term in the *Alphabetic Index*.

_____ Read and follow all inclusion, exclusion, and other instructional notes.

_____ Review the diagnostic statement for additional information concerning the main term.

Fill in the blank.

1. A condition that co-exists with the first-listed diagnosis and complicates the treatment of the first-listed diagnosis is called a _____.

2. A condition that co-exists with the first-listed diagnosis but does not directly affect the first-listed diagnosis outcome or treatment is called a _____.

3. Listing diagnostic codes in the correct order is known as _____.

4. Diagnostic codes must be selected to the highest level of _____.

5. Code only those conditions that are clearly _____ in the patient's medical record.

Write the main term and assign the correct ICD-9-CM code for each diagnosis.

1. Gastric influenza

   Main Term: _____ Code: _____

2. Laceration of the eyeball

   Main Term: _____ Code: _____

3. Acute pyogenic thyroiditis

   Main Term: _____ Code: _____

4. Malaria with hepatitis

   Main Term: _____ Code: _____

5. Recurrent bleeding peptic ulcer

   Main Term: _____ Code: _____

6. Hypoglycemia

   Main Term: _____ Code: _____

7. Lymphangitis, acute

   Main Term: _____ Code: _____

continued on the next page

continued from the previous page

8. Ectopic pregnancy

Main Term: _____ Code: _____

9. Arthritis due to psoriasis

Main Term: _____ Code: _____

10. Appendicitis with perforation

Main Term: _____ Code: _____

SUPPLEMENTARY CLASSIFICATIONS

The supplementary classifications of ICD-9-CM are located in *Volume 1*, the *Tabular List,* immediately following the 17 main chapters. These classifications are commonly called V codes and E codes. V codes are often used in physician office and ambulatory coding. E codes, which are for the most part optional, are used less often.

V Codes

V codes are found in the "Supplementary Classification of Factors Influencing Health Status and Contact with Health Services" section of the *Tabular List*. No wonder medical billers and coders refer to this section as the "V codes"! These codes apply to situations such as office visits for vaccinations, suture removal, and annual physical examinations.

Table 4–8 lists the *Alphabetic Index* main terms that lead to V codes.

Although V codes are sometimes used in hospitals, they are more frequently assigned in health care settings, such as physician offices, clinics, and outpatient services. As with all coding activities, the billing specialist must be certain that the patient record supports the selected code and that the selected code is the most appropriate for the services rendered.

> **EXAMPLE**
> Jolinda brings her two-year-old son in for a well-child visit. During the physical exam, the physician notices that Miguel's throat is quite red and takes a throat culture. The results indicate that Miguel has strep throat. Jolinda leaves the office with a prescription for an antibiotic.
>
> In this case, the V code for a well-child visit is listed as the reason for the encounter. The appropriate codes for strep throat and throat culture are also submitted for reimbursement.

There is no "magic list" of V codes that may be rejected by some or all third-party payers. Unacceptable V codes for Medicare and Medicaid patients are routinely updated. Fiscal intermediaries (insurance companies) may notify health care providers which V codes are unacceptable for reimbursement.

Table 4–9 lists the V code categories and titles. Information about each V code category follows Table 4–9.

TABLE 4–8

Alphabetic Index Main Terms that Lead to V Codes		
Admission (encounter)	Dialysis	Outcome of delivery
Aftercare	Donor	Pregnancy
Attention to	Examination	Problem
Boarder	Exposure	Prophylactic
Care (of)	Fitting (of)	Replacement by
Carrier (suspected) of	Follow-up	Resistance, resistant
Checking	Health	Screening
Contact	Healthy	Status
Contraception, contraceptive	History (personal) of	Supervision (of)
Convalescence	Maintenance	Test(s)
Counseling	Maladjustment	Therapy
Dependence	Newborn	Transplant, transplanted
	Observation	Vaccination

Categories V01–V06 Persons with Health Hazards Related to Communicable Diseases

Codes from categories V01 through V06 are assigned when the reason for the service includes vaccination and inoculation against a communicable disease. The patient may have been exposed to the disease or may fall into a high-risk category, as with flu shots for specific populations. *Alphabetic Index* terms such as "contact," "exposure," "prophylactic (preventive)," and "vaccination" lead to V01–V06 codes.

EXAMPLE

Abby was seen by the pediatrician for a DPT vaccination (immunization). DPT is a combination immunization for diphtheria, pertussis, and tetanus. Because this is the reason for the visit, code V06.1, "Vaccination and inoculation against combinations of diseases, diphtheria-tetanus-pertussis, combined," is the appropriate ICD-9-CM code.

Categories V07–V09 Persons with Need for Isolation, Other Potential Health Hazards and Prophylactic Measures

Codes from categories V07 through V09 are usually assigned as an additional code when a condition is classified or coded elsewhere.

EXAMPLE

Janelle was admitted to City Hospital and placed in isolation. Her diagnosis is necrotic septicemia due to vancomycin-resistant staphylococcus aureus (VRSA).

The diagnosis code for necrotic septicemia is assigned as the principal diagnosis. V07.0 (Isolation) and V09.8 (VRSA) may be assigned as additional codes.

TABLE 4–9

V Code Categories and Titles	
Categories	**Titles**
V01–V06	Persons with Potential Health Hazards Related to Communicable Diseases
V07–V09	Persons with Need for Isolation, Other Potential Health Hazards, and Prophylactic Measures
V10–V19	Persons with Potential Health Hazards Related to Personal and Family History
V20–V29	Persons Encountering Health Services in Circumstances Related to Reproduction and Development
V30–V39	Liveborn Infants According to Type of Birth
V40–V49	Persons with a Condition Influencing Their Health Status
V50–V59	Persons Encountering Health Services for Specific Procedures and Aftercare
V60–V69	Persons Encountering Health Services in Other Circumstances
V70–V82	Persons without Reported Diagnosis Encountered during Examination and Investigation of Individuals and Populations
V83–V84	Genetics
V85	Body Mass Index
V86	Estrogen Receptor Status
V87	Other Specified Personal Exposures and History Presenting Hazards to Health
V88	Acquired Absence of Other Organs and Tissue
V89	Other Suspected Conditions Not Found

Categories V10–V19 Persons with Potential Health Hazards Related to Personal and Family History

Codes from categories V10 through V19 are assigned when there is a personal or family history of malignant neoplasms, mental health problems, allergies, or other diseases. Codes from these categories provide additional information about the patient and are rarely, if ever, submitted for reimbursement as the sole reason for the encounter.

EXAMPLE

The patient is seen for a sinus infection. During the exam, the patient states, "I'm allergic to penicillin."

A sinus infection is the reason for the office visit. For billing purposes, the ICD-9-CM code for sinusitis is listed as the diagnostic code. The code V14.0, "Personal history of allergy to medicinal agents, penicillin," may be included as additional information, but it has no effect on reimbursement.

EXAMPLE

A healthy 30-year-old woman is seen for an employment physical. She states that her mother and her dad's sister had breast cancer in their 30s. The physician completes the employment physical and orders a baseline mammography.

In this case, the appropriate V code for an employment physical is selected as the first-listed diagnosis: V70.5, "General medical examination, preemployment screening." If no other problems are identified, that is the code submitted with the insurance claim. If problems are found during the physical, the appropriate ICD-9-CM codes are submitted as additional diagnoses.

The reason for the mammography is a family history of breast cancer. If the patient's insurance covers this service, the radiologist's billing specialist submits V16.3, "Family history of malignant neoplasm, breast," as the first-listed diagnosis. If the mammogram reveals any problems, the appropriate ICD-9-CM codes are also submitted with the insurance claim.

Categories V20–V29 Persons Encountering Health Services in Circumstances Related to Reproduction and Development

Codes from categories V20 through V29 describe all stages of pregnancy, child development, and birth control. These categories are commonly used in the physician office setting. Table 4–10 lists the conditions associated with codes V20 through V29. Application examples follow Table 4–10.

Codes from category V20 are assigned to routine health assessments of a healthy infant or child. Category V21 applies when the visit includes the identification of a specific developmental state.

EXAMPLE

Martin is seen for a routine preschool hearing and vision screening. The physician notes that Martin has experienced a growth spurt that was greater than expected. Although there is no problem at this time, Martin's parents are advised to monitor his growth.

Code V20.2, "Routine infant or child health check," is selected as the reason for the visit and submitted on the insurance claim. Code V21.0, "Period of rapid growth in childhood," may be included as an additional finding.

TABLE 4–10

Pregnancy, Child Development, Birth Control V Codes	
Condition	**V Codes**
Pregnancy, postpartum, procreative management	V22 Normal pregnancy
	V23 Supervision of high-risk pregnancy
	V24 Postpartum care and examination
	V26 Procreative management
	V27 Outcome of delivery
	V28 Encounter for antenatal screening of mother
Child development	V20 Health supervision of infant or child
	V21 Constitutional states in development
	V29 Observation and evaluation of newborns and infants for suspected condition not found
Birth control	V25 Encounter for contraceptive management

Codes from category V22 are assigned to supervision of a normal pregnancy. This category has three choices: "Supervision of a normal first pregnancy" is coded V22.0, and "Supervision of other [or subsequent] normal pregnancy" is coded V22.1. These codes are used in physician offices and clinics and can stand alone in those settings. Code V22.2, "Pregnant state, incidental," is assigned when the pregnancy is not the primary reason for the encounter.

EXAMPLE

Jolinda is seen for follow-up treatment and evaluation of psoriasis. She is six months pregnant and states she feels fine.

In this example, the reason for the visit is related to psoriasis. The appropriate ICD-9-CM diagnosis code for psoriasis is submitted with the insurance claim. Code V22.2, "Pregnant state, incidental," is optional, as long as follow-up for psoriasis is unrelated to the pregnancy and does not affect the management of the pregnancy.

EXAMPLE

Routine prenatal visit for Roberta, who is three months pregnant. Roberta has gained eight pounds and is pleased that she is doing better with her weight this time. During her last pregnancy, she gained 15 pounds in the first trimester.

In this example, code V22.1, "Supervision of other normal pregnancy," accurately describes the reason for this visit. In the absence of any other diagnostic statement, this code stands on its own.

Codes from category V23 are assigned when a condition is present that may add risk to the pregnancy. These codes are listed in the *Alphabetical Index* under "Pregnancy, supervision (of) (for)" or "Pregnancy, management affected by." The condition must be clearly identified in the patient's record and includes statements such as "pregnant with a history of neonatal death."

EXAMPLE

Given her history of two stillbirths in three pregnancies, Miranda was relieved when she heard strong fetal heart sounds. She is advised to continue with her current activity level and dietary program. Her next prenatal visit is scheduled in one month.

In this example, the patient has a history of stillbirths. This justifies the code V23.5, "Supervision of high-risk pregnancy, pregnancy with other poor reproductive history (stillbirth or neonatal death)." In the absence of any other diagnostic statement, this code stands alone.

Codes from category V24 are assigned for uncomplicated and routine postpartum care and examination. The postpartum period is six weeks following delivery. If a postpartum complication is identified during the visit, the code for the complication is selected as the first-listed diagnosis.

EXAMPLE

Martina is seen for a six-week appointment following delivery of a healthy baby girl. She offers no complaints, and no complications are noted.

This is an example of a routine postpartum visit. Code V24.2, "Routine postpartum follow-up," is the correct code, and it stands alone.

EXAMPLE

Sara is seen three weeks following delivery of a healthy baby boy. Examination today reveals a swollen red area surrounding the episiotomy site. There is no exudate from the wound. Sara states there is "itching and burning" in the area. A topical antibiotic cream is prescribed.

In this case, an infection developed within the postpartum period and involves the episiotomy site. The billing specialist selects the correct ICD-9-CM diagnostic code for a postpartum infection of the episiotomy site. Code 674.34, "Other complications of obstetrical surgical wounds, postpartum," includes this infection. A code from category V24 is not appropriate for this situation.

Codes from category V25 are assigned when the purpose of the office visit is related to contraceptive management, commonly called birth control. Many insurance companies do not cover health care encounters associated with birth control.

EXAMPLE

Darryl is seen for voluntary vasectomy for purposes of birth control. Darryl must return for a postvasectomy sperm count.

Code V25.2, "Sterilization, interruption of the vas deferens," is submitted with the insurance claim, provided the patient's insurance covers office visits related to voluntary sterilization.

Codes from category V26 apply to artificial insemination, repair of fallopian tubes or vas deferens following sterilization, genetic counseling, and other procreative treatments. Many of these treatments or procedures are classified as experimental and must be paid for by the patient. Fertility specialists may use these codes to tabulate statistics.

Codes from category V27 are intended to code the outcome of delivery in the mother's medical record. These codes are for statistical purposes only and are not used for reimbursement.

Codes from category V28 are assigned to screening activities that involve amniocentesis and ultrasound. While ultrasound has become a fairly common prenatal screening tool, its use must be clinically justified.

EXAMPLE

Denise, who began her pregnancy at a normal weight, is estimated at 30 weeks gestation and has gained only five pounds. Her obstetrician is concerned about fetal size compared with the estimated gestational age. An ultrasound is performed to evaluate fetal growth and development. No abnormalities are found.

In this case, code V28.4, "Antenatal screening, screening for fetal growth retardation using ultrasonics," is the correct diagnostic code. When the screening identifies an abnormal finding, then the abnormal condition is coded as the diagnostic statement.

Codes from category V29 are assigned to situations in which a newborn is suspected of having a particular condition that is ruled out after examination and observation. A newborn is an infant in the first 28 days of life (also called the neonatal period).

EXAMPLE

During her last trimester, Maureen developed a vaginal yeast infection. Conservative medical management controlled the symptoms. The normal vaginal delivery resulted in the birth of a healthy baby girl. Candidiasis is the organism that causes vaginal yeast infections and thrush. Maureen's family physician scheduled weekly appointments to monitor the newborn for thrush.

In this case, code V29.0, "Observation for suspected infectious condition," is the appropriate diagnostic code and is submitted with the insurance claim. If at any time during the observation period a diagnosis is identified, then the V29 code would no longer be appropriate.

REINFORCEMENT EXERCISES 4–9

Match the V code titles in Column A with the V code categories in Column B.

Column A   **Column B**

1. Encounter for antenatal screening of mother   _____   V20

2. Constitutional states in development   _____   V21

3. Contraceptive management   _____   V22

4. Health supervision, infant or child   _____   V23

5. Normal pregnancy   _____   V24

6. Observation and evaluation of newborns and infants   _____   V25

7. Outcome of delivery   _____   V26

8. Postpartum care and evaluation   _____   V27

9. Procreative management   _____   V28

10. Supervision of high-risk pregnancy   _____   V29

Provide a short answer for each statement or question.

1. Name the V code categories that are used to identify liveborn infants in the hospital setting.

   _____

   _____

   _____

2. List the V codes and their descriptions that are included in the supervision of a normal pregnancy category.

   _____

   _____

   _____

continued on the next page

continued from the previous page

3. When would the coder/biller assign V22.2, "Pregnancy state, incidental"?

_____

_____

_____

4. What is the purpose of codes from category V27, "Outcome of delivery"?

_____

_____

_____

5. Give an example of a condition that would justify selecting a code from category V23, "Supervision of high-risk pregnancy."

_____

_____

_____

Categories V30–V39 Liveborn Infants According to Type of Birth

Codes in categories V30–V39 are assigned to liveborn infants who are occupying a hospital crib or bassinet. Three-digit categories identify single, twin, or multiple births, and the status of the twin or multiple mates. Four digit subcategories identify whether or not the infant(s) was born in the hospital. Fifth digit subcategories identify delivery with or without mention of cesarean section.

EXAMPLE

Mrs. Cho gave birth to healthy twin girls by cesarean delivery. The mother's admission is coded as a live birth, cesarean delivery, twins. Each infant admission is assigned code V31.01, twin, mate born live, in the hospital by cesarean delivery.

Categories V40–V49 Persons with a Condition Influencing Their Health Status

Codes in categories V40 through V49 are used under the following circumstances:

- Nonspecific diagnoses that usually begin with the words "problem with"
- Postsurgical conditions involving organ transplants, artificial openings, and implanted devices
- Dependence on machines
- Problems with internal organs, head, neck, trunk, and limbs

These codes are typically assigned as additional diagnostic codes and can often explain or justify services that are rendered. Diagnostic statements for V codes 40–49 usually begin with "status post" or "dependence on."

EXAMPLE

Patient is seen with a diagnosis of umbilical hernia. Status post ileostomy. The umbilical hernia, 553.1, is coded as the reason for the visit with V44.2, "Artificial opening status post, ileostomy," as an additional code.

Categories V50–V59 Persons Encountering Health Services for Specific Procedures and Aftercare

Codes from categories V50–V59 can be assigned as the primary diagnosis in the physician office and clinic settings. These codes are selected in the following circumstances:

- To indicate a reason for care in patients who have already been treated for some disease or injury not now present or who are receiving care to consolidate treatment
- To deal with residual states
- To prevent recurrence

EXAMPLE

As a result of severe ulcerative colitis, a patient has a total proctocolectomy—removal of the rectum and entire large intestine—with construction of an ileostomy. The ulcerative colitis is now "cured." However, the patient may need treatment or services related to the ileostomy. Codes listed under V55, "Attention to artificial openings," apply to services related to an ileostomy.

Codes from category V50 are assigned to a wide variety of situations, such as hair transplant, circumcision, ear piercing, and prophylactic organ removal.

Codes from category V51 apply to aftercare involving the use of plastic surgery. Cosmetic plastic surgery and plastic surgery as a treatment for a current condition are excluded from category V51.

Codes from category V52 are assigned to services related to artificial limbs, eyes, dental devices, and breast prosthetics and implants.

EXAMPLE

After losing 50 pounds, a patient is measured and fitted with a new artificial leg. Code V52.1, "Fitting and adjustment of . . . [an] artificial leg," is the diagnostic code for the office visit.

Codes from category V53 cover nervous system and special sense devices; cardiac pacemakers and defibrillators; intestinal, urinary, and orthopedic devices; wheelchairs; and other unspecified devices.

Codes in category V54 cover orthopedic aftercare involving internal fixation devices, healing traumatic and pathologic fractures, and cast removal.

EXAMPLE

Eight weeks after a motor vehicle accident, the patient was seen in the office. The foot and leg cast was taken off, and the heel pin was removed. Codes V54.01, "Removal of . . . internal fixation device (pins)," and V54.89, "Removal of . . . cast," are the diagnostic codes for the office visit. These codes are submitted with the insurance claim.

Codes in category V55 are assigned to services related to artificial openings such as catheter care, closure of the opening, and passage of sounds or bougies. Problems with an external stoma are not covered in category V55.

EXAMPLE

The patient is seen for replacement of the cystostomy tube. Code V55.5, "Attention to artificial openings, cystostomy," is the diagnostic code for this office visit.

Codes in category V56 include services related to dialysis and dialysis catheter care. An additional code to identify the associated condition is required.

EXAMPLE

Victoria completed her peritoneal dialysis and returned home with a new supply of dialysis solution. She was diagnosed with renal failure in May of last year. Codes V56.8, "Encounter for . . . peritoneal dialysis," and 586, "Renal failure, unspecified," are the diagnostic codes for this visit.

Codes in category V57 are assigned when the service provided includes physical, occupational, vocational, and speech therapy. As with the dialysis V codes, this category requires an additional code to identify the underlying condition.

EXAMPLE

Melissa is seen for physical therapy for hemiplegia. Codes 342.90, "Hemiplegia, unspecified, affecting unspecified side," and V57.1, "Care involving . . . other physical therapy," are the diagnostic codes for the office visit.

Categories V60–V69 Persons Encountering Health Services in Other Circumstances

Codes from categories V60–V69 can be assigned as the primary diagnosis in the physician office and clinic settings. These codes cover a variety of circumstances—from homelessness (V60.0, "Lack of housing") to problems related to lifestyles (V69.3, "Gambling and betting").

Category V65 includes circumstances such as counseling sessions for dietary surveillance, HIV and other sexually transmitted diseases, exercise, and health education or instruction.

Category V66 often applies to long-term and hospice care following surgery, radiotherapy, or chemotherapy.

Category V67 is used for surveillance only following completed treatment. These codes are located in the *Alphabetic Index* under the phrases "Follow-up," "Encounter, for, follow-up," and "Admission, for, follow-up."

EXAMPLE

Rhonda is seen for an examination following successful treatment of pyoderma gangrenosum (purulent skin disease associated with ulcerative colitis) with Dapsone. Because Dapsone can cause liver damage, code V67.51, "Follow-up examination . . . following completed treatment with high-risk medication," is assigned as the reason for the follow-up visit.

Category V68 includes situations such as issuing a medical certificate, repeat prescriptions, and request for expert advice.

Category V69 covers lack of physical exercise, high-risk sexual behavior, gambling, and problems related to lifestyle.

REINFORCEMENT EXERCISE 4–10

Match the V codes in Column A with the titles in Column B.

Column A	Column B
1. V40–V49 _____	**a.** Administrative purposes
2. V50–V59 _____	**b.** Attention to artificial openings
3. V50 _____	**c.** Conditions influencing health status
4. V60–V69 _____	**d.** Dialysis and catheter care
5. V52 _____	**e.** Elective surgery
6. V55 _____	**f.** Encountering health services, other circumstances
7. V56 _____	**g.** Encountering health services, specific procedures and aftercare
8. V57 _____	**h.** Fitting and adjustment of prosthetic device and implant
9. V67 _____	**i.** Follow-up examinations
10. V68 _____	**j.** Rehabilitation procedures

Categories V70–V89 Persons Without Reported Diagnosis Encountered During Examination and Investigation of Individuals and Populations

Codes from categories V70–V89 include the following:

- All types of routine medical examinations
- Observation and evaluation for suspected conditions not found, such as mental illness, malignant neoplasms, rape, and other specified suspected conditions
- Special screening for sexually transmitted, bacterial, infectious, endocrine, nutritional, metabolic, viral, neurological, and immunity disorders and other body system diseases and malignant neoplasms

Most of the categories in this section are appropriate as stand-alone codes for the physician office or clinic setting. Abnormal findings disclosed at the time of these examinations must be coded to the appropriate ICD-9-CM chapter.

Category V70 includes codes that apply to routine visits and to preventive care when no complaints are present. Category V70 codes are located under the alphabetic entry "examination and examination, medical, for." When a specific condition, sign, or diagnosis is being evaluated, the code for the condition must be included on the insurance claim. Table 4–11 lists the general medical examination categories, titles, and examples.

TABLE 4–11

V70 General Medical Examinations	
V Code	**Title/Example**
V70.0	Routine general medical examination at a health care facility; excludes infant or child
V70.1	General psychiatric examination, requested by the authority
V70.2	General psychiatric examination, other and unspecified
V70.3	Other medical examination for administrative purposes; sports competition, driving license, adoption, marriage, etc.; excludes attendance for issuance of medical certificates, pre-employment screening
V70.4	Examination for medicolegal reasons; blood-alcohol tests, blood-drug testing, paternity testing; excludes accidents, assault, rape
V70.5	Health examination of defined subpopulations; armed forces personnel, occupational health, pre-employment screening, preschool children, etc.
V70.6	Health examinations in population surveys
V70.7	Examination of participant in clinical trial
V70.8	Other specified general medical examinations
V70.9	Unspecified general medical examination

EXAMPLE

Lance, an accomplished swimmer, is seen for completion of the required sports physical. No abnormalities are found, and no restrictions for participation are documented. Code V70.3, "Other medical examination for administrative purposes, . . . sports competition," is assigned as the reason for the encounter.

EXAMPLE

Phillip is seen for court-ordered paternity testing. Code V70.4, "Examination for medicolegal reasons, Paternity testing," is assigned as the reason for the visit. The blood test is also coded and included on the insurance claim.

Codes from category V71 are assigned when a person without a diagnosis is suspected of having an abnormal condition that requires examination and observation even if no signs or symptoms of the condition are present. Conditions in this category include examination of the victim or culprit following alleged rape or seduction (V71.5), observation for suspected tuberculosis (V71.2), and observation and evaluation of abuse and neglect (V71.81). If the suspected condition is not found, category V71 codes are assigned as the reason for the examination or observation.

Codes from category V72 include routine examination of specific systems, such as eyes and vision and ears and hearing as well as dental exams, annual or routine gynecological exams, and routine preoperative examinations. Diagnostic activities such as radiology, laboratory tests, and skin tests for allergies are coded to this category.

Categories V73 through V89 include codes to identify screening examinations for specific conditions and disorders that may or may not be found. These codes are located in the *Alphabetic Index* under the entry "Screening (for)." The conditions covered in these categories range from anemia to suspected maternal and fetal conditions. Table 4–12 lists categories V73 through V89, with examples.

TABLE 4–12

Categories V73 Through V89		
Code	Category Name	Examples
V73	Special screening examination for viral and chlamydial diseases	V73.0 Poliomyelitis V73.1 Smallpox V73.88 Other specified chlamydial diseases
V74	Special screening examination for bacterial and spirochetal diseases	V74.0 Cholera V74.1 Pulmonary tuberculosis V74.2 Leprosy (Hansen's disease)
V75	Special screening examination for other infectious diseases	V75.0 Rickettsial diseases V75.1 Malaria V75.2 Leishmaniasis
V76	Special screening for malignant neoplasms	V76.0 Respiratory organs V76.10 Breast screening, unspecified
V77	Special screening for endocrine, nutritional, metabolic, and immunity disorders	V77.0 Thyroid disorders V77.1 Diabetes mellitus V77.2 Malnutrition
V78	Special screening for disorders of blood and blood-forming organs	V78.0 Iron deficiency anemia V78.1 Other and unspecified deficiency anemia V78.2 Sickle cell disease or trait
V79	Special screening for mental disorders and developmental handicaps	V79.0 Depression V79.1 Alcoholism V79.2 Mental retardation
V80	Special screening for neurological, eye, and ear diseases	V80.0 Neurological conditions V80.1 Glaucoma V80.2 Other eye conditions
V81	Special screening for cardio-vascular, respiratory, and genitourinary diseases	V81.1 Ischemic heart V81.1 Hypertension V81.2 Other and unspecified cardiovascular conditions

continued on the next page

continued from the previous page

V82	Special screening for other conditions	V82.0 Skin conditions V82.1 Rheumatoid arthritis
V83	Genetic carrier status	V83.0 Hemophilia A carrier
V84	Genetic susceptibility to disease	V84.0 Genetic susceptibility to malignant neoplasm
V85	Body mass index (BMI)	V85.0 Body mass index less than 19, adult (adult is defined as persons over 20 years old) V85.1 Body mass index between 19–24, adult
V86	Estrogen receptor status	V86.0 Estrogen receptor positive status [ER+] V86.1 Estrogen receptor negative status [ER−]
V87	Other specified personal exposures and history present hazards to health	V87.01 Contact with arsenic V87.31 Exposure to mold
V88	Acquired absence of other organs and tissue	V88.01 Acquired absence of both cervix and uterus; status post total hysterectomy
V89	Other suspected conditions not found	V89.02 Suspected placental problem not found V89.03 Suspected fetal anomaly not found

REINFORCEMENT EXERCISES 4–11

Match the V codes in Column A with the statements in Column B.

Column A

1. V70 _____
2. V72 _____
3. V75 _____
4. V76 _____
5. V77 _____

Column B

a. dental examinations
b. general medical examinations
c. screening, endocrine disorders
d. screening, infectious diseases
e. screening, malignant neoplasms

Write the exclusions for the listed V code categories.

1. V70.0, "General medical examination at a health care facility"

_____

continued on the next page

continued from the previous page

2. V70.3, "Other medical examination for administrative purposes"

3. V70.4, "Examination for medicolegal reasons"

4. V70.6, "Health examination in population surveys"

5. V76.2, "Special screening for malignant neoplasms"

6. V80.2, "Special screening for . . . eye . . . diseases, Other eye conditions"

7. V81.4, "Special screening for respiratory conditions"

8. V82.4, "Postnatal screening for chromosomal anomalies"

9. V87.0, "Contact with and (suspected) exposure to hazardous metals"

10. V87.4, "Personal history of drug therapy"

E Codes

E codes are listed in the "Supplementary Classification of External Causes of Injury and Other Adverse Effects." As with V codes, health care professionals refer to this section simply as "E codes." E codes provide an avenue to classify environmental events, circumstances, and conditions that cause injury, poisoning, adverse effects, and other abnormal conditions.

E codes are intended to provide data for injury research and prevention. The codes capture information about the following:

- Cause: How the injury or poisoning occurred (fall, flood, explosion)
- Intent: Why the injury or poisoning occurred (accident, assault, suicide attempt)
- Place: Where the injury or poisoning occurred (home, public building, workplace)

The use of E codes in many health care settings is optional, except for categories E930 through E949. This section is titled "Drugs, Medicinal and Biological Substances Causing Adverse Effects in Therapeutic Use." A portion of this section is shown in Figure 4–10. Review the figure, and pay close attention to the inclusion and exclusion notes.

Includes: correct drug properly administered in therapeutic or prophylactic dosage, as the cause of any adverse effect including allergic or hypersensitivity reactions

Excludes: *accidental overdose of drug and wrong drug given or taken in error...*

accidents in the technique of administration of drug or biological substance...

administration with suicidal or homicidal intent or intent to harm...

E930   **Antibiotics**

Excludes: *that used as eye, ear, nose, and throat and local anti-infectives...*

E930.0   Penicillins
Natural
Synthetic
Semisynthetic...

E931   Other anti infectives

E932   Hormones and synthetic substitutes

E933   Primarily systemic agents

E934   Agents primarily affecting blood constituents

E935   Analgesics, antipyretics, and antirheumatics...

FIGURE 4–10 Drugs, Medicinal and Biological Substances Causing Adverse Effects in Therapeutic Use (E930–E949) (Permission to reuse granted by Ingenix)

Some state laws require the use of E codes, as in cases of firearms accidents, mass transport accidents, and other incidents related to public health and safety. E codes cannot be assigned as the only diagnostic code for a particular case. In most coding references, the alphabetic index for E codes, "Index to External Causes," follows the "Table of Drugs and Chemicals Index."

MISCELLANEOUS CODING GUIDELINES

Late effects, burns, and HIV/AIDS have coding guidelines unique to each condition. The guidelines are discussed individually.

Late Effects

There are a variety of illnesses and injuries that once treated result in a temporary or permanent medical problem or condition. This condition is called a **residual**.

EXAMPLE
A severe burn may result in a scar as a residual; a stroke may result in aphasia.

A **late effect** is the residual condition that remains after the acute phase of an illness or injury has been resolved. There is no definitive timetable for late effects. Documentation of late effects may include wording such as "residual of," "old," "sequela of," "late," and "due to" or "following" a previous illness or injury.

Late effects often require two codes: one for the residual condition that is currently affecting the patient and another code to describe the original injury or illness. The residual condition code is sequenced first. In some cases, there is a combination code that includes the residual condition and the underlying cause.

> **EXAMPLE**
>
> Keloid formation of the right forearm due to previous laceration. In this example, keloid is the residual late effect and is coded 701.4, "Keloid scar." The cause of the keloid, previous laceration, is coded 906.1, "Late effect of open wound of extremities without mention of tendon injury."

> **EXAMPLE**
>
> Hemiplegia due to old CVA. Code 438.20, "Late effects of cerebrovascular disease, hemiplegia affecting unspecified side," includes both the late effect and its cause.

When the diagnostic statement does not include the residual condition, code only the cause of the late effect. Late effect codes are located in the *Alphabetic Index* under the main term "Late" and the subterm "effect(s) (of)."

Burns

Codes from ICD-9-CM categories 940 through 949 apply to current unhealed burns with the exception of sunburn and friction burns. Sunburns are classified as dermatitis, and friction burns are classified as superficial injuries. Scars and contractures that remain when the burn has healed are coded as late effects.

> **EXAMPLE**
>
> Elizabeth is seen for treatment of sunburn. Code 692.71, "Contact dermatitis and other eczema, Due to solar radiation, Sunburn," is the correct diagnostic code.

> **EXAMPLE**
>
> Ronald is seen for an abrasion of the left leg due to skidding across the basketball court. Code 916.0, "Superficial injury of . . . leg . . . , Abrasion without mention of infection," is the correct diagnostic code.

> **EXAMPLE**
>
> Brett is seen for the assessment of contracture of three fingers on his left hand. Sequela of a previous grease burn. Codes 709.2, "Scar conditions and fibrosis of skin," and 906.6, "Late effect of burn, wrist or hand," are the correct diagnostic codes. The contracture code, 709.2, is sequenced first.

Burn diagnoses require at least two codes: one for the site and degree of the burn and another for the percentage of body surface affected. Category 948, "Burns classified according to extent of body surface involved," provides codes ranging from less than 10% of body surface (948.00) to 90% or more of the body surface (948.99). Body surface involvement is estimated based on the "rule of nines," which assigns a body surface burn percentage. Figure 4–11 illustrates the rule of nines.

The percentages are adjusted for infants, children, and adults with large buttocks, abdomens, or thighs. It is the physician or health care provider's responsibility to calculate the extent of the burn.

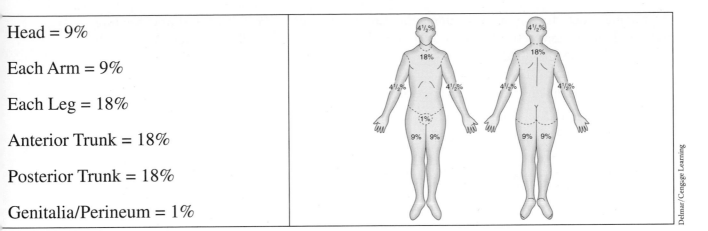

Head = 9%

Each Arm = 9%

Each Leg = 18%

Anterior Trunk = 18%

Posterior Trunk = 18%

Genitalia/Perineum = 1%

FIGURE 4–11 Rule of Nines

HIV/AIDS

Because of the prejudicial nature of HIV- and AIDS-related diagnoses, the patient must sign an Authorization for Release of HIV Status so these codes can be included on an insurance claim.

Category 042 is used to code acquired immunodeficiency syndrome (AIDS), AIDS-like syndrome, AIDS-related complex (ARC), and symptomatic HIV infection. Specific conditions, such as Kaposi's sarcoma, should also be coded.

Several V codes apply to HIV/AIDS conditions. Code V08, "Asymptomatic human immunodeficiency virus infection," is used when the patient has tested positive for HIV and displays no symptoms. Code V72.6, "Laboratory examination," is selected when the visit includes a lab test to rule out HIV infection. Code V73.89, "Other specified viral diseases," is selected when patient exposure to HIV is unknown. Code V01.7, "Contact with or exposure to . . . other viral diseases," is selected when the patient has been exposed to the AIDS virus.

There are two coding guidelines for reporting services rendered to HIV-infected and AIDS patients:

1. When treating or evaluating an HIV-related illness, the first-listed diagnosis code is 042. Codes related to other conditions or manifestations, such as Kaposi's sarcoma, are listed as secondary conditions.
2. When treating or evaluating a condition unrelated to HIV-related illnesses, the reason for the visit is coded and is the first-listed diagnosis. The HIV disease and related manifestations are sequenced as secondary diagnoses.

Do not assign an HIV or AIDS code to cases documented as "probable," "possible," or "questionable." Use V08 or 795.71, "nonspecific serological evidence of human immunodeficiency virus."

Volume 3: Tabular List and Alphabetic Index of Procedures

Volume 3, the *Tabular List and Alphabetic Index of Procedures,* is often referred to as the "Procedure Codes." The procedure codes in *Volume 3* are used to code and report services rendered during an inpatient or hospital episode of care. The organizational patterns, format, and conventions in *Volume 3* are nearly identical to those in *Volumes 1* and *2*. The few differences are presented after the overview of the components of *Volume 3*.

Volume 3 includes two main sections: the *Alphabetic Index to the Tabular List* of procedure codes and 18 chapters in the *Tabular List* of procedure codes. The specific characteristics of each section are described individually.

Alphabetic Index

The *Alphabetic Index* is a listing of procedures, tests, operations, surgeries, and other therapies. The organization of the *Alphabetic Index* to procedures is very similar to the format of the *Alphabetic Index of Diseases and Injuries* (*Volume* 2). Main terms are bolded and flush left. Main terms for the *Alphabetic Index* to procedures include the following:

- Eponyms, such as "Billroth II operation" (partial gastrectomy with gastrojejunostomy)
- Nouns, such as "examination," "bypass," "operation"
- Operations, such as diverticulectomy, gastrectomy, proctocolectomy
- Procedures or tests, such as amniocentesis, colonoscopy, scan
- Verbs, such as "closure," "excision," "repair"

Subterms associated with main terms and other subterms are indented and listed in alphabetic order—**except for** subterms that begin with the words "as," "by," and "with." These words are known as "connecting words" and immediately follow a main term or subterm entry as appropriate. Figure 4–12 is an example of an entry from the *Volume 3 Alphabetic Index.*

The entries in the *Alphabetic Index* are fairly comprehensive. A specific entry in the *Alphabetic Index* may in fact be coded to a less specific category in the *Tabular List* of procedures.

> **EXAMPLE**
> Following a motor vehicle accident, Caleb was admitted for a cervical spine injury and placed in a Thomas collar.

Incision (and drainage) ← main term

  with ← connecting word

    exploration–*see* Exploration

    removal of foreign body–*see* Removal, foreign body

  abdominal wall 54.0 ← subterm

    as operative approach–*omit code*

FIGURE 4–12 Volume 3 Alphabetic Index Entry

In this example, the Alphabetic Index lists "Thomas collar" as a subterm under the main term "Application." The code noted in the Index is 93.52. In the Tabular List, code 93.52 is "Application of neck support." Even though "Thomas collar" is not included in the list of neck supports noted under the code, the billing specialist or medical coder relies on the accuracy of the Tabular List and assigns 93.52 as the code for the application of a Thomas collar.

Tabular List

The *Tabular List* in *Volume 3* contains 18 chapters. With the exception of Chapter 1, "Procedures and Interventions Not Elsewhere Classified," Chapter 13, "Obstetrical Procedures," and Chapter 16, "Miscellaneous Diagnostic and Therapeutic Procedures," the chapters are organized by body systems and organs. Table 4–13 lists the *Tabular List* chapters and code categories.

Procedure codes in the *Tabular List* consist of three or four digits. Two digits precede a decimal point, and one or two digits follow the decimal point. As with disease and condition codes, a three-digit code cannot be used if a four-digit code is available. The third and fourth digits provide additional information about the procedure. The *Tabular List* includes important inclusion and exclusion notes. Figure 4–13 is an example of a *Tabular List* entry.

TABLE 4–13

Volume 3 Tabular List Chapters and Categories	
Chapter Titles	Categories
00. Procedures and Interventions, Not Elsewhere Classified	00–00.9
1. Operations on the Nervous System	01–05
2. Operations on the Endocrine System	06–07
3. Operations on the Eye	08–16
3A. Other Miscellaneous Diagnostic and Therapeutic Procedures	17
4. Operations on the Ear	18–20
5. Operations on the Nose, Mouth, and Pharynx	21–29
6. Operations on the Respiratory System	30–34
7. Operations on the Cardiovascular System	35–39
8. Operations on the Hemic and Lymphatic System	40–41
9. Operations on the Digestive System	42–54
10. Operations on the Urinary System	55–59
11. Operations on the Male Genital Organs	60–64
12. Operations on the Female Genital Organs	65–71
13. Obstetrical Procedures	72–75
14. Operations on the Musculoskeletal System	76–84
15. Operations on the Integumentary System	85–86
16. Miscellaneous Diagnostic and Therapeutic Procedures	87–99

---

7. OPERATIONS ON THE CARDIOVASCULAR SYSTEM (35–39)

35   **Operations on valves and septa of heart**

Includes: sternotomy (median)

(transverse)

thoracotomy

Code also cardiopulmonary bypass [extracorporeal circulation] [heart-lung machine] (39.61)

35.0   **Closed heart valvotomy**

| *Excludes:* | *percutaneous (balloon) valvuloplasty (35.96)* |

35.00   **Closed heart valvotomy, unspecified valve**

35.01   **Closed heart valvotomy, aortic valve**

35.02   **Closed heart valvotomy, mitral valve**

35.03   **Closed heart valvotomy, pulmonary valve**

35.04   **Closed heart valvotomy, tricuspid valve**

FIGURE 4–13 Volume 3 Tabular List Entry (Permission to reuse granted by Ingenix)

Volume 3 Coding Conventions

Most of the coding conventions discussed for *Volumes 1* and *2* also apply to *Volume 3*. The exceptions are "code also," "omit code," and slanted brackets [ ]. These conventions are discussed and examples are given here.

"Code also" means that additional procedures and use of special equipment must be coded and submitted with the insurance claim. "Code also" instructions provide a list of codes that are acceptable additional codes.

EXAMPLE

Pedro was admitted for a permanent colostomy. Colostomy is coded to subcategory 46.1, which includes the instruction to "code also any synchronous resection (45.49, 45.71–45.79, 45.8)." The permanent colostomy is coded as 46.13.

The operative report is reviewed to discover how much of the large intestine was removed (resected) during the colostomy procedure. The appropriate code from the "code also" list is assigned to the resection.

"Omit code" is found in both the *Tabular List* and *Alphabetic Index* of *Volume 3*. As the phrase implies, the instruction tells the billing specialist or medical coder not to assign a procedure code. "Omit code" usually applies to procedures that are

- Closures of given procedures
- Exploratory procedures that are incidental to another procedure that is carried out
- Lysis of adhesions by blunt, digital, manual, or mechanical methods
- Usual surgical approaches of a given procedure

Slanted brackets *[ ]* are found in the *Alphabetic Index* of *Volume 3*. Slanted brackets alert the billing specialist or medical coder that closely related procedures require two codes.

> **EXAMPLE**
> Becky was admitted for anastomosis of the bladder to the ileum.
> In this example, the entry in the Alphabetic Index is "**Anastomosis**, bladder to ileum 57.87 [45.51]." Because code 45.51 is in slanted brackets, the billing specialist or medical coder knows that two codes must be assigned for this procedure.

In the *Tabular List* of *Volume 3*, code 57.87, "Reconstruction of urinary bladder," includes the notation to "code also resection of intestine (45.50–45.52)." Code 45.51, the slanted bracket code, falls in the range of the "code also" instruction.

The anastomosis is coded to 57.87 and sequenced first. Code 45.51, "Isolation of segment of small intestine," is also selected and included on the health insurance claim.

ASSIGNING ICD-9-CM PROCEDURE CODES

Accurate procedure code assignment depends on three activities:

- Identifying the principal procedure
- Selecting and sequencing procedure codes
- Following applicable ICD-9-CM coding conventions and all instructions noted in *ICD-9-CM Volume 3*

As stated previously, ICD-9-CM procedure codes are used for coding and reporting inpatient or hospital episodes of care. Documentation in the patient's record must support all procedure codes submitted for reimbursement.

Identifying the Principal Procedure

The **principal procedure** is the procedure performed for definitive treatment rather than for diagnostic or exploratory purposes or the procedure performed to resolve a complication. If more than one procedure meets the definition of the principal procedure, the procedure most closely related to the principal diagnosis(es) is selected as the principal procedure.

EXAMPLE

Juanita, who was recently diagnosed with breast cancer, was admitted for a radical mastectomy, right breast. On the second postoperative day, she fell on the way to the bathroom and sustained a femoral neck (hip) fracture. The fracture was treated via open reduction with internal fixation.

In this case, the principal diagnosis is breast cancer. Radical mastectomy is the procedure most related to the principal diagnosis, and it is coded and sequenced first as the principal procedure. The femoral neck fracture is coded and sequenced after the principal diagnosis; the closed reduction with internal fixation is coded and sequenced after the principal procedure.

Selecting and Sequencing Procedure Codes

Codes assigned to the principal procedure are always sequenced first. In addition to the principal procedure, other significant procedures are coded. A **significant procedure** is surgical in nature, carries a procedural and/or anesthetic risk, and requires specialized training. Codes for significant procedures are sequenced *after* the principal procedure code.

The steps for selecting procedure codes are enumerated and discussed here. Examples are provided as needed. Refer to Figure 4–14 as you study procedure coding steps.

1. Identify the main term in the procedure statement. (In this example, the main term is in bold.)

   EXAMPLE
   Carotid **endarterectomy**

2. Locate the main term in the *Volume 3 Alphabetic Index*.

   EXAMPLE
   Locate **endarterectomy** in the Index.

3. Review the procedure statement for additional information about the main term.

   EXAMPLE
   Carotid refers to the carotid artery and identifies the anatomic location of the **endarterectomy.**

4. Review the subterms listed under the main term to determine if any entry matches the additional information in the procedure statement.

   EXAMPLE
   In this example, "carotid" is not listed as a subterm under the main term. Because the carotid artery is located in the neck, the subterms "head" and "neck" apply.

5. Follow any cross-reference instructions, such as "code also." If there are no cross-reference instructions, note the code listed with the applicable subterm entry.

   EXAMPLE
   In this example, there are no cross-reference instructions. The code for "endarterectomy, head and neck (open) NEC" is 38.12.

PROCEDURE: Carotid Endarterectomy

ALPHABETIC INDEX	TABULAR LIST
Endarterectomy (gas) (with patch graft) 38.10	**38 Incision, excision, and occlusion of vessels…**
abdominal 38.16	The following fourth-digit subclassification is for
aortic (arch) (ascending) (descending) 38.14	use with appropriate categories in sections 38.0,
coronary artery–*see* category 36.0	38.1, 38.3, 38.5, 38.6, and 38.8 according to site…
open chest approach 36.03	**0 unspecified site**
head and neck (open) NEC 38.12	**1 intracranial vessels**
percutaneous approach, intracranial	Cerebral (anterior) (middle)
vessel(s) 00.62	Circle of Willis
percutaneous approach, precerebral	Posterior communicating artery
(extracranial) vessels(s) 00.61	**2 other vessels of head and neck**
intracranial (open) NEC 38.11	Carotid artery (common) (external) (internal)
percutaneous approach, intracranial	Jugular vein (external) (internal)…
vessel(s) 00.62	**38.1 Endarterectomy**
percutaneous approach, precerebral	Endarterectomy with:
(extracranial) vessel(s) 00.61	embolectomy
lower limb 38.18	patch graft
thoracic NEC 38.15	temporary bypass during procedure
upper limb 38.13	thrombectomy

FIGURE 4–14 Selecting Procedure Codes

6. **Check the code listed in the *Alphabetic Index* with the description in the *Tabular List*.**

> **EXAMPLE**
> Section 38.1 in the Tabular List is "Endarterectomy."

7. Read and follow all inclusion, exclusion, and other instructional notes.

> **EXAMPLE**
> The instruction note for category 38 states that a fourth digit is required in sections 38.0, 38.1, and 38.3. "Endarterectomy" is in section 38.1, and a fourth digit is required to complete the code.

8. Assign the code(s) to the highest level of specificity by selecting a three-digit code only when no four-digit code is available.

> **EXAMPLE**
> A fourth digit is needed to complete the code. The fourth digit 2 indicates that the carotid artery is the site of the endarterectomy. The Tabular List confirms that the correct code for carotid endarterectomy is 38.12.

Step 6 is bolded here for the same reason it was bolded under diagnostic coding: A competent insurance billing specialist or medical coder *never* codes directly from the Alphabetic Index.

MISCELLANEOUS CODING GUIDELINES FOR PROCEDURES AND BIOPSIES

Additional coding guidelines cover the following situations: bilateral procedures; canceled, incomplete, or failed surgeries or procedures; and biopsies.

Bilateral Procedures

When a single code is available to describe a procedure as bilateral, the code is selected and listed once on the insurance claim.

> **EXAMPLE**
> Belinda was admitted for a bilateral oophorectomy, which is the removal of both ovaries. The surgeon completed the surgery, and Belinda was discharged in good condition.
> In this example, code 65.51, "bilateral oophorectomy, . . . Removal of both ovaries at same operative episode," accurately describes the procedure.

When a bilateral procedure code is not available and the same procedure is done bilaterally at the same time, the procedure code is selected and listed twice on the insurance claim.

> **EXAMPLE**
> Roland was admitted for bilateral orchiopexy, which is the surgical fixation of undescended testes into the scrotum.
> In this example, there is no code for bilateral orchiopexy. Code 62.5, "Orchiopexy," is selected and listed twice on the insurance claim.

Canceled, Incomplete, and Failed Procedures

When a scheduled surgery or procedure is not completed or is considered to have failed, codes are assigned to the level of service that was actually performed or completed. In these situations, the following general guidelines apply:

1. An endoscopic operative approach is coded as an exploratory endoscopy of the site.

2. An **open procedure**, defined as opening or entering a body cavity or space, is coded as an exploration of the anatomic site.

3. When only an incision is made, code the incision of the anatomic site.

4. A **failed procedure**, which is a procedure that did not achieve the desired result, is coded as a performed procedure.

5. V codes related to the reason for the incomplete or cancelled procedure may also be assigned.

6. A surgery or procedure that is cancelled before it begins is coded only to the appropriate V code related to the reason for canceling the surgery or procedure.

A careful review of the operative or procedure report provides information for accurate coding. Examples for these guidelines are given here.

EXAMPLE OF GUIDELINE 1

Maria was admitted for a laparoscopic, bilateral tubal ligation. After placement of the laparoscope, she developed tachycardia, and the procedure was cancelled.

In this example, the endoscopic operative approach is coded as an exploratory laparoscopy. Code 54.21, "diagnostic procedures of abdominal region, Laparoscopy," appropriately describes the level of service rendered and is coded as the principal procedure. The appropriate V code for the cancelled procedure is also assigned.

EXAMPLE OF GUIDELINE 2

Takeesha was admitted for a total abdominal hysterectomy due to persistent menorrhagia. After the pelvic cavity was opened and entered, the patient exhibited a drop in blood pressure and respiratory rate. The procedure was stopped, and the operative site was closed.

In this example, code 54.11, "Exploratory laparotomy," is assigned as the principal procedure code. The appropriate V code for the cancelled procedure is also assigned.

EXAMPLE FOR GUIDELINE 3

Takeesha was admitted for a total abdominal hysterectomy due to persistent menorrhagia. Shortly after the incision was made, she developed tachycardia. The procedure was stopped, and the incision was closed.

In this example, code 54.0, "Incision of abdominal wall," is assigned as the principal procedure code.

EXAMPLE FOR GUIDELINE 4

Gera was admitted for percutaneous transluminal angioplasty of the carotid artery. Immediately after the procedure, the artery again occluded.

In this case, the procedure was performed, but the desired result was not obtained. Code 00.61, "Percutaneous angioplasty or atherectomy of precerebral (extracranial) vessel(s)," is assigned as the principal procedure code.

EXAMPLE FOR GUIDELINE 5

Maria was admitted for a laparoscopic, bilateral tubal ligation. After placement of the laparoscope, she developed tachycardia, and the procedure was cancelled. The operative approach is coded as an exploratory laparoscopy and is the principal procedure. Code V64.1, "procedure not carried out because of contraindication," is also assigned.

EXAMPLE FOR GUIDELINE 6

Takeesha was admitted for a total abdominal hysterectomy due to persistent menorrhagia. Prior to surgery, she developed a low-grade fever, and the surgery was cancelled.

In this example, no procedure code is assigned. Menorrhagia is coded as the principal diagnosis, and V64.1 is assigned to identify that the procedure was not performed.

Biopsy Coding

When a biopsy is performed during an inpatient or hospital episode of care, codes from *ICD-9-CM Volume 3* are assigned. Biopsies are categorized as open or closed. An **open biopsy** is performed via an incision into the appropriate anatomic site or space, and tissue is taken for microscopic examination. A **closed biopsy** is performed without an incision. Tissue is taken percutaneously, endoscopically, by needle (often called "needle aspiration biopsy"), or by a bristle-type instrument called a brush (often called a "brush biopsy"). Figure 4–15 illustrates a biopsy entry in the *Tabular List* of *Volume 3*.

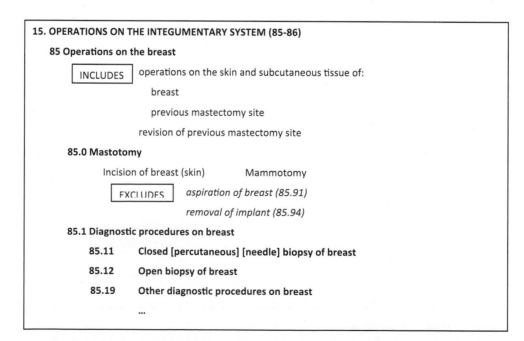

FIGURE 4–15 Volume 3 Tabular List Biopsy Entry (Permission to reuse granted by Ingenix)

General guidelines for coding biopsies include the following:

1. Endoscopic biopsies may be assigned to codes that identify both the endoscopic procedure and the biopsy.
2. Endoscopic biopsies that cannot be assigned to codes that identify both the endoscopic procedure and the biopsy are assigned separate codes for the endoscopy and the biopsy. The endoscopy is the principal procedure and is coded and sequenced first. The biopsy is coded and sequenced after the principal procedure.
3. When a biopsy is performed and immediately followed by a more extensive surgical procedure, the surgical procedure is the principal procedure and is coded and sequenced first. The biopsy is coded and sequenced after the principal procedure.
4. An open biopsy is coded as such. Because an incision is implicit in an open biopsy, do not assign a separate code for the incision.

A careful review of the procedure report provides information for accurate biopsy coding. Examples for these guidelines are given here.

EXAMPLE FOR GUIDELINE 1

During Pedro's recent hospitalization, he underwent a transbronchial lung biopsy. The pathology report was negative for malignant cells.

In this example, the transbronchial lung biopsy is assigned code 33.27, "Closed endoscopic biopsy of lung." This code identifies both the endoscopic procedure and the biopsy.

EXAMPLE FOR GUIDELINE 2

During Katerina's recent hospitalization, a mediastinoscopy with lymph tissue biopsy was performed. The pathology report was positive for cellular dysplasia.

In this example, there is no code that covers both the mediastinoscopy and the biopsy. Two codes are assigned. Code 34.22, "Mediastinoscopy," is sequenced before the biopsy code. The instruction note states, "Code also any lymph node biopsy, if performed." The biopsy is coded to 40.11, "Biopsy of lymphatic structure."

EXAMPLE FOR GUIDELINE 3

Pedro was hospitalized for an open lung biopsy with frozen section and possible pneumonectomy. The pathology report was positive for lung cancer, and the surgeon removed Pedro's right lung. The procedure statement was "open biopsy of the lung with frozen section and pneumonectomy, right lung."

In this case, the pneumonectomy is assigned code 32.59, "Other and unspecified pneumonectomy," and sequenced first. The open biopsy is coded to 33.28, "Open biopsy of lung."

EXAMPLE FOR GUIDELINE 4

Hazel was hospitalized for a wedge biopsy of the liver via laparotomy and for possible removal of the liver. The pathology report was negative.

In this case, laparotomy indicates that a wedge biopsy is an open biopsy. The laparotomy is the incision and is not coded. The wedge biopsy is coded to 50.12, "Open biopsy of liver."

ABBREVIATIONS

Table 4–14 lists the abbreviations presented in this chapter.

TABLE 4–14

Abbreviations and Meanings	
Abbreviation	Meaning
AHA	American Hospital Association
AHIMA	American Health Information Management Association
AIDS	acquired immunodeficiency syndrome
CMS	Center Medicare and Medicaid Services
CPT	Current Procedural Terminology
CVA	cerebrovascular accident
HIV	human immunodeficiency virus
ICD-9-CM	International Classification of Diseases, 9th Revision, Clinical Modification
ICD-10	International Classification of Diseases, 10th Revision
NCHS	National Center for Healthcare Statistics
NEC	not elsewhere classified
NOS	not otherwise specified

REINFORCEMENT EXERCISES 4–12

Fill in the blank.

1. *ICD-9-CM Volume 3* is commonly called the _____.

2. The _____ is a listing of procedures, tests, operations, surgeries, and therapies.

3. The subterms "as," "by," and "with" are known as _____.

4. The _____ in *ICD-9-CM Volume 3* has 18 chapters.

5. ICD-9-CM procedure codes consist of _____ or _____ digits.

6. _____ means that the use of special equipment must be coded.

7. _____ indicate that closely related procedures require two codes.

8. The _____ convention applies to the usual surgical approach of a given procedure.

9. In *Volume 3*, _____ are bolded and flush left.

10. The *Tabular List* is predominantly organized by _____ and _____.

continued on the next page

continued from the previous page

Rank each statement from 1 to 8. Place a 1 in front of the first step for selecting an ICD-9-CM procedure code and an 8 in front of the last step.

_____ Assign codes to the highest level of specificity.

_____ Check the code listed in the *Alphabetic Index* with the description in the *Tabular List*.

_____ Follow any cross-reference instructions, such as "code also."

_____ Identify the main term in the procedure statement.

_____ Locate the main term in the *Alphabetic Index*.

_____ Read and follow all inclusion, exclusion, and other instruction notes.

_____ Review the procedure statement for additional information about the main term.

_____ Review the subterms listed under the main term.

Mark each statement as True (T) or False (F).

1. _____ Bilateral procedure codes are available for all surgeries.

2. _____ Biopsy codes must be sequenced first.

3. _____ Closed biopsies are often accomplished via endoscopy.

4. _____ Incisions related to open biopsies are assigned a separate code.

5. _____ Two codes may be necessary for bilateral procedures.

6. _____ V codes are assigned to failed procedures.

7. _____ V codes may be assigned when a procedure is cancelled before it begins.

SUMMARY

This chapter included a review of ICD-9-CM diagnostic and procedure coding. The history of ICD-9-CM and the unique features of *Volume 1* (the *Tabular List of Diseases and Injuries*), *Volume 2* (the *Alphabetic Index of Diseases and Injuries*), and *Volume 3* (the *Tabular List and Alphabetic Index of Procedures*) were presented. Coding conventions were discussed, and examples of the conventions were given. Accurate coding has a direct effect on the financial health of all health care agencies. Inappropriate coding can result in rejected claims, inadequate reimbursement, and, in the worst case, charges of fraud or abuse.

REVIEW EXERCISES

Write a short answer for each statement.

1. A temporary or permanent medical problem or condition resulting from an illness or injury.

2. Residual condition that remains after the illness or injury has been resolved.

3. Used to calculate the extent of a burn injury.

4. Short name for ICD-9-CM Volume 1.

5. Short name for ICD-9-CM Volume 2.

6. Diseases, conditions, or injuries printed in bold and flush left in the *Alphabetic Index.*

7. Precedes subterms and is placed immediately after the main term.

8. Codes in the Neoplasm Table are arranged by

9. Direct the billing specialist or medical coder to look elsewhere.

10. Lists of conditions that are coded to the same ICD-9-CM code.

11. Lists of conditions not covered by a specific ICD-9-CM code.

12. Placing diagnostic codes in the correct order.

13. Supplementary classifications or codes that are frequently assigned in a clinic, office, and outpatient setting.

14. Directions and guidelines that assist in accurate code assignment.

15. Mandatory cross-reference term.

_____

16. Enclose nonessential modifiers.

_____

17. Abbreviation that means the same thing as "unspecified."

_____

18. Abbreviation indicating that a specific diagnosis does not have a separate code.

_____

19. Connect a list or series of descriptions or diagnoses to a common main term or code.

_____

20. Enclose a manifestation code.

_____

21. A(n) _____ procedure indicates that an incision is necessary to enter a body cavity or space.

22. A(n) _____ procedure indicates that the procedure was done and the desired result was not achieved.

23. Tissue taken by a bristle-type instrument is called a(n) _____ biopsy.

24. In *Volume 3*, the phrase _____ applies to the usual surgical approach of a given procedure.

25. The _____ procedure is performed for definitive treatment rather than for diagnostic or exploratory purposes.

ICD-9-CM CODING PRACTICE SETS

The best way to learn how to code is to practice coding. The ICD-9-CM coding practice sets are organized by *Tabular List* chapters. The practice sets are *not* all-inclusive, nor do they cover all coding situations. The goal of this section is to present a variety of diagnostic statements for coding.

Write the main term and then assign the correct ICD-9-CM code(s) for each diagnostic statement. Include E codes where applicable.

General

1. Asian flu (influenza) shot (vaccination). _____

2. Viral hepatitis inoculation. _____

3. Pre-employment physical (examination). _____

4. Sports physical. _____

5. Routine prenatal visit, first pregnancy. _____

6. Removal of leg cast. _____

7. Screening for diabetes mellitus. _____

8. Exposure to HIV. _____

9. Patient stepped on a broken bottle and sustained a three-inch laceration, requiring seven sutures. Instructed to return in 10 days for suture removal.

_____

10. This four-year-old patient is being evaluated for delayed development due to the toxic effect of lead paint ingested over the past two years.

_____

Symptoms, Signs, and Ill-Defined Conditions

1. Abdominal pain. _____

2. Anorexia. _____

3. Chest pain, unspecified. _____

4. Diarrhea. _____

5. Labile hypertension. _____

6. Syncope. _____

7. Cardiogenic shock. _____

8. Functional heart murmur. _____

9. Abnormal mammogram. _____

10. Right lower quadrant abdominal pain, with nausea and vomiting.

_____

Infectious and Parasitic Diseases

1. Aseptic meningitis. _____

2. Gastroenteritis due to salmonella. _____

3. Rotavirus enteritis. _____

4. Cystitis, acute, due to Escherichia coli (E. coli).

_____

5. Viral hepatitis, type A. _____

6. Primary genital syphilis. _____

7. Anthrax pneumonia. _____

Endocrine, Nutritional and Metabolic Diseases, and Immunity Diseases

1. Type 1 diabetes with ketoacidosis. _____

2. Gouty arthritis. _____

3. Diabetic hypoglycemia. _____

4. Cushing's syndrome. _____

5. Familial hypercholesterolemia. _____

6. AIDS-related complex. _____

7. Salmoneliosis. _____

8. Hyperthyroidism. _____

9. This 10-year-old female is seen today for continued treatment of cystic fibrosis. She has gained three pounds and is in the 45th percentile for weight. Mom was advised to continue supplemental nutrition. _____

10. This 35-year-old male is seen today for exogenous obesity. Weight loss this visit was three pounds. Total weight loss is 45 pounds. Patient was advised to continue with his weight reduction program. _____

Nervous System and Sense Organs

1. Rheumatoid arthritis. _____

2. Acute follicular conjunctivitis. _____

3. Classical migraine. _____

4. Bacterial meningitis. _____

5. Trigeminal neuralgia. _____

6. Senile macular degeneration. _____

7. This three-year-old female is seen today rubbing and tugging at her right ear and in minimal distress. Inspection of the ear canals reveals acute suppurative otitis media on the right; the left is clear. Tympanic membranes are intact.

   _____

8. Routine eye examination revealed a partial retinal detachment, with a single defect noted.

   _____

Circulatory System

1. Unstable angina pectoris. _____

2. Arteriosclerotic heart disease. _____

3. Thrombophlebitis of deep femoral vein. _____

4. Hemorrhoids. _____

5. Orthostatic hypotension. _____

6. Hypertensive cardiovascular disease, malignant.

_____

7. Bilateral thrombosis of carotid artery. _____

8. Atrial fibrillation. _____

9. This 55-year-old female is seen with complaints of nocturnal angina pectoris that is relieved with nitroglycerin tablets, sublingual.

_____

10. During the patient's physical examination, heart sounds were consistent with mitral valve insufficiency.

_____

Respiratory System

1. Obstructive chronic bronchitis. _____

2. Chronic maxillary sinusitis. _____

3. Hay fever due to pollen. _____

4. Chronic obstructive pulmonary disease. _____

5. Pneumonia due to SARS-associated coronavirus.

_____

6. Hypertrophy of tonsils and adenoids. _____

7. Purulent bronchitis. _____

8. Unilateral, vesicular emphysema. _____

9. This 45-year-old male is seen for shortness of breath, low-grade fever, and general malaise. Examination revealed an acute upper respiratory infection with influenza.

_____

Digestive System

1. Ulcerative stomatitis. _____

2. Bleeding gastric ulcer. _____

3. Reflux esophagitis. _____

4. Hiatal hernia. _____

5. Acute gastroenteritis. _____

6. Acute cholecystitis with choledocholithiasis.

7. Diverticulosis of the large intestine. _____

8. Alcoholic cirrhosis of the liver. _____

9. Recurrent left inguinal hernia. _____

10. This 36-year-old female has been seen for repeated episodes of explosive diarrhea, severe cramping, and lack of bowel control. Colonoscopy today reveals moderate ulcerative colitis of the sigmoid colon and rectum.

Genitourinary System

1. Hematuria. _____

2. Urinary tract infection. _____

3. Benign prostatic hypertrophy. _____

4. Vaginitis. _____

5. Urethritis. _____

6. Spermatocele. _____

7. Premenstrual syndrome. _____

8. Nephrolithiasis. _____

9. Endometriosis of the ovary. _____

10. This 30-year-old female patient is seen today to discuss the results of her recent Pap test, which revealed dysplasia of the cervix (uteri).

Write the main term and then assign the correct ICD-9-CM code(s) for each procedure.

1. Coronary artery bypass graft of three vessels.

2. Cholecystectomy, open. _____

3. Total proctocolectomy with permanent exterior ileostomy.

4. Endoscopic removal of common bile duct calculi.

5. Temporary tracheostomy and insertion of tracheal tube.

_____

6. Revision of ileostomy stoma. _____

7. Radical nephrectomy of right kidney due to polycystic kidney disease.

_____

8. Bilateral breast reduction. _____

9. Bilateral total knee replacement of both knee joints.

_____

10. Bilateral myringtomy, placement of tympanostomy tubes, general anesthesia.

_____

11. Phillip was admitted to the hospital for repair of a deviated nasal septum and collapsed nasal cartilage. The operative report states, "Nasoseptal repair with cartilage graft to the nasal tip."

_____

12. While playing in a championship basketball game, Margaret sustained a knee injury. She was admitted for an arthroscopic examination of her left knee. The procedure report included the following information:

PREOPERATIVE DIAGNOSIS: Tear of medial meniscus, left knee.

POSTOPERATIVE DIAGNOSIS: Tear of medial meniscus, left knee.

OPERATION PERFORMED: Arthroscopic examination of the left knee and arthroscopic partial medial meniscectomy.

_____

CODING CHALLENGE

Read the following medical reports and write the diagnoses and procedures in the space provided. Assign the correct ICD-9-CM diagnosis and procedure codes. Sequence the codes according to principal diagnosis and principal procedure guidelines. These cases relate to inpatient episodes of care.

1. DISCHARGE SUMMARY

PATIENT: Walker, Lamar
ADMISSION DATE: November 16, 20xx
DISCHARGE DATE: November 18, 20xx
ADMITTING DIAGNOSES: 1. Urinary retention secondary to benign prostatic hypertrophy. 2. Chronic obstructive pulmonary disease.
DISCHARGE DIAGNOSES: 1. Benign prostatic hypertrophy, secondary urinary retention. 2. Chronic obstructive pulmonary disease.

continued on the next page

continued from the previous page

PROCEDURES: 1. Transurethral resection of the prostate. 2. Percutaneous suprapubic cystostomy.

HISTORY: The patient is a 72-year-old gentleman with a recent history of recurrent urinary retention. A cystoscopy performed in the office demonstrated a large obstructed prostate. Given his problems with recurrent urinary retention, the patient agreed to a transurethral resection of the prostate. Remainder of the patient's history is available in the admitting note.

HOSPITAL COURSE: Following admission, the patient was taken to the operating room and underwent a complicated transurethral resection of the prostate and a percutaneous suprapubic cystostomy. There was moderate hemorrhage, and the patient received one unit of packed red blood cells intraoperatively. His postoperative hemoglobin was stable at 10.3.

During the postoperative period, he remained afebrile, and his urine gradually cleared. The Foley catheter was removed on the third postoperative day. At discharge, the patient was ambulating without assistance, able to void without difficulty, and tolerating a regular diet.

DISCHARGE INSTRUCTIONS: 1. Postoperative follow-up in my office in two weeks. 2. Normal activities, as tolerated. 3. Notify my office if clots appear in the urine.

PRINCIPAL DIAGNOSIS: _____

PRINCIPAL PROCEDURE: _____

OTHER DIAGNOSIS(ES): _____

OTHER PROCEDURE(S): _____

2. DISCHARGE SUMMARY

PATIENT: Mowafi, Ayeesha
ADMISSION DATE: December 10, 20xx
DISCHARGE DATE: December 13, 20xx
ADMITTING DIAGNOSES: 1. Ruptured left ectopic (tubal) pregnancy.
DISCHARGE DIAGNOSES: 1. Ruptured left ectopic (tubal) pregnancy. 2. Endometriosis.

PROCEDURES: 1. Laparoscopic left salpingectomy, partial.

HISTORY: The patient is a 30-year-old gravida I, para 0 female who presented in the emergency department with acute abdominal pain. A serum pregnancy test was positive. Pelvic ultrasound was negative for an intrauterine pregnancy. The patient had pelvic and left lower-quadrant tenderness. No pelvic mass was palpated. The patient has endometriosis.

HOSPITAL COURSE: The patient was admitted and taken to the operating room. Culdocentesis was positive. She underwent laparoscopic partial left salpingectomy. The patient tolerated the procedure well. She was discharged on the third postoperative day, tolerating a regular diet, ambulating without difficulty, and passing flatus.

DISCHARGE INSTRUCTIONS: 1. Postoperative follow-up in my office in two weeks. 2. Normal activities, as tolerated. 3. Return to the emergency department for swelling, elevated temperature, or pelvic pain.

PRINCIPAL DIAGNOSIS: _____

PRINCIPAL PROCEDURE: _____

OTHER DIAGNOSIS(ES): _____

OTHER PROCEDURE(S): _____

3. DISCHARGE SUMMARY

PATIENT: Mehrotra, Basu
ADMISSION DATE: May 20, 20xx
DISCHARGE DATE: May 26, 20xx
ADMITTING DIAGNOSES: 1. Right index finger infection.
DISCHARGE DIAGNOSES: 1. Suppurative tenosynovitis and osteomyelitis, right index finger. 2. Peripheral vascular disease.
PROCEDURES: 1. Incision and drainage of distal phalanx, open amputation of distal phalanx, and placement of flexor tendon sheath catheter for irrigation. 2. Debridement of bone and soft tissue.
HISTORY: The patient is a 48-year-old male who presented with a necrotic infection of the right index finger. See the admission history and physical for complete details.
HOSPITAL COURSE: The patient was admitted and started on intravenous antibiotics with poor results. He was taken to the operating room and underwent drainage and debridement of necrotic tissue, right index finger. The operative procedure revealed suppuration of the soft tissues and osteomyelitic involvement of the distal phalangeal remnant and distal portion of the middle phalanx. The distal phalanx was amputated. Purulent material was present in the distal portion of the flexor tendon sheath. A catheter was placed in the flexor tendon sheath for irrigation.

The patient's general condition remained stable. The acute infection in the right index finger resolved. On the fifth postoperative day, he returned to the operating room for further debridement of necrotic tissue. He tolerated this procedure well and was discharged on the next postoperative day.
DISCHARGE MEDICATIONS: Keflex 500 mg every six hours.
DISCHARGE INSTRUCTIONS: 1. Keep the index finger dressing intact until seen by me in follow-up in five days. 2. Diet and activities as tolerated. 3. Return to the emergency department for swelling, elevated temperature, or discharge from the site.

PRINCIPAL DIAGNOSIS: _____

PRINCIPAL PROCEDURE: _____

OTHER DIAGNOSIS(ES): _____

OTHER PROCEDURE(S): _____

4. DISCHARGE SUMMARY

PATIENT: Wellington, Martha
ADMISSION DATE: June 10, 20xx
DISCHARGE DATE: June 18, 20xx
ADMITTING DIAGNOSES: Possible pulmonary abscess due to pneumonia.
DISCHARGE DIAGNOSES: Pulmonary abscess, right lower lobe, due to pneumonia.
PROCEDURES: 1. Right thoracotomy. 2. Decortication and wedge resection, right lower lobe of the lung.
HISTORY: The patient is a 43-year-old female with complaints of increasing right chest pain and shortness of breath for several days prior to admission. Initially, the patient had been diagnosed with left pleurisy that had resolved. About one month ago, the patient had complaints of shortness of breath, green and blood-tinged sputum, 102-degree fever, and night sweats. She denies any tuberculosis exposure.
HOSPITAL COURSE: The patient was admitted and treated on the medical unit with intravenous fluid and intravenous antibiotics, including Timentin and Flagy. Her condition did not appreciably improve, and she was transferred to the surgical unit. She subsequently underwent a right thoracotomy, decortication, and wedge resection of the right lower lobe of the lung. Two chest tubes were placed. The anterior tube was removed on the second postoperative day. The posterior tube was removed on the day prior to discharge. The patient's condition improved, and chest x-rays taken just prior to discharge revealed a small amount of right-sided pleural effusion. The left lung was clear. No pneumothorax was seen. The lungs were free of active infiltrate. The cardiac size was within normal limits. The patient continued on antibiotics until the day before discharge. She was discharged on the sixth postoperative day in good condition.
DISCHARGE MEDICATIONS: Tylenol #3, one to two tablets every four hours as needed.
DISCHARGE INSTRUCTIONS: 1. No heavy lifting for six weeks. 2. Sponge baths. 3. See me in my office in two days for staple removal and wound check. 4. Return to the emergency department for shortness of breath, elevated temperature, or discharge from the site.

PRINCIPAL DIAGNOSIS: _____

PRINCIPAL PROCEDURE: _____

OTHER DIAGNOSIS(ES): _____

OTHER PROCEDURE(S): _____

5. OPERATIVE REPORT

PATIENT: Kempanin, Salmi
DATE OF OPERATION: July 10, 20xx
PREOPERATIVE DIAGNOSIS: Possible intermittent left testicular torsion.
POSTOPERATIVE DIAGNOSES: 1. Torsion and necrosis of left appendix testis.
  2. Hydrocele.
OPERATION PERFORMED: 1. Excision of left appendix testis. 2. Left
  hydro-celectomy. 3. Bilateral orchiopexy.
DESCRIPTION: The patient was brought to the operating room, placed in the supine
  position, and general anesthesia was administered. The genital area was prepped and
  draped in the usual sterile manner. A midline scrotal incision was made through the
  dartos layers, revealing a necrotic appendix testis that was subsequently resected.
  A 3-0 Prolene suture was taken through the dependent portion of the testicle to the
  dartos layer to prevent subsequent torsion. Fluid was drained from the hydrocele, and
  the hydrocele sac was removed completely. Through the same incision, a 3-0 Prolene
  suture was used to fix the right testicle in position to prevent torsion on that side. The
  wound was closed in two layers of running 4-0 Dexon, and a modified pressure dressing was applied. The patient was returned to the recovery room in satisfactory condition. Blood loss was negligible. Sponge and needle counts were correct × 2.

PRINCIPAL DIAGNOSIS: _____

PRINCIPAL PROCEDURE: _____

OTHER DIAGNOSIS(ES): _____

OTHER PROCEDURE(S): _____

WEBSITES

American Health Information Management Association: www.ahima.org
American Hospital Association: www.aha.org
American Medical Association: www.ama-assn.org
Centers for Medicare and Medicaid Services: www.cms.hhs.gov
National Center for Health Statistics: www.cdc.gov/nchs

CHAPTER 5

International Classification of Diseases, Tenth Revision, Clinical Modification (ICD-10-CM)

LEARNING OBJECTIVES

Upon successfully completing this chapter, the reader should have the knowledge to:

1. Identify the organization responsible for developing ICD-10.
2. Describe three differences between ICD-9-CM and ICD-10-CM.
3. Define the alphanumeric characters in ICD-10-PCS codes.
4. Discuss the challenges of implementing ICD-10-CM and ICD-10-PCS.

KEY TERMS

Alphabetic Index
Approach
Body system
Centers for Medicare
   and Medicaid Services
   (CMS)
Combination code
Common procedure term
Essential modifier
Excludes 1
Excludes 2
First listed code
Includes
International Classification of
   Diseases, Tenth Revision,

Clinical Modification
   (ICD-10-CM)
International Classification of
   Diseases, Tenth Revision,
   Procedure Coding System
   (ICD-10-PCS)
List of codes
Main term
National Center for Health
   Statistics (NCHS)
Nonessential modifier
Not elsewhere classified
   (NEC)
Parentheses ( )
Placeholder *x*

Point dash (.-)
Principal diagnosis
Qualifier
Root operation
7th character extension
Square brackets [ ]
Subterm
Tables
Tabular List
U.S. Centers for Disease
   Control (CDC)
U.S. Department of Health
   and Human Services
   (HHS)

OVERVIEW

The *International Statistical Classification of Diseases and Related Health Problems* (ICD-10) was published by the World Health Organization (WHO) between 1992 and 1994. Except for the United States, every country in the world that participates in maintaining health care statistics has

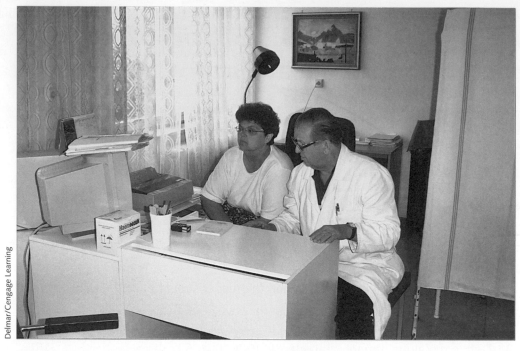

FIGURE 5–1 Reviewing ICD-10 in Podhorod, Slovakia (2004)

adopted ICD-10. In Figure 5–1, the author and Dr. Fedor Rosocha review ICD-10 codes at his clinic in Podhorod, Slovakia.

As published by the WHO, ICD-10 consists of three volumes:

- *Volume 1: Tabular List*—a list of alphanumeric codes, organized diseases, conditions, disorders, external causes of diseases and conditions, and factors influencing health status
- *Volume 2: Instruction Manual*—a compilation of rules, guidelines, and coding conventions
- *Volume 3: Alphabetic Index*—an alphabetic index to the conditions in *Volume 1*

Overall, ICD-10 provides more clinical detail for the diseases included than ICD-9 does, and it also includes codes for diseases discovered since the last revision of ICD-9.

The **National Center for Health Statistics (NCHS)**, a division of the **U.S. Centers for Disease Control (CDC)**, is responsible for developing the clinical modification of ICD-10. In 2003, the NCHS published a pre-release draft of the **International Classification of Diseases, Tenth Revision, Clinical Modification (ICD-10-CM)**. ICD-10-CM is intended to replace ICD-9-CM. When this text was published, the anticipated implementation date for ICD-10-CM was 2013. Current information about ICD-10-CM is available on the CDC website: www.cdc.gov/nchs/icd/icd10cm.htm.

While the National Center for Health Statistics is responsible for developing ICD-10-CM, the **Centers for Medicare and Medicaid Services (CMS)**, a division of the **U.S. Department of Health and Human Services (HHS)**, is responsible for developing a replacement for *ICD-9-CM Volume 3* procedure codes. The new procedure classification system is called the **International Classification of Diseases, Tenth Revision, Procedure Coding System (ICD-10-PCS)**. ICD-10-PCS was completed in 1998 and has been updated annually since then. When this text was published, an implementation date for ICD-10-PCS was not established. Current information about ICD-10-PCS is available on the CMS website: www.cms.hhs.gov. At the CMS home page, use ICD10-PCS as the search term.

The purpose of this chapter is to provide an introduction to the components of both ICD-10-CM and ICD-10-PCS. The unique characteristics of both coding classification systems are presented individually.

INTERNATIONAL CLASSIFICATION OF DISEASES, TENTH REVISION, CLINICAL MODIFICATION (ICD-10-CM)

The format and organizational features of ICD-10-CM will remain fairly consistent with those found in ICD-9-CM. The major difference between ICD-9-CM and ICD-10-CM is that ICD-10-CM codes are alphanumeric and have up to seven characters. Each ICD-10-CM code begins with a letter that may be followed by up to six characters. The components of ICD-10-CM are discussed individually.

ICD-10-CM Volumes

The ICD-10-CM consists of two volumes:

- **The *Tabular List*:** A list of alphanumeric codes organized by organ systems, etiology, external causes, or other criteria such as symptoms and signs. Coding conventions and instructions are included in the *Tabular List*
- **The *Alphabetic Index*:** An alphabetic index to the conditions in the *Tabular List*

Tabular List

The *Tabular List* consists of 21 chapters, which are listed in Table 5–1. Note that the first character of the ICD-10-CM code is a capital letter. Except for the letters D and H, each letter is associated with a particular chapter. Review Table 5–1 to identify the chapters that use the letters D and H.

TABLE 5–1

ICD-10-CM Chapters with Code Ranges	
Chapter	**Title and Code Ranges**
Chapter 1	Certain Infectious and Parasitic Diseases (A00–B99)
Chapter 2	Neoplasms (C00–D48)
Chapter 3	Diseases of the Blood and Blood-Forming Organs and Certain Diseases Involving the Immune Mechanism (D50–D89)
Chapter 4	Endocrine, Nutritional, and Metabolic Diseases (E00–E90)
Chapter 5	Mental and Behavioral Disorders (F01–F99)
Chapter 6	Diseases of the Nervous System (G00–G99)[†]
Chapter 7	Diseases of the Eye and Adnexa (H00–H59)[†]
Chapter 8	Diseases of the Ear and Mastoid Process (H60–H95)[†]

continued on the next page

continued from the previous page

ICD-10-CM Chapters with Code Ranges	
Chapter	**Title and Code Ranges**
Chapter 9	Diseases of the Circulatory System (I00–I99)
Chapter 10	Diseases of the Respiratory System (J00–J99)
Chapter 11	Diseases of the Digestive System (K00–K93)
Chapter 12	Diseases of the Skin and Subcutaneous Tissue (L00–L99)
Chapter 13	Diseases of the Musculoskeletal System and Connective Tissue (M00–M99)
Chapter 14	Diseases of the Genitourinary System (N00–N99)
Chapter 15	Pregnancy, Childbirth, and the Puerperium (O00–O99)
Chapter 16	Certain Conditions Originating in the Perinatal Period (P04–P96)
Chapter 17	Congenital Malformations, Deformations, and Chromosomal Abnormalities (Q00–Q99)
Chapter 18	Symptoms, Signs, and Abnormal Clinical and Laboratory Findings, Not Elsewhere Classified (R00–R99)
Chapter 19	Injury, Poisoning, and Certain Other Consequences of External Causes (S00–T98)*
Chapter 20	External Causes of Morbidity (V01–Y98)*
Chapter 21	Factors Influencing Health Status and Contact with Health Services (Z00–Z99)**

†Included in Chapter 6, "Diseases of the Nervous System and Sense Organs," in ICD-9-CM.
*Listed in ICD-9-CM as E-codes, "Supplementary Classification of External Causes of Injury and Poisoning."
**Listed in ICD-9-CM as V-codes, "Supplementary Classification of Factors Influencing Health Status and Contact with Health Services."

ICD-10-CM *Tabular List* chapters are organized into blocks of three-character categories that cover similar or closely related conditions. Each chapter begins with a summary of the category blocks contained in the chapter. Figure 5–2 illustrates this feature.

Codes in the *Tabular List* may include up to seven characters, which include **three-character category** codes; **four-character subcategory** codes; **five-character subcategory** codes; **six-character subcategory** codes; **7th character extensions**; and the **placeholder** *x*. Each type of code is described individually. Refer to Figure 5–3 for examples of ICD-10-CM codes. Note that the first character in any ICD-10-CM code is a capital letter that identifies the chapter.

- **Three-character category (code):** A capital letter with two digits that represents a single disease or a group of closely related conditions. While most three-character categories are further divided into four-character subcategories, there are some conditions that are coded to a three-character category.

CHAPTER 9

Diseases of the Circulatory System (I00–I99) ...

This chapter contains the following blocks:

I00–I02	Acute rheumatic fever
I05–I09	Chronic rheumatic fever
I10–I15	Hypertensive diseases
I20–I25	Ischemic heart diseases
I26–I28	Pulmonary heart disease and diseases of pulmonary circulation
I30–I52	Other forms of heart disease
I60–I69	Cerebrovascular diseases
I70–I79	Diseases of arteries, arterioles, and capillaries
I80–I89	Diseases of veins, lymphatic vessels, and lymph nodes, not elsewhere classified
I95–I99	Other and unspecified disorders of the circulatory system

Delmar/Cengage Learning

FIGURE 5–2 Category Blocks

- **Four-character subcategory (code):** A three-character category followed by a period/decimal point and one additional digit. The fourth digit provides more information or specificity for the description of the condition. In most cases, the fourth digit 8 (.8) means that even though the diagnostic statement may include some specific information, there is no other code available for the condition. The fourth digit 9 (.9) usually means that the diagnostic statement does not include enough information to select a more specific code.
- **Five-character subcategory (code):** A three-character category followed by a period/decimal point and two additional digits. A five-character subcategory code is a subdivision of a four-character subcategory code.
- **Six-character subcategory (code):** A three-character category followed by a period/decimal point and three additional digits. A six-character subcategory code is a subdivision of a five-character subcategory code.
- **7th character extension:** Many ICD-10-CM codes require an additional character, called an "extension," to provide additional information about the patient's condition. An extension is always the seventh and final character in a code. Letters and numbers are used as 7th character extensions. ICD-10-CM Chapters 18 through 21 make extensive use of 7th character extensions.

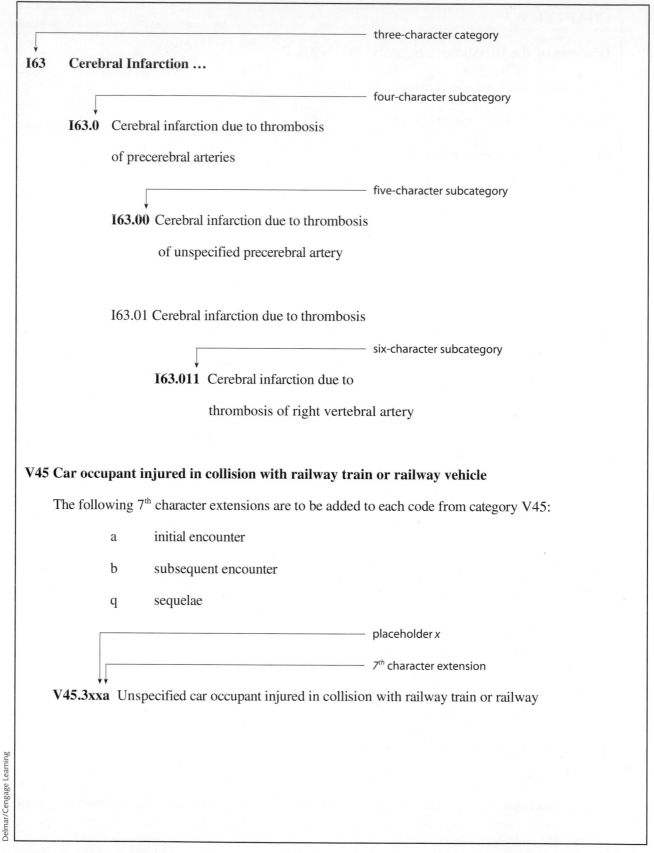

three-character category

I63   **Cerebral Infarction ...**

four-character subcategory

I63.0   Cerebral infarction due to thrombosis

of precerebral arteries

five-character subcategory

I63.00 Cerebral infarction due to thrombosis

of unspecified precerebral artery

I63.01 Cerebral infarction due to thrombosis

six-character subcategory

I63.011 Cerebral infarction due to

thrombosis of right vertebral artery

V45 Car occupant injured in collision with railway train or railway vehicle

The following 7th character extensions are to be added to each code from category V45:

a   initial encounter

b   subsequent encounter

q   sequelae

placeholder *x*

7th character extension

V45.3xxa Unspecified car occupant injured in collision with railway train or railway

Delmar/Cengage Learning

FIGURE 5–3 *Tabular List* Codes

- **Placeholder *x*:** Also called the "dummy x," this is used in conjunction with codes that require a 7th character extension. When a code with fewer than six characters requires a seventh character, the placeholder *x* is used to create a six-character code.

ICD-10-CM TABULAR LIST CONVENTIONS

Tabular List coding conventions affect accurate code assignment. The conventions include instructional notations, punctuation, and symbols. The abbreviation NOS (not otherwise specified) is used in the *Tabular List* and *Alphabetic Index*. The coding conventions are described here. Following the descriptions, Table 5–2 gives examples of the conventions.

TABLE 5–2

Tabular List Coding Conventions	
Convention	**Example**
And	A18.4 Tuberculosis of skin **and** subcutaneous tissue Tuberculosis of skin, or subcutaneous tissue, or skin and subcutaneous tissue included in this code
Code first	I32 Pericarditis in diseases classified elsewhere **Code first** underlying disease such as: uremia (N19)
Colon (:)	Pericarditis (in): Coxsackie (virus) (B33.23)
Excludes 1	I31 Other diseases of pericardium **Excludes 1:** postcardiotomy syndrome (I97.0)
Excludes 2	Diseases of the circulatory system (I00–I99) **Excludes 2:** neoplasms (C00–D48)
Includes	I63 Cerebral Infarction **Includes:** occlusion and stenosis of cerebral and precerebral arteries, resulting in cerebral infarction
Parentheses ( )	I10 Essential **(primary)** hypertension The parentheses enclose a nonessential modifier.
Point dash (.-)	Diseases of esophagus, stomach, and duodenum (K20–K31) Excludes 2: hiatus hernia (K44.-)
Square brackets [ ]	B00 Herpes viral **[herpes simplex]** infections
Use additional code	K20 Esophagitis **Use additional code** to identify alcohol abuse and dependence (F10.-).
With	K21.0 Gastro-esophageal reflux disease **with** esophagitis

- **And; with:** The word "and," as used in the *Tabular List*, means "and/or." This notation indicates that either condition may be assigned to a given code. The word "with" indicates that more than one condition (usually two) is included in a given code.
- **Code first/Use additional (secondary) code:** This means that the patient's condition is a manifestation of an underlying condition. The underlying disease or condition must be coded and sequenced first. The manifestation of the underlying disease or condition is coded and sequenced after the underlying condition. "Use additional code" means that another code may be needed to completely describe the patient's condition.
- **Colon (:):** This is placed after words or phrases that apply to the indented information that follows the colon.
- **Excludes 1:** This notation indicates diagnoses that cannot be coded to a given category. This type of note indicates that the excluded code is never used at the same time as the code listed above the "excludes 1" note.
- **Excludes 2:** This notation means that the excluded condition is not a part of the condition represented by a given code. The "excludes 2" notation may also indicate that more than one code is needed to accurately describe the patient's condition.
- **Includes:** This word appears immediately under category codes to further define or give examples of diagnostic statements included in the category.
- **Parentheses ( ):** These enclose the following types of information: **nonessential modifiers** (words or statements in the diagnosis that do not affect the code); codes that are excluded from a particular category; and the range of codes included in a chapter or category block of codes.
- **Point dash (.-):** This indicates that the code is incomplete and an additional digit (or digits) is needed.
- **Square brackets [ ]:** Square brackets enclose synonyms, alternate wordings, and explanatory phrases.

Alphabetic Index

The *Alphabetic Index* for ICD-10-CM includes the following:

- An index to diseases and conditions coded to Chapters 1 through 19 and Chapter 21
- A Table of Neoplasms arranged alphabetically by anatomic site with codes for malignant, benign, in situ, uncertain behavior, or unspecified behavior neoplasms
- An index to the terms related to the external causes of morbidity and terms in Chapter 20, "External Causes of Morbidity (V01–Y99)"
- A Table of Drugs and Chemicals, used to code poisonings and adverse effects of drugs classified in Chapter 19, "Injury, Poisoning, and Certain Other Consequences of External Causes (S00–T98)," and Chapter 20

The *Alphabetic Index* is organized by **main terms** that are bolded and flush left. Main terms are usually conditions rather than anatomic sites. Main terms for Chapter 21, "Factors Influencing Health Status and Contact with Health Services," include "admission (for)," "aftercare," "boarder," "convalescence," "examination," "history," "prescription," "problem," "state of," "status," and "vaccination."

Main term entries include **subterms** (also called **essential modifiers**) that are indented under the main term. **Subterm** modifiers are indented under the applicable subterm. Figure 5–4 is an example of an *Alphabetic List* entry.

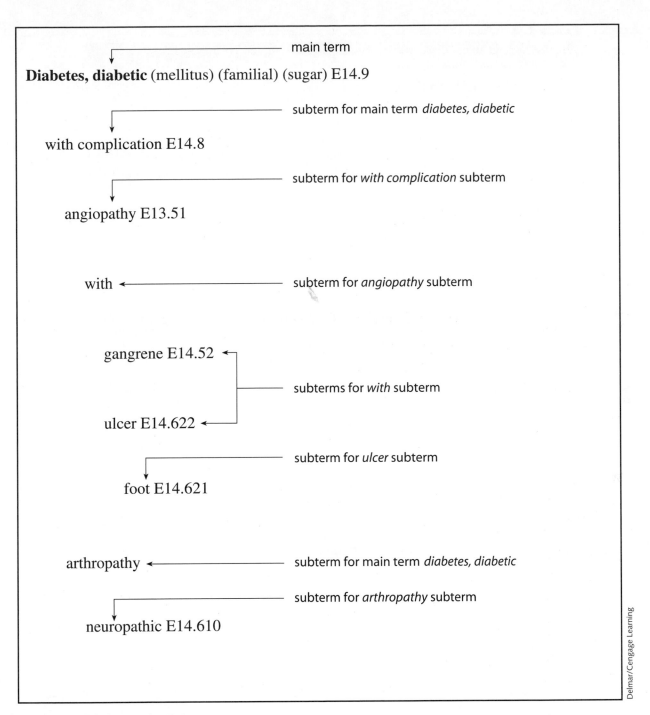

FIGURE 5–4 Alphabetic Index Entry

See, see also, and the abbreviation **NEC (not elsewhere classified)** are *Alphabetic Index* coding conventions. Review the descriptions below, and refer to Table 5–3 for examples of the coding conventions.

- **See; See also:** Cross-reference conventions that direct the billing specialist or medical coder to another main term or to another category or code
- **NEC:** Indicates that the code applies when a more specific code is not available

TABLE 5-3

Alphabetic Index Coding Conventions	
Convention	Example
See	**Diabetes, diabetic** (mellitus) (familial) (sugar) E14.9. . . brittle—**see** Diabetes, type 1 If the diagnostic statement is "brittle diabetes," the "see" cross-reference directs the coder to the Diabetes, type 1, *Alphabetic Index* entry.
See also	**Diarrhea, diarrheal** (disease) (infantile) (inflammatory) R19.7 . . . amebic (**see also** Amebiasis) A06.0 If the diagnostic statement is "amebic diarrhea," the "see also" cross-reference directs the coder to the Amebiasis *Alphabetic Index* entry.

NEC	**Diarrhea, diarrheal** (disease) (infantile) (inflammatory) R19.7. . .
	
	 due to
	
	    bacteria A04.9
	
	       specified **NEC** A04.8

If the diagnosis is "bacterial diarrhea" and the bacterium is specified but there is no code for the specified bacterium, the NEC (not elsewhere classified) code is assigned.

REINFORCEMENT EXERCISES 5-1

Spell out each of the listed abbreviations.

1. CDC

_____

2. CMS

_____

3. ICD-10-CM

_____

4. ICD-10-PCS

_____

5. NCHS

_____

continued on the next page

continued from the previous page

Fill in the blank.

1. The _____ is a list of alphanumeric codes organized by etiology and other criteria.

2. A(n) _____ is used in conjunction with codes that require a 7th character extension.

3. A(n) _____ notation means a given diagnosis cannot be coded to a given category.

4. The _____ indicates that a code is incomplete and additional digits are required.

5. Subterms are also known as _____.

ASSIGNING ICD-10-CM DIAGNOSES CODES

Assigning ICD-10-CM diagnoses codes involves the same steps as ICD-9-CM code assignment. The steps include selecting and sequencing the code(s) and following both the ICD-10-CM coding conventions and the *ICD-10-CM Official Guidelines for Coding and Reporting for Acute Short-Term and Long-Term Hospital Inpatient and Physician Office and Other Outpatient Encounters.* The *Official Guidelines* complement the conventions and instructions within the ICD-10-CM. The ICD-10-CM conventions and instructions take precedence over the *Guidelines.*

The *Official Guidelines* are organized into these sections:

- **Section I:** Structure and conventions of ICD-10-CM; general guidelines that apply to the entire classification; chapter-specific guidelines for each ICD-10-CM chapter
- **Section II:** Guidelines for selecting the principal diagnosis for non-outpatient settings
- **Section III:** Guidelines for reporting additional diagnoses in non-outpatient settings
- **Section IV:** Coding and reporting for outpatient settings

It is beyond the scope of this text to cover the *ICD-10-CM Official Guidelines* in detail. The current version of the *Guidelines* is posted on the CDC website.

Selecting Diagnoses Codes

Accurate diagnoses code selection requires the use of both the *Alphabetic Index* and the *Tabular List.* The codes for diagnoses documented in the patient's medical record are located in the *Alphabetic Index* and confirmed in the *Tabular List.* In most cases, a symptom code should not be used in the presence of a confirmed diagnosis. Symptoms may be coded if they are not associated with the confirmed diagnosis(es).

Diagnoses must be coded to the highest level of specificity. This means that a three-character code cannot be selected when a four-character code is available; a four-character code cannot be selected when a five-character code is available; and a five-character code cannot be selected when a six-character code is available.

A **combination code**—defined as a single code used to classify two diagnoses, or to classify a diagnosis with an associated sign or symptom, or to classify a diagnosis with an associated complication—is selected when the combination code accurately identifies the diagnostic conditions. When the diagnostic conditions cannot be coded to a combination code, multiple codes that accurately identify the conditions may be selected.

Finally—and most importantly—documentation in the patient's medical record must clearly support the selected codes.

Sequencing Diagnoses Codes

When health services are provided in an inpatient setting, the **principal diagnosis** is sequenced (listed) first. The principal diagnosis is the condition established after study to be chiefly responsible for occasioning the admission of the patient to the hospital for care. In all other health care settings, the condition(s) that describes the main reason for providing care is known as the **first listed diagnosis**.

The sequencing guidelines given in ICD-10-CM coding conventions and instructional notes *must* be adhered to first. General sequencing guidelines, as presented in the *ICD-10-CM Official Guidelines,* include the following:

- Sign or symptom codes are not usually sequenced as the principal diagnosis.
- Sign or symptom codes may be sequenced as the first listed diagnosis when no definitive diagnosis is established.
- The underlying condition associated with an acute manifestation (condition) is usually sequenced first, unless the acute manifestation is immediately life-threatening and primary treatment is directed at the acute manifestation.
- When two or more confirmed diagnoses equally meet the criteria for principal/first-listed diagnosis and Index, Tabular List, and coding guidelines do not provide sequencing direction, any one of the diagnoses may be sequenced first.
- When the scheduled treatment is not carried out, the code that identifies the condition or diagnosis that was planned to be treated is sequenced first.
- When a patient is admitted for treatment of a complication of surgery or medical care, the code that identifies the complication is sequenced first.
- Additional or secondary conditions or diagnoses are coded and sequenced after the principal/first listed diagnosis.
- Diagnoses related to previous or resolved medical conditions that have no impact on a patient's current condition may be coded. These codes are *not* submitted (reported) on the health insurance claim.

Because ICD-10-CM is significantly different from ICD-9-CM, replacing ICD-9-CM with ICD-10-CM presents many challenges. In order to prepare for the change, health care agencies must have enough time to train (or retrain) billing specialists and medical coders; update electronic coding programs (encoders); and educate physicians and other health care providers about the documentation requirements needed for accurate ICD-10-CM coding.

INTERNATIONAL CLASSIFICATION OF DISEASES, TENTH REVISION, PROCEDURE CODING SYSTEM (ICD-10-PCS)

The *International Classification of Diseases, Tenth Revision, Procedure Coding System* (ICD-10-PCS) was developed to replace *ICD-9-CM Volume 3* procedure codes. Once implemented, ICD-10-PCS will be used to code and report inpatient surgical and diagnostic procedures. ICD-10-PCS was designed and developed by 3M Health Information Systems under contract with the Centers for Medicare and Medicaid Services (CMS).

TABLE 5–4

ICD-10-PCS Sections	
Character	Section
0	Medical and Surgical
1	Obstetrics
2	Placement
3	Administration
4	Measurement and Monitoring
5	Extracorporeal Assistance and Performance
6	Extracorporeal Therapies
7	Osteopathies
8	Other Procedures
9	Chiropractic
B	Imaging
C	Nuclear Medicine
D	Radiation Oncology
F	Physical Rehabilitation and Diagnostic Audiology
G	Mental Health
H	Substance Abuse Treatment

ICD-10-PCS Code Structure

All codes in ICD-10-PCS have seven alphanumeric characters. Digits 0–9 and letters A–H, J–N, and P–Z are used. The letters O and I are not used, avoiding confusion with digits 0 and 1. The first character in any code *always* relates to a procedure section. Under ICD-10-PCS, procedures are divided into 16 sections according to the type of procedure performed. Each section is assigned an alphabetic or numeric character. Table 5–4 lists the procedure sections and related characters.

The code for procedures that are included in Section 0, "Medical and Surgical," *always* begins with the character 0; obstetrics procedures *always* begin with the character 1; chiropractic procedures *always* begin with the character G; and so forth.

The remaining six characters of an ICD-10-PCS code have a standard meaning *within* a given section. Because the same characters are used in all 16 sections, the meaning of the characters may change depending on the section.

To provide an example of the ICD-10-PCS, the meanings of the characters used to construct procedure codes found in the "Medical Surgical" section are presented here.

Medical and Surgical Section (0)

The majority of inpatient procedures are coded to Section 0, "Medical and Surgical." As stated previously, the first character of these procedure codes is 0. The remaining characters for medical

TABLE 5–5

Character 2, Body Systems			
Digit/Letter	Body System	Digit/Letter	Body System
0	Central Nervous System	J	Subcutaneous Tissue and Fascia
1	Peripheral Nervous System	K	Muscles
2	Heart and Great Vessels	L	Tendons
3	Upper Arteries	M	Bursae and Ligaments
4	Lower Arteries	N	Head and Facial Bones
5	Upper Veins	P	Upper Bones
6	Lower Veins	Q	Lower Bones
7	Lymphatic and Hemic System	R	Upper Joints
8	Eye	S	Lower Joints
9	Ear, Nose, Sinus	T	Urinary System
B	Respiratory System	U	Female Reproductive System
C	Mouth and Throat	V	Male Reproductive System
D	Gastrointestinal System	W	Anatomical Regions, General
F	Hepatobiliary System and Pancreas	X	Anatomical Regions, Upper Extremities
G	Endocrine System	Y	Anatomical Regions, Lower Extremities
H	Skin and Breast		

and surgical procedures are described on the following pages. Keep in mind that the meanings for each character apply to codes in the "Medical and Surgical" section.

Character 2 identifies the body system, which is the general physiological system or anatomical region involved in the procedure. Table 5–5 lists the digits and letters associated with character 2.

Character 3 identifies the **root operation**, which is a specific term that identifies the objective of the procedure. The "Medical and Surgical" section includes 31 different root operations, from alteration to transplantation. Table 5–6 lists examples of root operations.

Character 4 identifies the body part on which the procedure was performed. Digits and letters assigned to character 4 depend on the body system involved in the procedure. Table 5–7 gives examples of digits and letters assigned to body parts in two **body systems**.

By applying the information presented in Tables 5–4 through 5–7, the first four characters of the ICD-10-PCS code for a **hemigastrectomy** (excision of half of the stomach) are 0DB6:

- **0:** "Medical and Surgical" section
- **D:** Gastrointestinal System
- **B:** Excision (root operation)
- **6:** Stomach (body part)

TABLE 5–6

Character 3, Root Operations	
Root Operation	**Definition**
0 Alteration	Modifying the natural anatomic structure of a body part without affecting the function of the body part (e.g., breast reduction)
1 Bypass	Altering the route of passage of the contents of a tubular body part (e.g., coronary artery bypass)
2 Change	Taking out or off a device from a body part and putting back an identical or similar device in or on the same body part without cutting or puncturing the skin or a mucous membrane
3 Control	Stopping or attempting to stop postprocedural bleeding
4 Creation	Making a new genital structure that does not take over the function of a body part
5 Destruction	Physical eradication of all or a portion of a body part by the direct use of energy, force, or a destructive agent
6 Detachment	Cutting off all or part of the upper or lower extremities
7 Dilation	Expanding the orifice or the lumen of a tubular body part
8 Division	Cutting into a body part without draining fluids and/or gases from the body part in order to separate or transect a body part
9 Drainage	Taking or letting out fluids and/or gases from a body part
B Excision	Cutting out or off, without replacement, a portion of a body part

TABLE 5–7

Character 4, Body Parts			
Body Parts (Character 4): Gastrointestinal System			
Digit/Letter	**Body Part**	**Digit/Letter**	**Body Part**
0	Esophagus	G	Large Intestine, Left
1	Esophagus, Upper	H	Cecum
2	Esophagus, Middle	J	Appendix
3	Esophagus, Lower	K	Ascending Colon
4	Esophagogastric Junction	L	Transverse Colon
5	Upper Intestinal Tract	M	Descending Colon
6	Stomach	N	Sigmoid Colon
7	Stomach, Pylorus	P	Rectum
8	Small Intestine	Q	Anus

continued on the next page

continued from the previous page

Character 4, Body Parts			
Body Parts (Character 4): Gastrointestinal System			
Digit/Letter	**Body Part**	**Digit/Letter**	**Body Part**
9	Duodenum	R	Anal Sphincter
A	Jejunum	S	Greater Omentum
B	Ileum	T	Lesser Omentum
C	Ileocecal Valve	V	Mesentery
D	Large Intestine	W	Peritoneum
F	Large Intestine, Right		
Body Parts (Character 4): Hepatobiliary System and Pancreas			
Digit/Letter	**Body Part**	**Digit/Letter**	**Body Part**
0	Liver	7	Hepatic Duct, Caudate
1	Liver, Right Lobe	8	Cystic Duct
2	Liver, Left Lobe	9	Common Bile Duct
3	Liver, Caudate Lobe	B	Ampulla of Vater
4	Gallbladder	C	Pancreatic Duct
5	Hepatic Duct, Right	D	Pancreatic Duct, Accessory
6	Hepatic Duct, Left	F	Pancreas

Character 5 identifies the **approach**, which is the technique or method used to reach the procedure site. There are several approaches associated with the "Medical and Surgical" section. Table 5–8 lists five approaches with definitions and examples.

Character 6 in the "Medical and Surgical" section defines any device that was left in place when the procedure was completed. Four general types of devices exist:

- Biological or synthetic material that takes the place of all or a portion of a body part (skin grafts and joint prosthesis)
- Biological or synthetic material that assists or prevents a physiological function (intrauterine device, IUD)
- Therapeutic material that is not absorbed by, eliminated by, or incorporated into a body part (radioactive implant)
- Mechanical or electronic appliances used to assist, monitor, take the place of, or prevent a physiological function (pacemaker)

Table 5–9 lists examples of the "Medical and Surgical" section devices.

TABLE 5–8

Character 5, Approach	
Approach	Description
0 Open	Cutting through the skin or mucous membrane and as many body layers as necessary to expose the site of the procedure (e.g., abdominal hysterectomy)
3 Percutaneous	Entry, by puncture or minor incision, of instrumentation through the skin or mucous membrane and any other body layers as necessary to reach the site of the procedure (e.g., needle aspiration biopsy)
4 Percutaneous Endoscopic	Entry, by puncture or minor incision, of instrumentation through the skin or mucous membrane and any other body layers as necessary to reach and visualize the site of the procedure (e.g., arthroscopy)
8 Transorifice Intraluminal **Endoscopic**	Entry of instrumentation through a natural or artificial external orifice into the lumen of the connected tubular body part to reach the site of the procedure (e.g., colonoscopy)
X External	Procedures performed directly on the skin or mucous membrane and procedures performed indirectly by the application of external force through the skin or mucous membrane (e.g., closed reduction of fracture)

TABLE 5–9

Character 6, Device	
Digit/Letter	Device
0	Drainage device: Penrose drain
1	Radioactive element: "Seeds" placed for cancer treatment
2	Monitoring device: Pacemaker
3	Infusion device: Percutaneous infusion catheter (PIC line)
7	Autograft: Tissue transplanted from one part of the body to another in the same individual
8	Zoograft: Animal tissue transplanted to a human
J	Synthetic substitute: Teflon joint
K	Tissue substitute: "Mesh" used for hernia repair
M	Stimulator: Cerebral implants
Y	Device NEC: New devices not yet assigned a digit or letter
Z	None: Indicates no devices were used

Character 7 is called a **qualifier**, which identifies an additional attribute of a given procedure. Qualifiers are unique to each section and, in some cases to procedures within a section, of ICD-10-PCS. In the "Medical and Surgical" section, qualifiers identify the revision of a previous procedure, the type of transplant, a second site for a transplant, or the type of fluid taken out during drainage. When there is no specific qualifier for a procedure, the letter Z—which means "no qualifier"—is used for the seventh character of the code.

By applying the information presented in Tables 5–4 to 5–8 and the description of a qualifier, the last three characters of the ICD-10-PCS code for a **hemigastrectomy** (excision of half of the stomach) are 0ZZ:

- **0:** Open approach, which is the method used to excise all or part of the stomach
- **Z:** No device
- **Z:** No qualifier

The complete code for hemigastrectomy is 0DB60ZZ.

The ICD-10-PCS explanations, tables, and character definitions presented in this chapter are limited to the "Medical and Surgical" section. There are fifteen more sections in ICD-10-PCS, and it is beyond the scope of this chapter to cover all sections.

ICD-10-PCS Manual

Features of the ICD-10-PCS manual are presented here. The complete manual is available on the CMS website.

The ICD-10-PCS manual includes the following three sections:

- **Tables:** These are organized by section and include the information for assigning procedure codes. The ICD-10-PCS tables serve the same purpose as the ICD-9-CM Volume 3 *Tabular List*. Billing specialists and medical coders *must* use the tables for accurate code assignment.
- **Index:** This is an alphabetic index of procedures that directs the billing specialist and medical coder to the table that is used to assign a given procedure code. The types of terms listed in the Index are **main terms**, which include root operation and body system terms, and **common procedure terms**, which are names of procedures, such as appendectomy and cholecystectomy. The index provides the first three or four characters of the seven-character code.
- **List of Codes:** This is an alphanumeric list of all valid codes. Entries in the List of Codes include the seven-character code and the full text description of the code.

The steps involved in assigning ICD-10-PCS codes are no different from assigning ICD-9-CM codes. The patient's medical record is the source document for accurate code assignment. The billing specialist and medical coder locate the procedure in the ICD-10-PCS index; refer to the appropriate table by using the three or four characters given in the index; and assign the remaining characters by using the information from the table.

REINFORCEMENT EXERCISES 5–2

Fill in the blank.

1. All ICD-10-PCS codes consist of _____ alphanumeric characters.

2. The first character of an ICD-10-PCS code relates to a _____.

3. _____ is cutting out or off all of a body part without replacement.

4. A(n) _____ is cutting out or off a portion of a body part without replacement.

5. Visually or manually exploring a body part is known as _____.

6. A(n) _____ approach involves cutting through the skin or other body layers.

7. A closed reduction of a fracture is an example of a(n) _____ approach.

8. A _____ is always the seventh character of an ICD-10-PCS code.

9. The letter _____ is used to indicate that no qualifier or no device is associated with the procedure or code.

10. The _____ includes all valid ICD-10-PCS codes, with a description of each code.

ABBREVIATIONS

Table 5–10 lists the abbreviations in this chapter.

TABLE 5–10

Abbreviations and Meanings	
Abbreviation	**Meaning**
CDC	Centers for Disease Control
CMS	Center for Medicare and Medicaid Services
HHS	Department of Health and Human Services
ICD-10	*International Classification of Diseases, Tenth Revision*
ICD-10-PCS	*International Classification of Diseases, Tenth Revision, Procedure Coding System*
NCHS	National Center for Health Statistics
NEC	not elsewhere classified
WHO	World Health Organization

SUMMARY

This chapter provided an introduction to ICD-10-CM, the *International Classification of Diseases, Tenth Revision, Clinical Modification,* and ICD-10-PCS, the *International Classification of Diseases, Tenth Revision, Procedure Coding System.* These classification and coding systems are scheduled for implementation on October 1, 2013.

Both ICD-10-CM and ICD-10-PCS are substantially different from ICD-9-CM. The new coding systems are expanded for increased specificity, and codes consist of alphanumeric characters. Once implemented, ICD-10-CM will be used by all health care agencies for coding and reporting. ICD-10-PCS is intended to be used by hospitals and other inpatient health care agencies for coding and reporting procedures. Because of the specific nature of both systems, documentation in the patient's medical record will be subjected to an increasing level of scrutiny.

REVIEW EXERCISES

Multiple Choice

1. The International Statistical Classification of Diseases and Related Health Problems is published by

    a. NCHS.

    b. WHO.

    c. AMA.

    d. CMS.

2. The organization responsible for developing ICD-10-CM is the

    a. AMA.

    b. CMS.

    c. NCHS.

    d. WHO.

3. The objective of a procedure is known as a(n)

    a. approach.

    b. root operation.

    c. essential modifier.

    d. qualifier.

4. An ICD-10-CM code that represents a single disease or a group of closely related conditions is known as a

   a. three-character category code.

   b. classification code.

   c. four-character subcategory code.

   d. V code.

5. Which pair of coding conventions is not included in ICD-10-CM?

   a. brackets and braces

   b. colons and commas

   c. braces and section marks

   d. commas and braces

Short Answer

1. Explain the purpose of the point dash (.-).

2. Discuss the differences between ICD-9-CM and ICD-10-CM.

3. Describe the purpose of the tables that are included in ICD-10-PCS.

4. Identify the ICD-10-CM chapter, name, and code ranges for the ICD-9-CM V codes.

5. Name the ICD-10-CM chapter and code ranges for the ICD-9-CM E codes.

_____

_____

_____

WEBSITES

Centers for Disease Control (CDC): www.cdc.gov
National Center for Health Statistics: www.cdc.gov/nchs
World Health Organization (WHO): www.who.int/en

Current Procedural Terminology (CPT) and Healthcare Common Procedure Coding System (HCPCS)

LEARNING OBJECTIVES

Upon successfully completing this chapter, the reader should have the knowledge to:

1. Identify the two organizations responsible for maintaining and updating the CPT and HCPCS coding systems.
2. Describe the contents of the six sections of the *Current Procedural Terminology* coding reference.
3. Define the two levels of HCPCS codes.
4. Explain the difference between the ICD-9-CM, CPT, and HCPCS coding systems.
5. Interpret the meaning of symbols used in CPT coding.
6. Illustrate the use of CPT modifiers.
7. Define the cross-reference terms used in CPT coding.
8. Accurately assign CPT and HCPCS codes.

KEY TERMS

Add-on code
Ambulatory surgery center (ASC)
Bullet (•)
Category/subsection
Centers for Medicare and Medicaid Services (CMS)
Circle (○)
Circled bullet (⊙)
Consultation
Current Procedural Terminology (CPT)

Department of Health and Human Services (HHS)
Downcoding
Durable medical equipment (DME)
"Evaluation and Management" section (E/M)
Examination
Facing triangles (►◄)
Flash symbol (✔)
Global surgery concept

Health Insurance Portability and Accountability Act (HIPAA)
Healthcare Common Procedure Coding System (HCPCS)
History
Instructional note
Level II codes
Main term
Medical decision-making
Moderate sedation

Modifier	Referral	Subcategory
National codes	Section	Surgical package
Null zero (∅)	Section guideline	Technical component
Physical status modifier	*See*	Triangle (▲)
Plus sign (+)	*See also*	Unbundling
Procedure/service	Semicolon (;)	Upcoding
Professional component	Separate procedure	Universal no code (∅)

OVERVIEW

Current Procedural Terminology (CPT) and the *Healthcare Common Procedure Coding System* (HCPCS) are used to code the treatment a patient receives at a physician or provider's office, at an **ambulatory surgery center (ASC)**, or as a hospital outpatient. CPT is updated and published by the American Medical Association (AMA). HCPCS was developed by the **Centers for Medicare and Medicaid Services (CMS)** to complement the CPT coding system. CPT codes are also called HCPCS level I codes. The alphanumeric HCPCS codes are also called HCPCS level II codes. CMS is a division of the U.S. **Department of Health and Human Services (HHS)**.

CPT and HCPCS codes are used in conjunction with ICD-9-CM diagnosis codes to communicate patient services to insurance carriers (also called fiscal intermediaries) and to government and regulatory agencies. Both diagnoses and procedure codes are used to determine provider reimbursement. The documentation in the patient's medical record must clearly support *all* codes.

Inaccurate coding results in delayed or denied reimbursement. Intentional coding errors can lead to charges of insurance fraud, whereas unintentional coding errors can lead to charges of insurance abuse. Both fraud and abuse can result in civil and criminal penalties. Because reimbursement is based on the codes submitted, all health insurance companies and CMS have increased monitoring and auditing activities related to coding.

This chapter is an introduction to CPT and HCPCS coding conventions and applications and is not intended to be a comprehensive presentation of either system.

CURRENT PROCEDURAL TERMINOLOGY

The AMA developed *Current Procedural Terminology* (CPT) to provide a uniform language to accurately describe physician and provider services. The first edition was published in 1966 and consisted primarily of codes for surgical procedures and limited codes for other services, such as radiology, laboratory, and pathology. Over the years, CPT has been revised and expanded, and it is now the accepted coding system for nearly all provider services in ambulatory or outpatient settings and for some provider services related to hospital and long-term care.

CPT is updated annually by the CPT editorial panel. An advisory committee, which includes physicians and other health care professionals, assists the editorial panel with the annual revision. The annual revision is released late in the fall of each year, and the codes become effective on January 1. CPT codes answer this question: What did the provider do for the patient's problems? Billing specialists and medical coders need the most current edition of CPT to ensure accurate code assignment. Many physicians' offices have CPT codes printed on the encounter form (or route slip). The codes on the encounter form must be revised as needed.

Table 6-1

CPT Components and Description
Introduction: The introduction includes instructions for using the CPT manual, definitions of terms, and roots, prefixes, and suffixes for medical terms. Some CPT editions also include anatomical illustrations and procedural illustrations.
Main Sections: CPT main sections include guidelines for each section, the range of codes for the section, definitions of terms, and, in some editions, illustrations of selected services.
Appendices: CPT appendices provide a quick reference for modifier descriptions; clinical examples of evaluation and management (E/M) codes; summaries of CPT code changes, deletions, and additions; CPT add-on codes; CPT codes exempt from modifier -51; CPT codes exempt from modifier -63; CPT codes that include moderate (conscious) sedation; an alphabetic index of performance measures; genetic testing code modifiers; electrodiagnostic medicine codes; products pending Food and Drug Administration (FDA) approval codes; vascular families; and a crosswalk to deleted CPT codes.
Category II Codes: Category II codes are supplemental tracking codes that can be used for performance measurement. These codes are intended to facilitate data collection related to quality of care. The use of these codes is optional.
Category III Codes: Category III codes are temporary codes for emerging technology, services, and procedures that have not yet been assigned a Category I CPT code. If a Category III code is available for a specific technology, service, or procedure, it must be used instead of a Category I unlisted code. Category III codes consist of four numeric characters and one alpha character as the fifth character.
Alphabetic Index: The CPT alphabetic index is the key to locating codes in the main sections. The index is organized by main terms that include the type of procedure or service; by the organ or anatomical site; by the condition, such as "fracture"; or by synonyms, eponyms, and abbreviations, such as EEG and Pomeroy's operation.

CPT Components

The CPT code book has an Introduction, six main **sections**, 13 appendices, a list of CPT category II codes, a list of CPT category III codes, and an alphabetic index. Table 6–1 lists the CPT components with a brief description.

CPT Main Sections

Each CPT main section is preceded by guidelines that explain the unique coding conventions for the section. A specific range of codes relates to each of the six main sections. CPT codes—each of which is a five-digit number—represent a specific service. The six main sections and their ranges of codes are:

- "Evaluation and Management (E/M)": 99201 through 99499
- "Anesthesia": 00100 through 01999
- "Surgery": 10021 through 69990
- "Radiology": 70010 through 79999
- "Pathology and Laboratory": 80047 through 89398
- "Medicine": 90281 through 99199 and 99500 through 99607

TABLE 6–2

CPT Sections and Subdivisions			
Section	Category	Subcategory	Service/Procedure
Evaluation/ Management	Office or Other Outpatient Services	New Patient	99201: New patient office visit; presenting problem is self-limited or minor
Surgery	Urinary System	Kidney	50205: Renal biopsy; by surgical exposure of kidney
Medicine	Cardiovascular	Cardiography	93040: Rhythm ECG, 1-3 leads; interpretation and report

The main sections are divided into **categories** or **subsections**, **subcategories**, and **procedures** or **services**. The section divisions are used to identify services, procedures or therapies, examinations or tests, body systems, or anatomic sites. Table 6–2 is an example of the divisions of CPT main sections.

CPT Appendices

The CPT appendices include:

- **Appendix A:** "Modifiers"—A list of **modifiers** that may be added to a five-digit code to further explain the service provided
- **Appendix B:** "Summary of Additions, Deletions, and Revisions"—A summarization of CPT codes that have been added, deleted, and revised
- **Appendix C:** "Clinical Examples"—Clinical examples of services that represent "Evaluation and Management" CPT codes
- **Appendix D:** "Summary of CPT Add-on Codes"—A list of add-on codes, which are CPT codes that are used in conjunction with another CPT code
- **Appendix E:** "Summary of CPT Codes Exempt from Modifier 51"—A list of codes that may not be used with modifier -51
- **Appendix F:** "Summary of CPT Codes Exempt from Modifier 63"—A list of codes that may not be used with modifier -63
- **Appendix G:** "Summary of CPT Codes that Include Moderate (Conscious) Sedation"—A list of CPT procedure codes that include moderate (conscious) sedation as a part of the procedure
- **Appendix H:** "Alphabetic Index of Performance Measures by Clinical Condition or Topic"—A list of treatment/performance services by clinical condition
- **Appendix I:** "Genetic Testing Code Modifiers"—A list of modifiers that apply to molecular laboratory procedures related to genetic testing
- **Appendix J:** "Electrodiagnostic Medicine Listing of Sensory, Motory and Mixed Nerves"—A list of codes that apply to each sensory, motor, and mixed nerve. Each nerve constitutes one unit of service. These codes are used to enhance codes 95900, 95903, and 95904.

- **Appendix K:** "Product Pending FDA Approval"—A list of codes for some vaccine products that are pending FDA approval
- **Appendix L:** "Vascular Families"—A summary of the branches of vascular families when the starting point of intravascular catheterization is the aorta
- **Appendix M:** "Crosswalk to Deleted CPT Codes"—A summary of deleted CPT codes that can be crosswalked to new or revised codes

The appendices provide the billing specialist with a quick reference to CPT code changes and updates.

CPT Alphabetic Index

The CPT alphabetic index is organized by **main terms**, also called main entries. Main terms are printed in bold. There are four (4) types of main terms:

- Procedure or service: Laparoscopy, repair, cast
- Organ or anatomic site: Heart, skin, thyroid gland
- Condition: Fracture, ectopic pregnancy, pressure ulcer (decubitus)
- Synonyms, eponyms, and abbreviations: EEG, Caldwell-Luc procedure, Pomeroy's operation

Main terms may be followed by a series of indented terms that modify the main term and affect code selection.

In Figure 6–1, note that the main term "fracture" has several modifying terms. The billing specialist compares the procedure statement with the main term and then reviews the modifying terms to locate the code that best matches the procedure's description. For "intertrochanteric

---

Fracture

Ankle

    Bimalleolar...............27808–27814

    Closed...............27816–27818

    Lateral...............27786–27814, 27792

Femur

    Closed Treatment...........27230, 27238–27240, 27246, 27267–272–68,

        27500–27503, 27508, 27510, 27516–27517

    with manipulation...............27232

    without manipulation...............27267

FIGURE 6–1 Modifying Terms for Fracture

fracture of the femur, with implant," the billing specialist selects code 27245 and verifies the code with the full description found in the "Musculoskeletal" chapter.

The instructions for using the CPT index include a description of code ranges and modifying terms. The billing specialist and medical coder are clearly instructed *not* to assign codes from the index. *Always* refer to the main sections to ensure coding accuracy.

REINFORCEMENT EXERCISES 6–1

Spell out the abbreviations.

1. CPT

   _____

2. HCPCS

   _____

3. ASC

   _____

4. HHS

   _____

5. AHA

   _____

Provide a short answer for each item.

1. How often is CPT updated?

   _____

   _____

   _____

2. What agency requires the use of HCPCS codes?

   _____

   _____

   _____

3. Identify and define three CPT appendices.

   _____

   _____

   _____

continued on the next page

---

continued from the previous page

4. Identify the effective date of revised CPT codes.

_____

_____

_____

5. List the six main sections of the CPT code book.

_____

_____

_____

CPT Coding Conventions

CPT coding conventions include symbols and cross-references. The symbols are semicolons (;), bullets (•) and triangles (▲), facing triangles (►◄), plus signs (+), circles (○), circled bullets (☉), null zero or universal no code (Ø), and the flash symbol (※). The cross-references are "see" and "see also."

Semicolon

The **semicolon** (;) is used to identify the common part or main entry for indented modifying terms or descriptions. When several codes and descriptions refer to a specific procedure or have a shared beginning description, a semicolon follows the shared portion. Figure 6–2 is an example of CPT semicolon use.

In Figure 6–2, the procedure is colonoscopy, and there are several descriptions and codes that apply to variations of that procedure. "Colonoscopy, flexible, proximal to splenic flexure" is the common description shared by codes 45378 through 45382. Therefore, the full description for CPT code 45380 is "Colonoscopy, flexible, proximal to splenic flexure; with biopsy, single or multiple." Note that the full description for CPT code 45378 is "Colonoscopy, flexible, proximal to splenic flexure; diagnostic, with or without collection of specimen(s) by brushing or washing,

Endoscopy

☉**45378** Colonoscopy, flexible, proximal to splenic flexure; diagnostic, with or without collection of specimen(s) by brushing or washing, with or without colon decompression (separate procedure)

☉**45379** with removal of foreign body

☉**45380** with biopsy, single or multiple...

☉**45382** with control of bleeding...

Delmar/Cengage Learning

FIGURE 6–2 Semicolon Use

with or without colon decompression (separate procedure)." The description following the semicolon applies only to code 45378.

The billing specialist carefully reviews the patient's record to ensure that the correct code is selected.

EXAMPLE

Dr. Johnson circled *"colonoscopy"* on the route slip. The billing specialist reviewed the patient's record and discovered that the procedure note states, "Bleeding was controlled by cauterization." Colonoscopy with no mention of bleeding or specimen collection is coded as 45378. Based on the information in the procedure note, the correct code is 45381 "colonoscopy. . .*with control of bleeding... .*"

Because the reimbursement for colonoscopy with control of bleeding is more than the reimbursement for colonoscopy with no mention of bleeding, the record review in this case helped ensure appropriate payment for the service provided.

The indented statements following the semicolon may provide additional diagnostic information, additional or other anatomic sites, additional or other procedures, or additional codes for extensive procedures. These semicolon applications are shown in examples A through D.

EXAMPLE

A. *Additional Diagnostic Information*
   49585 Repair umbilical hernia, age 5 years or over; reducible
   49587 incarcerated or strangulated
Code 49587 is used when the diagnostic statement includes additional information about the hernia.

B. *Additional or Other Anatomic Sites*
   27050 Arthrotomy, with biopsy; sacroiliac joint
   27052 hip joint
Code 27052 is used when the arthrotomy, with biopsy is performed on a hip joint.

C. *Additional Procedures*
   44155 Colectomy, total, abdominal, with proctectomy; with ileostomy
   44156 with continent ileostomy
Code 44156 is used when the total abdominal colectomy and proctectomy includes a continent ileostomy.

D. *Additional Codes for Extensive Procedures*
   11040 Debridement; skin, partial thickness
   11041 skin, full thickness
   11042 skin, and subcutaneous tissue
   11043 skin, subcutaneous tissue, and muscle
Codes 11041 through 11042 are used when the debridement includes the tissues mentioned with each code.

Bullets and Triangles

A **bullet** (•) placed before a CPT code identifies the code as a new addition or new code. A **triangle** (▲) placed before a code identifies a revision in the narrative description of the code.

2010 Current Procedural Terminology © 2009 American Medical Association. All Rights Reserved.

EXAMPLE

A. *New Code*
- 21011   Excision, tumor, soft tissue of face or scalp, subcutaneous; less than 2 cm

B. *Revised Code*
- ▲ 21930   Excision, tumor, soft tissue of back or flank, subcutaneous; less than 3 cm

Appendix B of the CPT manual is a numerical list of additions, revisions, and deletions.

Facing Triangles

Facing triangles (►◄) are used to set off new or revised information in the CPT guidelines, the beginning of each main section, and throughout the CPT manual wherever descriptions have been changed.

EXAMPLE

Surgery/Mediastinum and Diaphragm
Diaphragm Repair
39520 Repair, diaphragmatic hernia (esophageal hiatal); transthoracic
►*(For laparoscopic paraesophageal hernia repair, see 43281, 43282)*◄

Plus Sign

The **plus sign** (+), which is placed in front of a five-digit CPT code, identifies an **add-on code**. Add-on codes are CPT codes that must be used with a related procedure code. In addition to the plus sign, the narrative description of add-on codes includes instructional notes as reminders that the codes must be used with another code. The following example illustrates how to apply add-on codes.

EXAMPLE

Surgery/Integumentary System
Excision—Debridement
11000   Debridement of extensive eczematous or infected skin; up to 10% of body surface
+11001   each additional 10% of the body surface, or part thereof (List separately in addition to code for primary procedure)
   (Use 11001 in conjunction with code 11000)

   Dr. Romero debrides the eczema from 30% of Loretta's body surface, which includes her trunk and legs. Code 11000 is selected to indicate that 10% of [the] body surface was debrided. Code 11001 is selected twice to indicate that an additional 20% of [the] body surface was also debrided. Three codes, 11000, 11001, and 11001, are used to accurately describe what Dr. Romero did for this patient.

Circle

A **circle** (○) is placed before a CPT code to indicate that the code has been reinstated or recycled.

Circled Bullets

A **circled bullet** (⊙) is placed before a CPT code to indicate that the service or procedure includes the use of **moderate** (conscious) **sedation**. Moderate sedation is the use of sedatives or pain relievers to minimize pain and discomfort without causing complete unconsciousness. Patients under moderate sedation are usually able to respond to verbal cues and communicate discomfort during the procedure. According to CPT coding guidelines, the physician who performs a procedure that includes moderate sedation should not submit a separate claim for the moderate sedation. When anesthesia services—moderate sedation or otherwise—are performed by someone other than the physician performing the procedure, the anesthesia code should be reported.

Null Zero or Universal No Code

The **null zero** or **universal no code** (∅) identifies CPT codes that may not be used with **modifier -51**. Modifier -51 is used when multiple procedures are performed by the same provider during a single encounter.

A CPT **modifier** is a two-digit number that is added to the five-digit CPT code or a five-digit number that is reported in addition to the CPT code. The modifier provides additional information about the procedure. Modifiers and their descriptions are presented with "Surgery" section codes.

Flash symbol

The **flash symbol** (✗) identifies CPT codes that classify products pending FDA approval.

See and See Also

The cross-references *see* and *see also* are found in CPT's main sections and alphabetic index. These references tell the billing specialist or medical coder to look at other CPT codes or sections. Accurate CPT code assignment depends on compliance with the "see" and "see also" instructions. Figure 6–3 shows examples of these instructions.

A. "See"

ALPHABETIC INDEX

Abbe-Eslander Procedure

See Reconstruction; Repair, Cleft Lip

B. "See Also"

MAIN SECTION

Anus/Incision

46050 Incision and drainage, perianal abscess, superficial

> (*See also* 45020, 46060)

FIGURE 6–3 *See* and *See Also* Instructional Notes

Delmar/Cengage Learning

Instructional Notes

In addition to symbols and cross-references used as coding conventions, CPT has extensive **instructional notes** and **section guidelines**. Instructional notes, which provide the billing specialist or coder with details about code selection, are located at the beginning of a heading, in parentheses before or after a code, or in parentheses as part of the code's description. Section guidelines are located at the beginning of each CPT section.

Heading Notes

Instructional notes located at the beginning of a CPT heading provide information about the following:

- Components of a service or procedure
- Definitions of terms and codes
- Directions for additional code assignment

Figure 6–4 lists an example of each heading instructional note.

Notes Before/After CPT Codes

Instructional notes placed before or after the CPT code primarily consist of additional, alternate, or deleted codes as well as other general information. Table 6–3 gives examples of before and after instructional notes.

Section Guidelines

The **section guidelines** precede each of the six main CPT sections and are clearly labeled. The guidelines can be brief, as with the "Anesthesia Guidelines," or extensive, as with the "Evaluation and Management (E/M) Guidelines."

The guidelines provide the billing specialist and medical coder with information that increases coding accuracy. Guidelines are discussed with each main section.

SERVICE AND/OR PROCEDURE COMPONENTS
Instructional notes under **Esophagus**, **Endoscopy** in the digestive system surgery codes direct the coder to select the code based on anatomical site, and surgical endoscopy always includes the diagnostic endoscopy.

DEFINITIONS OF TERMS AND CODES
The instructional notes under the **Vestibule of Mouth** heading in the digestive surgery codes describe the **vestibule** as "the part of the oral cavity outside the dentoalveolar structures; [including] the mucosal and submucosal tissue of lips and cheeks."

ADDITIONAL CODE ASSIGNMENT
The instructional notes under **Repair, Hernioplasty, Herniorrhaphy, Herniotomy** in the digestive surgery codes direct the billing specialist or coder to use an additional code for the repair of strangulated organs or structures.

Delmar/Cengage Learning

FIGURE 6–4 CPT Heading Instructional Notes

TABLE 6–3

Instructional Notes Before and After CPT Codes
Alternative Codes The note (For excision of pilonidal cyst, see 11770–11772) located under code 10081, "Incision and drainage of pilonidal cyst; complicated," directs the coder to the correct codes for "excision" of a pilonidal cyst.
Additional Codes The note (List 41114 in addition to code 41112 or 41113) located under code 41114 "Excision of lesion of tongue with closure; with local tongue flap," indicates that code 41114 is an additional code for codes 41112, "Excision of lesion of tongue with closure; anterior two-thirds," and 41113, "Excision of lesion of tongue with closure; posterior one-third."
Deleted Codes The note ►(78460–78465 have been deleted. To report, see 78451–78454)◄, which is located after code 78459, instructs the billing specialist or coder to use codes 78451–78454 for procedures previously coded to 78460–78465. The facing triangles highlight this note as new information.

REINFORCEMENT EXERCISES 6–2

Fill in the blank.

1. A(n) _____ is used to identify the main entry for indented modifying terms or descriptions.

2. A new CPT code is identified by a(n) _____ placed in front of the code.

3. Revised CPT code descriptions have a(n) _____ placed in front of the code.

4. _____ are used to set off new or revised information in CPT guidelines and main sections.

5. Add-on CPT codes are identified by a(n) _____ placed in front of the code.

6. A(n) _____ placed before a CPT code means that moderate sedation is included in the procedure.

7. The _____ identifies CPT codes that may not be used with modifier -51.

8. A _____ is a two-digit number that is added to the CPT code.

9. A reinstated or recycled CPT code is preceded by a(n) _____.

10. A _____ symbol indicates a product that is pending FDA approval.

FIGURE 6–5 Take a Deep Breath

Delmar/Cengage Learning

"EVALUATION AND MANAGEMENT" SECTION

CPT **"Evaluation and Management"** section (E/M) (99201–99499) codes are divided into three broad categories of provider services: office visits, hospital visits, and consultations. E/M codes capture information about medical services, as opposed to surgical services. As the name implies, evaluation and management codes are used to report physician or provider activities associated with evaluating an individual's health status and managing or implementing a plan of care related to that status. Evaluation and management services range from a routine sports physical to planning and implementing care for critically ill or injured individuals. Figure 6–5 illustrates a physician examining a patient.

There are several pages of "Evaluation and Management Services Guidelines." This chapter includes a brief discussion of the definitions of commonly used E/M terms and a detailed discussion of the instructions for selecting evaluation and management CPT codes. Refer to the CPT manual for a complete review of the E/M guidelines.

Commonly Used Terms

Certain keywords and phrases are used throughout the E/M section. The "Evaluation and Management Guidelines" provide a definition or description of the commonly used terms and phrases. Table 6–4 summarizes the definitions for CPT key terms and phrases.

TABLE 6–4

Evaluation and Management Definitions
Chief Complaint: A description of the problem that caused the patient to seek treatment, usually stated in the patient's words
Clinical Examples: Examples of the clinical situations associated with various E/M services that are listed in Appendix C
Concurrent Care: The provision of similar services to the same patient on the same day by more than one physician or provider
Counseling: A discussion with the patient or family about one or more of the following: diagnostic results, impressions, and recommendations; prognosis; risks and benefits of treatment options; treatment or follow-up instructions; importance of compliance with treatment options; reducing risk factors; and patient and family education. (Psychotherapy counseling; see 90804–90857)
Established Patient: A person who has received professional services within the past three years from physicians of the same specialty who belong to the same group practice
Face-to-Face Time: The time a physician spends face-to-face with the patient or family; a component of E/M codes
Family History: A review of medical events in the patient's family that includes significant information about the health status or cause of death of parents, siblings, and children and about diseases that may be hereditary or place the patient at risk
History of Present Illness: A chronological description of the patient's current problem, from the first sign or symptom to the time the patient seeks treatment
New Patient: A person who has not received professional services within the past three years from physicians of the same specialty who belong to the same group practice
Non–Face-to-Face Time: The time spent doing work before and after seeing the patient or family; not a component of E/M codes
Past Medical History: A narrative of the patient's past illnesses, injuries, treatments, operations, hospitalizations, allergies, and other age-appropriate information
Professional Services: Face-to-face services rendered by a physician and reported by one or more specific CPT codes. This definition of professional services is used only to distinguish between new and established patients
Social History: An age-appropriate review of marital status, employment history, substance use and abuse, sexual history, and level of education
Special Report: Documentation that supports the necessity for providing services that are unusual or not listed in the CPT manual
System Review (Review of Systems; ROS): An inventory of body systems through a series of questions to help define the problem, clarify the differential diagnosis, identify needed testing, or provide baseline patient data

continued on the next page

continued from the previous page

> **Unit/Floor Time:** The time the physician is present on the patient's hospital unit and at the bedside for the purpose of rendering service to the patient that is a component of E/M codes. Unit/floor time applies to hospital observation services, inpatient hospital care, initial and follow-up hospital consultations, and nursing facility visits.

> **Unlisted Service:** An evaluation or management service provided to the patient that does not have an associated CPT code

In addition to the terms listed in Table 6–4, CPT guidelines make a clear distinction between consultation and referral services. However, many physicians use these terms interchangeably.

According to CPT guidelines, a **consultation** is a "service provided by a physician whose opinion or advice regarding evaluation and/or management of a specific problem is requested by another physician or other appropriate source."

Under consultation guidelines, the physician or provider who requests the consultation retains the responsibility for managing the patient's care. Recommendations and requests for consultations are documented in the patient's record. For insurance billing purposes, CPT codes 99241 through 99255 apply to consultations.

A **referral** is the transfer of the management of patient care from one physician to another. A referral usually applies to a problem that requires the expertise of a specialist. Activities associated with referring a patient to another provider are documented in the patient's medical record.

There are no CPT categories or codes that apply to referrals. When a provider accepts a patient as a referral, the service is coded to the appropriate CPT category. The following example illustrates this point.

EXAMPLE
Dr. French has treated Marissa for gastrointestinal problems. A recent fiberoptic sigmoidoscopy indicates that Marissa has ulcerative colitis. Dr. French recommends that Marissa continue treatment with a gastroenterologist, and Marissa agrees.

Dr. French refers Marissa to Dr. Skopes, who is a gastroenterologist. During Marissa's first office visit with Dr. Skopes, he recommends a colonoscopy.

In this example, Marissa is a new patient to Dr. Skopes. The correct CPT category is Office/Other Outpatient Services, new patient, and the code range is 99201 through 99205. If Marissa had been referred to Dr. Skopes while she was in the hospital, the correct CPT category would have been Hospital Inpatient Services, code range 99221 through 99239.

E/M Categories

There are 22 categories of evaluation and management codes, which range from office visits to work-related and medical disability evaluation services. Each category has specific guidelines that describe the type of services that fall into the category. Table 6–5 lists the E/M categories, and Table 6–6 summarizes the guidelines for each category. The complete guidelines and instructions are found in the CPT manual.

TABLE 6–5

Evaluation and Management Categories	
Category	Range of Codes
Office/Other Outpatient Services	99201–99215
Hospital Observation Services	99217–99220
Hospital Inpatient Services	99221–99239
Consultations	99241–99255
Emergency Department Services	99281–99288
Critical Care Services	99291, 99292
Nursing Facility Services	99304–99318
Domiciliary, Rest Home (e.g., Boarding Home), or Custodial Care Services	99324–99337
Domiciliary, Rest Home (e.g., Assisted Living Facility), or Home Care Plan Oversight Services	99339–99340
Home Services	99341–99350
Prolonged Services	99354–99359
Physician Standby Services	99360
Case Management Services	99363–99368
Care Plan Oversight Services	99374–99380
Preventive Medicine Services	99381–99397
Counseling Risk Factor Reduction and Behavior Change Intervention	99401–99429
Non–Face-to-Face Physician Services	99441–99444
Special E/M Services (Basic Life and/or Disability Evaluation Services and Work-Related or Medical Disability Evaluation Services)	99450–99456
Newborn Care Services	99460–99465
Inpatient Neonatal Intensive Care Services and Pediatric and Neonatal Critical Services	99466–99480
Other Evaluation and Management Services (unlisted evaluation and management services)	99499

TABLE 6–6

E/M Category Guidelines
Office or Other Outpatient Services (99201–99215)
CPT codes from this category are used to report evaluation and management services provided in the physician or provider's office or in an outpatient or other ambulatory facility. The patient is an outpatient until admission to an inpatient facility occurs. Codes are divided between new and established patient services, and code selection depends on the complexity of the service provided.
Hospital Observation Services (99217–99220)
CPT codes from this category are used to report evaluation and management services provided to individuals who are admitted to an inpatient facility as "observation status." Discharge services and initial observation care codes are included in this category. The codes for new and established patients are the same, and code selection depends on the complexity of the service provided.
Hospital Inpatient Services (99221–99239)
CPT codes from this category are used to report evaluation and management services provided to hospital inpatients. Initial hospital care, subsequent hospital care, same-day admission and discharge, and hospital discharge codes are included in this category. The codes for new and established patients are the same, and code selection depends on the complexity of the service provided.
Consultations (99241–99255)
CPT codes from this category are used to report four types of consultations: office or other outpatient, initial inpatient, follow-up inpatient, and confirmatory. Consultation codes for new or established patients are the same, and code selection depends on the complexity of the service provided.
Emergency Department Services (99281–99288)
CPT codes from this category are used to report evaluation and management services to individuals who seek treatment at an emergency room or department. An emergency department is an organized hospital-based facility that is available 24 hours a day for the provision of unscheduled health care services to patients who need immediate medical attention. Codes for new or established patients are the same, and code selection depends on the complexity of the service provided.
Critical Care Services (99291, 99292)
CPT codes for critical care services depend on the total amount of time the physician devoted solely to providing services directly to the critically ill patient. The physician cannot provide services to any other patient during this time. The first 74 minutes of critical care services are covered by code 99291, and code +99292 (an add-on code) is used to report each additional 30 minutes of critical care services. The guidelines for this category are extensive and fully explained in the CPT manual.

continued on the next page

continued from the previous page

E/M Category Guidelines

Nursing Facility Services (99304–99318)

CPT codes from this category are used to report evaluation and management services provided to patients in nursing facilities, intermediate care facilities, or long-term care facilities. Comprehensive nursing facility assessments, subsequent nursing facility care, and nursing facility discharge services are included in this category. Codes for new or established patients are the same, and code selection depends on the complexity of the service provided.

Domiciliary, Rest Home (e.g., Boarding Home), or Custodial Care Services (99324–99337)

CPT codes from this category are used to report evaluation and management services rendered to individuals who live in a facility that provides room, board, and other personal assistance. There are separate codes for new and established patients, and code selection depends on the complexity of the evaluation and management services.

Domiciliary, Rest Home (e.g., Assisted Living Facility), or Home Care Plan Oversight Services (99339–99340)

CPT codes from this category are used to report physician services related to overseeing an individual's plan of care.

Home Services (99341–99350)

CPT codes from this category are used to report evaluation and management services provided to individuals in their homes or other private residences. There are separate codes for new and established patients, and code selection depends on the complexity of the evaluation and management services.

Prolonged Services (99354–99359)

CPT codes from this category are reported as add-on codes in conjunction with other E/M codes. Prolonged services can be provided with or without direct patient contact, must be more than 30 minutes, and are reported at 30-minute intervals after the first 74 minutes.

Physician Standby Services (99360)

This CPT code is used to report physician standby services when the standby is requested by another physician. The standby physician may not treat other patients during this time, and services are reported at every full 30 minute interval *after* the first 30 minutes. Standby service of less than 30 minutes on a given date is not reported separately.

Case Management Services (99363–99368)

CPT codes for team conferences and telephone consultations are included in this section. Team conferences are usually related to physician participation on an interdisciplinary health care team that plans and coordinates patient care services. Telephone consultations are usually initiated by a physician and directed to other health care professionals to provide patient care.

Care Plan Oversight Services (99374–99380)

These services usually include a review of clinical information and communication with other professionals involved in the patient's care; no more than one service within a calendar month; and only one physician may report services for the given timeframe.

continued on the next page

continued from the previous page

Preventive Medicine Services (99381–99397)

CPT codes from this category are used to report services provided to individuals to promote health and prevent illness or injury. These services may not be a part of other evaluation and management services. There are separate codes for preventive medicine services for new and established patients.

Counseling Risk Factor Reduction and Behavior Change Intervention (99401–99429)

CPT codes from this section are used to report services related to health promotion and illness or injury prevention. These codes apply to both new and established patients.

Non–Face-to-Face Physician Services (99441–99444)

CPT codes in this category include services provided via the telephone or online means.

Special Evaluation and Management Services (Basic Life and/or Disability Evaluation Services and Work-Related or Medical Disability Evaluation Services) (99450–99456)

CPT codes in this section are used to report evaluations performed when the patient or individual is applying for life or disability insurance. Under these codes, there is no active management of the problem or problems identified.

Newborn Care (99460–99465)

CPT codes from this section are used to report services provided to newborns in several different settings. Most codes relate to services rendered to a normal newborn.

Inpatient Neonatal Intensive Care Services and Pediatric and Neonatal Critical Services (99466–99480)

CPT codes in this category are used to report services provided to individuals from less than 28 days of age through 5 years of age. The CPT manual provides extensive instructions for these codes.

Other Evaluation and Management Services (99499)

This CPT code is used to report E/M services not covered elsewhere. Selection of this code usually requires the physician to provide a written report explaining the service and the reason for it.

REINFORCEMENT EXERCISES 6–3

Provide a short answer for each item.

1. List three broad categories of CPT evaluation and management services.

_____

_____

_____

continued on the next page

continued from the previous page

2. Describe the purpose of E/M codes.

_____

_____

_____

3. What is the difference between a consultation and a referral?

_____

_____

_____

Fill in the blank.

1. A(n) _____ is a person who has not received professional services within the past three years.

2. A(n) _____ is a person who has received professional services within the last three years.

3. The _____ is a description of the problem that caused the patient to seek treatment.

4. _____ is the time the physician is present on the patient's hospital unit and at the bedside.

5. A service provided to the patient that does not have an associated CPT code is called a(n) _____.

6. Services provided to promote health and prevent illness are called _____.

7. The _____ is a chronological description of the patient's current problem.

8. Team conferences and telephone consultations are included in the _____ services E/M codes.

Levels of Service

Most evaluation and management categories and subcategories have several codes that represent different levels of service. Levels of service are related to the nature of the patient's problem(s) and the complexity of the provider's evaluation. The following example lists five office visit codes, identifies the level of each code, and briefly describes the nature of the patient's problems.

EXAMPLE

OFFICE/OTHER OUTPATIENT VISITS: 99201 through 99205

Code	Level	Description
99201	I	Self-limited or minor problem(s)
99202	II	Low to moderately severe problem(s)

TABLE 6–7

Description of E/M Code Components
Component with Description
History: A chronological review of the individual's past medical and surgical history, family history, and social history as well as a review of one or more body systems. E/M codes that reflect a higher level of service require a more comprehensive history.
Examination: A physical examination of the individual that includes an assessment of one or more body systems or organ function. E/M codes that reflect a higher level of service require an examination of more body systems.
Medical Decision-Making: The complexity of establishing a diagnosis or selecting a management option based on the number of possible diagnoses; the amount of medical information obtained, reviewed, and analyzed; and the risk of complications or death. E/M codes that reflect a higher level of service require an increased complexity of medical decision-making.
Counseling: A discussion with the individual about diagnoses, treatment options, risks and benefits, follow-up, risk factor reduction, and compliance with treatment plans.
Coordination of Care: Activities related to ordering, referring, and discussing the patient's treatment with other providers, agencies, and the patient.
Nature of Presenting Problem: The level of severity or complexity of the individual's problem, disease, condition, illness, injury, symptom, or complaint; ranges from minimal severity to high severity.
Time: The number of minutes a provider spends with the individual; the number of minutes the provider spends reviewing tests, records, and other patient-related information.

99203	III	Moderately severe problem(s)
99204	IV	Moderate to severe problem(s)
99205	V	Moderate to severe problem(s) with high complexity

This example shows the relationship between the E/M code and the level of service.

There are seven factors that contribute to E/M levels of service and affect E/M code selection. The CPT manual calls these factors "components." Table 6–7 provides a list and brief descriptions of the factors or components.

The CPT manual has a complete discussion of the seven components.

Not all seven components are needed for every E/M code. E/M guidelines identify three **key components**—history, examination, and medical decision-making—that are required for most E/M codes. Because the three key components affect many E/M codes, they are described in detail.

History

This is information about the patient's previous health care encounters, family health, and lifestyle. In general, a history includes a chief complaint (CC); history of present illness (HPI); review of systems (ROS); and past, family, and social history. CPT describes four types of history that are defined as follows:

- **Problem-focused:** Consists of a chief complaint and a brief history of present illness or problem
- **Expanded problem-focused:** Consists of a chief complaint, brief history of present illness, and a review of the systems that relate to the patient's problem

Delmar/Cengage Learning

FIGURE 6–6 Types of History

- **Detailed:** Consists of a chief complaint; extended history of present illness; a review of the systems that relate to the patient's problem as well as a review of a limited number of additional systems; and a past, family, and social history directly related to the patient's problems
- **Comprehensive:** Consists of a chief complaint; extended history of present illness; review of all body systems; and a complete past, family, and social history

Figure 6–6 illustrates each type of history.

Examination

This is the physical examination of the patient. As with history, there are four types of examination:

- **Problem-focused:** A limited examination of the affected body area or organ
- **Expanded problem-focused:** A limited examination of the affected body area or organ system and other symptomatic or related organ system(s)
- **Detailed:** An extended examination of the affected body area(s) and other symptomatic or related organ system(s)
- **Comprehensive:** A general multisystem examination or a complete examination of a single organ system

Medical Decision-Making

This is the complexity of establishing a diagnosis and selecting a management or treatment option. Medical decision-making depends on the following conditions:

- The number of possible diagnoses or the number of management options that must be considered
- The amount or complexity of medical records, diagnostic tests, and other information that must be obtained, reviewed, and analyzed

- The risk of significant complications, morbidity, or mortality as well as comorbidities associated with the patient's presenting problem(s), the diagnostic procedure(s), or the possible management options

In order to qualify for a specific type of medical decision-making, two of the three conditions must be met. Based on these conditions, there are four types of medical decision-making:

- **Straightforward:** Indicating a minimal number of diagnoses; a minimal amount of information to be reviewed; and a minimal risk of complication, morbidity, or mortality; basically, an uncomplicated presenting problem.
- **Low complexity:** Indicating a limited number of diagnoses; a limited amount of information to be reviewed; and a low risk of complication, morbidity, or mortality; includes a controlled chronic disease.
- **Moderate complexity:** Indicating multiple diagnoses; a moderate amount of information to be reviewed/analyzed; and a moderate risk of complication, morbidity, or mortality; a multiple or in-depth system review is associated with this level of complexity.
- **High complexity:** Indicating extensive diagnoses; extensive amounts of information to be reviewed/analyzed; and a high risk of complications, morbidity, or mortality; complicated, multisystem problems are associated with this level of complexity.

Table 6–8 summarizes the conditions that contribute to each type of medical decision-making.

Remember, in order to qualify for a particular type of medical decision-making, two of the three conditions must be documented in the patient's record. Examples A through D illustrate each type of medical decision-making.

EXAMPLE

A. Straightforward Medical Decision-Making

Mrs. Pelletier is seen today with a rash and itching. She had contact within the last 48 hours with poison ivy. Diagnosis: Contact dermatitis.

B. Low-Complexity Medical Decision-Making

Mr. Victor is seen today with mild irritation of the eyes, tearing, light sensitivity, and blurred vision. After slit-lamp examination and vision testing, opacity in both corneas was noted. Fluorescein strip staining of the eyes revealed

TABLE 6–8

Types of Medical Decision-Making			
Type of Medical Decision-Making	Number of Diagnoses or Management Options	Amount or Complexity of Information to Be Reviewed	Risk of Complications, Morbidity, or Mortality
Straightforward	Minimal	Minimal or none	Minimal
Low Complexity	Limited	Limited	Low
Moderate Complexity	Multiple	Moderate	Moderate
High Complexity	Extensive	Extensive	High

chronic dendritic keratitis requiring long-term topical treatment.
Diagnosis: Chronic dendritic keratitis.

C. Moderate-Complexity Medical Decision-Making

Mr. Weller, a 77-year-old-male, presents today in mild distress. He relates a three-month history of substernal chest pain, episodic in nature. His hypertension has been fairly well controlled with his current medication. Mr. Weller states that the pain seems to be brought on by exertion. Diagnosis: No clear-cut diagnosis; several tests must be done to determine the cause of the substernal chest pain.

D. High-Complexity Medical Decision-Making

Ms. Yoha is a 70-year-old woman with diabetes mellitus and hypertension. She is accompanied by her sister, who explains that for the past two months, "my sister" has been experiencing agitation, confusion, and short-term memory loss. Glucose monitoring at home indicates sporadic control of the diabetes, and Ms. Yoha's blood pressure today is 190/110. Diagnoses: Diabetes mellitus and hypertension, poorly controlled. Possible transient ischemic attacks, cerebrovascular accident, or basal artery insufficiency.

Some E/M codes require documentation of all three key components, and others require only two of the three key components. Table 6–9 lists E/M subcategories that require two or three of the key components.

TABLE 6–9

E/M Categories and Number of Key Components		
Category	**E/M Codes**	**Key Components**
Office or Other Outpatient Services—*New Patient*	99201–99205	3
Office or Other Outpatient Services—*Established Patient*	99212–99215	2
Initial Hospital Observation Care—*New/Established Patient*	99218–99220	3
Initial Hospital Care—*New or Established Patient*	99221–99223	3
Subsequent Hospital Care	99231–99233	2
Observation or Inpatient Care Services—*Patients admitted and discharged on the same day*	99234–99236	3
Office or Other Outpatient Consultations—*New/Established Patients*	99241–99245	3
Initial Inpatient Consultation—*New/Established Patient*	99251–99255	3
Follow-up Inpatient Consultation—*Established Patient*	99261–99263	2

continued on the next page

continued from the previous page

Emergency Department Services—*New or Established Patient*	99281–99285	3
Initial Nursing Facility Care—*New or Established Patient*	99304–99306	3
Subsequent Nursing Facility Care—*New/Established Patient*	99307–99310	2
Domiciliary, Rest Home (e.g., Boarding Home), or Custodial Care Services—*New Patient*	99324–99328	3
Domiciliary, Rest Home (e.g., Boarding Home), or Custodial Care Services—*Established Patient*	99334–99337	2
Home Services—*New Patient*	99341–99345	3
Home Services—*Established Patient*	99347–99350	2

Documentation Requirements

Selecting the appropriate evaluation and management CPT code is a complex clinical decision that is the responsibility of the physician or provider. Many providers document the E/M code by circling or checking one of the E/M codes that are preprinted on the encounter form or route slip. Figure 6–7 is a sample encounter form with the E/M and diagnosis codes circled.

The encounter form is routed to the billing office, and the billing specialist submits an insurance claim by using the codes noted on the form. However, with the passage of the 1996 **Health Insurance Portability and Accountability Act (HIPAA)**, insurance carriers are closely monitoring evaluation and management codes. The documentation in the patient's record must clearly support evaluation and management codes as well as the diagnoses codes.

In today's health care environment, billing specialists and medical coders are often expected to review the patient's record for documentation and additional information that may affect coding accuracy. In some practices, the billing specialist or medical coder codes "from the record" and compares the results with the encounter form codes. The following example illustrates this activity.

EXAMPLE

Brenda, the billing specialist in Dr. Hamilton's office, is preparing an insurance claim for Jenny Lind. On Ms. Lind's encounter form, Dr. Hamilton selected 99213 as the E/M code and urinary tract infection as the diagnosis.

Brenda checks the key components for 99213 and notes that this code requires two of the three key components: an expanded problem-focused history, an expanded problem-focused exam, and low-complexity medical decision-making. The only documentation related to this visit is a progress note that states: "Patient seen today for pain on urination. Urinalysis ordered. Pending results, will start the patient on amoxicillin."

Based on the progress note in this example, the billing specialist alerts the provider that code 99213 requires documentation of either a history or exam related to the problem. In addition, the billing specialist also checks the patient's record for the urinalysis lab slip. If it is in the record,

ELIZABETH FOY, MD
CHARLES FRENCH, MD
ROBERT HOWARD, MD
DENZEL HAMILTON, MD
ROBERTA PHARYNGEAL, MD
HENRY ROMERO, MD

SUPERIORLAND CLINIC
714 HENNEPIN AVENUE
BLUEBERRY, ME 49855
PHONE: (906) 336-4600   FAX: (906) 336-4020

NEW PATIENT	CODE	FEE	LAB TEST	CODE	FEE	LAB TEST	CODE	FEE
Level I	99201		AST	84450		LDH	83615	
Level II	99202		Albumin	82040		Lipid Panel	80061	
Level III	99203		Alk Phos	84075		Metabolic Panel	80053	
Level IV	99204		BUN	84520		Obstetric Panel	80055	
Level V	99205		CBC	85027		Occult Blood	82270	
ESTABLISHED PATIENT			CBC/diff	85025		PAP smear	88150	
Level I	99211		CK/CPK	82550		PPD Skin Test	86580	
Level II	99212		Drug Screen	80100		Prothrombin Time	85610	
Level III	99213		Electrolyte Panel	80051		PSA	84152	
Level IV	99214		Estrogen	82671		Rapid Strep Screen	87880	
Level V	99215		Glucose/blood	82947		Sed Rate	85651	
OFFICE CONSULTATION			GTT	82951		TSH	84443	
Level I	99241		HgbA1C	83036		Urinalysis	81000	
Level II	99242		Hepatitis Panel	80074				
Level III	99243		HIV Screen	86703				
Level IV	99244							
Level V	99245		**OTHER TESTS**			**OTHER TESTS**		
HOSPITAL INPATIENT			A/P Chest X-ray			Holter/24 hr		
Initial/Complex	99223		DXA Scan	77080		Sigmoidoscopy	45330	
Subsequent	99231		EKG Int/Report	93000		Stress Test	93015	
EMERGENCY DEPARTMENT SERV.			Rhythm EKG	93040				
Level I	99281							
Level II	99282							
Level III	99283		**TREATMENTS**	CODE	FEE	**TREATMENTS**	CODE	FEE
Level IV	99284		Flu Shot	90658				
Level V	99285							

DIAGNOSIS

Abdominal Pain	789.00	Gastritis	535.50	OTHER DIAGNOSIS		CODE
Angina Pectoris, Unspec.	413.9	Hemorrhoids, NOS	455.6			
Asthma, Unspecified	493.90	Hiatal hernia	553.3			
Bronchitis, Acute	466.0	Hyperlipidemia, NOS	272.4			
Bursitis	727.3	Hypertension, Unspec.	401.9			
CHF	428.0	Hyperthyroidism	242.90	REFERRAL/COMMENTS		
Colon polyp	211.3	Hypothyroidism	244.9			
Conjunctivitis, Unspec.	372.00	Osteoarthritis, Unspec	715.99			
Diabetes Mellitus, Type I	250.01	Osteoporosis, postmen.	733.01			
Diabetes Mellitus, Type II	250.00	Pleurisy	511.0			
Diverticulosis, colon	562.10	Serious Otitis Media, Acute	381.01			
Emphysema	492.8	UTI	599.0			

DATE	PATIENT NAME	DOB	CHARGES	PAYMENT	BALANCE

I authorize my insurance benefits to be paid directly to the above named physician. I understand that I am obligated to pay deductibles, copayments, and charges for non-covered services. I authorize release of my medical information for billing purposes.

PATIENT SIGNATURE: **DATE:**

Delmar/Cengage Learning

FIGURE 6–7 Encounter Form

urinalysis should be checked on the encounter form, and the insurance claim should include a charge for that service.

It is important to emphasize that the billing specialist and medical coder do not challenge the clinical judgment of the physician. Rather, the record review is a method to ensure that the documentation in the patient record supports the physician- or provider-selected code.

Approaching the provider about the accuracy of a selected code may be difficult. However, it is better to clarify the code before submitting the insurance claim. Insurance carriers and regulatory agencies monitor E/M codes for **upcoding** and **downcoding**. Upcoding is selecting codes at a higher level than the level substantiated by the patient's record. Downcoding is selecting codes at a lower level than the service requires. Upcoding results in overpayment for services rendered. Some providers downcode under the mistaken assumption that this prevents insurance carrier or regulatory agency audits. In fact, both upcoding and downcoding can be categorized as insurance fraud or abuse.

Documentation guidelines for evaluation and management codes are covered in the CPT manual. In addition to those guidelines, the CMS and the AMA have developed an extensive set of guidelines for E/M codes. The guidelines are available from the CMS website and several commercial vendors.

The CMS/AMA guidelines are substantial. It is beyond the scope of this text to cover or reproduce these guidelines in their entirety. Tables 6–10 through 6–12 summarize the documentation requirements for each of the key components of evaluation and management codes.

Table 6–10 summarizes the history documentation requirements.

Table 6–11 summarizes the examination documentation requirements.

Table 6–12 summarizes the medical decision-making documentation requirements.

TABLE 6–10

History Documentation Requirements				
Type of History	Chief Complaint	History of Present Illness	Review of Systems	Past, Family, and Social History
Problem-Focused	Required	*Brief	Not required	Not required
Expanded Problem-Focused	Required	*Brief	Problem pertinent; all systems that pertain to the problem	Not required
Detailed	Required	**Extended	Extended; all systems directly related to the problem and a limited number of additional systems; review of two to nine body systems is documented	Pertinent; at least one of the following is documented: past history, family history, or social history
Comprehensive Required		**Extended	Complete; all systems related to the problem and all additional body systems; review of 10 organ systems is documented	Complete; two or three of the following are documented: past history, family history, or social history

*Includes one to three of the following: location, severity, quality, duration, timing, context, modifying factors, and associated signs and symptoms that relate to the patient's present problem or illness.

**Includes at least four of the following: location, severity, quality, duration, timing, context, modifying factors, and associated signs and symptoms that relate to the patient's present problem or illness; or the status of at least three chronic or inactive conditions.

TABLE 6–11

Examination Documentation Requirements	
Type of Examination	**Documentation Requirements**
Problem-Focused Exam	A limited examination of the affected body area* or organ system that includes documentation of the results of assessing one to five structures or functions of the affected area or organ system**
Expanded Problem-Focused Exam	A limited examination of the affected body area or organ system and other symptomatic or related systems that includes documentation of the results of assessing at least six structures or functions of one or more body areas or systems
Detailed Exam	An extended examination of the affected body areas and other symptomatic or related organ systems that includes documentation of the results of assessing at least two structures or functions in six organ systems or the results of assessing at least twelve structures or functions in two or more organ systems
Comprehensive Exam	A general multisystem exam that includes documentation of the results of assessing at least two structures or functions in nine organ systems or the results of assessing all structures and functions in the affected organ system and at least one structure or function of the remaining organ systems

*CPT body areas include head and face; neck; chest, breast, axilla; abdomen; genitalia, groin, buttocks; back; and each extremity.

**CPT organ systems include eyes; ears, nose, mouth, throat; cardiovascular; respiratory; gastrointestinal; genitourinary; musculoskeletal; skin; neurologic; psychiatric; and hematologic, lymphatic, and immunologic systems.

TABLE 6–12

Medical Decision-Making Documentation Requirements
Types of Medical Decision-Making with Documentation Requirements
Straightforward: Documentation of a self-limited problem or diagnosis that presents a minimal risk for complications, development of additional problems, loss of organ structure or function, or death; review of a *minimal amount* of clinical data (e.g., previous medical records, routine lab, and x-ray results)
Low complexity: Documentation of two or more self-limited problems, a stable chronic condition, or an acute, uncomplicated illness or injury that presents a low risk for complications, development of additional problems, loss of organ structure or function, or death; review of a limited amount of clinical data (e.g., previous medical records, lab tests, superficial needle biopsies)

continued on the next page

continued from the previous page

> **Moderate complexity:** Documentation of multiple problems or diagnoses, chronic illnesses with mild increase in progression, uncertain new diagnoses requiring additional tests, or acute illness that affects several body systems that present a moderate risk for complications, development of additional problems, loss of organ structure or function, or death; review of a moderate amount of clinical data (e.g., stress tests or invasive diagnostic procedures, such as endoscopies, cardiac catheterization, lumbar puncture)

> **High complexity:** Documentation of extensive problems or diagnoses, chronic illness with a severe increase in progression, acute or chronic illness or injuries that threaten the patient's life or body function that present a high risk for complications, development of additional problems, loss of organ structure or function, or death; review of extensive amounts of clinical data that results in major elective or emergency surgery, poor prognosis, or other management options associated with high-risk illness, injury, or disease

After reviewing the documentation requirement tables, it is obvious that E/M coding is a complex clinical process. In order to receive appropriate reimbursement, the provider must be sure that the requirements for each E/M code or level of service are clearly noted in the patient's record. The familiar saying "If it isn't documented, it hasn't been done" applies more than ever. Given the increased focus on reducing health care costs, the increased focus on insurance claims fraud or abuse, and the increased availability of electronic monitoring by CMS and insurance carriers, providers should welcome the billing specialist's efforts related to reviewing patient records for documentation and coding purposes.

REINFORCEMENT EXERCISES 6–4

Write a short answer for each item.

1. Identify the three key components that are required for many E/M codes.

_____

_____

_____

2. Identify the four types of history and examination.

_____

_____

_____

3. What are the required elements of a problem-focused history?

_____

_____

_____

continued on the next page

continued from the previous page

4. Identify the elements of a comprehensive history.

_____

_____

_____

5. List the three conditions that affect medical decision-making.

_____

_____

_____

6. List the four types of medical decision-making.

_____

_____

_____

7. Identify two requirements for high-complexity medical decision-making.

_____

_____

_____

8. What are two of the three requirements for moderate-complexity medical decision-making?

_____

_____

_____

9. Briefly define upcoding.

_____

_____

_____

10. Briefly define downcoding.

_____

_____

_____

continued on the next page

continued from the previous page

> ### Fill in the blank.
>
> **1.** The complexity of establishing diagnoses and selecting treatment options is called _____.
>
> **2.** A(n) _____ exam is limited to the affected body area or organ.
>
> **3.** A(n) _____ examination consists of a limited examination of the affected body area or organ system and other symptomatic or related organ systems.
>
> **4.** An extended examination of the affected body area(s) and other symptomatic or related organ system(s) is called a(n) _____ examination.
>
> **5.** A(n) _____ examination consists of a general multisystem examination or a complete examination of a single organ system.

Selecting Evaluation and Management Codes

Evaluation and management codes are listed in the CPT alphabetic index by type of service. For example, office visit codes are listed under "Office and/or Other Outpatient Services"; consultations under "Consultation"; hospital visits under "Hospital Services"; and so forth.

When services are provided in the physician or provider's office, the CPT code is usually on the encounter form or route slip. The physician selects the CPT code, and the billing specialist uses that code for insurance billing.

Even though CPT code assignment is the provider's responsibility, the billing specialist or medical coder reviews the encounter form and patient record to determine if the evaluation and management CPT code accurately describes the diagnosis or service rendered.

> **EXAMPLE**
>
> The billing specialist receives the encounter form/route slip for a new patient recently treated for acute sinusitis. The provider selected code 99203, "Office or other outpatient visit," which requires the three key components of a detailed history, a detailed examination, and medical decision-making of low complexity. The billing specialist knows that this type of service has often been coded as 99202 and takes the following steps:
>
> - Reviews the patient's medical record for additional information
> - Reviews the clinical examples for codes 99202 and 99203 in Appendix C of the CPT manual for a similar situation
>
> In this case, the CPT manual has an example for acute maxillary sinusitis, which is assigned to code 99202. If the patient's record does not furnish additional information, the billing specialist asks the provider for clarification.

There also are situations in which a higher-level E/M code should have been selected. In those situations, the billing specialist takes the same steps to verify the accuracy of the selected code. Appendix C, "Clinical Examples," of the CPT manual is a valuable reference because it provides the billing specialist with examples of clinical documentation for the following E/M codes:

- Office or Other Outpatient Services: 99201–99215
- Hospital Inpatient Services: 99221–99233
- Consultations: 99241–99255
- Emergency Department Services: 99281–99285
- Critical Care Services: 99291
- Prolonged Services: 99354, 99355, 99356, 99358, 99359
- Physician Standby Services: 99360
- Care Plan Oversight Services: 99375

The introduction to Appendix C clearly states that the clinical examples are just that—examples—and the required number of key components must be documented in the patient's medical record to select or report a particular evaluation and management code.

When services are provided outside the provider's office, as with hospital services, the provider notes the service and brings the information to the billing specialist or medical coder. In this situation, the billing specialist may be expected to select the appropriate code for insurance billing. Review the following examples and follow the coding steps by using a CPT reference—if you have one available.

EXAMPLE

Dr. Rodriguez arrives at the office after making hospital rounds and gives the billing specialist the following list of hospital visits:

A. John Wu—initial inpatient evaluation, detailed H&P, low complexity.
B. Elizabeth Brooks—discharged, 30 minutes.
C. Erik Gervais—hospital visit, second day, detailed exam, high complexity.

A. The billing specialist or medical coder locates Hospital Services in the CPT index. The first entry is "Inpatient Services," which is further indented with descriptions of hospital inpatient services. The range of codes for "Initial Care, new or established patient" is 99221–99233. For John Wu, the billing specialist refers to that range of codes in the "Evaluation and Management" section and selects 99221, "Initial hospital care: detailed or comprehensive history and examination; medical decision-making, straightforward or low complexity." All three components are required.

B. The range of codes for "Discharge Services" is 99238–99239. For Elizabeth Brooks, the billing specialist refers to that range of codes in the "Evaluation and Management" section and selects 99238, "Hospital discharge day management; 30 minutes or less."

C. The range of codes for "Subsequent Hospital Care" is 99231–99233. For Erik Gervais, the billing specialist refers to that range of codes in the "Evaluation and Management" section and selects 99233, "Subsequent hospital care; detailed interval history; detailed examination; medical decision-making, high complexity." Two of the three components are required.

Selecting and verifying the accuracy of E/M codes has a positive effect on the financial health of the provider's practice. Accurate codes ensure timely and appropriate reimbursement for services rendered. Inaccurate coding results in payment delays or denials and may even lead to an investigation for fraud or abuse.

Evaluation and Management Modifiers

Although most modifiers apply to surgery or procedure codes, there are three modifiers that are used with E/M codes. Each modifier is listed and described, and an application example follows the descriptions. The modifiers are:

- **-24: Unrelated Evaluation and Management Service by the Same Physician [Provider] during a Postoperative Period.** Modifier -24 is used to signify that an E/M service unrelated to the original procedure was performed during the procedure's postoperative period.
- **-25: Significant, Separately Identifiable Evaluation and Management Service by the Same Physician on the Same Day of the Procedure or Other Service.** Modifier -25 is used to identify that an E/M service was performed on the same day of a procedure and that the E/M service was above and beyond the usual preoperative or postoperative care. The E/M service may be prompted by the condition that necessitated the procedure.
- **-57: Decision for Surgery.** Modifier -57 is used to identify that an E/M service resulted in the initial decision to perform surgery.

> **EXAMPLE**
> Modifier -24: Unrelated Evaluation and Management Service by the Same Physician during a Postoperative Period
> Roger Dodger sees Dr. Pharyngeal for a routine postoperative office visit and suture removal for his recent carpal tunnel surgery. During the visit, Roger tells Dr. Pharyngeal that he has noticed bright red blood in his stools. Dr. Pharyngeal does a rectal exam and notes that Roger has external hemorrhoids. She prescribes a topical medication.

In this example, the correct E/M code is 99212 with modifier -24 to indicate that the physician provided a service unrelated to the suture removal. The billing specialist submits the insurance claim and lists the ICD-9-CM code for hemorrhoids as the first diagnosis and 99212-24 as the first CPT code.

V58.32 is the diagnosis code for the suture removal, and the CPT code is 99212. Because suture removal is included as part of the routine postoperative care, there is no charge for the services related to suture removal.

> **EXAMPLE**
> Modifier -25: Significant, Separately Identifiable Evaluation and Management Service by the Same Physician on the Same Day of the Procedure or Other Service
> Mr. Wattson was hospitalized for a total hip replacement. After returning to his room after surgery, he attempted to get out of bed and fell. Dr. Romero, the surgeon who performed the surgery, was making rounds and assessed Mr. Wattson's injuries and the operative site. Fortunately, Mr. Wattson only suffered a minor bruise on the nonsurgical buttock.

In this example, the correct E/M code is 99232 with modifier -25 to indicate that the assessment of the fall was separate and distinct from the operative service. The physician provides the billing specialist with documentation of the assessment, including a diagnosis. The billing specialist submits an insurance claim with hematoma as the diagnosis and code 99232-25 as the evaluation and management code.

EXAMPLE

Modifier -57: Decision for Surgery

Jacqueline Beckwith, a seven-year-old girl, is seen for a sore throat. Rapid culture results indicate that Jacqueline has strep throat. This is her fourth episode in six months. Dr. French is concerned that Jacqueline is developing a high tolerance for antibiotic therapy and recommends a tonsillectomy. The parents agree, the surgery is scheduled for the next day, and the doctor completes a preoperative assessment. The Beckwiths' insurance plan includes preoperative services the day before surgery as part of the reimbursement for the surgery.

In this example, the correct E/M code is 99212 with modifier -57 to indicate that the office visit resulted in the initial decision for surgery. The billing specialist submits an insurance claim with the correct ICD-9-CM diagnosis for strep throat and CPT code 99212-57 as the office visit code.

REINFORCEMENT EXERCISES 6–5

Select the correct CPT E/M code for the following services.

1. Office consultation, established patient, with a detailed history and examination, and medical decision-making of low complexity. _____

2. New patient office visit, with a problem-focused history and examination, and straightforward medical decision-making. _____

3. Initial neonatal intensive care for a critically ill infant. _____

4. New patient home visit with a problem-focused history and examination and straightforward medical decision-making. _____

5. Office visit for a 65-year-old female, established patient, seen for her B-12 injection by the nurse. _____

6. Emergency department visit for a 16-year-old male, who was thrown from his bike, suffered a brief loss of consciousness, and presents with a 4-inch separation of his lower lip and skin from gingival tissue. _____

7. Follow-up consultation for 45-year-old female, status post total proctocolectomy this admission, with terminal ileus requiring revision of stoma, excessive blood loss during second surgery, transfused 5 units of whole blood; recent history of femoral artery blood clot treated with coumadin. _____

Anesthesia Section

Anesthesia is the pharmacological suppression of nerve function that is administered by general, regional, or local method. The CPT codes for anesthesia (00100–01999) are used to report the administration of anesthesia by an anesthesiologist or nurse anesthetist under the responsible supervision of an anesthesiologist. Anesthesia codes include the following services:

- General, regional, and local anesthesia
- Other support services deemed necessary by the anesthesiologist during the procedure

- Preoperative and postoperative visits by the anesthesiologist
- Care during the procedure
- Monitoring of vital signs
- Administration of blood or any other fluid

Unusual forms of monitoring, such as intra-arterial, central venous, and Swan-Ganz, are not included in the anesthesia codes and should be reported separately.

Moderate (conscious) sedation, with or without analgesia, is reported by using codes 99413–99150 in CPT's "Medicine" section. These codes apply when the physician performing the procedure also provides the moderate sedation. When another physician provides the anesthesia service, the anesthesia codes are used to report the service.

Anesthesia codes are primarily organized by anatomic site. Table 6–13 lists the anesthesia code categories.

TABLE 6–13

Anesthesia Categories	
Anesthesia Category	**CPT Code Range**
Head	00100–00222
Neck	00300–00352
Thorax (Chest Wall and Shoulder Girdle)	00400–00474
Intrathoracic	00500–00580
Spine and Spinal Cord	00600–00670
Upper Abdomen	00700–00797
Lower Abdomen	00800–00882
Perineum	00902–00952
Pelvis (Except Hip)	01112–01190
Upper Leg (Except Knee)	01200–01274
Knee and Popliteal Area	01320–01444
Lower Leg (Below Knee, Ankle, and Foot)	01462–01522
Shoulder and Axilla	01610–01682
Upper Arm and Elbow	01710–01782
Forearm, Wrist, and Hand	01810–01860

continued on the next page

continued from the previous page

Anesthesia Categories	
Anesthesia Category	**CPT Code Range**
Radiological Procedures	01916–01936
Burn Excisions or Debridement	01951–01953
Obstetrics	01958–01969
Other Procedures	01990–01999

Radiological procedure codes (01916–01936) are used to report anesthesia services related to radiography procedures, such as myelography and diskography.

Other procedure codes (01990–01999) are used to report anesthesia for maintaining organ health when harvesting organs from a brain-dead patient, for administering a local anesthetic or other medication to an upper or lower extremity, and for daily management of administering medication into the epidural or subarachnoid spaces of the meninges.

Anesthesia Modifiers

Anesthesia services are reported with a five-digit CPT code plus the addition of a **physical status modifier** that addresses the overall health status of the patient. Table 6–14 lists the modifiers and their meanings.

In addition to the physical status modifiers, other CPT modifiers apply to anesthesia codes. Examples follow the modifier descriptions. The modifiers are:

- **-23: Unusual Anesthesia.** Modifier -23 is used to identify situations in which general anesthesia is administered during a procedure that is usually done with no anesthesia or with local anesthesia.

TABLE 6–14

Anesthesia Physical Status Modifiers	
Anesthesia Modifier	**Description**
P1	Normal healthy patient
P2	Patient with mild systemic disease
P3	Patient with severe systemic disease
P4	Patient with severe systemic disease that is a constant threat to life
P5	A moribund patient who is not expected to survive without the operation
P6	A declared brain-dead patient whose organs are being removed for donor purposes

- **-51: Multiple Procedures.** Modifier -51 is used to identify situations in which multiple anesthesia services were provided on the same day or during the same operative episode.
- **-53: Discontinued Procedure.** Modifier -53 is used to identify situations in which the physician elects to terminate or discontinue a procedure because of risk to the patient's health. Do not use this modifier when the procedure is cancelled before the patient is prepped for the procedure or anesthesia is started.

EXAMPLE

Modifier -23: Unusual Anesthesia

Mrs. Coder's six-year-old daughter, Melanie, is seen in the emergency department because she pushed a pebble into her left nostril. Although the object can be reached with a snare, Melanie is very agitated and will not allow the physician to remove the pebble. The nurse anesthetist administers a general anesthetic, and the pebble is removed.

In this example, the correct anesthesia code is 00160, "Anesthesia for procedures on nose...," with modifier -23 to signify that the procedure does not usually require anesthesia and this is an unusual case. The billing specialist submits an insurance claim for the physician with the ICD-9-CM code for presence of a foreign object and the CPT code 30310 for removal of a foreign body, intranasal requiring general anesthesia. Modifier -23 may be added to the CPT code. The anesthesiologist's billing specialist submits an insurance claim with the ICD-9-CM code for presence of a foreign object and the CPT code 00160 with modifier -23 to identify that the anesthesia services were provided under unusual circumstances.

EXAMPLE

Modifier -51: Multiple Procedures

Victoria Gervais, a 67-year-old female, was hospitalized for a total hip replacement. Within 12 hours of surgery, she developed "trash foot" syndrome, and it was determined that she had an embolus in her external iliac artery. She was returned to the OR for a direct embolectomy.

In this example, the correct anesthesia code is 01502, "Anesthesia ... embolectomy direct...," with modifier -51 to identify that this anesthesia service was provided on the same day as another anesthesia service. The billing specialist submits the insurance claim with the diagnosis and anesthesia codes for the total hip replacement listed first and the diagnosis and anesthesia codes for the embolectomy listed next.

EXAMPLE

Modifier -53: Discontinued Procedure

Ron Lawrence is scheduled for a unilateral radical abdominal orchiectomy for testicular cancer.

During the first 10 minutes of the procedure, Mr. Lawrence's blood pressure "bottoms out," and the surgeon decides to close immediately and reschedule the surgery.

In this example, the correct anesthesia code is 00928, "Anesthesia ... radical orchiectomy abdominal," with modifier -53 to identify that the procedure was discontinued after the induction of the anesthetic agent. The billing specialist submits an insurance claim with the ICD-9-CM code that describes why the procedure was discontinued and the anesthesia code 00928-53.

Anesthesia Add-On Codes

Anesthesia add-on codes are used to describe very difficult circumstances that significantly affect the anesthesia service. The circumstances include extraordinary condition of the patient, notable operative conditions, and unusual risk factors. Add-on codes are not reported alone but in addition to the selected anesthesia CPT code.

Table 6–15 shows the add-on codes and their meanings.

For purposes of the anesthesia add-on codes, an emergency exists when a delay in treatment would lead to a significant increase in the threat to the patient's life or body part.

Anesthesia Code Selection and Reporting

CPT codes from the anesthesia section must be reported on all Medicare insurance claims. Some insurance carriers require anesthesia services to be reported with the applicable surgery code. The billing specialist follows the insurance carrier's guidelines in determining which CPT codes are appropriate for reporting anesthesia services.

> **EXAMPLE**
>
> Ray Bourque underwent a thromboendarterectomy of the right carotid artery.
>
> Medicare Claim: 00350, "Anesthesia for procedures on major vessels of [the] neck; not otherwise specified."
>
> Non-Medicare Claim: 35301, "Thromboendarterectomy, including patch graft, if performed; carotid, vertebral, subclavian [arteries], by neck incision."

In this example, if the patient is covered by Medicare, the anesthesia code 00350-P1 ("Anesthesia for procedures for major vessels of neck; not otherwise specified—normal healthy patient") is submitted with the insurance claim. However, if the patient is covered by an insurance plan that requires anesthesia services to be reported with the CPT code that describes the procedure performed, the procedure code 35301-P1 ("Thromboendarterectomy, including patch graft, if performed; carotid, verterbral subclavian, by neck incision—normal healthy patient") is submitted with the insurance claim. Note that both codes have the modifier -P1, which is a physical status modifier.

TABLE 6–15

Anesthesia Add-on Codes	
Add-on Code	**Description**
+99100	Anesthesia for patients of extreme age (i.e., under 1 year and over 70)
+99116	Anesthesia complicated by utilization of total body hypothermia
+99135	Anesthesia complicated by utilization of controlled hypotension
+99140	Anesthesia complicated by emergency conditions; specify the emergency conditions

When a physician provides anesthesia for surgery that she performs, the appropriate codes from the "Surgery" section are reported with the addition of modifier -47, "Anesthesia by surgeon." Physicians who provide services with moderate sedation, which is sedation with or without analgesia, report the sedation services by using codes 99143–99150, located in the CPT "Medicine" section.

REINFORCEMENT EXERCISES 6–6

Provide a short answer for each item.

A. When is it appropriate to use moderate (conscious) sedation codes from the "Medicine" section?

_____

_____

_____

B. What is the purpose of anesthesia modifiers that begin with the letter P?

_____

_____

_____

C. Write brief definitions for anesthesia modifiers -23, -51, and -53.

_____

_____

_____

D. Briefly describe when it is appropriate to use anesthesia add-on codes.

_____

_____

_____

"Surgery" Section

The CPT "Surgery" section includes codes for procedures performed by physicians of any specialty, such as general surgeons, ophthalmologists, dermatologists, and gynecologists. CPT defines surgical procedures in the broadest possible sense of the term, from heart transplant to cystoscopy. The "Surgery" section is organized by body system. Table 6–16 lists the surgery categories and code ranges.

Nearly all surgical categories have several subcategories organized by specific organ, anatomical site, and type of procedure. Accurate code selection depends on a careful review and application of category and subcategory instructions. As with all coding, the patient's medical record must

TABLE 6–16

Surgery Categories	
Surgery Category	**Code Range**
General	10021–10022
Integumentary System	10040–19499
Musculoskeletal System	20000–29999
Respiratory System	30000–32999
Cardiovascular System	33010–37799
Hemic and Lymphatic Systems	38100–38999
Mediastinum and Diaphragm	39000–39599
Digestive System	40490–49999
Urinary System	50010–53899
Male Genital System	54000–55920
Intersex Surgery	55970–55980
Female Genital System	56405–58999
Maternity Care and Delivery	59000–59899
Endocrine System	60000–60699
Nervous System	61000–64999
Eye and Ocular Adnexa	65091–68899
Auditory System	69000–69979
Operating Microscope	69990

clearly support the selected procedure or surgical CPT code. The physician's notes and operative or procedure report are source documents when identifying the service rendered.

Surgical and procedure codes are listed in the CPT alphabetic index by the specific name of the procedure (e.g., cystoscopy); the type of procedure (incision, excision, repair, removal); or anatomic site. The insurance billing specialist or medical coder first checks the alphabetic index for a given surgery or procedure. Once the code or range of codes is identified, go to the appropriate surgical category or subcategory and then select the CPT code that best conforms with the information in the patient's medical record.

Surgical Package

A **surgical package**, called a **global surgery concept** by Medicare, is the range of services that is included in a surgical intervention. According to CPT guidelines, a surgical package includes:

- Administration of local infiltration, metacarpal/metatarsal/digital block, or topical anesthesia

- Following the decision for surgery, one related evaluation and management encounter on the date of surgery or the day immediately before surgery
- Immediate postoperative care, such as dictating operative notes or talking with the family and other physicians
- Writing orders
- Evaluating the patient in the postanesthesia recovery area
- Typical postoperative follow-up care

For reimbursement purposes, a surgical package is reported under the appropriate surgery or procedure code. For documentation or administrative purposes, the postoperative follow-up office visit is coded and reported with no charge.

EXAMPLE

Following a motor vehicle accident, Marilyn underwent an open reduction, internal fixation for a fractured calcaneus, code 28415. She is seen today for cast removal.

In this example, there is no charge for the cast removal because the service is included in the normal, uncomplicated follow-up care for the open reduction and internal fixation of the fracture. Figure 6–8 illustrates no charge for cast removal.

FIGURE 6–8 No Charge for Cast Removal

When the postoperative follow-up visits require treatment for surgical complications, the appropriate E/M code is reported for reimbursement for services related to the complication. The ICD-9-CM code related to the complication is submitted with the insurance claim.

> **EXAMPLE**
> Following a motor vehicle accident, Marilyn underwent an open reduction, internal fixation for a fractured calcaneus, code 28415. She is seen today and states that her foot feels hot. The physician removes a portion of the cast and notes that the surgical site is red and warm to the touch, and he prescribes an antibiotic for a suspected postoperative infection.

In this example, if the third-party payer allows payment for services related to postoperative complications, the billing specialist submits an insurance claim for this office visit. The diagnosis codes are 998.59, "Other postoperative infection," and 686.9, "Unspecified local infection of the skin and subcutaneous tissue." The CPT code is 99213, "Established patient office visit."

Third-party payers may have a different definition of the surgical package. For patients covered by Medicare, the surgical package is called a global surgery concept. For major surgeries, the Medicare global surgery definition includes the following:

- Preoperative services provided one day prior to surgery or the day of surgery, except when the preoperative service resulted in the initial decision to perform the surgery or when the service provided by the same physician during a postoperative period is unrelated to the original procedure
- The actual surgical procedure
- Postoperative services provided within 90 days of the surgical procedure, except when the service is unrelated to the surgical procedure
- Postoperative services that do not require a return to the operating room, such as dressing changes and care of the operative incision site; removal of sutures, staples, wires, lines, tubes, drains, casts, and splints; urinary catheter care; and care of other postoperative tubes and intravenous lines

For minor and endoscopic procedures, the Medicare global surgery definition includes:

- Preoperative services provided one day prior to surgery or the day of surgery, except when the preoperative service resulted in the initial decision to perform the surgery or when the service provided by the same physician during a postoperative period is unrelated to the original procedure
- The actual procedure
- Postoperative services provided within 10 days of the surgical procedure, except when the service is unrelated to the surgical procedure

Services that are part of a surgical package or global surgery concept cannot be billed individually. This practice is called **unbundling** and constitutes fraud. Unbundling results in additional reimbursement to the provider for services that are covered by one fee. The billing specialist never unbundles services that are included in a surgical package.

REINFORCEMENT EXERCISES 6–7

Write a short answer for each item.

A. List three ways surgical and procedure codes can be located in the CPT manual alphabetic index.

_____

_____

_____

B. Identify the services included in the CPT definition of a surgical package.

_____

_____

_____

C. What is included in the Medicare global surgery concept?

_____

_____

_____

D. Briefly define unbundling.

_____

_____

_____

Separate Procedures

CPT codes designated as **separate procedures** are usually carried out as a component of another more comprehensive procedure and under that circumstance cannot be billed separately. In fact, it is fraudulent to attempt to secure reimbursement for a separate procedure when it is part of a more comprehensive procedure or service.

EXAMPLE

Maria Delgado is hospitalized for a total abdominal hysterectomy, which is to include removal of the ovaries and fallopian tubes.

The billing specialist submits an insurance claim for this procedure. Only one procedure code—58150, "Total abdominal hysterectomy (corpus and cervix) with or without removal of tube(s), with or without removal of ovary or ovaries"—is entered on the claim form.

The billing specialist must not code the removal of each organ as a separate procedure (i.e., removal of the cervix, removal of the ovaries, and removal of the fallopian tubes).

However, if the separate procedure is actually performed independently, it may be coded and billed as such.

> **EXAMPLE**
>
> Maria Delgado is hospitalized for removal of ovaries and fallopian tubes. Her uterus and cervix are left intact.
>
> The billing specialist submits an insurance claim for this procedure. The procedure is coded as 58720, "Salpingo-oophorectomy, complete or partial, unilateral or bilateral (separate procedure)." "Modifier -59, distinct service," may be added to the code to explain that the procedure was not performed as a component of a larger procedure.

Modifiers

As previously stated, modifiers provide additional information about a service or procedure. Modifiers are used to communicate the following:

- A service or procedure has both a professional and a technical component.
- A service or procedure was performed by more than one physician or in more than one location.
- A service or procedure has been increased or reduced.
- Only part of a service was performed.
- An adjunctive service was performed.
- A bilateral procedure was performed.
- A service or procedure was provided more than once.
- Unusual events occurred.

Modifiers are expressed as either a two-digit or a five-digit number, depending on the preference of the third-party payer. A five-digit modifier always begins with 099, and it is the last two digits that distinguish one modifier from another. A hyphen precedes a two-digit modifier. Therefore, modifier -47 and 09947, "Anesthesia by Surgeon," indicates that the surgeon provided regional or general anesthesia for a surgical procedure. Table 6–17 lists the modifiers that can be

TABLE 6–17

Surgery Modifiers
Modifier with Description
-22: Unusual Procedural Services. The service provided is greater than the service usually associated with a specific procedure.
-26: Professional Component. The provider/physician delivers the professional component only of a given procedure or service.
-32: Mandated Service. The service is provided because a third party—e.g., insurance carrier, regulatory agency—requires it.
-47: Anesthesia by Surgeon. The surgeon provided the regional or general (not local) anesthesia for a surgical procedure.

continued on the next page

continued from the previous page

-50: Bilateral Procedure. Bilateral procedures are performed during the same operative episode; with the exception of procedures that are specified as bilateral.

-51: Multiple Procedures. Multiple procedures are performed on the same day or during the same operative episode; list the primary procedure first; secondary procedures with modifier -51.

-52: Reduced Services. Part of the procedure or service is reduced or eliminated at the discretion of the physician; applies to inpatient procedures or services.

-53: Discontinued Procedure. The procedure is discontinued because of a risk to the patient's well-being; not to be used if an elective procedure is canceled prior to surgical preparation or induction of anesthesia; applies to inpatient procedures or services.

-54: Surgical Care Only. One physician performs the procedure only; a different physician provides the preoperative and postoperative care.

-55: Postoperative Management Only. The physician provides preoperative services only.

-56: Preoperative Management Only. The physician provides postoperative services only.

-57: Decision for Surgery. The evaluation and management service results in the initial decision to perform surgery.

-58: Staged or Related Procedure or Service by the Same Physician during the Postoperative Period. An additional procedure related to the original procedure is performed during the postoperative period of the original procedure; the same physician must provide the additional procedure.

-59: Distinct Procedural Service. A procedure or service that is distinct from the original services is provided on the same day as the original services; usually requires a different operative site or organ, a separate incision or excision, or a separate lesion or injury; do not use this modifier if another modifier is more applicable to the situation.

-62: Two Surgeons. Two surgeons are required to perform the procedure; both surgeons must report the service with modifier -62; does not apply to assistant surgeon(s) (see modifier -80).

-63: Procedure Performed on Infants Less than 4 Kilograms. This applies to procedures performed on neonates and infants up to a present body weight of 4 kilograms.

-66: Surgical Team. Procedure is performed by a surgical team; applies to very complex procedures (e.g., organ transplants).

-76: Repeat Procedure or Service by Same Physician. A procedure is repeated by the same physician who performed the original procedure.

-77: Repeat Procedure by Another Physician. The procedure is repeated by a physician different from the one who performed the original procedure.

-78: Uplanned Return to the Operating/Procedure Room by the Same Physician Following Initial Procedure for a Related Procedure during the Postoperative Period. A procedure related to the original procedure is performed during the original procedure's postoperative period (e.g., return to the operating room for malunion of a compound fracture that required surgery). For repeat procedures on the same day, see modifier -76.

continued on the next page

continued from the previous page

Surgery Modifiers
Modifier with Description
-79: Unrelated Procedure or Service by the Same Physician during the Postoperative Period. A procedure or service that is unrelated to the original procedure is performed during the original procedure's postoperative period. For repeat procedures on the same day, see modifier -76.
-80: Assistant Surgeon. The physician who assists a surgeon during a particular procedure reports the procedure with modifier -80; the operating surgeon does not use modifier -80.
-81: Minimum Assistant Surgeon. The physician who provided minimal assistance to the operating surgeon reports the procedure with modifier -81; the operating surgeon does not use modifier -81.
-82: Assistant Surgeon (when a qualified resident surgeon is not available. This applies primarily to teaching hospitals, where surgical residents are often the assistant surgeon; when a surgical resident is not available, another physician may assist the operating surgeon; the operating surgeon does not use modifier -82.
-90: Reference (Outside) Laboratory. This signifies that laboratory procedures/tests were performed by a lab outside the control of the reporting physician.
-91: Repeat Clinical Diagnostic Laboratory Test. This signifies the need to repeat a lab test on the same day that the original test is done; used when multiple test results are necessary to establish a diagnosis; do not use modifier -91 when a test is repeated because of specimen or equipment problems or when the test itself requires multiple results.
-99: Multiple Modifiers. Alerts insurance carriers that more than one modifier is being submitted on a claim; many insurance carriers have a limit on the number of modifiers that are reported.

used with surgery codes. A complete list of all CPT modifiers, with complete descriptions and examples, is located in Appendix A of the CPT manual. Selected examples follow the table.

EXAMPLE

Modifier -47: Anesthesia by Surgeon

Geralyn Adamski, who is in the hospital for delivery of her second child, develops complications that require an emergency cesarean section. The obstetrician administers a saddle block, a regional anesthesia that acts on the perineum and buttocks, and performs the c-section.

In this example, the correct codes are 59514 with modifier -47 to signify that the obstetrician performed the cesarean section and administered the regional anesthesia and 62311, "Injection. . . (including anesthetic). . . lumbar . . .," which applies to the saddle block.

EXAMPLE

Modifier -50: Bilateral Procedure

Durwin Rogers, who has experienced recurrent reducible inguinal hernias for the past year, is seen as an outpatient for bilateral hernia repair. The procedure is successful, and Durwin is discharged home within 18 hours.

In this example, the correct code is 49520 with modifier -50 to signify that two hernia repairs were done during the same procedure. The billing specialist submits an insurance claim with the ICD-9-CM code for the bilateral recurrent inguinal hernias and with the CPT code 49520-50.

EXAMPLE
Modifier -51: Multiple Procedures
    René Jean was seen for wide excision of basal cell carcinoma, left cheek, and full-thickness skin graft from the right thigh. The skin graft was removed from the patient and the wound closed. The basal cell carcinoma was excised, and the lesion measured 3.0 cm. The wound was covered with the full-thickness graft. All sites were secured with 5-0 Prolene sutures.

In this example, the correct CPT codes are 11643 with modifier -51 to signify that the basal cell carcinoma was excised and that another procedure was done at the same time and 15220 to signify the full-thickness skin graft. The modifier is not applied to code 15220.

EXAMPLE
Modifier -80: Assistant Surgeon
    Dr. Heubert performs a suboccipital craniectomy with cervical laminectomy for decompression of the medulla and spinal cord, with a dural graft. Dr. Crush assists with this surgery, which is done to correct a malformation of the spine.

In this example, the correct code for reporting Dr. Heubert's service is 61343, "Craniectomy, suboccipital with cervical laminectomy . . . with or without dural graft . . . ." No modifier is used with Dr. Heubert's bill. Dr. Crush's billing specialist submits an insurance claim with the ICD-9-CM code for the malformation problem and CPT code 61343-80 to show that he was the assistant surgeon for this procedure.

Ambulatory Surgery Center Modifiers

Several CPT modifiers are approved for use with procedures provided in ambulatory surgery centers (ASC) and hospital outpatient departments. CPT modifiers that apply to ASC and hospital outpatient departments include the following:

- **-25:** Significant, Separately Identifiable Evaluation and Management Service by the Same Physician on the Same Day of the Procedure or Other Service
- **-27:** Multiple Outpatient Hospital E/M Encounters on the Same Date
- **-50:** Bilateral Procedure
- **-52:** Reduced Services
- **-58:** Staged or Related Procedure or Service by the Same Physician during the Postoperative Period
- **-59:** Distinct Procedural Service
- **-73:** Discontinued Outpatient Hospital/Ambulatory Surgery Center Procedure Prior to Administration of Anesthesia
- **-74:** Discontinued Outpatient Hospital/Ambulatory Surgery Center Procedure after Administration of Anesthesia
- **-76:** Repeat Procedure by Same Physician
- **-77:** Repeat Procedure by Another Physician
- **-78:** Unplanned Return to the Operating/Procedure Room by the Same Physician Following Initial Procedure for a Related Procedure during the Postoperative Period
- **-79:** Unrelated Procedure or Service by the Same Physician during the Postoperative Period
- **-91:** Repeat Clinical Diagnostic Laboratory Test

Except for modifier -27, the description and examples for modifiers that apply to ambulatory surgery centers are found on the previous pages and in Table 6–17. For hospital outpatient reporting purposes, modifier -27 may be used to report separate and distinct evaluation and management encounters or services performed in multiple outpatient hospital settings on the same day. Modifier -27 is *not* to be used for services provided by the same physician on the same date in multiple outpatient settings.

REINFORCEMENT EXERCISES 6–8

Fill in the blank.

1. CPT codes designated as _____ are usually part of a more comprehensive procedure.

2. Modifiers are written as a(n) _____ or _____ number.

3. A five-digit modifier always begins with _____.

4. A(n) _____ precedes a two-digit modifier.

Supply the correct CPT code for each procedure.

1. Incisional biopsy of the breast. _____

2. Flexible sigmoidoscopy. _____

3. Repair of bilateral inguinal hernia for a 40-year-old patient. _____

4. Total abdominal proctocolectomy with ileostomy. _____

5. Removal of four benign skin lesions from the back, laser procedure. _____

6. Closed reduction of proximal humerus fracture. _____

7. After falling down a short flight of stairs, Reggie underwent a limited arthroscopic synovectomy of the left knee. The procedure went well, and Reggie is scheduled for discharge this afternoon. _____

8. Myra, a four-year-old female, has had recurrent episodes of otitis media, difficult to treat with antibiotic therapy. Based on her pediatrician's recommendation, Myra's parents authorized a bilateral myringotomy with placement of tympanostomy tubes. The procedure was done under general anesthetic. _____

9. Willa's abdominal ultrasound revealed the presence of an abdominal aortic aneurysm. Surgical intervention was required, and Willa successfully underwent a repair of the aneurysm. Her prognosis is good. _____

10. Because of failure to pass the kidney stones under medical management, Hank agreed to an ESWL (extracorporeal shock wave lithotripsy). _____

"Radiology" Section (70010–79999)

Radiology procedures are also known as diagnostic imaging procedures. Radiologists and radiology technicians provide radiology services. The radiologist's services are called the **professional component**, and the radiology technician's services are known as the **technical component**. The professional component includes supervising the service, reading and interpreting the results, and documenting the interpretation in a report. The technical component includes activities associated with actually doing the diagnostic imaging and the expenses for supplies and equipment. A radiologist may perform both the professional and technical components.

"Radiology" section codes are organized by type of imaging and anatomic site. "Radiology" subsections include instructional notes that contribute to coding accuracy. The billing specialist or medical coder must pay close attention to these instructional notes. Table 6–18 lists the categories of radiology services and code ranges.

Several conventions and guidelines discussed earlier in this chapter also apply to the "Radiology" section and are not repeated here.

"Radiology" codes are listed in the alphabetic index by type of exam and anatomic site. For example, brachial angiography is indexed under "Angiography, brachial" and "Artery, brachial angiography."

Radiological Supervision and Interpretation

Many codes in the "Radiology" section include the phrase "radiological supervision and interpretation." When a physician performs the procedure and also provides the supervision and interpretation, two codes are needed. One code relates to the actual radiology service, and the other relates to the injection or introduction of a contrast medium with a needle or catheter.

EXAMPLE

Bill Hobbs, a local high school football player, is seen for an arthrography of the knee with contrast. Dr. Pierce, an orthopedic physician, injects the contrast medium, completes the arthrography, reviews the film, and documents the findings.

TABLE 6–18

Radiology Categories	
Radiology Category	**Code Range**
Diagnostic Radiology (Diagnostic Imaging)	70010–76499
Diagnostic Ultrasound	76506–76999
Radiologic Guidance	77001-77263
Radiation Oncology	77280–77799
Nuclear Medicine	78000–79999

In this example, two CPT codes are needed to fully describe physician services. Code 73580 identifies the supervision, interpretation, and documentation of the findings. Code 27370 identifies the injection of the contrast medium. The billing specialist submits an insurance claim with the ICD-9-CM code that describes the problem and CPT codes 73580 and 27370.

When the radiologist interprets and documents the results of a radiographic procedure, modifier -26, "Professional component," is used to identify the service.

> **EXAMPLE**
>
> Rita Hobbs had a mammogram as part of her annual physical. The radiology technician did a bilateral mammography with two views of each breast. Dr. Watts, a radiologist, reviewed and interpreted the films and documented that there were no changes from the previous films. Dr. Watts sent a copy of the report to Rita's family physician.

In this example, the correct radiology code is 77057, "Screen mammography, bilateral, two views of each breast," with modifier -26 to identify that the radiologist completed the professional component of the mammography. The radiologist's billing specialist submits an insurance claim with the appropriate ICD-9-CM code and CPT radiology code 77057-26.

"Pathology and Laboratory" Section

The "Pathology and Laboratory" section (80047–89398) of CPT includes services by a physician or by technicians under the responsible supervision of a physician. This section includes codes for services and procedures that range from a straightforward urinalysis to the more complex cytogenetic studies. Table 6–19 lists the categories of pathology and laboratory services and code ranges.

Pathology and laboratory codes are listed in the CPT alphabetic index by the specific name of the test; specific substance, specimen, or sample being tested; and the method used to gather the sample or conduct the test.

> **EXAMPLE**
>
> Complete blood count is indexed under "complete blood count"; bone marrow biopsy is indexed under "bone marrow" and "biopsy, bone marrow"; and fine needle aspiration of thyroid tissue is indexed under "fine needle aspiration."

CPT coding conventions discussed earlier in the chapter also apply to the "Pathology and Laboratory" section. There is one CPT modifier that is unique to this section. Modifier -90, "Reference (Outside) Laboratory," is used to indicate that another party besides the reporting physician performed the actual laboratory procedure.

Providers who operate a clinical lab within the office practice include frequently ordered lab tests and related CPT codes on the preprinted encounter form. The insurance billing specialist or medical coder must make certain that these codes are updated annually.

"Medicine" Section

The "Medicine" section (90281–99607) includes a wide range of medical services and procedures, from routine childhood vaccinations to renal dialysis. Table 6–20 lists and briefly describes the categories of medical services and procedures.

Table 6–19

Pathology and Laboratory Categories	
Pathology/Laboratory Category	**Code Range**
Organ- or Disease-Oriented Panels	80047–80076
Drug Screening Testing	80100–80103
Therapeutic Drug Assays	80150–80299
Evocative/Suppression Testing	80400–80440
Consultations (Clinical Pathology)	80500–80502
Urinalysis	81000–81099
Chemistry	82000–84999
Hematology and Coagulation	85002–85999
Immunology	86000–86849
Transfusion Medicine	86850–86999
Microbiology	87001–87999
Anatomic Pathology	88000–88099
Cytopathology	88104–88199
Cytogenetic Studies	88230–88299
Surgical Pathology	88300–88399
In Vivo (e.g., Transcutaneous) Laboratory Procedures	88720–88741
Other Procedures	89049–89240
Reproductive Medicine Procedures	89250–89398

Table 6–20

Medicine Categories
Medicine Category with Description
Immune Globulins (90281–90399): Codes apply only to the immune globulin product; report with the administration code.
Immunization Administration for Vaccines/Toxoids (90465–90474): Codes apply to administration only; report with the correct vaccine or toxoid code.
Vaccines, Toxoids (90476–90749): Codes apply to vaccine or toxoid products only.

continued on the next page

continued from the previous page

Medicine Category with Description
Psychiatry (90801–90899): Includes a variety of psychotherapy modalities in various health care settings.
Biofeedback (90901–90911): Codes for using biofeedback to retrain sphincter muscles.
Dialysis (90935–90999): Codes for end-stage renal disease services, hemodialysis, and miscellaneous dialysis procedures.
Gastroenterology (91000–91299): Codes for various tests related to esophageal, gastric motility, and gastric secretions.
Ophthalmology (92002–92499): Codes related to ophthalmology services, including supplies.
Special Otorhinolaryngologic Services (92502–92700): Codes for services related to hearing, vision, and laryngeal functioning.
Cardiovascular (92950–93799): Codes for therapeutic and diagnostic tests related to the heart and its vessels.
Noninvasive Vascular Diagnostic Studies (93875–93990): Codes for diagnostic tests related to the function of arteries and veins.
Pulmonary (94002–94799): Codes for a variety of pulmonary and respiratory function tests.
Allergy and Clinical Immunology (95004–95199): Codes for a variety of allergy tests and allergy immunotherapy.
Endocrinology (95250-95251): Code for 72-hour glucose monitoring.
Neurology and Neuromuscular Procedures (95803–96020): Codes for a variety of nerve and muscle function tests (e.g., sleep testing, electromyography, and seizure studies).
Medical Cenetics and Genetic Counseling Services (96040): This code applies to genetic counseling services for each 30 minutes of face-to-face time with the patient or family.
Central Nervous System Assessments/Tests (96101–96125): Codes apply to services related to CNS function tests (e.g., MMPI, Developmental Screening Test II, and Early Language Milestone Screen).
Health and Behavior Assessment/Intervention (96150–96155): Codes for assessments related to biopsychosocial factors of physical health problems.
Hydration, Therapeutic, Prophylactic, Diagnostic Injections and Infusions, and Chemotherapy and Other Highly Complex Drug or Highly Complex Biologic Agent Administration (96360–96549): Codes apply to administration of chemotherapeutic agents by several methods.
Photodynamic Therapy (96567–96571): Codes for the application of light to destroy lesions.
Special Dermatological Procedures (96900–96999): Codes apply to dermatology services not covered elsewhere.
Physical Medicine and Rehabilitation (97001–97799): Codes apply to various services related to physical therapy, occupational therapy, tests and measurements, and other services related to rehabilitation medicine.
Medical Nutrition Therapy (97802–97804): Codes apply to assessment and intervention related to nutrition.
Acupuncture (97810–97814): Codes apply to acupuncture with or without electrical stimulation.
Osteopathic Manipulative Treatment (98925–98929): Codes apply to services provided by an osteopathic physician.
Chiropractic Manipulative Treatment (98940–98943): Codes apply to services provided by a chiropractor.

continued on the next page

continued from the previous page

Education and Training for Patient Self-Management (98960-98962): Codes apply to patient education services prescribed by a physician and provided by a qualified nonphysician health care provider using a standardized curriculum.
Non-Face-to-Face Nonphysician Services (98966-98969): Codes apply to telephone and online medical services provided by a nonphysician health care professional.
Special Services, Procedures, and Reports (99000-99091): Codes apply to a variety of services not covered elsewhere.
Qualifying Circumstances for Anesthesia (99100–99140): Codes related to complicated anesthesia situations.
Moderate (Conscious) Sedation (99143–99150): Codes apply to cases when the patient must be able to respond to stimulation or verbal commands during a procedure; a trained observer must be present to assist the physician in monitoring the patient's level of consciousness.
Other Services and Procedures (99170–99199): Various codes for services not covered elsewhere.
Home Health Procedures/Services (99500–99602): Codes apply to nonphysician health care professionals providing services in the patient's home.
Medication Therapy Management Services (99605-99607): Codes apply to a face-to-face assessment between a pharmacist and a patient that is related to the patient's medication regiment.

Medicine codes are listed in the CPT alphabetic index by type of service and anatomic site. For example, heart catheterization is indexed under "Catheterization, cardiac, left heart, right heart," and "Heart, catheterization."

When a physician or provider renders more than one service on the same day or during the same office or other outpatient visit, each service is coded and submitted for reimbursement.

EXAMPLE

Scott Williamson, a 45-year-old male, is seen for follow-up of the effectiveness of a new hypertension medication and receives a hepatitis B vaccination. The office visit, established patient, is coded as 99212. The hepatitis B vaccination requires two codes, one for the vaccine and one for the administration of the vaccine: 90746, "hepatitis B vaccine, adult dosage, for intramuscular use" and 90471, "immunization administration . . . one vaccine."

In this example, the billing specialist submits an insurance claim for the office visit and vaccination that includes all three codes. As with all insurance billing activities, the patient's record must have sufficient documentation to support all reported services.

REINFORCEMENT EXERCISES 6–9

Fill in the blank.

1. The _____ component of radiology services includes expenses for supplies and equipment.

2. Reading and interpreting the results of a radiology film are part of the _____ component of the service.

continued on the next page

continued from the previous page

3. Modifier _____ identifies the professional component of a radiology service.

4. Modifier _____ is unique to the "Pathology and Laboratory" section of the CPT manual.

Assign the correct CPT codes.

A. A/P and lateral view of the chest. _____

B. Barium enema. _____

C. Follow-up ultrasound, pregnant uterus. _____

D. Blood glucose tolerance test to confirm diabetes mellitus. Three specimens are drawn. _____

E. Gross and microscopic autopsy, without the brain and spinal cord. _____

F. Gross and microscopic examination of prostate tissue following transurethral resection of the prostate. _____

G. Based on Lyle's symptoms, Dr. Howard ordered a blood test to confirm the presence of Epstein-Barr virus or related antibodies. _____

H. Prior to employment, Ellen was vaccinated for hepatitis B. _____

I. Following a stroke, Marty Jones was seen for physical and occupational therapy evaluations. _____

J. Mrs. Shaski, who is diagnosed with end-stage renal disease, and her daughter completed training for peritoneal dialysis with an automated cycler. _____

HEALTHCARE COMMON PROCEDURE CODING SYSTEM (HCPCS)

The information presented here is a brief introduction to the **Healthcare Common Procedure Coding System (HCPCS)**. Two levels of codes are associated with HCPCS. HCPCS level I codes are the **Current Procedural Terminology (CPT)** codes. HCPCS level II codes, also called HCPCS national codes, were developed by the *Centers for Medicare and Medicaid Services (CMS)*. HCPCS level II codes are required by Medicare insurance carriers as well as other health insurance companies. Bulletins provided by Medicare and private insurance carriers alert the agency to the mandated HCPCS codes.

HCPCS level II codes (or HCPCS national codes) are used to report physician and nonphysician services, such as ambulance services, chiropractic services, dental procedures, drugs and medications, and **durable medical equipment (DME)**. Complete listings of HCPCS codes may be purchased from the U.S. Government Printing office, the local Medicare insurance carrier, or commercial publishers. The American Dental Association has copyrighted the D codes, which apply to dental services. A list of D codes must be purchased from that association.

HCPCS Level II: National Codes

Level II HCPCS codes consist of five-digit alphanumeric characters, beginning with a letter and ending with four numbers. Table 6–21 lists the HCPCS sections.

TABLE 6-21

HCPCS Level II Sections	
Section	Description
A codes	Transportation Services, Including Ambulance, Medical and Surgical Supplies, Administrative, Miscellaneous, and Investigational Services
B codes	Enteral and Parenteral Therapy
C codes	Temporary Codes for Use with Outpatient Prospective Payment System
D codes	Dental Procedures
E codes	Durable Medical Equipment (DME) (e.g., wheelchair)
G codes	Procedures/Professional Services (Temporary)
H codes	Alcohol and Drug Abuse Treatment Services
J codes	Drugs Administered Other than Oral Method
K codes	Temporary Codes (Durable Medical Equipment codes established by Medicare Administrative Contractors)
L codes	Orthotic Procedures and Devices
M codes	Medical Services
P codes	Pathology and Laboratory Services
Q codes	Miscellaneous Services (Temporary Codes)
R codes	Diagnostic Radiology Services
S codes	Temporary National Codes (Non-Medicare)
T codes	National T Codes Established for State Medicaid Agencies
V codes	Vision Services

HCPCS Level II Modifiers

In addition to the alphanumeric codes, HCPCS uses modifiers that provide further information about services provided to the patient. For Medicare claims, HCPCS Level II modifiers may be used with either HCPCS or CPT codes. Private insurance carriers may also allow Level II modifiers to be combined with CPT codes. Modifiers do not change the basic definition of the service/procedure and are used to describe the following types of information:

- The service was provided by an anesthesiologist.
- The service was performed by a nonphysician health care professional (clinical psychologist, nurse practitioner, physician assistant).
- The service was provided as part of a specific government program.
- Equipment was purchased or rented.
- Single or multiple patients were seen during nursing home visits.

There are literally hundreds of modifiers, and they are updated as needed. Tables 6-22 and 6-23 list some of the more commonly used modifiers. Table 6-22 includes modifiers associated with services and procedures. Table 6-23 includes modifiers associated with

TABLE 6–22

HCPCS Modifiers for Services/Treatment	
Modifier	Description
-AA	Anesthesia services furnished by anesthesiologist
-AH	Clinical psychologist
-AJ	Clinical social worker
-AS	Physician assistant, nurse practitioner, or clinical nurse specialist for assistant at surgery
-E1	Eyelid, upper left
-F1	Left hand, second digit
-F5	Right hand, thumb
-LC	Left circumflex coronary artery (Hospitals use with codes 92980–92984, 92995, 92996)
-LT	Left side
-NU	New equipment
-RC	Right coronary artery (Hospitals use with codes 92980–92984, 92995, 92996)
-RT	Right side
-TD	Registered nurse
-T1	Left foot, second digit
-T5	Right foot, great toe

transportation or ambulance services that identify the point of origin and the point of destination of the ambulance.

EXAMPLE

Marissa was recently diagnosed with obsessive-compulsive disorder (OCD). She meets with a clinical psychologist for a 30-minute individual counseling session.

In this example, the billing specialist submits the insurance claim with the code 90804-AH. CPT code 90804 means the patient received up to 30 minutes of face-to-face counseling, and the modifier -AH means the service was provided by a clinical psychologist.

EXAMPLE

Vicki Gervais went into insulin shock and was transported by ambulance from her home to the local hospital.

In this example, the appropriate HCPCS code for ambulance service is modified with the letters RH. The first letter, R, identifies the point of origin as the patient's home (residence), and the letter H identifies the destination as a hospital. For transportation modifiers, the point of origin character is first and the destination character is second.

Figure 6–9 gives examples of CPT codes that include HCPCS modifiers.

TABLE 6–23

HCPCS Transportation Modifiers	
Modifier	**Description**
D	Diagnostic or therapeutic site other than P or H when these are used as origin codes
E	Residential, domiciliary, custodial facility (except skilled nursing facility)
G	Hospital-based End-Stage Renal Disease (ESRD) facility
H	Hospital
I	Site of transfer (e.g., airport or helicopter pad) between modes of ambulance transport
J	Free-Standing ESRD facility
N	Skilled nursing facility (SNF)
P	Physician's office
R	Residence (e.g., patient's home)
S	Scene of accident or acute event
X	Destination code only. Intermediate stop at physician's office (includes nonhospital facility or clinic) en route to the hospital

Rebecca Stone, a 70-year-old Medicare patient, underwent excision of tendons, right palm and left middle finger.

The correct CPT codes are 26180, *excision of tendon, finger, flexor (separate procedure), each tendon*; and 26170, *excision of tendon, palm, flexor, single (separate procedure), each [tendon]*.

Since these codes are noted as "separate procedures," CPT modifier -59 is needed to indicate that the procedures were distinct and unrelated.

HCPCS modifiers -F2, *third digit, left hand* and -RT, *right side,* are needed to clarify the location of each procedure.

The billing specialist submits an insurance claim with the following codes:
    26180-F2, *excision of tendon, finger, flexor…, each tendon, third digit, left hand.*

    26170-59-RT, *excision of tendon, palm flexor, single…, each, distinct procedural service, right side.*

Delmar/Cengage Learning

FIGURE 6–9 CPT/HCPCS Modifiers

ABBREVIATIONS

Table 6–24 lists the abbreviations in this chapter.

TABLE 6–24

Abbreviations and Meanings	
Abbreviation	Meaning
ASC	Ambulatory Surgery Center
CC	chief complaint
CPT	Current Procedural Terminology
DME	durable medical equipment
E/M	Evaluation and Management
FH	family history
HCPCS	Healthcare Common Procedure Coding System
HHS	Department of Health and Human Services
HPI	history of present illness
PMH	past medical history
ROS	review of systems
SH	social history

SUMMARY

Current Procedural Terminology is the accepted coding system for nearly all provider services in ambulatory or outpatient settings and some provider services associated with hospital and long-term care. CPT is maintained and published by the American Medical Association.

The CPT manual and codes are updated annually. Billing specialists and medical coders must use the most current version so accurate codes are assigned. There are extensive instructions throughout the CPT manual that provide guidelines for code assignment. CPT's six main sections are "Evaluation and Management," "Anesthesia," "Surgery," "Radiology," "Pathology and Laboratory," and "Medicine." Each section has additional instructions that are unique to the section.

Coding conventions for CPT include semicolons, bullets, triangles, facing triangles, plus signs, circled bullets, null zero or the universal no code symbol, and the cross-reference terms "see" and "see also." The conventions provide information about a specific code. Modifiers, which are expressed as a two-digit number preceded by a hyphen, play an important role in CPT code selection. Modifiers are reported with the main CPT code and indicate that special circumstances affected the provided service.

HCPCS, a common procedure coding system, is maintained and published by the Centers for Medicare and Medicaid Services. HCPCS includes Level I, CPT codes, and Level II, national codes.

Level II codes are used to report services such as drugs, chiropractic services, dental procedures, and durable medical equipment. There are over 3,000 Level II codes, each consisting of a five-digit alphanumeric number. Level II HCPCS codes have over 100 modifiers that indicate special circumstances related to the Level II codes.

CPT and HCPCS codes are used in conjunction with ICD-9-CM diagnosis codes to communicate patient services to insurance carriers. These codes determine provider reimbursement, and the documentation in the patient record must clearly support all codes.

All insurance carriers closely monitor CPT and HCPCS codes for accuracy. Medicare insurance carriers are bound by law to report any suspected fraudulent or abusive billing practices, which are often associated with inaccurate coding. Upcoding, downcoding, and unbundling are three examples of fraudulent activities associated with coding. The billing specialist and medical coder play an important role in ensuring coding accuracy by reviewing the patient's record for documentation that supports the provider-selected code.

REVIEW EXERCISES

CPT CODING EXERCISES

Assign the correct CPT code to each statement or case. Use modifiers as necessary.

1. Laparoscopic cholecystectomy with cholangiography. _____

2. Diagnostic arthroscopy followed by removal of the medial meniscus by arthrotomy. _____

3. Cardiac catheterization, right side only, with conscious sedation, IV. _____

4. Influenza vaccine, intramuscular, 65-year-old patient. _____

5. GI series x-ray, with small bowel and air studies, without KUB. _____

6. Retrograde pyelography with KUB. _____

7. Stool for occult blood. _____

8. Throat culture, bacterial. _____

9. Home visit, problem-focused, established. _____

10. Initial hospital visit, new patient, high complexity. _____

11. Office consultation for an established patient, high complexity with surgery scheduled for tomorrow. _____

12. Assistant surgeon, cesarean section, delivery only. _____

13. Abdominal hysterectomy, surgery only. _____

14. Postoperative management of vaginal hysterectomy. _____

15. Mrs. Rogers, a new patient, is seen for a complete physical examination. She has osteoarthritis, hypertension, and insulin-dependent diabetes mellitus. A detailed history and exam was performed with medical decision making of low complexity. _____

16. Normal newborn history and physical examination. _____

17. Routine well-baby care for six-month-old infant, previously seen at six-week checkup. _____

18. Cardiovascular stress test on a 56-year-old male with recent EKG changes, physician supervision only. _____

19. Dr. Chen performed an ultrasound on a pregnant woman, 16 weeks gestation, for complete fetal and maternal evaluation (first pregnancy). _____

20. Endometrial biopsy for postmenopausal bleeding on a new patient. _____

21. Syphilis test qualitative. _____

22. MaryAnn Parrish is seen in the office today for a blood pressure check, which is performed by the nurse under the physician's supervision. _____

23. Tonia Zeebart, a 45-year-old female, is seen in the office today for an annual physical. She is in good health and has no complaints. Dr. Roy performs a comprehensive history and physical and counsels Tonia on proper diet and exercise. Tonia is a new patient. _____

24. Left nasal endoscopy for control of epistaxis. _____

25. Flexible fiber-optic laryngoscopy performed for removal of a dime that was stuck in the patient's larynx. _____

26. Active immunization with live measles, mumps, and rubella virus vaccine during an annual preventive medicine visit on a five-year-old, established patient. _____

27. Bonita Matilda arrives at the emergency department by ambulance. She was involved in a motor vehicle accident. The ED physician performs a comprehensive physical examination and notes swelling of the left foot at the medial and lateral malleolus with ecchymosis on the dorsal surface of the foot. There is tenderness at both malleoli and on the heel portion of the foot. The extensor tendon sheaths appear swollen. X-ray of the left foot and thigh show a lateral malleolus avulsion and a lateral calcaneus comminuted fracture. Dr. Footloose is called for a surgical consultation. He examines Bonita and admits her to the operating room for an open reduction, pin fixation of the fractured calcaneus. _____

28. Rashael Kroll, a 10-year-old female, was chasing her younger sister Chelsea and fell through a sliding glass door. Rashael sustained two lacerations: Left knee, 5.5 cm laceration involving deep subcutaneous tissue and fascia, repaired with layered closure using 1% lidocaine local anesthesia; left hand, 2.5 cm laceration of the dermis, repaired with simple closure under local anesthesia. Follow-up in 10 days for suture removal. _____

CODING CHALLENGE

Read the following procedure reports and write the diagnosis and procedures in the space provided. Assign the correct ICD-9-CM diagnosis codes and CPT procedure codes. These cases relate to outpatient or ambulatory episodes of care.

1. PROCEDURE REPORT

PATIENT NAME: Loonsfoot, Peter
DATE OF PROCEDURE: January 11, 20xx
PROCEDURE: Sigmoidoscopy and hemorrhoidectomy.
INDICATIONS: Mr. Loonsfoot developed perianal discomfort, itching, and a palpable perianal mass. There was no history of blood loss.
DESCRIPTION: The patient was brought to the operating room, placed in the recumbent position, and general anesthesia was induced. He was then placed in the lithotomy position. Proctosigmoidoscopy was carried out with a rigid scope and inserted to approximately 25 centimeters. No mucosal lesions were seen. One prolapsed and thrombosed hemorrhoid was revealed. The scope was withdrawn and the perianal area prepped and draped in the usual manner. The hemorrhoid was grasped with a clamp and placed in traction. An elliptical incision was made and the hemorrhoid was resected without difficulty. Several bleeders were electrocoagulated, but no significant bleeding occurred. The area was prepped and a Nupercainal impregnated sponge was placed in the anal canal. Sterile dressings were applied. The patient was taken to recover in good condition.
FINDINGS: Internal hemorrhoid with prolapse and partial thrombosis.

DIAGNOSIS(ES): _____

PROCEDURE(S): _____

2. PROCEDURE REPORT

PATIENT NAME: Estrada, Justin
DATE OF PROCEDURE: February 20, 20xx
DIAGNOSIS: Family medical history of colon cancer, 1st degree relative.
PROCEDURE: Colonoscopy with polypectomy.
INDICATIONS: Mr. Estrada is a 60-year-old male with a family history of colon cancer. His father died at age 68 from colon cancer.
DESCRIPTION: The patient was brought to the procedure room and was put into conscious sedation. He was placed in the left lateral decubitus position, and the colonoscope was introduced through the anus and advanced to the cecum. The quality of the prep was good, and the colon was clean. The colonoscope was slowly withdrawn, and visual inspection revealed a 2 mm sessile polyp in the ascending colon. No bleeding was present. Polypectomy was performed with hot forceps. Resection was complete and all tissue retrieved. Examination of the sigmoid colon revealed the presence of a few diverticula.
FINDINGS: 1. Single polyp, all tissue removed. 2. Diverticulosis.
OUTCOME/INSTRUCTIONS: The patient tolerated the procedure well. There were no complications, and he was discharged to his wife. The patient was advised not to drive or operate any equipment or machinery for 24 hours. He should immediately report any bloating, rectal bleeding, or fever.

DIAGNOSIS(ES): _____

PROCEDURE(S): _____

3. PROCEDURE REPORT

PATIENT NAME: Fishbone, Wanda
DATE OF PROCEDURE: March 20, 20xx
DIAGNOSIS: Nuclear cataract with cortical spoking, right eye.
PROCEDURE: Extracapsular cataract extraction (ECCE) with a posterior chamber intraocular lens implant, right eye.
DESCRIPTION: The patient was brought to the procedure room and placed in the supine position. Periorbital akinesia and anesthesia were achieved with a 50/50 mixture of 2% Xylocaine and 0.75% Marcain given in a retrobulbar fashion. A total of 3 cc of solution was used. The patient's periorbital areas were prepped and the right eye was draped in the usual fashion. The lids of the right eye were retracted, and an 8-0 black silk bridle suture was passed under the superior rectus tendon, and the globe was retracted downward. A conjunctival peritomy was then performed for 180 degrees. Hemostasis was obtained with wet-field cautery. A corneoscleral groove was then formed approximately 2 mm posterior to the surgical limbus and beveled anteriorly. The anterior chamber was entered with a razor blade incision and filled with Healon. The anterior capsulotomy was then performed using a can-opener technique. The wound was opened to its full extent with scissors. The nucleus was expressed without difficulty. A model 6741-B, 23 diopter, posterior chamber lens was irrigated and inserted into the capsular bag without difficulty. The surgical site was closed in the usual manner.

The patient tolerated the procedure well and was transferred to the recovery area in excellent condition. Barring any difficulties, she will be discharged home early this evening.

DIAGNOSIS(ES): _____

PROCEDURE(S): _____

4. PROCEDURE REPORT

PATIENT NAME: Applewood, Cedric
DATE OF PROCEDURE: March 20, 20xx
PROCEDURE: Catheterization of the left heart with left ventricular angiography.
INDICATIONS: Mr. Applewood presented in the ER with unstable angina pectoris, symptomatically.
DESCRIPTION: The patient was brought to the catheterization laboratory, and the right groin was prepped, draped, and anesthetized. The right femoral artery was accessed. A #7 French sheath was introduced and a #7 French JL4 catheter was advanced to the left coronary artery and was visualized. This was then exchanged for an Amplatz R1 catheter, and the right coronary artery was visualized in different views. This was then exchanged for a #7 French pigtail, and left ventricular angiograms were obtained. The patient tolerated the procedure well, and the sheaths were left in place.
FINDINGS: 1. Mild coronary artery disease with 30% occlusion of the left circumflex artery, native. 2. A 20% occlusion of the right coronary artery, native, and a 30% stenosis of the left anterior descending artery, native. 3. Left ventricular angiography revealed a normal size left ventricle and no mitral regurgitation.

DIAGNOSIS(ES): _____

PROCEDURE(S): _____

5. PROCEDURE REPORT

PATIENT NAME: Brindley, Sandra
DATE OF PROCEDURE: April 15, 20xx
INDICATIONS: Recurrent epigastric distress.
PROCEDURE PERFORMED: Esophagogastroduodenoscopy (EGD) with removal of foreign bodies (bezoar), biopsy of the duodenum and stomach.
DESCRIPTION: Under sedation, the patient's throat was anesthetized with Cetacaine spray, and the Olympus video endoscope was introduced. The gastroesophageal junction was encountered, and the stomach was entered, insufflated, and examined. The bezoar was immediately noted. The bezoar was plucked with biopsy forceps and flushed. It was suctioned and gently irrigated in the distal duodenum. The duodenal bulb was examined. The scope was withdrawn into the stomach, and remaining bezoar material was identified and removed. The scope was then reintroduced into the pylorus, and duodenal and bulbar biopsies were obtained. Mild bleeding was noted and hemostasis achieved. The patient tolerated the procedure well and was taken to the recovery room in excellent condition.
FINDINGS: At the gastroesophageal junction, there was minimal erythema, consistent with grade I gastroesophageal reflux disease. Underlying diffuse gastritis was present. Pyloric and duodenal bulb ulcerations were present. Biopsies of the duodenal bulb, gastric pylorus, and gastric antrum were obtained after removal of the bezoar.

DIAGNOSIS(ES): _____

PROCEDURE(S): _____

CHALLENGE EXERCISE

1. Obtain copies of various physician office encounter forms. Review the forms for CPT codes and check the codes against the current CPT manual. Are any codes on the encounter form outdated? Are there typographical errors in the code section? As the billing specialist, how would you approach the manager or provider in order to solve these problems?

WEBSITES

American Medical Association: www.ama-assn.org
Centers for Medicare and Medicaid Services: www.cms.gov/hcpcs

CHAPTER 7

Developing an Insurance Claim

KEY TERMS

Adult primary policy
Adult secondary policy
Allowed charge
Charge slip
Clean claim
CMS-1500
Co-insurance
Co-insurance payment
Co-pay
Co-payment
Custodial parent

Daily accounts receivable journal
Daily transaction journal
Day sheet
Delinquent claim
Dirty claim
Electronic health (medical) record (EHR; EMR)
Encounter form
Explanation of benefits (EOB)

Health care claim summary
New patient
Noncustodial parent
Patient account ledger
Pending claim
Primary payer
Remittance advice (RA)
Routing form
Superbill

OVERVIEW

The health care industry exists primarily to provide health and medical services to patients. From the largest university-based hospital to the solo physician practice, members of a health care team take pride in their ability to provide quality patient care. However, it is important to remember that all health care agencies must receive payment for services rendered. If the hospital, physician office, or clinic cannot remain solvent, everybody loses. Patients lose services, employees lose jobs, and the community loses the services of the agency and the benefits of the revenue generated by the agency.

Insurance claim processing is the avenue for the agency to be paid. Processing claims is a service provided to the patient by the health care agency. The patient must give complete and accurate information in order to take advantage of this service. Reimbursement, which means receiving payment for services rendered, is everybody's business.

To ensure a positive cash flow, each staff member must do his or her part to facilitate appropriate and timely reimbursement. The reception/front desk staff contributes by helping the patient complete a comprehensive registration form, the clinical staff contributes by documenting all services rendered, and the insurance billing specialist contributes by completing, submitting, and following up insurance claims in a timely manner. From the moment the patient enters the office until the insurance claim is submitted and paid, complete and accurate information must be captured.

This chapter covers the three general activities associated with developing an insurance claim. The activities are patient registration, clinical assessment and treatment, and patient departure procedures. Patient registration and insurance billing are often the first steps taken to implement an **electronic health (medical) record (EHR; EMR)**.

EXAMPLE

Patient registration is accomplished by entering the patient's name and demographics into a database. The database is updated as necessary. Charges for the visit are entered, and the computer program generates various forms such as a route slip, current account statement, and the insurance billing document.

Whether the office uses a manual or computer system, the process remains the same. In fact, the agency must have a well-organized manual system prior to adopting an electronic health record. If the manual system is faulty, the problems will carry over to the electronic system. The old saying "garbage in, garbage out" remains true today!

PATIENT REGISTRATION

Developing an insurance claim begins when an individual calls to schedule an appointment. If the individual is a new patient, preliminary information must be taken to be sure that the physician can provide the appropriate services. If the individual is an established patient, the appointment is scheduled.

The Health Insurance Portability and Accountability Act (HIPAA) privacy and security rules have a direct impact on patient registration procedures. Most offices have installed "privacy" windows in the registration area to prevent patients who are waiting to be seen from overhearing staff conversations and phone calls. Patient sign-in sheets are modified so that only a blank line is available. This prevents patients from seeing the names of individuals who were seen throughout the day. Computer monitors are fitted with privacy shields so that information on a computer screen is visible only to the individual using the computer. HIPAA privacy and security rules are discussed in Chapter 2.

New Patient Procedures

A **new patient** is defined as a person who is being seen by a physician for the first time or a person who has not received services within the past three years. In a multispecialty clinic, a new patient is a person who is being seen for the first time or who has not received services from any physician or provider of the same specialty within the past three years.

When a new patient calls for an appointment, the receptionist asks for the following information:

- Patient's name, address, phone number, and birth date; if the patient is a minor, the name and phone number of the parent or guardian
- The reason for the appointment
- Name of the insurance company, identification numbers, insured's name, and the employer's name (if the insurance is provided through the employer)

When the insurance plan is unfamiliar to the office staff or when there is a question about which physician the patient should see, offer to return the patient's call within a specific time-frame. This gives the insurance billing specialist time to verify insurance eligibility and benefit coverage. Clinical staff can use this time to determine if the patient should be seen and to identify the health care professional who can best provide the service.

> **EXAMPLE**
>
> Yolanda calls and asks for an appointment with Dr. Small. Yolanda is new to the area, and a neighbor has recommended this physician. Yolanda has diabetes and has ABC insurance through her employer. Dr. Small, an internist, usually does not see people with diabetes. Another physician, Dr. Large, takes those cases. In addition, the practice has no experience with ABC insurance.
>
> The receptionist offers to return the call and explains that Dr. Large usually takes new patients with a diabetes diagnosis. The receptionist then discusses the new patient request with the physician and routes the insurance information to the billing specialist. The billing specialist calls the insurance carrier and inquires about deductibles, co-payments, and benefit coverage.

Once the physician has agreed to take the new patient and insurance information is verified, the receptionist calls the individual and schedules an appointment. At this time, the receptionist should:

1. Ask the patient about previous medical treatment. The patient should arrange to supply medical records before the initial appointment. If this is not possible, the patient must sign an authorization to release information when he or she registers as a new patient.
2. Remind the patient to bring insurance verification, which is usually an insurance identification card.

Discuss the provider's payment policy. For example, some providers collect the co-pay or co-insurance on the day of the appointment. Many practices expect payment if the charges are less than a certain amount, regardless of insurance coverage. If the physician is a nonparticipating or out-of-network provider, the patient will likely be responsible for a greater percentage, if not all, of the bill. Individuals enrolled in a managed care plan and who expect the managed care plan to pay for services must have preauthorization from the primary care physician in order to see a specialist. Preauthorization can be a referral form or letter from the primary care physician or a phone call from a case manager who provides verbal authorization. The referral can be faxed to the specialist's office or hand-carried by the patient. Individuals enrolled in a managed care plan may see a specialist at their own expense without preauthorization.

Patient Registration Form and Authorizations: New Patient

Many offices ask new patients to come in a few minutes before the scheduled appointment. When the patient arrives, the receptionist provides a copy of the patient registration form and makes a copy, front and back, of the insurance card. The patient registration form completes the information taken during the initial phone call. When the registration form is completed, the receptionist checks for any unanswered questions. Figure 7–1 is a sample patient registration form.

In an electronic environment, the receptionist retrieves the information taken when the appointment was scheduled. The receptionist verifies that demographic information is correct. The patient's insurance card may be scanned into the patient's electronic record. Some health care providers also require some form of identification, such as a driver's license, which is also scanned into the electronic record.

If previous medical records are needed, the patient signs an authorization to release information for each office or hospital that has the medical information. The patient also signs an authorization to release information to the insurance company. Without this authorization, an insurance claim cannot be processed. A sample release of information form for medical records is shown in Chapter 2. Figure 7–2 is a sample authorization for insurance billing.

In a manual system, the registration form is a source document for the patient's medical, account, and insurance billing records. In an electronic environment, the information in the patient's database is immediately available to administrative and clinical staff.

Established Patient Procedures

When an established patient requests an appointment, the appointment is scheduled, and the receptionist may update the patient's database at that time. The patient is instructed to bring his or her insurance card, especially if the patient has a new or different insurance plan. At the time of the appointment, demographic and insurance information is updated or verified as necessary. If the insurance plan has changed, the new insurance card is either copied (front and back) or scanned into the database. The patient must also sign an authorization to release information to the new insurance company.

Primary and Secondary Insurance Policies

Patients may have more than one health insurance policy. The insurance billing specialist identifies the **primary payer**, the insurance company that is billed first. Once the primary payer has fulfilled its responsibility, the claim is submitted to the secondary payer. Insurance benefits must be coordinated so the total amount paid does not exceed 100% of the charges.

Determining primary and secondary payer status depends on whether the patient is an adult or a child. When the patient is an adult, the **adult primary policy** is the insurance policy that lists the patient as the subscriber, insured, or dependent on the primary insurance plan. The **adult secondary policy** is the insurance policy that lists the patient as the subscriber, insured, or dependent on the secondary insurance plan.

SUPERIORLAND CLINIC
714 Hennepin Avenue
Blueberry, ME 49855

PATIENT REGISTRATION

DATE: 06/05/20xx

PATIENT INFORMATION

PATIENT'S LAST NAME:	FIRST NAME:	MIDDLE INITIAL:	DOB:
HELLMAN	ABIGAIL	M	10/30/1960

PATIENT'S ADDRESS:	PHONE: Home: (906) 555-2345
714 HENNEPIN ANYTOWN ME 49855	Work: (906) 555-3456

SINGLE: MARRIED: X WIDOWED:	MALE: FEMALE: X

OCCUPATION:	EMPLOYER/ADDRESS:	EMPLOYER PHONE:
TEACHER	ANYTOWN ELEMENTARY SCHOOL 301 W SPRUCE ANYTOWN ME 49855	(906) 555-3456

EMERGENCY CONTACT:	RELATIONSHIP TO PATIENT:	PHONE: Home: (906) 555-2345
PAUL HELLMAN	HUSBAND	Work: (906) 555-6066

REASON FOR TODAY'S VISIT:
SORE THROAT

WORK RELATED INJURY/ILLNESS? YES: NO: X DATE:	AUTO ACCIDENT? YES: NO: X DATE:	OTHER ACCIDENT? YES: NO: X DATE:

INSURANCE INFORMATION

INSURANCE CO.	GROUP NO:	INSURED'S ID NO:
AETNA	87000	503529750

INSURED'S NAME:	INSURED'S DOB:	RELATIONSHIP TO INSURED:
ABIGAIL HELLMAN	10/30/1960	SELF: X SPOUSE: CHILD: OTHER:

INSURED'S ADDRESS:	INSURED'S PHONE:	INSURED'S EMPLOYER:
SAME	SAME	SEE ABOVE

OTHER INSURANCE

SECONDARY INSURANCE:	GROUP NO:	ID NUMBER:	EMPLOYER:
CIGNA	89000	614630861	QUALITY CONTRACTORS

OTHER INSURED'S NAME:	OTHER INSURED'S DOB:	RELATIONSHIP TO PATIENT:
PAUL HELLMAN	11/12/1959	SPOUSE

OTHER INSURED'S ADDRESS:	OTHER INSURED'S PHONE:
SAME	SAME

AUTHORIZATION

I hereby authorize my insurance company benefits to be paid directly to the physician. I realize that I am responsible to pay for any non-covered services. I hereby authorize the release of pertinent medical information to the insurance company.

Patient/Legal Representative Signature: *Abigail Hellman* Date: 06/05/20xx

FIGURE 7–1 Patient Registration Form

(Practice Letterhead Here)

*Authorization for Release of Medical Information to the Insurance Carrier
and Assignment of Benefits to Physician*

COMMERCIAL INSURANCE

I hereby authorize release of medical information necessary to file a claim with my insurance company and ASSIGN BENEFITS OTHERWISE PAYABLE TO ME TO _____(fill in physician's name)_____ MD, PA.

I understand that I am financially responsible for any balance not covered by my insurance carrier. A copy of this signature is as valid as the original.

Signature of patient or guardian_____   Date _____

MEDICARE INSURANCE

BENEFICIARY _____   MEDICARE NUMBER_____

I request that payment of authorized Medicare benefits be made either to me or on my behalf to ____(fill in physician's name)____ for any services furnished to me by that physician. I authorize any holder of medical information about me to release to the Centers for Medicare and Medicaid Services and its agents any information needed to determine these benefits or the benefits payable for related services.

Beneficiary Signature _____   Date _____

MEDICARE SUPPLEMENTAL INSURANCE

BENEFICIARY _____   Medicare Number _____

Medigap ID Number _____

I hereby give (name of physician or practice) permission to ask for Medicare Supplemental Insurance payments for my medical care.

I understand that (name of Medicare supplemental insurance carrier) needs information about me and my medical condition to make a decision about these payments. I give permission for that information to go to (name of Medicare supplemental insurance company).

I request that payment of authorized Medicare supplemental benefits be made either to me or on my behalf to (name of physician or practice) for any services furnished me by that physician. I authorize any holder of medical information about me to release to (name of Medicare supplemental insurance company) any information required to determine and pay these benefits.

Beneficiary Signature _____   Date _____

Delmar/Cengage Learning

FIGURE 7–2 Authorization for Insurance Billing

EXAMPLE

Roger is employed at Penelope Paints. His employer provides health insurance. Roger is identified as the subscriber on his company insurance policy. Roger's wife, Helen, who is employed by Rhoda Rooter, Inc., lists Roger as a dependent on her company insurance policy.

In this example, the billing specialist sends an insurance claim to Roger's insurance company first. Once payment is received, the balance is submitted to Helen's insurance company. If Helen is listed as a dependent on Roger's health plan, her medical bills are sent to her insurance company first, and the balance is submitted to Roger's. If neither Roger nor Helen lists the other as a dependent, Roger's claim is submitted to his insurance company and Helen's is submitted to hers.

Determination of the primary and secondary payer for children depends on the marital and custodial status of the parents. When the parents are divorced, the health insurance plan of the **custodial parent**—the parent the child lives with—is primary, unless the divorce decree states otherwise. If the parents remarry, the custodial parent plan is primary, the custodial stepparent plan is secondary, and the health insurance plan of the **noncustodial parent** is third. However, the divorce decree may assign responsibility for medical expenses to either parent.

For children living with both parents—and if both parents have insurance coverage—primary and secondary payer status is determined by the birthday rule. Under the birthday rule, the primary payer is the insurance policy of the parent whose birth month and day come earlier in the calendar year. The year of the birth is not a factor in determining primary and secondary payer status.

REINFORCEMENT EXERCISES 7–1

Briefly describe how the listed individuals contribute to insurance claims processing.

1. Patient

   _____

   _____

   _____

2. Receptionist

   _____

   _____

   _____

3. Clinical staff

   _____

   _____

   _____

4. Insurance billing specialist

   _____

   _____

   _____

continued on the next page

continued from the previous page

Provide a brief definition for each term or a short answer for each question.

1. New patient

_____

_____

_____

2. Patient registration form

_____

_____

_____

3. List the three instructions that the receptionist should give to a new patient when an appointment is scheduled.

_____

_____

_____

4. Name the two types of forms that a new patient completes during the first encounter.

_____

_____

_____

Fill in the blank with the correct term or phrase.

1. The insurance company billed first is called the _____.

2. The insurance company billed second is called the _____.

3. For children, the health insurance plan of the _____ is billed first when parents are divorced, unless the divorce decree states otherwise.

4. The _____ is the insurance policy that lists the patient as the subscriber or policyholder.

5. The patient's _____ is verification of insurance coverage.

Encounter Form: New and Established Patients

Once the registration process is completed, an **encounter form**—also called a **charge slip, routing form**, or **superbill**—is generated. The encounter form is one of the source documents for financial, diagnostic, and treatment information. The patient's medical record also provides diagnostic and treatment information. The encounter form is attached to the patient record and routed to the examination room.

Most offices and clinics use a preprinted encounter form. The form can be generic, intended for general use, or customized (developed for a specific type of practice or clinic). Figure 7–3 is an example of an encounter form developed for use by internal medicine specialists. Refer to this figure as you read about each section of the encounter form.

ELIZABETH FOY, MD CHARLES FRENCH, MD ROBERT HOWARD, MD DENZEL HAMILTON, MD ROBERTA PHARYNGEAL, MD HENRY ROMERO, MD				**SUPERIORLAND CLINIC** 714 HENNEPIN AVENUE BLUEBERRY, ME 49855 PHONE: (906) 336-4600 FAX: (906) 336-4020					
NEW PATIENT	**CODE**	**FEE**	**LAB TEST**	**CODE**	**FEE**	**LAB TEST**	**CODE**	**FEE**
Level I	99201		AST	84450		LDH	83615	
Level II	99202		Albumin	82040		Lipid Panel	80061	
Level III	99203		Alk Phos	84075		Metabolic Panel	80053	
Level IV	99204		BUN	84520		Obstetric Panel	80055	
Level V	99205		CBC	85027		Occult Blood	82270	
ESTABLISHED PATIENT			CBC/diff	85025		PAP smear	88150	
Level I	99211		CK/CPK	82550		PPD Skin Test	86580	
Level II	99212		Drug Screen	80100		Prothrombin Time	85610	
Level III	99213		Electrolyte Panel	80051		PSA	84152	
Level IV	99214		Estrogen	82671		Rapid Strep Screen	87880	
Level V	99215		Glucose/blood	82947		Sed Rate	85651	
OFFICE CONSULTATION			GTT	82951		TSH	84443	
Level I	99241		HgbA1C	83036		Urinalysis	81000	
Level II	99242		Hepatitis Panel	80074				
Level III	99243		HIV Screen	86703				
Level IV	99244							
Level V	99245		**OTHER TESTS**			**OTHER TESTS**		
HOSPITAL INPATIENT			A/P Chest X-ray			Holter/24 hr		
Initial/Complex	99223		DXA Scan	77080		Sigmoidoscopy	45330	
Subsequent	99231		EKG Int/Report	93000		Stress Test	93015	
EMERGENCY DEPARTMENT SERV.			Rhythm EKG	93040				
Level I	99281							
Level II	99282							
Level III	99283		**TREATMENTS**	**CODE**	**FEE**	**TREATMENTS**	**CODE**	**FEE**
Level IV	99284		Flu Shot	90658				
Level V	99285							

DIAGNOSIS						
Abdominal Pain	789.00	Gastritis	535.50	OTHER DIAGNOSIS		CODE
Angina Pectoris, Unspec.	413.9	Hemorrhoids, NOS	455.6			
Asthma, Unspecified	493.90	Hiatal hernia	553.3			
Bronchitis, Acute	466.0	Hyperlipidemia, NOS	272.4			
Bursitis	727.3	Hypertension, Unspec.	401.9			
CHF	428.0	Hyperthyroidism	242.90	REFERRAL/COMMENTS		
Colon polyp	211.3	Hypothyroidism	244.9			
Conjunctivitis, Unspec.	372.00	Osteoarthritis, Unspec	715.90			
Diabetes Mellitus, Type I	250. 01	Osteoporosis, postmen.	733.01			
Diabetes Mellitus, Type II	250.00	Pleurisy	511.0			
Diverticulosis, colon	562.10	Serious Otitis Media, Acute	381.01			
Emphysema	492.8	UTI	599.0			

DATE	**PATIENT NAME**	**DOB**	**CHARGES**	**PAYMENT**	**BALANCE**

I authorize my insurance benefits to be paid directly to the above named physician. I understand that I am obligated to pay deductibles, copayments, and charges for non-covered services. I authorize release of my medical information for billing purposes.

PATIENT SIGNATURE: **DATE:**

FIGURE 7–3 Encounter Form

Heading

The heading of the form usually includes the name, address, phone number, and fax number of the agency. Health care provider names may also be included in the heading. The receptionist circles the name of the individual treating the patient. In an electronic environment, the name of the treating physician may be printed when the form is generated.

Examination and Treatment Section

The examination and treatment section includes the following information: types of encounters, laboratory or diagnostic tests ordered or performed, *Current Procedural Terminology* (CPT) codes, and fees. Encounters are categorized as new patient, established patient, office consultation, hospital inpatient, and emergency department service. There are different levels of services listed under each of these headings. The CPT code for each level is preprinted on the encounter form. Criteria for the levels of service are explained in Chapter 6. The physician or health care provider checks the box (or circles the code) that identifies the level of service the patient received during the encounter or visit.

Treatments are categorized as lab tests, other tests, and treatments. The names of frequently provided or ordered tests and treatments and the associated CPT codes are preprinted on the encounter form. The physician or health care provider checks the boxes (or circles the codes) that identify the tests and treatments associated with the encounter or visit. The blank spaces under these headings allow the provider to write in the names of additional tests and treatments. The referral/comments area is used to note infrequently ordered tests and treatments.

The billing clerk enters the current charges in the fee column for the encounter, tests, and treatments completed during the patient's visit. The patient receives a copy of the encounter form before leaving the office.

Because CPT codes are updated annually, the encounter form should be reviewed each year to ensure that the preprinted CPT codes for the levels of service, tests, and treatments are accurate.

Diagnosis

The diagnosis section lists diagnoses that are commonly identified in a particular practice. The diagnoses are listed alphabetically and include the *International Classification of Diseases, Ninth Revision, Clinical Modification* (ICD-9-CM) code for each diagnosis. Because ICD-9-CM codes are also updated annually, the encounter form must be updated to include any changes. There is a space available for entering any diagnosis not listed. The health care provider circles all diagnoses related to the current visit.

Referral/Comments

The physician or provider makes note of referrals, the timeframe for follow-up appointments, or other comments in the space labeled "Referral/Comments." The authorization statement to pay the physician directly and to release medical information to insurance carriers must be signed by the patient.

Demographic and Billing Information

The encounter form usually has a section for the date of the encounter, the patient's name and date of birth, charges for the current visit, payments, and the balance. In a paper environment, the balance is usually the balance due for the current visit. In an electronic environment, the balance may be the sum of a previous balance and the current balance.

REINFORCEMENT EXERCISES 7–2

Provide a short answer for each item.

1. List three synonyms for encounter form.

   _____

   _____

   _____

2. What is the purpose of the encounter form?

   _____

   _____

   _____

3. Briefly describe the information associated with encounter form sections.

   a. Heading

   _____

   _____

   _____

   b. Examination and treatment section

   _____

   _____

   _____

   c. Diagnosis

   _____

   _____

   _____

   d. Demographic information

   _____

   _____

   _____

CLINICAL ASSESSMENT AND TREATMENT

Once registration is completed, the patient is ready to be seen by the health care provider. The patient's concerns and reason for the appointment are assessed. The assessment can be a brief medication review or a comprehensive physical examination. Diagnostic and laboratory tests may be ordered or completed during the visit. The health care provider is responsible for documenting all aspects of patient care and treatment.

The health care provider enters sufficient information in the patient's medical record to justify the services provided and the charges billed. Written clinical justification is required for every diagnostic test and treatment. The health care provider also completes the clinical sections of the encounter form, which include examinations, laboratory tests, and diagnosis. Comments or referrals are entered in the appropriate section, and the timeframe for the next appointment is noted. At the conclusion of the visit, the patient is instructed to take the encounter form to the reception desk.

PATIENT DEPARTURE PROCEDURES: NEW AND ESTABLISHED PATIENTS

Patient departure procedures include scheduling another appointment if necessary; computing the charges for current services; posting charges and payments; assigning numeric codes to all procedures and diagnoses; and generating and submitting the insurance claim form. Professional attention to all departure procedures ensures that the patient will receive follow-up care and that the agency will receive reimbursement for services rendered.

Scheduling and Billing

After seeing the health care provider, the patient is directed to the reception area, and if necessary, another appointment is scheduled. The receptionist may also enter today's charges on the encounter form and ask the patient if he or she intends to make a payment. The patient signs the authorization statement on the encounter form. In many offices, once the receptionist has taken care of appointments or referrals, the patient is directed to the billing clerk. The billing clerk enters the current charges and inquires about a payment. When a payment is made, the balance due is entered in the appropriate space. In an electronic environment, the patient may sign an electronic signature pad. The billing clerk then prints a copy of the encounter form for the patient.

Patients without insurance are responsible for the entire charge. The agency may require full payment for charges under a specific dollar amount. This information should be clearly posted or communicated to the patient when the appointment is scheduled. Charges that exceed the full-payment threshold are billed to the patient. Some agencies have a payment schedule that includes a monthly finance charge for the unpaid balance.

Patients with health insurance may be required to pay a portion of the charge. Most insurance policies stipulate a **co-payment**, also called **co-pay**, or a **co-insurance payment**, also called **co-insurance**. A co-payment is a specific dollar amount that the patient must pay the provider for each encounter. A co-insurance payment is a specific percentage of the charge that the patient must pay. Example A illustrates co-payment, and example B illustrates co-insurance.

> **EXAMPLE A**
> ABC Insurance Company requires a $20 co-payment for each encounter. The patient is responsible for $20, and the remainder is submitted to the insurance company. In this example, the co-payment should be collected during the departure procedures.

EXAMPLE B

ABC Insurance Company pays 80% of all charges, and the patient is responsible for the remaining 20% as a co-insurance payment. In this example, the billing specialist has two options: (1) compute the patient's share of the charge and collect all or a portion of that amount or (2) inform the patient that once the insurance payment is received, the patient will receive a bill for the balance.

Posting Charges and Payments

The billing department is responsible for posting (entering) all charges and payments to the patient's account. Encounter forms are the source documents for charges. Checks, receipts, and insurance statements are the source documents for payments. Charges and payments are posted to the **patient account ledger**, which is a permanent record of financial transactions between the patient and the agency, and to the **daily accounts receivable journal**, which is also called a **day sheet** or **daily transaction journal**. The transaction journal is a summary of charges, payments, and current balance for a given day.

Most health care agencies use a computerized billing system. The billing system may be an application of the electronic health record software or a separate software program. In the electronic environment, charges, payments, and other billing information is entered into the patient's database. Each patient is assigned an identification number that allows any information to be entered or retrieved by that number. Once the billing information is entered, the software simultaneously updates patient accounts and other financial records. The billing specialist can generate statements, receipts, insurance claim forms, patient account ledgers, accounts receivable journals, and other financial reports as needed. Figure 7–4 shows a patient account ledger displayed on a computer screen.

File   Charges   Payments   Print Statement   Print Receipt   Print History   Help

ACCT NO	482609872		NAME	HELLMAN, ABIGAIL M		BAL	450.00

30 DAY BAL 300.00	60 DAY BAL 100.00	90 DAY BAL 50.00	120 DAY BAL

DATE	SERVICE		CHARGE	PREV BAL	NEW BAL
052020xx	99213 OV		45.00	450.00	495.00

DATE	PAYMENT	AMOUNT	PREV BAL	NEW BAL
052020xx	PT CHK 2123	50.00	495.00	445.00
062020xx	BC/BS OV 052020xx	40.00	445.00	405.00

PRIMARY INS NAME ID	SECONDARY INS NAME ID	OTHER INS NAME ID
BCBS WVP467902345	AETNA AH45678	

Delmar/Cengage Learning

FIGURE 7–4 Patient Account Ledger

SUPERIORLAND CLINIC		TRANSACTIONS JOURNAL			06/25/20XX	
PATIENT ID	PATIENT	DESCRIPTION	PREV BAL	CHARGE	PAYMENT	NEW BAL
121548	HELLMAN A	99213 OV	450.00	45.00	50.00	445.00
121548	HELLMAN A	BCBS PAYMENT	445.00		45.00	405.00
121550	BURLESON T	AETNA PAYMENT	100.00		50.00	50.00
121551	SMART I	PT CHCK 3234	50.00		50.00	0.00
121552	LIGHTFOOT C	99205 OV	0.00	75.00		75.00
121552	LIGHTFOOT C	LAB TESTS	75.00	200.00		275.00
121552	LIGHTFOOT C	PT CHCK 501	275.00		60.00	215.00
TOTAL			1395.00	320.00	255.00	1460.00

FIGURE 7–5 Sample Transaction Journal

After all charges and payments are entered into the system, the billing specialist can generate a daily transaction journal (day sheet). The transaction journal summarizes the charges, payments, and current balance for a specific day. Figure 7–5 is an example of a transaction journal.

Assigning Numeric Codes

Accurate treatment, procedure, and diagnosis codes are needed for reimbursement. The provider is responsible for circling all applicable preprinted codes on the encounter form. At a minimum, the billing specialist uses those codes for insurance claims. However, the provider may add diagnoses or treatments such as lab tests, which may not be printed on the encounter form. The provider may also note diagnostic and treatment information in the patient's medical record. Before submitting only the circled preprinted codes, the billing specialist must review the encounter form and the patient's medical record for additional diagnostic and treatment information.

When additional diagnoses and treatments are included on the encounter form or in the patient's medical record, they are assigned the appropriate numeric code. The additional codes may not affect the amount of reimbursement, but they can prevent payment denials or delays.

EXAMPLE

Marilyn is seen for an infected insect bite. The physician examines the area and writes a prescription for a topical antibiotic. Marilyn has diabetes and is concerned about the accuracy of her glucometer. The physician orders a blood glucose lab test. "Infected insect bite" is written on the encounter form, and the glucose lab test and related code are circled.

If the billing specialist submits the insurance claim with the codes for an infected insect bite diagnosis and a blood glucose lab test, there is a good chance the claim will be denied. A blood glucose test is not related to an infected insect bite. In order to receive payment for the blood test, the appropriate diabetes code must be included on the insurance claim.

Diagnostic and procedure codes are submitted with the insurance claim and may be included with the charges posted to the patient's account. Chapter 4 covers ICD-9-CM coding for diagnoses and Chapter 6 covers *Current Procedure Terminology* (CPT) coding for treatments and procedures.

REINFORCEMENT EXERCISES 7–3

Provide a brief definition for each term or a short answer for each question.

1. What is the difference between co-payment and co-insurance?

_____

_____

_____

2. Patient account ledger

_____

_____

_____

3. Transaction journal

_____

_____

_____

4. What is the purpose of assigning numeric codes to patient services?

_____

_____

_____

5. List and describe three activities associated with patient departure procedures.

_____

_____

_____

INSURANCE CLAIM FORM: GENERATION AND SUBMISSION

Once charges and payments are posted and diagnoses and procedures are coded, the billing specialist generates an insurance claim form. The **CMS-1500** is the most commonly used insurance claim form. The CMS-1500, which was developed by the Centers for Medicare and Medicaid Services (CMS) and approved by the American Medical Association (AMA), has been in use for many years. Most major health insurance companies require the CMS-1500 for reporting provider services. Figure 7–6 is a sample of the CMS-1500.

(1500)

HEALTH INSURANCE CLAIM FORM

APPROVED BY NATIONAL UNIFORM CLAIM COMMITTEE 08/05

| | PICA | | | | | | | PICA | | |

1. MEDICARE ☐ (Medicare #) MEDICAID ☐ (Medicaid #) TRICARE CHAMPUS ☐ (Sponsor's SSN) CHAMPVA ☐ (Member ID #) GROUP HEALTH PLAN ☐ (SSN or ID) FECA BLK LUNG ☐ (SSN) OTHER ☐ (ID)

1a. INSURED'S I.D. NUMBER   (For Program in Item 1)

2. PATIENT'S NAME (Last Name, First Name, Middle Initial)

3. PATIENT'S BIRTH DATE   MM DD YY   SEX   M ☐ F ☐

4. INSURED'S NAME (Last Name, First Name, Middle Initial)

5. PATIENT'S ADDRESS (No., Street)

6. PATIENT RELATIONSHIP TO INSURED   Self ☐ Spouse ☐ Child ☐ Other ☐

7. INSURED'S ADDRESS (No., Street)

CITY   STATE

8. PATIENT STATUS   Single ☐   Married ☐   Other ☐

CITY   STATE

ZIP CODE   TELEPHONE (Include Area Code)   (   )

Employed ☐   Full-Time Student ☐   Part-Time Student ☐

ZIP CODE   TELEPHONE (Include Area Code)   (   )

9. OTHER INSURED'S NAME (Last Name, First Name, Middle Initial)

10. IS PATIENT'S CONDITION RELATED TO:

11. INSURED'S POLICY GROUP OR FECA NUMBER

a. OTHER INSURED'S POLICY OR GROUP NUMBER

a. EMPLOYMENT? (Current or Previous)   YES ☐   NO ☐

a. INSURED'S DATE OF BIRTH   MM DD YY   SEX   M ☐ F ☐

b. OTHER INSURED'S DATE OF BIRTH   MM DD YY   SEX   M ☐ F ☐

b. AUTO ACCIDENT?   PLACE (State)   YES ☐   NO ☐

b. EMPLOYER'S NAME OR SCHOOL NAME

c. EMPLOYER'S NAME OR SCHOOL NAME

c. OTHER ACCIDENT?   YES ☐   NO ☐

c. INSURANCE PLAN NAME OR PROGRAM NAME

d. INSURANCE PLAN NAME OR PROGRAM NAME

10d. RESERVED FOR LOCAL USE

d. IS THERE ANOTHER HEALTH BENEFIT PLAN?   YES ☐   NO ☐   **If yes**, return to and complete item 9 a-d.

READ BACK OF FORM BEFORE COMPLETING & SIGNING THIS FORM.
12. PATIENT'S OR AUTHORIZED PERSON'S SIGNATURE I authorize the release of any medical or other information necessary to process this claim. I also request payment of government benefits either to myself or to the party who accepts assignment below.

SIGNED _____   DATE _____

13. INSURED'S OR AUTHORIZED PERSON'S SIGNATURE I authorize payment of medical benefits to the undersigned physician or supplier for services described below.

SIGNED _____

14. DATE OF CURRENT: MM DD YY ◄ ILLNESS (First symptom) OR INJURY (Accident) OR PREGNANCY (LMP)

15. IF PATIENT HAS HAD SAME OR SIMILAR ILLNESS, GIVE FIRST DATE MM DD YY

16. DATES PATIENT UNABLE TO WORK IN CURRENT OCCUPATION   MM DD YY   FROM   TO   MM DD YY

17. NAME OF REFERRING PROVIDER OR OTHER SOURCE

17a.
17b. NPI

18. HOSPITALIZATION DATES RELATED TO CURRENT SERVICES   MM DD YY   FROM   TO   MM DD YY

19. RESERVED FOR LOCAL USE

20. OUTSIDE LAB?   YES ☐   NO ☐ $ CHARGES

21. DIAGNOSIS OR NATURE OF ILLNESS OR INJURY (Relate Items 1, 2, 3, or 4 to Item 24E by Line)

1. |___.___| 3. |___.___|

2. |___.___| 4. |___.___|

22. MEDICAID RESUBMISSION   CODE   ORIGINAL REF. NO.

23. PRIOR AUTHORIZATION NUMBER

24. A. DATE(S) OF SERVICE						B. PLACE OF SERVICE	C. EMG	D. PROCEDURES, SERVICES, OR SUPPLIES (Explain Unusual Circumstances) CPT/HCPCS MODIFIER	E. DIAGNOSIS POINTER	F. $ CHARGES	G. DAYS OR UNITS	H. EPSDT Family Plan	I. ID. QUAL.	J. RENDERING PROVIDER ID. #
From MM	DD	YY	To MM	DD	YY									
1														NPI
2														NPI
3														NPI
4														NPI
5														NPI
6														NPI

25. FEDERAL TAX I.D. NUMBER   SSN ☐ EIN ☐

26. PATIENT'S ACCOUNT NO.

27. ACCEPT ASSIGNMENT? (For govt. claims, see back)   YES ☐   NO ☐

28. TOTAL CHARGE $

29. AMOUNT PAID $

30. BALANCE DUE $

31. SIGNATURE OF PHYSICIAN OR SUPPLIER INCLUDING DEGREES OR CREDENTIALS (I certify that the statements on the reverse apply to this bill and are made a part thereof.)

SIGNED _____   DATE _____

32. SERVICE FACILITY LOCATION INFORMATION

a.   b.

33. BILLING PROVIDER INFO & PH # (   )

a.   b.

NUCC Instruction Manual available at: www.nucc.org

APPROVED OMB-0938-0999 FORM CMS-1500 (08-05)

CARRIER / PATIENT AND INSURED INFORMATION / PHYSICIAN OR SUPPLIER INFORMATION

FIGURE 7–6 Sample CMS-1500 (For instructional use only. Courtesy of the Centers for Medicare and Medicaid Services, www.cms.hhs.gov)

TABLE 7–1

Essential Information for CMS-1500	
Type of Information	**Description**
Insurance Plan/Program	• Name of insurance company • Contract numbers—group number and insured number, primary policy • Insured's complete name, address, date of birth, and employer • Secondary insurance policy information—insured's name, date of birth, and employer
Patient Information	• Complete name, address, date of birth, sex, and relationship to the insured • Account number, if assigned
Diagnostic and Treatment Information	• Type of illness or injury—job-related or accident related • Complete diagnostic codes for conditions treated and noted on the submitted claim • Dates of service, procedure codes, charges, and total charges for services rendered
Provider Information	• Name, address, identifying codes, and signature

Source documents for CMS-1500 information include a copy of the patient's insurance ID card, the patient registration form, the encounter form, and the patient's medical and account records. Table 7–1 lists essential information for completing the insurance claim form.

Information captured on the CMS-1500 is divided into two sections: (1) patient and insured information (items 1 through 13) and (2) treatment and provider information (items 14 through 33). The sections are presented with a table that describes each item and identifies the source document for the information. This is a brief introduction to the content of the CMS-1500. Chapter 8 covers the CMS-1500 in detail, and Chapters 11–15 explain CMS-1500 completion guidelines for various insurance programs.

Patient and Insured Information: Blocks 1–13

Figure 7–7 is a sample of the CMS-1500 patient and insured information section, blocks 1 through 13. Refer to each block number as you review Table 7–2, which describes the content of this section.

Treatment and Provider Information: Blocks 14–33

Figure 7–8 is a sample of the CMS-1500 treatment and provider information section, blocks 14 through 33. Refer to each item number as you review Table 7–3, which describes the content of this section.

The insurance claim form can be submitted electronically or by mail. In either case, the provider authenticates the claim with a signature. Authentication includes an actual signature or a typed, stamped, or electronic signature approved by the insurance carrier. Some claims may

```
( 1500 )
HEALTH INSURANCE CLAIM FORM
APPROVED BY NATIONAL UNIFORM CLAIM COMMITTEE 08/05
```

☐☐☐ PICA		PICA ☐☐☐

1. MEDICARE ☐ (Medicare #) MEDICAID ☐ (Medicaid #) TRICARE CHAMPUS ☐ (Sponsor's SSN) CHAMPVA ☐ (Member ID #) GROUP HEALTH PLAN ☒ (SSN or ID) FECA BLK LUNG ☐ (SSN) OTHER ☐ (ID) **1a.** INSURED'S I.D. NUMBER (For Program in Item 1) 503529750

2. PATIENT'S NAME (Last Name, First Name, Middle Initial) HELLMAN, ABIGAIL, M

3. PATIENT'S BIRTH DATE MM 10 DD 30 YY 19XX SEX M ☐ F ☒

4. INSURED'S NAME (Last Name, First Name, Middle Initial) HELLMAN, ABIGAIL, M

5. PATIENT'S ADDRESS (No., Street) 724 HENNEPIN

6. PATIENT RELATIONSHIP TO INSURED Self ☒ Spouse ☐ Child ☐ Other ☐

7. INSURED'S ADDRESS (No., Street) 724 HENNPIN

CITY ANYTOWN STATE ME

8. PATIENT STATUS Single ☐ Married ☒ Other ☐

CITY ANYTOWN STATE ME

ZIP CODE 49855 TELEPHONE (Include Area Code) (906) 555 2345

Employed ☒ Full-Time Student ☐ Part-Time Student ☐

ZIP CODE 49855 TELEPHONE (Include Area Code) (906) 555 2345

9. OTHER INSURED'S NAME (Last Name, First Name, Middle Initial) HELLMAN PAUL

10. IS PATIENT'S CONDITION RELATED TO:

11. INSURED'S POLICY GROUP OR FECA NUMBER 87000

a. OTHER INSURED'S POLICY OR GROUP NUMBER 614630861

a. EMPLOYMENT? (Current or Previous) YES ☐ NO ☒

a. INSURED'S DATE OF BIRTH MM 10 DD 30 YY 19XX SEX M ☐ F ☒

b. OTHER INSURED'S DATE OF BIRTH MM 11 DD 12 YY 19XX SEX M ☒ F ☐

b. AUTO ACCIDENT? YES ☐ NO ☒ PLACE (State)

b. EMPLOYER'S NAME OR SCHOOL NAME ANYTOWN ELEMENTARY SCHOOL

c. EMPLOYER'S NAME OR SCHOOL NAME QUALITY CONTRACTORS

c. OTHER ACCIDENT? YES ☐ NO ☒

c. INSURANCE PLAN NAME OR PROGRAM NAME AETNA

d. INSURANCE PLAN NAME OR PROGRAM NAME CIGNA

10d. RESERVED FOR LOCAL USE

d. IS THERE ANOTHER HEALTH BENEFIT PLAN? ☒ YES ☐ NO *If yes,* return to and complete item 9 a-d.

READ BACK OF FORM BEFORE COMPLETING & SIGNING THIS FORM.
12. PATIENT'S OR AUTHORIZED PERSON'S SIGNATURE I authorize the release of any medical or other information necessary to process this claim. I also request payment of government benefits either to myself or to the party who accepts assignment below.

SIGNED SIGNATURE ON FILE   DATE MM DD YY

13. INSURED'S OR AUTHORIZED PERSON'S SIGNATURE I authorize payment of medical benefits to the undersigned physician or supplier for services described below.

SIGNED SIGNATURE ON FILE

CARRIER ↑↓ PATIENT AND INSURED INFORMATION ↑↓

FIGURE 7–7 CMS-1500 Blocks 1–13 (For instructional use only. Courtesy of the Centers for Medicare and Medicaid Services, www.cms.hhs.gov)

TABLE 7–2

Description of CMS-1500 Blocks 1–13		
Block	**Description**	**Source Document**
1, 1a	Type of insurance and insured's ID number	Insurance ID card
2, 3, 5, 6	Patient's name, date of birth, address, telephone number, and relationship to the insured	Registration form; patient's medical record
4, 7	Insured's name and address; may or may not be same as patient's	Registration form; patient's medical record
8	Patient status: marital, employed, student	Registration form; patient's medical record
9, 9a–9d	Other insured's name and information (policies that may supplement the primary policy)	Registration form; patient's medical record
10a–c	Identifies if the patient's condition is related to an accident or employment	Registration form; patient's medical record
11, 11a–d	Primary insurance policy information; insurance billed first	Registration form; patient's medical record
12	Authorization to release information; patient or legal representative signature	Patient's medical record and registration form; encounter form
13	Authorization to pay benefits to the provider; patient or legal representative signature or **a** signature on file	Assignment of benefits forms; encounter form; patient's medical record

14. DATE OF CURRENT: ILLNESS (First symptom) OR		15. IF PATIENT HAS HAD SAME OR SIMILAR ILLNESS,	16. DATES PATIENT UNABLE TO WORK IN CURRENT OCCUPATION	

14. DATE OF CURRENT: MM DD YY 06 04 20YY — ILLNESS (First symptom) OR INJURY (Accident) OR PREGNANCY (LMP)

15. IF PATIENT HAS HAD SAME OR SIMILAR ILLNESS, GIVE FIRST DATE MM DD YY

16. DATES PATIENT UNABLE TO WORK IN CURRENT OCCUPATION MM DD YY FROM TO MM DD YY

17. NAME OF REFERRING PROVIDER OR OTHER SOURCE HELEN SHASKI

17a.
17b. NPI 0123456789

18. HOSPITALIZATION DATES RELATED TO CURRENT SERVICES MM DD YY FROM TO MM DD YY

19. RESERVED FOR LOCAL USE

20. OUTSIDE LAB? ☐ YES ☒ NO $ CHARGES

21. DIAGNOSIS OR NATURE OF ILLNESS OR INJURY (Relate Items 1, 2, 3, or 4 to Item 24E by Line)
1. 034 . 0
2. ___ . ___
3. ___ . ___
4. ___ . ___

22. MEDICAID RESUBMISSION CODE   ORIGINAL REF. NO.

23. PRIOR AUTHORIZATION NUMBER

24. A. DATE(S) OF SERVICE From MM DD YY — To MM DD YY	B. PLACE OF SERVICE	C. EMG	D. PROCEDURES, SERVICES, OR SUPPLIES (Explain Unusual Circumstances) CPT/HCPCS | MODIFIER	E. DIAGNOSIS POINTER	F. $ CHARGES	G. DAYS OR UNITS	H. EPSDT Family Plan	I. ID. QUAL.	J. RENDERING PROVIDER ID. #
1	06 04 YY 06 04 YY	11		99212		1	45 00	1		NPI	2345678910
2	06 04 YY 06 04 YY	11		87880		1	50 00	1		NPI	2345678910
3										NPI	
4										NPI	
5										NPI	
6										NPI	

25. FEDERAL TAX I.D. NUMBER SSN ☐ EIN ☒ — 494134726

26. PATIENT'S ACCOUNT NO. 900281

27. ACCEPT ASSIGNMENT? (For govt. claims, see back) ☒ YES ☐ NO

28. TOTAL CHARGE $ 95 00

29. AMOUNT PAID $ 10 00

30. BALANCE DUE $ 85 00

31. SIGNATURE OF PHYSICIAN OR SUPPLIER INCLUDING DEGREES OR CREDENTIALS (I certify that the statements on the reverse apply to this bill and are made a part thereof.)
SIGNATURE ON FILE
SIGNED   DATE MM DD YY

32. SERVICE FACILITY LOCATION INFORMATION
a.   b.

33. BILLING PROVIDER INFO & PH # (906) 336 4600
SUPERIORLAND CLINIC
714 HENNEPIN AVENUE
BLUEBERRY ME 49855
a. 0987654321   b.

PHYSICIAN OR SUPPLIER INFORMATION

NUCC Instruction Manual available at: www.nucc.org   APPROVED OMB-0938-0999 FORM CMS-1500 (08-05)

FIGURE 7–8 CMS-1500 Blocks 14–33 (For instructional use only. Courtesy of the Centers for Medicare and Medicaid Services, www.cms.hhs.gov)

require attachments, such as an operative report or prior authorization documentation. The majority of insurance claims are submitted electronically. In these situations, the CMS-1500 is computer-generated and authenticated by an electronic signature. Chapter 10 covers electronic claims submissions.

Insurance claims files should be maintained for the period of time directed by state and federal statutes. Government insurance claim forms must be retained for six years. According to a CMS ruling in March 1992, providers and billing services filing claims electronically must retain the source documents that generated the claim as well as the daily summary of claims transmitted and received. Earlier in this chapter, source documents were defined as the encounter form and the patient's medical and financial records. Patient medical and financial records must be retained according to prevailing state and federal statutes. The six-year CMS rule applies *only* to the encounter form and the daily summary of transmitted and received insurance claims.

Insurance Carrier Procedures

Once the insurance carrier receives a claim, it is reviewed for errors and omissions. Standard error edits, which are part of the insurance company's computer program, search for the following:

- Patient and policy identification to validate that the patient is covered by the policy
- CPT codes to determine if the services are covered by the policy
- ICD-9-CM codes to confirm the medical necessity of the services and treatment

TABLE 7–3

Description of CMS-1500 Blocks 14–33		
Block	**Description**	**Source Document**
14	Date of first symptom, current illness; accident date; pregnancy, last menstrual period (LMP)	Patient's medical record
15	First date of same or similar illness	Patient's medical record
16	Dates patient was unable to work	Patient's medical record
17	Referring physician	Patient's medical record
17a	Referring physician ID number assigned by the insurance plan	Insurance plan
17b	Referring physician NPI number	National provider identification number; universal physician or provider identification number; office, clinic, agency records
18	Hospitalization dates	Patient's medical record
19	Insurance company–specific information	Insurance company manual
20	Identifies usage of an outside lab	Patient's medical record; patient account record
21	Diagnostic codes (ICD-9-CM or current revision)	Encounter form; code books
22	Medicaid cases only	Medicaid insurance carrier
23	Prior authorization number	Patient's medical record; insurance plan authorization communication (letter, fax, verbal)
24A–J	Information entered in the unshaded area for each line in 24A–24J; one service per line	See the description for each field below.
24A	Dates of services or procedures	Patient's medical record
24B	Place of service	Insurance carrier instructions
24C	Identifies the service as an emergency	Patient's medical record
24D	Procedure, service, supply codes	*Current Procedural Terminology* (CPT) code books; HCPCS codes
24E	Diagnosis code related to the procedure, service, supply	CMS-1500, block 21
24F	Charges for each service	Encounter form; patient account

continued on the next page

continued from the previous page

24G	Number of times the service was provided	Encounter form; patient account
24H	EPSDT (early and periodic screening for diagnosis and treatment)	Patient's medical record; Medicaid guidelines
24I	ID Qualifier (shaded area) NPI (preprinted)	Insurance carrier; provider qualifier
24J	Shaded area Unshaded area (10-digit national provider identification number)	Office records Office records
25	SSN (provider's Social Security number) or EIN (employer identification number	Office record
26	Patient's account number, if assigned	Patient's account
27	Identifies if the provider accepts insurance payment as payment in full	Provider policy
28–30	Total charges; amount paid; balance due	Patient's account
31	Provider signature and date; manual, electronic, signature stamp	Insurance company procedures; office policy
32	Identifies service locations such as an outside lab, a hospital, or a nursing home	Patient's medical record; patient's account
33	Provider's billing name, address, telephone number NPI (preprinted)	Office, clinic, agency records Office, clinic, agency records
33a	**National Provider Identification number**	
33b	Other billing ID number	Insurance carrier; often left blank

Insurance carriers may have other standard edits unique to a specific insurance policy. For example, if the patient is a full-time student between the ages of 19 and 23, an edit function could request verification of enrollment. Discrepancies between gender and condition may be reviewed. For example, a patient coded as "male" has a postmenopausal syndrome diagnosis.

If the claim is accepted, the insurance carrier computes the payment due to the provider or patient. Payment is sent to the provider when the provider has a participating contract with the insurance carrier or accepts assignment or when the patient assigns benefits directly to the provider. When none of these conditions exist, the payment is sent to the patient. Payment depends on the deductible, co-payment, co-insurance, and the **allowed charge**, which is the maximum amount the insurance company pays for a service. Allowed charges are based on a variety of factors, which may include the following:

- The average or usual and customary fee in a geographic area for a specific service
- The average or usual and customary fee by provider type for a specific service
- A percentage of the average or usual and customary fee
- The amount negotiated between the insurance carrier and the policyholder, employer, or provider
- An arbitrary amount set by the insurance policy or carrier

Allowed charges may be equal to but are almost always less than the provider fee. Allowed charges are *never* more than the provider fee.

The insurance company generates an **explanation of benefits (EOB)**, which explains how the reimbursement is determined. An EOB is always sent to the patient and provider. The provider's EOB, also called **remittance advice (RA)**, is a summary of all benefits paid to the provider within a certain timeframe for all patients covered by a specific insurance policy. Figure 7–9 is an example of a generic provider EOB. Note that more than one patient is listed on the EOB.

In Figure 7–9, there are 11 entries, and each entry includes the patient's name, procedure code, date of service, charges, approved amounts, amount the patient (subscriber) may owe the provider, and the amount that the insurance policy paid toward the bill. Few, if any, insurance plans pay 100% of the original charges. The difference between the amount charged and the amount paid may be billed to the patient. However, several government-sponsored health insurance programs do not allow the physician to bill the balance to the patient.

The patient also receives an EOB, also called a **health care claim summary**. The EOB summarizes how the insurance company determined the reimbursement for the services the patient received. The reverse side of an EOB often has answers to commonly asked questions about the EOB, an antifraud hotline number, and definitions for terms used in the EOB. Figure 7–10 is a sample patient EOB. In this example the provider participates in the insurance carrier's reimbursement program and agrees to accept the insurance benefit as payment in full. Note that the form is clearly marked with the statement "This Is Not a Bill."

Review the EOB in Figure 7–10 and note the following:

- The name of the provider for each service is listed.
- Provider charges are itemized.
- The insurance payment is subtracted from the total charge.
- The balance of the charge not covered in the payment is highlighted (boxed).
- The explanation statement tells the patient why a certain amount was not paid.

The EOB provides a toll-free number and an address for patient inquiries.

Insurance Claim Follow-Up

Once the insurance claim is filed or submitted, the billing specialist establishes an insurance claim follow-up file. The file—manual or computer-generated—is used to keep track of claims as they are paid.

At a minimum, the insurance claim follow-up file includes the date of service, patient name and identification, insurance carrier, service code, the amount filed, and the date the claim was filed.

Any Insurance   EXPLANATION OF BENEFITS   Check # 88099
Company, USA   Check Voucher   Provider: 007

PATIENT NAME	PROCEDURE CODE	SERVICE DATE	ORIGINAL CHARGES	APPROVED AMOUNT	SUBSCRIBER MAY OWE	ANY INSURANCE PAID	
APPLE A1230	99215	06-28-xxxx	193.99	161.09	16.10	144.99	
						sub total:	144.99
BELL B4560	85023	06-24-xxxx	36.75	28.96	.00	28.96	
	83718	06-24-xxxx	59.06	10.27	.00	10.27	
	81000	06-24-xxxx	21.00	16.05	.00	16.05	
	36415	06-24-xxxx	6.04	5.37	.00	5.37	
	80016	06-24-xxxx	51.45	36.85	.00	36.85	
						sub total:	97.50
CHAMP C7890	85023	06-25-xxxx	36.75	28.96	.00	28.96	
	83718	06-25-xxxx	59.06	10.27	.00	10.27	
	81000	06-25-xxxx	21.00	16.05	.00	16.05	
	36415	06-25-xxxx	6.04	5.37	.00	5.37	
	80016	06-25-xxxx	51.45	36.85	.00	36.85	
						sub total:	97.50
DELL D0120	99215	06-29-xxxx	193.99	161.09	16.10	144.99	
	85641	06-29-xxxx	25.20	17.12	.00	17.12	
	81000	06-29-xxxx	21.00	16.05	.00	16.05	
	36415	06-29-xxxx	6.04	5.37	.00	5.37	
						sub total:	183.53
ECHO E0340	45330	06-22-xxxx	241.24	217.96	.00	217.96	
						sub total:	217.96
FRANK F0560	85023	06-29-xxxx	36.75	28.96	.00	28.96	
	80002	06-29-xxxx	40.52	30.54	.00	30.54	
						sub total:	59.50
GRAY G0780	36415	06-24-xxxx	6.04	5.37	1.07	4.30	
						sub total:	4.30
HEATH H0900	76075	06-28-xxxx	253.05	185.15	.00	185.15	
	36415	06-28-xxxx	6.04	5.37	.00	5.37	
						sub total:	190.52
INCH	81000	06-22-xxxx	21.00	16.05	1.60	14.45	
						sub total:	14.45
JAVA	82270	06-22-xxxx	28.35	8.95	1.79	7.16	
						sub total:	7.16
KELLY	82270	06-28-xxxx	28.35	8.95	.00	8.95	
						sub total:	8.95

Check Date: 07-07-xxxx   Provider Code: 0 F3 7149   Page Total   1026.36

FOR INQUIRIES PLEASE USE YOUR ANY INSURANCE COMPANY TOLL FREE SERVICE NUMBER

FIGURE 7–9 Provider Explanation of Benefits. CPT © 2009 American Medical Association. All Rights Reserved.

ID NO	406-76-1759	DATE	JUN 08, 20xx

HEALTH CARE CLAIM SUMMARY

This summary shows claims processed for the insured of   Baril, Viola   ID NUMBER   406-7

Any payments shown were made during the period of   JUN 01, 20xx   through   JUN 08, 20xx

TOTAL CHARGES PROCESSED	$400.00

TOTAL PAID TO YOU	$.00	TOTAL PAID TO PROVIDER	$360.00

TOTAL AMOUNT NOT PAID	$40.00

This amount is the sum of the LESS DEDUCTIBLE column plus the AMOUNT NOT PAID column

PLEASE REFER TO THE CODES IN THE EXPL COLUMN AND THEIR EXPLANATIONS.

CLAIM NUMBER	PATIENT	PROVIDER (PROV)	TYPE OF SERVICE	SERVICE DATES FROM	TO	TOTAL CHARGES	BASIC PAYS YOU OR PROVIDER	ELIGIBLE CHARGES	MAJOR MEDICAL LESS DEDUCT-IBLE	PAYS YOU OR PROVIDER	AMOUNT NOT PAID
8138064538	BARIL	H. Sleeper	ANESTHESIA	040300	040300	400.00		400.00		360.00PROV	40.00
						400.00	.00PROV	400.00	.00	360.00PROV	40.00

IF YOUR BENEFIT SUMMARY INCLUDES CHARGES YOU DON'T RECOGNIZE, IT COULD BE THE RESULT OF A MISHANDLED OR FRAUDULENT CLAIM. PLEASE NOTIFY YOUR CUSTOMER SERVICE REPRESENTATIVE.

EXPLANATION:
872 THIS AMOUNT IS THE COINSURANCE (SHARE) THAT IS YOUR RESPONSIBILITY UNDER YOUR POLICY

THIS IS NOT A BILL

FOR CUSTOMER ASSISTANCE CALL TOLL FREE 1-800-553-2084
SEND WRITTEN INQUIRIES TO: ANTHEM INSURANCE COMPANIES, INC, PO BOX 590, GREENWOOD IN 46142-0590

DEAR INSURED: This summary of claims received on behalf of you and any other persons covered under your policy. We are providing it to you to help you better understand how your coverage is working to protect you.

CONTACT US AT THE PHONE OR ADDRESS SHOWN ABOVE:
IF YOU HAVE MOVED; we will correct your address.
IF YOUR IDENTIFICATION CARD HAS BEEN LOST OR STOLEN; we will replace it.
IF YOU HAVE ANY QUESTIONS ABOUT THIS CLAIM SUMMARY OR YOUR COVERAGE; we will be glad to answer them.

ADDITIONAL REMINDERS:
• WE CANNOT RETURN ANY PAPERS YOU SEND US. If you need to send us this summary or any other papers, please make photocopies beforehand. You may need them for income tax purposes.
• YOU HAVE THE RIGHT TO APPEAL ANY CLAIM WE DON'T PAY OR PAY ONLY IN PART. Mail us a request to review your claim within sixty (60) days of the date you received this summary.

32N-0233 r3(09-90) D

Delmar/Cengage Learning

FIGURE 7–10 Sample Explanation of Benefits

When an insurance company sends a remittance check and EOB to the provider, the billing specialist enters the payments into the billing system. Claims that are paid on the first submission are often called **clean claims**. Unfortunately, all insurance claims do not fall into this category. The billing specialist must work with a variety of problem claims.

Problem Claims

Problem claims include denied and delinquent claims. Claims that are denied or rejected are often called **dirty claims**. Reasons for denied claims fall into two categories: technical errors and insurance policy coverage issues. Technical errors include missing or incorrect information. Common errors or omissions include:

- Transposed numbers
- Incorrect patient insurance identification number
- Incorrect or incomplete CPT or ICD-9-CM codes
- Incorrect or inconsistent dates of service
- Incorrect year of service
- Missing information such as place of service, provider address, or identification
- Mathematical errors

These types of errors are easily corrected, and the claim can be resubmitted.

Denials based on insurance policy coverage issues are more complex and often require involving the patient in the resolution of the problem. Denied claims are usually related to insurance coverage issues, which may include the following:

- The service rendered is not covered by the policy.
- The patient was not covered by the policy at the time the service was rendered.
- The service was related to a pre-existing condition not covered by the policy.
- The insurance carrier determines that the service was not medically necessary.
- Precertification was required and was not obtained.

When a claim is denied, the billing specialist contacts the insurance carrier to find out if additional steps must be taken in order for the claim to be paid. The insurance carrier may request additional documentation to support the medical necessity of the service or may direct the billing specialist to submit a written appeal. The billing specialist complies with the insurance carrier's instructions and resubmits the claim.

If a claim is denied because the service is not covered by the policy or because the patient was not covered when the service was rendered, the billing specialist notifies the patient that the claim was denied. A phone call, followed by written notification that includes a copy of the claims denial, alerts the patient that the charges may be billed to the patient. The insurance company also notifies the patient that a claim has been denied and the reason for denial.

Delinquent claims, also called **pending claims**, are those claims that are neither rejected nor denied but for which payment is overdue. The most common reason for a pending claim is that the claim is lost or misplaced. Paper claims can be lost in the mail. Electronic claims can be lost because of transmission problems, computer hardware and software problems, or electrical power outages. The claim can even be lost once it has reached the insurance carrier.

When the billing specialist identifies a delinquent claim, the insurance company is queried as to the status of the claim. The inquiry is made by phone, electronically (e-mail), or in writing. Written inquiries may be submitted by using an insurance claim tracer form, as shown in Figure 7–11.

An electronic or written inquiry must include a copy of the original claim. The insurance carrier is obligated to respond to inquiries about delinquent claims.

INSURANCE COMPANY_____ DATE _____

ADDRESS:_____

PATIENT NAME_____ NAME OF INSURED_____

IDENTIFICATION NUMBER_____

EMPLOYER NAME & ADDRESS_____

DATE CLAIM FILED_____ CLAIM AMOUNT_____

Attached is a copy of the original claim submitted to you on _____. We have not yet received a request for additional information and still await payment of this claim. Please review the attached duplicate and process it for payment.

If there are any questions regarding this claim, please answer the following and return this letter to our office.

IF CLAIM HAS BEEN PAID:

        Date of payment: _____

        Amount of payment: _____

        Payment made to: _____

IF CLAIM HAS BEEN DENIED:

        Reason for denial: _____

                           _____

        Has the patient been notified?   ☐ Yes   ☐ No

IF CLAIM IS STILL PENDING:

        Please state reason why.

        _____

        _____

Sincerely,

Judy Jolly, **CMA**
Insurance Specialist

Delmar/Cengage Learning

FIGURE 7–11 Insurance Claims Tracer

State Insurance Commission

Insurance carrier business practices are subject to both state and federal laws. These laws range from compliance with fair employment practices to paying benefits in a timely fashion. Each state has a department or agency, often called the State Insurance Commission, responsible for monitoring insurance company activities. Responsibilities of the State Insurance Commission include the following:

- Monitoring the financial strength of insurance companies
- Protecting the interests of the insured and policyholders
- Verifying that insurance contracts are executed in good faith

- Releasing information about the number of complaints that are filed against a specific insurance company in a year
- Resolving insurance conflicts

The head of the agency is usually called the state insurance commissioner.

The insurance billing specialist has an interest in the role of the state insurance commissioner as related to benefit payments. If a provider consistently has problems obtaining reimbursement from a particular insurance carrier and all direct attempts to resolve the problem fail, the billing specialist may file a formal complaint with the State Insurance Commission. Types of problems that should be referred to the State Insurance Commission are

- The improper denial, delay, or reduction of payment for services
- The inability of two insurance carriers to reach an agreement about primary payer status

The provider or the patient may submit a written request or complaint to the insurance commissioner. In some states, the request or complaint must come from the insured or patient. The billing specialist may assist the insured or patient in this process. The request should include the following information:

- The name, address, and telephone number of the person submitting the request or complaint
- The name, address, and telephone number of the insured and the patient
- The name and address of the insurance company
- The name, address, and telephone number of the insurance agent, if known
- The dates the insurance coverage was in effect
- A copy of the policy, if possible
- A narrative description of the problem, including the date the claim was submitted
- Copies of related correspondence

If the billing specialist assists the patient in preparing the complaint, the patient or the insured should sign the cover letter.

Insurance companies are highly motivated to avoid insurance commission complaints and usually work directly with the provider, patient, or insured to resolve delinquent claim problems. A high number of complaints or requests for review will negatively affect an insurance company's ability to do business in a given state. Most insurance billing specialists can work their entire careers without ever becoming involved with the insurance commission complaint process.

REINFORCEMENT EXERCISES 7–4

Provide a short answer for each item.

1. What is the CMS-1500?

_____

_____

_____

continued on the next page

continued from the previous page

2. Name the two sections of the CMS-1500.

_____

_____

_____

3. Briefly describe the phrase "allowed charge."

_____

_____

_____

4. What is the purpose of an EOB?

_____

_____

_____

5. List five items that are included on an insurance claim follow-up file.

_____

_____

_____

_____

6. List three reasons why an insurance claim may be denied.

_____

_____

_____

7. Briefly describe the role of the state insurance commission.

_____

_____

_____

Fill in the blank with the correct term or phrase.

1. Claims that are paid on the first submission are called _____.

2. Claims that are denied or rejected are called _____.

3. Claims that have no action taken are called _____.

4. CMS is the abbreviation for _____.

5. _____ are assigned to all diagnoses, tests, and procedures.

ABBREVIATIONS

Table 7–4 lists the abbreviations in this chapter.

TABLE 7–4

Abbreviations and Meanings	
Abbreviation	Meaning
CMS	Centers for Medicare and Medicaid Services
EHR	electronic health record
EIN	employer identification number
EMR	electronic medical record
EOB	explanation of benefits
NPI	national provider identification (number)
RA	remittance advice
SSN	social security number

SUMMARY

Although the health care industry exists primarily to provide health and medical services to patients, the industry must remain solvent. Insurance claim processing is one way health care agencies receive payment for services rendered. Processing claims is a service provided to the patient. The three general activities associated with developing an insurance claim are patient registration, clinical assessment and treatment, and patient departure procedures. The patient's medical and financial records, registration form, and encounter form are the source documents for insurance claim processing. The CMS-1500 is a standardized form used to submit health insurance claims.

Once a claim has been received and accepted, the insurance carrier generates an explanation of benefits (EOB). Both the patient and the provider receive an EOB, which explains how the insurance carrier determined the amount paid for the services rendered. The insurance billing specialist maintains an insurance claim register, which is used to keep track of the payment status of insurance claims.

REVIEW EXERCISES

Write a brief definition for each term or answer the question.

1. Co-payment

_____

_____

_____

2. Transaction journal

_____

_____

_____

3. Encounter form

_____

_____

_____

4. New patient

_____

_____

_____

5. Patient account ledger

_____

_____

_____

6. Patient registration form

_____

_____

_____

7. Pending or delinquent claims

_____

_____

_____

8. List three reasons why a claim may be rejected.

_____

_____

_____

9. Describe the insurance coverage issues that may result in denied claims.

_____

_____

_____

10. Arrange the patient registration activities in chronological order. Place number 1 by the first step, 2 by the second, and so on.

a. _____ Check the registration form for unanswered questions.

b. _____ Copy the front and back of the insurance card.

c. _____ Obtain authorization to bill the insurance company.

d. _____ The patient fills out the registration form.

e. _____ The patient signs authorization to obtain previous medical records.

f. _____ Review the payment policy.

11. Arrange the patient departure activities in chronological order. Place number 1 by the first step, 2 by the second, and so on.

a. _____ Assign numeric codes to procedures and diagnoses.

b. _____ Collect the payment from the patient.

c. _____ Enter the total charges on the encounter form.

d. _____ Generate the insurance claim form.

e. _____ Post charges and payments to the day sheet.

f. _____ Post charges and payments to the patient's account ledger.

g. _____ The provider authenticates the claim form.

h. _____ Schedule another appointment if necessary.

i. _____ Submit the claim form to the insurance company.

Fill in the blank with the appropriate term.

1. The _____ is a standardized insurance claim form.

2. An insurance company document that describes the amount paid for services rendered is called a(n) _____.

3. The _____ is the maximum amount the insurance carrier pays for a service.

4. Another term for the provider's EOB is _____.

5. A _____ is a specific amount a patient with health insurance must pay for a service.

Write True or False on the line following each statement.

1. Diagnostic codes are seldom included on the CMS-1500. _____

2. An insurance ID card is a valuable source document. _____

3. Secondary insurance policy information should be included on the CMS-1500.

_____

4. Authentication ensures that all codes are accurate. _____

5. An insurance claim is paid within 30 days. _____

6. The insurance carrier reviews each claim for errors. _____

7. An allowed charge is the maximum amount the insurance company pays for a service. _____

8. Both the patient and the provider receive an explanation of benefits (EOB). _____

9. Insurance information must be retained indefinitely. _____

CHALLENGE EXERCISES

1. Develop a telephone procedure that includes the types of questions the receptionist should ask a new patient.
2. Review an explanation of benefits that has been sent to you or a family member. Is the EOB easy to read and understand? Is it clearly marked "This Is Not a Bill"? How would you improve the EOB?

WEBSITE

Centers for Medicare and Medicaid Services: www.cms.hhs.gov/CMSForms

CHAPTER 8

Common CMS-1500 Completion Guidelines

LEARNING OBJECTIVES

Upon successfully completing this chapter, the reader should have the knowledge to:

1. Accurately complete the CMS-1500 data fields.
2. List 10 guidelines for submitting optically scanned CMS-1500 claim forms.
3. Describe seven common errors that are made when completing the CMS-1500.
4. Abstract information from a case study to complete the CMS-1500 form.

KEY TERMS

CMS-1500
Early and Periodic Screening for Diagnosis and Treatment (EPSDT)
Employer identification number (EIN)

Federal Employees' Compensation Act (FECA)
Last menstrual period (LMP)

National provider identification (NPI)
Signature on File (SOF)
Social security number (SSN)

OVERVIEW

The **CMS-1500** is an insurance billing form that is used by physicians, other health care providers, and medical suppliers to submit claims for services or items provided to patients who are not hospitalized. The CMS-1500 is accepted by Medicare, Medicaid, TRICARE/CHAMPUS (Office of Civilian Health and Medical Programs of the Uniformed Services), CHAMPVA (Civilian Health and Medical Programs of the Department of Veterans Affairs), **FECA (Federal Employees' Compensation Act)**, and most private insurance companies. Figure 8–1 is an example of the CMS-1500.

Chapter 7 introduced the CMS-1500 and briefly described the data items included on the form. This chapter provides detailed guidelines for completing the form. These guidelines are common to most commercial health insurance companies, such as Aetna, United Health Care, Prudential,

FIGURE 8–1 Sample CMS-1500 (For instructional use only. Courtesy of the Centers for Medicare and Medicaid Services, www.cms.hhs.gov)

Cigna, and others. Instructions for government insurance programs, Blue Cross/BlueShield, and workers' compensation cases are presented in separate chapters.

Accurate data entry skills and attention to detail are essential for completing the CMS-1500. Filing guidelines for the CMS-1500 claim form are subject to change. The insurance billing specialist must obtain and read updated billing manuals, newsletters, and brochures that explain the changes as they become effective. Filing claims according to outdated guidelines results in denied claims or delayed reimbursement.

OPTICAL SCANNING GUIDELINES

The CMS-1500 is printed in red to allow for optical scanning. In order for insurance carriers to process the scannable CMS-1500, data must be entered according to the following guidelines:

- All data must be entered within the borders of each field (box).
- Data should be typed (or keyed). For paper claims submission, provider and patient signatures are acceptable.
- Enter all alphabetic characters in uppercase letters.
- Enter a space for the following, which are preprinted on the form:
  - Dollar sign or decimal in all charges or totals
  - Decimal point in a diagnosis code number, except for E codes
  - Parentheses surrounding the area code in a telephone number
- Enter commas between the patient or policyholder's last name, first name, and middle initial. This guideline applies to optical scanning. Most electronic claims software does not require commas.
- Enter two zeros in the cents column of monetary fields when the fee or charge is in whole dollars.
- Enter birth dates as an eight-digit number with spaces between the digits for the month, date, and year; two digits are used for the month and date, and four digits are used for the year (MM DD YYYY). Entering a space between the sets of digits keeps the numbers within the designated block or field. This guideline applies to optical scanning. Most electronic claims software does not require spaces between digits.
- Enter other dates as six- or eight-digit numbers as directed by the insurance carrier. Six-digit dates are entered as MMDDYY (two-digit month, two-digit date, and two-digit year). Eight-digit dates are entered as MMDDYYYY (two-digit month, two-digit date, and four-digit year). Spaces between sets of number may or may not be required.
- Do not key the letter O for the number zero.
- Do not enter a hyphen between CPT and HCPCS code and a modifier. Enter a space between the code and modifier. If multiple modifiers are used, enter a space between modifiers.
- Do not enter hyphens or spaces in a **social security number (SSN)** or in an **employer identification number (EIN)**.
- Do not use punctuation in the names entered on the form, except for a hyphenated last name, which is known as a compound name.

Do not use designations of birth order (e.g., Jr., III) unless such designations are on the patient's insurance ID card.

CMS-1500 GUIDELINES

Instructions for completing the CMS-1500 are divided into two major categories: (1) patient information and (2) treatment and provider information. Each section of the CMS-1500 is highlighted in a figure that corresponds to the discussion of the section. Refer to the figures as you read the explanation. Because most claims are now filed electronically, the following guidelines do *not* include commas between names or spaces between dates.

CMS-1500 PATIENT INFORMATION

The first 13 CMS-1500 blocks or fields capture information about the patient and the patient's health insurance policy. Figure 8–2 shows the top of the form, including blocks 1 and 1a.

Block 1: Insurance Plan

Enter an X in the box that describes the type of insurance plan. Group Health Plan and Other are used to identify most private and commercial insurance programs. Medicare, Medicaid, TRICARE /CHAMPUS, CHAMPVA, and FECA/Black Lung are government-sponsored programs.

Block 1a: Insured's I.D. Number

Enter the health insurance identification number as it appears on the patient's insurance card. Do not enter hyphens or spaces in the number.

Blocks 2 through 8 capture patient and insured identification information. The patient and the insured may or may not be the same individual. When the patient is a dependent child, the insured is the name of the individual who has the insurance policy that covers the child. A wife covered by her husband's health plan is listed as the patient, and the insured is her husband. When the patient is the individual who has the insurance policy, then the patient and the insured are the same. Figure 8–3 highlights blocks 2 through 8.

FIGURE 8–2 Blocks 1 and 1a CMS-1500 (For instructional use only. Courtesy of the Centers for Medicare and Medicaid Services, www.cms.hhs.gov)

FIGURE 8–3 CMS-1500 Blocks 2–8 (For instructional use only. Courtesy of the Centers for Medicare and Medicaid Services, www.cms.hhs.gov)

Block 2: Patient's Name

Enter the patient's last name, first name, and middle initial in uppercase letters. Do not include titles or birth designations such as Sr. or Jr. unless the patient's insurance ID has that information.

Block 3: Patient's Birth Date and Sex (Gender)

Enter the patient's eight-digit birth date as MMDDYYYY. Enter an X in the appropriate box to indicate male or female. If the patient's gender is unknown, leave blank.

Block 4: Insured's Name

Enter the insured's (policyholder's) last name, first name, and middle initial. Some insurance companies allow you to enter SAME in block 4 when the patient and the insured are the same person, some will not. To be certain of acceptance by all carriers, enter Insured's Information again in block 4.

Block 5: Patient's Address

Enter the patient's mailing address and ZIP code. Enter a hyphen to separate the first five and last four numbers of a nine-digit ZIP code. Enter the patient's telephone number. Do not put parentheses around the area code. The area code may automatically fill the preprinted parentheses.

Block 6: Patient Relationship to Insured

Enter an X in the appropriate box to indicate the patient's relationship to the insured: Self when the patient and insured are the same person; Spouse when the patient is married to the insured; Child when the patient is the child or stepchild of the insured; and Other if the patient is the insured's unmarried domestic partner.

Block 7: Insured's Address

Enter the insured's (policyholder's) full address. Some commercial insurance companies allow you to enter SAME in block 7 when the patient's and insured's address are the same.

Block 8: Patient Status

Enter an X in the box that indicates the patient's marital status. If the patient is an unmarried domestic partner, enter an X in Other.

Enter an X in Employed if the patient has a job. Enter an X in the appropriate box to indicate the patient's status as a student. Student status, full- or part-time, applies to patients between the ages of 19 and 23 who are the insured's dependents. Some insurance policies cover only full-time students. The insurance company may require written acknowledgment of the student's status from the school, college, or university.

If the patient is unemployed and/or not a full- or part-time student, leave blank.

Blocks 9–11: Other Insured's Name; Is Patient Condition Related To; Insured's Policy Group or FECA Number

Block 9 is completed when the patient is covered by more than one health insurance plan. Blocks 10 and 11 are completed for all patients. Figure 8–4 shows blocks 9 through 11.

Blocks 9–9d: Other Insured's Name; Policy Number; Date of Birth; Employer's or School Name; Insurance Plan Name or Program Name

Blocks 9–9d are completed when the patient is covered by more than one health insurance policy. The secondary (or supplemental) insurance policy information is entered in Blocks 9–9d. If there is no secondary or supplemental insurance policy, leave blocks 9–9d blank.

<table>
<tr>
<td colspan="2">

9. OTHER INSURED'S NAME (Last Name, First Name, Middle Initial)

BARIL, PHILIP, L

</td>
<td colspan="2">10. IS PATIENT'S CONDITION RELATED TO:</td>
<td colspan="2">

11. INSURED'S POLICY GROUP OR FECA NUMBER

51000

</td>
</tr>
<tr>
<td colspan="2">

a. OTHER INSURED'S POLICY OR GROUP NUMBER

89000

</td>
<td colspan="2">

a. EMPLOYMENT? (Current or Previous)

☐ YES ☒ NO

</td>
<td colspan="2">

a. INSURED'S DATE OF BIRTH   SEX
MM | DD | YY
12 | 15 | 1960   M☐   F☒

</td>
</tr>
<tr>
<td colspan="2">

b. OTHER INSURED'S DATE OF BIRTH   SEX
MM | DD | YY
10 | 30 | 1959   M☒   F☐

</td>
<td colspan="2">

b. AUTO ACCIDENT?   PLACE (State)

☐ YES ☒ NO ____

</td>
<td colspan="2">

b. EMPLOYER'S NAME OR SCHOOL NAME

NORTH WEST INDUSTRY

</td>
</tr>
<tr>
<td colspan="2">

c. EMPLOYER'S NAME OR SCHOOL NAME

BELL MEDICAL

</td>
<td colspan="2">

c. OTHER ACCIDENT?

☐ YES ☒ NO

</td>
<td colspan="2">

c. INSURANCE PLAN NAME OR PROGRAM NAME

CIGNA

</td>
</tr>
<tr>
<td colspan="2">

d. INSURANCE PLAN NAME OR PROGRAM NAME

AETNA

</td>
<td colspan="2">10d. RESERVED FOR LOCAL USE</td>
<td colspan="2">

d. IS THERE ANOTHER HEALTH BENEFIT PLAN?

☒ YES   ☐ NO   **If yes,** return to and complete item 9 a-d.

</td>
</tr>
</table>

FIGURE 8–4 CMS-1500 Blocks 9–11 (For instructional use only. Courtesy of the Centers for Medicare and Medicaid Services, www.cms.hhs.gov)

Block 9: Other Insured's Name

Enter the insured's (policyholder's) last name, first name, and middle initial.

Block 9a: Other Insured's Policy or Group Number

Enter the policy or group number.

Block 9b: Other Insured's Birth Date

Enter the insured's (policyholder's) eight-digit birth date as MMDDYYYY. Enter an X in the appropriate box to indicate the policyholder's gender. If the gender is unknown, leave this blank.

Block 9c: Employer's Name or School Name

Enter the insured's (policyholder's) employer name, if employed. If the insured is unemployed and a full- or part-time student, enter the name of the school. Otherwise, leave this blank.

Block 9d: Insurance Plan Name or Program Name

Enter the name of the secondary or supplemental health insurance plan.

Blocks 10–10d: Is Patient's Condition Related To

Enter an X in the appropriate box to indicate if the patient's condition is related to work, an auto accident, or other accident.

Block 10a: Employment? (Current or Previous)

Enter an X in YES if the condition is work-related; otherwise, enter an X in NO. A work-related injury falls under workers' compensation insurance.

Block 10b: Auto Accident? Place (State)

Enter an X in YES if the condition is the result of an automobile accident; otherwise, enter an X in NO. If yes, enter the two-character abbreviation for the state of the patient's residence. Treatment of injuries sustained during an auto accident may be billed to the automobile insurance company.

Block 10c: Other Accident

Enter an X in YES if the condition is a result of an accident not related to employment or automobile; otherwise, enter an X in NO. Payment for treating injuries sustained on private or business properties may be the responsibility of a homeowner's or business insurance policy.

EXAMPLE A: HOMEOWNERS INSURANCE

At a neighborhood picnic, Janelle's three-year-old son falls off the neighbor's jungle gym and sustains a broken arm. The neighbor's homeowner's insurance may be liable for medical expenses related to the child's injury.

EXAMPLE B: BUSINESS INSURANCE

Mr. Howard slips on the ice in front of the local department store and sustains a sprained ankle. The store's liability insurance may be liable for medical expenses related to treating Mr. Howard's injury.

Block 10d: Reserved For Local Use

Leave this blank.

Block 11–11d: Insured's Policy Group Number or FECA Number; Insured's Date of Birth; Employer's Name or School Name; Insurance Plan Name or Program; Is There Another Health Benefit Plan?

Blocks 11–11c are used to gather additional information about the insured's (the individual (the individual named in block 4) health insurance policy. Block 11d. identifies whether or not the patient is covered by another insurance plan.

Block 11: Insured's Policy Group or FECA Number

Enter the insured's (named in block 4) health insurance policy number or group number. Do not enter hyphens or spaces in the policy or group number.

Enter the Federal Employees' Compensation Act (FECA) number, if applicable. The FECA number is assigned to a patient who is covered by the workers' compensation program for individuals employed by the federal government.

EXAMPLE

Coal miners with black lung disease and the federal workers injured in the 1995 Oklahoma City bombing tragedy are covered under FECA.

Block 11a: Insured's Date of Birth

Enter the insured's (named in block 4) eight-digit birth date as MM DD YYYY. Enter an X in the appropriate box to indicate the insured's gender. If the gender is unknown, leave this blank.

Block 11b: Employer Name or School Name

Enter the name of the insured's (named in block 4) employer, if employed. Enter the name of the school if the insured is unemployed and considered to be a full- or part-time student. Otherwise, leave this blank.

Block 11c: Insurance Plan Name or Program

Enter the name of the insured's (named in block 4) health insurance plan or program.

Block 11d: Is There Another Health Benefit Plan?

Enter an X in NO when the patient is covered by only one insurance plan. Enter an X in YES when the patient is covered by a secondary or supplemental health insurance plan. If YES is marked, blocks 9–9d must be completed.

Blocks 12 and 13: Patient Authorization

Blocks 12 and 13 document the patient's authorization to release information and assign insurance benefits to the provider. These blocks are shown in Figure 8–5.

12. PATIENT'S OR AUTHORIZED PERSON'S SIGNATURE I authorize the release of any medical or other information necessary to process this claim. I also request payment of government benefits either to myself or to the party who accepts assignment below.	13. INSURED'S OR AUTHORIZED PERSON'S SIGNATURE I authorize payment of medical benefits to the undersigned physician or supplier for services described below.
SIGNED SIGNATURE ON FILE DATE MM DD YY	SIGNED SIGNATURE ON FILE

READ BACK OF FORM BEFORE COMPLETING & SIGNING THIS FORM.

FIGURE 8–5 CMS-1500 Blocks 12 and 13 (For instructional use only. Courtesy of the Centers for Medicare and Medicaid Services, www.cms.hhs.gov)

Block 12: Patients or Authorized Persons Signature

The patient or authorized person's signature or the phrase SIGNATURE ON FILE must be entered to allow the release of medical information necessary for claims processing. SIGNATURE ON FILE means that the patient has signed an authorization form, which is kept on file.

Block 13: Insured's or Authorized Person's Signature

The insured's or authorized person's signature or the phrase SIGNATURE ON FILE must be entered to allow the insurance company to send payment directly to the provider.

REINFORCEMENT EXERCISES 8–1

Complete blocks 1–13 of the CMS-1500 form (Figure 8–6) by using the information on the patient registration form (Figure 8–7).

FIGURE 8–6 CMS-1500 Blocks 1–13 (For instructional use only. Courtesy of the Centers for Medicare and Medicaid Services, www.cms.hhs.gov)

FAMILY MD
800 Medical Drive
Anytown, ME 49855

PATIENT REGISTRATION

DATE: 06/04/20xx

PATIENT INFORMATION

PATIENT'S LAST NAME:	FIRST NAME:	MIDDLE INITIAL:	DOB:
HELLMAN	ABIGAIL	M.	10/30/19xx

PATIENT'S ADDRESS:	PHONE:
724 HENNEPIN ANYTOWN ME 49855	Home: (906) 555-2345 Work: (906) 555-3456

SINGLE: MARRIED: X WIDOWED:	MALE: FEMALE: X

OCCUPATION:	EMPLOYER/ADDRESS:	EMPLOYER PHONE:
TEACHER	ANYTOWN ELEMENTARY SCHOOL 301 W. SPRUCE ANYTOWN, ME 49855	(906) 555-3456

EMERGENCY CONTACT:	RELATIONSHIP TO PATIENT:	PHONE:
PAUL HELLMAN	SPOUSE	(906) 555-2345 (906) 250-6066

REASON FOR TODAY'S VISIT:

SORE THROAT

WORK RELATED INJURY/ILLNESS? YES: NO: X DATE:	AUTO ACCIDENT? YES: NO: X DATE:	OTHER ACCIDENT? YES: NO: X DATE:

INSURANCE INFORMATION

INSURANCE CO.	GROUP NO:
AETNA	87000

INSURED'S NAME:	INSURED'S ID NO:	RELATIONSHIP TO INSURED:
ABIGAIL M. HELLMAN	**503529750**	SELF: X SPOUSE: CHILD: OTHER:

INSURED'S ADDRESS:	INSURED'S PHONE:
SAME	SAME

OTHER INSURANCE

SECONDARY INSURANCE:	GROUP NO:	ID NUMBER:	EMPLOYER:
CIGNA	89000	614630861	QUALITY CONTRACTORS

OTHER INSURED'S NAME:	OTHER INSURED'S DOB:	RELATIONSHIP TO PATIENT:
PAUL HELLMAN	11/12/19xx	SPOUSE

OTHER INSURED'S ADDRESS:	OTHER INSURED'S PHONE:
SAME	(H) (906) 555-2345 (W) (906) 250-6066

AUTHORIZATION

I hereby authorize my insurance company benefits to be paid directly to the physician. I realize that I am responsible to pay for any non-covered services. I hereby authorize the release of pertinent medical information to the insurance company.

Patient/Legal Representative Signature: **Date:**

Delmar/Cengage Learning

FIGURE 8–7 Patient Registration Form

CMS-1500 TREATMENT AND PROVIDER INFORMATION

Treatment and provider information begins with block 14, Date of Current Illness, and continues through block 33, Billing Provider Info & PH #. Diagnostic and treatment information must be supported by documentation in the patient's medical record. Insurance carriers closely monitor diagnosis and treatment codes. Inconsistencies, errors, or questionable codes result in delayed processing or denied payment. In the worst-case scenario, coding errors may lead to fraud or abuse investigations.

Blocks 14, 15, 16, and 18 refer to dates related to the onset of illness, hospitalization, and the estimated time a patient is unable to work. Figure 8–8 shows blocks 14 through 18.

Block 14: Date of Current: Illness (First symptom) OR Injury (Accident) OR Pregnancy (LMP)

Block 14 is used in four different ways: (1) Date of Current Illness—enter the date of the current episode of care or service; (2) First Symptom—enter the date that the symptoms of the current illness/problem first appeared; (3) Injury—for workers' compensation and other problems that resulted form an accident, enter the date that the injury first occurred; (4) Pregnancy (LMP)—enter the date of the patient's **last menstrual period (LMP)**. The patient's medical record is the source document for dates related to first symptom, injury, or pregnancy. The date is entered as an eight-digit (MMDDYYYY) or six-digit (MMDDYY) number, depending on insurance carrier preference.

> **EXAMPLE**
>
> First Symptom: A note dated 3/8/20YY states that the patient exhibited symptoms two months ago. The date of current illness (first symptom) is 010820YY.
>
> For a sprained wrist sustained after falling off a jungle gym two weeks ago." The date of current injury is 060520YY.
>
> Pregnancy (LMP): A note dated 7/20/20YY states that "the patient is seen today to confirm pregnancy. LMP was 5/20/20YY. The date of LMP is 052020YY.

Block 15: If Patient Has Had Same or Similar Illness, Give First Date

Enter the date, either six or eight digits, if the patient has had the same or similar illness and the previous illness is documented in the patient's record. Otherwise, leave this blank. Previous pregnancies are not a similar illness.

Block 16: Dates Patient Unable to Work In Current Occupation

Enter the date, either six or eight digits, that the patient is/was unable to work in his or her current occupation. Otherwise, leave this blank. Block 16 is especially significant for short- or long-term disability claims.

14. DATE OF CURRENT: ILLNESS (First symptom) OR INJURY (Accident) OR PREGNANCY (LMP) MM DD YY 06 12 20YY	15. IF PATIENT HAS HAD SAME OR SIMILAR ILLNESS, GIVE FIRST DATE MM DD YY	16. DATES PATIENT UNABLE TO WORK IN CURRENT OCCUPATION MM DD YY MM DD YY FROM TO
17. NAME OF REFERRING PROVIDER OR OTHER SOURCE	17a. 17b. NPI	18. HOSPITALIZATION DATES RELATED TO CURRENT SERVICES MM DD YY MM DD YY FROM TO

FIGURE 8–8 CMS-1500 Blocks 14, 15, 16, and 18 (For instructional use only. Courtesy of the Centers for Medicare and Medicaid Services, www.cms.hhs.gov)

17. NAME OF REFERRING PROVIDER OR OTHER SOURCE	17a.		18. HOSPITALIZATION DATES RELATED TO CURRENT SERVICES
ROBERT CIMA MD	17b. NPI 1234567890		FROM MM DD YY TO MM DD YY
19. RESERVED FOR LOCAL USE			20. OUTSIDE LAB? $ CHARGES
			[X] YES [ ] NO 300 00

FIGURE 8–9 CMS-1500 Blocks 17, 19, and 20 (For instructional use only. Courtesy of the Centers for Medicare and Medicaid Services, www.cms.hhs.gov)

Block 18: Hospitalization Dates Related to Current Services

Enter the hospital admission (FROM) and discharge (TO) dates, either six or eight digits, if the patient received inpatient services (e.g., hospital, skilled nursing facility). If the patient has not been discharged at the time the claim is submitted, leave the discharge date (TO) blank. If there is no hospitalization related to the current services, leave this blank.

Blocks 17, 19, and 20

Blocks 17, 19, and 20 are used to record information about a referring provider, specific local or insurance carrier data, and outside laboratory services. Figure 8–9 shows these blocks.

Block 17: Name of Referring Provider or Other Source

Enter the first name, middle initial (if known), last name, and credentials of the professional who referred or ordered health care services or supplies reported on the claim. Do not use punctuation. If there is no referring provider, leave this blank.

Block 17a (no title, shaded):

This block is used when the insurance carrier or other entity assigns a unique identifier to provider. Enter the unique identifier for the provider entered in block 17. In many cases, block 17a is left blank. A unique identifier may be an **employer identification number (EIN)** or a **physician/provider identification number (PIN)** assigned by the insurance company.

Block 17b: NPI (unshaded)

Enter the 10-digit national provider identifier (NPI) of the provider entered in block 17. Otherwise, leave this blank. CMS developed a **national provider identification (NPI)** number for all providers who submit claims to government-sponsored health insurance programs. Non-government health insurance carriers may also require the NPI.

Block 19: Reserved For Local Use

Block 19 is often left blank.

Block 20: Outside Lab?

Enter an X in the NO box if all laboratory procedures reported on the claim were performed in the provider's office. Enter an X in the YES box if the laboratory procedures reported on the claim were performed by an outside laboratory and billed to the provider.

When YES is checked, enter the total amount charged by the outside laboratory in $ CHARGES. Enter the outside laboratory's name, mailing address, and NPI in blocks 32 and 32a, respectively. If the outside laboratory has an identification number other than the NPI, enter that number in block 32b.

21. DIAGNOSIS OR NATURE OF ILLNESS OR INJURY (Relate Items 1, 2, 3, or 4 to Item 24E by Line)		22. MEDICAID RESUBMISSION CODE	ORIGINAL REF. NO.
1. |491 .21	3. |485 .__		
2. |788 .1	4. |__ .__	23. PRIOR AUTHORIZATION NUMBER	

FIGURE 8–10 CMS-1500 Blocks 21, 22, and 23 (For instructional use only. Courtesy of the Centers for Medicare and Medicaid Services, www.cms.hhs.gov)

Block 21: Diagnosis or Nature of Illness or Injury (Relate Items 1, 2, 3 or 4 to Item 24E by Line)

Block 21 is used to record ICD-9-CM diagnosis codes. Figure 8–10 illustrates block 21.

Enter ICD-9-CM (or current ICD) diagnosis codes as follows: 1. First-listed (primary) diagnosis code; and other diagnoses in items 2 through 4. All codes are entered to the highest degree of specificity. Enter the fourth and fifth digit, when applicable, to the right of the preprinted period in items 1 through 4. Each service/treatment code entered in Block 24D must be related to at least one of the diagnosis codes in block 21.

Block 22: Medicaid Resubmission Code

Leave this blank. Reserved for Medicaid claims. See Figure 8–10.

Block 23: Prior Authorization Number

This block is used when the patient must obtain preauthorization from an insurance program representative in order for the insurance carrier to pay the claim. Managed care health insurance plans often require preauthorization for elective or unusually expensive services or procedures. Enter the prior authorization number or leave this blank. See Figure 8–10.

REINFORCEMENT EXERCISES 8–2

Read the following progress note and complete blocks 14–23 of the CMS-1500 (Figure 8–11). Use June 12, 20YY, as the date of service.

PROGRESS NOTE: Viola is seen today for a sore throat that first presented three days ago. The patient has a low-grade fever of 100.2°F. Physical examination was essentially normal with the exception of an inflamed throat. Swab culture was taken and confirmed the presence of streptococcus for a diagnosis of streptococcal pharyngitis. Erythromycin was prescribed. The patient is to return in 10 days for follow-up. Office visit code is 99212. Signed by: Roberta Pharyngeal, MD.

DIAGNOSIS CODE: Streptococcal pharyngitis, 034.0.

CPT CODE: Throat culture, 87081.

14. DATE OF CURRENT: ILLNESS (First symptom) OR INJURY (Accident) OR PREGNANCY (LMP) MM DD YY	15. IF PATIENT HAS HAD SAME OR SIMILAR ILLNESS, GIVE FIRST DATE MM DD YY	16. DATES PATIENT UNABLE TO WORK IN CURRENT OCCUPATION MM DD YY MM DD YY FROM TO
17. NAME OF REFERRING PROVIDER OR OTHER SOURCE	17a. 17b. NPI	18. HOSPITALIZATION DATES RELATED TO CURRENT SERVICES MM DD YY MM DD YY FROM TO
19. RESERVED FOR LOCAL USE		20. OUTSIDE LAB? $ CHARGES ☐ YES ☐ NO
21. DIAGNOSIS OR NATURE OF ILLNESS OR INJURY (Relate Items 1, 2, 3, or 4 to Item 24E by Line) 1. |__ .__ 3. |__ .__		22. MEDICAID RESUBMISSION CODE ORIGINAL REF. NO.
2. |__ .__ 4. |__ .__		23. PRIOR AUTHORIZATION NUMBER

FIGURE 8–11 CMS-1500 Blocks 14–23 (For instructional use only. Courtesy of the Centers for Medicare and Medicaid Services, www.cms.hhs.gov)

FIGURE 8–12 CMS-1500 Block 24A–J (For instructional use only. Courtesy of the Centers for Medicare and Medicaid Services, www.cms.hhs.gov)

Blocks 24A–J: Dates of Service; Procedures; Charges; Miscellaneous

Blocks 24A–J is a multi-item block used to record the date, place, charge, and treatment codes for services rendered to the patient. Only six services can be submitted on one claim form. Complete each horizontal line (A–J) before entering data into the next line. Required fields in this block may vary by insurance carrier. Figure 8–12 illustrates one line of blocks 24A–J.

Block 24A: Dates of Service

Enter the date the procedure or service was performed in the From column. A six-digit date is entered as MMDDYY; an eight-digit date is entered as MMDDYYYY without spaces. When a specific service is provided on one date, insurance carriers may require the date to be entered in the From and To fields or only in the From field. When the same service is performed on consecutive days, insurance carriers usually require the range of dates to be entered in the From and To fields.

Block 24B: Place of Service

Enter the appropriate two-digit Place of Service (POS) code to identify where the patient received the service—e.g., a physician's office. Table 8–1 lists Place of Service codes.

Block 24C: EMG

Enter a Y (for yes) in this block when the patient receives emergency treatment. An emergency is usually defined as a condition or injury that without immediate treatment is likely to result in loss of life or serious impairment of organ structure or function. Otherwise, leave this blank. Receiving treatment in an emergency department does *not* in itself constitute an emergency.

Block 24D: Procedures, Services, or Supplies

Enter the CPT or HCPCS level II code, plus required modifiers as applicable, for the services or procedures performed on the date(s) included in block 24A. Four modifiers can be entered for each CPT/HCPCS code. Note the separate fields for CPT/HCPCS codes and four modifiers.

Block 24E: Diagnosis Code

Enter the diagnosis pointer number (1 through 4) from block 21 for the diagnosis that best justifies the medical necessity for the service listed in block 24D.

TABLE 8–1

CMS-1500 Place of Service Codes	
Place of Service	**Code**
Pharmacy	01
School	03
Homeless Shelter	04
Indian Health Service Free-Standing Facility	05
Indian Health Service Provider-Based Facility	06
Tribal 638 Free-Standing Facility	07
Tribal 638 Provider-Based Facility	08
Prison Correctional Facility	09
Provider's Office	11
Patient's Home	12
Assisted Living Facility	13
Group Home	14
Mobile Home	15
Urgent Care Facility	20
Inpatient Hospital	21
Outpatient Hospital	22
Emergency Room Hospital	23
Ambulatory Surgery Center	24
Birthing Center	25
Military Treatment Facility or Uniformed Service Treatment Facility	26
Skilled Nursing Facility	31
Nursing Facility	32
Custodial Care Facility	33
Hospice	34
Ambulance–Land	41
Ambulance–Air or Water	42
Independent Clinic	49
Federally Qualified Health Center	50
Inpatient Psychiatric Facility	51

continued on the next page

continued from the previous page

Psychiatric Facility–Partial Hospitalization	52
Community Mental Health Center	53
Intermediate Care Facility/Mentally Retarded	54
Residential Substance Abuse Treatment Center	55
Psychiatric Residential Treatment Center	56
Nonresidential Substance Abuse Treatment Facility	57
Mass Immunization Facility	60
Comprehensive Inpatient Rehabilitation Facility	61
Comprehensive Outpatient Rehabilitation Facility	62
End-Stage Renal Disease Treatment Facility	65
Public Health Clinic	71
Rural Health Clinic	72
Independent Laboratory	81
Other Places of Service	99

Block 24F: Charges

Enter the fee charged for each reported procedure or service. See Figure 8–12. When the same procedure is performed on consecutive days and reported on one line or when the same procedure is performed more than once during a single encounter, enter the total charges in block 24F. Do not enter commas, periods, or dollar signs. Do not enter negative amounts. Enter 00 in the cents area if the amount is a whole number.

EXAMPLE

Mrs. Britley is seen on three consecutive days for a brief office visit and receives a series of injections. The fee for each visit is $50. If these encounters are reported on one line of block 24, then the total charge of 150 00 is entered in block 24F.

EXAMPLE

Mr. Rodriguez provides three separate urine samples for three separate urinalysis tests over a period of 12 hours. The fee for each urinalysis is $25. The total charge of 75 00 is entered in block 24F.

Block 24G: Days or Units

Enter the number of days or units for procedures or services reported in block 24D. If just one procedure or service is reported in block 24D, enter a 1 in block 24G. Other considerations for completing block 24G include:

- Anesthesia services are reported as the number of minutes the patient received anesthesia. Therefore, two hours of anesthesia services are reported as 120 minutes in block 24G.
- Bilateral and multiple procedures are listed as individual procedures in block 24D and reported as one unit each in block 24G.

- Inclusive dates for the same service or procedure are reported in block 24G as the number of days identified in block 24A—Dates of Service, From and To. Therefore, brief office visits from January 1 to January 5 are reported as five units in block 24G.
- Identical radiology studies performed more than once during the same day are counted as individual units. Therefore, three chest x-rays taken on the same day are reported as three units in block 24G. Do not report the number of x-ray views taken for a specific radiology study. For example, a posteroanterior and lateral view of the chest, which is one chest x-ray with two views, is reported as one unit in block 24G.

Block 24H: EPSDT Family Plan (Early and Periodic Screening for Diagnosis and Treatment)

Leave this blank. This block is used to identify services provided under the Medicaid EPSDT program.

Block 24I: ID. QUAL. (shaded area)

Enter the provider's type of identification number as assigned by the insurance carrier. This may be a provider identification number (PIN), employer identification number (EIN), or another unique identification number. Otherwise, leave this blank.

NPI (national provider identification) is preprinted in the unshaded area of block 24I.

Block 24J: Rendering Provider ID # (shaded area)

Enter the provider's identification number as assigned by the insurance carrier. Otherwise, leave this blank.

Block 24J: Rendering Provider ID # NPI (unshaded area)

If the provider who performed the service is a member of a group practice, enter the provider's 10-digit NPI. Leave this blank if the provider is a solo practitioner. Other NPIs may be required, such as the NPI for an outside laboratory or durable medical equipment providers.

REINFORCEMENT EXERCISES 8–3

Use the following information to complete block 24A–24J of the CMS-1500 (Figure 8–13). Use June 12, 20YY, as the date of service.

OFFICE VISIT CODE: Established patient office visit, 99212.
PLACE OF SERVICE: Provider's office, 11.
DIAGNOSIS CODE: Streptococcal pharyngitis, 034.0.
CPT CODE: Throat culture, 87081.
CHARGES: Office visit, $45; throat culture, $25.
PROVIDER NPI: 2345678901.

Blocks 25–33: Provider and Billing Entity Identification; Charges

Blocks 25 through 33 are used to record provider and billing identification information and the total charges for services rendered. Accurate information is essential for prompt and adequate reimbursement. Figure 8–14 shows the CMS-1500, blocks 25 through 33.

FIGURE 8–13 CMS-1500 Block 24A–J (For instructional use only. Courtesy of the Centers for Medicare and Medicaid Services, www.cms.hhs.gov)

FIGURE 8–14 CMS-1500 Blocks 25–33 (For instructional use only. Courtesy of the Centers for Medicare and Medicaid Services, www.cms.hhs.gov)

Block 25: Federal Tax I.D. Number

Enter the provider's Social Security number (SSN) or employer (tax) identification number (EIN). Do not enter hyphens or spaces in the number. Enter an X in the appropriate box.

Block 26: Patient's Account No.

Enter the patient's account number as assigned by the provider. This block is sometimes left blank.

Block 27: Accept Assignment?

Enter an X in the YES box if the provider accepts the insurance payment as payment in full. Enter an X in the NO box if the provider does not accept the insurance payment as payment in full.

Block 28: Total Charges

Enter the total amount for all charges listed in block 24F on one claim form. If more than one claim is submitted for the same patient, each form must have its own total charge entered in block 28.

Block 29: Amount Paid

Enter the total amount the patient (or another payer) paid toward services covered by the insurance plan. If no payment was made, leave this blank.

Block 30: Balance Due

Subtract the amount paid (block 29) from the total charges (block 28) and then enter the difference in block 30. Do not enter a negative amount or a credit due to the patient.

Block 31: Signature of Physician or Supplier

Enter the provider's first name, last name, and credentials without punctuation. Enter the six- (MMDDYY) or eight-digit (MMDDYYYY) date that the claim was completed. Many insurance companies also accept the statement SIGNATURE ON FILE or SOF.

When using SIGNATURE ON FILE, the practice or facility must maintain a current signature file that has the written signature of every provider or physician. Signature stamps may be used when an arrangement has been made with the insurance carrier to accept the stamps.

Blocks 32–32b: Name and Address of Facility Where Services Were Rendered

Enter the name and address where procedures or services were provided, if the location is other than the provider's office or patient's home. Other locations include a hospital, outside laboratory, skilled nursing facility, or durable medical equipment providers. Otherwise, leave this blank. Enter the name of the facility on the first line, the address on the second line, and the city, state, and ZIP code on the third line. For a nine-digit ZIP code, enter a hyphen between the first five digits and the last four digits.

Block 32a (unshaded)

Enter the 10-digit NPI for the facility entered in block 32a.

Block 32b (shaded)

Leave this blank.

Block 33: Billing Provider Info & PH

- Enter the provider's billing name, address, and telephone number as follows: For all providers, enter the phone number in the space to the left of the block title. Do not enter parentheses for the area code; the area code may automatically fill the preprinted parentheses.
- For a solo practitioner, enter the provider's first name, middle initial (if known), last name, and credential on the first line (do not use punctuation); enter the provider's address on the second line; enter the city, state, and ZIP code on the third line. For a nine-digit ZIP code, enter a hyphen between the first five digits and the last four digits.
- For practitioners in a group practice, enter the name of the practice or agency on the first line; enter the address on the second line; and enter the city, state, and ZIP code on the third line. For a nine-digit ZIP code, enter a hyphen between the first five digits and the last four digits.

Block 33a (unshaded)

Enter the 10-digit NPI of the billing provider. For a solo practitioner, enter the practitioner's NPI number; for a group practice, enter the 10-digit NPI of the group practice (e.g., clinic, agency).

Block 33b (shaded)

Leave this blank.

25. FEDERAL TAX I.D. NUMBER	SSN EIN	26. PATIENT'S ACCOUNT NO.	27. ACCEPT ASSIGNMENT? (For govt. claims, see back) ☐ YES ☐ NO	28. TOTAL CHARGE $	29. AMOUNT PAID $	30. BALANCE DUE $
31. SIGNATURE OF PHYSICIAN OR SUPPLIER INCLUDING DEGREES OR CREDENTIALS (I certify that the statements on the reverse apply to this bill and are made a part thereof.)		32. SERVICE FACILITY LOCATION INFORMATION		33. BILLING PROVIDER INFO & PH # ( )		
SIGNED DATE		a. b.		a. b.		

NUCC Instruction Manual available at: www.nucc.org   APPROVED OMB-0938-0999 FORM CMS-1500 (08-05)

FIGURE 8–15 CMS-1500 Blocks 25–33 (For instructional use only. Courtesy of the Centers for Medicare and Medicaid Services, www.cms.hhs.gov)

REINFORCEMENT EXERCISES 8–4

Use the following information to complete blocks 25–33 of the CMS-1500 (Figure 8–15).

PROGRESS NOTE 6/12/20YY: Viola is seen today for a sore throat that first presented three days ago. The patient has a low-grade fever of 100.2°F. Physical examination was essentially normal, with the exception of an inflamed throat. Swab culture was taken and confirmed the presence of streptococcus for a diagnosis of streptococcal pharyngitis. Erythromycin was prescribed. The patient is to return in 10 days for follow-up. Office visit code is 99212. Signed by: Roberta Pharyngeal, MD.
DIAGNOSIS CODE: Streptococcal pharyngitis, 034.0.
CPT CODE: Throat culture, 87081.
CHARGES: Office visit, $50.00; throat culture, $20.00 (office lab).
GROUP PRACTICE: Family MD; 800 Medical Drive; Anytown, MI 49855. Phone: (906) 555-8181
PHYSICIAN FEDERAL TAX ID NUMBER: EIN 49-2134726.
PHYSICIAN NPI: 0051551500.
GROUP PRACTICE NPI: 4985543258.
The physician accepts assignment.
The patient paid the 20% co-pay.

COMMON ERRORS MADE WHEN COMPLETING THE CMS-1500

The insurance billing specialist must take great care to ensure the accuracy of all CMS-1500 data fields (blocks). Even the simplest mistake can cause delayed or denied reimbursement. Some common errors associated with CMS-1500 completion are:

- Incorrect patient insurance identification number
- Incorrect CPT code or failure to use a modifier
- Incorrect ICD-9-CM code or missing fourth or fifth digits
- ICD-9-CM code that does not validate that the service or procedure was medically necessary
- Absence of referring physician name and identification when required
- Mathematical errors related to charges and total amount due
- Incorrect, missing, or duplicate dates of service
- Incomplete provider information

Figure 8–16 is an example of a completed CMS-1500.

(1500)

HEALTH INSURANCE CLAIM FORM

APPROVED BY NATIONAL UNIFORM CLAIM COMMITTEE 08/05

◄── CARRIER

| | | PICA | | | | | | PICA | | |

1. MEDICARE	MEDICAID	TRICARE CHAMPUS	CHAMPVA	GROUP HEALTH PLAN	FECA BLK LUNG	OTHER	1a. INSURED'S I.D. NUMBER (For Program in Item 1)
☐ (Medicare #)	☐ (Medicaid #)	☐ (Sponsor's SSN)	☐ (Member ID #)	☐ (SSN or ID)	☐ (SSN)	☒ (ID)	453897

2. PATIENT'S NAME (Last Name, First Name, Middle Initial)	3. PATIENT'S BIRTH DATE	SEX	4. INSURED'S NAME (Last Name, First Name, Middle Initial)
BARIL, VIOLA, M	MM 12 DD 15 YY 1960 M ☐ F ☒		BARIL, VIOLA, M

5. PATIENT'S ADDRESS (No., Street)	6. PATIENT RELATIONSHIP TO INSURED	7. INSURED'S ADDRESS (No., Street)
123 PANSY LANE	Self ☐ Spouse ☐ Child ☐ Other ☐	123 PANSY LANE

CITY	STATE	8. PATIENT STATUS	CITY	STATE
ANYTOWN	ME	Single ☐ Married ☒ Other ☐	ANYTOWN	ME

ZIP CODE	TELEPHONE (Include Area Code)		ZIP CODE	TELEPHONE (Include Area Code)
49855	(906)	Employed ☒ Full-Time Student ☐ Part-Time Student ☐	49855	(906) 2222222

9. OTHER INSURED'S NAME (Last Name, First Name, Middle Initial)	10. IS PATIENT'S CONDITION RELATED TO:	11. INSURED'S POLICY GROUP OR FECA NUMBER
BARIL, PHILIP, L		51000

a. OTHER INSURED'S POLICY OR GROUP NUMBER	a. EMPLOYMENT? (Current or Previous)	a. INSURED'S DATE OF BIRTH	SEX
89000	☐ YES ☒ NO	MM 12 DD 15 YY 1960	M ☐ F ☒

b. OTHER INSURED'S DATE OF BIRTH	SEX	b. AUTO ACCIDENT?	PLACE (State)	b. EMPLOYER'S NAME OR SCHOOL NAME
MM 10 DD 30 YY 1959	M ☒ F ☐	☐ YES ☒ NO		NORTHWEST INDUSTRY

c. EMPLOYER'S NAME OR SCHOOL NAME	c. OTHER ACCIDENT?	c. INSURANCE PLAN NAME OR PROGRAM NAME
BELL MEDICAL	☐ YES ☒ NO	CIGNA

d. INSURANCE PLAN NAME OR PROGRAM NAME	10d. RESERVED FOR LOCAL USE	d. IS THERE ANOTHER HEALTH BENEFIT PLAN?
AETNA		☒ YES ☐ NO **If yes,** return to and complete item 9 a-d.

READ BACK OF FORM BEFORE COMPLETING & SIGNING THIS FORM.

12. PATIENT'S OR AUTHORIZED PERSON'S SIGNATURE I authorize the release of any medical or other information necessary to process this claim. I also request payment of government benefits either to myself or to the party who accepts assignment below.

SIGNED   SIGNATURE ON FILE   DATE   MM DD YY

13. INSURED'S OR AUTHORIZED PERSON'S SIGNATURE I authorize payment of medical benefits to the undersigned physician or supplier for services described below.

SIGNED   SIGNATURE ON FILE

◄── PATIENT AND INSURED INFORMATION

14. DATE OF CURRENT: ILLNESS (First symptom) OR INJURY (Accident) OR PREGNANCY (LMP)	15. IF PATIENT HAS HAD SAME OR SIMILAR ILLNESS, GIVE FIRST DATE MM DD YY	16. DATES PATIENT UNABLE TO WORK IN CURRENT OCCUPATION
MM 06 DD 12 YY		FROM MM DD YY TO MM DD YY

17. NAME OF REFERRING PROVIDER OR OTHER SOURCE	17a.	18. HOSPITALIZATION DATES RELATED TO CURRENT SERVICES
	17b. NPI 1234567890	FROM MM DD YY TO MM DD YY

19. RESERVED FOR LOCAL USE	20. OUTSIDE LAB?	$ CHARGES
	☒ YES ☐ NO	300 | 00

21. DIAGNOSIS OR NATURE OF ILLNESS OR INJURY (Relate Items 1, 2, 3, or 4 to Item 24E by Line)	22. MEDICAID RESUBMISSION CODE ORIGINAL REF. NO.
1. 491 . 21 3. 485 . ___	
2. 788 . 1 4. ___ . ___	23. PRIOR AUTHORIZATION NUMBER

24. A. DATE(S) OF SERVICE						B. PLACE OF SERVICE	C. EMG	D. PROCEDURES, SERVICES, OR SUPPLIES (Explain Unusual Circumstances)		E. DIAGNOSIS POINTER	F. $ CHARGES	G. DAYS OR UNITS	H. EPSDT Family Plan	I. ID. QUAL.	J. RENDERING PROVIDER ID. #
	From			To				CPT/HCPCS	MODIFIER						
MM	DD	YY	MM	DD	YY										
1	06	12	YY				11		99214		1	80 | 00	1		NPI	0123456789
2															NPI	
3															NPI	
4															NPI	
5															NPI	
6															NPI	

25. FEDERAL TAX I.D. NUMBER	SSN EIN	26. PATIENT'S ACCOUNT NO.	27. ACCEPT ASSIGNMENT? (For govt. claims, see back)	28. TOTAL CHARGE	29. AMOUNT PAID	30. BALANCE DUE
11123341	☒		☒ YES ☐ NO	$ 80 | 00	$ 8 | 00	$ 72 | 00

31. SIGNATURE OF PHYSICIAN OR SUPPLIER INCLUDING DEGREES OR CREDENTIALS (I certify that the statements on the reverse apply to this bill and are made a part thereof.)	32. SERVICE FACILITY LOCATION INFORMATION	33. BILLING PROVIDER INFO & PH # (906) 555 8181
SIGNATURE ON FILE	DIAGNOSTIC SERVICES 700 LAB DRIVE NEWBERRY MI 49868	FAMILY MD 800 MEDICAL DRIVE ANYTOWN ME 49855
SIGNED DATE 06 12 YY	a. 4986832147 b.	a. 4985543258 b.

◄── PHYSICIAN OR SUPPLIER INFORMATION

NUCC Instruction Manual available at: www.nucc.org

APPROVED OMB-0938-0999 FORM CMS-1500 (08-05)

FIGURE 8–16 Completed CMS-1500 Form (For instructional use only. Courtesy of the Centers for Medicare and Medicaid Services, www.cms.hhs.gov)

ABBREVIATIONS

Table 8–2 lists the abbreviations with their meanings presented in this chapter.

TABLE 8–2

Abbreviations and Meanings	
Abbreviation	Meaning
CHAMPUS	Civilian Health and Medical Program of the Uniformed Services
CHAMPVA	Civilian Health and Medical Program of the Department of Veterans Affairs
CMS	Centers for Medicare and Medicaid Services
LMP	last menstrual period
NPI	national provider identification
POS	place of service
SOF	signature on file

SUMMARY

This chapter provides a review of the general directions for completing the CMS-1500, the universal insurance claim form. Optical scanning guidelines are included. Common errors associated with CMS-1500 completion are listed and described.

REVIEW EXERCISES

Select the Correct Answer

Circle the term or phrase that accurately completes each statement.

1. *Do* or *Do not* include titles in block 2, Patient's Name.
2. The national provider identification number (NPI) was developed by the *Social Security Administration* or *CMS*.
3. The NPI will always apply to *government* or *nongovernment* health insurance programs.
4. Prior authorization numbers are most often associated with *primary care physicians* or *managed care plans.*
5. Block 21 has room for up to four diagnostic codes that are recorded as *ICD-9 CM* codes or *CPT/HCPCS* codes.
6. Block 24H, EPSDT, is associated with the *Medicare* or *Medicaid* health insurance program.

True or False

Write True or False on the line following each statement.

1. Note all monetary entries with the appropriate dollar or cents symbol. _____

2. Compound names may be hyphenated. _____

3. Do not use any punctuation in the patient's name. _____

4. Use two zeros in the cent column when the fee is listed in whole dollars. _____

5. Separate the patient's last name, first name, and middle initial with commas. _____

6. Use both lowercase and uppercase letters for alphabetic characters. _____

 CHALLENGE EXERCISE

1. Interview the billing specialist at a local physician's office about CMS-1500 completion do's and don'ts. Based on the information from the interview, develop a handout to share with the other students in your class.

WEBSITE

National Uniform Claim Committee: www.nucc.org

CHAPTER 9

Common UB-04 (CMS-1450) Completion Guidelines

LEARNING OBJECTIVES

Upon successfully completing this chapter, the reader should have the knowledge to:

1. Accurately describe key terms and abbreviations.
2. Discuss a brief history of the UB-04.
3. Describe information reported in five sections of the UB-04.
4. Accurately complete UB-04 data fields.
5. Discuss the role of the health insurance billing specialist.

KEY TERMS

Accommodation code
Admitting diagnosis
Ambulatory payment
  classification (APC)
Ancillary services code
Assignment of benefits
Attending physician
Complication/co-morbidity
  (CC)
Centers for Medicare and
  Medicaid Services (CMS)
Chargemaster
Clean claim
Clearinghouse
CMS-1450
Co-insurance days
Condition code
Covered days
Critical access hospital (CAH)
Current Procedural
  Terminology (CPT)

Department of Health and
  Human Services (HHS)
Diagnosis related group
  (DRG)
Dirty claim
Electronic claims submission
  (ECS)
Electronic health record
  (EHR)
Encoder
Florida Shared System (FSS)
Form locator (FL)
Healthcare Common Procedure
  Coding System (HCPCS)
Health Care Finance
  Administration (HCFA)
Health insurance claim
  number (HICN)
Health Insurance Portability
  and Accountability Act
  (HIPAA)

Inpatient prospective
  payment system (IPPS)
Insured
Intermediate care facility
  (ICF)
International Classification of
  Diseases, Ninth Revision,
  Clinical Modification
  (ICD-9-CM)
Length of stay (LOS)
Lifetime reserve day
Major complication/
  co-morbidity (MCC)
Medicare-severity diagnosis
  related group (MS-DRG)
National Provider
  Identification number
  (NPI)
National Uniform Billing
  Committee (NUBC)
Occurrence code

Outpatient prospective
   payment system
   (OPPS)
Primary payer
Principal diagnosis
Principal procedure

Prospective payment system
   (PPS)
Secondary payer
Skilled nursing facility (SNF)
Subscriber
Taxonomy code

Tertiary payer
UB-04
Uniform Hospital
   Discharge Data Set
   (UHDDS)
Value code

OVERVIEW

This chapter is an introduction to the complex world of hospital insurance claims processing. Major topics include hospital reimbursement, developing the insurance claim, and guidelines for completing the hospital claims submission form. The universal hospital claims submission form is the **CMS-1450**, commonly called the UB-04.

Since 1974, the U.S. **Department of Health and Human Services (HHS)**, then known as the Department of Health, Education, and Welfare, has required hospitals to report a minimum, common core of information for all hospital discharges. The **Uniform Hospital Discharge Data Set (UHDDS)** was implemented in 1974 and is periodically revised. The original purpose of the UHDDS was to capture uniform and comparable information related to hospital services provided to Medicare and Medicaid beneficiaries. Because the UB-04 includes data elements required by the UHDDS, all health insurance programs capture uniform and comparable information related to hospital services. Table 9–1 lists the UHDDS elements that are captured on the UB-04.

TABLE 9–1

Uniform Hospital Discharge Data Set
Uniform Hospital Discharge Data Set with Explanations
Personal identification: A unique number assigned to each patient that distinguishes the patient and the patient's health record from all others
Date of birth: Patient's date of birth
Sex: Patient's sex (male, female, or unknown)
Residence: ZIP code or code for foreign residence
Hospital identification: A unique number assigned to each facility
Admission and discharge dates: Dates the patient was admitted and discharged from the hospital
Physician identification: A unique number assigned to each physician; **attending physician** and operating physician, if applicable
Disposition of patient: The condition or way in which the patient left the hospital (e.g., discharged home; left against medical advice; died)
Expected payer for most of the bill: The major source that the patient expects to pay the bill (e.g., Blue Cross/Blue Shield, Medicare, Medicaid, workers' compensation)

continued on the next page

continued from the previous page

Diagnoses: All diagnoses affecting the current hospital stay
Principal diagnosis: The condition determined after study to be chiefly responsible for the patient's admission to the hospital
Secondary or Other diagnoses: Diagnoses that affect the length of stay, develop during the length of stay, or affect the treatment received
Complication: An additional diagnosis that arises after the beginning of hospital care that modifies the course of the patient's illness or required medical care
Co-morbidity: A pre-existing condition that because of its presence with a specific principal diagnosis, will cause an increase in the patient's length of stay
Procedures and dates: All significant procedures identified as surgical in nature, carrying a procedural risk, carrying an anesthetic risk, or requiring specialized training
Principal procedure: Procedure performed for definitive treatment rather than for diagnostic or exploratory purposes or procedure deemed necessary to take care of a complication. When two procedures appear to be principal, the procedure most closely related to the principal diagnosis should be selected as the principal procedure.

HOSPITAL REIMBURSEMENT

In the past, insurance companies paid the hospital based on the patient's **length of stay (LOS)** and the charges associated with the length of stay. The length of stay is defined as the number of days of service from admission to discharge date. Payment was usually a percentage of the total charges, and the patient was held responsible for the balance. This type of reimbursement is known as per-diem or fee-for-service payment. Under per diem and fee for service, there was little incentive to control the cost of hospital care.

During the 1970s, rising health care costs threatened the financial stability of the Medicare program. As a result of this threat, the **Centers for Medicare and Medicaid Services (CMS)**, then called the **Health Care Finance Administration (HCFA)**, established a new hospital reimbursement system. In 1983, CMS implemented a **prospective payment system (PPS)** for hospital inpatient services provided to Medicare beneficiaries. Under the original PPS, hospital reimbursement was based on **diagnosis related groups (DRGs)**. DRGs categorized or grouped diagnoses that were medically related, required similar treatments, and had similar lengths of stay. Each DRG had a preset reimbursement amount that the hospital received for each case that fell into a specific DRG. Therefore, under the original prospective payment system, the patient's diagnosis determined the amount a hospital received for providing treatment. The prospective payment system for inpatients is called the **inpatient prospective payment system (IPPS)**.

On October 1, 2007, CMS approved an extensive restructuring of the diagnostic related groups for the inpatient prospective payment system (IPPS). The original DRGs were replaced with **Medicare-severity diagnosis related groups (MS-DRG)**. Implementation of MS-DRGs was phased in between October 1, 2007, and October 1, 2009. MS-DRGs are based on the patient's principal diagnosis, secondary diagnosis, procedures performed, sex, discharge status (alive or expired),

TABLE 9–2

MS-DRGs for Heart Failure		
MS-DRG	MS-DRG Title	Reimbursement Rate
MS-DRG 291	Heart failure w (with) MCC	$6,246.00
MS-DRG 291	Heart failure w CC	$5,030.00
MS-DRG 292	Heart failure w/o (without) CC/MCC	$4,350.00

the presence of a **complication/co-morbidity (CC)** or a **major complication/co-morbidity (MCC)**, or the absence of a CC or MCC. For purposes of MS-DRG assignment, a CC is defined as a condition that substantially increases the use of hospital resources. An MCC is a more severe complication/co-morbidity. Each MS-DRG has a preset reimbursement amount that the hospital receives for each case that falls into a specific MS-DRG. Table 9–2 lists three MS-DRGs for heart failure and a sample reimbursement rate based on CCs and MCCs.

Note the difference between the reimbursement rates for heart failure with or without a CC or MCC. Accurate MS-DRG assignment is dependent on accurate diagnosis and procedure codes, and accurate medical coding depends on the documentation in the patient's medical record. Other factors that affect MS-DRG assignment include the patient's gender and discharge status (e.g., alive or expired).

Several *International Classification of Diseases, Ninth Revision, Clinical Modification* **(ICD-9-CM)** diagnosis and procedure codes are related to each MS-DRG. For example, ICD-9-CM codes 428.0 through 428.9, with fifth digits as appropriate, represent about 15 different diagnoses related to heart failure. Each of these codes would be grouped into one of the three MS-DRGs for heart failure. Encoders—computer programs used to assign diagnostic and procedure codes—are able to assign MS-DRGs based on the diagnostic and procedure codes and other data entered into the program.

In addition to hospital inpatient prospective payment, the Centers for Medicare and Medicaid Services have implemented an **outpatient prospective payment system (OPPS)**. This system applies to hospital outpatient/ambulatory procedures and ambulatory surgery centers. Under OPPS, outpatient/ambulatory services provided to Medicare patients have a preset reimbursement rate. The payment rates are based on the **ambulatory payment classification (APC)** system. The ambulatory payment classification system groups diagnostic and therapeutic procedures that are similar in nature and that consume similar resources. There are over 9,000 ambulatory payment classification categories, and each APC is assigned a unique number. Several *Current Procedural Terminology* **(CPT)** codes are related to each APC. For example, APC 154, "Hernia/Hydrocele Procedures," includes the CPT codes for over 30 hernia repairs, ranging from reducing a hernia present in a premature infant to repairing a hernia with mesh placement. As with the inpatient prospective payment system, accurate coding is crucial to accurate APC assignment. Table 9–3 lists a few APCs with related or included procedures.

In a hospital, medical coders are responsible for assigning the appropriate ICD-9-CM, CPT, and Level II *Healthcare Common Procedure Coding System* **(HCPCS)** codes for both inpatient and outpatient services. Medical coders are usually part of the health information or medical record department. Billing specialists and medical coders work together to ensure that insurance claims are filed in a timely manner.

TABLE 9–3

APCs with Procedures
APC with Procedures
APC 105, "Revision/Removal of Pacemakers": Removal of pacemaker system; removal of pacemaker electrode; removal of pulse generator
APC 113, "Excision, Lymphatic System": Excision of lymph channels; removal of lymph nodes, neck; removal of lymph nodes, groin; biopsy/removal of lymph nodes
APC 142, "Small Intestine Endoscopy": Endoscopy, including duodenum; endoscopy, including ileum; endoscopy, removal of polyps; endoscopy, removal of foreign object
APC 154, "Hernia/Hydrocele Procedure": Repair of inguinal hernia; repair/reduction of umbilical hernia; repair/reduction of epigastric hernia; repair/reduction of inguinal hernia, premature infant; repair/reduction of ventral hernia
APC 254, "Level IV Ear, Nose, Throat Procedures": Excision of mouth lesion; excision of tongue lesion; reconstruction of the mouth; partial removal of the tongue

DEVELOPING THE INSURANCE CLAIM

Developing an insurance claim for inpatient and outpatient services includes the following activities:

- Registering the patient
- Capturing charges for services provided to the patient
- Assigning diagnosis and procedure codes

All activities associated with developing the insurance claim are equally important. The billing specialist is usually the last person to review and edit insurance claim information. When information is missing, incomplete, or inaccurate, the billing specialist works with other departments to resolve the problem.

Patient Registration

Developing an insurance claim begins when the patient comes to the facility for services. The admission staff is responsible for registering the patient. The registration process begins with a valid order for services that includes a diagnosis and physician signature. Admission staff collects the patient's demographic and insurance information, makes a copy of the patient's insurance identification card (both front and back), and enters the information into the hospital's database. For an **electronic health record (EHR)**, the insurance card may be scanned, front and back, into the database. The information is entered with the patient's hospital or billing identification number. Registration information is the foundation for the health insurance claim.

When the patient is covered by more than one insurance plan, the admitting staff collects information that is used to determine the **primary** or **secondary payer**. A primary payer is the health insurance plan that is billed first. A secondary payer is the health insurance plan that is billed after payment is received from the primary payer.

When a Medicare beneficiary presents for hospital inpatient services and there is a question as to whether the services will be covered by Medicare, the admitting staff must give the beneficiary written notification of noncoverage. The notification must include the service(s) that may not be covered; the patient's responsibility for the cost of the noncovered services; the name and address of the organization for the beneficiary to appeal the notice; the time frame for an appeal; and the beneficiary's signature as well as date and time that the beneficiary received the notification. The beneficiary's legal representative, such as a guardian, may act on behalf of the beneficiary. Figure 9–1 is a sample notice of noncoverage admission or preadmission.

Capturing Charges for Services Rendered

The charges for services provided to the patient must be entered into the hospital's database with the patient's hospital or billing identification number. Each hospital department enters the type of service or supply provided to the patient. For an electronic health record, supply items, such as medications, special dressings, and catheterization kits, have a bar code identification number that is scanned. If there is no bar code for the service or supply, the identification number is keyed (typed) into the database. All entries for a specific patient must include the patient's hospital or billing identification number. Once the entry is made, the hospital's **chargemaster** adds the correct charge for the service or supply. The chargemaster is a computer program or database that contains the charges and CPT and HCPCS codes for services and supplies. Charges range from the room rate for a specific hospital unit to the price for a blood test.

> **EXAMPLE**
> On March 10, 20YY, Rosa is admitted to Mercy Hospital for a radical mastectomy. During preoperative preparation, an intravenous line is placed, preoperative sedation is administered, and a urinary catheter is placed. The bar codes for the intravenous line, sedation medication, and catheter line are scanned, and Rosa's patient identification number is entered into the database. After surgery, Rosa is returned to her hospital room. Twenty-four hours later, Rosa develops a fever, and the surgeon orders a postoperative complete blood count (CBC), with a white blood cell differentiation. Once the blood test is completed, the identification code for the test and Rosa's patient identification number are entered into the database. Rosa is discharged on March 15, 20YY.

At the end of the hospital inpatient or ambulatory/outpatient stay, the discharge date is entered into the database. The admission and discharge dates are used to determine the patient's length of stay. The length of stay is determined by the number of days that the patient was an inpatient at midnight. The length of stay is used to calculate the total room charges for the number of days the patient occupied a hospital bed. The discharge date is *not* included in the length of stay. The length of stay can be calculated by subtracting the admission date from the discharge date or by counting each day from the admission date to the day before the discharge date. If a patient dies or is transferred to another facility on the day of admission, the facility may bill for one day of service.

> **EXAMPLE**
> Rosa was admitted on March 10 and discharged on March 15. Rosa occupied a hospital bed from March 10 through March 14, which is five days. The discharge day, March 15, is not counted as an occupied bed. Therefore, Rosa's length of stay is five days.

Superiorland Hospital
835 Marquette Drive
Blueberry, ME 49855
(906) 312-9446

NOTICE OF NONCOVERAGE ADMISSION OR PREADMISSION

March 21, 20YY
Date of Notice

March 21, 20YY
Admission Date

Akiko Park
Patient/Representative Name

491884766A
Health Insurance Claim Number

15 High Place, Blueberry ME 49855
Address

Elmer Mattson, MD
Attending Physician

Superiorland Hospital finds that your admission for bronchopneumonia is not covered under Medicare because inpatient treatment for bronchopneumonia is medically unnecessary or could be safely rendered in another setting. This determination was based on Superiorland's understanding and interpretation of available Medicare coverage policies and guidelines. You should discuss other arrangements with your physician. If you decide to be admitted to Superiorland Hospital, you will be financially responsible for all charges related to your inpatient treatment.

This notice, however, is not an official Medicare determination. Maine Peer Review, Inc., is authorized by the Medicare program to review inpatient hospital services provided to Medicare beneficiaries. **If you disagree with our conclusion, you should contact** Maine Peer Review, Inc., **to have your case reviewed**. The following options are available:

1. **Preadmission Review:** Within three days of receipt of this notice, or if you choose to be admitted at any point during the stay, request an *immediate review* of the facts in your case. You may make this request through the hospital or directly to Maine Peer Review.

2. **Admission Review:** Immediately, or at any point during your hospital stay, request an *immediate review* of the facts in your case. You may make this request through the hospital or directly to Maine Peer Review, Inc., at the address listed below.

3. **If you do not wish for an immediate review, you may still request a review within 30 calendar days from the date of receipt of this notice. You may contact** Maine Peer Review **by telephone or in writing.**

MAINE PEER REVIEW 336 BAGGS ROAD BLUEBERRY, ME 57446 1-800-555-5900

1. Maine Peer Review will send you a **formal determination** of the medical necessity and appropriateness of your hospitalization, and will inform you of your reconsideration and appeal rights.

2. If Maine Peer Review **disagrees with the hospital**, you will be refunded any money you paid the hospital except for any amounts for deductible, coinsurance, and convenience services or items normally not covered by Medicare.

3. If Maine Peer Review **agrees with the hospital**, you are responsible for payment for all services beginning on (fill in the date when the patient is responsible for the bill).

ACKNOWLEDGEMENT OF RECEIPT OF NOTICE

I understand that my signature does not indicate that I agree with this notice of noncoverage of benefits. It indicates only that I have received a copy of the notice.

Signature of Beneficiary or Legal Representative   Date   Time

Delmar/Cengage Learning

FIGURE 9–1 Notice of Noncoverage Admission or Preadmission

Assigning Diagnosis and Procedure Codes

As stated previously, medical coders are responsible for assigning the appropriate diagnosis and procedure codes related to hospital services. The patient's medical record is the source document for this activity. In the past, medical coders manually assigned the appropriate ICD-9-CM, CPT, or HCPCS Level II codes. In today's electronic age, hospitals have invested in high-quality computer-assisted coding programs called **encoders**. Several commercial vendors market encoders, and the hospital is able to select the product that best meets its needs.

Encoders are valuable tools, but they cannot replace qualified medical coders. The medical coder carefully reviews the patient's record for the principal diagnosis, the principal procedure, and additional diagnoses and procedures that affect the current hospital stay. Documentation in the patient's record *must* clearly support every code assigned to the case. If the documentation is incomplete or questionable, the medical coder communicates with the appropriate physician or hospital department for additional information.

The medical coder enters diagnostic and procedure information into the encoder. The encoder program delivers on-screen prompts that provide the coder with instructional notes similar to those available in the coding reference books. The medical coder must also follow all coding conventions and regulatory guidelines. Diagnosis and procedure codes are entered into the hospital's database by using the patient identification number. After the codes are entered, patient information is released to the billing department for insurance claim processing.

REINFORCEMENT EXERCISES 9–1

Spell out the following abbreviations.

1. APC

   _____

2. CC

   _____

3. CMS

   _____

4. HHS

   _____

5. LOS

   _____

6. MCC

   _____

---

continued on the next page

continued from the previous page

7. MS-DRG

_____

8. OPPS

_____

9. IPPS

_____

10. UHDDS

_____

11. EHR

_____

Briefly define or describe the following terms.

1. Chargemaster

_____

_____

_____

2. Co-morbidity

_____

_____

_____

3. Complication

_____

_____

_____

4. Disposition of patient

_____

_____

_____

continued on the next page

continued from the previous page

5. Encoder

_____

_____

_____

6. Primary payer

_____

_____

_____

7. Principal diagnosis

_____

_____

_____

8. Principal procedure

_____

_____

_____

9. Secondary payer

_____

_____

_____

10. Uniform Bill 04 (UB-04)

_____

_____

_____

UB-04 COMPLETION GUIDELINES

As stated earlier, the UB-04 is a universal claims submission form that is accepted by nearly all health insurance companies. The UB-04 was developed and is revised by the **National Uniform Billing Committee (NUBC)**. The NUBC was established to develop a claims submission form that could replace the many billing forms hospitals were required to use. The UB-04 is designed

to capture information for reimbursement and statistical purposes. The most current information about the UB-04 form can be found on the NUBC or CMS websites.

General guidelines for completing the UB-04 include the following:

- All information should be keyed or typed.
- Dates are usually entered by using eight digits to represent the month, day, and year.
- Key all alphabetic characters in uppercase letters.
- Leave one blank space between last name, first name, and middle initial.
- Do not key the letter O for the number zero.
- Do not use punctuation in the patient/policyholder's name, except for a hyphen in a compound name.
- Do not use designations such as Sr. or Jr.
- Do not use dollar signs, decimals, or commas in any monetary field. Two zeros in the cents column are acceptable.
- Do not include the decimal in medical codes.
- Do not add a dash in front of a procedure code modifier.

Insurance carriers provide guidelines for completing the UB-04 by way of manuals, newsletters, e-mails, and online instruction guides. Guidelines for Medicare claims processing are found in the *Medicare Claims Processing Manual*, Chapter 25, "Completing and Processing [the] UB-04." These guidelines are available at the CMS website. The completion guidelines in this chapter are based on Medicare guidelines and interviews with several billing specialists. The information relates primarily to hospital claims submission.

There are 81 fields on the UB-04. Each field, known as a **form locator (FL)**, has a number, and most fields have a name or title. Instructions for completing the UB-04 are divided into five general sections: (1) patient and provider information; (2) conditions, events, and additional information that may affect claims payment; (3) services provided and related charges; (4) insurance company (payer), insured, and employer information; and (5) medical codes and physician identification information. Each section is presented in a figure that corresponds to the discussion of the section. Refer to the figures as you read the explanations. All fields are keyed in uppercase letters.

UB-04 Patient and Provider Information (FL 1–17)

The first 17 fields capture information about the hospital and the patient. Figure 9–2 shows FL 1 through FL 17. Refer to Figure 9–2 as you learn about these fields.

FIGURE 9–2 UB-04 FL 1–17 (For instructional use only. Courtesy of the Centers for Medicare and Medicaid Services, www.cms.hhs.gov)

FL 1: Provider Name, Address, and Telephone Number (Untitled)

Enter the following hospital information on four lines: (a) hospital name; (b) street address or post office box number; (c) city, state, and ZIP code; (d) telephone number with area code, fax number, and the country code, if applicable. Lines a–c are required by all insurance carriers.

FL 2: Pay-to Name, Address, (Untitled)

If the claim is paid to an entity other than the billing provider named in FL1, enter the name, address, city, state, and ZIP code of the pay-to entity.

FL 3a: Patient Control Number

The patient control number is assigned by the hospital and is also known as the "account number" or "billing number." An account number is assigned each time a patient is admitted. This number is referenced on the remittance advice form that is received from the insurance carrier. The patient control number may consist of alphanumeric or only numeric characters.

FL 3b: Medical Record Number

Enter the patient's medical record number, which is assigned by the provider.

FL 4: Type of Bill (TOB)

This field is required by all third-party payers. The type of bill is a three-digit number, and each digit has a specific meaning. The first digit tells the insurance carrier where the service was provided (type of facility). Table 9–4 lists the type of facility associated with the first digit.

TABLE 9–4

FL 4 TOB First Digit/Type of Facility	
TOB First Digit	**Type of Facility**
1	Hospital—facility licensed to provide inpatient treatment
2	Skilled nursing facility (SNF)—facility or distinct part of a hospital that is licensed to provide skilled nursing care or rehabilitation services
3	Home health agency (HHA)—provider licensed to provide skilled nursing and other therapeutic services, usually in the patient's home
4	Religious nonmedical hospital
5	Reserved for national assignment
6	**Intermediate care facility (ICF)**—facility that provides services to patients who do not need skilled nursing care
7	Clinic or hospital-based renal dialysis facility—an outpatient facility that provides scheduled diagnostic, treatment, rehabilitative, and educational services for ambulatory patients
8	Specialty facility or ambulatory surgery center (ASC)—facility that provides some type of specialty services or is licensed to perform surgical procedures that do not require inpatient hospitalization
9	Reserved for national assignment

TABLE 9-5

FL 4 TOB Second Digit for Hospitals	
TOB Second Digit	**Description**
1	Inpatient—services provided from admission to discharge. For Medicare, this applies to services covered by Part A (hospital) insurance.
2	Inpatient—services provided from admission to discharge that are covered by Medicare Part B insurance
3	Outpatient—services including outpatient/ambulatory surgeries, diagnostic tests or procedures, and various therapies
4	Other—diagnostic tests provided as a result of a referral from a provider/physician not directly associated with the hospital or skilled nursing facility (e.g., a family physician orders a mammography and the individual has the test done at the hospital's radiology department)
8	Swing bed—skilled or intermediate nursing care provided in an acute care hospital. This applies to Medicare cases; the hospital must have a swing bed agreement with the Medicare fiscal intermediary.

The second digit represents the type of care provided, which is also known as the "billing classification." Table 9–5 includes a brief description for each second digit associated with services provided by a hospital.

The third digit, which is called the "frequency of bill," identifies special conditions related to the claim, such as late charges, replacement of a prior claim, or a cancellation of a prior claim. When a patient is scheduled to receive a series of services, such as physical therapy treatments, the facility may submit interim claims from the date the therapy begins until the date it ends. Third digits 2, 3, and 4 tell the insurance carrier that the bill is related to a series of services. The number 4 is used to identify the final interim claim related to a series of services. More than one unit of service may be reported on each interim claim. Table 9–6 follows the example and provides a brief description of commonly used third digits.

EXAMPLE

Following a stroke, Martha is scheduled for rehabilitative physical therapy as a hospital outpatient. She participates in a variety of physical therapy treatments three days per week for 12 weeks, for a total of 36 treatments. The hospital submits three claims (about once a month or every four weeks) for the physical therapy services. The TOB first and second digit for each claim is 13, which indicates that the services were provided in a hospital outpatient setting. The type of bill code on the first claim is 132. The third digit (2) indicates that the claim being submitted relates to a series of treatments. The type of bill code on the second claim is 133. The third digit (3) identifies the claim as an interim claim related to a series of treatments. The type of bill code on the third claim is 134. The third digit (4) identifies the claim as the final interim claim related to a series of treatments.

TABLE 9–6

TOB Frequency of Bill/Special Conditions	
TOB Third Digit	**Description**
1	Hospital inpatient from admission through discharge
2, 3	Interim claim for a series of services
4	Final interim claim for a series of services
5	Late charge claim
7	Replacement claim—applies to claims submitted for under- or overpayment adjustments; original claim is null and void.
8	Void/cancel of a prior claim—used to change the provider identification number, or health insurance claim number, or to refund a duplicate payment

FL 5: Federal Tax Number
Enter the facility's nine-digit federal tax identification number with a hyphen between the second and third digits (xx-xxxxxxx). Some insurance carriers do not allow a hyphen between the second and third digits.

FL 6: Statement Covers Period
This field captures the beginning and ending dates of service, usually the admission and discharge dates. Dates are entered with eight digits. The eight-digit form is MMDDYYYY. Enter the admission date under the word "from" and the discharge date under the word "through."

FL 7: Untitled Reserved for Future Use

FL 8: Patient Name
FL 8a: This field is completed when the patient has a unique identification number assigned by the insurance plan, such as a case number for a workers' compensation claim.
FL 8b: Enter the patient's last name, first name, and middle initial (if known).

FL 9: Patient Address
FL 9a: Enter the patient's street address. Enter an apartment number, if applicable.
FL 9b: Enter the name of the city, town, or other municipality.
FL 9c: Enter the two-character state abbreviation.
FL 9d: Enter the ZIP code.
FL 9e: Enter the country code, when applicable.

FL 10: Patient's Birth Date
Enter the patient's birth date in the eight-digit format (MMDDYYYY).

FL 11: Sex
Enter an M for male or an F for Female. Some insurance companies allow U for unknown.

REINFORCEMENT EXERCISES 9–2

Provide a brief explanation for each term.

1. Form locator (FL)

_____

_____

_____

2. NUBC

_____

_____

_____

3. Patient control number

_____

_____

_____

4. TOB

_____

_____

_____

5. TOB 1st digit

_____

6. TOB 2nd digit

_____

7. TOB 3rd digit

_____

FL 12: Admission Date

Enter the date the patient was admitted for inpatient care or outpatient services or enter the home health care start date. The date is entered in an eight-digit format. Do not use any punctuation between the year, month, and day.

FL 13: Admission Hour

When the insurance plan requires this field, enter the hour the patient was admitted to the facility. Hours are reported in military time, sometimes called the 24-hour clock. Midnight is noted as 00; 1 A.M. as 01; 2 A.M. as 02; and so forth. Noon is noted as 12; 1 P.M. as 13; 2 P.M. as 14; and so forth. The hospital's registration/admission software may automatically enter the hour of admission.

FL 14: Type of Admission

Enter the number that identifies the priority of the admission as follows:

- **01: Emergency:** The patient required immediate medical intervention as a result of severe, life-threatening, or potentially disabling conditions.
- **02: Urgent:** The patient required immediate attention.
- **03: Elective:** The patient's condition permitted adequate time to schedule the admission.
- **04: Newborn**
- **05: Trauma Center:** Admission to a licensed trauma center
- **06–08: Reserved for local use**
- **09:** Information not available

Codes for this field are supplied by the insurance company or fiscal intermediary.

TABLE 9–7

Source of Admission Codes	
Code	Description
1	Physician referral—inpatient admission because of the recommendation of the personal physician; outpatient services requested by personal physician or by self-referral
2	Clinic referral—admission on the recommendation of the facility's clinic physician
3	Managed Care Plan Referral—admission on the recommendation of a Managed Care Plan physician
4	Hospital transfer—admission because of the transfer from an acute care facility
5	Skilled nursing facility transfer—admission because of the transfer from a skilled nursing facility (SNF)
6	Transfer from another health care facility—admission because of the transfer from a facility other than an acute care hospital or skilled nursing facility
7	Emergency room—admission on the recommendation of the facility's emergency room/department physician
8	Court/law enforcement—admission because of the action of a court or law enforcement agency representative (e.g., psychiatric inpatient admission)
9	Information not available—means by which the patient was admitted to this facility is not known
A	Transfer from a critical care access hospital (CAH)—admission because of the transfer from a critical care access hospital, usually to a larger hospital or regional medical center

FL 15: Source of Admission (SRC)

Enter the number that identifies the circumstances of the patient's admission. This field is required by Medicare and may be required by other insurance carriers. Table 9–7 lists some source of admission codes with descriptions.

FL 16: Discharge Hour (DHR)

Enter the time that the patient was discharged. When this field is required, hours are reported in military time, as described in FL 13.

FL 17: Patient Status (STAT)

Enter the status of the patient at the time of discharge. This two-digit code is required by all payers. Table 9–8 lists the codes with their meanings. Codes 08; 10–19; 21–29; 31–39; 44–49; 52–50; and 67–99 are reserved for national assignment or for use by states or other reporting agencies.

TABLE 9–8

Discharge Status Codes and Descriptions	
Code	**Description**
01	Discharged; home, self
02	Discharged/transferred; other inpatient hospital
03	Discharged/transferred to a Medicare certified SNF
04	Discharged/transferred to an ICF
05	Discharged/transferred to another type of institution not defined elsewhere
06	Discharged/transferred; home health agency
07	Discharged against medical advice
20	Expired or did not recover (religious nonmedical health care facility)
40	Expired, home; hospice claims only
41	Expired in a medical facility, such as a hospital, SNF, ICF, or freestanding hospice; hospice claims only
42	Expired, place unknown; hospice claims only
43	Discharged/transferred to a federal health care facility
50	Discharged; home hospice care
51	Discharged; medical facility hospice care
61	Discharged/transferred; swing bed, same facility
62	Discharged/transferred; rehabilitation facility
63	Discharged/transferred; long-term care hospital
64	Discharged/transferred to a Medicaid certified nursing facility
65	Discharged/transferred to a psychiatric hospital or psychiatric distinct part unit of a hospital
66	Discharged/transferred to a **Critical Access Hospital (CAH)**

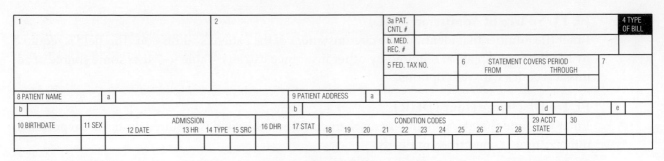

FIGURE 9–3 UB–04 FL 1–17 (For instructional use only. Courtesy of the Centers for Medicare and Medicaid Services, www.cms.hhs.gov)

REINFORCEMENT EXERCISES 9–3

Complete FL 1 through FL 17 in Figure 9–3 by using the information in the following paragraph.

Alex Franks was admitted to Memorial Hospital at 1 P.M. on March 20, 20YY. He underwent scheduled surgery for total knee replacement, as recommended by his family physician. His medical record number is 381509 and his account number is 492618. He was discharged at 10 A.M. on March 25, 20YY, and went home. He lives at 825 Maplewood Avenue in Huntsville, Texas 59855. Alex was born on June 5, 1956. Alex has Blue Cross health insurance through his employer, Texas Software Corporation. His hospital stay is covered, and there are no co-insurance days. Memorial Hospital is located in Huntsville at 101 International Drive; its phone number is (919) 555-1010. Memorial's federal tax number is 50-3729492. The type of bill code for this admission is 111, which means hospital (1) inpatient (1) from admission to discharge (1).

UB-04 Condition and Event Information (FL 18–41)

Fields 18 through 41 capture additional information about conditions and events that affect payment of the claim. There are three major categories in this section: (1) **condition codes** (FL 18–28), which relate to the patient's insurance eligibility and primary or secondary insurance coverage; (2) **occurrence codes** (FL 31–36), which identify specific events that determine liability for paying the claim, including coordinating health insurance benefits; and (3) **value codes** and amounts (FL 39–41), which identify actual dollar amounts that affect the patient's insurance benefits. Fields 29, 30, 37, and 38 are also described in this section. Figure 9–4 illustrates FL 18 through 41. Refer to the figure as you read about these fields.

Condition Codes (FL18–28)

This section of the UB-04 should be labeled "financial condition codes" because the information is used to determine the patient's insurance benefits, primary and secondary insurance coverage, and insurance liability other than the patient's health insurance carrier. There are literally hundreds of condition codes. It is beyond the scope of this text to define all of them. Some of the more commonly used condition codes are listed here:

- **02:** Condition is employment related; workers' compensation may be the primary payer.
- **09:** Neither the patient nor spouse is employed; required by Medicare when the patient and spouse are not employed and do not have insurance coverage with an employer

1 SUPERIORLAND HOSPITAL 835 MARQUETTE DRIVE BLUEBERRY ME 49855 906 312 9446 FAX 906 447 5131	2		3a PAT. CNTL # 457247112		4 TYPE OF BILL
			b. MED. REC. # 457247		111
			5 FED. TAX NO.	6 STATEMENT COVERS PERIOD FROM THROUGH	7
			49-2610830	1012YY 1017YY	

8 PATIENT NAME	a		9 PATIENT ADDRESS	a 609 OSBORN			
b SHATSKI STEPHAN M			b BLUEBERRY		c ME	d 49855	e

10 BIRTHDATE	11 SEX	12 DATE	ADMISSION 13 HR	14 TYPE	15 SRC	16 DHR	17 STAT	18	19	20	21	CONDITION CODES 22	23	24	25	26	27	28	29 ACDT STATE	30
12151966	M	1012YY	13	03	1	10	01													

31 OCCURRENCE CODE DATE	32 OCCURRENCE CODE DATE	33 OCCURRENCE CODE DATE	34 OCCURRENCE CODE DATE	35 OCCURRENCE SPAN CODE FROM THROUGH	36 OCCURRENCE SPAN CODE FROM THROUGH	37
a						a
b						b

38 SHATSKI STEPHAN M 609 OSBORN BLUEBERRY ME 49855	39 VALUE CODES CODE AMOUNT	40 VALUE CODES CODE AMOUNT	41 VALUE CODES CODE AMOUNT
	a A3	01 350 00	50 75 00
	b		
	c		
	d		

FIGURE 9–4 UB-04 FL 18–41 (For instructional use only. Courtesy of the Centers for Medicare and Medicaid Services, www.cms.hhs.gov)

- **10:** Patient or spouse is employed, but no employer-sponsored group health insurance program coverage exists; required by Medicare when the patient or spouse is employed but does not have health insurance with the employer
- **21:** Billing for denial notice; hospital knows that the service is not covered but needs a denial notice from Medicare in order to bill another insurance carrier
- **28:** Patient and/or spouse's employer-sponsored group health plan is secondary to Medicare
- **39:** Private room medically necessary; most insurance coverage pays for a semiprivate room (two patients per room); medical necessity must be documented, and the insurance carrier may require such documentation.

Enter as many codes as necessary to accurately describe the patient's financial condition related to health insurance coverage. These codes are usually associated with determining whether Medicare is the primary or secondary payer.

Although fields FL 29 and FL 30 are not condition codes, they are described here.

FL 29: Accident State (ACDT STATE)

If the admission is a result of an automobile accident, enter the two-character abbreviation for the state where the accident took place.

FL 30: (Untitled)

This is reserved for future use.

Occurrence Codes and Dates (FL 31–34)

Occurrence codes define a specific event, such as an auto accident, that affects payment of the claim. The date of the occurrence must also be reported. Complete the unshaded portions, FL 31a–FL 34a, before entering information in the shaded, FL 31b–FL 34b, portions. Enter dates in the eight-digit format (MMDDYYYY). Some of the more commonly used occurrence codes are listed here:

- **01:** Auto accident
- **02:** No-fault insurance
- **03:** Other accident, non-auto accident
- **04:** Accident, employment related

- **06:** Crime victim
- **11:** Onset of symptoms/illness; required when outpatient therapy services, such as physical therapy, are provided; include the date that the patient first became aware of the symptoms
- **16:** Date of last therapy; indicates the last day of therapy services such as physical, occupational, or speech therapy
- **18:** Date of retirement of the patient/beneficiary; required by Medicare
- **19:** Date of retirement of spouse; required by Medicare
- **24:** Date insurance denied; date that an insurance carrier other than Medicare denied payment of the claim
- **32:** Date beneficiary is notified of intent to bill for procedures or treatments; required by Medicare when the patient is covered by Medicare and elects to undergo a procedure or treatment that is not covered by Medicare. The patient must be given a written Advance Beneficiary Notice that describes the procedure and the cost and tells the patient that Medicare will not pay for the procedure.

If there are more than eight occurrences, use FL 35 and 36 to enter additional codes and dates. Leave the "through" block blank.

FL 35 and 36: Occurrence Span Codes and Date

This field is used to identify occurrences that happen over a period of time (e.g., a series of outpatient services, such as physical therapy). Enter the first and last date of the outpatient service in the From and Through fields. Dates are entered in the eight-digit format.

Although fields 37 and 38 are not occurrence codes, they are described here.

FL 37: (Untitled)

This is reserved for future use.

FL 38: Responsible Party (Untitled)

Enter the name and address of the person who is responsible for paying the bill. Patients who have reached the age of majority or who are emancipated minors are responsible for the bill, regardless of insurance coverage. When the patient is covered by health insurance, the responsible party pays the amount not covered by insurance. This field does not apply to individuals who are covered by Medicaid. All providers must accept Medicaid payment and are not allowed to bill the patient for the remaining balance.

Value Codes (FL 39–41)

A value code is a two-character numeric, alphabetic, or alphanumeric code that identifies the following information:

- An estimated amount that will be paid by the patient's insurance carrier
- The semiprivate room rate
- Co-insurance, co-payments, and deductibles that are the patient's responsibility
- Services that are not covered by the patient's health insurance

When more than one value code is needed, enter data in lines 39a through 41a first; in lines 39b through 41b second; and so forth. Enter the value codes in alphanumeric order. Table 9–9 lists and describes commonly used value codes.

TABLE 9–9

Value Codes with Descriptions	
Code	Description
01	Most common semiprivate room rate
14	No-fault auto or other insurance
15	Workers' compensation
32	Multiple patient ambulance transport (more than one patient, single ambulance)
37	Pints of blood furnished
47	Any liability insurance (accident, lawsuit, product liability suit)
50	Physical therapy visits
80	**Covered days**; number of days covered by health insurance; for Medicare claims, the admission staff or billing specialist can determine how many covered days are available to a Medicare beneficiary by accessing a regional Medicare Common Working File (CWF) database. The **Florida Shared System (FSS)** is one of the regional databases that serves this purpose.
81	Noncovered days; number of days not covered by health insurance
82	Co-insurance days; number of days that the patient must pay a co-insurance fee Medicare co-insurance days are counted from the 61st hospital day to the 150th hospital day; the co-insurance amount from the 61st day to the 90th day is 25% of the Medicare deductible; the coinsurance amount from the 91st day to the 150th day is 50% of the Medicare deductible. Other insurance plans may also have co-insurance day requirements.
83	**Lifetime reserve days**; number of days from the patient's Medicare lifetime reserve days (60 days maximum) for inpatient hospital care. The number of lifetime reserve days for a Medicare beneficiary is available by accessing one of the nine regional CWF databases. Lifetime reserve days can be used after the 90th day of hospitalization.
A1	Estimated deductible, Payer A (primary payer) (patient's responsibility)
A3	Estimated payment from Payer A (primary payer)
B3	Estimated payment from Payer B (secondary payer)

EXAMPLE

Travis was admitted for a total hip replacement and was in the hospital for five days. The semiprivate room rate for an orthopedic bed is $450 per day. Other charges for this hospitalization were $6,000, and the total bill was $8,250. Travis's insurance coverage requires a $500 deductible.

The billing specialist enters the following information in FL 39 through FL 41: value code 01 in line 39a under the heading "Code"; 450 00 in line 39a under the heading "Amount"; value code A1 in line 40a under the heading "Code";

500 00 in line 40a under the heading "Amount"; value code A3 in line 41a under the heading "Code"; and 7750 00 in line 41a under the heading "Amount."

Value code 01 identifies the entry as the semiprivate room rate; value code A1 identifies the entry as the patient's deductible; and value code A3 identifies the estimated payment expected from the insurance carrier.

There are hundreds of value codes representing services ranging from units of blood to co-insurance days. Requirements for completing FL 39–41 vary by insurance carrier. However, nearly all insurance carriers require information related to the semiprivate room rate, the estimated payment from the insurance carrier, co-insurance, co-payments, and deductibles. Secondary payers require value codes and amounts that are paid by a primary payer.

REINFORCEMENT EXERCISES 9–4

Write a brief description of the following terms.

1. Condition codes

_____

_____

2. Occurrence codes

_____

_____

3. Value codes

_____

_____

4. Occurrence span codes

_____

_____

5. Common working file

_____

_____

6. Co-insurance days

_____

_____

7. Lifetime reserve days

_____

_____

continued on the next page

continued from the previous page

Identify each of the following codes and descriptions as a condition code, an occurrence code, or a value code.

1. A3: Estimated payment from the primary payer _____

2. 01: Auto accident _____

3. 01: Most common semiprivate room rate _____

4. 06: Crime victim _____

5. 09: Neither patient nor spouse is employed _____

6. 15: Workers' compensation _____

7. 16: Date of last therapy _____

8. 21: Billing for denial _____

9. 39: Private room medically necessary _____

10. 83: Lifetime reserve days _____

42 REV. CD.	43 DESCRIPTION	44 HCPCS / RATES	45 SERV. DATE	46 SERV. UNITS	47 TOTAL CHARGES	48 NON-COVERED CHARGES	49	
120	R/B SEMI	350 00		5	1750 00			1
250	PHARMACY				750 00			2
258	IV SOLUTIONS				5 00			3
274	PROSTHETIC DEVICE				400 00			4
301	LAB / CHEMISTRY				350 00			5
324	DX CHEST / XRAY				75 00	75 00		6
360	OR SERVICES				1500 00			7
370	ANESTHESIA				200 00			8
421	PHYS THERAP / VISIT				75 00			9
710	RECOVERY ROOM				120 00			10
730	EKG/ECG				95 00			11
								12
								13
								14
								15
								16
								17
								18
								19
								20
								21
								22
001	TOTAL CHARGES			5	5320 00	75 00		23

FIGURE 9–5 UB-04 FL 42–49 (For instructional use only. Courtesy of the Centers for Medicare and Medicaid Services, www.cms.hhs.gov)

FL 42 and 43: Revenue Code (REV. CD.) and Description

Revenue codes are three- or four-digit numbers that identify services provided to the patient. When the insurance carrier requires a four-digit entry in this field, the first digit is always 0. Each revenue code has a narrative description that is entered in FL 43. The last entry in FL 42–43 is *always* revenue code 001, with the description "total charges" in FL 43. The total charges must equal the sum of both covered and noncovered charges. There are nearly 1,000 revenue codes that are used by all insurance carriers.

Revenue codes are divided into two categories: accommodation codes and ancillary services codes. **Accommodation codes** identify the type of bed—such as medical/surgical, pediatric, or psychiatric—that the patient occupies in a hospital room. A hospital room is classified as follows: "private," a single-bed room; "semiprivate," two beds per room or three and four beds per room; and "ward," five or more beds per room. Room and board charges/rates vary by room classification and type of bed. A private room in an intensive care unit (ICU) will have a higher room rate than a ward in a medical/surgical unit. The room and board rate includes items and services such as routine linens, towels, nightgowns, meals, and routine nursing care associated with the specific unit. Table 9–10 lists some of the accommodation revenue codes with descriptions.

TABLE 9–10

Accommodation Revenue Codes (FL 42)	
Accommodation Code	**Definition**
114	Psychiatric, private room
116	Detoxification unit, private room
120	General medical, semiprivate room
121	Medical/surgical, gynecology (GYN), semiprivate room
122	Obstetrics (OB), semiprivate room
123	Pediatric, semiprivate room
124	Psychiatric, semiprivate room
151	Medical/surgical, gynecology, ward
171	Newborn nursery, Level I, routine newborn care
174	Newborn nursery, Level IV, newborn intensive care
201	Intensive care unit (ICU), surgical care
206	Intermediate intensive care unit, post ICU, also called step down
211	Coronary care unit (CCU), myocardial infarction care
212	Coronary care unit, pulmonary care
213	Coronary care unit, heart transplant care

Ancillary services codes identify services and supplies that are not included in the room and board charges. Items and services such as an egg-crate mattress, pharmacy, laboratory tests, and radiology services are separate entries in FL 42 and 43. Table 9–11 lists some of the ancillary services revenue codes with descriptions.

TABLE 9–11

Ancillary Services Revenue Codes (FL 42)	
Ancillary Services Code	Description
250	Pharmacy, general
258	Intravenous (IV) solutions
261	IV therapy, infusion pump
264	IV therapy/supplies
274	Prosthetic device
275	Pacemaker
276	Intraocular lens
301	Laboratory, blood chemistry tests
306	Lab/bacteriology and microbiology blood tests
311	Lab/pathological, cytology; laboratory tests on cells
312	Lab/pathological, histology; laboratory tests on tissue
314	Lab/pathological, biopsy
321	Radiology/diagnostic, angiocardiography
322	Radiology/diagnostic, arthrography
324	Chest x-ray
331	Radiology/therapeutic, chemotherapy—injected
333	Radiology/therapeutic, radiation therapy
341	Nuclear medicine, diagnostic procedures
342	Nuclear medicine, therapeutic procedures
352	Computerized tomography (CT) scans, whole body
360	Operating room services
370	Anesthesia, general
402	Other imaging services, ultrasound
421	Physical therapy visit
710	Recovery room
730	EKG/ECG (electrocardiogram)

When a UB-04 is generated, the hospital's billing software (chargemaster) enters the revenue codes in FL 42. A narrative description of the revenue code is simultaneously entered in FL 43. The billing specialist reviews the revenue codes and descriptions to determine if entries are complete and accurate.

> **EXAMPLE**
>
> Jane Li reviews the UB-04 for a patient who underwent a total hip replacement. She notes that a general anesthesia revenue code (370) and an operating room service code (360) are listed in FL 42 and 43. A code for recovery room services is not included on the UB-04. Jane knows that a general anesthesia code should be billed with a recovery room code (710). Jane puts a hold on the claim and notifies the surgical department that a recovery room revenue code is needed. Surgical department staff enters the revenue code. Jane retrieves the UB-04, completes the editing process, and releases the claim for submission.

FL 44: HCPCS/Rates/HIPPS Code

FL 44 is used to report three types of information: 1) the CPT or HCPCS code for the services identified in FL 42 and 43; 2) the per-day room rate for inpatient care for the type of accommodation identified in FL 42 and 43; and 3) the Health Insurance Prospective Payment System (HIPPS) rate that apply to skilled nursing facilities.

For inpatient hospital claims, the first line of FL 42 is the accommodation code, the FL 43 is a narrative description of the accommodation (see Figure 9–5), and the per-day room rate is entered in FL 44. For inpatient ancillary services identified in FL 42 and 43, such as pharmacy and IV solutions, FL 44 is left blank (see Figure 9–5).

For outpatient (ambulatory) claims, FL 44 is used to report either the *Current Procedural Terminology* (CPT) codes or the *Healthcare Common Procedure Coding System* (HCPCS) codes that apply to the ancillary services revenue codes identified in FL 42 and 43. The CPT or HCPCS codes identify the *specific* service provided to the patient. For example, there are about 50 blood chemistry tests associated with revenue code 301 (laboratory, chemistry). When different blood chemistry tests are done, the revenue code is always 301, and the CPT or HCPCS code tells the insurance carrier exactly which tests the patient received. CPT or HCPCS codes are required entries for Medicare outpatient claims.

FL 45: Service Date (SERV. DATE)

For inpatient services, this field is often not required; leave it blank. Some insurance carriers require this field for outpatient services, such as diagnostic tests. Enter the eight-digit date on which each service identified in FL 42-44 was provided, if required.

FL 46: Service Units (SERV. UNITS)

This field is used to report the number of services identified in FL 42–44 that were provided. Units of service include items such as the number of days in the type of accommodation (hospital room), pints of blood, number of tests performed, and number of therapeutic activities or treatments. Therapeutic activity units of service are measured in 15- or 30-minute increments, which means that every 15 or 30 minutes of therapy is equal to one unit of service. For example, if a patient spends 38 minutes in physical therapy and a unit of service is 30 minutes, enter 1 in FL 46.

FL 47: Total Charges

Enter the total charges for the services identified in FL 42.

FL 48: Noncovered Charges
Enter the charges for the services identified in FL 42 that are *not* covered by the insurance carrier. The noncovered charges are included in the dollar amount entered in FL 47.

FL 49: Untitled
This is for future use.

REINFORCEMENT EXERCISES 9–5

Fill in the blank.

1. _____ is the description for the last entry in FL 43.

2. The type of bed occupied by the patient is identified by a(n) _____.

3. _____ identify services and supplies not included in the room and board rates.

4. _____ identify a specific service that was provided during an outpatient episode of care.

5. Therapeutic activity units of service are measured in _____.

Insurance and Employer Information (FL 50–65)

This section of the UB-04 captures information related to insurance plans, the patient or insured, and employer identification. Accurate insurance information ensures that the primary payer is billed first and that all other payers, especially Medicare, are subsequently billed in the correct order. Insurance information is captured at the time of registration and is entered into the hospital's database. Figure 9–6 illustrates FL 50–65. Refer to this figure as you read the descriptions.

FL 50: Payer Name
Enter the name(s) of the health insurance plan(s) that provide payment for services. The primary payer's (first billed) name is entered on line A; the secondary payer's name is entered on line B; and the tertiary (third) payer's name is entered on line C. If Medicare is the primary payer, enter MEDICARE on line A.

FL 51: Health Plan No.
Enter the plan number for the payer named in FL 50. The health plan number, which is on the insurance card, is captured during the patient registration process.

50 PAYER NAME	51 HEALTH PLAN ID	52 REL INFO.	53 ASG BEN.	54 PRIOR PAYMENTS	55 EST. AMOUNT DUE	56 NPI	8901234567
AETNA	9101003777	Y	Y		5245 00	57 OTHER PRV ID	

58 INSURED'S NAME	59 P. REL.	60 INSURED'S UNIQUE ID	61 GROUP NAME	62 INSURANCE GROUP NO.
SHATSKI STEPHAN M	18	MSB 902332438	NMU	8100

63 TREATMENT AUTHORIZATION CODES	64 DOCUMENT CONTROL NUMBER	65 EMPLOYER NAME
		NORTHERN MAINE UNIVERSITY

FIGURE 9–6 UB-04 FL 50–65 (For instructional use only. Courtesy of the Centers for Medicare and Medicaid Services, www.cms.hhs.gov)

FL 52: Release of Information (REL INFO)

This field tells the payer that the provider has the patient's signature on file to authorize the release of information necessary to process the insurance claim. The patient signs the release of information authorization at the time of registration/admission. Enter one of the following:

- **Y** for "yes": The patient agrees to release information
- **R** for "restricted": The patient places some restrictions on the release
- **N** for "no": The patient refuses to release information

The patient may restrict the release of certain types of information, such as HIV status, substance abuse, or any information not related to the current admission. When the patient refuses to release information, registration staff informs the patient that an insurance claim cannot be submitted and the patient must pay the bill.

FL 53: Assignment of Benefits (ASG BEN)

Assignment of benefits means that the patient authorizes the insurance carrier to send payment to the facility. The patient may also choose not to assign benefits, and in that case, payment is sent to the patient. Admission staff enters Y for "yes" or N for "no," depending on the patient's choice.

FL 54: Prior Payments

Payments received before the claim is submitted to an insurance plan are entered in FL 54. This includes deductibles and co-payments collected from the patient. When a claim is submitted to more than one payer, the billing specialist enters the payment received from other payers. For example, a claim submitted to the secondary payer must include the payment received from the primary payer. Claims submitted to a tertiary payer must include the payments received from the primary and secondary payers. Use lines A, B, and C to record payments received from the insurance carriers identified in lines A, B, and C in FL 50.

FL 55: Estimated Amount Due

Enter the amount that represents the estimated payment expected from a payer listed in FL 50 A, B, or C. The amount(s) entered in FL 55 A, B, or C must correspond to the insurance carriers noted in FL 50.

FL 56: NPI (National Provider Identification Number)

Enter the billing provider's 10-digit NPI. The billing provider is the agency that submits the claim and receives payment for services rendered.

FL 57: Other Provider ID

In some cases, the insurance company assigns a unique identification number to providers. If the payer identified in FL 50 A, B, or C has assigned an identification number to the billing provider, enter that number in FL 57 A, B, or C. The identification number in FL 57 must correspond to the insurance company name in FL 50.

FL 58: Insured's Name

Enter the full name—last, first, and middle initial (if required)—of the insured or **subscriber**, defined as the individual who has the insurance. If more than one insurance plan is listed in FL 50, enter the subscriber's name on FL 58 A, B, and C that corresponds to the insurance company in FL 50 A, B, and C. When the patient is the subscriber, the names are the same. If the patient is covered

Table 9–12

Relationship Codes		
HIPAA Code	Explanation	Previous Code
01	Spouse	02
10	Foster child	06
15	Ward (patient is ward of insured)	07
17	Stepchild (son or daughter)	05
18	Self (patient is the insured)	01
19	Child (patient is natural child of the insured)	03
20	Employee (patient is an employee of the insured	08
22	Handicapped dependent (dependent child whose coverage extends beyond usual termination age limits)	10
41	Injured plaintiff (patient is claiming insurance as a result of injury covered by the insured)	15
53	Life partner; domestic partner; significant other	20

by another individual's insurance, the subscriber's name is different from the patient's name. For Medicaid claims, the patient is always the subscriber because all Medicaid recipients have their own ID card. For Medicare claims, enter the name that appears on the patient's Medicare ID card.

FL 59: Patient's Relationship to Insured (P. REL)
Enter the code that accurately reflects the patient's relationship to the individuals named in FL 58 A, B, and C. In October 2003, Medicare implemented **Health Insurance Portability and Accountability Act (HIPAA)** security codes for this field. Other insurance carriers require either the HIPAA or previous relationship codes. Some frequently used relationship codes are listed in Table 9–12.

FL 60: Insured's Unique ID
Enter the insured's ID number *exactly* as it appears on the patient's health insurance identification card. Medicare beneficiaries are assigned a **health insurance claim number (HICN)** as the insured's ID number. If more than one insurance plan is listed in FL 50, enter the insured's ID number in FL 60 A, B, and C that corresponds to the insurance plans in FL 50 A, B, and C.

FL 61, 62: Group Name, Insurance Group Number
Enter the name and insurance group number of the group or plan that provides health insurance coverage to the insured in FL 61 and 62, respectively. This may be the name of the insured's employer, a fraternal or professional association, or other organization. If more than one insurance plan is listed in FL 50, enter the group or plan name on FL 61 A, B, and C that corresponds to the insurance plans in FL 50 A, B, and C. Likewise, enter the insurance group number on FL 62 A, B, and C that corresponds to the insurance plans in FL 50 A, B, and C. When Medicare is the primary payer, leave FL 61 and 62 blank.

EXAMPLE

Rhonda is employed by UP University (UUU), which provides health insurance for over 6,000 employees. Rhonda's insurance identification number is XYZ123456. UUU's health insurance plan is administered through the Teacher's Health Insurance Company (THIC), and the plan number is UU5559. In this example, the group or plan name, UP University, is entered in FL 61 and the insurance plan number, UU5559, is entered in FL 62.

FL 63: Treatment Authorization Codes

When the insurance plan requires prior authorization for services, enter the authorization code assigned by the payer or insurance plan. The primary payer's authorization code is entered on line FL 63A. Secondary and tertiary payer authorization codes may be entered on lines FL 63B and FL 63C, respectively, or in the Remarks section (FL 80).

FL 64: Document Control Number

This field is used when the current claim is related to or a replacement for previous claim that was submitted to a payer. The previous claim number is entered in FL 64. The entry in FL 64A should refer to the payer identified in FL 50A; FL 64B to FL 50B; and FL 64C to FL 50C.

FL 65: Employer Name

If required by the insurance plan, enter the name of the employer(s) of the insured individual(s) entered in FL 58 A, B, and C in FL 65. For FL 65, line A corresponds to the primary payer identified in FL 50A; line B corresponds to the secondary payer (FL 50B); and line C corresponds to the tertiary payer (FL 50C). The employer's name is often needed or required for workers' compensation claims.

REINFORCEMENT EXERCISES 9–6

Write a brief description for each term.

1. assignment of benefits

_____

2. HICN

_____

3. relationship code

_____

4. billing provider

_____

5. treatment authorization code

_____

Medical Codes and Physician Identification (FL 66–81)

This section of the UB-04 captures the diagnosis and procedure codes that identify the patient's medical condition(s) and related treatment(s). At a minimum, inaccurate coding has a negative impact on reimbursement. Intentional coding errors can lead to charges of insurance fraud, whereas unintentional coding errors can lead to charges of insurance abuse. As previously stated, documentation in the patient's record must clearly support all medical codes submitted with the insurance claim.

Diagnoses related to hospital inpatient and outpatient insurance claims are reported by the *International Classification of Diseases, Ninth Revision, Clinical Modification* (ICD-9-CM) coding system. The ICD-9-CM codes must be assigned to the highest level of specificity, which means diagnoses codes consist of three to five digits.

Depending on the requirements of the insurance carrier, procedures are reported by either ICD-9-CM procedure codes or *Healthcare Common Procedure Coding System* (HCPCS) codes. For inpatient claims, procedures are reported by ICD-9-CM codes. For outpatient claims, Medicare and Medicaid require HCPCS procedure codes, which are entered in FL 44. Other payers (insurance carriers) may also require HCPCS procedure codes for outpatient procedures.

HCPCS codes are divided into two categories: Level I and Level II. Level I HCPCS procedure codes are the same as the *Current Procedural Terminology* (CPT) codes. Therefore, outpatient procedures for Medicare, Medicaid, and other payers as required are reported by CPT codes. Level II HCPCS codes, also called "national codes," are used to report services such as ambulance services, chiropractic services, dental procedures, drugs and medications, and durable medical equipment.

Figure 9–7 illustrates FL 66–81. Refer to this figure as you learn about these fields.

FL 66: DX (Diagnosis and Procedure Code Qualifier)

Enter the number that identifies the version of the *International Classification of Diseases* (ICD) used to report medical codes. Enter a 9 to denote ICD-9-CM. When ICD-10 is implemented, the qualifier will be 10.

FL 67: Preprinted 67 (Principle Diagnosis Code)

For inpatient claims, the **principal diagnosis** is the condition established after study to be chiefly responsible for the patient's admission. Enter the ICD-9-CM code for the condition or diagnosis that meets the definition of "principal diagnosis." The ICD-9-CM diagnosis code must be reported to the highest level of specificity, which means the code may consist of three to five digits. Do not

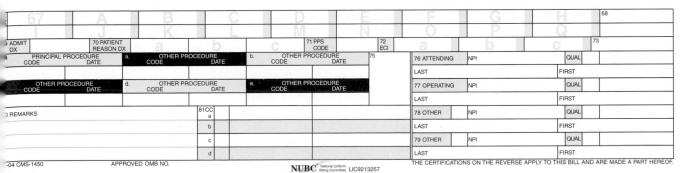

FIGURE 9–7 UB-04 FL 66–81 (For instructional use only. Courtesy of the Centers for Medicare and Medicaid Services, www.cms.hhs.gov)

use a period or decimal point to separate the third and fourth digits. Physicians and medical coders are responsible for identifying the principal diagnosis. The billing specialist works closely with the medical coder—and the physician if necessary—to resolve any questions concerning the principal diagnosis.

For outpatient claims, enter the ICD-9-CM code that identifies the diagnosis or symptom that is chiefly responsible for the outpatient service. If the outpatient service results in a definitive diagnosis, enter the ICD-9-CM code for the definitive diagnosis.

> **EXAMPLE A (OUTPATIENT CLAIM)**
> Chiquita is admitted as an outpatient for a colonoscopy to evaluate the cause of frequent episodes of cramping and diarrhea. The colonoscopy is negative, and the physician tells Chiquita to increase fiber in her diet. In this example, the principal diagnosis is diarrhea, and the appropriate ICD-9-CM code is entered in FL 67.

> **EXAMPLE B (OUTPATIENT CLAIM)**
> Chiquita is admitted as an outpatient for a colonoscopy to evaluate the cause of frequent episodes of cramping and diarrhea. The colonoscopy reveals ulcerative colitis. The physician prescribes medication and tells Chiquita to call her if the symptoms do not subside in three days. In this example, ulcerative colitis is the definitive diagnosis, and the appropriate ICD-9-CM code is entered in FL 67.

FL 67A–Q: Preprinted (Other Diagnosis Codes)

Enter the ICD-9-CM diagnosis codes for additional problems or conditions that either co-exist at the time of admission or develop during the patient's length of stay and affect the treatment and services provided. Do not use a period or decimal point between the third and fourth digits.

FL 68: Untitled

This is for future use.

FL 69: Admitting Diagnosis (Admit Dx)

The **admitting diagnosis** is the diagnosis, condition, symptom, or other reason that required hospitalization. The admitting diagnosis is identified by the physician. Third-party payers use the admitting diagnosis to determine if the inpatient admission or outpatient service was justified. Enter the ICD-9-CM code for the admitting diagnosis. The admitting diagnosis may be called the chief complaint or the provisional diagnosis.

FL 70a–c: Patient's Reason for Visit (Patient Reason Dx)

These fields are used for unscheduled outpatient visits. Enter the diagnosis code for the patient's reason for seeking treatment.

FL 71: Prospective Payment System Code (PPS Code)

If required by the insurance plan, enter the MS-DRG or the APC code in this field.

FL 72: External Cause of Injury Code (ECI)

E codes, which are part of the ICD-9-CM coding system, identify external causes of injury, such as accidents, poisonings, or other adverse affects. FL 72 is an optional field and is completed according to facility policy or insurance carrier requirements. When this field is used, enter the E code, and do not use a period or decimal point between the third and fourth digits.

FL 73: Untitled
Reserve this for future use.

FL 74: Principal Procedure Code and Date
For inpatient claims, the **principal procedure** is the procedure performed for definitive treatment rather than for diagnostic or exploratory purposes. If two or more procedures appear to meet this definition, the procedure most closely related to the principal diagnosis is selected as the principal procedure. The hospital's medical coders are responsible for identifying the principal procedure and assigning the correct code. The billing specialist works closely with the medical coder to resolve any questions concerning the principal procedure. Enter the ICD-9-CM three- or four-digit code that identifies the principal procedure. Do not include a period or decimal point between the second and third digits. Enter the date of the procedure in the eight-digit format.

For outpatient claims, the principal procedure is the procedure performed during the outpatient encounter. Outpatient procedures are coded with ICD-9-CM procedure codes. Enter the three- or four-digit procedure code without a period or decimal point between the second and third digits. Although the provider may capture the ICD-9-CM procedure code for internal use, for Medicare, Medicaid, and other third-party payers for outpatient claims, the CPT (Level I HCPCS code) *must* be listed in FL 44. For electronic claims, the claims submission software automatically deletes the ICD-9-CM procedure codes *before* the claim is sent to the Medicare and Medicaid insurance carrier.

FL 74a–e: Other Procedure Code and Date
This field is used to report additional significant procedures related to the current episode of care. Both diagnostic and treatment procedures that relate to the principal diagnosis are included on the UB-04. For inpatient claims, enter the ICD-9-CM code for the additional diagnostic and treatment procedures. For outpatient claims, the HCPCS code *must* be listed in FL 44.

FL 75: Untitled
This is reserved for future use.

FL 76: Attending Physician (Provider) Name and Identification (Attending NPI; QUAL)
Enter the NPI number for the physician (provider) with overall responsibility for the patient's care and treatment. For other identification numbers, enter the two-digit qualifier (0B = State License Number; 1G = Unique provider identification number (UPIN); or G2 Provider Commercial Number) in the unshaded QUAL block. Enter the other identification number to the right of the two-digit qualifier.

Enter the physician's last and first name in the blocks below the identification numbers.

FL 77: Operating Provider Name and Identification Number (Operating)
Enter the surgeon's name and identification number following the same guidelines for the attending physician (provider) as described in FL 76.

FL 78–79: Other Provider Name and Identification Number (Other)
These fields are used to report the name and identification number of other physicians who provided services to the patient. Enter the other physician/provider name and identification number, as described in FL 76.

EXAMPLE

Carlos is admitted for coronary bypass surgery. During the postoperative period, he develops four-limb paresis, and a neurologist is called in to evaluate Carlos's condition. The surgeon and neurologist both provide treatment until Carlos is discharged. In this example, the neurologist's ID number and name are entered in FL 78 or FL 79.

FL 80: Remarks

This field is used to report additional information required by the payer to assist in claims processing. The information may include the address of the insured when it is not the same as the patient's address; narrative description of unlisted procedure codes; date a Medicare beneficiary received an Advance Beneficiary Notice; reason for billing Medicare prior to receiving payment from the primary payer; reasons that a claim is cancelled or voided; or other comments required by the payer.

FL 81a–d: Code-Code (CC)

This field is used to report additional codes related to a Form Locator, such as FL 39 value codes. FL 81 is also used to report the hospital's **taxonomy code**. A taxonomy code is a 10-digit alphanumeric number that identifies the provider's specialty or provider type. These codes were developed to facilitate electronic claims processing that comply with HIPAA requirements. According to the CMS website, health care providers, including hospitals, select a taxonomy code that most closely represents the services offered by the individual practitioner or facility. For example, taxonomy code 282N00000X identifies a general acute care hospital. Some insurance plans require the taxonomy code for insurance claims processing. Figure 9–8 is an example of a completed UB-04.

REINFORCEMENT EXERCISES 9–7

Fill in the blank.

1. _____ codes are used to report all diagnoses.

2. Level I HCPCS procedure codes are the same as _____ codes.

3. The _____ diagnosis is the reason that caused the patient to seek treatment.

4. _____ identify external causes of injury and may or may not be included on the UB-04.

5. The _____ is performed for definitive treatment rather than for exploratory purposes.

6. The _____ is primarily responsible for the patient's medical care and treatment.

7. Level II HCPCS codes are also called _____.

8. For Medicare outpatient claims, the _____ must be listed in FL 44.

9. A _____ code is an alphanumeric number that is used to facilitate electronic claims processing.

10. ICD-9-CM codes must be reported to the highest level of _____.

1 SUPERIORLAND HOSPITAL 835 MARQUETTE DRIVE BLUEBERRY ME 49855 906 312 9446 FAX 906 447 5131	2		3a PAT. CNTL # 457247112		4 TYPE OF BILL
			b. MED. REC. # 457247		111
			5 FED. TAX NO.	6 STATEMENT COVERS PERIOD FROM THROUGH	7
			49-2610830	1012YY 1017YY	

8 PATIENT NAME: b SHATSKI STEPHAN M
9 PATIENT ADDRESS: a 609 OSBORN b BLUEBERRY c ME d 49855

10 BIRTHDATE 12151966 | 11 SEX M | ADMISSION 12 DATE 1012YY 13 HR 13 14 TYPE 03 15 SRC 1 | 16 DHR 10 | 17 STAT 01

CONDITION CODES 18-28; 29 ACDT STATE; 30

31-37 OCCURRENCE / OCCURRENCE SPAN

38 SHATSKI STEPHAN M
609 OSBORN
BLUEBERRY ME 49855

39 CODE AMOUNT	40 CODE AMOUNT	41 CODE AMOUNT
A3 5245 00	01 350 00	50 75 00

42 REV CD.	43 DESCRIPTION	44 HCPCS/RATE/HIPPS CODE	45 SERV. DATE	46 SERV. UNITS	47 TOTAL CHARGES	48 NON-COVERED CHARGES	49
120	R/B SEMI	350 00		5	1750 00		1
250	PHARMACY				750 00		2
258	IV SOLUTIONS				5 00		3
274	PROSTHETIC DEVICE				400 00		4
301	LAB/CHEMISTRY				350 00		5
324	DX CHEST XRAY				75 00	75 00	6
360	OR SERVICES				1500 00		7
370	ANESTHESIA				200 00		8
421	PHYS/THERAP/VISIT				75 00		9
710	RECOVERY ROOM				120 00		10
730	EKG/ECG				95 00		11
001	TOTAL CHARGES			5	5320 00	75 00	22

PAGE ___ OF ___ | CREATION DATE | TOTALS →

50 PAYER NAME	51 HEALTH PLAN ID	52 REL INFO.	53 ASG BEN.	54 PRIOR PAYMENTS	55 EST. AMOUNT DUE	56 NPI 8901234567
A AETNA	9101003777	Y	Y		5245 00	57 OTHER PRV ID

58 INSURED'S NAME	59 P. REL.	60 INSURED'S UNIQUE ID	61 GROUP NAME	62 INSURANCE GROUP NO.
SHATSKI STEPHAN M	18	MSB 902332438	NMU	8100

63 TREATMENT AUTHORIZATION CODES | 64 DOCUMENT CONTROL NUMBER | 65 EMPLOYER NAME NORTHERN MAINE UNIVERSITY

66 DX 71516 250 00 | 68
9

69 ADMIT DX 71516 | 70 PATIENT REASON DX | 71 PPS CODE | 72 ECI | 73

74 PRINCIPAL PROCEDURE CODE DATE 8154 1013YY | a. OTHER PROCEDURE | b. OTHER PROCEDURE | 75 | 76 ATTENDING NPI 5584547890 QUAL LAST SOROCHUK FIRST OLENA

c. OTHER PROCEDURE | d. OTHER PROCEDURE | e. OTHER PROCEDURE | 77 OPERATING NPI 6695678681 QUAL LAST HOWARD FIRST ROBERT

80 REMARKS | 81CC a 282N00000X | 78 OTHER NPI QUAL LAST FIRST | 79 OTHER NPI QUAL LAST FIRST

UB-04 CMS-1450 | APPROVED OMB NO. 0938-0997 | NUBC™ NATIONAL UNIFORM BILLING COMMITTEE | THE CERTIFICATIONS ON THE REVERSE APPLY TO THIS BILL AND ARE MADE A PART HEREOF.

FIGURE 9–8 Completed UB–04 (For instructional use only. Courtesy of the Centers for Medicare and Medicaid Services, www.cms.hhs.gov)

SUBMITTING THE INSURANCE CLAIM

Most insurance claims are submitted electronically. The hospital may use direct claims submission, which means the billing specialist sends the claim directly to the insurance carrier. Many health care providers, including hospitals, use a clearinghouse for electronic claims submission. A **clearinghouse** is an organization that accepts electronic claims, edits the claims, provides the billing specialist with error-edit messages, and subsequently distributes the claims to the appropriate insurance carriers. Chapter 10 includes a more detailed discussion of direct and clearinghouse **electronic claims submission (ECS)**. The information presented here relates to clearinghouse ECS.

Once the patient is discharged and medical codes are assigned, patient information is released or downloaded to the electronic billing system. The billing specialist can access the claims by payer type, service type, or individual claim with the patient's name and patient control number. The UB-04 for the individual patient is displayed. The billing specialist checks the UB-04 to determine if all required fields are completed. Special attention is given to the following information:

- The patient's name and sex appear to be consistent.
- ICD-9-CM and HCPCS codes are properly located on the UB-04.
- Insurance/payer information is present.

Billing specialists are often assigned one or two payers for insurance claims processing. The billing specialist then becomes very familiar with the requirements of the assigned payers and can readily identify problems that may cause a claim to be delayed or denied.

> **EXAMPLE**
>
> Marcus is the billing specialist for Aetna, and he is reviewing a claim for a patient who received outpatient physical therapy treatments. Marcus knows that when the patient receives outpatient physical therapy services, Aetna requires occurrence code 11 and a corresponding date in FL 32. Occurrence code 11 indicates that outpatient physical therapy services were provided, and the date identifies when the patient first became aware of the symptoms. As Marcus checks the UB-04, he notes that FL 32 is not completed, and there are charges for physical therapy treatments in FL 42 through FL 47. Marcus puts a hold on the claim, which prevents the claim from being sent to the clearinghouse. He also phones or e-mails the physical therapist and requests the needed date. When Marcus receives the date, he brings up the patient's UB-04, adds the occurrence code and date, and releases the claim for further processing.

When the billing specialist releases the insurance claim, the hospital can submit the claim to the clearinghouse. Some hospitals submit claims in batches at regular intervals, while others allow submission at the time the billing specialist releases the claim. The clearinghouse software programs review and edit the claim for compliance with specific payer requirements and for HIPAA compliance as well. A **clean claim** has no errors and is submitted to the appropriate insurance company. A **dirty claim** has errors or omissions that would cause the claim to be delayed or denied. The clearinghouse places a hold on dirty claims and sends error messages to the billing department.

The billing specialist receives the error messages for all claims that have errors or omissions. The error message lists the claims by patient control number and name and includes a detailed list of problems for each claim. More than one claim is included on the error message. The billing specialist retrieves each claim and makes the corrections.

More often than not, the billing specialist can readily correct errors involving these:

- The patient's age, sex, and marital status
- Simple data entry (typographical) mistakes
- Health Plan ID number(s) (FL 51)
- The provider NPI or ID number (FL 56 or FL 57)
- The insurance group number (FL 62)
- Physician NPI or other ID numbers (FL 77–79)

When the error messages relate to invalid codes, the billing specialist contacts the health information (medical record) department or medical coders and requests the correct codes for the claim.

EXAMPLE

Hannah is a billing specialist for Blueberry Memorial Hospital. She works primarily with Medicare inpatient claims and is in the process of reviewing error messages from the insurance carrier. The error message for Mr. Smith's claim states "invalid code, principal procedure." Mr. Smith was hospitalized for a total proctocolectomy due to severe universal ulcerative colitis. Hannah checks the ICD-9-CM diagnosis code listed as the principal diagnosis in FL 67. The code is 787.91, which is the code for diarrhea. In this case, the principal procedure is not consistent with the principal diagnosis. Hannah contacts a medical coder and requests clarification of the principal diagnosis. The medical coder reviews the patient's record and notes that the code for ulcerative colitis was omitted. Ulcerative colitis is the principal diagnosis and is consistent with the principal procedure. The coder enters the code 556.6 for universal ulcerative colitis into the database. After the code is entered, Hannah releases the claim for resubmission.

In some cases, an experienced billing specialist knows that a specific treatment is included in an overall code and the specific treatment cannot be billed separately.

EXAMPLE

Katka is a billing specialist for Superiorland Hospital. She handles all Blue Cross claims and recently received an error message for a patient who had several outpatient physical therapy treatments. The error message states "invalid code, physical therapy services." Katka retrieves the claim and reviews the charges. She notes that the claim includes six entries for physical therapy services and six entries for "cryotherapy." Cryotherapy is a specific type of physical therapy. Katka knows that cryotherapy cannot be billed separately and is included as part of the charge for the physical therapy service. Katka edits the claim, and the separate charges for cryotherapy are deleted. Katka releases the claim for resubmission.

The insurance carrier may also reject claims and send error messages to the billing department. The error message, sometimes called a "facility claim correction message," for a given date or time period lists all claims that need corrections. The billing specialist clicks on the claim identification number, and a window opens that describes the error. As with clearinghouse errors, the billing specialist is often able to correct the errors and resubmit the claim. At times, the billing specialist must contact the insurance carrier to resolve issues related to rejected or denied claims.

Billing specialists rely on nearly every department in the hospital to capture accurate information for insurance claims processing. Although the information is electronically stored, retrieved, and submitted, it is initially entered by people—and people can make mistakes. In order to correct data entry errors, mistakes, and omissions, the successful billing specialist must be detail-oriented and able to communicate and work with others.

ABBREVIATIONS

Table 9–13 lists the abbreviations with meanings in this chapter.

TABLE 9–13

Abbreviations and Meanings	
Abbreviation	Meaning
APC	Ambulatory Payment Classification (system)
CC	complication/co-morbidity
CMS	Centers for Medicare and Medicaid Services
DRG	diagnosis related group
ECS	electronic claims submission
FL	field locator
HHS	Department of Health and Human Services
HICN	health insurance claim number
IPPS	inpatient prospective payment system
LOS	length of stay
MCC	major complication/co-morbidity
MS-DRG	medical-severity diagnosis related group
NUBC	National Uniform Billing Committee
OPPS	outpatient prospective payment system
UB-04	Uniform Bill (2004 revision)
UHDDS	Uniform Hospital Discharge Data Set

SUMMARY

This chapter introduces the student to the UB-04, which is the universal hospital claims submission form. The UB-04 is used for hospital inpatient and outpatient claims, skilled nursing facility claims, and home health agency claims. There are 81 fields on the UB-04, and completion requirements vary by third-party payers, also known as insurance carriers. Although most insurance claims are filed electronically, there are times when a paper claim must be submitted. The billing specialist is usually the last—and sometimes the only—person to review and edit the complete UB-04 before it is submitted. In addition, the billing specialist works with various hospital departments and staff to correct or resolve erroneous or inaccurate claims information.

REVIEW EXERCISES

Abbreviations

Spell out each abbreviation.

1. APC _____

2. CMS _____

3. CPT _____

4. HHS _____

5. MS-DRG _____

6. DCN _____

7. FL _____

8. HCPCS _____

9. HICN _____

10. LOS _____

11. NUBC _____

12. OPPS _____

13. UHDDS _____

14. NPI _____

Short Answer

Write a brief description for each term.

1. Admitting diagnosis

   _____

   _____

   _____

2. Chargemaster

   _____

   _____

   _____

3. Primary payer

   _____

   _____

   _____

4. Principal diagnosis

   _____

   _____

   _____

5. Principal procedure

   _____

   _____

   _____

6. Florida Shared System

   _____

   _____

   _____

7. Clean claim

   _____

   _____

   _____

8. Dirty claim

_____

_____

_____

Multiple Choice

Circle the best answer from the choices provided.

1. The universal hospital claims form is called the
   a. CMS-1450.
   b. CMS-1500.
   c. UB-04.
   d. a and c
   e. none of the above

2. Diagnosis related groups were developed as part of the
   a. outpatient prospective payment system.
   b. inpatient prospective payment system.
   c. CMS discharge data set.
   d. ICD-9-CM coding system.
   e. all the above

3. Ambulatory payment classifications were developed as part of the
   a. outpatient prospective payment system.
   b. inpatient prospective payment system.
   c. CMS discharge data set.
   d. CPT coding system.
   e. all the above

4. Developing an insurance claim includes all *except* one of the following:
   a. patient registration
   b. capturing charges for services provided to the patient
   c. completing the UB-04
   d. assigning diagnosis and procedure codes
   e. making a copy of the patient's insurance card

5. The "patient control number" is
   a. assigned by the hospital.
   b. used to enter charges and services provided to the patient.
   c. known as the account or billing number.
   d. referenced on the insurance company's remittance advice form.
   e. all the above.

6. "Lifetime reserve days" apply to
   a. Medicare beneficiaries.
   b. outpatient treatment days.
   c. Medicaid beneficiaries.
   d. military treatment centers.
   e. a and c

7. A "condition code" identifies which of the following?
   a. actual dollar amounts that affect the patient's insurance benefits
   b. the condition of the patient at the time of admission
   c. the condition of the patient at the time of discharge
   d. specific events that determine health insurance liability
   e. primary and secondary insurance coverage

8. "Occurrence codes" include all *except* one of the following:
   a. auto accidents
   b. admission date
   c. onset of symptoms/illness
   d. date insurance payment was denied
   e. employment-related accident

9. A "value code" is used to identify which of the following?
   a. the semiprivate room rate
   b. primary payer
   c. secondary payer
   d. lifetime reserve days
   e. b and c

10. "Ancillary services" codes include which of the following patient services?
    a. routine nursing care
    b. operating room services
    c. room and board
    d. intensive care unit services
    e. none of the above

11. Submitting an insurance claim includes all *except* which of the following?
    a. reviewing the UB-04
    b. correcting data entry errors
    c. responding to error-edit messages
    d. making a copy of the patient's insurance card
    e. b and d

1 MEMORIAL HOSPITAL 101 INTERNATIONAL DRIVE HUNTSVILLE TX 59855 919 555 1010	2		3a PAT. CNTL # 492160341		4 TYPE OF BILL
			b. MED. REC. # 492160		111

5 FED. TAX NO.	6 STATEMENT COVERS PERIOD FROM THROUGH	7
50-3729492	0320YY 0325YY	

8 PATIENT NAME a	9 PATIENT ADDRESS a 825 MAPLEWOOD AVE			
b FRANKS ALEX	b HUNTSVILLE	c TX	d 59855	e

10 BIRTHDATE	11 SEX	ADMISSION 12 DATE	13 HR	14 TYPE	15 SRC	16 DHR	17 STAT	CONDITION CODES 18 19 20 21 22 23 24 25 26 27 28	29 ACDT STATE	30
06051956	M	0320YY	13	03	1	10	01			

31 OCCURRENCE CODE DATE	32 OCCURRENCE CODE DATE	33 OCCURRENCE CODE DATE	34 OCCURRENCE CODE DATE	35 OCCURRENCE SPAN CODE FROM THROUGH	36 OCCURRENCE SPAN CODE FROM THROUGH	37
a						
b						

38	39 VALUE CODES CODE AMOUNT	40 VALUE CODES CODE AMOUNT	41 VALUE CODES CODE AMOUNT
	a		
	b		
	c		
	d		

42 REV CD.	43 DESCRIPTION	44 HCPCS/RATE/HIPPS CODE	45 SERV. DATE	46 SERV. UNITS	47 TOTAL CHARGES	48 NON-COVERED CHARGES	49
1							1
2							2
3							3
4							4
5							5
6							6
7							7
8							8
9							9
10							10
11							11
12							12
13							13
14							14
15							15
16							16
17							17
18							18
19							19
20							20
21							21
22							22
23	PAGE ___ OF ___ CREATION DATE		TOTALS →				23

50 PAYER NAME	51 HEALTH PLAN ID	52 REL INFO.	53 ASG BEN.	54 PRIOR PAYMENTS	55 EST. AMOUNT DUE	56 NPI	
A							
B							57 OTHER PRV ID
C							

58 INSURED'S NAME	59 P. REL.	60 INSURED'S UNIQUE ID	61 GROUP NAME	62 INSURANCE GROUP NO.
A				
B				
C				

63 TREATMENT AUTHORIZATION CODES	64 DOCUMENT CONTROL NUMBER	65 EMPLOYER NAME
A		
B		
C		

66 DX								68

69 ADMIT DX	70 PATIENT REASON DX	71 PPS CODE	72 ECI	73

74 PRINCIPAL PROCEDURE CODE DATE	a. OTHER PROCEDURE CODE DATE	b. OTHER PROCEDURE CODE DATE	75	76 ATTENDING NPI QUAL
				LAST FIRST
c. OTHER PROCEDURE CODE DATE	d. OTHER PROCEDURE CODE DATE	e. OTHER PROCEDURE CODE DATE		77 OPERATING NPI QUAL
				LAST FIRST

80 REMARKS	81CC a	78 OTHER NPI QUAL
	b	LAST FIRST
	c	79 OTHER NPI QUAL
	d	LAST FIRST

UB-04 CMS-1450   APPROVED OMB NO. 0938-0997   NUBC™ NATIONAL UNIFORM BILLING COMMITTEE   THE CERTIFICATIONS ON THE REVERSE APPLY TO THIS BILL AND ARE MADE A PART HEREOF.

FIGURE 9–9 UB-04 (For instructional use only. Courtesy of the Centers for Medicare and Medicaid Services, www.cms.hhs.gov)

APPLICATION EXERCISE

Review the UB-04 in Figure 9–9. Complete FL 18 through FL 81, as necessary, by using the information provided. Refer to Tables 9–8, 9–9, and 9–10 for value and revenue codes.

PATIENT NAME: Alex Franks; Health Insurance ID: FA22306

EMPLOYER: Texas Software Corporation; Huntsville, Texas 59855

INSURANCE: Blue Cross; health plan, ID BC999; group name, Texas Software; insurance group number, 881

HOSPITAL: Memorial Hospital; provider NPI, 1234567890

ATTENDING PHYSICIAN: Takeesha Johnson, MD; NPI, 2345678901

SURGEON: Enrique Shaver, MD; NPI, 3456789012

SERVICES: Semiprivate room, $540 per day; operating room services, $1,500; blood chemistry tests, three (3), $50 each; chest x-ray, $90; general anesthesia, $200; recovery room, $50; pharmacy, $250; prosthetic device, $150.

ADMITTING AND PRINCIPAL DIAGNOSIS: Degenerative joint disease, knee, 715.16

PROCEDURE: Total knee replacement, 81.54; Done on March 21, 20YY

NOTE: Mr. Franks has signed a release of information for insurance payment and assignment of benefits.

CHALLENGE EXERCISES

1. Interview a billing specialist at your local hospital. Ask about the challenges related to hospital billing, such as frequent changes to UB-04 guidelines, the most common insurance claim errors, and the length of time between the patient's discharge and submitting the insurance claim.
2. Visit the National Uniform Billing Committee website at www.nubc.org or the Centers for Medicare and Medicaid Services website at www.cms.gov for current information about the UB-04. Does either website provide a sample of the UB-04?

WEBSITES

Centers for Medicare and Medicaid Services: www.cms.hhs.gov
National Uniform Billing Committee: www.nubc.org

CHAPTER 10

Electronic Data Interchange (EDI)

LEARNING OBJECTIVES

Upon successfully completing this chapter, the reader should have the knowledge to:

1. Define all key terms and abbreviations.
2. Describe the difference between carrier-direct and clearinghouse electronic claims submission.
3. List five considerations for establishing an electronic data interchange.
4. Discuss the advantages of electronic claims submission.
5. List four confidentiality safeguards related to electronic claims submission.

KEY TERMS

Carrier-direct
Centers for Medicare and
   Medicaid Services (CMS)
Clearinghouse
Compliance monitoring
Electronic claim
Electronic claims
   submission (ECS)

Electronic data
   interchange (EDI)
Error-edit
Health Insurance Portability
   and Accountability
   Act (HIPAA)
Interactive communication
   and transactions

Protected health
   information (PHI)
Remittance
Third-party
   administrator (TPA)
Turnaround time

OVERVIEW

Electronic data interchange (EDI) is a process that sends information back and forth between two or more individuals by computer linkages. The individuals or organizations can function as both sender and receiver. An electronic claim is one that is submitted to the insurance carrier by computer modem or computer download or upload via the Internet. Large hospitals have used electronic claims submission since the 1960s. Figure 10–1 illustrates electronic data interchange.

Delmar/Cengage Learning

FIGURE 10–1 Electronic Data Interchange

This chapter is an introduction to **electronic claims submission (ECS)**, which has been the method of choice for filing insurance claims since the 1980s. During the implementation of the Health Insurance Portability and Accountability Act (HIPAA) regulations and rules, Medicare insurance carriers were encouraged to develop HIPAA-compliant ECS policies and practices. As a result of this effort, 98 percent of all Medicare claims in 2004 were electronically submitted according to the regulations set forth in HIPAA. In fact, the standard format adopted for national use under HIPAA meets the billing requirements for all U.S. health care payers.

The **Centers for Medicare and Medicaid Services (CMS)** is one of the driving forces behind electronic claims submission. CMS promotes the advantages of using electronic data interchange (EDI). According to CMS publications, the advantages include:

- Faster payment, as electronic claims submitted in the HIPAA standard format can be paid as early as the 14th day after the date of receipt, whereas paper claims and electronic claims submitted in a non-HIPAA format cannot be paid earlier than the 27th day after the date of receipt.
- Reduced opportunity for errors.
- Lower administrative, postage, and handling costs than paper claims.
- Online and immediate acknowledgement that the insurance carrier received the claim.
- The standard format meets billing requirements for all U.S. health care payers who must comply with HIPAA.
- Electronic **remittance** (payment for services rendered) can be sent to a provider-preferred location (e.g., the provider's/facility's business bank account).

There are disadvantages to ECS, most of which relate to the electronic part of the process. Power outages and computer hardware and software problems will bring ECS to a halt. Because ECS is a two-way street, problems on either end of the connection may affect both the provider and the insurance carrier. A reliable backup system for electronic records is a necessity. ECS poses unique challenges concerning health information security, confidentiality, and privacy. Regardless of the disadvantages or challenges, the electronic exchange of information is a fact of life for the insurance billing specialist.

ELECTRONIC CLAIMS SUBMISSION OPTIONS

There are two options for electronic claims submission:

- **Carrier-direct:** This option allows the billing specialist to submit claims directly to the insurance carrier.
- **Clearinghouse** or **third-party administrator** (**TPA**): Under this option, insurance claim information is submitted to an organization that in turn distributes the claims to the appropriate insurance company.

There are advantages and disadvantages to both options.

Carrier-Direct Claims Submission

In order to implement the carrier-direct option, the provider must establish electronic claims processing agreements with each insurance carrier associated with the provider's practice. The agreements or contracts must clearly identify provider/agency and insurance carrier responsibilities regarding the following: information security, compliance monitoring, equipment and software, staff training, and turnaround time.

The **Health Insurance Portability and Accountability Act (HIPAA)** privacy and security rules mandate that electronic **protected health information (PHI)** must be secure. In order to comply with HIPAA, electronic claims processing agreements must describe how insurance information is submitted; who has access to the information; the security features or software that protect information when a wireless network is used; non-redisclosure policies; and the storage and retention policies for information once the insurance claim is processed.

Compliance monitoring activities include coding accuracy, verification of services provided, and accountability to regulatory agencies when errors are made. Because billing errors can result in charges of insurance fraud or abuse, the electronic claims processing agreement must identify provider and insurance carrier responsibilities related to compliance monitoring.

The agreement must include provisions for teaching the provider's staff how to use the claims submission software and whether there is a training fee. The agreement must also include answers to questions such as these: Where is training conducted—onsite or offsite? Is there a limit on the number of staff who can participate in training? Will retraining be offered when the software is updated?

Turnaround time is the length of time from claims submission to claims payment. As stated earlier, Medicare claims submitted electronically by using the HIPAA standard format can be paid as early as the 14th day after the date of receipt. The agreement should describe the turnaround time for clean claims and the provider's recourse when the expected turnaround time is not met.

The advantages of carrier-direct electronic claims submission are (1) the provider retains control of claims submission; (2) patient medical records are readily available when needed; and (3) the billing specialist can immediately respond to error-edit messages. The carrier-direct claims submission software includes an **error-edit** feature that identifies errors that would cause the claim to be rejected or denied. Error-edit messages flag incomplete required data fields, invalid health insurance claim numbers, and discrepancies between a patient's sex and diagnoses codes. The billing specialist is able to make corrections before the claim is transmitted.

The disadvantages of carrier-direct electronic claims submission are (1) the costs associated with purchasing or leasing equipment and software; (2) hiring and training staff to process the claims; and (3) establishing claims processing agreements with each insurance carrier.

Clearinghouse Claims Submission

As stated earlier, the clearinghouse claims submission method involves an intermediate step. The provider submits insurance claims to a processing center called a clearinghouse or third-party administrator (TPA). The clearinghouse redistributes the claims to the appropriate insurance carriers. Clearinghouses charge a fee for processing insurance claims. The fee can be assessed per claim or as a percentage of the dollar amount of all processed claims.

Insurance claims are submitted to the clearinghouse via electronic files. Each insurance company has a unique identifier assigned by the clearinghouse. The unique identifier tells the clearinghouse the insurance company (carrier) that must receive the claim. Claims are submitted to the clearinghouse periodically depending on the volume of claims or provider preference. Once claims are submitted, the clearinghouse edits the claims for accuracy; reformats the claims according to the current HIPAA guidelines; and transmits the claims to the appropriate insurance carrier. When a claim clears the editing process, commonly called a *clean claim*, the insurance carrier sends the payment to the provider or the patient.

When a claim fails to pass the clearinghouse edits, an electronic report is sent to the provider. These reports are commonly called error-edit messages. Claims may fail due to format issues, coding inaccuracies, or other missing or incorrect information. The billing specialist corrects the error and resubmits the claim to the clearinghouse.

In addition to submitting insurance claims via electronic files, a clearinghouse also handles paper claims for the provider. When the provider is required to submit a paper claim, the billing specialist completes the CMS-1500 and sends it to the clearinghouse. As with electronic claims submission, the clearinghouse transmits paper claims to the appropriate insurance carrier.

As with carrier-direct claims submission, the provider must have a written contract that identifies provider/agency and clearinghouse responsibilities regarding information security, compliance monitoring, equipment or software, and turnaround time. Staff training is usually minimal.

The two main advantages of using a clearinghouse for electronic claims submission are: (1) The provider must establish only one contract/agreement and (2) the financial investment for equipment, software, and additional staff is usually less than the costs associated with the carrier-direct option.

The disadvantages of contracting with a clearinghouse are: (1) The initial set-up of insurance company format requirements may create problems if the clearinghouse has not previously submitted claims to the company; (2) the provider does not have direct control of claims submission; and (3) cash flow is directly affected by the efficiency of the clearinghouse.

REINFORCEMENT EXERCISES 10–1

Fill in the blank.

1. A(n) _Electronic Claims_ is submitted to the insurance carrier via the Internet.

2. A(n) _Clearing house or TPA_ distributes claims to the appropriate insurance carrier.

3. The _Direct Claim submission_ electronic claims submission method allows the provider to communicate directly with the insurance company.

4. _Clearing house_ is a process that checks the claim for accuracy and completeness.

5. The clearinghouse assigns a(n) _Unique Identifier_ to each insurance company (carrier).

Provide a short answer for each item.

1. Briefly describe two components of an electronic claims processing agreement.

   Carrier-direct - Direcly submit claim to Insura Co
   Clearing houses. The biling Spenir submit
   Claim to clearihon The edi a and send to Insuran Co.

2. List three components of an electronic claims processing agreement required by HIPAA.

   _____

   _____

   _____

3. Describe the differences between carrier-direct and clearinghouse electronic claims submission options.

   _____

   _____

   _____

COMPLETING THE HEALTH INSURANCE CLAIM

When a provider contracts with a clearinghouse, the billing specialist does not complete the CMS-1500 insurance claim form. Insurance claim information is transmitted to the clearinghouse via an electronic file. Billing information is retrieved from the patient's database or from source documents, such as the encounter form, patient registration documents, and the patient's record. When patient information is maintained in an electronic database or electronic medical record, information is retrieved from those sources. As previously stated, the clearinghouse receives the electronic file and subsequently submits the CMS-1500 to the insurance carrier.

The billing specialist retrieves information for the electronic file according to clearinghouse and insurance carrier requirements. Although all carriers require much of the same information—such as patient demographic information, insurance program information, and treatment or clinical information—there may be data items that are mandated by an individual insurance carrier. The billing specialist must have access to and comply with requirements mandated by a specific insurance carrier. As with paper claims submission, attention to detail and accuracy are the keys to successful claims submission.

The provider's billing software should include edits for accurate claims processing that include the following elements:

- Invalid diagnoses and treatments related to genderoprostatitis for a female patient
- Invalid diagnoses and treatments related to ageopregnancy-related diagnosis for a 92-year-old woman
- Invalid diagnosis and treatment codesodiagnosis code requires a third, fourth, or fifth digit; deleted CPT code

Billing software may also include edits that alert the billing specialist that the evaluation and management (E/M) code is not supported by the diagnosis and treatment codes. This feature is extremely valuable as a quality assurance monitor. The billing specialist can immediately resolve this type of error by reviewing the patient record for additional information or by asking the physician for clarification of the E/M code.

Patient and Physician Signature Requirements

Electronic claims submission makes it impossible to have a written physician signature on each claim. Most insurance carriers accept the statement SIGNATURE ON FILE in fields that require a signature. The health care agency must maintain a current file that includes the written signatures of all individuals who provide services to patients.

The patient's signature is required for assignment of benefits and release of confidential health information to insurance carriers. To accommodate this requirement for electronic claims submission, the health care agency must obtain a signed authorization from the patient. The authorization is updated at each visit—monthly, annually, or as frequently as required by the insurance plan, the insurance carrier, or other regulatory agency.

In the physician office setting, the authorizations are obtained when the patient registers for an appointment or when the patient presents the encounter form to the billing specialist at the conclusion of the appointment. In the inpatient or outpatient hospital setting, the authorizations are obtained as part of the registration/admission process. Once the patient has signed the necessary authorization, the phrase SIGNATURE ON FILE may be entered in fields that require the patient's signature.

Coding

One of the most valuable features of electronic claims processing software is the error-edit function for coding. Most electronic claims processing programs identify invalid codes, age conflicts, sex conflicts, and procedure code versus diagnostic code conflicts. Because coding systems are updated annually, it is important that the agency purchases the current version of the coding systems. Billing software often includes annual coding updates either at no charge or for an additional fee.

Incorrect codes result in denied or delayed payment of claims. A pattern of coding errors can trigger an investigation of fraud or abuse.

Interactive Communication

One of the greatest benefits of EDI and electronic claims submission is the capacity for **interactive communication and transactions**. Interactive communication is the ability to share information online.

> **EXAMPLE**
>
> The billing specialist can query the clearinghouse or insurance carrier's electronic files regarding the status of any claim that was submitted. The billing specialist enters necessary information—usually the patient's name, claim number, date of submission, and the office or agency's unique and secure identification number. The billing specialist receives immediate feedback that may allow the billing specialist to resolve the problem.

Interactive communication is an efficient way to monitor the following claims information:

- Delayed payment of claims
- Reasons for claims denial
- Verification of insurance eligibility
- Status of patient's deductible

When a query is made, the insurance billing specialist may be able to correct any inaccurate information and immediately resubmit the claim. If this is not possible, the billing specialist prints a hard copy of the status of the claim, tracks down the problem, and resubmits the claim when the error is corrected.

Some of the more common problems with insurance claims are incomplete diagnostic codes, missing data items, obsolete codes, and insufficient information to justify the services rendered to the patient. When coding and data item errors are corrected, the claim can be electronically resubmitted. If the insurance carrier needs additional documentation to justify the services rendered, the billing specialist can send the required medical reports. In either situation, electronic communication reduces the amount of time it takes to identify and correct problems with insurance claims.

REINFORCEMENT EXERCISES 10–2

Provide a short answer for each item.

1. List three types of information required by nearly all insurance carriers.

demographic information

Insurance program information

treatment and clinical information

2. Describe two edits often included in insurance billing software.

Invalid diagnoses and treatment relate to gender

Invalid diagnosis age - 92 year old.

continued on the next page

continued from the previous page

3. Identify sources and source documents for retrieving information for electronic claims submission.

_____

_____

_____

Write true or false for each statement.

1. The CMS-1500 is made obsolete when using electronic claims submission. _____

2. Electronic claims submission software programs edit insurance claims data for accuracy. _____

3. A pattern of coding errors can trigger an investigation of fraud or abuse. _____

4. The provider is responsible for assigning accurate diagnostic and procedure codes. _____

5. Interactive communication is a time-consuming way to identify and correct insurance claims data. _____

CONFIDENTIALITY AND ELECTRONIC CLAIMS PROCESSING

As defined in Chapter 2, confidential information is not open to public inspection. In the age of electronic communication, confidentiality laws and guidelines that apply to the paper medical record may seem outdated. Nothing could be further from the truth. As discussed in Chapter 2, the agency's policies and procedures that govern release of confidential information must include safeguards related to any form of electronic communication. Review Chapter 2 for a complete discussion of confidentiality and release of information. Additional confidentiality safeguards related to electronic claims submission and electronic records include the following:

- Assign a unique identifier (password) to staff members who submit or access electronic claims and records.
- Change passwords periodically.
- Delete passwords of individuals who are no longer employed by the agency.
- Enforce written policies and disciplinary actions that address sharing passwords among staff.
- Never save confidential information on the computer hard drive.
- Store media containing backup files in a locked and fireproof location.

These safeguards are reasonable and relatively easy to implement. Whatever steps are taken to ensure confidential treatment of patient-specific insurance information, the insurance billing specialist should insist on a written policy that addresses electronic claims submission and confidentiality. The billing specialist could even take the initiative and draft this type of policy. Figure 10–2

ELECTRONIC CLAIMS SUBMISSION POLICY

A. CONFIDENTIALITY
- Information submitted electronically is subject to the same confidentiality policies as all other patient information.
- Passwords are assigned to individuals who submit claims, and they are changed every three months.
- Do not share your password or allow other staff access to the ECS program with your password.
- Computer monitor privacy screens will be used at all times.

B. SECURITY
- Close the ECS program when you are away from the workstation. NO EXCEPTIONS.
- Visitors are not allowed in the billing department.

C. STAFF TRAINING
- Employees working with ECS must attend training sessions as directed by the supervisor.
- Administrative leave with pay is granted to employees who attend ECS training.

D. EDI CONTRACTS
- The billing department supervisor maintains ECS contracts.
- The billing department supervisor is responsible for sharing contract changes with the billing staff.

Delmar/Cengage Learning

FIGURE 10–2 Electronic Claims Submission Policy Components

lists some of the items to include in an electronic claims submission policy. The policy must be updated as technology changes.

ELECTRONIC RECORD MANAGEMENT

Components of a record management system for paper files include filing, storage, retrieval, retention, and protection. Electronic record management addresses these same components—but with a different twist.

EXAMPLE

Paper records are stored as is, usually in a file cabinet or on a shelf. There is no need to make a second copy. Electronic records can be stored on a variety of electronic media that become obsolete. For example, "floppy" and "hard" disks commonly used in the past are nearly useless now. Electronic records should be backed up regularly. Some hospitals maintain two servers: one for current or active records and one that is used as a backup. The University of Utah Health Science Center maintains this type of backup system. According to a recent medical student's experience, one server "went down," and within 15 minutes, the backup server had restored all electronic records.

Table 10–1 summarizes the components of a record management system and lists some considerations unique to electronic records.

REINFORCEMENT EXERCISES 10–3

Write true or false for each statement.

1. Confidentiality laws for paper records do not apply to electronic records. _____

2. Staff members should share a common password for efficient access to insurance files. _____F_____

3. Confidential information should never be stored on a computer's hard drive. _____T_____

4. A written policy should address electronic claims submission and confidentiality. _____T_____

5. Electronic records management systems include the same components as a record management system for paper files. _____T_____

Fill in the blank.

1. Electronic records are usually filed _____.

2. _____ must be backed up regularly.

3. All records—either electronic or paper—must be stored in a(n) _____ area.

4. Computer monitor _____ are one of the tools available to protect confidential information.

5. _____ assigned to previous employees should be deleted from all electronic or computer program files.

TABLE 10–1

Record Management	
Record Management	**Electronic Record Considerations**
FILING • Alphabetic by patient name • Numeric by medical record number	Electronic records are usually filed by a unique patient identification number and patient name.
STORAGE • Paper or electronic storage • Location of storage area • Storage area security	Electronic records are stored on electronic media. The storage area must have appropriate safeguards against natural disasters and theft.
RETRIEVAL • Retrieval is the key to record management • Active vs. inactive records • Twenty-four-hour access or limited access • Information that cannot be retrieved is useless.	Electronic records must have a reliable backup system. Active and inactive records need not be separated because electronic media hold large amounts of data.

ABBREVIATIONS

Table 10–2 lists the abbreviations in this chapter.

TABLE 10–2

Abbreviations and Meanings	
Abbreviation	**Meaning**
CMS	Centers for Medicare and Medicaid Services
ECS	electronic claims submission
EDI	electronic data interchange
HIPAA	Health Insurance Portability and Accountability Act
PHI	protected health information
TPA	third-party administrator

SUMMARY

Electronic claims submission (ECS) is an efficient way to submit health insurance claims. A carrier-direct electronic claims submission program means the provider establishes ECS contracts with each insurance company or carrier. A clearinghouse electronic claims submission program means the agency or provider contracts with a third party who receives claims information from the provider and transmits the claim to the appropriate insurance carrier.

Electronic claims submission and interactive communication allow the billing specialist to edit insurance claim information and make corrections via the Internet. The status of insurance claims can be monitored online. Denied and delayed claims can be accessed, and problems can be corrected immediately. Confidentiality and record management issues related to electronic records are similar to those related to paper records. Patient information is confidential, no matter how it is transmitted or stored. The agency should have a written policy that complies with HIPAA security rules related to electronic health information.

REVIEW EXERCISES

Multiple Choice

Circle the correct answer from the choices provided.

1. The identification of provider and insurance carrier responsibilities for accurate coding is part of

    a. quality assurance.

    b. compliance monitoring.

    c. staff training.

    d. pending legislation.

2. The length of time from claims submission to claims payment is known as

    a. wait time.

    b. real time.

    c. time sharing.

    d. turnaround time.

3. In order to establish electronic claims submission, the provider must

    a. receive approval from the practice manager.

    b. hire an electronic claims processor.

    c. execute a contract with insurance carriers or a clearinghouse.

    d. execute a contract with CMS.

4. Confidentiality safeguards for electronic claims submission include

    a. creating a paper backup for each electronic claim.

    b. assigning and periodically changing passwords.

    c. filing electronic records by patient name.

    d. hiring an electronic claims processor.

5. The process of sending information between two or more individuals via computer linkage is called

   a. electronic data interchange.

   b. carrier-direct ECS.

   c. clearinghouse ECS.

   d. electronic claims submission.

Fill in the Blank

1. Another name for clearinghouse is ___TPA___.

2. For electronic claims submission, the phrase _____ is printed in place of the patient or provider signatures.

3. As with paper claims submission, _____ is the most important factor in ECS.

4. The _____ function of electronic claims processing software identifies invalid procedure codes.

5. _____ is defined as the ability to share information online.

Short Answer

Provide a brief definition for each term or a short answer for each question.

1. Identify four advantages of electronic claims submission. Explain why you believe your choices are advantages.

   _____

   _____

   _____

2. Discuss HIPAA's impact on electronic claims submission.

   _____

   _____

   _____

CHALLENGE ACTIVITY

1. Using the Internet, find a software company that sells electronic claims processing or billing software. What keywords should you use for the search? Use the online demo if one is available.

WEBSITE

Centers for Medicare and Medicaid Services: www.cms.hhs.gov

CHAPTER 11

Blue Cross/Blue Shield

LEARNING OBJECTIVES

Upon successfully completing this chapter, the reader should have the knowledge to:

1. Define all key terms and abbreviations presented in the chapter.
2. Describe three pieces of information provided by Blue Cross/Blue Shield insurance identification cards.
3. Define the most commonly used Blue Cross/Blue Shield payment method.
4. List three differences between a participating provider and a nonparticipating provider.
5. Accurately complete the CMS-1500 data fields.

KEY TERMS

Allowable charge
Blue Choice Point of Service (POS)
Blue Cross and Blue Shield Association (BCBSA)
Blue Cross Traditional
Blue Cross/Blue Shield (BC/BS)
Blue Preferred PPO
BlueCard Program
Customary fee
Durable medical equipment (DME)
Enrollee

Enrollment code
Family coverage
Federal Employee Health Benefit Program (FEHB)
Federal Employee Program (FEP)
Group number
Member
Participating provider (PAR)
Personal care physician (PCP)
Plan code
Point of service (POS)

Preferred provider organization (PPO)
Reasonable fee
Relative value scale (RVS) fee
Single coverage
Subscribers
Subscriber identification (ID)
Usual fee
Usual, customary, and reasonable (UCR) fee
Web-DENIS
Write-off

OVERVIEW

Blue Cross/Blue Shield (BC/BS) is a nationwide federation of nonprofit health insurance companies. Blue Cross/Blue Shield is often called the "Blues." Blue Cross health insurance usually covers hospital charges, and Blue Shield health insurance usually covers physician or provider charges. However, between the two plans, services such as outpatient surgery, long-term care, **durable medical equipment (DME)**, and prescription medications are also often covered. Durable medical equipment is nondisposable medical devices such as crutches, prostheses, and wheelchairs. A patient may be enrolled in one or both of the Blues plans.

Blue Cross traces its history to a 1933 St. Paul, Minnesota, hospitalization insurance plan—the first insurance plan to use the blue cross symbol. In 1933, the American Hospital Association (AHA) adopted the symbol when the AHA became the agency for accrediting new prepaid hospitalization plans. In 1978, the AHA deeded the right to both the Blue Cross name and symbol to the Blue Cross Association. The symbol was updated at that time and is a registered trademark.

Blue Shield traces its history to a 1938 American Medical Association (AMA) meeting. At this meeting, the AMA House of Delegates passed a resolution supporting the concept of voluntary health insurance that encouraged physicians to cooperate in prepaid health plans. The first such plan, established in Palo Alto, California, in 1939, was called the California Physicians' Service. Individuals who enrolled in the plan were called **subscribers**. Physician fees for subscribers with an annual income of less than $3,000 were paid in full by the insurance plan. Subscribers with an annual income in excess of $3,000 paid a small percentage of the physician fee, and the insurance plan paid the rest. This practice was the forerunner of patient coinsurance. Individuals enrolled in BC/BS plans are called subscribers or enrollees.

The blue shield was first used as a trademark in 1939 by the Buffalo, New York, medical care plan. In 1948, the symbol was formally adopted by the Associated Medical Care Plans, which was the approving agency for accreditation of new physician prepaid health insurance plans. In 1951, the Associated Medical Care Plans changed its name to the National Association of Blue Shield Plans and retained the blue shield symbol.

In 1977, the membership of both Blue Cross and Blue Shield voted to combine their two staffs under one president. By 1986, the board of directors for each association had merged to form the **Blue Cross and Blue Shield Association (BCBSA)**. Although the BCBSA represents the Blues on a national level, some Blue Cross and Blue Shield plans maintain separate corporate identities. In most states, however, Blue Cross and Blue Shield plans function as a single corporation.

Whether they function as separate corporations or as a single corporation, both Blue Cross and Blue Shield are bound by state laws and insurance regulations. Blue Cross and Blue Shield of Michigan operates according to the Michigan laws and regulations that apply to health insurance companies; BC/BS of Hawaii operates according to the laws and regulations of that state; and so forth.

Blue Cross/Blue Shield offers a wide variety of health insurance plans. Therefore, this chapter is limited to general information related to BC/BS plans. The insurance billing specialist must follow the specific state or local BC/BS guidelines that apply to the provider's patient population.

Some state BC/BS offices offer an electronic inquiry system that gives providers online access to information related to BC/BS subscribers and other claims processing information. For example, Blue Cross/Blue Shield of Michigan developed **Web-DENIS**, which allows providers immediate access to subscriber information such as deductible and co-payment amounts. BC/BS manuals, publications, and insurance claims tracking are also available via Web-DENIS.

This chapter covers the following topics: general types of Blue Cross/Blue Shield health insurance plans; participating vs. nonparticipating providers; payment methods; and general insurance claims procedures. Because state or regional Blue Cross/Blue Shield plans may have unique requirements for claims submission, always check with the local BC/BS office for current guidelines.

BLUE CROSS/BLUE SHIELD HEALTH INSURANCE PLANS

Blue Cross/Blue Shield offers a variety of health insurance plans, ranging from individual insurance to health maintenance organization coverage. Under Blue Cross/Blue Shield health insurance plans, the **subscriber** is the individual enrolled with the BC/BS plan. The subscriber, also known as the **enrollee**, is usually named on the health insurance identification (ID) card. A **member** is usually the subscriber's spouse or dependent who is eligible for insurance coverage. Members are not named on the health insurance ID card. The general plans discussed here include **Blue Cross Traditional, Blue Preferred PPO, Blue Choice Point of Service (POS), BlueCard program, and Blue Cross Federal Employee Program (FEP)**.

Blue Cross Traditional

Blue Cross Traditional is a health insurance plan that is available to individuals and groups. Coverage includes hospital, surgical, and medical care. Subscribers are not required to have a **personal care physician (PCP)** and may obtain services from a specialist by self-referral. A personal care physician, also called a primary care physician or provider, is responsible for the overall management of an individual's medical care.

Blue Preferred Provider Organization

Blue Preferred Provider Organization (PPO) is a health insurance plan that is available to individuals and groups. Under this plan, subscribers and members are encouraged to obtain services from health care providers who have a contract with the plan. A preferred provider is a health care facility or professional who agrees to treat subscribers for a reduced fee. Members who receive health care services from the plan's network of preferred providers have lower out-of-pocket costs. Members are not required to have a personal care physician and do not need a referral to see another PPO network provider. If a member chooses to receive services from an out-of-network provider, co-payments are higher and some services are not covered. PPO plans are very common, especially when an employer provides health insurance benefits. Figure 11–1 is a sample PPO identification card.

The identification card is usually labeled with a PPO logo. The **subscriber identification (ID)** consists of letters and numbers. The three letters identify the plan as a PPO. The subscriber ID is a unique identifier assigned by Blue Cross. Since the implementation of the Health Insurance Portability and Accountability Act (HIPAA), the subscriber's Social Security number is no longer used as the ID number.

The **group number** identifies the name of the employer or group that provides health insurance. The **plan code** identifies the local (state) BCBS plan that provides the insurance. Other information on the identification card may include the effective date of coverage, prescription benefit code, and the co-payment for office visits.

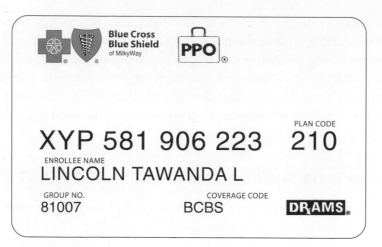

FIGURE 11–1 BC/BS Group Plan, PPO Identification Card (Courtesy of Blue Cross/Blue Shield of Maryland)

Blue Choice Point of Service

Blue Choice Point of Service (POS) plans are available only through group coverage. Under a Blue Choice program, members choose a personal care physician (PCP) who manages the members' treatment. The PCP also makes referrals to other providers, if necessary. Members do not pay any deductible when they receive care from their PCP. Members who seek services from another provider without first seeing their personal care physician pay deductibles and higher co-payments.

BlueCard Program

The **BlueCard Program** is available to individuals who are members of other Blue Cross insurance plans. This program provides members with access to a network of traditional inpatient, outpatient, and professional health care providers around the world. In non-emergency situations, the member is advised to call the BlueCard Worldwide Service Center to arrange for services at a BlueCard Worldwide hospital or to schedule a physician appointment.

For inpatient care at a BlueCard Worldwide hospital, the member pays the deductible, the co-pay, and the fee for noncovered services. The provider files the health insurance claim. The member may have to pay the hospital and submit a claim when inpatient care is obtained from a non-BlueCard Worldwide hospital. For all outpatient and other professional services (office visit), the member pays the provider and submits the insurance claim. To submit a claim, the member completes the BlueCard International Claim form and sends it to the BlueCard Worldwide Service Center.

Blue Cross Federal Employee Program

The **Federal Employee Health Benefit Program (FEHB)** is a health insurance program that applies to federal government employees, retirees, spouses, and dependents. Government employees and retirees can choose **single coverage**, which means that only the employee/retiree has insurance, or **family coverage**, which means spouses and dependents also have insurance.

In many areas, Blue Cross/Blue Shield is the insurance carrier for this health plan and is responsible for providing identification cards and processing insurance claims. The FEHB is also known as the **Federal Employee Program (FEP)**. Figure 11–2 is an example of a Blue Cross/Blue Shield FEP health insurance card. Note that the card is clearly labeled as an FEP health

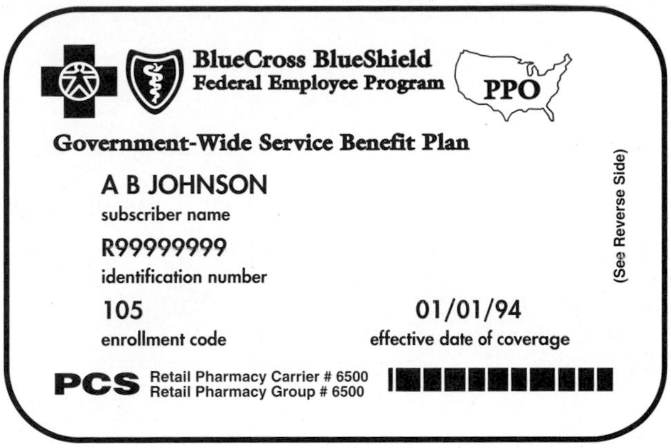

FIGURE 11–2 BC/BS Federal Employee Plan Identification Card (Courtesy of Blue Cross/Blue Shield of Maryland)

insurance card. The subscriber's name and ID number are self-explanatory. The **enrollment code** signifies whether the subscriber has single or family coverage. Single coverage enrollment codes are 111, basic coverage, and 104, standard coverage. Family coverage codes are 112, basic coverage, and 105, standard coverage. More services are covered by standard insurance plans than are covered by basic insurance plans. The FEP card shows the effective date of coverage in the lower-right corner. The billing specialist notes this date to ensure that charges for services rendered before the date of coverage are not submitted to the FEP plan.

Blue Cross/Blue Shield identification cards provide the billing specialist with important information about the patient's insurance plan and coverage. This is one reason it is necessary to keep an updated copy, both front and back, of the patient's insurance card on file.

REINFORCEMENT EXERCISES 11–1

Spell out the abbreviations.

1. BCBSA

_____

2. DME

_____

3. FEHB

_____

4. PCP

_____

5. POS

_____

continued on the next page

continued from the previous page

Fill in the blank.

1. The _____ is the individual enrolled with a Blue Cross/Blue Shield plan.

2. On the BC/BS PPO card, the _____ represents the name of the employer/ group that provides health insurance for the enrollee.

3. Blue Cross insurance usually covers _____ charges.

4. Blue Shield usually covers _____ charges.

Provide a short answer for each question.

1. Briefly describe the BlueCard Program.

2. What are two differences between the Blue Preferred PPO plan and the Blue Choice POS plan?

PARTICIPATING AND NONPARTICIPATING PROVIDERS

As with other insurance companies, Blue Cross/Blue Shield offers health care providers the opportunity to become **participating providers (PAR)**. Contracts are negotiated between the provider and BC/BS. Benefits of becoming a BC/BS participating provider include the following:

- Insurance payments are sent directly to the provider.
- Claim-filing assistance is made available to the provider's staff.
- Training seminars, manuals, and newsletters are furnished to the provider's staff.
- The provider's name, address, and specialty are published in the BC/BS participating provider directory, which is distributed to all BC/BS subscribers and participating providers.

In return for these benefits, participating providers agree to do the following:

- Submit claims for all BC/BS subscribers.
- Adjust the difference between the amount charged by the provider and the approved or allowed fee on all covered services, which are identified in the insurance plan.
- Bill patients for only the deductible or co-payment amounts that are based on the BC/BS allowed fee for covered services.

TABLE 11–1

Fee Adjustment and Co-Payments			
Fee Adjustment			
Provider Fee	Allowed Fee Covered Service	Adjustment	Adjusted Fee
$100	$80	−$20	$80
Co-Payment Based on Allowed Fee: Covered Service			
Allowed Fee	Copayment 10 Percent of Allowed Fee	Bill Patient	Bill Insurance
$80	$8	$8	$72*

*Payment is sent directly to participating provider.

Table 11–1 illustrates an adjusted fee and a co-payment based on the BC/BS allowed fee.

When a provider agrees to adjust his or her fees, the difference between the full fee and the allowed fee is called an adjustment or **write-off**. Write-offs have important business and income tax implications. Patient accounts must clearly document all fee adjustments and write-offs. The billing specialist is often responsible for entering adjustments or write-offs into the patient's account. The provider's business manager or accountant is responsible for reporting adjustments and write-offs in accordance with local, state, and federal tax laws.

Nonparticipating providers are health care providers who do not have a contract with a BC/BS plan. Nonparticipating providers charge the patient the provider's full fee for services rendered. The patient may be expected to pay all or part of the fee at the time of service. Either the nonparticipating provider or the patient files an insurance claim. For nonparticipating providers, the patient may receive the payment, and the provider must bill the patient. Many providers sign participation agreements because they receive the insurance payment directly.

For nonparticipating providers, the billing specialist should make every effort to collect deductibles and co-payments when services are rendered. Many providers expect payment in full for charges up to specific amount. When charges exceed the provider's threshold the billing specialist sets up a payment schedule with the patient.

PROVIDER REIMBURSEMENT

Provider reimbursement or payment is often based on the **usual, customary,** and **reasonable (UCR) fee** and the **relative value scale (RVS)** amount.

Usual, Customary, and Reasonable (UCR) Fees

Usual, customary, and reasonable fees are defined as:

- **Usual fee:** The fee the provider usually charges for a given service.
- **Customary fee:** The fee that other providers, in the same geographic area and with similar training, charge for the same service. The customary fee is an average of the fees charged by other providers or the fee that falls in the 90th percentile of the fees charged by other providers.
- **Reasonable fee:** A fee that is higher than the usual or customary fee and can be justified by the patient's condition. The insurance carrier determines whether there is sufficient justification for the higher fee. The following example illustrates a reasonable fee.

TABLE 11–2

Usual, Customary, and Reasonable Fees
Usual Fee Dr. Pedal, a dermatologist, charges all patients $250 for the removal of three skin tags.
Customary Fee The other dermatologists in Dr. Pedal's geographic area have a range of fees for the removal of three skin tags. The 90th percentile of all the fees for this service is $290. Under the 90th percentile rule, $290 is the customary fee for removal of three skin tags.
Reasonable Fee Dr. Pedal removes three skin tags. The patient has a reaction to the local anesthetic, which requires additional medical attention. Dr. Pedal charges $300, which is $50 more than his usual fee and $10 more than the customary fee. Due to the complication, the insurance carrier determines that $300 is a reasonable fee.

EXAMPLE

Marlena, who is pregnant, is scheduled for a cesarean section. She has been taking Coumadin, an anticoagulant, due to a recent episode of blood clotting. The usual and customary fee for a cesarean section is $500. Because of Marlena's anticoagulant therapy, the procedure requires additional resources, and the provider charges $600. The insurance company reviews the reason for the additional fee and determines that $600 is a reasonable fee in Marlena's case, so it agrees to pay the claim based on a $600 fee rather than a $500 fee.

Usual, customary, and reasonable fees are the primary method for determining provider reimbursement. If the provider's fee exceeds the usual and customary fee, the insurance carrier reviews all documentation related to the service. The information in the patient's medical record must clearly identify the extenuating circumstances related to the increased fee. Review Table 11–2 for examples of usual, customary, and reasonable fees.

Usual, customary, and reasonable fees are not automatically paid in full. Most insurance plans pay only a percentage of the UCR fee. The maximum amount the insurance carrier will pay for specific services is called the **allowable charge** or **allowable fee**. The billing specialist maintains a file of the allowable charges for each insurance carrier. The insurance carrier notifies the provider of any changes in allowable charges.

Figure 11–3 illustrates the patient account for each of the following examples.

EXAMPLE A: NONPARTICIPATING PROVIDER

Mr. Smith's BC/BS group plan pays 80 percent of the UCR, leaving Mr. Smith with a 20 percent co-payment. His physician does not participate in the plan. Mr. Smith is charged $125 for today's office visit. The UCR for an office visit is $100. The allowable charge, 80 percent of the UCR, is $80. Mr. Smith pays $45 at the time of service—the $25 that exceeds the UCR and 20 percent of the UCR, which is $20. The billing specialist submits a claim for the remaining $80. Because the physician is nonparticipating, the $80 insurance payment may be sent to Mr. Smith, and the physician's office must send a bill or statement in order to collect the balance due.

A. NONPARTICIPATING PROVIDER

ACCOUNT NO.	PATIENT NAME	DOB	INSURANCE	MED REC NO.
456789112	SMITH PHILIP M.	10/15/1957	BCBS XYZ44442121	456789

PATIENT ADDRESS	909 DAISY LANE FLOWERS MD 20000	HOME 906 555 8800	WORK 906 555 5678

DOS	PRVD	CPT CODE	DESCRIPTION	CHARGE		CREDIT		BALANCE	
05/20/20YY	007	99213	OFFICE VISIT	125	00				
05/20/20YY			PT. CHK 10234			45	00	80	00
05/22/20YY			INS. FILED						

B. PARTICIPATING PROVIDER

ACCOUNT NO.	PATIENT NAME	DOB	INSURANCE	MED REC NO.
456789112	SMITH PHILIP M.	10/15/1957	BCBS XYZ44442121	456789

PATIENT ADDRESS	909 DAISY LANE FLOWERS MD 20000	HOME 906 555 8800	WORK 906 555 5678

DOS	PRVD	CPT CODE	DESCRIPTION	CHARGE		CREDIT		BALANCE	
05/20/20YY	007	99213	OFFICE VISIT	125	00				
05/20/20YY			BCBS ADJUSTMENT			25	00	100	00
05/20/20YY			PT CHK 10234			20	00	80	00
05/22/20YY			INS. FILED						

FIGURE 11–3 Patient Account Entries

EXAMPLE B: PARTICIPATING PROVIDER

If Mr. Smith's physician was a participating provider, the $25 is entered as an adjustment. If Mr. Smith pays the $20 co-payment, the billing specialist submits a claim for $80. If Mr. Smith does not pay the $20 co-payment, the billing specialist submits a claim for $100. The $80 insurance payment is sent directly to the provider. Mr. Smith is then billed for the remaining $20.

The same process applies to a reasonable fee. If the insurance carrier determines that a fee in excess of the usual and customary fee is reasonable, a participating provider receives 80 percent of the reasonable fee, and the patient is responsible for the 20 percent co-payment. Keep in mind that the co-payment varies according to the insurance plan.

Blue Cross/Blue Shield preferred provider contracts establish a fee for each covered service through negotiations between the insurance plan and the provider. The provider's full fee, the UCR fee, and other factors enter into the negotiated fees. The negotiated fees are always less than the provider's full fees and may be less than UCR fees. Because a PPO contract is intended to direct PPO plan subscribers to participating providers, the lower fees are offset by an increase in the number of patients.

Relative Value Scale (RVS) Amount

The **relative value scale (RVS) amount** is an insurance company calculation that establishes fees based on the provider's time, skill, and overhead costs associated with providing a service. The time, skill, and overhead costs are converted into numeric units, and each service is assigned a numeric unit value based on the relative value of the service.

> **EXAMPLE**
>
> A pre-employment physical may be assigned a relative value unit of .5, and a comprehensive physical examination may be assigned a relative value unit of 1.

The second part of the calculation is a fixed dollar amount per relative value unit. The fixed dollar amount is calculated on the basis of provider charges. Insurance companies maintain extensive databases of provider charges for services rendered. The fixed dollar amount is multiplied by the numeric unit, which results in the fee for a particular service. The fixed dollar amount is part of the contract negotiated between the insurance company and the provider.

> **EXAMPLE**
>
> The pre-employment physical has a relative value unit of .5. When you multiply the fixed dollar amount of $100 by .5, the fee is $50. The comprehensive physical has a relative value unit of 1. When you multiply the fixed dollar amount of $100 by 1, the fee is $100.

Each CPT code—a five-digit code assigned to physician and provider services—is assigned a relative value unit. Table 11–3 is an example of provider fees based on $100 per relative value unit.

Blue Cross/Blue Shield furnishes each provider with the relative value scale fees. As with UCR fees, most insurance plans pay a percentage of the fee, and the patient is responsible for the remainder.

> **EXAMPLE**
>
> Marie's BC/BS individual insurance plan pays 70 percent of the RVS fee. Marie undergoes a total abdominal colectomy. Her insurance pays 70 percent of the $2,391, which is $1,673.70. Marie's co-pay is 30 percent, which is $717.30.

TABLE 11–3

CPT Code	Description	Fixed Dollar Amount/RVU	RVU	Fee
45380	Colonoscopy and biopsy	$100	4.43	$443
54150	Newborn circumcision	$100	1.8	$180
44150	Total abdominal colectomy	$100	23.91	$2,391
19101	Incisional breast biopsy	$100	3.18	$318
58260	Vaginal hysterectomy, uterus	$100	12.96	$1,296

The billing specialist discusses the co-pay with Marie and establishes a payment plan. If the surgeon is a participating provider, the billing specialist submits a claim for $1,673.70, and the payment is sent directly to the provider. The billing specialist for a nonparticipating provider establishes a payment plan for the $717.30 co-pay and may submit the claim for the patient. If the patient assigns benefits to the provider, the payment is sent to the provider. If the patient does not assign benefits to the provider, the payment is sent to the patient. The patient must be billed for the remaining balance.

Some providers require full payment of the co-pay before the service is performed. In the case of nonparticipating physicians, it is not unusual for the patient to prepay up to 50 percent of the cost of the service. These payment arrangements are especially important when the service—usually some type of elective surgery—has a high cost. The billing specialist discusses the provider's payment policy with the patient.

REINFORCEMENT EXERCISES 11–2

Write a short answer for each item.

1. List three benefits of being a participating provider.

2. List three obligations of participating providers.

3. What is meant by the phrase "usual fee"?

4. Briefly describe the phrase "customary fee."

continued on the next page

continued from the previous page

5. Under what circumstances is a provider paid a reasonable fee?

_____

_____

_____

6. What is a write-off?

_____

_____

_____

7. List three factors that affect RVS fees.

_____

_____

_____

CMS-1500 COMPLETION: BLUE CROSS/BLUE SHIELD

Most Blue Cross/Blue Shield insurance plans use the CMS-1500 claim form. Check with the local carrier or plan representative if there is any doubt that the CMS-1500 is the correct form. BC/BS will not process an insurance claim submitted on the wrong form. BC/BS plans set time limits for claim submission that range from 90 days to one year. In order to ensure prompt reimbursement, claims should be submitted within 30 days.

General CMS-1500 completion instructions for Blue Cross/Blue Shield claims are presented here. Claims submission requirements are revised regularly. The local or regional BC/BS office can provide the billing specialist with the most current requirements. General guidelines for completing the CMS-1500 for Blue Cross/Blue Shield plans include the following:

- Enter all insurance identification numbers exactly as they appear on the insurance card.
- The word "insured" on the CMS-1500 form is the same as "subscriber" or "enrollee." BC/BS identification cards use the term "subscriber" or "enrollee" for "insured."
- Prior to the year 2000, birth dates were entered as MM/DD/YY. Many insurance carriers now require four digits for the year: MM/DD/YYYY.
- When entering monetary information, always include both dollars and cents, even if the cents notation is 00. Do not use decimals or dollar signs.

Figure 11–4 is an example of a completed claim form when BC/BS is the primary payer. Refer to Figure 11–4 as you review the instructions. The BC/BS health insurance card in Figure 11–1 is the source document for information in blocks 1a, 2, and 11.

(1500)

HEALTH INSURANCE CLAIM FORM

APPROVED BY NATIONAL UNIFORM CLAIM COMMITTEE 08/05

| | PICA | | | | | | | PICA | | |

1. MEDICARE	MEDICAID	TRICARE CHAMPUS	CHAMPVA	GROUP HEALTH PLAN	FECA BLK LUNG	OTHER	1a. INSURED'S I.D. NUMBER (For Program in Item 1)
☐ (Medicare #)	☐ (Medicaid #)	☐ (Sponsor's SSN)	☐ (Member ID #)	☐ (SSN or ID)	☐ (SSN)	☒ (ID)	XYP581906223

2. PATIENT'S NAME (Last Name, First Name, Middle Initial)	3. PATIENT'S BIRTH DATE	SEX	4. INSURED'S NAME (Last Name, First Name, Middle Initial)
LINCOLN TAWANDA L	MM 12 DD 15 YY 1948	M ☐ F ☒	LINCOLN TAWANDA L

5. PATIENT'S ADDRESS (No., Street)	6. PATIENT RELATIONSHIP TO INSURED	7. INSURED'S ADDRESS (No., Street)
714 HENNEPIN ROAD	Self ☒ Spouse ☐ Child ☐ Other ☐	714 HENNEPIN ROAD

CITY	STATE	8. PATIENT STATUS	CITY	STATE
CHICAGO	IL	Single ☐ Married ☒ Other ☐	CHICAGO	IL

ZIP CODE	TELEPHONE (Include Area Code)		ZIP CODE	TELEPHONE (Include Area Code)
49855	(806) 2263336	Employed ☒ Full-Time Student ☐ Part-Time Student ☐	49855	(806) 226 3336

9. OTHER INSURED'S NAME (Last Name, First Name, Middle Initial)	10. IS PATIENT'S CONDITION RELATED TO:	11. INSURED'S POLICY GROUP OR FECA NUMBER
		81007

a. OTHER INSURED'S POLICY OR GROUP NUMBER	a. EMPLOYMENT? (Current or Previous) ☐ YES ☒ NO	a. INSURED'S DATE OF BIRTH MM 12 DD 15 YY 1948 M ☐ F ☒

b. OTHER INSURED'S DATE OF BIRTH MM DD YY M ☐ F ☐	b. AUTO ACCIDENT? PLACE (State) ☐ YES ☒ NO	b. EMPLOYER'S NAME OR SCHOOL NAME

c. EMPLOYER'S NAME OR SCHOOL NAME	c. OTHER ACCIDENT? ☐ YES ☒ NO	c. INSURANCE PLAN NAME OR PROGRAM NAME BCBS MI

d. INSURANCE PLAN NAME OR PROGRAM NAME	10d. RESERVED FOR LOCAL USE	d. IS THERE ANOTHER HEALTH BENEFIT PLAN? ☐ YES ☒ NO If yes, return to and complete item 9 a-d.

READ BACK OF FORM BEFORE COMPLETING & SIGNING THIS FORM.

12. PATIENT'S OR AUTHORIZED PERSON'S SIGNATURE I authorize the release of any medical or other information necessary to process this claim. I also request payment of government benefits either to myself or to the party who accepts assignment below.

SIGNED _____ DATE _____

13. INSURED'S OR AUTHORIZED PERSON'S SIGNATURE I authorize payment of medical benefits to the undersigned physician or supplier for services described below.

SIGNED _____

14. DATE OF CURRENT: ILLNESS (First symptom) OR INJURY (Accident) OR PREGNANCY (LMP) MM 01 DD 04 YY 20YY	15. IF PATIENT HAS HAD SAME OR SIMILAR ILLNESS, GIVE FIRST DATE MM DD YY	16. DATES PATIENT UNABLE TO WORK IN CURRENT OCCUPATION FROM MM DD YY TO MM DD YY

17. NAME OF REFERRING PROVIDER OR OTHER SOURCE LILY ROBERTS MD	17a. 17b. NPI 9012345678	18. HOSPITALIZATION DATES RELATED TO CURRENT SERVICES FROM MM DD YY TO MM DD YY

19. RESERVED FOR LOCAL USE	20. OUTSIDE LAB? ☐ YES ☒ NO $ CHARGES

21. DIAGNOSIS OR NATURE OF ILLNESS OR INJURY (Relate Items 1, 2, 3, or 4 to Item 24E by Line)	22. MEDICAID RESUBMISSION CODE ORIGINAL REF. NO.
1. 786 .50 3. __ . __	23. PRIOR AUTHORIZATION NUMBER
2. __ . __ 4. __ . __	

24. A. DATE(S) OF SERVICE From MM DD YY To MM DD YY	B. PLACE OF SERVICE	C. EMG	D. PROCEDURES, SERVICES, OR SUPPLIES (Explain Unusual Circumstances) CPT/HCPCS MODIFIER	E. DIAGNOSIS POINTER	F. $ CHARGES	G. DAYS OR UNITS	H. EPSDT Family Plan	I. ID. QUAL.	J. RENDERING PROVIDER ID. #
1	01 04 YY	11		99212	1	30 00	1		NPI	0123456789
2									NPI	
3									NPI	
4									NPI	
5									NPI	
6									NPI	

25. FEDERAL TAX I.D. NUMBER SSN EIN	26. PATIENT'S ACCOUNT NO.	27. ACCEPT ASSIGNMENT? (For govt. claims, see back)	28. TOTAL CHARGE	29. AMOUNT PAID	30. BALANCE DUE
495245837 ☒		☒ YES ☐ NO	$ 30 00	$	$ 30 00

31. SIGNATURE OF PHYSICIAN OR SUPPLIER INCLUDING DEGREES OR CREDENTIALS (I certify that the statements on the reverse apply to this bill and are made a part thereof.) RONALD W GERVAIS MD SIGNED DATE 01 06 20YY	32. SERVICE FACILITY LOCATION INFORMATION a. b.	33. BILLING PROVIDER INFO & PH # (806) 7529118 MEDICAL CLINC 6 GREENWAY DRIVE CHICAGO IL 49855 a. 8901234567 b.

NUCC Instruction Manual available at: www.nucc.org

APPROVED OMB-0938-0999 FORM CMS-1500 (08-05)

FIGURE 11–4 BC/BS Primary Payer CMS-1500 (For instructional use only. Courtesy of the Centers for Medicare and Medicaid Services, www.cms.hhs.gov)

Block 1	Enter X in Other.
Block 1a	Enter the subscriber's identification number as it appears on the insurance card.
Block 2	Enter the patient's name—last, first, middle initial—in uppercase letters.
Block 3	Enter the patient's eight-digit birth date. Enter an X in M or F. If the gender is unknown, leave this blank.
Block 4	Enter the subscriber/enrollee's name as it appears on the insurance card.
Block 5	Enter the patient's permanent mailing address and telephone number.
Block 6	Enter an X in the box that describes the relationship of the patient to the subscriber (insured). If the patient is an unmarried domestic partner, enter an X in Other.
Block 7	Enter the subscriber/enrollee's address and telephone number, including the area code.
Block 8	Enter an X in the appropriate box to indicate the patient's marital status. If the patient is an unmarried domestic partner, enter an X in Other. Enter an X in the appropriate box to indicate the patient's employment or student status. If the patient is unemployed and/or not a full- or part-time student, leave this blank.
Blocks 9–9d	**NOTE:** Complete Blocks 9–9d when the patient is covered by more than one insurance plan.
Block 9	Enter the other insured person's name—last, first, and middle initial—in uppercase letters.
Block 9a	Enter the other insured person's policy or group number.
Block 9b	Enter the other insured person's eight-digit birth date.
Block 9c	Enter the other insured person's employer or school name.
Block 9d	Enter the other insured person's insurance plan or program name.
Blocks 10a–10c	Enter X in Yes or No as applicable. If the patient's condition is the result of an auto accident (10b), enter the two-character abbreviation of the state where the accident occurred.
Block 10d	Leave this blank.
Block 11	Enter the subscriber/enrollee's group number exactly as it appears on the insurance card.
Block 11a	Enter the subscriber's eight-digit date of birth. Enter an X in the appropriate box to indicate the subscriber's gender. If the gender is unknown, leave this blank.
Block 11b	Leave this blank.
Block 11c	Enter the subscriber's insurance plan name, including the name of the state (i.e., BCBS MI).

continued on the next page

continued from the previous page

Block 11d	Enter an X in the appropriate box to indicate if there is another health insurance plan. If YES, complete blocks 9 through 9D.
Block 12	Leave this blank.
Block 13	Leave this blank.
Block 14	Enter an eight-digit date, usually the date of service. For injury, accident, or trauma follow-up care, enter the date of the injury, accident, or trauma. For end-stage renal disease, enter the date of the kidney transplant or first maintenance dialysis. For pregnancy-related services, enter the date of the last menstrual period or the estimated date of conception.
Block 15	Enter an eight-digit date, if applicable. Otherwise, leave this blank.
Block 16	Enter an eight-digit date, if applicable. Otherwise, leave this blank.
Block 17	If there is a referring physician/provider, enter the first name, middle initial (if known), last name, and credential. Otherwise leave this blank.
Block 17a	Leave this blank.
Block 17b	Enter the 10-digit NPI number for the referring physician/provider named in block 17.
Block 18	Enter the eight-digit admission and discharge dates if services were provided during a hospital inpatient episode of care.
Block 19	Leave this blank.
Block 20	Enter an X in the NO box if all laboratory services reported on the claim were performed in the provider's office. Enter an X in the YES box if laboratory services were performed by an outside laboratory. Enter the total amount charged by the outside laboratory.
Block 21	Enter the ICD-9-CM diagnosis codes to the highest level of specificity. Enter the primary (first-listed) diagnosis in line 1.
Block 22	Leave this blank.
Block 23	Leave this blank.
Block 24A	Enter the date the service was performed, in the eight-digit format, in the FROM column. If the service was performed on consecutive days during a range of dates, enter an eight-digit date in the TO column. **EXAMPLE** Hilda visits the physician on September 7, 8, and 9, 20YY, for a series of prednisone injections. Enter 0907YY in the FROM column and 0909YY in the TO column.
Block 24B	Enter the two-digit code that identifies where the service was provided. (See "Place of Service Codes" in Chapter 8.)
Block 24C	Enter Y for YES if the service was an emergency. Otherwise, leave this blank.

continued on the next page

continued from the previous page

Block 24D	Enter the CPT/HCPCS code and applicable modifier(s) for procedures and services.
Block 24E	Enter the diagnosis reference code from block 21 that relates to the procedure/service performed on the date of service.
Block 24F	Enter the total charge for the service(s) listed on each line.
Block 24G	Enter the number of days or units for procedures or services reported in Block 24D. If just one procedure or service was performed, enter 1 in block 24G.
Block 24H	Leave this blank.
Block 24I	Leave this blank.
Block 24J	Enter the 10-digit NPI number in the unshaded area of block 24J for the provider who performed the service or procedure.
Block 25	Enter the provider's social security number (SSN) or employer identification number (EIN). Do not enter hyphens or spaces in the number. Enter an X in the appropriate box to identify which number is reported.
Block 26	Enter the patient's account number as assigned by the provider. Otherwise, leave this blank.
Block 27	Enter an X in YES for providers who accept assignment. Otherwise, enter an X in NO.
Block 28	Enter the total charges for all services on lines 1 through 6.
Block 29	Enter the amount paid by the patient. Do not enter any amount paid by Medicare or other insurance.
Block 30	Enter the difference between the total charges and the amount paid. Otherwise, leave this blank.
Block 31	Enter the provider's name and credential (e.g., LETIA JOHNSON MD) and the date the claim was completed (MMDDYYYY). Do not enter spaces in the date.
Block 32	Enter the name and address where procedures or services were provided, if at a location other than the provider's office. If YES is checked in block 20, enter the name and address of the facility that performed the laboratory service.
Block 32a	Enter the 10-digit NPI number of the facility entered in block 32.
Block 32b	Leave this blank.
Block 33	Enter the provider's billing name, address, and phone number, including the area code. Enter the phone number in the area next to the block title. Do not enter parentheses for the area code. Enter the name on line 1, the address on line 2, and the city, state, and ZIP code on line 3. For a nine-digit ZIP code, enter the hyphen.
Block 33a	Enter the 10-digit NPI number of the billing provider. If the provider is a solo practitioner, enter the individual's NPI number. If the provider is part of a group practice, enter the group practice NPI number.
Block 33b	Leave this blank.

ABBREVIATIONS

Table 11–4 lists the abbreviations and meanings in this chapter.

TABLE 11–4

Abbreviations and Meanings	
Abbreviation	Meaning
AHA	American Hospital Association
AMA	American Medical Association
BC/BS	Blue Cross/Blue Shield
BCBSA	Blue Cross Blue Shield Association
DME	durable medical equipment
FEHBP	Federal Employees Health Benefit Program
FEP	Federal Employees Program
nonPAR	nonparticipating provider
PAR	participating provider
PCP	primary care provider
POS	point of service
PPO	preferred provider organization
RVU	relative value unit
UCR	usual, customary, and reasonable (fee)

The completed claim is submitted to the local Blue Cross/Blue Shield claims processing center. Most claims are filed electronically.

SUMMARY

Blue Cross/Blue Shield is recognized in all countries that deal with private health insurance plans. In the past, Blue Cross plans covered hospital services, and Blue Shield covered physician or provider services. Today, the two companies cover services such as outpatient surgery, long-term care, and prescription medication.

Blue Cross/Blue Shield identification cards are a source of important information. The billing specialist needs a copy, both front and back, of the patient's current ID card. The insured's name, identification number, insurance group number, and plan code are found on the ID card.

Blue Cross/Blue Shield offers several benefits to participating providers, including sending the insurance payment directly to the provider. Staff training and claims-filing assistance are other services available to participating providers' staff.

Blue Cross/Blue Shield uses two payment methods: UCR fees and RVS fees. BC/BS calculates an allowed charge for covered services. Insurance claims for provider services are submitted electronically or manually by using the CMS-1500 form.

REVIEW EXERCISES

Use the following information to complete a CMS-1500 for submission to BC/BS as the primary payer. Your instructor will tell you how to obtain the form.

PATIENT NAME: Charles Wu
DOB: 11/12/46
ADDRESS: 507 East Osborn; Blueberry, ME 49855
HOME PHONE: (906) 555-6997
WORK PHONE: (906) 555-1234
SPOUSE: Janis Wu
ADDRESS: 507 East Osborn; Blueberry, ME 49855
EMPLOYER: Sawyer Lumber Mill, County Road 550, Blueberry, ME 49855
INSURANCE INFORMATION: BC/BS ID: XYP 692107334 GROUP #: 92118
PLAN: 421
OTHER INSURANCE: No
SUPERIORLAND CLINIC
714 HENNEPIN AVE.
BLUEBERRY, ME 49855
TAX ID # 49-4134726
SUPERIORLAND CLINIC PHONE: (806) 555-6060
SUPERIORLAND CLINIC NPI: 4567890123
PROGRESS NOTE
DATE: March 15, 20YY
MR. Wu is seen today for recurrent pain in the right shoulder. On examination, there is moderate range of motion accompanied by pain with movement. CBC was essentially normal. Right shoulder x-ray taken two days ago revealed changes consistent with bursitis. He is to take 600 mg of ibuprofen q.i.d. and return in three weeks for follow-up. He should call the office if the pain worsens. SIGNED BY: Henry Romero, MD. NPI: 2311287891.
OFFICE VISIT/ESTABLISHED PATIENT: 99212
CBC: 85025
DIAGNOSIS: Bursitis, code 727.3
CHARGES: Office visit, $45; CBC, $24
NOTE: Dr. Romero is a participating physician and accepts assignment.

Multiple Choice

Circle the correct answer from the choices provided.

1. Individuals who are covered by BC/BS plans are often referred to as

    a. recipients.

    b. insurees.

    c. subscribers.

    d. members.

2. Blue Cross insurance plans usually cover

   a. hospital charges.

   b. physician charges.

   c. prescription medication charges.

   d. home health charges.

3. Blue Shield insurance plans usually cover

   a. hospital charges.

   b. home health charges.

   c. prescription medication charges.

   d. physician charges.

4. The maximum amount an insurance company pays for a specific service is called the

   a. covered fee.

   b. allowable fee.

   c. UCR fee.

   d. user fee.

5. BC/BS provider payments are primarily based on the

   a. UCR fee.

   b. physician's fee.

   c. prevailing fee.

   d. customary fee.

6. The BlueCard Program

   a. allows the patient to see any provider.

   b. is accepted by participating providers throughout the United States.

   c. limits the patient to preferred providers only.

   d. covers care in a specified geographic area only.

7. A write-off is best described as

   a. a bad debt.

   b. a letter informing the patient of an insurance denial.

   c. the difference between the insurance payment and the provider's charge.

   d. a handwritten progress note.

8. As a PPO, BC/BS establishes

   a. fee schedules for provider payments.

   b. group health insurance plans.

   c. contracts between health care providers and organizations that provide health insurance.

   d. contracts between employers and health insurance companies.

9. BC/BS participating provider benefits include

   a. enhanced reimbursement rates.

   b. inclusion in national advertising campaigns.

   c. guaranteed number of patient visits.

   d. direct payments from the insurance company.

10. "Covered services" refers to

    a. services provided by a physician.

    b. services identified in the insurance plan.

    c. services that are medically necessary.

    d. services requested by the patient.

CHALLENGE ACTIVITY

1. Schedule an interview with a BC/BS customer representative. Prior to the interview, develop questions that will help you gather information about the training or education needed to work as a customer representative, the most rewarding aspects of the job, the least rewarding aspects, regulatory pressures from the state and federal governments, working with providers, and working with subscribers. Share the information, as a paper or presentation, with your class or instructor.

WEBSITES

Blue Cross and Blue Shield Association: www.bcbs.com
Blue Cross/Blue Shield of Michigan (Medicare Advantage): www.bcbsm.com/Medicare
Centers for Medicare and Medicaid Programs: www.cms.hhs.gov

CHAPTER 12

Medicare

LEARNING OBJECTIVES

Upon successfully completing this chapter, the reader should have the knowledge to:

1. Describe the difference between Medicare Parts A, B, C, and D.
2. Identify the eligibility requirements for Medicare.
3. List 10 examples of services covered by Medicare Part B.
4. Define all key terms and abbreviations.
5. Describe the differences between a participating and a nonparticipating provider.
6. Discuss the incentives for becoming a participating provider.
7. Differentiate between Medicare as the primary and the secondary payer.
8. Successfully complete the CMS-1500 according to Medicare guidelines.

KEY TERMS

Abdominal Aortic Aneurysm (AAA)

Advance Beneficiary Notice (ABN)

Balance-bill

Benefit period

Centers for Medicare and Medicaid Services (CMS)

Conditional primary payer status

Coordination of Benefits Administrator (COBA)

Durable medical equipment (DME)

Durable medical equipment Medicare Administrative Contractor (DME MAC)

Elective surgery

Formulary

Geographic adjustment factor (GAF)

Health Insurance Claim Number (HICN)

Health Maintenance Organization (HMO)

Lifetime reserve days

Limiting fee

Medical Savings Account (MSA)

Medicare

Medicare Administrative Contractor (MAC)

Medicare Advantage (MA)

Medicare Advantage Prescription Drug Plan (MA-PDP)

Medicare fee schedule (MFS)

Medicare-Medicaid Crossover Program

Medicare Part A

Medicare Part B

Medicare Part C

Medicare Part D

Medicare Summary Notice (MSN)

Medicare supplemental plan, Medicare secondary payer (MSP)

Medicare Special Needs Plan
  (SNP)
Medigap
National conversion factor
  (CF)
National Correct Coding
  Initiative (NCCI)
National provider
  identification (NPI)
Nonparticipating provider
  (NonPAR)

Ordering physician
Out-of-pocket expenses
Participating provider
  (PAR)
Physician extender
Preferred Provider
  Organization (PPO)
Prescription drug plan
  (PDP)
Private Fee-for-Service
  (PFFS)

Qualified Medicare
  Beneficiary (QMB)
Qualifying Individuals (QI)
Referring physician
Relative value unit (RVU)
Remittance notice
Resource-based relative value
  scale (RBRVS)
Specified Low-Income
  Medicare Beneficiary
  (SLMB)

OVERVIEW

Medicare is a federal health insurance program created in 1965 as Title 18 of the Social Security Act (SSA). It is managed by the **Centers for Medicare and Medicaid Services (CMS)**. Medicare is the nation's largest health insurance program and covers millions of Americans. Medicare benefits are divided into **Medicare Part A, Medicare Part B, Medicare Part C, and Medicare Part D**. Medicare Part A helps pay for care received in hospitals and skilled nursing facilities and for home health and hospice care. Medicare Part B helps pay for physician services, outpatient hospital care, and other medical services, such as clinical laboratory services; physical, occupational, and speech therapy; and durable medical equipment (DME). Medicare Part C, also known as **Medicare Advantage (MA)**, is an alternative to the original Medicare fee-for-service plan. Under Medicare Part C, private insurance companies pay for health services that would be covered by Medicare Part A, B, and D. Medicare Part D is a prescription drug (medication) plan that offers insurance benefits for prescription drugs. Medicare Part A is usually premium-free. Other Medicare plans are available for a monthly premium.

Medicare is generally available to individuals who are:

- Age 65 years and older
- Citizens or permanent residents of the United States
- Retired or who have worked at least 10 years in Medicare-covered employment
- The spouse or widow(er) of an individual who has worked for at least 10 years in Medicare-covered employment

Individuals younger than age 65 may qualify for Medicare if they are:

- Disabled and have received Social Security Disability Insurance (SSDI) benefits for two years
- Diagnosed with end-stage renal disease (ESRD)
- Kidney donors when the donated kidney is transplanted to an individual with end-stage renal disease

Medicare beneficiaries with incomes below the federal poverty level may be eligible for the **Qualified Medicare Beneficiary (QMB)** program. The QMB program is a Medicaid program for beneficiaries who need help paying for Medicare services. The QMB program pays Medicare Part A and Part B premiums, deductibles, and coinsurance amounts.

Medicare beneficiaries with incomes slightly above the federal poverty level may be eligible for the **Specified Low-Income Medicare Beneficiary (SLMB)** program or the **Qualifying Individual (QI)** program. The SLMB is a Medicaid program that pays Medicare Part B premiums for beneficiaries who are enrolled in Medicare Part A. The Qualifying Individual program is a Medicaid program that pays all or a portion of the Medicare Part B premiums for beneficiaries who are enrolled in Medicare Part A and who are not otherwise eligible for Medicaid.

The Medicare Health Insurance Program is constantly changing. Insurance billing specialists must keep up with the changes. The local Social Security office has current Medicare information. Several government websites offer nearly up-to-the-minute changes. The Centers for Medicare and Medicaid Services can be reached online at http://www.cms.gov, and the Medicare web site address is http://www.medicare.gov.

Although CMS manages the Medicare program, it does not directly pay for services rendered to Medicare patients. Companies that handle payments for Medicare are called **Medicare Administrative Contractors (MAC)**, formerly known as insurance carriers or fiscal intermediaries. Medicare Administrative Contractors provide updated information about Medicare changes and regulations.

This chapter covers information related to Medicare Part A, Part B, Part C, and Part D. Topics include services covered, reimbursement issues for participating (PAR) and nonparticipating (NonPAR) providers for Medicare Part B, the Medicare fee schedule, Medicare as the primary and secondary payer, Medicare Advantage plans, and claim submission procedures.

MEDICARE PART A

An individual is eligible for premium-free Medicare Part A if the person meets the general requirements listed in the previous section.

Enrollment in Medicare Part A is handled in two ways: automatically or by application. Individuals who are not yet 65 and are already receiving Social Security or Railroad Retirement benefits are automatically enrolled in Medicare Part A. A Medicare card is mailed to these individuals about three months before their 65th birthday. Disabled individuals are also automatically enrolled in Medicare Part A beginning in the 25th month of their disability. A Medicare card is mailed to these individuals about three months before they are entitled to Medicare benefits or three months before the 25th month of their disability. Retired and disabled individuals are also automatically enrolled in Medicare Part B, but they may refuse this insurance.

Individuals who are not receiving Social Security or Railroad Retirement benefits must apply for Medicare three months before their 65th birthday. Individuals on kidney dialysis or who are waiting for a kidney transplant must also apply for Medicare.

Individuals enrolled in Medicare or Railroad Retirement Medicare receive an identification card. Figure 12–1 shows a sample Medicare card. The Railroad Retirement Medicare card is nearly identical to the standard Medicare ID card. The toll-free number for the Social Security Administration is replaced with the heading Railroad Retirement Board. The number for the Board is on the back of the card.

Note that the Medicare identification card includes the beneficiary's name, sex, type of coverage (Part A, Part B, or both), effective date, and Medicare claim number. The Medicare claim number is called the **health insurance claim number (HICN)**. This number is the social security number of the wage earner. A one- or two-character suffix follows the Social Security number. The suffix identifies the beneficiary status of the individual named on the ID card. For example, an

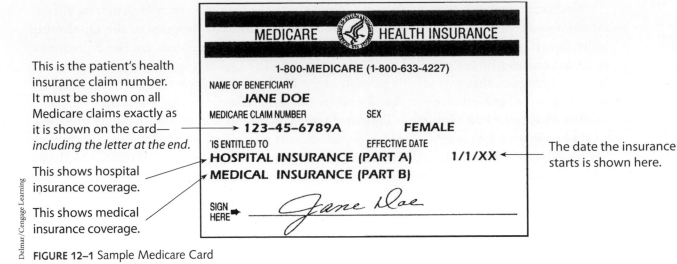

This is the patient's health insurance claim number. It must be shown on all Medicare claims exactly as it is shown on the card—*including the letter at the end.*

This shows hospital insurance coverage.

This shows medical insurance coverage.

The date the insurance starts is shown here.

Delmar/Cengage Learning

FIGURE 12–1 Sample Medicare Card

HICN that ends with the letter A means that the beneficiary is the wage earner; the letter B indicates the wife of the wage earner; B1 is the husband of the wage earner; and D is the widow of the wage earner. All HICN suffixes are available on the Medicare website.

Medicare Part A: Covered Services

Medicare Part A, commonly known as hospital insurance, provides health insurance coverage for care provided by hospitals, skilled nursing homes, home health care, and hospice. Some of the services covered by Medicare Part A are listed:

- **Hospital Stays:** Semiprivate room, meals, usual nursing care, and ancillary services and supplies that are medically necessary. Medicare does cover a private room, such as an intensive care unit, if medically necessary.
- **Skilled Nursing Facility:** Semiprivate room, meals, and skilled nursing and rehabilitative services. Skilled nursing facility care includes services such as intravenous injections and physical therapy that cannot be provided on an outpatient basis.
- **Home Health Care:** Covered services must be ordered by a physician and are limited to reasonable and necessary intermittent skilled nursing care, physical therapy, occupational therapy, speech-language therapy, and home health aide services. Wheelchairs, hospital beds, oxygen, and other medical supplies and services may also be covered.
- **Hospice Care:** For the terminally ill, Medicare covers medications for symptom control and pain relief; physician care; nursing services; and medical supplies.

It is impossible to list every service covered by Medicare Part A. However, in order for any service to be covered, the service must be medically necessary. This means the service must be appropriate for the diagnosis and treatment of the beneficiary's medical condition.

Medicare Part A: Deductibles and Co-payments

Like any health insurance plan, Medicare Part A has deductibles and copayments. In 2009, the deductible for the first 60 days of inpatient hospital care was approximately $1068. From the 61st to 150th day of inpatient hospital care, the beneficiary is responsible for daily co-payments. The 2009 co-payment for the 61st to 90th day of inpatient hospital care was $267 per day and

$534 per day from the 91st to 150th day. The deductible for the 91st to 150th hospital day applies only when the beneficiary uses his or her lifetime reserve days to help pay for an extended hospitalization. Lifetime reserve days are described later in this section. The beneficiary is responsible for all charges after the 150th day of care.

For skilled nursing facility care, the beneficiary pays nothing for the first 20 days. In 2009, the co-payment for skilled nursing care from the 21st to 100th day of care was about $134 per day. After the 100th day, the beneficiary is responsible for all charges.

Medicare Part A deductibles and co-payments are based on the beneficiary's **benefit period**. A benefit period begins when an individual is admitted to a hospital or skilled nursing facility and ends 60 days after discharge. Benefit periods are important because the beneficiary must pay the inpatient hospital deductible and the skilled nursing care co-payments for *each* benefit period. There is no limit to the number of benefit periods available to Medicare Part A beneficiaries. Example A illustrates how the benefit period affects inpatient hospital deductibles, and Example B illustrates how the benefit period affects skilled nursing facility co-payments.

EXAMPLE A: INPATIENT HOSPITAL DEDUCTIBLE

David Brindley, a 70-year-old retired teacher, is admitted to Blueberry Medical Center on June 1 and discharged on June 15. He returns to his home and does well until October, when he trips over a scatter rug, fractures a hip, and is hospitalized from October 12 through October 30. Because 60 days elapsed between hospitalizations, Mr. Brindley received services during two (2) benefit periods and is responsible for $1068 of the hospital bill for June and $1068 of the hospital bill for October. Medicare Part A would cover the remainder of each hospital bill.

EXAMPLE B: SKILLED NURSING FACILITY COPAYMENTS

After hip surgery, Mr. Brindley is transferred to a skilled nursing facility for postoperative rehabilitation. He stays at the facility for two weeks (14 days). Because Mr. Brindley's skilled nursing stay was less than 20 days, Medicare Part A covers the entire 14 days, and he does not pay a deductible. After being home for a week, he is readmitted to the skilled nursing facility for further rehabilitative care. This time, Mr. Brindley's length of stay is 21 days. Because 60 days did not elapse between the two admissions, Mr. Brindley is in the same benefit period. His first length of stay, 14 days, is deducted from the co-payment-free 20 days, which leaves 6 days in Mr. Brindley's benefit period. Medicare Part A pays for the 6 days of his second episode of care. For the remaining 15 days, Mr. Brindley must pay the deductible for each day. In 2009, the deductible was $134 per day, which means Mr. Brindley is responsible for $2018 of the second episode of care.

The benefit period concept may seem complicated. Simply put, Medicare Part A beneficiaries must have a 60-day break between hospital inpatient or skilled nursing facility episodes of care to trigger a new benefit period.

The benefit period formula does not apply to Medicare-approved home health care services, such as physician and nursing services. When a beneficiary qualifies for home health care, there is no deductible. There is a 20 percent co-payment of the Medicare-approved amount for **durable medical equipment (DME)**. Durable medical equipment includes items such as a wheelchair or hospital bed.

Lifetime Reserve Days

Lifetime reserve days are a fixed number of days that Medicare will cover when a beneficiary is hospitalized for more than 90 days during a benefit period. Under the original Medicare plan, beneficiaries are allowed 60 lifetime reserve days that may be used only once during the beneficiary's lifetime. For each lifetime reserve day used, Medicare pays all covered services *except* the per-day deductible, which was $534 in 2009. Lifetime reserve days apply only to inpatient hospital care. The following example illustrates Medicare coverage when using lifetime reserve days.

EXAMPLE

Violet is a 79-year-old woman who has several health problems but is able to live in her own home. She was admitted to Blueberry Memorial Hospital on August 1, 20YY, with necrotizing cellulitis. She was placed on intravenous therapy and other appropriate treatments. She did not respond well to medical therapy and underwent several debridements of necrotic tissue. Gangrene became a problem, and she had three toes amputated. Violet was discharged on September 2, 20YY. Her length of stay was 32 days. Medicare Part A covered all approved charges except the $1068 deductible. Within two weeks, Violet had a setback, and she returned to the hospital. The cellulitis continued to worsen, and she developed several life-threatening complications. Violet was hospitalized from September 14 through November 23, 20YY—a 70-day length of stay. She was discharged to her daughter's home and continued with antibiotic treatment. Violet had a total of 102 hospital days between the two episodes of care.

Because Violet returned to the hospital within two weeks, her benefit period continued from her first admission in August. Medicare Part A covered the cost of the first 28 days of her second admission. There was no deductible because Violet met the deductible for the benefit period during her first hospitalization. On the 61st hospital day, Violet was responsible for the $267-per-day co-payment until her 90th hospital day.

The hospital social worker visited Violet on November 18 to discuss the possibility of using lifetime reserve days, should the need arise. Violet agreed, and from her 91st hospital day until her discharge, she used 11 of her lifetime reserve days and was also responsible for the $534-per-day deductible. Medicare Part A paid the cost of all covered services except the per-day deductible.

By the time Violet was discharged on November 23, she had received 102 days of inpatient hospital care in one benefit period and had used 11 of her lifetime reserve days. Her deductibles and co-payments totaled $14,952.00.

Violet recovered and was able to return to her own home after spending Christmas with her daughter's family. On March 15 of the following year, Violet fell in the shower and sustained a femoral neck hip fracture. She was admitted to Blueberry Memorial Hospital and underwent a total hip replacement. Because 60 days had elapsed since her last hospitalization, Violet began a new benefit period. She was in the hospital for 10 days. Medicare Part A paid the cost of all covered services, and Violet was responsible for the $1068 deductible.

Additional information about Medicare Part A is available on the Medicare website at http://www.medicare.gov. Another good resource is the annual publication *Medicare and You*, which is sent to Medicare beneficiaries and is available at your local Social Security Administration office.

REINFORCEMENT EXERCISES 12–1

Write a short answer for each question or statement.

1. Name the government agency that manages Medicare.

_____

_____

_____

2. Who is eligible for Medicare?

_____

_____

_____

3. Briefly describe the differences between Medicare Part A, Part B, Part C, and Part D.

_____

_____

_____

4. Define the term "benefit period."

_____

_____

_____

5. Explain the purpose of Medicare Part A "lifetime reserve days."

_____

_____

_____

Write Out Each Abbreviation.

1. CMS

_____

continued on the next page

continued from the previous page

2. QMB

_____

3. SLMB

_____

4. MAC

_____

5. HICN

_____

MEDICARE PART B

Individuals who qualify for Medicare Part A also qualify for Medicare Part B. Participation in Medicare Part B is optional. Beneficiaries pay a monthly premium based on income. In 2009, the standard Medicare Part B premium was $96.40, and the annual deductible was $135. The monthly premium increases according to an individual's or couple's annual income. For example, an individual with an annual income over $85,000 but less than $107,000 pays $134.90 per month. A couple with an annual income between $170,000 and $214,000 pays $134.50 per month each, for a total of $265. Part B premiums are deducted from an individual's monthly Social Security check. If an individual does not receive Social Security, the monthly premium is billed to the individual.

In addition to the annual deductible, beneficiaries are required to pay co-insurance for Part B covered services. The co-insurance for most services is 20% of the Medicare-allowed charge. Some services have a higher co-insurance. For example, co-insurance for most outpatient mental health services is 50 percent. Federal law obligates providers to collect the deductible and coinsurance payment.

Medicare Part B: Covered Services

Like most health insurance plans, Medicare Part B does not pay for every available medical service. Medicare is only required to pay for services and supplies that are reasonable, medically necessary, and consistent with the patient's diagnosis. Medicare does not pay for procedures or treatments that are considered experimental or still in the investigative or trial stage.

Medicare Part B is intended to help defray the cost of a variety of diagnostic, treatment, and preventive health care services. Table 12–1 describes examples of diagnostic and treatment services, and Table 12–2 describes examples of preventive services.

In addition to the services listed in Tables 12–1 and 12–2, Medicare Part B helps cover the cost of artificial limbs and eyes, breast prostheses following mastectomy, and one pair of eyeglasses after cataract surgery with an intraocular lens.

The Medicare co-insurance payment may vary depending on the type of service. While many services require a 20 percent co-insurance/co-payment, mental health, physical, and occupational therapy services may have a higher co-payment. Billing specialists receive current information via the Medicare Administrative Contractor and Medicare bulletins and transmittals.

TABLE 12–1

Diagnostic and Treatment Services
Medical and Other Services: Physicians' services except for routine physical exams; outpatient medical and surgical services and supplies; diagnostic tests; ambulatory surgery center facility fees for approved procedures; durable medical equipment such as wheelchairs, hospital beds, oxygen, and walkers; outpatient physical and occupational therapy, including speech-language therapy and mental health services
Clinical Laboratory Service: Blood tests, urinalysis, and more
Home Health Care: Part-time skilled care, home health aide services, durable medical equipment when supplied by a home health agency while getting Medicare-covered home health care, and other supplies and services as approved by Medicare
Outpatient Hospital Services: Services for the diagnosis or treatment of an illness or injury
Diabetes Supplies: Blood sugar testing monitors, blood sugar test strips, lancets and more; insulin and certain medical supplies used to inject insulin may be covered by Medicare Part D
Blood: Pints of blood needed as an outpatient or as a component of a Part-B-covered service

TABLE 12–2

Preventive Services	
Preventive Service	**Eligible Beneficiaries**
Abdominal Aortic Aneurysm Screening (AAA) A one-time screening ultrasound. Medicare only covers this screening if you get a referral as a result of your "Welcome to Medicare" physical.	Beneficiaries at risk for having an AAA
Bone Mass Measurement (Bone Density) Once every 24 months or as indicated by the patient's condition	Beneficiaries at risk for losing bone mass
Cardiovascular Screening Monitoring plasma cholesterol, lipid, and triglyceride levels, as indicated by the patient's condition	All beneficiaries
Colorectal Cancer Screening • Fecal occult blood tests every 12 months • Flexible sigmoidoscopy every 48 months • Colonoscopy generally once every 120 months; every 24 months for high-risk individuals • Barium enema once every 48 months when substituted for sigmoidoscopy or colonoscopy	All beneficiaries age 50 and older; no age limit for colonoscopy

continued on the next page

continued from the previous page

Preventive Services	
Preventive Service	**Eligible Beneficiaries**
Diabetes Screening	Medicare beneficiaries with any of the following risk factors: • high blood pressure • history of abnormal cholesterol and triglyceride levels • obesity • history of high blood sugar
Flu Shots	All beneficiaries
Glaucoma Screening Once every 12 months	Medicare beneficiaries at risk for glaucoma
Mammogram Screening • Once every 12 months • One baseline screening mammogram	All women with Medicare age 40 and older Women between 35 and 39
Pap Smear and Pelvic Exam • Once every 24 months • Once every 12 months for high-risk individuals or women of childbearing age with an abnormal Pap smear in the past three years	Medicare beneficiaries
Physical Examination (one-time "Welcome to Medicare" Physical) One preventive physical examination within the first 12 months of the date of enrollment	All Medicare beneficiaries
Pneumococcal Shot Pneumonia shot; once in a lifetime	All beneficiaries
Prostate Cancer Screening • Prostate-specific antigen (PSA) test once every 12 months	Beneficiaries age 50 and older
Smoking Cessation Eight face-to-face visits in a 12-month period	Medicare beneficiaries diagnosed with an illness caused or complicated by tobacco use

Although Medicare pays only for services and supplies that are considered reasonable and medically necessary, there may be situations in which the provider believes a service is necessary, but it may be denied by Medicare. When this situation occurs, the insurance billing specialist must have the patient sign an **Advance Beneficiary Notice (ABN)**. The ABN must be completed *before* the service is performed. The notice must contain information that is clear and accurate so the patient can make an informed choice about accepting the service and paying for it. According to CMS guidelines, the ABN must include the following:

- Date of service
- Cost of service
- Narrative of the particular service in language the patient understands
- Provider's statement that Medicare is likely to deny payment
- Reason(s) why the provider believes payment will be denied
- Patient's signature and date of signature

Figure 12–2 is a sample Advance Beneficiary Notice form.

Even though the provider believes Medicare will deny a service, a claim is submitted and a copy of the Advanced Notice agreement is sent with the claim. There is always a chance that payment may be approved. Failure to have the patient complete the notice *before* providing the service results in the following:

- Physicians who do not accept Medicare payment must refund any denied charges collected from the patient.
- Physicians who accept Medicare will not receive payment for denied services and must refund any money collected from the patient.

Medicare Part B: Providers

Health care providers may choose whether to participate in Medicare. Physicians who elect to be Medicare **participating providers (PARs)** contract with Medicare and agree to accept the Medicare-approved payment rate for services rendered to all Medicare patients. A **nonparticipating provider (NonPAR)** does not contract with Medicare and therefore does not agree to accept the Medicare-approved payment rate for services rendered to all Medicare patients.

Participating Providers

Under Medicare Part B, a participating provider (PAR) agrees to be enrolled in the Medicare program. The Medicare Administrative Contractor remits payment directly to the provider's office and not to the beneficiary. PARs agree to accept assignment for Medicare patients. The provider files claims for services and accepts the Medicare-approved payment rate for services rendered to Medicare patients. The provider receives 80 percent of the approved rate from Medicare and 20 percent of the approved rate from the patient. The participating provider also collects the deductible, if applicable. As a PAR, the physician or provider cannot **balance-bill** the patient for the difference between the Medicare-approved amount and the provider's usual fee for the service. Table 12–3 is an example of a PAR fee and payment rate.

To increase the number of participating providers, Congress has mandated several incentives:

- Direct payment of all claims
- An approved payment rate that is 5 percent higher than for NonPAR physicians
- Providing PAR directories, a list of all participating physicians, to Medicare patients
- A message included on the **Medicare Summary Notice (MSN)** sent to patients who are treated by NonPAR providers that **out-of-pocket expenses** (the amount of money the patient must pay for a service) are reduced if services are received from a participating provider

(A) Notifier(s):

(B) Patient Name: **(C) Identification Number:**

ADVANCE BENEFICIARY NOTICE OF NONCOVERAGE (ABN)

<u>NOTE:</u> If Medicare doesn't pay for **(D)**_____ below, you may have to pay.

Medicare does not pay for everything, even some care that you or your health care provider have good reason to think you need. We expect Medicare may not pay for the **(D)**_____ below.

(D)_____	**(E) Reason Medicare May Not Pay:**	**(F) Estimated Cost:**

WHAT YOU NEED TO DO NOW:

- Read this notice, so you can make an informed decision about your care.
- Ask us any questions that you may have after you finish reading.
- Choose an option below about whether to receive the **(D)**_____ listed above.
  Note: If you choose Option 1 or 2, we may help you to use any other insurance that you might have, but Medicare cannot require us to do this.

(G) OPTIONS: Check only one box. We cannot choose a box for you.
☐ **OPTION 1. I** want the **(D)**_____ listed above. You may ask to be paid now, but I also want Medicare billed for an official decision on payment, which is sent to me on a Medicare Summary Notice (MSN). I understand that if Medicare doesn't pay, I am responsible for payment, but **I can appeal to Medicare** by following the directions on the MSN. If Medicare does pay, you will refund any payments I made to you, less co-pays or deductibles.
☐ **OPTION 2. I** want the **(D)**_____ listed above, but do not bill Medicare. You may ask to be paid now as I am responsible for payment. **I cannot appeal if Medicare is not billed.**
☐ **OPTION 3. I** don't want the **(D)**_____ listed above. I understand with this choice I am **not** responsible for payment, and **I cannot appeal to see if Medicare would pay.**

(H) Additional Information:

This notice gives our opinion, not an official Medicare decision. If you have other questions on this notice or Medicare billing, call **1-800-MEDICARE** (1-800-633-4227/**TTY:** 1-877-486-2048). Signing below means that you have received and understand this notice. You also receive a copy.

(I) Signature:	**(J) Date:**

According to the Paperwork Reduction Act of 1995, no persons are required to respond to a collection of information unless it displays a valid OMB control number. The valid OMB control number for this information collection is 0938-0566. The time required to complete this information collection is estimated to average 7 minutes per response, including the time to review instructions, search existing data resources, gather the data needed, and complete and review the information collection. If you have comments concerning the accuracy of the time estimate or suggestions for improving this form, please write to: CMS, 7500 Security Boulevard, Attn: PRA Reports Clearance Officer, Baltimore, Maryland 21244-1850.

Form CMS-R-131 (03/08)   Form Approved OMB No. 0938-0566

FIGURE 12–2 Advance Beneficiary Notice. (Courtesy of the Centers for Medicare and Medicaid Services, www.cms.hhs.gov)

TABLE 12–3

Participating Provider Payment	
PAR fee	$125
PAR Medicare-approved rate	$100
PAR receives 80 percent from Medicare	$80
Patient pays PAR 20 percent	$20
PAR adjusts/writes off the difference	$25

The Medicare Summary Notice, also called an explanation of benefits (EOB) or remittance advice, provides detailed payment information. Figure 12–3 is a sample of a Medicare Summary Notice.

Nonparticipating Providers (NonPARs)

A nonparticipating provider (NonPAR) is a physician or other health care provider who does not enroll in the Medicare program. NonPARs can accept assignment on a claim-by-claim basis, but they are subject to several restrictions:

- Medicare does not send payments directly to NonPARs. Payments are sent to the patients.
- On nonassigned claims, NonPARs are restricted to charging the patient no more than the **limiting fee**, defined as a maximum of 15 percent above the NonPAR Medicare-approved rate.
- On assigned claims, only the deductible and co-insurance due at the time of service can be collected.
- Balance-billing the patient is against the law in some states.
- NonPARs must accept assignment on clinical laboratory charges.
- NonPARs must file all Medicare claims regardless of assignment status.

Computing the NonPAR approved rate and limiting fee appears complicated. Basically, the NonPAR approved rate is set at 5 percent below the PAR approved rate. However, a Non-PAR physician who does not accept assignment may charge a maximum of 15 percent above the NonPAR approved rate. The NonPAR physician must then collect the difference from the patient.

> **EXAMPLE**
>
> The Medicare PAR approved rate for a particular service is $100. The Medicare NonPAR approved rate for the same service is $95. The NonPAR physician can charge up to 15 percent above the NonPAR approved rate as the limiting fee for this service—in this case, $109.25. The NonPAR physician receives 80 percent of the NonPAR approved rate from Medicare ($95 × .80 = $76). The patient owes the physician the difference between the limiting fee and the NonPAR approved rate—in this case, $14.25—and 20 percent of the Non-PAR approved rate—in this case, $19. The patient's total liability is $33.25. Table 12–4 illustrates NonPAR payment.

Patients who receive services from nonparticipating providers have higher out-of-pocket expenses than patients who receive services from participating providers.

Medicare Summary Notice ①

June 16, 20YY

④
John Beneficiary
609 Osborn
Blueberry, ME 49855

②

CUSTOMER SERVICE INFORMATION

Your Medicare Number: 222-22-2222A ③

If you have questions, write or call
Medicare (#12345)
555 Medicare Blvd
Suite 200
Medicare Building
Medicare, US XXXXX-XXXX

Call: 1-800-MEDICARE (1-800-633-4227)
Ask for Doctor Services
TTY users should call: 1-877-486-2048

⑤
BE INFORMED: Protect
your Medicare Number as you
would a credit card number.

This is a summary of claims processed from 5/15/20YY through 8/15/20YY

⑥
PART B MEDICAL INSURANCE – ASSIGNED CLAIMS

Dates of Service	Services Provided	Amount Charged	Medicare Approved	Medicare Paid Provider	You May Be Billed	See Notes Section
⑦ Claim number 12345-84956 ⑧ Paul Jones, MD 123 West Street Blueberry, ME 49855		⑩	⑪	⑫	⑬	⑭ a
		$55.00	$44.35	$0.00	$44.35	b
⑨ 04/07/20YY	1 Office/Outpatient Visit, ES (99214)					

⑮ **THIS IS NOT A BILL**– Keep this notice for your records.

Delmar/Cengage Learning

1. **Date:** Date MSN was sent.
2. **Customer Service Information:** Who to contact with questions about the MSN.
   Your Medicare number (3).
3. **Medicare Number:** The number on your Medicare card.

FIGURE 12–3 Medicare Summary Notice

Notes Section:

a This information is being sent to your private insurer(s). Send any questions regarding your benefits to them.

b This approved amount has been applied toward your deductible.

⑰ **Deductible Information:**

You have now met $44.35 of your $XXX.XX Part B deductible for 20xx.

⑱ **General Information:**

Please notify us if your address has changed are incorrect as shown on this notice.

⑲ **Appeals Information – Part B**

If you disagree with any claims decision on this notice, your appeal must be Received by **November 1, 20xx.**

Follow the instructions below:

1) Circle the item(s) you disagree with and explain why you disagree.
2) Send this notice, or a copy, to the address in the "Customer Service Information" box on Page 1.
3) Sign here_____ Phone Number _____

Delmar/Cengage Learning

4. **Name and Address:** If incorrect, contact the company listed in (2), and the Social Security Administration immediately.
5. **Be Informed:** Messages about ways to protect yourself and Medicare from fraud and abuse.
6. **Part B Medical Insurance = Assigned Claims:** Type of service. See the back of MSN for Information about assignment. (**Please note:** For unassigned services, this section is called **"Part B Medical Insurance – Unassigned Claims."**)
7. **Claim Number:** Number that identifies this specific claim.
8. **Provider's Name and Address:** Doctor (may show clinic, group, and/or referring doctor) or Provider's name and billing address. The referring doctor's name may also be shown if the service was ordered or referred by another doctor. The address shown is the billing address and may be different from where you received the services.
9. **Dates of Service:** Date service or supply was received. You may use these dates to compare with the dates shown on the bill you receive from your doctor.

FIGURE 12–3 *continued*

10. **Amount Charged:** Amount the provider billed Medicare.

11. **Medicare Approved:** Amount Medicare approves for this service or supply.

12. **Medicare Paid Provider:** Amount Medicare paid to the provider. (**Please Note:** For unassigned services, this column is called "**Medicare Paid You.**")

13. **You May be Billed:** The total amount the provider may bill you, including deductibles, coinsurance, and noncovered charges. Medicare supplement (Medigap) policies may pay all or part of this amount.

14. **See Notes Section:** Explains letters in (14) for more detailed information about your claim.

15. **This is not a bill:** This is not a bill.

16. **Notes Section:** Explains letters in (14) for more detailed information about your claim.

17. **Deductible Information:** How much of your yearly deductible you have met.

18. **General Information:** Important Medicare news and information.

19. **Appeals Information:** How and when to request an appeal.

FIGURE 12–3 *continued*

NonPARs who accept assignment on a particular case are not restricted to billing the limiting fee. Medicare reimbursement is still based on the NonPAR approved rate. NonPARs who submit claims for an assigned case may collect the deductible, if applicable, and the 20 percent coinsurance. If the full fee is collected at the time of service, the assigned status of the claim is void.

Nonparticipating physicians who do not accept assignment for **elective surgery** must provide the patient with a Medicare Surgical Financial Disclosure Statement. Elective surgery is a surgical procedure that is not an emergency and is scheduled in advance and where failure to have the surgery is not life-threatening. The financial disclosure statement must include the following:

- Type of surgery
- Estimated charges
- Medicare estimated payment
- Estimated balance due from the patient

A sample disclosure statement is shown in Figure 12–4.

TABLE 12–4

NonPAR Payment		
NonPAR approved rate		$ 95.00
NonPAR limiting fee (15 percent above NonPAR approved rate)		$109.25
Medicare pays 80 percent of NonPAR approved rate		$ 76.00
Total amount patient owes physician		$ 33.25
20 percent of NonPAR approved rate	($19.00)	
Difference between approved rate and limiting fee	($14.25)	

Practice Letterhead

Dear Patient:

As previously discussed, I do not plan to accept assignment for your surgery. The Medicare law requires that I give a Surgery Financial Disclosure Statement to all Medicare patients who are having elective surgery. These estimates assume that you have met the $135.00 annual Medicare Part B deductible.

Type of surgery: *Cholecystectomy*

Estimated charge:	$ *1,000.00*
Medicare estimated payment:	$ *750.00*
Your estimated payment:	$ *250.00*

Date: *3/31/20xx*   Beneficiary Signature *Viola Baril*

Delmar/Cengage Learning

FIGURE 12–4 Medicare Disclosure Statement

Failure to provide the disclosure statement may result in a substantial fine. In addition, assistant surgeon fees may be limited to a specific percentage rate. Check with the local Medicare Administrative Contractor for the current rate.

Nonparticipating providers who do not accept assignment collect fees from Medicare patients the same way that they collect fees from other patients. Co-pays and deductibles, if known, are collected at the time of service. If the practice's billing policy requires payment at the time of service up to a certain dollar amount, the policy applies to Medicare patients.

EXAMPLE

A nonparticipating physician who does not accept assignment treats Regina, a 68-year-old Medicare patient. The billing policy states that any balance due of $50 or less is expected at the time of service. Regina's bill is $110, the NonPAR limiting fee. The NonPAR approved fee is $95. Regina pays the 20 percent co-pay of the NonPAR approved rate ($19) as well as the $15 difference between the limiting fee and the approved rate, for a total of $34. Regina's balance is $76. The billing specialist submits the claim to the Medicare insurance carrier and, because the insurance carrier will send the payment to Regina, sends Regina a bill for the remaining $76.

Additional information about Medicare Part B is available on the Medicare website at http://www.medicare.gov. Another good resource is the annual publication *Medicare and You*, which is sent to Medicare beneficiaries and is available at your local Social Security Administration office.

REINFORCEMENT EXERCISES 12–2

Write Out the Abbreviations.

1. PAR

_____

2. NonPAR

_____

3. ABN

_____

4. MSN

_____

5. AAA

_____

Identify Each Service with D for Diagnostic/Treatment or P for Preventative.

1. Flu shot _____

2. Pints of blood _____

3. Oxygen _____

4. Pneumococcal shot _____

5. Wheelchair _____

Write a Short Answer for Each Question.

1. What is the purpose of an ABN?

_____

_____

_____

2. List three advantages of being a PAR.

_____

_____

_____

3. Define the term "limiting fee."

_____

_____

_____

MEDICARE PART C

Medicare Part C, also known as **Medicare Advantage (MA)**, is an alternative to the original fee-for-service Medicare program. Medicare sponsors MA plans and pays private insurance companies to provide health insurance products to individuals who qualify for Medicare. MA plan enrollees are still on Medicare and retain full rights and protections entitled to all Medicare beneficiaries. Under a MA plan, the individual:

- Must be enrolled in Medicare Part A and Part B
- Must continue paying the monthly premium for Medicare Part B
- May pay a monthly premium for additional benefits offered by the MA plan
- May have prescription drug coverage through the MA plan

Simply put, individuals who choose a MA plan are essentially buying their Medicare coverage from a private insurance company.

Individuals enrolled in a MA plan receive an insurance identification card from the insurance company that administers the plan. For example, Blue Cross/Blue Shield of Michigan offers an MA called Medicare Plus Blue. Enrollees are issued an ID card with the BC/BS logo. Medicare Plus Blue is a private fee-for-service plan that includes Medicare Part A, Part B, and Part D.

There are several types of MA plans. Three are discussed in this text: Medicare **Health Maintenance Organization (HMO)**; **Preferred Provider Organizations (PPO)**; and **Private Fee-for-Service (PFFS)** plans. Table 12–5 lists the features of HMOs and PPOs.

Medicare Advantage Private Fee-for-Service (PFFS) Plans

Medicare Advantage PFFS plans are offered by private insurance companies. The private insurance company (not Medicare) decides how much to pay providers and the co-pay amount for enrollees. Enrollees pay a monthly premium, which is based on the deductible and co-payment. An individual who chooses a high deductible has a lower monthly premium.

Under a Medicare Advantage PFFS, the enrollee is allowed to receive services from any provider or hospital, as long as the provider or hospital accepts the payment terms established by the insurance plan. Private Fee-for-Service plans do *not* contract with health care providers and do *not* distinguish between participating and nonparticipating providers. The enrollee must be sure that the provider will accept the plan's payment terms *before receiving services*. Enrollees may not use a Medicare supplemental insurance plan to cover the cost of co-payments and deductibles. Medicare Advantage PFFSs may include a prescription drug plan. If not, the enrollee is allowed to join a separate Medicare prescription drug plan.

Providers can choose to accept the insurance plan on a case-by-case basis. When a provider agrees to accept the insurance plan, the enrollee is responsible for any co-payment or deductible. Providers submit the insurance claim to the private insurance company that manages the PFFS plan.

The Medicare Part C information presented in this text is a brief overview of MA insurance plans. Additional and updated information is available on the Medicare web site at http://www.medicare.gov.

TABLE 12–5

Medicare Advantage HMO and PPO Features	
Medicare HMO Features	**Medicare PPO Features**
• Primary care physician manages health care; makes referrals to specialists (except for OB/GYN)	• May or may not assign a primary care physician
• Must receive services from providers who contract with the HMO; exception: emergency care, out-of-area urgent care, or pre-approved referral	• Lower co-payment for receiving services from a provider in the PPO network (preferred or in-network provider)
• Does not cover services received from providers outside of the plan, unless exceptions noted above apply. Note: Enrollees must pay for these services.	• Covers services received from an out-of-network provider; enrollee has a higher co-pay for out-of-network provider services. Note: Emergency care may be exempt from an out-of-network penalty.
• may offer prescription drug plan Note: If the HMO does not offer a prescription drug plan, enrollees generally cannot get other prescription drug coverage.	• generally no referral is necessary for a specialist Note: Enrollees have a lower co-pay for in-network specialists
• May offer an option that allows enrollees to receive services from providers outside the plan; there is usually a charge for this option, and limits may be set for using the option.	• Enrollees may be required to meet a deductible before coverage begins.

MEDICARE PART D: PRESCRIPTION DRUG BENEFIT

Under **Medicare Part D**, Medicare beneficiaries regardless of income, health status, or current prescription expenses have the opportunity to enroll in a **prescription drug plan (PDP)** to help defray the cost of prescription medications. Beneficiaries will generally have two main options for receiving the prescription drug benefit:

- Beneficiaries who stay with the traditional Medicare health plan may choose to join a stand-alone PDP, and drug benefits are added to their regular Medicare coverage.
- Beneficiaries who choose to receive their medical and drug benefits from one source may join an MA plan and choose a prescription drug plan associated with the MA plan. The **Medicare Advantage prescription drug plan (MA-PDP)** provides integrated benefit coverage for hospital, physician, and medication costs.

Prescription drug plans are available from many health-related companies. For example, in 2009, approximately 20 companies offered more than 51 different prescription drug coverage plans to Medicare beneficiaries in Michigan. Beneficiaries can learn about the plans available in their state from the following resources: their local Social Security Administration office, notices sent to them by the Centers for Medicare and Medicaid Services (CMS), information provided by their Medicare insurance carrier, visiting the Medicare Prescription Drug Plan Finder website, or attending one of the many informational meetings hosted by various groups and organizations.

Prescription Coverage

All prescription drug plans are required to offer basic drug coverage, which is also called "standard prescription drug coverage." Some PDPs offer additional coverage for an additional premium.

Medicare prescription drug plans cover generic and brand-name medications. Each PDP has a list of medications that are covered by the plan. This list of medications is called a **formulary**. The PDP formulary must always meet Medicare requirements. However, Medicare does not require any PDP to include all prescription medications. Medicare beneficiaries must research the prescription drug plans in their area to learn which plans cover their specific medications. If a plan decides to remove a drug from its formulary, it must provide 60 days' notice to beneficiaries affected by the change. In this situation, beneficiaries have the following options: (1) With the help of their physician, apply for an exception that allows beneficiaries to continue to use the medication as part of their covered drug benefits; (2) ask their physician if another medication from the PDP formulary can be substituted for the current drug; or (3) continue taking the medication and pay for it out of pocket.

Prescription Drug Plan Enrollment

Enrollment in a prescription drug plan is entirely voluntary. Beneficiaries who already have prescription drug coverage through a former employer, union, or other source may keep that coverage and choose not to enroll in the Medicare drug plan. Beneficiaries are allowed to join, change, or withdraw from a Medicare drug plan when they are first eligible for Medicare or between November 15 and December 31 each year. In most cases, a beneficiary remains enrolled for the entire calendar year. There are circumstances under which a beneficiary is allowed to change a Medicare drug plan, such as moving out of the service area or losing other credible drug coverage. A late enrollment penalty may be added to the monthly premium if a beneficiary does not join a PDP when first eligible.

Medicare beneficiaries can enroll in a prescription drug plan by completing an application form provided by the company that offers the plan, completing the company's online application, or calling the company that offers the plan.

Prescription Drug Plan Premiums, Deductibles, and Co-Payments

Beneficiaries who enroll in a prescription drug plan pay premiums, deductibles, and co-payments. Monthly premiums vary according to the coverage offered by the plan. According to CMS, the average monthly premium in 2009 was about $28, and the annual deductible was $295. The deductible is established by CMS and may be adjusted each year. Once the deductible is met, the plan pays 75 percent and the beneficiary pays 25 percent of the next $2,250 prescription drug costs. The beneficiary must pay 100 percent of the next $2,850 drug costs. Once the beneficiary spends $3,600 out-of-pocket, the beneficiary pays 5 percent and the plan pays 95 percent of prescription drug costs for the rest of the calendar year. The following example illustrates out-of-pocket expenses for a basic prescription drug plan.

EXAMPLE

Juanita takes six prescription medications daily. She pays $300 per month, for a total of $3,600 per year for her medications. Juanita decides to enroll in a basic prescription drug plan to help pay these costs. The premiums are $36 per month or $432 per year. She must pay the $295 deductible each year, which leaves her with $3,305 in annual drug costs. Juanita pays 25 percent of the next $2,250 ($562.50), which leaves her with $1,055 of the remaining cost. Juanita pays 100 percent of the remaining cost, up to $2,850. Juanita's annual out-of-pocket expense for her prescription drug coverage is $2,344.50. This figure includes the following: $482 for annual premiums; a $295 annual deductible; the 25 percent co-payment for $2,250 worth of drug costs, which is $562.50; and 100 percent of the remaining $1,055.

Juanita's prescription drug plan saves her $1,255.50 per year, which is the difference between her annual medication cost of $3,600 and her out-of-pocket expense of $2,344.50, which is required by her plan.

Monthly premiums, deductibles, and co-payment rates or ranges may be adjusted annually. Increases in these out-of-pocket expenses will have an effect on the beneficiary's overall savings.

Individuals with limited income and resources may be eligible for additional help to pay the out-of-pocket expenses of a prescription drug plan. Working together, the Social Security Administration and CMS have developed criteria that allow qualified individuals to receive about $2,000 to pay premiums, annual deductibles, and co-payments. Medicare Part A or Part B beneficiaries who meet the following criteria should apply for this benefit:

- Resources do not exceed $12,510 for a single person or $25,010 for a married person living with a spouse
- Annual income of less than $16,245 for a single person or a combined annual income of $21,855 for a married person living with a spouse
- Resident of one of the 50 states or the District of Columbia

Applying for this benefit does not automatically enroll an individual in a prescription drug plan. Medicare beneficiaries who qualify for this additional help must also enroll in a PDP.

The information presented here is a brief overview of Medicare Part D. Additional and updated information is available on the Medicare website at http://www.medicare.gov.

OTHER MEDICARE HEALTH PLAN CHOICES

Some of the MA plans were discussed under Medicare Part C. Other Medicare health plans include **Medicare special needs plans (SNP)** and **Medicare** medical savings account (MSA) plans.

Medicare special needs plans are a type of MA Plan that usually limits membership to individuals with specific diseases or conditions. Medicare SNPs tailor their benefits, choose providers, and create drug **formularies** (list of medications covered by the plan) to best meet the specific needs of the individuals enrolled in the plan. Most Medicare SNPs serve the following:

- Individuals with specific diseases such as diabetes, HIV/AIDS, or congestive heart failure
- Individuals who require nursing home care, either in a facility or in their own home
- Individuals who qualify for Medicare and Medicaid

Medicare Special Needs Plans are administered by private health insurance companies who establish the criteria for joining the plan. Medicare beneficiaries who enroll in a SNP continue to pay the Medicare Part B premium. There may also be a monthly premium for the SNP.

Medicare Medical Savings Accounts have been available since November 1998. Under an MSA, the Medicare beneficiary chooses a Medicare-approved insurance policy that has a high annual deductible. Medicare pays a set amount of money to private health insurance companies that contract with Medicare to offer the plan. At the beginning of each year, the private company deposits money from Medicare into the savings account. Individuals enrolled (member or enrollee) in the plan cannot deposit their own money into the account. The enrollee uses the account to pay for medical services until the deductible is met. Once the deductible is met, the MSA insurance plan is billed for medical expenses during the remainder of the calendar year.

Once enrolled in a MSA plan, the Medicare beneficiary must stay in the plan for a full year. If the MSA is exhausted before the deductible is met, the beneficiary pays the rest of the deductible out of pocket. Any balance left at the end of the year can be carried over to the next year, and the Medicare deposited amount is added to the balance. The beneficiary also has the option of withdrawing MSA money for nonmedical reasons, but that money is then taxed.

Individuals with both Medicare Part A and Part B can enroll in an MSA plan. Medicare beneficiaries with other types of health insurance, such as TRICARE or a group health plan, generally cannot enroll. MSA plans do not offer Medicare Part D prescription drug coverage. However, MSA enrollees can join a stand-alone prescription drug plan.

REINFORCEMENT EXERCISES 12–3

Write Out Each Abbreviation.

1. HMO _____

2. MA _____

3. PDP _____

4. PFFS _____

5. PPO _____

Write a Short Answer for Each Statement.

1. Describe three differences between an MA HMO and PPO.

_____

_____

_____

2. List three features of a Medicare PFFS plan.

_____

_____

_____

3. Define the term "formulary."

_____

_____

_____

continued on the next page

continued from the previous page

---

4. What is a Medicare Special Needs Plan?

_____

_____

_____

5. Describe three features of a Medicare Medical Saving Account.

_____

_____

_____

MEDICARE FEE SCHEDULE (MFS)

The **Medicare fee schedule (MFS)**, a list of Medicare-approved fees for physician/provider services, is based on a fairly complex calculation called the **resource-based relative value scale (RBRVS)**. The RBRVS system calculates approved fees based on the following variables:

- A **relative value unit (RVU)**, which includes physician work, practice expenses, and malpractice costs
- A **geographic adjustment factor (GAF)**, which adjusts the fees according to variations in regional costs
- A **national conversion factor (CF)**, a figure that is multiplied by the RVU to convert the RVU into a payment amount

The Medicare fee schedule is calculated on an annual basis. Medicare Administrative Contractors send the revised schedule to physicians in the region covered by the contractor. The fee schedule includes the Medicare payment rates for participating physicians and nonparticipating physicians and the limiting fee or charge for approved services. Figure 12–5 is an illustrative example of a Medicare fee schedule.

Note that the sample Medicare fee schedule includes the physician's usual fee and three Medicare fees. For purposes of this example, fees are calculated as follows:

- The Medicare fee for participating providers (PARs) is 80 percent of the physician fee.
- The Medicare fee for nonparticipating providers (NonPARs) is 5 percent less than the participating provider fee.
- The limiting fee/charge for NonPARs who do not accept assignment is 15 percent above the NonPAR fee.

The NonPAR limiting fee is the maximum amount a nonparticipating provider can legally charge a Medicare patient.

Considering the complexity of figuring out Medicare fees and that RBRVS are calculated annually, insurance billing specialists appreciate receiving an updated Medicare fee schedule from the Centers for Medicare and Medicaid Services or the Medicare Administrative Contractor.

| SERVICE | PHYSICIAN | MEDICARE FEE | | |
CODE/DESCRIPTION	USUAL FEE	PAR APPROVED	NonPAR APPROVED	LIMITING* FEE
EVALUATION AND MANAGEMENT				
Office Visit, New Patient				
99201 Level I	30.00	24.00	22.80	26.22
99202 Level II	50.00	40.00	38.00	43.70
99203 Level III	75.00	60.00	57.00	65.55
99204 Level IV	125.00	100.00	95.00	109.25
99205 Level V	150.00	120.00	114.00	131.10
Office Visit, Established Patient				
99211 Level I	20.00	16.00	15.20	17.48
99212 Level II	40.00	32.00	30.40	34.56
99213 Level III	65.00	52.00	49.40	56.81
99214 Level IV	80.00	64.00	60.80	69.92
99215 Level V	100.00	80.00	76.00	87.40

*Maximum amount NonPAR provider may charge Medicare patients

Delmar/Cengage Learning

FIGURE 12–5 Sample Medicare Fee Schedule

NATIONAL CORRECT CODING INITIATIVE (NCCI)

The Medicare insurance program pays nearly half a million physicians about $50 *billion* per year for services provided to Medicare beneficiaries. Because diagnosis and procedure codes have a direct impact on physician and provider payment, the Centers for Medicare and Medicaid Services (CMS) has a financial incentive to ensure coding accuracy.

In 1996, CMS implemented the **National Correct Coding Initiative (NCCI)**. The NCCI has two major goals:

- To promote physician and provider compliance with Medicare diagnosis and procedure coding guidelines
- To ensure appropriate payment (reimbursement) for physician and provider services

All claims submitted to Medicare insurance carriers are edited by an electronic screening process that verifies the following: (1) The patient is a Medicare beneficiary; (2) all co-payments and deductibles have been met; (3) Medicare is the primary payer; and (4) diagnosis and procedure codes are accurate.

NCCI edits identify invalid diagnosis codes, such as (ICD-9-CM) E codes, and discrepancies between the diagnosis code and the patient's age or sex. For example, a claim submitted for a male patient with the code for ovarian failure or a claim submitted for a female patient with the code for prostate hypertrophy will be returned to the provider without payment.

NCCI edits identify the following types of procedure coding errors:

- **Mutually exclusive procedures:** Reporting two procedures that cannot possibly be performed at the same time, such as a laminectomy (removal of the bony arches of a vertebra) and a total hip replacement
- **Component part coding:** Submitting separate or multiple codes for a procedure that is covered by a single code, such as reporting a separate code for a laparotomy (incision into the abdomen) that was done as part of an appendectomy
- **Unbundling:** Submitting separate or multiple codes for services that are part of a global surgery package, such as routine postoperative services
- **Invalid modifier:** Assigning the wrong modifier to a *Current Procedural Terminology* (CPT) code or a *Healthcare Common Procedure Coding System* (HCPCS) Level II code. For example, CPT modifier -52, "Reduced Services," applies only to procedures or services provided on an inpatient basis and may not be assigned to outpatient or ambulatory surgery center procedure codes.

When NCCI edits identify coding errors, the provider is notified that the claim is rejected. A pattern of coding errors may prompt the Medicare Administrative Contractor to audit a significant sample of all Medicare claims. A consistent pattern of coding errors may lead to charges of Medicare insurance fraud or abuse. The implications of fraud and abuse are discussed in Chapter 2.

Many commercial billing software programs are equipped with edit features that identify errors before the claim is submitted. The billing specialist can prevent claims submission errors by:

- Accurately completing all required fields of the insurance claim form
- Following Medicare claims submission guidelines
- Updating insurance billing references, which are sent to providers via bulletins or transmittals
- Attending training sessions related to changes for submitting Medicare claims
- Checking all CPT and HCPCS Level II modifiers
- Reviewing the patient's medical record or asking the physician for clarification when there are questions related to diagnosis and procedure codes
- Alerting the office manager or physician when there is a concern related to coding accuracy

Because insurance billing specialists are actively involved in insurance claims submission, they have a vested interest in the accuracy, validity, and legality of that process.

REINFORCEMENT EXERCISES 12–4

Write out Each Abbreviation.

1. MFS_____

2. NCCI_____

3. RBRVS_____

continued on the next page

continued from the previous page

Briefly Define Each Term or Phrase.

1. Mutually exclusive procedure

_____

_____

_____

2. Component part coding

_____

_____

_____

3. Unbundling

_____

_____

_____

4. Invalid modifier

_____

_____

_____

Provide a Short Answer for Each Question.

1. Describe three steps the insurance billing specialist can take to prevent claims submission errors.

_____

_____

_____

2. What is the purpose of the NCCI?

_____

_____

_____

MEDICARE CLAIMS SUBMISSION

CMS provides extensive guidelines for submitting health insurance claims in the *Medicare Claims Processing Manual*, which is available on the CMS website. Current information is sent to providers via Medicare transmittals and communication with the regional Medicare Administrative Contractor (MAC). MACs are responsible for processing Medicare claims in a specific jurisdiction. Table 12–6 lists the CMS jurisdictions; states and U.S. territories included in each jurisdiction; and the MAC in effect at the time of publication.

Information about the MACs is available on their respective websites. The Medicare Administrative Contractors for the 15 jurisdictions process Medicare Part A and Part B claims and are also known as **A/B MAC**s.

CMS has identified four durable medical equipment (DME) jurisdictions and awarded Medicare administrative contracts for processing claims related to DME. The contractors are known

TABLE 12–6

CMS Jurisdictions, States/U.S. Territories, and MACs		
Jurisdiction	States/U.S. Territories	MAC
1	American Samoa, California, Guam, Hawaii, Nevada, Northern Mariana Islands	Palmetto Government Benefits Administrator
2	Alaska, Idaho, Oregon, Washington	National Heritage Insurance Corp.
3	Arizona, Montana, North Dakota, South Dakota, Utah, Wyoming	Noridian Administrative Services
4	Colorado, New Mexico, Oklahoma, Texas	Trailblazer Health Enterprises
5	Iowa, Kansas, Missouri, Nebraska	Wisconsin Physician Services
6	Illinois, Minnesota, Wisconsin	Noridian Administrative Services
7	Arkansas, Louisiana, Mississippi	Trailblazer Health Enterprises
8	Indiana, Michigan	National Government Services
9	Florida, Puerto Rico, U.S. Virgin Islands	First Coast Service Options, Inc.
10	Alabama, Georgia, Tennessee	Cahaba Government Benefit Administrators
11	North Carolina, South Carolina, Virginia, West Virginia	Palmetto Government Benefits Administrator
12	Delaware, District of Columbia, Maryland, New Jersey, Pennsylvania	Highmark Medicare Services
13	Connecticut, New York	National Government Services
14	Maine, Massachusetts, New Hampshire, Rhode Island, Vermont	National Heritage Insurance Corp.
15	Kentucky, Ohio	Highmark Medicare Services

TABLE 12–7

CMS Jurisdictions, States/U.S. Territories, and DME MACs		
CMS Jurisdiction	States/U.S. Territories	DME MAC
A	Connecticut, Delaware, District of Columbia, Maine, Maryland, Massachusetts, New Hampshire, New Jersey, New York, Pennsylvania, Rhode Island, Vermont	National Heritage Insurance Corp.
B	Illinois, Indiana, Kentucky, Michigan, Minnesota, Ohio, Wisconsin	AdminaStar Federal, Inc.
C	Alabama, Arkansas, Colorado, Florida, Georgia, Louisiana, Mississippi, New Mexico, North Carolina, Oklahoma, Puerto Rico, South Carolina, Tennessee, Texas, U.S. Virgin Islands, Virginia, West Virginia	CIGNA Government Services
D	Alaska, American Samoa, Arizona, California, Guam, Hawaii, Idaho, Iowa, Kansas, Missouri, Montana, Nebraska, Nevada, North Dakota, Northern Mariana Islands, Oregon, South Dakota, Utah, Washington, Wyoming	Noridian Administrative Services

as **DME MAC**s (Durable Medical Equipment Medicare Administrative Contractor). Table 12–7 lists the CMS jurisdictions; states and U.S. territories included in the jurisdictions; and the DME MAC in effect at the time of publication.

Information about the DME MACs is available on their respective websites.

General Guidelines for Medicare Claims Submission

General guidelines apply to all Medicare claims submission activities. The guidelines include:

- The CMS-1500 is used for Medicare Part B claims.
- All providers are required to file claims for Medicare beneficiaries.
- Dates are entered in a six- or eight-digit format.
- Claims must be filed within specified deadlines, usually one year from the date of service or December 31 of the year following the date of service.
- With few exceptions, Medicare claims are filed electronically.

CMS-1500 completion instructions depend on Medicare's status as primary or secondary payer.

Medicare as Primary Payer

Medicare is the primary payer for nearly all provider services. Insurance coverage information is captured during the patient registration process. If there is any question about Medicare payer status, the insurance billing specialist clarifies the status *before* submitting a claim. Billing Medicare as primary when the status is secondary can result in sanctions ranging from an audit of the provider's billing practices to charges of Medicare fraud or abuse.

Medicare is considered the primary payer when the following circumstances exist:

- The individual is eligible for an employer-sponsored group health plan but has declined to enroll or recently dropped coverage.
- The individual is currently employed but is not yet eligible for employer-sponsored group plan coverage or has exhausted benefits under the group plan.
- The individual is covered by TRICARE/CHAMPUS.
- The individual is under age 65 and has Medicare due to disability or end-stage renal disease and is not covered by an employer-sponsored plan.
- The patient has both Medicare and Medicaid.

Certain situations do allow Medicare to be billed as the primary payer for a temporary period of time. This is known as Medicare **conditional primary payer status**. Conditional primary payer status may be appropriate under the following conditions:

- Another insurance plan that is normally considered primary to Medicare issues a denial of payment that is being appealed.
- A physically or mentally impaired individual does not file a claim to the primary insurance plan.
- A workers' compensation claim is denied and moving through the appeal process.
- The primary payer does not respond within 120 days of filing a claim.

Conditional primary payer status allows the provider to be reimbursed for services rendered. If payment is received from the primary carrier at a later date, the billing specialist must immediately return payments made by the Medicare Administrative Contractor.

REINFORCEMENT EXERCISES 12–5

Fill in the blank.

1. The _____ is used for Medicare Part B claims.

2. The regional _____ furnish providers with an up-to-date Medicare fee schedule.

3. Medicare is the _____ payer when an individual qualifies for Medicare and Medicaid.

4. CMS has identified _____ MAC jurisdictions.

5. A/B MACs process claims for _____ and _____.

Provide a Short Answer for Each Question.

1. What is the difference between A/B MACs and DME MACs?

   _____

   _____

2. Describe two situations that allow Medicare to be billed as a conditional primary status.

   _____

   _____

Completing the CMS-1500: Medicare as Primary Payer

The following block-by-block instructions for completing the CMS-1500 apply to Medicare as the primary payer.

Block 1	Enter an X in the Medicare box.
Block 1a	Enter the patient's **health insurance claim number (HICN)** exactly as it appears on the Medicare ID card.
Block 2	Enter the patient's last name, first name, and middle initial in uppercase letters exactly as they appear on the Medicare ID card.
Block 3	Enter the patient's eight-digit birth date (MMDDYYYY); enter an X in M or F.
Block 4	Leave this blank.
Block 5	Enter the patient's current mailing address and telephone number. On the first line, enter the street address; the second line, the city and state; the third line, the ZIP code and phone number.
Blocks 6, 7	Leave this blank.
Block 8	Enter an X in the appropriate box for the patient's marital, employment, and student status.
Blocks 9–9d	Leave this blank.
Block 10a	Enter an X in YES or NO. If YES, another insurance may be primary to Medicare.
Block 10b	Enter an X in YES or NO. If YES, enter the two character abbreviation for the state where the accident occurred. If YES, another insurance may be primary to Medicare.
Block 10c	Enter an X in YES or NO. If YES, another insurance may be primary to Medicare.
Block 10d	Leave this blank.
Block 11	Enter NONE and then go to Block 12.
Blocks 11a–11d	Leave this blank.
Block 12	Enter SIGNATURE ON FILE.
Block 13	Enter SIGNATURE ON FILE.
Block 14	Enter the eight-digit date of current illness/service, the date an injury first occurred, and the last menstrual period or estimated date of pregnancy. When the patient is being treated by a chiropractor, enter the date that treatment was initiated. In block 19, enter the date of the x-ray that justifies the course of treatment.

continued on the next page

continued from the previous page

Block 15	Leave this blank.
Block 16	Enter the eight-digit dates that indicate the timeframe the patient is unable to work. Otherwise, leave this blank.
Block 17	Enter the last name, first name, and middle initial of the referring or ordering physician if the service or item was ordered or referred by a physician. (See Special Notes.)

Special Notes:

- The term "physician" includes a doctor of medicine, osteopathy, dental surgery, dental medicine, podiatric medicine, optometry, and chiropractor.
- **Referring physician:** A physician who requests an item or service for a beneficiary that will be provided by another physician, and the item or service may be covered under the Medicare program.
- **Ordering physician:** A physician or, when appropriate, a nonphysician practitioner, who orders nonphysician services, such as diagnostic laboratory tests, pharmaceutical services, or durable medical equipment (DME).
- **Ordered/Referred services:** Diagnostic, laboratory, and radiology services; consultant services; durable medical equipment; parenteral and enteral nutrition; immunosuppressive drug claims; physical and occupational therapy; prosthesis; and orthotic devices. Enter the ordering physician's name in block 17.
- **Physician extenders:** A physician's assistant, nurse practitioner, or other limited license practitioner. When these individuals refer a patient for consultant services, the name of the supervising physician is entered in block 17.
- **Surgeon:** When a physician refers the patient to a surgeon, enter the referring physician's name in block 17. If there is no referring physician, enter the surgeon's name in block 17.
- **Assistant surgeon:** When the claim is filed for an assistant surgeon, enter the surgeon's name in block 17.
- **Ordering/performing physician:** When the ordering physician is the performing physician, which is often the case with intra-office clinical laboratory tests, enter the performing physician's name in block 17.
- **Diagnostic service:** When a physician refers the patient to another physician who then orders and performs a diagnostic service, a separate claim form is required for the diagnostic service. On the first claim form, enter the original ordering/referring physician's name in block 17. On the second claim form, enter the performing physician's name.

Block 17a	Leave this blank.
Block 17b	Enter the NPI of the referring/ordering physician listed in block 17.
Block 18	Enter the dates of hospitalization in an eight-digit format.
Block 19	Medicare guidelines state that this block is used for the following:

- For independent physical or occupational therapist and all podiatrist claims, enter the eight-digit date the patient was last seen and the NPI number of the attending physician. Do not enter spaces in the date (MMDDYYYY).
- For chiropractic claims, enter the eight-digit date of the required x-ray.
- For not otherwise classified (NOC) drug claims, enter the name and dosage of the drug.
- For unlisted procedure or not otherwise classified code, enter a concise description of the service. If the description does not fit in block 19, submit an attachment with the claim.
- **Modifier -99 in block 24D:** Enter all modifiers that are covered in block 24D by the multiple modifier -99. If more than one -99 is used on the claim, enter the line number being reported followed by an equal sign and all modifiers that apply to that line. *Example:* 1 = 20 50 80 indicates that modifiers 20, 50, and 80 apply to the first line in block 24D.
- **Homebound:** Enter this term when an independent laboratory renders an EKG tracing or obtains a specimen from a homebound or institutionalized patient.
- **Patient refuses to assign benefits:** Enter this statement when the Medicare beneficiary absolutely refuses to assign benefits to a participating provider. In this case, payment can only be made directly to the beneficiary.
- **Testing for hearing aid:** Enter this statement to receive an intentional Medicare denial as primary when a secondary payer is involved.
- **Dental examination claim:** Enter the specific surgery for which the dental exam is being performed.
- **Low osmolar contrast material claim:** Enter the specific name and dosage when there is no HCPCS code for the material used as a contrast.
- When providers share the postoperative care for a global surgery, enter the date the care was assumed or relinquished. *Example:* Dr. Jones provides postoperative care through June 10, 20xx. Dr. Bones provides postoperative care from June 11 through June 15. Dr. Jones's billing specialist enters the relinquished date 061020xx in block 19, and Dr. Bones's billing specialist enters the assumed date 061120xx in block 19.

Block 20	Enter an X in NO when the laboratory tests are performed in the provider's office. Enter an X in YES if an outside laboratory performed the tests listed on the claim and the provider filing the claim was billed for the tests and is passing the fee on to the patient. The total cost is entered in the CHARGES section of block 20. The name and address of the outside laboratory is entered in block 32.
Block 21	Enter up to four ICD-9-CM diagnostic codes that describe the patient's condition. Enter the first-listed diagnosis code in 1. Enter other diagnoses in priority order. All narrative diagnoses for nonphysician specialties must be submitted as an attachment. Do not use any decimal points.
Block 22	Leave this blank.

continued on the next page

continued from the previous page

Block 23	Only one condition may be reported in block 23.
	Enter a prior authorization code if one is assigned.
	Enter the investigational device exemption (IDE) when an investigational device is used in an FDA-approved clinical trial.
	Enter the NPI of the home health agency or hospice when CPT code G0181 or G0182 is billed; applies when a physician is providing care plan oversight services.
	Enter the 10-digit Clinical Laboratory Improvement Act (CLIA) certification number for laboratory services billed by an entity performing CLIA covered tests.
Block 24A	Enter the eight-digit date for each procedure, service, or supply. When from and to dates are shown for a series of identical services, enter the number of days or units in column G.
Block 24B	Enter the place of service code. (See Chapter 8.)
Block 24C	Leave this blank.
Block 24D	Enter the CPT or HCPCS codes and required modifiers. Enter the specific procedure code without narrative description. *Exception:* When reporting an unlisted procedure code or not otherwise classified (NOC) code, include a narrative description in block 19 or submit an attachment. Do not place a hyphen before the modifier.
Block 24E	Enter one diagnosis reference number (1 through 4) for the ICD-9-CM diagnosis code in block 21 that best justifies the medical necessity for services identified in block 24D. Use only one reference number per line.
Block 24F	Enter the fee for each listed service. Do not use dollar signs or decimal points; always include cents. If the same service was performed on consecutive days, enter the fee for one service in block 24F and the number of times the service was performed in block 24G.
Block 24G	Enter the number of days or units. This block is most commonly used for multiple visits, units of supplies, or anesthesia minutes of oxygen volume. If only one service is performed, enter 1.
Block 24H	Leave this blank.
Block 24I	Enter the ID qualifier 1C in the shaded portion.
Block 24J	Leave the shaded portion blank.
	Enter the rendering physician's NPI number in the unshaded portion.
Block 25	Enter the provider's Federal Tax ID number (Employer Tax Identification Number [EIN]) or Social Security Number (SSN).
	Enter an X in the appropriate box.
Block 26	Enter the patient account number, as assigned by the provider, if applicable.

continued on the next page

continued from the previous page

Block 27	Enter an X in YES if the physician accepts assignment of benefits. Enter an X in NO if the physician does not accept assignment.
Block 28	Enter total charges for all services submitted on a claim.
Block 29	Enter the total amount the patient paid on the covered services only.
Block 30	Leave this blank.
Block 31	Enter SIGNATURE ON FILE or a computer-generated signature. Electronic claims submission software may automatically enter the date the claim is completed or submitted.
Block 32	Enter the name, address, and ZIP code of the service location for all services other than those furnished in place of service home (12).
Block 32a	If required by the Medicare claims processing policy, enter the NPI of the service facility. Otherwise, leave this blank.
Block 32b	Leave this blank.
Block 33	Enter the provider's billing name, address, ZIP code, and telephone number.
Block 33a	For solo-practice providers, enter the NPI of the provider/physician. For group-practice providers, enter the NPI of the group practice.
Block 33b	Leave this blank.

Figure 12–6 is a sample of a completed CMS-1500 form when Medicare is the primary payer and the patient has no supplemental insurance.

REINFORCEMENT EXERCISES 12–6

Using the patient and provider information given here, complete a CMS-1500 for a Medicare as primary payer claim. Your instructor can tell you how to obtain the CMS-1500.

Patient Information

Name: Matthew Mattson—married, male, birth date January 3, 1927
Address: 109 Spruce Street, Blueberry, ME 49966
Phone: (906) 555-3336
Insurance: Medicare 388579728A
Employment Status: Retired
Diagnosis/Code: Pleurisy, 511.0; atrial tachycardia, 427.89
Services/Code: Office visit, 99212; chest x-ray, two views, 71020
Date of Service: March 3, 20xx
Charges: Office visit, $50; chest x-ray, $50

continued on the next page

continued from the previous page

Provider Information

Superiorland Clinic
714 Hennepin Ave.
Blueberry, ME 49966
Phone: (906) 337-8778
Superiorland Clinic NPI : 4567890123
Sara M. Gervais, MD
Physician NPI : 0987654321
EIN: 11-234567
Dr. Gervais is a participating provider.

Medicare as Primary with Supplemental Insurance

Because Medicare does not cover all medical services, some people choose to supplement their Medicare insurance with additional health insurance. There are a number of insurance companies that advertise Medicare supplemental policies. As with any advertised product, the consumer must carefully scrutinize these plans before entering into a contractual arrangement.

There are three general types of Medicare supplemental insurance plans:

- Medigap
- Employer-sponsored Medicare supplemental health insurance
- Medicare-Medicaid Crossover Program

These plans, called **Medicare supplemental plans (MSPs)**, cover the patient's Medicare deductible and co-insurance costs. Each supplemental plan is discussed individually.

Medigap Insurance Plans

Medigap insurance is specifically designed to supplement Medicare's benefits and is regulated by federal and state law. A Medigap insurance plan is clearly identified as Medicare supplemental insurance, and it provides specific benefits that fill in the gaps of Medicare coverage. The federal government has approved 12 standard Medigap policies. Each policy is labeled with the letters A through L, and it provides coverage for a variety of health services. The services covered by each of the 12 government-approved Medigap plans are listed in Table 12–8.

A check mark in a column means that the Medigap policy pays 100 percent of the described benefit. A percentage in the column indicates the percentage of the described benefit paid by the Medigap plan. Medigap plans cover co-insurance payments only after the deductible has been met, unless the Medigap plan also covers the deductible.

Note that Medigap policies pay most, if not all, Medicare co-insurance amounts and may provide coverage for Medicare's deductibles. Other services covered by some Medigap policies include prescription drugs, preventive screening, and emergency medical care while traveling outside the United States. Although the federal government regulates the Medigap benefits, the individual company sets the cost or premium for the policy. Premiums can vary widely even in the same geographic location.

FIGURE 12–6 Medicare Primary Payer CMS-1500 (For instructional use only. Courtesy of the Centers for Medicare and Medicaid Services, www.cms.hhs.gov)

TABLE 12–8

Medigap Plans A through L												
Medigap Benefits	A	B	C	D	E	F	G	H	I	J	K	L
Medicare Part A co-insurance and all costs after hospital benefits are exhausted	√	√	√	√	√	√	√	√	√	√	√	√
Medicare Part B co-insurance or co-payment for services, except preventative services	√	√	√	√	√	√	√	√	√	√	50 percent	75 percent
Blood, first three pints	√	√	√	√	√	√	√	√	√	√	50 percent	75 percent
Hospice care co-insurance or co-payment											50 percent	75 percent
Skilled nursing facility care coinsurance		√	√	√	√	√	√	√	√	√	50 percent	75 percent
Medicare Part A deductible		√	√	√	√	√	√	√	√	√	50 percent	75 percent
Medicare Part B deductible		√	√		√							
Medicare Part B excess charges						√	80 percent		√	√		
Foreign travel emergency, up to plan limits			√	√	√	√	√	√	√	√		
At-home recovery, up to plan limits				√			√		√	√		
Medicare preventative care Part B co-insurance	√	√	√	√	√	√	√	√	√	√	√	√
Preventative care not covered by Medicare, up to $120					√					√		

Processing Medigap Claims

Medigap claim processing depends on the status of the provider. Participating provider (PAR) Medigap claims are electronically transferred from the Medicare insurance carrier to the Medigap insurance carrier. The insurance billing specialist enters Medigap carrier and policyholder information in the CMS-1500 blocks 9 through 9d and block 13 when filing the Medicare claim. If the Medigap carrier is not able to process claims electronically, the insurance billing specialist makes a copy of the Medicare remittance or summary notice and attaches it to the claim that is sent to the Medigap insurance carrier.

Nonparticipating (NonPAR) providers are not required to include Medigap information on the claim form. If the NonPAR provider agrees to file a Medigap claim, the patient must provide a copy of the Medicare Summary Notice to the provider.

Completing the CMS-1500: Medicare Primary with Medigap

The patient must sign an authorization to release Medigap benefits to the provider so the insurance billing specialist can properly complete the CMS-1500 Medicare claim. When the patient is a Medicare beneficiary and has Medigap supplemental insurance and the provider participates in Medicare, the insurance billing specialist completes the CMS-1500 claim according to the following instructions. These instructions do not apply to employer-sponsored Medicare supplemental plans or to nonparticipating providers.

Blocks 1 through 8	No change from Medicare as primary payer
Block 9	Enter SAME if the patient is the Medigap insured.
	Enter the last name, first name, and middle initial of the Medigap insured if the name is different from the name in Block 2.
Block 9a	Enter MEDIGAP, MG, or MGAP followed by the policy number and group number. If there is no group, enter the policy number only.
Block 9b	Enter the Medigap insured's eight-digit birth date.
	Enter an X in M or F.
Block 9c	Leave this blank if the Medigap claim-based identification number is entered in 9d. Otherwise, enter the claims processing address of the Medigap insurer.
	EXAMPLE 714 Hennepin Road, Blueberry, ME 49966 is written as 714 HENNEPIN RD ME 49966.
Block 9d	Enter the **COBA (coordination of benefits administrator)** Medigap claim-based ID number.
	The COBA ID, a five-digit number that begins with a 5, allows the beneficiary's claim to be electronically sent to Medigap insurer. This service is available to participating providers.
Blocks 10–12	No change from Medicare as primary payer

continued on the next page

continued from the previous page

Block 13	Enter SIGNATURE ON FILE. Note: The provider must obtain an authorization that specifically includes the name of the Medigap insurance plan so payment is sent to the provider.
Blocks 14–33	No change from the instructions for Medicare as primary payer

Figure 12–7 is an example of a completed CMS-1500 for Medicare patients with Medigap insurance.

REINFORCEMENT EXERCISE 12–7

Use the patient information from Reinforcement Exercises 12–6 for Matthew Mattson, with the Addition of Medigap group and COBA ID numbers, and the following provider information to complete a CMS-1500 for Medicare with Medigap. Your instructor can tell you where to get the form.

Medigap Numbers

Group # 23110; COBA ID: 50505

Provider Information

Superiorland Clinic
714 Hennepin Ave.
Blueberry, ME 49966
Phone: (906) 337-8778
Superiorland Clinic NPI: 4567890123
Sara M. Gervais, MD
Physician NPI: 0987654321
EIN: 11-234567
Dr. Gervais is a participating provider.

Employer-Sponsored Medicare Supplemental Plans

Some employers offer their retired employees an insurance plan that is intended to supplement the retiree's Medicare coverage. These plans do not qualify for designation as a Medigap policy. Employer-sponsored plans are not regulated by the federal government and are subject to the same conditions established in the employer's employee health insurance plans. Premiums for an employer-sponsored supplemental plan are paid by or through the employer.

Health care providers are not required to file employer-sponsored Medicare supplemental insurance claims. Because these plans are not designated as Medigap policies, the insurance billing specialist does not include the plan's insurance information in blocks 9 through 9d on a Medicare claim.

Some employers provide the Medicare insurance carrier with monthly information about retirees who are covered by Medicare supplemental plans. When this is the case, information is electronically transferred from the Medicare insurance carrier to the supplemental plan insurance

(1500)

HEALTH INSURANCE CLAIM FORM

APPROVED BY NATIONAL UNIFORM CLAIM COMMITTEE 08/05

☐☐ PICA   PICA ☐☐

| 1. MEDICARE [X] (Medicare #)   MEDICAID ☐ (Medicaid #)   TRICARE CHAMPUS ☐ (Sponsor's SSN)   CHAMPVA ☐ (Member ID #)   GROUP HEALTH PLAN ☐ (SSN or ID)   FECA BLK LUNG ☐ (SSN)   OTHER ☐ (ID) | 1a. INSURED'S I.D. NUMBER (For Program in Item 1) 11234980A |

2. PATIENT'S NAME (Last Name, First Name, Middle Initial)
PUBLIC JOHN Q

3. PATIENT'S BIRTH DATE MM 09 | DD 25 | YY 1930   SEX M [X]   F ☐

4. INSURED'S NAME (Last Name, First Name, Middle Initial)

5. PATIENT'S ADDRESS (No., Street)
108 SENATE AVE

6. PATIENT RELATIONSHIP TO INSURED
Self ☐   Spouse ☐   Child ☐   Other ☐

7. INSURED'S ADDRESS (No., Street)

CITY ANYWHERE   STATE US

8. PATIENT STATUS
Single [X]   Married ☐   Other ☐

Employed ☐   Full-Time Student ☐   Part-Time Student ☐

CITY   STATE

ZIP CODE 12345   TELEPHONE (Include Area Code) (101) 201 7891

ZIP CODE   TELEPHONE (Include Area Code) ( )

9. OTHER INSURED'S NAME (Last Name, First Name, Middle Initial)
SAME

10. IS PATIENT'S CONDITION RELATED TO:

11. INSURED'S POLICY GROUP OR FECA NUMBER

a. OTHER INSURED'S POLICY OR GROUP NUMBER
MEDIGAP 486901

a. EMPLOYMENT? (Current or Previous)
☐ YES   [X] NO

a. INSURED'S DATE OF BIRTH MM | DD | YY   SEX M ☐ F ☐

b. OTHER INSURED'S DATE OF BIRTH MM 09 | DD 25 | YY 1930   SEX M [X]   F ☐

b. AUTO ACCIDENT?   PLACE (State)
☐ YES   [X] NO

b. EMPLOYER'S NAME OR SCHOOL NAME

c. EMPLOYER'S NAME OR SCHOOL NAME

c. OTHER ACCIDENT?
☐ YES   [X] NO

c. INSURANCE PLAN NAME OR PROGRAM NAME

d. INSURANCE PLAN NAME OR PROGRAM NAME
59999

10d. RESERVED FOR LOCAL USE

d. IS THERE ANOTHER HEALTH BENEFIT PLAN?
☐ YES   ☐ NO   *If yes*, return to and complete item 9 a-d.

READ BACK OF FORM BEFORE COMPLETING & SIGNING THIS FORM.

12. PATIENT'S OR AUTHORIZED PERSON'S SIGNATURE I authorize the release of any medical or other information necessary to process this claim. I also request payment of government benefits either to myself or to the party who accepts assignment below.

SIGNED SIGNATURE ON FILE   DATE

13. INSURED'S OR AUTHORIZED PERSON'S SIGNATURE I authorize payment of medical benefits to the undersigned physician or supplier for services described below.

SIGNED SIGNATURE ON FILE

14. DATE OF CURRENT: MM 04 | DD 12 | YY 20XX   ILLNESS (First symptom) OR INJURY (Accident) OR PREGNANCY (LMP)

15. IF PATIENT HAS HAD SAME OR SIMILAR ILLNESS, GIVE FIRST DATE MM | DD | YY

16. DATES PATIENT UNABLE TO WORK IN CURRENT OCCUPATION FROM MM | DD | YY   TO MM | DD | YY

17. NAME OF REFERRING PROVIDER OR OTHER SOURCE
17a.
17b. NPI

18. HOSPITALIZATION DATES RELATED TO CURRENT SERVICES FROM MM | DD | YY   TO MM | DD | YY

19. RESERVED FOR LOCAL USE

20. OUTSIDE LAB? ☐ YES   [X] NO $ CHARGES

21. DIAGNOSIS OR NATURE OF ILLNESS OR INJURY (Relate Items 1, 2, 3, or 4 to Item 24E by Line)
1. 540 . 0
2. _____ . _____
3. _____ . _____
4. _____ . _____

22. MEDICAID RESUBMISSION CODE   ORIGINAL REF. NO.

23. PRIOR AUTHORIZATION NUMBER

24. A. DATE(S) OF SERVICE From MM DD YY — To MM DD YY	B. PLACE OF SERVICE	C. EMG	D. PROCEDURES, SERVICES, OR SUPPLIES (Explain Unusual Circumstances) CPT/HCPCS — MODIFIER	E. DIAGNOSIS POINTER	F. $ CHARGES	G. DAYS OR UNITS	H. EPSDT Family Plan	I. ID. QUAL.	J. RENDERING PROVIDER ID. #
1	04 12 20XX 04 12 20XX	11		99213	1	75 00	1		IC / NPI	7865432107
2	04 12 20XX 04 12 20XX	11		71020	1	50 00	1		IC / NPI	7865432107
3									NPI	
4									NPI	
5									NPI	
6									NPI	

25. FEDERAL TAX I.D. NUMBER 11-123441   SSN ☐ EIN [X]

26. PATIENT'S ACCOUNT NO.

27. ACCEPT ASSIGNMENT? (For govt. claims, see back) [X] YES   ☐ NO

28. TOTAL CHARGE $ 125 00

29. AMOUNT PAID $ 25 00

30. BALANCE DUE $

31. SIGNATURE OF PHYSICIAN OR SUPPLIER INCLUDING DEGREES OR CREDENTIALS (I certify that the statements on the reverse apply to this bill and are made a part thereof.)
SIGNATURE ON FILE
SIGNED   DATE

32. SERVICE FACILITY LOCATION INFORMATION
MEDICARE EAST
1201 MEDIC DRIVE
ANYWHERE US 12345
a. 5687812403   b.

33. BILLING PROVIDER INFO & PH # (101) 111 1234
MEDICARE EAST
1201 MEDIC DRIVE
ANYWHERE US 12345
a. 5687812403   b.

NUCC Instruction Manual available at: www.nucc.org   APPROVED OMB-0938-0999 FORM CMS-1500 (08-05)

CARRIER — PATIENT AND INSURED INFORMATION — PHYSICIAN OR SUPPLIER INFORMATION

FIGURE 12–7 Medicare/Medigap CMS-1500 (For instructional use only. Courtesy of the Centers for Medicare and Medicaid Services, www.cms.hhs.gov)

carrier. If electronic transfer is not an option, the patient must file for benefits after receiving the Medicare Summary Notice.

Medicare-Medicaid Crossover Program

The **Medicare-Medicaid Crossover Program**, a combination of the Medicare and Medicaid health insurance plans, is available to these groups:

- Medicare-eligible individuals with incomes below the federal poverty level, the Qualified Medicare Beneficiary program
- Individuals who are eligible for Medicare's Specified Low-Income Medicare Beneficiary program

Crossover program claims are also known as Medi/Medi claims, Care/Caid claims, or 18/19 claims, which refers to Title 18 and Title 19 of the Social Security Act Amendments of 1965.

Processing Medicare-Medicaid Crossover Claims

All health care providers must accept assignment on Medicare-Medicaid crossover claims. If assignment is not accepted, the Medicare payment is likely to be sent to the patient, and the Medicaid payment is either sent to the patient or denied.

The insurance billing specialist enters the designation MCD in block 10d of the CMS-1500 claim that is submitted to the Medicare Administrative Contractor. The MAC electronically transfers the Medicare claim and payment information to the Medicaid insurance carrier. The Medicaid carrier processes payment for the patient's Medicare deductible and co-payment and services covered by Medicaid. The payments are sent directly to the provider.

Completing the CMS-1500: Medicare-Medicaid Crossover Claims

Medicare-Medicaid crossover claim completion guidelines apply to Medicare patients who have Medicaid coverage that is not part of a health maintenance organization. In other words, the following CMS-1500 instructions apply to patients who receive services on a fee-for-service basis.

Patients with Medicaid must present a current Medicaid identification card. The billing specialist or receptionist makes a copy of the card, front and back, so the Medicaid ID number is available for inclusion on the CMS-1500.

Block 1	Enter an X in the Medicare and Medicaid boxes.
Blocks 1a–10c	No change from the instructions for Medicare as primary payer
Block 10d	Enter the abbreviation MCD followed by the patient's Medicaid ID number.
Blocks 11–26	No change from the instructions for Medicare as primary payer
Block 27	Enter an X in YES. All providers must accept assignment.
Blocks 28–33	No change from the instructions for Medicare as primary payer

Figure 12–8 is an example of a Medicare-Medicaid crossover claim.

(1500)

HEALTH INSURANCE CLAIM FORM

APPROVED BY NATIONAL UNIFORM CLAIM COMMITTEE 08/05

☐☐☐ PICA | PICA ☐☐☐

1. MEDICARE [X] (Medicare #) MEDICAID [X] (Medicaid #) TRICARE CHAMPUS ☐ (Sponsor's SSN) CHAMPVA ☐ (Member ID #) GROUP HEALTH PLAN ☐ (SSN or ID) FECA BLK LUNG ☐ (SSN) OTHER ☐ (ID)	1a. INSURED'S I.D. NUMBER (For Program in Item 1) 00128743D

2. PATIENT'S NAME (Last Name, First Name, Middle Initial) PATIENT MARY S	3. PATIENT'S BIRTH DATE MM DD YY 03 08 1933 SEX M ☐ F [X]	4. INSURED'S NAME (Last Name, First Name, Middle Initial)

| 5. PATIENT'S ADDRESS (No., Street) 91 HOME STREET | 6. PATIENT RELATIONSHIP TO INSURED Self ☐ Spouse ☐ Child ☐ Other ☐ | 7. INSURED'S ADDRESS (No., Street) |

CITY NOWHERE | STATE US | 8. PATIENT STATUS Single ☐ Married [X] Other ☐ | CITY | STATE

ZIP CODE 12367 | TELEPHONE (Include Area Code) (101) 201 8989 | Employed ☐ Full-Time Student ☐ Part-Time Student ☐ | ZIP CODE | TELEPHONE (Include Area Code) ( )

9. OTHER INSURED'S NAME (Last Name, First Name, Middle Initial)	10. IS PATIENT'S CONDITION RELATED TO:	11. INSURED'S POLICY GROUP OR FECA NUMBER

a. OTHER INSURED'S POLICY OR GROUP NUMBER | a. EMPLOYMENT? (Current or Previous) ☐ YES [X] NO | a. INSURED'S DATE OF BIRTH MM DD YY SEX M ☐ F ☐

b. OTHER INSURED'S DATE OF BIRTH MM DD YY SEX M ☐ F ☐ | b. AUTO ACCIDENT? PLACE (State) ☐ YES [X] NO | b. EMPLOYER'S NAME OR SCHOOL NAME

c. EMPLOYER'S NAME OR SCHOOL NAME | c. OTHER ACCIDENT? ☐ YES [X] NO | c. INSURANCE PLAN NAME OR PROGRAM NAME

d. INSURANCE PLAN NAME OR PROGRAM NAME | 10d. RESERVED FOR LOCAL USE MCD1012345XT | d. IS THERE ANOTHER HEALTH BENEFIT PLAN? ☐ YES [X] NO If yes, return to and complete item 9 a-d.

READ BACK OF FORM BEFORE COMPLETING & SIGNING THIS FORM.
12. PATIENT'S OR AUTHORIZED PERSON'S SIGNATURE I authorize the release of any medical or other information necessary to process this claim. I also request payment of government benefits either to myself or to the party who accepts assignment below.

SIGNED SIGNATURE ON FILE DATE _____

13. INSURED'S OR AUTHORIZED PERSON'S SIGNATURE I authorize payment of medical benefits to the undersigned physician or supplier for services described below.

SIGNED SIGNATURE ON FILE

14. DATE OF CURRENT: MM DD YY 01 28 20XX ◄ ILLNESS (First symptom) OR INJURY (Accident) OR PREGNANCY (LMP)	15. IF PATIENT HAS HAD SAME OR SIMILAR ILLNESS, GIVE FIRST DATE MM DD YY	16. DATES PATIENT UNABLE TO WORK IN CURRENT OCCUPATION MM DD YY MM DD YY FROM TO

17. NAME OF REFERRING PROVIDER OR OTHER SOURCE | 17a. | 17b. NPI | 18. HOSPITALIZATION DATES RELATED TO CURRENT SERVICES MM DD YY MM DD YY FROM TO

19. RESERVED FOR LOCAL USE | 20. OUTSIDE LAB? ☐ YES [X] NO $ CHARGES

21. DIAGNOSIS OR NATURE OF ILLNESS OR INJURY (Relate Items 1, 2, 3, or 4 to Item 24E by Line)
1. 511.10
2. 427.89
3. V12.51
4. ___.___

22. MEDICAID RESUBMISSION CODE ORIGINAL REF. NO.

23. PRIOR AUTHORIZATION NUMBER

24. A. DATE(S) OF SERVICE From MM DD YY To MM DD YY	B. PLACE OF SERVICE	C. EMG	D. PROCEDURES, SERVICES, OR SUPPLIES (Explain Unusual Circumstances) CPT/HCPCS MODIFIER	E. DIAGNOSIS POINTER	F. $ CHARGES	G. DAYS OR UNITS	H. EPSDT Family Plan	I. ID. QUAL.	J. RENDERING PROVIDER ID. #
1	01 28 20XX 01 28 20XX	11		99248	1	150 00			IC NPI	6878901234
2	01 28 20XX 01 28 20XX	11		71020	1	50 00			IC NPI	6878901234
3	01 28 20XX 01 28 20XX	11		93000	1	50 00			IC NPI	6878901234
4									NPI	
5									NPI	
6									NPI	

25. FEDERAL TAX I.D. NUMBER SSN EIN 11-123391 [X]	26. PATIENT'S ACCOUNT NO.	27. ACCEPT ASSIGNMENT? (For govt. claims, see back) [X] YES ☐ NO	28. TOTAL CHARGE $ 250 00	29. AMOUNT PAID $ 25 00	30. BALANCE DUE $

31. SIGNATURE OF PHYSICIAN OR SUPPLIER INCLUDING DEGREES OR CREDENTIALS (I certify that the statements on the reverse apply to this bill and are made a part thereof.) SIGNATURE ON FILE SIGNED DATE	32. SERVICE FACILITY LOCATION INFORMATION MEDICARE EAST 1201 MEDIC DRIVE NOWHERE US 12367 a. 5432109897 b.	33. BILLING PROVIDER INFO & PH # (909) 555 8888 MEDICARE EAST 1201 MEDIC DRIVE NOWHERE US 12367 a. 5432109897 b.

NUCC Instruction Manual available at: www.nucc.org | APPROVED OMB-0938-0999 FORM CMS-1500 (08-05)

FIGURE 12–8 Medicare/Medicaid Crossover CMS-1500 (For instructional use only. Courtesy of the Centers for Medicare and Medicaid Services, www.cms.hhs.gov)

CARRIER

PATIENT AND INSURED INFORMATION

PHYSICIAN OR SUPPLIER INFORMATION

REINFORCEMENT EXERCISE 12–8

Using the following patient and provider information, complete a CMS-1500 for a Medicare/Medicaid crossover claim. Your instructor can tell you where to get the form.

Patient Information

Name: Joline Pellitier, single, female
Birth Date: January 4, 1928
Address: 609 Osborn, Blueberry, ME 49966
Phone: (906) 338-2612
Insurance: Medicare 499680839A; Medicaid 212345602XT
Employment Status: Retired
Diagnosis/Code: Gastritis, 535.50
Service/Code: Office visit, 99212; CBC 85025
Date of Service: March 4, 20YY
Charges: Office visit, $50; CBC, $45

Provider Information

Superiorland Clinic
714 Hennepin Ave.
Blueberry, ME 49966
Phone: (906) 337-8778
Superiorland Clinic NPI: 4567890123
Barbara Dollar, MD
Physician NPI: 9876543210
EIN: 50-3816934
Dr. Dollar accepts assignment.

Medicare as Secondary Payer (MSP)

Medicare is the secondary payer when a Medicare patient is covered by one or more of the following health insurance plans:

- An employer-sponsored group health plan with more than 20 covered employees
- Disability coverage through an employer-sponsored health plan with more than 100 covered employees
- Liability coverage when a person is involved in an automobile or another type of accident
- Illness or injury that falls under workers' compensation
- End-stage renal disease covered by an employer-sponsored group health plan of any size during the first 18 months of the patient's eligibility for Medicare
- Veterans Administration (VA) preauthorized services for an individual eligible for both VA benefits and Medicare
- Coal miners, either currently or formerly employed, who have problems that are directly related to black lung disorder and other disorders on the Department of Labor's list of acceptable diagnoses

All primary insurance plans must be billed before Medicare claims are submitted. Providers who routinely bill Medicare as primary when Medicare is the secondary payer may be subject to disciplinary fines and/or penalties. Providers are not required to file Medicare secondary claims unless the patient specifically requests this service.

In order to identify whether a Medicare patient has an insurance plan that is primary to Medicare, the billing specialist may ask the patient to complete a detailed questionnaire related to other insurance coverage. The questionnaire is incorporated into patient registration procedures, and the information is updated at each subsequent encounter. Figure 12–9 is an example of a detailed insurance coverage questionnaire.

When Medicare is the secondary payer, a copy of the EOB from the primary plan must be attached to the Medicare claim. In order for the provider to receive payment and an EOB from the primary insurance company, the patient must assign the primary payer benefits to the provider. Once the patient assigns benefits, the billing specialist is able to submit the insurance claim to the primary payer.

If the patient does not assign the primary plan benefits, the billing specialist explains the provider's payment policy, collects fees due at the time of service, and informs the patient that he or she must file the insurance claim. The billing specialist also informs the patient that Medicare cannot be billed as a secondary payer until the patient provides the office with a copy of the primary payer's EOB.

Completing the CMS-1500: Medicare Secondary

After payment is received from the primary payer—either directly through assignment of benefits or from the patient when the patient receives the insurance payment and then passes it on to the provider—the billing specialist completes a CMS-1500 for Medicare, secondary payer. As previously stated, a copy of the EOB from the primary payer is attached to the CMS-1500. Guidelines for CMS-1500 completion are listed here.

Block 1	Enter an X in the Medicare box.
Block 1a	Enter the patient's Medicare ID number.
Block 2	Enter the patient's name as instructed.
Block 3	Enter the patient's birth date and sex.
Block 4	Enter the name of the insured for the policy that is primary to Medicare. If the patient is the insured, enter SAME.
Block 5	Enter the patient's address, phone number, and ZIP code.
Block 6	Enter an X in the box that identifies the patient's relationship to the person named in block 4.
Block 7	Enter the address and phone number of the person named in block 4. If the person in block 4 is the patient, enter SAME.

continued on the next page

continued from the previous page

Block 8	Enter an X in the boxes that describe the patient's marital and employment status.
Block 9–9d	Leave this blank.
Blocks 10a–10c	Check YES or NO as appropriate.
	If 10b is YES, enter the two-character abbreviation for the state where the accident occurred.
Block 10d	Leave this blank.
Block 11	Enter the insured's policy or group number.
Block 11a	Enter the birth date and sex of the person who has the primary insurance if different from block 3.
Block 11b	Enter the name of the employer who provides the primary insurance. If there is no employer, leave this blank.
	If the insured is retired, enter RETIRED and the eight-digit date of retirement.
Block 11c	Enter the PAYERID number of the primary insurance plan. If the PAYERID number is not known, enter the name of the primary insurance plan.
Block 11d	Leave this blank.
Blocks 12–28	No change from the instructions for Medicare as primary
Block 29	Enter only the amount the patient has paid. Attach the primary insurance plan's EOB to show the amount paid by the primary payer.
Blocks 30–33	No change from the instructions for Medicare as primary

Figure 12–10 is an example of a CMS-1500, Medicare as secondary payer claim.

REINFORCEMENT EXERCISE 12–9

Using the following patient and provider information, complete a CMS-1500 for a Medicare as secondary payer claim. Your instructor can tell you where to get the form.

Patient Information

Name: Viola Baril, married, female
Birth Date: January 5, 1929
Address: 301 West Spruce, Blueberry, ME 49966
Phone: (906) 338-3943
Insurance: Medicare 511919402B
Other Insurance: Husband's BC/BS

continued on the next page

Practice Letterhead

All Medicare Patients:

In order for us to comply with the Medicare as Secondary Payer laws you must fill out this Medicare Data Sheet before we can properly process your insurance claim.

Please complete this questionnaire and return it to the desk. We will also need to make photocopies of all your insurance identification cards. Do not hesitate to ask for clarification of any item on this form.

CHECK ALL ITEMS THAT DESCRIBE YOUR HEALTH INSURANCE COVERAGE

1. I am working full-time _____ part-time _____ I retired on ___/___/___.

   _____ I am enrolled in a Medicare HMO plan.

2. _____ I am entitled to black lung benefits.

   _____ I had a job-related injury on ___/___/___.

   _____ I have a fee service card from the VA.

   _____ I had an organ transplant on ___/___/___.

   _____ I have been on kidney dialysis since ___/___/___.

   _____ I am being treated for an injury received in a car accident _____

   _____ other vehicle. Other type of accident (please identify)_____

   _____

3. _____ I am employed/My spouse is employed and I am covered by an employer-sponsored health care program covering more than 20 employees. Name of policy:

   _____

4. _____ I/My spouse has purchased a private insurance policy to supplement Medicare. Name of policy:

   _____

5. _____ I have health insurance through my/my spouse's previous employer or union. Name of previous employer or union:

   _____

6. _____ I am covered by Medicaid and my ID number is: _____

7. _____ I am retired and covered by an employer-sponsored retiree health care plan. Name of plan:

   _____

8. _____ I am retired but have been called back temporarily and have employee health benefits while I am working. Name of plan:

   _____

Patient Signature _____ Date ___/___/___.

FIGURE 12–9 Detailed Insurance Questionnaire

continued from the previous page

Employment Status: Retired
Date of Service: June 20, 20YY
Diagnosis/Code: Colon polyp, 211.3
Service/Code: Office visit, 99214; Sigmoidoscopy, 45330
Charges: Office visit, $90; Sigmoidoscopy, $150

Spouse

Name: Eugene Baril
Birth Date: May 20, 1935
Employed by: Westland Community College
Insurance: BC/BS R2345678 214
PAYERID: 446543712

Provider Information

Superiorland Clinic
714 Hennepin Ave.
Blueberry, ME 49966
Phone: (906) 337-8778
Superiorland Clinic NPI: 4567890123
Mark Beckwith, MD
Physician NPI: 4444098765
EIN: 61-4927045

PROCESSING MEDICARE PAYMENTS

Once the billing specialist submits claims to the Medicare Administrative Contractor, participating providers receive payments directly from the carrier on a regular basis. Payments are not claim-specific; rather, the provider receives a remittance check that covers several claims. A **remittance notice** is included with the payment. The provider's Medicare remittance notice is a document that recaps, by patient, the services rendered, the amount billed, the allowed amount, co-insurance, and the amount the provider was paid. Figure 12–11 is a sample Medicare remittance notice.

The billing specialist enters or posts payment information to each patient's account. For participating providers, the difference between the amount charged and amount allowed is written off as an adjustment. If the patient has not already paid the co-insurance or deductible, a statement is generated and sent to the patient.

The remittance notice may include information about denied claims. The billing specialist pulls the financial and medical records for each denied claim, reviews this information, and resubmits the claim as appropriate. For example, the insurance billing specialist may discover a coding error, correct the error, and resubmit the claim.

(1500)

HEALTH INSURANCE CLAIM FORM

APPROVED BY NATIONAL UNIFORM CLAIM COMMITTEE 08/05

CARRIER

| | PICA | | | | | | | | PICA | |

1. MEDICARE	MEDICAID	TRICARE CHAMPUS	CHAMPVA	GROUP HEALTH PLAN	FECA BLK LUNG	OTHER	1a. INSURED'S I.D. NUMBER (For Program in Item 1)
[X] (Medicare #)	(Medicaid #)	(Sponsor's SSN)	(Member ID #)	(SSN or ID)	(SSN)	(ID)	111223344A

2. PATIENT'S NAME (Last Name, First Name, Middle Initial)	3. PATIENT'S BIRTH DATE / SEX	4. INSURED'S NAME (Last Name, First Name, Middle Initial)
NEELY JACK L	MM 11 DD 04 YY 1940 M [X] F	NEELY MARY A

5. PATIENT'S ADDRESS (No., Street)	6. PATIENT RELATIONSHIP TO INSURED	7. INSURED'S ADDRESS (No., Street)
129 WATER STREET	Self [ ] Spouse [X] Child [ ] Other [ ]	129 WATER STREET

CITY	STATE	8. PATIENT STATUS	CITY	STATE
NOWHERE	US	Single [ ] Married [X] Other [ ]	NOWHERE	US

ZIP CODE	TELEPHONE (Include Area Code)		ZIP CODE	TELEPHONE (Include Area Code)
12367	(101) 202 1278	Employed [ ] Full-Time Student [ ] Part-Time Student [ ]	12367	(101) 202 1278

9. OTHER INSURED'S NAME (Last Name, First Name, Middle Initial)	10. IS PATIENT'S CONDITION RELATED TO:	11. INSURED'S POLICY GROUP OR FECA NUMBER
		R1234567

a. OTHER INSURED'S POLICY OR GROUP NUMBER	a. EMPLOYMENT? (Current or Previous) [ ] YES [X] NO	a. INSURED'S DATE OF BIRTH MM 03 DD 19 YY 1942 SEX M [ ] F [X]

b. OTHER INSURED'S DATE OF BIRTH MM DD YY SEX M [ ] F [ ]	b. AUTO ACCIDENT? [ ] YES [X] NO PLACE (State)	b. EMPLOYER'S NAME OR SCHOOL NAME FEDERAL DEPT INVESTIGATIONS

c. EMPLOYER'S NAME OR SCHOOL NAME	c. OTHER ACCIDENT? [ ] YES [X] NO	c. INSURANCE PLAN NAME OR PROGRAM NAME BCBS FEDERAL

d. INSURANCE PLAN NAME OR PROGRAM NAME	10d. RESERVED FOR LOCAL USE	d. IS THERE ANOTHER HEALTH BENEFIT PLAN? [ ] YES [ ] NO If yes, return to and complete item 9 a-d.

READ BACK OF FORM BEFORE COMPLETING & SIGNING THIS FORM.

12. PATIENT'S OR AUTHORIZED PERSON'S SIGNATURE I authorize the release of any medical or other information necessary to process this claim. I also request payment of government benefits either to myself or to the party who accepts assignment below.

SIGNED **SIGNATURE ON FILE** DATE _____

13. INSURED'S OR AUTHORIZED PERSON'S SIGNATURE I authorize payment of medical benefits to the undersigned physician or supplier for services described below.

SIGNED **SIGNATURE ON FILE**

14. DATE OF CURRENT: ILLNESS (First symptom) OR INJURY (Accident) OR PREGNANCY (LMP) MM 01 DD 05 YY 20XX	15. IF PATIENT HAS HAD SAME OR SIMILAR ILLNESS. GIVE FIRST DATE MM DD YY	16. DATES PATIENT UNABLE TO WORK IN CURRENT OCCUPATION MM DD YY FROM TO MM DD YY

17. NAME OF REFERRING PROVIDER OR OTHER SOURCE	17a.	18. HOSPITALIZATION DATES RELATED TO CURRENT SERVICES MM DD YY FROM TO MM DD YY
	17b. NPI	

19. RESERVED FOR LOCAL USE	20. OUTSIDE LAB? [ ] YES [X] NO $ CHARGES

21. DIAGNOSIS OR NATURE OF ILLNESS OR INJURY (Relate Items 1, 2, 3, or 4 to Item 24E by Line)	22. MEDICAID RESUBMISSION CODE ORIGINAL REF. NO.
1. 569 3 3. _____	
2. V10 05 4. _____	23. PRIOR AUTHORIZATION NUMBER

24. A. DATE(S) OF SERVICE From MM DD YY To MM DD YY	B. PLACE OF SERVICE	C. EMG	D. PROCEDURES, SERVICES, OR SUPPLIES (Explain Unusual Circumstances) CPT/HCPCS MODIFIER	E. DIAGNOSIS POINTER	F. $ CHARGES	G. DAYS OR UNITS	H. EPSDT Family Plan	I. ID. QUAL.	J. RENDERING PROVIDER ID. #
1	01 05 20XX 01 05 20XX	24		45378	1	700 00	1		IC NPI	5432876019
2									NPI	
3									NPI	
4									NPI	
5									NPI	
6									NPI	

25. FEDERAL TAX I.D. NUMBER SSN EIN	26. PATIENT'S ACCOUNT NO.	27. ACCEPT ASSIGNMENT? (For govt. claims, see back) [X] YES [ ] NO	28. TOTAL CHARGE $ 700 00	29. AMOUNT PAID $ 50 00	30. BALANCE DUE $
11-123341 [X]					

31. SIGNATURE OF PHYSICIAN OR SUPPLIER INCLUDING DEGREES OR CREDENTIALS (I certify that the statements on the reverse apply to this bill and are made a part thereof.) SIGNATURE ON FILE SIGNED DATE	32. SERVICE FACILITY LOCATION INFORMATION AMBULATORY SURGERY CENTER 101 PARK STREET NOWHERE US 12367 a. 6512987120 b.	33. BILLING PROVIDER INFO & PH # (101) 111 1234 MEDICARE WEST 1201 MEDIC DRIVE NOWHERE US 12367 a. 6521210908 b.

NUCC Instruction Manual available at: www.nucc.org

APPROVED OMB-0938-0999 FORM CMS-1500 (08-05)

FIGURE 12–10 Medicare as Secondary Payer CMS-1500 (For instructional use only. Courtesy of the Centers for Medicare and Medicaid Services, www.cms.hhs.gov)

① MEDICARE INSURANCE CARRIER
PROVIDER # G1616 ②
③ CHECK # 10298

④ 09/21/2000

MEDICARE
REMITTANCE
NOTICE ⑫

⑥ ⑦ ⑧ ⑨ ⑩ ⑪

NAME	SERVICE DATE	PROCEDURE	BILLED	ALLOWED	COINS	ADJUST.	PROV PD
ACE, Wm. ⑤	09032000	99214	62.87	62.87	12.57		50.30
	09032000	93000	27.68	27.68	5.54		22.14
	09032000	85025	36.75	10.73	0.00	26.02	10.73
	09032000	84153	57.75	25.42	0.00	32.33	25.42
	09032000	81000	21.00	4.37	0.00	16.63	4.37
	09032000	G0001	6.04	3.00	0.00	3.04	3.00
		CLAIM TOT	212.09	134.07	18.11	78.02	115.96
DEUCE, M	09032000	80054	51.45	11.45	0.00	40.40	11.05
	09032000	80061	68.25	14.65	0.00	53.60	14.65
		CLAIM TOT	119.70	25.70	0.00	94.00	25.70
TREY, R	09022000	99214	62.87	62.87	12.57		50.30
	09022000	85025	36.75	10.73	0.00	26.02	10.73
	09022000	84439	36.75	12.46	0.00	24.29	12.46
	09022000	85651	25.20	4.91	0.00	20.29	4.91
	09022000	84443	80.32	23.21	0.00	57.11	23.21
	09022000	G0001	6.04	3.00	0.00	3.04	3.00
		CLAIM TOT	247.93	117.18	12.57	130.75	104.61
QUIP, L	09022000	80058	35.40	6.35	0.00	29.05	6.35
	09022000	80051	31.50	5.65	0.00	25.82	5.65
		CLAIM TOT	66.90	12.00	0.00	54.90	12.00
RAYS, P	09022000	99213	41.08	41.08	8.22		32.86
		CLAIM TOT	41.08	41.08	8.22	0.00	32.86
SETH, M	09022000	45330	106.27	106.27	21.25		85.02
	09022000	85025	36.75	10.73	0.00	26.02	10.73
	09022000	G0001	6.04	3.00	0.00	3.04	3.00
	09022000	80054	51.45	14.39	0.00	37.06	14.39
		CLAIM TOT	200.51	134.39	21.25	66.12	113.14
BEST, T	09022000	85027	26.25	6.43	0.00	19.82	6.43
	09022000	G0001	6.04	3.00	0.00	3.04	3.00
		CLAIM TOT	63.79	9.43	0.00	22.86	9.43
WURST, L	09022000	84153	57.75	25.42	0.00	32.33	25.42
	09022000	G0001	6.04	3.00	0.00	3.04	3.00
		CLAIM TOT	63.79	28.42	0.00	35.37	28.42
LOVE, I	09022000	85025	36.75	10.73	0.00	26.02	10.73
	09022000	81000	21.00	4.37	0.00	16.63	4.37
	09022000	G0001	6.04	3.00	0.00	3.04	3.00
		CLAIM TOT	63.79	18.10	0.00	45.69	18.10
HART, C	09032000	99211	16.36	16.36	3.27		13.09
		CLAIM TOT	16.36	16.36	3.27	0.00	13.09

FIGURE 12–11 Sample Medicare Remittance Notice 2010 CPT codes (C) 2009 American Medical Association. All rights reserved.

1. Name of Medicare insurance carrier.
2. Provider number.
3. Check number for the check included with the remittance notice.
4. Date remittance notice was generated.
5. Beneficiary name.
6. Date the service was rendered.
7. CPT code.
8. Amount the provider billed Medicare for the service.
9. Medicare-approved or -allowed amount for the service.
10. Beneficiary's coinsurance responsibility.
11. Adjustment amount a participating provider takes on the beneficiary's bill.
12. Amount the Medicare insurance carrier paid the provider.

FIGURE 12–11 *continued*

ABBREVIATIONS

Table 12–9 lists the abbreviations and meanings in this chapter.

TABLE 12–9

Abbreviations and Meanings	
Abbreviation	Meaning
ABN	advance beneficiary notice
A/B MAC	Part A and Part B Medicare Administrative Contractor
CF	(national) conversion factor
CMS	Centers for Medicare and Medicaid Services
DME	durable medical equipment
DME MAC	durable medical equipment Medicare Administrative Contractor
EOB	explanation of benefits
ESRD	end-stage renal disease
GAF	geographic adjustment factor
HICN	health insurance claim number
HMO	health maintenance organization
MA	Medicare Advantage

continued on the next page

continued from the previous page

MAC	Medicare Administrative Contractor
MA-PD	Medicare Advantage Prescription Drug Plan
MFS	Medicare Fee Schedule
MSA	medical savings account
MSN	Medicare Summary Notice
MSP	Medicare as secondary payer
NCCI	National Correct Coding Initiative
NonPAR	nonparticipating provider
NPI	national provider identification (number)
PAR	participating provider
PDP	prescription drug plan
PFFS	private fee-for-service
PPO	preferred provider organization
QI	qualified individual
QMB	qualified Medicare beneficiary
RVU	relative value unit
SLIMB	specified low-income Medicare beneficiary
SNP	(Medicare) Special Need Program

SUMMARY

Medicare is the nation's largest health insurance program, covering millions of Americans. Hospital, institutional, home health, and hospice costs are paid under Part A. Physician services, outpatient hospital care, laboratory tests, and other medical costs are paid under Part B. In general, Medicare Part A is available to people (and their spouses) who have worked for at least 10 years in Medicare-covered employment, are 65 years old, and are citizens or permanent residents of the United States. Most people do not pay for Medicare Part A.

Medicare Part B is voluntary, and individuals who choose to enroll pay a monthly premium. The premium is adjusted annually. Medicare Part B covers a wide variety of medical services that are reasonable, necessary, and consistent with the patient's diagnoses or problems. In addition to the monthly premium, Medicare Part B beneficiaries pay an annual deductible and 20 percent of the allowed charge on all covered services.

Medicare Part D, the prescription drug benefit, provides all Medicare beneficiaries with the opportunity to voluntarily enroll in a prescription drug plan. The purpose of all PDPs is to help defray the costs associated with prescription medications. The plans cover generic and brand-name drugs. Individuals who enroll in a PDP pay premiums, deductibles, and co-payments. Additional financial assistance is available for individuals with limited resources and incomes.

Health care providers can choose whether to participate in Medicare Part B. Participating providers agree to accept the Medicare-approved payment rate as payment in full. Participating providers collect the 20 percent co-payment from the beneficiary, are obligated to submit Medicare claims to the insurance carrier, receive payment directly from the insurance carrier, and may not bill the beneficiary for any amount that exceeds the approved payment rate. Nonparticipating providers must also submit Medicare claims to the insurance carrier, are not paid directly, and are restricted to charging fees that are 15 percent above the nonparticipating provider approved fee.

The Centers for Medicare and Medicaid Services (CMS) developed the National Correct Coding Initiative (NCCI) program. The purpose of the program is to promote accurate coding and appropriate insurance claims payments. The NCCI edits Medicare insurance claims and identifies errors that have a direct impact on reimbursement.

Medicare can be either the primary or the secondary payer for beneficiaries' medical expenses. Medicare is usually the primary payer, even when the patient has Medigap, other Medicare supplemental insurance, or Medicaid. Medicare is the secondary payer when the patient is covered by an employer-sponsored group health plan with more than 20 covered employees, by an employer-sponsored disability insurance plan, by other insurance due to an accident or workers' compensation, by Veterans Administration preauthorized services, or by the FECA black lung insurance plan.

Medicare offers additional health plan choices called Medicare Advantage plans, which include managed care, preferred provider organizations, private fee-for-service, special needs plans, and Medical Savings Accounts. The goal of the plans is to provide Medicare beneficiaries with quality health care in a cost-effective manner. Medicare Advantage plans are also called Medicare Part C.

REVIEW EXERCISES

Fill in the Blank

1. Medicare _____ covers care received in hospitals and nursing homes.

2. Medicare _____ covers physician services and outpatient hospital care.

3. Medicare beneficiaries with low incomes and limited resources may be eligible for the _____ program.

4. Health insurance companies that handle payments for Medicare Part B are called _____.

5. _____ contract with Medicare and agree to accept the Medicare-approved payment rate.

6. _____ are limited in the amount they can charge for rendering services to Medicare beneficiaries.

7. The _____ is a list of Medicare-approved fees for provider services.

8. A(n) _____ is sent to the provider and recaps services rendered and payments received.

Covered Services

Place an X next to services covered by Medicare.

1. Annual physical exams. _____

2. Breast augmentation. _____

3. Clinical laboratory tests. _____

4. Cosmetic surgery. _____

5. Flu shots. _____

6. Physical therapy. _____

7. Prostate cancer screening. _____

8. Wheelchair. _____

Abbreviations

Spell out the following abbreviations.

1. DME _____

2. MFS _____

3. MSN _____

4. MSP _____

5. NonPAR _____

6. PAR _____

7. QI _____

8. QMB _____

9. RVU _____

10. SLMB _____

11. NCCI _____

12. MA _____

13. DME MAC _____

14. ABN _____

15. PFFS _____

True or False

Write True or False on the line following each statement.

1. Individuals age 65 or older qualify for Medicare. _____

2. Enrollment in Medicare Part B is automatic. _____

3. Most retirees are eligible for premium-free Medicare Part A. _____

4. Medicare beneficiaries must pay a premium for Medicare Part B. _____

5. Providers are allowed to waive the deductible and co-pay for Medicare beneficiaries. _____

6. Participating providers may not balance-bill Medicare beneficiaries. _____

7. The limiting fee applies to both PARs and NonPARs. _____

8. Elective surgery is defined as surgery that is scheduled in advance. _____

9. The RBRVS system is used to calculate Medicare-approved fees. _____

10. Medicare is the primary payer when the patient has both Medicare and Medicaid coverage. _____

11. NPI stands for "national provider identifier." _____

Multiple Choice

Circle the correct answer from the choices provided.

1. Which governmental agency manages the Medicare program?

   a. CMS

   b. Social Security Administration

   c. Department of Health and Human Services

   d. Medicare Integrity Program

2. The Medicare Summary Notice is also known as the

   a. Advanced Notice Medicare Beneficiary Agreement.

   b. Medicare Surgical Financial Disclosure Statement.

   c. explanation of benefits.

   d. Medicare fee schedule.

3. The deadline for filing Medicare claims is

   a. one year from the date of service.

   b. December 31 of the year following the date of service.

   c. six months from the date of service.

   d. one year from the date the patient expires.

4. Conditional primary payer status may apply when

   a. a workers' compensation claim is being appealed.

   b. the patient's 65th birthday is within three days of the date of service.

   c. the billing specialist submits the claim within six months of the date of service.

   d. the patient's disability determination is pending.

5. The ordering physician is the one who

   a. oversees or manages the patient's treatment plan.

   b. orders nonphysician services.

   c. requests an item or service covered by Medicare.

   d. treats the patient.

6. Medicare is the secondary payer when the patient is covered by

   a. Medigap.

   b. Medicaid.

   c. VA-preauthorized services.

   d. TRICARE.

7. Medicare Advantage plans include all but one of the following:

   a. PDPs.

   b. HMOs.

   c. PFFSs.

   d. PPOs.

8. Prescription drug plans are required to cover

   a. all prescription medications.

   b. generic and brand-name medications.

   c. medications listed on the Medicare formulary.

   d. 75 percent of the cost of prescription medications.

9. A PDP's list of medications is known as

   a. the formulary.

   b. covered drugs.

   c. standard prescription coverage.

   d. basic prescription coverage.

10. NPIs were developed by the

    a. AMA.

    b. AHA.

    c. NCCI.

    d. CMS.

CHALLENGE ACTIVITIES

1. With the instructor's permission, invite a billing specialist from a local physician's office to talk to your class about Medicare claim submission.
2. Prepare a reference booklet that includes a sample of a CMS-1500 that is correctly completed for each type of Medicare claim presented in this chapter.

WEBSITES

AdminaStar Federal, Inc.: www.adminastar.com
Cahaba Government Benefit Administrators: www.cahabagba.com
CIGNA Government Services: www.cignagovernmentservices.com
First Coast Service Options, Inc.: www.fcso.com
Highmark Medicare Services: www.highmarkmedicareservices.com
Medicare: www.medicare.gov
National Government Services: www.adminastar.com
National Heritage Insurance Corp.: www.medicarenhic.com
Noridian Administrative Services: www.noridianmedicare.com
Palmetto Government Benefits Administrator: www.palmettogba.com
Trailblazer Health Enterprises: www.trailblazerhealth.com
Wisconsin Physician Services: www.wpsmedicare.com

CHAPTER 13

Medicaid

LEARNING OBJECTIVES

Upon successfully completing this chapter, the reader should have the knowledge to:

1. Define all terms and abbreviations presented in the chapter.
2. Describe three differences between Medicare and Medicaid.
3. Identify two pieces of federal legislation that apply to Medicaid.
4. Accurately complete the CMS-1500 according to Medicaid guidelines.
5. List two circumstances under which Medicaid is the secondary payer.

KEY TERMS

18/19
Aid to Families with
   Dependent Children
   (AFDC)
Care/Caid
Early and Periodic Screening,
   Diagnostic, and Treatment
   Services (EPSDT)
Enrollee
Fiscal agents

Medi/Medi
Medicaid
Medicaid expansion program
Medicare/Medicaid Crossover
   Program (MCD)
Participant
Payer of last resort
Qualified Medicare
   Beneficiary Program
   (QMB)

Recipient
Remittance advice (RA)
State Children's Health
   Insurance Program
   (SCHIP)
Supplemental Security
   Income (SSI)
Title 19
Title 21

OVERVIEW

In 1965, Congress passed **Title 19**, an amendment to the Social Security Act that established a federal medical assistance program called **Medicaid**. Medicaid is a joint venture between federal and state governments. Coverage and benefits vary from state to state, but basic Medicaid eligibility requirements apply to all programs. The purpose of Medicaid is to provide health insurance for specific populations. Medicaid services can be covered under health maintenance organization (HMO) or preferred provider organization (PPO) programs. Individuals enrolled in Medicaid programs are known as **recipients**, **participants**, and **enrollees**. Medicaid eligibility

TABLE 13–1

Medicaid Populations	
Population	Description
Medically indigent, low-income individuals and families	• Individuals and families who meet the income levels established by the state in which they live • Individuals and families without health insurance
Aged and disabled persons covered by **Supplemental Security Income (SSI)**	• SSI is a federal income assistance program that provides cash payments to blind, disabled, or aged individuals.
Persons covered by the **Qualified Medicare Beneficiary (QMB) Program**	• QMB pays Medicare premiums, deductibles, and patient co-payments for Medicare-eligible persons with low incomes—usually a percentage of the federal poverty guidelines.
Persons covered by **Aid to Families with Dependent Children (AFDC)**	• AFDC provides financial assistance to children and families who meet specific income levels and to pregnant women who meet the income requirements and would qualify if their babies were already born.
Persons receiving institutional or other long-term care	• Long-term care facilities, including nursing homes, adult foster care homes, and state psychiatric facilities

does not depend on age, except for programs that are intended to provide services to children and pregnant women. Income is the primary screening tool. Table 13–1 lists the populations eligible for Medicaid.

In the past, the federal government imposed many requirements on states in order to qualify for Medicaid funds. In 1997, **Title 21** of the Social Security Act was amended to allow states to create a health insurance program for children of low-income working families, who are often described as "the working poor." The amendment is known as the **State Children's Health Insurance Program (SCHIP)**. Under SCHIP, the federal government provides additional Medicaid funds to states that are willing to expand their Medicaid program health insurance options or develop new health insurance plans to cover more children. Families do not have to qualify for Aid to Families with Dependent Children in order to participate in SCHIP programs.

Individual states have different names for Medicaid programs, such as Medi-Cal in California. In Michigan, MICHILD is a Medicaid program for individuals age 19 and younger and pregnant women of any age. MICHILD is a **Medicaid expansion program**, which is any federal/state health insurance program that is funded by Medicaid legislation with the specific intent of providing additional or expanded services to Medicaid recipients.

MEDICAID COVERAGE

Although Medicaid coverage varies from state to state, basic health care services include:

- Hospitalization—preauthorization for non-emergency hospitalization is usually required.
- Outpatient hospital services

- Diagnostic tests
- Skilled nursing care
- Home health care
- Physician's office visits—specialist referrals are made by the patient's primary care physician.
- Surgical care
- Dental care
- Obstetric and prenatal care provided by a midwife or certified nurse practitioner

Individual states may offer Medicaid coverage for additional services, such as:

- Vision screening and glasses
- Mental health care
- Prescription medication benefits
- Hearing screening and hearing aids
- Family planning services
- Substance abuse treatment
- Medical supplies and equipment
- Immunizations

An individual who qualifies for Medicaid health insurance receives an identification card. The card is issued monthly, according to changes in the individual's income. Most states require Medicaid participants to report income changes within 10 days of the change. If no change is reported, Medicaid coverage is continued and a new ID card is sent to the individual. The billing specialist carefully checks the date on the identification card to ensure that the services provided fall within the current coverage period.

In 1967, Congress passed the **Early and Periodic Screening, Diagnostic, and Treatment Services (EPSDT)** law. EPSDT mandates that states must provide routine pediatric checkups to all children enrolled in Medicaid. In 1989, the EPSDT law was revised to include definitions for terms such as "screening," "vision," "dental," and "hearing services." In addition, a new requirement was added that mandated that states provide treatment for any problems identified by the screening services.

Unlike Medicare, Medicaid participants do not pay premiums or deductibles. Over the past several years, Medicaid established a co-payment (co-pay) plan for Medicaid recipients. A co-payment is a fee that the patient pays for services. When this text was published, Medicaid co-payments ranged from $1 to $5. For example, the Medicaid co-pay for a prescription may be $1, and the co-pay for an office visit may be $3.

REINFORCEMENT EXERCISES 13–1

Write True or False on the line following each statement.

1. Medicaid is available to individuals aged 65 and older. _____

2. Medicaid is a social welfare program. _____

3. Title 18 is the section of the Social Security Act that applies to Medicaid. _____

continued on the next page

continued from the previous page

4. Individuals who receive SSI do not need Medicaid health insurance coverage. _____

5. SCHIP is an amendment to the Social Security Act. _____

Provide a short answer for each item.

1. List four basic health care services included in all Medicaid programs.

_____

_____

_____

2. List four additional health care services offered by individual states.

_____

_____

_____

3. How often is a Medicaid ID card issued?

_____

_____

_____

4. What is the primary screening tool for Medicaid eligibility?

_____

_____

_____

5. What is EPSDT?

_____

_____

_____

MEDICAID BILLING

Providers who treat Medicaid patients are obligated to accept the Medicaid payment as payment in full. By law, the provider may not bill or balance-bill the patient for the cost of a Medicaid-covered service. Medicaid fees are typically much lower than other insurance programs, and reimbursement can be delayed for several months. Because of these issues, many providers limit the number of Medicaid patients they treat. Some providers choose not to participate in Medicaid programs.

When a provider chooses not to participate in Medicaid programs, office staff communicates this information in a nonbiased manner.

EXAMPLE

Part of the screening process for new patients includes questions about insurance coverage. When a prospective patient identifies Medicaid as the health insurance program, the receptionist or billing specialist simply tells the individual that the provider does not participate in Medicaid. It is helpful to have a list of area physicians who do participate and to refer the individual to those physicians.

If the provider agrees to participate in Medicaid programs, the billing specialist and all agency staff must treat Medicaid patients with the same dignity and respect afforded other patients. Medicaid is a social welfare program; however, the negative stereotypes that may be associated with welfare programs have no place in a professional setting.

Billing specialists who work for providers who participate in Medicaid must have current information about Medicaid coverage and benefits. The information is available from Medicaid insurance carriers, also called **fiscal agents**, which reimburse the provider for services rendered. Many states have established a website for providers who treat Medicaid recipients. These websites offer information ranging from eligibility verification to claims submission guidelines. Providers who participate in the Medicaid program have access to online information. In fact, several states include their Medicaid policy manual via the web.

Medicaid is called the **payer of last resort**. This means that payment for services rendered is collected from all other sources *before* a claim is submitted to Medicaid.

Medicaid Claims Submission

Most states use the CMS-1500 as the insurance claim form. Instructions for completing the CMS-1500 when Medicaid is the only insurance program are given here. These instructions are generic. Each state's Medicaid policy manual has the instructions for that specific state.

Block 1	Enter an X in Medicaid.
Block 1a	Enter the patient's Medicaid identification number.
Block 2	Enter the patient's last name, first name, and middle initial, if known.
Block 3	Enter the patient's eight-digit birth date. Enter an X in the appropriate gender box.
Block 4	Leave this blank.
Block 5	Enter the patient's address and phone number.
Block 6	Leave this blank.
Block 7	Leave this blank.
Block 8	Enter an X in the box that describes the patient's marital status and whether the patient is employed or a student.
Blocks 9–9d	Leave this blank.

continued on the next page

continued from the previous page

Block 10a	Enter an X in YES or NO.
Block 10b	Enter an X in YES or NO. If YES, enter the two-character abbreviation for the state where the accident occurred. Enter the date of the accident in block 14.
Block 10c	Enter an X in YES or NO. If YES, enter the date of the accident in block 14.
Block 10d	Leave this blank.
Blocks 11–11d	Leave this blank.
Block 12	Leave this blank. The patient's Medicaid application authorizes release of medical information for billing purposes.
Block 13	Leave this blank. Payment is made directly to participating providers.
Block 14	Enter the eight-digit date as appropriate. If YES was answered in item 10b or 10c, enter the eight-digit date of the accident.
Blocks 15 and 16	Leave these blank.
Block 17	Enter the referring/ordering provider's first and last name and professional credential.
Block 17a	Leave this blank.
Block 17b	Enter the national provider identification (NPI) number of the provider named in block 17.
Block 18	Enter the admission and discharge dates in the six- or eight-digit format, if applicable. Otherwise, leave this blank.
Block 19	Enter special remarks, if necessary. Otherwise, leave this blank.
Block 20	Leave this blank.
Block 21	Enter ICD-9-CM diagnoses codes to the highest level of specificity. Enter the first-listed diagnosis code in item 1. Enter other diagnosis codes in items 2, 3, and 4 in descending priority.
Block 22	Complete only when resubmitting a Medicaid claim; otherwise, leave this blank. To submit a replacement, voided, or cancelled claim, enter the resubmission code in the left side of block 22 and then enter the claim reference number (CRN) of the paid claim being replaced, voided, or cancelled. Resubmission codes are available in the Medicaid policy manual.
Block 23	Enter the Medicaid prior authorization number, if applicable. Prior authorization is often required for elective inpatient services, transplant services, and other services described in the Medicaid policy manual.
Blocks 24A–J	Complete the unshaded areas of blocks 24A-24J according to the guidelines given below.

continued on the next page

continued from the previous page

Block 24A	Enter a six- or eight-digit date of service in the From and To columns.
Block 24B	Enter the place of service code. Use the Medicare place of service codes.
Block 24C	Enter a Y if the service was an emergency or an N for non-emergency services.
Block 24D	Enter CPT procedure codes, with modifiers as necessary.
Block 24E	Enter the one diagnosis reference number from block 21 that best justifies the medical necessity for each service listed in block 24D.
Block 24F	Enter the charge for the service rendered.
Block 24G	Enter the number of units of service. If only one service is performed, enter 1.
Block 24H	Leave this blank.
Block 24I	Leave this blank.
Block 24J	Enter the provider's 10-digit NPI number in the unshaded area of this block.
Block 25	Enter the billing entity's Employer's Federal Tax Identification Number. Enter an X in the EIN box.
Block 26	Enter the patient's account number, if one is assigned. This number will be referenced on the remittance advice (RA) form or explanation of benefits (EOB).
Block 27	Leave this blank. Providers treating Medicaid patients must accept assignment.
Block 28	Enter the total charges for services listed on lines one through six.
Block 29	Leave this blank.
Block 30	Enter the balance due from Medicaid by subtracting the amount in block 29 from the amount in block 28.
Block 31	Enter SIGNATURE ON FILE (for electronic claims). The provider's signature or signature stamp may also be required or accepted.
Block 32	Enter the name and address of the facility where services were rendered. Enter the facility's NPI number in Block 32a. Leave Block 32b blank.
Block 33	Enter the provider's billing name, address, and phone number. Enter the NPI number in Block 33a of the individual or entity identified in Block 33.
Block 33b	Leave this blank.

Figure 13–1 is an example of a completed claim form when Medicaid is the patient's only insurance plan.

FIGURE 13–1 Completed CMS-1500 for Medicaid (For instructional use only. Courtesy of the Centers for Medicare and Medicaid Services, www.cms.hhs.gov)

Medicaid Secondary Payer

It is possible that a Medicaid patient has another health insurance plan. In that case, the other insurance plan is the primary payer and is billed first. The billing specialist completes the CMS-1500 according to the primary payer guidelines and submits the claim to the primary payer. Once payment is received from the primary payer, the billing specialist submits a claim to Medicaid under any one of the following conditions:

- The primary payer denies payment.
- Reimbursement from the primary payer is less than the Medicaid payment.
- Medicaid covers services that are not covered by the primary payer.

The billing specialist completes another CMS-1500 for Medicaid, attaches a copy of the explanation of benefits from the primary payer, and submits the claim to the Medicaid fiscal agent. When the Medicaid beneficiary has one private or group health plan, including Medicare, CMS-1500 instructions are as follows:

Blocks 1–3	No change from the instructions when Medicaid is the only payer
Block 4	Enter the insured's name for the private or group health insurance plan covering the beneficiary. If the insured and the patient are the same, enter the word SAME.
Block 5	No change from the instructions when Medicaid is the only payer
Block 6	When block 4 is completed, enter an X in the box that describes the patients relationship to the individual named in block 4.
Block 7	When blocks 4 and 11 are completed, enter the insured's address and telephone number. When the address is the same as the patient's, enter the word SAME.
Blocks 8–10d	No change from the instructions when Medicaid is the only payer
Block 11	Enter the insured's policy or group number or Medicare health insurance claim number (HICN).
Block 11a	When the insured is *not* the patient, enter the insured's eight-digit birth date and an X appropriate gender. When the insured *is* the patient, leave this blank. This information is captured in block 3.
Block 11b	Enter the employer's name or school name, if applicable.
Block 11c	Enter the complete insurance plan or program name.
Block 11d	Enter an X in NO.
Blocks 12–28	No change from the instructions when Medicaid is the only payer
Block 29	Enter the amount paid by the primary insurance plan.
Block 30–33b	No change from the instructions when Medicaid is the only payer

Figure 13–2 is a sample CMS-1500 when Medicaid is the secondary payer.

(1500)

HEALTH INSURANCE CLAIM FORM

APPROVED BY NATIONAL UNIFORM CLAIM COMMITTEE 08/05

| | PICA | | | | | PICA | |

1. MEDICARE	MEDICAID	TRICARE CHAMPUS	CHAMPVA	GROUP HEALTH PLAN	FECA BLK LUNG	OTHER	1a. INSURED'S I.D. NUMBER (For Program in Item 1)
(Medicare #)	[X] (Medicaid #)	(Sponsor's SSN)	(Member ID #)	(SSN or ID)	(SSN)	(ID)	257885301

2. PATIENT'S NAME (Last Name, First Name, Middle Initial)
ROZWELL, MARTIN, L

3. PATIENT'S BIRTH DATE MM DD YY 10 10 1990 **SEX** M [X] F [ ]

4. INSURED'S NAME (Last Name, First Name, Middle Initial)
ROZWELL, JOHN, M

5. PATIENT'S ADDRESS (No., Street)
409 CACTUS DRIVE

6. PATIENT RELATIONSHIP TO INSURED
Self [ ] Spouse [ ] Child [X] Other [ ]

7. INSURED'S ADDRESS (No., Street)
SAME

CITY DESERT	STATE AZ	8. PATIENT STATUS Single [X] Married [ ] Other [ ]	CITY	STATE

| ZIP CODE 69075 | TELEPHONE (Include Area Code) (822) 361 6578 | Employed [ ] Full-Time Student [ ] Part-Time Student [ ] | ZIP CODE | TELEPHONE (Include Area Code) ( ) |

9. OTHER INSURED'S NAME (Last Name, First Name, Middle Initial)

10. IS PATIENT'S CONDITION RELATED TO:

11. INSURED'S POLICY GROUP OR FECA NUMBER
81007

a. OTHER INSURED'S POLICY OR GROUP NUMBER

a. EMPLOYMENT? (Current or Previous) YES [ ] NO [X]

a. INSURED'S DATE OF BIRTH MM DD YY 06 04 1960 **SEX** M [X] F [ ]

b. OTHER INSURED'S DATE OF BIRTH MM DD YY SEX M [ ] F [ ]

b. AUTO ACCIDENT? YES [ ] NO [X] PLACE (State)

b. EMPLOYER'S NAME OR SCHOOL NAME
DYNAMIC COMPUTERS

c. EMPLOYER'S NAME OR SCHOOL NAME

c. OTHER ACCIDENT? YES [ ] NO [X]

c. INSURANCE PLAN NAME OR PROGRAM NAME
BCBS

d. INSURANCE PLAN NAME OR PROGRAM NAME

10d. RESERVED FOR LOCAL USE

d. IS THERE ANOTHER HEALTH BENEFIT PLAN?
YES [ ] NO [X] *If yes,* return to and complete item 9 a-d.

READ BACK OF FORM BEFORE COMPLETING & SIGNING THIS FORM.

12. PATIENT'S OR AUTHORIZED PERSON'S SIGNATURE I authorize the release of any medical or other information necessary to process this claim. I also request payment of government benefits either to myself or to the party who accepts assignment below.

SIGNED _____ DATE _____

13. INSURED'S OR AUTHORIZED PERSON'S SIGNATURE I authorize payment of medical benefits to the undersigned physician or supplier for services described below.

SIGNED _____

14. DATE OF CURRENT: MM DD YY 02 03 20YY ILLNESS (First symptom) OR INJURY (Accident) OR PREGNANCY (LMP)	15. IF PATIENT HAS HAD SAME OR SIMILAR ILLNESS, GIVE FIRST DATE MM DD YY	16. DATES PATIENT UNABLE TO WORK IN CURRENT OCCUPATION MM DD YY FROM TO MM DD YY

17. NAME OF REFERRING PROVIDER OR OTHER SOURCE	17a. _____ 17b. NPI	18. HOSPITALIZATION DATES RELATED TO CURRENT SERVICES MM DD YY FROM TO MM DD YY

19. RESERVED FOR LOCAL USE	20. OUTSIDE LAB? YES [ ] NO [ ]	$ CHARGES

21. DIAGNOSIS OR NATURE OF ILLNESS OR INJURY (Relate Items 1, 2, 3, or 4 to Item 24E by Line)

1. 782 . 1
2. ___ . ___
3. ___ . ___
4. ___ . ___

22. MEDICAID RESUBMISSION CODE _____ **ORIGINAL REF. NO.** _____

23. PRIOR AUTHORIZATION NUMBER

24. A. DATE(S) OF SERVICE From MM DD YY	To MM DD YY	B. PLACE OF SERVICE	C. EMG	D. PROCEDURES, SERVICES, OR SUPPLIES (Explain Unusual Circumstances) CPT/HCPCS	MODIFIER	E. DIAGNOSIS POINTER	F. $ CHARGES	G. DAYS OR UNITS	H. EPSDT Family Plan	I. ID. QUAL.	J. RENDERING PROVIDER ID. #
02 03 YY	02 03 YY	11	N	99212		1	45 00	1		NPI	7890123456
										NPI	
										NPI	
										NPI	
										NPI	
										NPI	

25. FEDERAL TAX I.D. NUMBER 494134726 SSN [ ] EIN [X]	26. PATIENT'S ACCOUNT NO. 277885	27. ACCEPT ASSIGNMENT? (For govt. claims, see back) YES [ ] NO [ ]	28. TOTAL CHARGE $ 45 00	29. AMOUNT PAID $ 0 00	30. BALANCE DUE $ 45 00

31. SIGNATURE OF PHYSICIAN OR SUPPLIER INCLUDING DEGREES OR CREDENTIALS (I certify that the statements on the reverse apply to this bill and are made a part thereof.)
SIGNATURE ON FILE
SIGNED _____ DATE _____

32. SERVICE FACILITY LOCATION INFORMATION
OUTREACH CLINIC
608 SAGEBUSH
DESERT AZ 69075
a. 7770123456 b.

33. BILLING PROVIDER INFO & PH # (822) 7529118
OUTREACH CLINIC
608 SAGEBUSH
DESERT AZ 69075
a. 7770123456 b.

NUCC Instruction Manual available at: www.nucc.org

APPROVED OMB-0938-0999 FORM CMS-1500 (08-05)

FIGURE 13–2 CMS-1500 Medicaid as Secondary Payer (For instructional use only. Courtesy of the Centers for Medicare and Medicaid Services, www.cms.hhs.gov)

In the unusual circumstance when the Medicaid recipient has more than one private or group insurance plan, including Medicare, a claim must be submitted to both insurance plans *before* a claim is submitted to Medicaid. Once payment is received from both payers, the billing specialist submits a claim to Medicaid under any one of the conditions previously cited. The billing specialist completes another CMS-1500 for Medicaid, attaches the EOBs from both payers, and submits the claim to the Medicaid fiscal agent. Information for the primary private or group health plan is entered in blocks 11–11d, and information for the second private or group health plan is entered in blocks 9–9d. Complete blocks 9–9d as follows:

Block 9	Enter the insured's name for the secondary commercial or private insurance plan.
Block 9a	Enter the secondary insurance plan policy or group number.
Block 9b	Enter the insured's eight-digit birth date. Enter an X in the appropriate gender box.
Block 9c	Enter the employer name or school name, if applicable.
Block 9d	Enter the plan or program name of the secondary insurance plan.

In addition to completing blocks 9–9d, the insurance billing specialist enters the total amount received from both payers in block 29. The remaining CMS-1500 blocks are completed according to Medicaid as secondary payer guidelines.

Medicare/Medicaid Crossover Program

The **Medicare/Medicaid Crossover Program (MCD)** is a combination of the Medicare and Medicaid programs. This plan is available to Medicare-eligible individuals who also qualify for Medicaid. This program is sometimes called **Medi/Medi, Care/Caid,** or **18/19** claims. The 18/19 name refers to Title 18 (Medicare) and Title 19 (Medicaid) of the Social Security Act.

When a patient qualifies for both Medicare and Medicaid, the billing specialist submits the claim to the Medicare insurance carrier. The CMS-1500 is completed according to Medicare guidelines, with the following changes:

- Enter an X in Medicare and Medicaid in block 1.
- Enter the initials MCD and the patient's Medicaid ID number in block 10d.

MCD indicates that the claim should be handled as a Medicare/Medicaid crossover. The billing specialist ensures that the claim is filed within the stated deadline. Most Medicare/Medicaid crossover claims follow the Medicare filing deadline, which is December 31 of the year following the date of service. In some states, crossover claims are submitted within the Medicaid filing deadline.

The Medicare insurance carrier pays its portion of the claim and then electronically transfers the claim to the Medicaid fiscal agent. The provider receives payment from Medicare and Medicaid for services covered by each program.

The provider must accept assignment for Medicare/Medicaid crossover claims. If assignment is not accepted, the Medicare payment is usually sent to the patient. The Medicaid payment is either sent to the patient or denied, according to state Medicaid policy.

Processing Medicaid Payments

Medicaid payments are sent directly to the provider. The billing specialist receives a **remittance advice (RA)**, which is a detailed explanation of claims denial or approval, sometimes called an explanation of benefits (EOB). Many providers still use the term "EOB," although "remittance advice" is more current.

The remittance advice lists the payment activity for several patients. Payment activity falls under these categories: adjustment, approval, denial, suspension, and audit/refund. Most states use these or similar terms to describe how payment decisions are made. Table 13–2 gives a brief description of each payment activity category.

Claims are rarely paid without some of them being adjusted, denied, or suspended. Figure 13–3 is a sample Medicaid remittance advice form.

Table 13–2

Medicaid Payment Activities		
Payment Activity	**Description**	**Example**
Adjustment	Adjustments are made to the approved Medicaid fee. Reasons for the adjustment are explained or coded on the remittance advice form.	Provider was overpaid or underpaid for services rendered to a specific patient. The adjustment is made on the next claim submitted for that patient.
Approval	Payment is made at the maximum allowable Medicaid rate.	Provider receives the allowed Medicaid payment, with no adjustments.
Denial	Denial of the approved Medicaid fee is noted, with an explanation, on the RA form.	Reasons for denial include: the service is not covered by Medicaid, claims submission errors, the patient is no longer eligible for Medicaid, and required or requested documentation was not attached to the claim.
Suspension	Payment is suspended while the claim is being reviewed; this is neither an approval nor a denial. An explanation is included on the RA form.	Suspension occurs when a procedure or service is questioned but cannot be summarily denied; additional documentation is needed; or administrative problems prevent the timely payment of claims.

MEDICAID
REMITTANCE ADVICE

Roberta Pharyngeal MD
714 Hennepin Avenue
Blueberry, ME 49855

| PROVIDER NUMBER RBP74911 | CLAIM TYPE MEDICAL | CHECK NUMBER 490678 | DATE 05/01/20xx | | | PAGE 1 of 2 pages | |

RECIPIENT NAME	RECIPIENT MEDICAID ID NO.	SERVICE DATE	PROCEDURE CODE		AMOUNT BILLED	AMOUNT ALLOWED	AMOUNT PAID	EXPL. CODE
APPROVED CLAIMS								
ACE, Wm.	730698276	02/10/20xx	99214		60.00	51.00	51.00	
	730698276	02/10/20xx	93000		20.00	16.22	16.22	
	730698276	02/10/20xx	G0001		3.00	0.00	0.00	0499
				TOTAL	83.00	67.22	67.22	
DUECE, M	841709387	02/11/20xx	99214		60.00	51.00	51.00	
				TOTAL	60.00	51.00	51.00	
				TOTAL FOR APPROVED	140.00	118.22	118.22	
DENIED CLAIMS								
TREY, R	942810498	02/12/20xx	99214		60.00			0401
	942810498	02/12/20xx	85025		36.75			
				TOTAL FOR DENIED	96.75			
SUSPENDED CLAIMS								
QUIP, L	053921309	02/13/20xx	99213		41.00			0399
	053921309	02/13/20xx	85027		26.25			0399
				TOTAL	67.25			
RAYS, P	164032410	02/15/20xx	99213		41.00			0399
SETH, M	275143521	02/15/20xx	45330		106.27			0399
	275143521	02/15/20xx	85025		36.75			0399
				TOTAL	143.02			
				TOTAL SUSPENDED	251.27			

EXPLANATION OF DENIAL, SUSPENSION, ADJUSTMENT CODES

0499 SERVICE NOT COVERED BY MEDICAID
0401 PATIENT NOT ELIGIBLE FOR MEDICAID
0399 ADDITIONAL DOCUMENTATION UNDER REVIEW

Delmar/Cengage Learning

FIGURE 13–3 Medicaid Remittance Advice

REINFORCEMENT EXERCISES 13–2

Write True or False on the line following each statement.

1. Providers who treat Medicaid patients are obligated by law to accept assignment. _____

2. Medicaid does not offer coverage under HMOs or PPOs. _____

3. Medicaid is a social welfare program. _____

4. Physicians are obligated to treat a certain number of Medicaid recipients. _____

5. Medicaid is the payer of last resort. _____

Provide a short answer for each item.

1. List three situations that prompt a Medicaid claims submission when the patient has other health insurance.

_____

_____

_____

2. Briefly define the Medicare/Medicaid Crossover Program.

_____

_____

_____

3. Describe the unique characteristic of the Medicare/Medicaid Crossover Program.

_____

_____

_____

4. List three reasons why a provider chooses not to participate in Medicaid programs.

_____

_____

_____

ABBREVIATIONS

Table 13–3 lists the abbreviations and meanings in this chapter.

TABLE 13-3

Abbreviations and Meanings	
Abbreviation	**Meaning**
AFDC	Aid to Families with Dependent Children
EOB	explanation of benefits
EPSDT	Early and Periodic Screening, Diagnosis, and Treatment Services
HMO	health maintenance organization
MCD	Medicare/Medicaid Crossover Program
PPO	preferred provider organization
QMB	qualified Medicare beneficiary
RA	remittance advice
SCHIP	State Children's Health Insurance Program
SSI	Supplemental Security Income

SUMMARY

Medicaid is a joint venture between federal and state governments that provides health insurance for specific populations, such as individuals and families with low incomes, aged and disabled persons, and persons covered by Aid to Families with Dependent Children (AFDC).

Medicaid coverage varies from state to state, but basic health services are a feature of all Medicaid programs. Medicaid participants pay no premiums for the coverage, and there are usually no deductibles or co-payments. Most Medicaid claims are filed by using the CMS-1500 claim form.

Medicaid is the payer of last resort. Therefore, other insurance programs are billed first. When a patient has both Medicare and Medicaid, information is electronically exchanged between the Medicare and Medicaid insurance carriers.

REVIEW EXERCISES

CASE STUDY

Read the following case study. From the information provided, complete a CMS-1500 claim form for Medicaid submission. Your instructor can tell you where to obtain the form.

NAME: Ralph English
DOB: 10/3/1952
ADDRESS: 1312 W. Easterday, Blueberry, ME 49855
PHONE: (H) (906) 555-4444; (W) (906) 555-7777
SPOUSE: Rita English
INSURANCE: Medicaid; ID: 3689964123
Superiorland Clinic

continued on the next page

continued from the previous page

714 Hennepin Ave.
Blueberry, ME 49855
PHONE: (906) 336-4600
Tax ID #: 49-4134726
Superiorland Clinic NPI: 4567890123
Elizabeth Foy NPI: 7890123456
PROGRESS NOTE
Date: July 7, 20yy

Ralph is seen today with complaints of difficulty breathing, low-grade fever, and fatigue.
On examination, his blood pressure was 140/80, and he appeared to be in some respira-
tory distress. Chest sounds were consistent with bronchitis. I recommended rest, fluids,
and a nonaspirin pain reliever. In addition, I prescribed clarithromycin 300 mg b.i.d. for
10 days. Ralph is to call if his symptoms worsen. Return in two weeks for follow-up.
SIGNED: Elizabeth Foy, MD
OFFICE VISIT: 99212; $40
DIAGNOSIS: acute bronchitis; 466.0

Abbreviations

Spell out each abbreviation.

1. AFDC _____

2. SCHIP _____

3. EPSDT _____

4. QMB _____

5. SSI _____

Fill in the Blank

1. _____ is a joint federal and state government health insurance program.

2. Individuals enrolled in Medicaid programs are known as _____.

3. A(n) _____ is any federal/state health insurance that is intended to provide additional
   Medicaid services to Medicaid recipients.

4. Providers who _____ in the Medicaid program must accept Medicaid fees as payment
   in full.

5. Medicaid insurance carriers are also called _____.

6. A(n) _____-digit number is used to enter the patients' birth dates on the CMS-1500.

7. A copy of the primary payer's _____ must be attached to the CMS-1500 when
   submitting the claim to Medicaid.

8. Medicaid is the _____ of last resort.

9. The initials MCD in block 10d of the CMS-1500 mean the claim is a(n) _____.

10. A detailed explanation of Medicaid claims denial or approval is called a(n) _____.

Multiple Choice

Circle the correct answer from the choices provided.

1. A provider may choose not to participate in Medicaid because
   a. Medicaid is a welfare program.
   b. participation is limited to physicians.
   c. payments are sent directly to the patient.
   d. reimbursement is limited.

2. The Medicaid remittance advice form
   a. is sent to the patient.
   b. lists the payment activity for several patients.
   c. provides claims submission guidelines.
   d. defines eligibility requirements for Medicaid.

3. Titles 18, 19, and 21 are
   a. amendments to the Social Security Act.
   b. a series of references for federal insurance programs.
   c. numeric references to special Medicare guidelines.
   d. Medicaid laws enacted by Congress.

4. Medicaid is the secondary payer
   a. when the primary payer denies payment for services.
   b. never because Medicaid is the payer of last resort.
   c. after the patient pays the first $50 of any charges.
   d. after a claim is submitted to the SCHIP program.

5. Which service is *not* covered under the Medicaid EPSDT program?
   a. pediatric examinations for children
   b. family planning
   c. amniocentesis to detect birth defects
   d. vision screening for children

6. Under the SCHIP program,
   a. patients must chip in to pay for health care services.
   b. families must qualify for AFDC.
   c. states are encouraged to expand health insurance programs for children.
   d. parents receive additional funds for child care expenses.

7. Individuals enrolled in Medicaid programs are called
   a. patients.
   b. recipients.
   c. members.
   d. subscribers.

8. Current Medicaid billing instructions are obtained from
   a. other providers who participate in Medicaid.
   b. the Medicaid information center in Washington, D.C.
   c. the state insurance commission.
   d. the Medicaid insurance carrier.

9. Suspension of Medicaid payment occurs when
   a. additional documentation is needed.
   b. the provider's charge exceeds the Medicaid fee.
   c. the service is not covered by Medicaid.
   d. the patient's income exceeds Medicaid limits.

CHALLENGE ACTIVITIES

1. Create a grid that compares how the CMS-1500 is completed block by block for Medicaid and private or commercial insurance programs. What are the main differences? Which blocks are the same?
2. Find out the name of the state agency in your area that administers the Medicaid program. Obtain a copy of the Medicaid application form and then fill it out. Is the form complicated? Which questions are the most unusual? Are there any questions that you think are unnecessary? Ask your instructor if you can discuss the application form in class.

WEBSITES

Centers for Medicare and Medicaid Services: www.cms.hhs.gov/Medicaid
MIChild (Michigan): www.michigan.gov/mdch

CHAPTER 14

TRICARE and CHAMPVA

LEARNING OBJECTIVES

Upon successfully completing this chapter, the reader should have the knowledge to:

1. Define all terms and abbreviations presented in the chapter.
2. Describe the difference between TRICARE and CHAMPVA.
3. Identify four eligibility requirements each for TRICARE and CHAMPVA.
4. Accurately complete the CMS-1500 according to TRICARE and CHAMPVA guidelines.
5. List three distinguishing characteristics of TRICARE Standard, TRICARE Prime, and TRICARE Extra.

KEY TERMS

Allowable charge
Authorized provider
Beneficiary
CHAMPUS Maximum
    Allowable Charge
    (CMAC)
Civilian Health and Medical
    Program of the Uniformed
    Services (CHAMPUS)
Civilian Health and
    Medical Program of the
    Veterans Administration
    (CHAMPVA)
Cost sharing
Defense Enrollment
    Eligibility and Reporting
    System (DEERS)

Department of Defense
    (DoD)
Durable medical equipment
    (DME)
Health Administration
    Center (HAC)
Health care finder
Limited charge
Locality code
Maximum allowable charge
Military treatment facility
    (MTF)
National Oceanic
    and Atmospheric
    Administration (NOAA)
North Atlantic Treaty
    Organization (NATO)

Primary care manager
    (PCM)
Program Integrity Office
Sponsor
TRICARE
TRICARE contractor
TRICARE Extra
TRICARE for Life (TFL)
TRICARE Management
    Agency (TMA)
TRICARE Plus
TRICARE Prime
TRICARE Standard
Uniformed services
Veteran

OVERVIEW

In 1966, Congress created the **Civilian Health and Medical Program of the Uniformed Services (CHAMPUS)**, a federally funded comprehensive health benefits program for dependents of personnel serving in the **uniformed services**. Uniformed services include the Army, Navy, Air Force, Marines, Coast Guard, Public Health Service, **National Oceanic and Atmospheric Administration (NOAA)**, and the **North Atlantic Treaty Organization (NATO)**. In 1993, the **Department of Defense (DoD)** changed the name from CHAMPUS to **TRICARE**. TRICARE is a health care benefits program available to active duty members, retirees, and their dependents. TRICARE programs include the following:

- **TRICARE Prime:** A managed care program that allows beneficiaries to receive services from a military treatment facility (MTF) or contracted civilian medical providers in a preferred provider network (PPN)
- **TRICARE Plus:** A primary care enrollment option for Military Health System beneficiaries who are not enrolled in TRICARE Prime, a civilian HMO, or a Medicare HMO. Beneficiaries receive services at military treatment facilities (MTFs).
- **TRICARE Extra:** A network of health care providers that dependents can use on a case-by-case basis without a required enrollment
- **TRICARE Standard:** The original health benefit program that allows more choice of health care providers but with higher out-of-pocket expenses than TRICARE Prime and TRICARE Extra plans
- **TRICARE for Life (TFL):** A health benefit program available to TRICARE beneficiaries who are eligible for Medicare

The **Civilian Health and Medical Program of the Veterans Administration (CHAMPVA)** serves the needs of dependent spouses and children of disabled veterans and surviving spouses and dependent children of veterans who died in the line of duty or as a result of disabilities connected to the uniformed services. Because of the similarity between CHAMPVA and TRICARE, the programs are often mistaken for each other. The programs are completely separate and serve totally different beneficiary populations. Information about CHAMPVA is presented later in this chapter. Individuals who are part of TRICARE are not eligible for CHAMPVA.

Dependents who are eligible for TRICARE or CHAMPVA are called **beneficiaries**. The active-duty service member is called the **sponsor**. A **veteran** is an individual who served in the U.S. armed forces, is no longer in the service, and was honorabley discharged.

TRICARE HEALTH BENEFITS PROGRAMS

Three TRICARE programs are discussed in this chapter: TRICARE Prime, TRICARE Extra, and TRICARE Standard.

TRICARE Prime

Under TRICARE Prime, most health care services are provided by a **military treatment facility (MTF)**. Additional services, when necessary, are provided by the TRICARE contractor's preferred provider network (PPN). Active-duty personnel must enroll in TRICARE Prime. Enrollment is accomplished by registering with the **Defense Enrollment Eligibility and Reporting System (DEERS)**. Other individuals who may enroll in TRICARE Prime include:

- Family members and survivors of active-duty personnel
- Retirees and their family members and survivors under age 65

Individuals enrolled in TRICARE Prime are assigned a **primary care manager (PCM)**, who coordinates the individual's care, maintains health records, and makes referrals to specialists.

Civilian health care providers are allowed to treat TRICARE Prime beneficiaries under the following circumstances:

- The civilian health care provider is a member of the TRICARE contractor's preferred provider network.
- The primary care manager refers the beneficiary to a civilian provider.
- Emergency treatment is needed, and the civilian emergency room is the nearest available facility.
- The beneficiary chooses a civilian health care provider without the PCM's approval.

If a beneficiary seeks treatment from a civilian provider without approval, the beneficiary is responsible for 50 percent of the cost of the service after the deductible is met.

TRICARE Extra

Under TRICARE Extra, beneficiaries must choose health care providers who are listed in the TRICARE *Provider Directory*. TRICARE Extra is an option available to all individuals who are eligible for TRICARE Standard. Active-duty personnel are not eligible for TRICARE Standard and therefore are not eligible for TRICARE Extra. Civilian health care providers who are listed in the TRICARE *Provider Directory* may provide treatment for TRICARE Extra enrollees.

TRICARE Standard

TRICARE Standard is the current name for the traditional CHAMPUS program. Under this plan, the beneficiary receives treatment from any **authorized provider**. An authorized provider is a hospital, institution, physician, or other professional who meets the licensing and certification requirements of TRICARE and is practicing within the scope of that license. Out-of-pocket expenses are higher with TRICARE Standard than with TRICARE Prime or TRICARE Extra. Table 14–1 summarizes the eligibility requirements for TRICARE Standard, TRICARE Extra, and TRICARE Prime.

TABLE 14–1

TRICARE Program Eligibility
TRICARE Standard and TRICARE Extra
• Dependents of active-duty military, Public Health Service, NOAA, and NATO personnel
• Retired military, Public Health Service, NOAA, and NATO personnel and their dependents
• Surviving family members of active-duty members or retired personnel
TRICARE Prime
• Active duty personnel
• Individuals eligible for TRICARE Standard and TRICARE Extra

The Defense Enrollment Eligibility and Reporting System (DEERS) is a database used to verify beneficiary eligibility. The billing specialist should ask patients with TRICARE Standard coverage if they are enrolled in DEERS. Patients can verify their enrollment by calling the nearest personnel office of any service or by calling the DEERS center. Providers may not directly verify DEERS enrollment because of the Federal Privacy Act. If the patient is not sure about enrollment, the billing specialist makes a telephone available so the patient can call DEERS. TRICARE claims processors (insurance carriers) verify eligibility via DEERS, and payment is denied if a patient is not enrolled.

Civilian health care providers often treat TRICARE Standard beneficiaries and, as stated earlier, may treat TRICARE Extra beneficiaries. TRICARE reimbursement issues include the following:

- Participating vs. nonparticipating provider status
- Covered and noncovered services
- Prior authorization for some services
- Durable medical equipment criteria
- Verification of TRICARE eligibility
- Deductibles and **cost sharing**, which is the same as co-payment and co-insurance
- Allowable charge and **(CHAMPUS) Maximum Allowable Charge (CMAC)**, which is the maximum amount TRICARE will pay for a service
- Timely claims submission
- Fraud and abuse

Each topic is discussed throughout the remainder of this chapter.

REINFORCEMENT EXERCISES 14–1

Spell out the full name for each abbreviation provided.

1. CHAMPUS

_____

2. DoD

_____

3. NATO

_____

4. CHAMPVA

_____

5. MTF

_____

continued on the next page

continued from the previous page

6. PCM

_____

7. CMAC

_____

8. DEERS

_____

Provide a brief definition for each term.

1. TRICARE Standard

_____

_____

_____

2. TRICARE Prime

_____

_____

_____

3. TRICARE Extra

_____

_____

_____

4. beneficiary

_____

_____

_____

5. sponsor

_____

_____

_____

continued on the next page

continued from the previous page

6. veteran

_____

_____

_____

7. authorized provider

_____

_____

_____

8. cost sharing

_____

_____

_____

9. DEERS

_____

_____

_____

PARTICIPATING AND NONPARTICIPATING PROVIDERS

TRICARE Standard encourages providers to participate in the program and accept assignment. The provider agrees to accept the TRICARE-determined allowable charge as the full fee, even if it is less than the billed amount. TRICARE Standard pays the allowable charge, less the patient cost-share and outpatient deductible. Payment is sent directly to the provider. Participation can be on a case-by-case basis. Participating providers may charge the patient for noncovered services.

When a provider agrees to participate, first determine if the service is covered. For covered services, the billing specialist requests that the cost sharing amount be paid at the time of service. The balance is submitted to the TRICARE insurance carrier. For noncovered services, the billing specialist informs the patient that he or she is responsible for the bill.

Nonparticipating providers may or may not submit the insurance claim for TRICARE beneficiaries. If the nonparticipating provider does not submit the claim, payment is sent to the beneficiary. By federal law, nonparticipating providers may charge 15 percent more than the TRICARE allowable charge. The 15 percent of the allowable charge is called the **limited charge**. This charge must be paid by the TRICARE Standard beneficiary.

EXAMPLE

Sara is the daughter of a retired army colonel. She is covered by TRICARE Standard and had her tonsils removed as an outpatient. The allowable charge for tonsillectomy is $500. Sara's surgeon is nonparticipating and charges $600 for a tonsillectomy. Sara's parents are responsible for the co-payment and 15 percent of the TRICARE allowable charge.

In this case, the co-payment is 20 percent of the allowable charge, which is $100. Fifteen percent of the allowable charge is $75. Sara's parents must pay $175 out of pocket. The remaining $400 is billed to TRICARE. The surgeon receives a total of $575 for the procedure and cannot bill Sara's parents for the remaining $25. If the provider's office submits the claim, payment is sent directly to the provider. Otherwise, payment is sent to the beneficiary, and the provider must bill the patient.

By participating in TRICARE, providers have the benefit of collecting payment directly from the insurance carrier. The costs related to billing the patient are minimized.

COVERED AND NONCOVERED SERVICES

It is impossible to list all TRICARE covered and noncovered services. Table 14–2 lists examples of covered services. Table 14–3 lists examples of noncovered services. Note that some covered services are limited.

EXAMPLE

Breast reconstruction is a covered service that is limited to reconstruction that is necessary because a mastectomy was performed due to breast cancer.

There may be limits on the number of services, such as with Pap smears. For a healthy individual, TRICARE may pay for an annual Pap smear. When the initial Pap is abnormal, follow-up exams may be covered.

The most current information about covered services, including any limits, is available from the TRICARE regional administrator or in the TRICARE *Provider Manual*.

Noncovered services are not payable by TRICARE. However, there are exceptions. Table 14–3 identifies cosmetic surgery and routine physical exams as noncovered services that may at times be covered by TRICARE.

EXAMPLE

Blepharoplasty, surgical repair of the eyelid, is often done for cosmetic purposes, such as achieving a more youthful appearance. However, if blepharoplasty is done to correct or repair a defect of the eyelid, TRICARE may cover part of the cost.

As with covered services, information about exceptions to noncovered services is available from the TRICARE regional administrator or in the *Provider Manual*. Participating providers receive a copy of and updates to the *Provider Manual*.

TABLE 14-2

TRICARE Standard Covered Services			
Service	Limits	Service	Limits
Ambulance		Medical supplies and dressings	
Ambulatory surgery		Mental health care	Yes
Anesthesia		Morbid obesity	Yes
Breast reconstruction	Yes	Outpatient care	
Chronic renal disease		Oxygen	
Consultation services		Pap smears	Yes
CT scans		Percutaneous transluminal coronary angioplasty	
Diagnostic testing		Physical therapy	
Durable medical equipment		Prescription drugs and medicines	
Family planning; prescription contraceptives		Prosthetic devices	
Free-standing birthing centers		Speech therapy	Yes
Hospice	Yes	Sterilization	
Immunizations	Yes	Radiation therapy services	
Inpatient care		Surgery (preoperative and postoperative care)	
In-home cardio-respiratory monitors		Transplants	Yes
Laboratory and pathology		Well-child care (birth to 17 years)	
Magnetic resonance imaging	Yes	X-ray services	
Mammograms	Yes		
Maternity care			

TABLE 14–3

TRICARE Noncovered Services			
Service	**Exceptions**	**Service**	**Exceptions**
Acupuncture		Naturopaths	
Anesthesia by surgeon		Routine physical exams	Yes
Artificial insemination		Radial keratotomy	
Breast reduction or augmentation (cosmetic purposes)		Routine foot care	
Cosmetic surgery	Yes	Sterilization reversal	
Custodial care		Vitamins	
Domiciliary care		Weight reduction programs	
Electrolysis		Unproven procedures or treatments	
Exercise programs			

PREAUTHORIZATION

TRICARE Standard requires preauthorization for a number of procedures. Table 14–4 lists examples of some of the procedures requiring preauthorization. The list is not all-inclusive.

High-cost procedures usually require preauthorization. The insurance carrier or **health care finder**—a health care specialist who assists beneficiaries and providers with preauthorizations—can provide information about the preauthorization status of a specific procedure.

TABLE 14–4

Procedures Requiring TRICARE Preauthorization	
Procedure	**Procedure**
Arthroscopy (shoulder, elbow, wrist, knee, ligament, ankle)	Laparoscopic cholecystectomy
Breast mass or tumor excision	Ligation/transection of fallopian tubes
Cardiac catheterization	Magnetic resonance imaging
Cataract removal	Myringotomy or tympanostomy
Cystoscopy	Neuroplasty
Diagnostic laparoscopy	Rhinoplasty or septoplasty
D&C for diagnostic or therapeutic reasons	Strabismus repair
Hernia repair	Tonsillectomy or adenoidectomy
	Upper gastrointestinal endoscopy

TRICARE Standard does not provide preauthorization for cosmetic, plastic, or reconstructive surgery. These types of surgery are covered when the purpose is:

- To restore function
- To correct a serious birth defect
- To restore body form or structure after an accidental injury
- To improve appearance after severe disfigurement or extensive scarring from surgery or cancer
- For breast reconstruction following a mastectomy

Additional documentation establishing the medical necessity for cosmetic, plastic, or reconstructive procedures may be required when submitting a claim.

DURABLE MEDICAL EQUIPMENT (DME)

According to TRICARE guidelines, **durable medical equipment (DME)** is equipment that improves function, prevents further deterioration of a physical condition, and provides a medical function and not simply transportation. DME examples include wheelchairs, prostheses, oxygen, and braces.

Items such as eyeglasses, contact lenses, hearing aids, and other communication devices do not qualify for reimbursement as durable medical equipment. Other noncovered items include exercise equipment, spas, whirlpools, hot tubs, swimming pools, or similar equipment. Air conditioners, humidifiers, dehumidifiers, and air filters are also excluded.

Providers who supply durable medical equipment as rentals, lease/purchases, or outright purchases may be reimbursed by TRICARE Standard. In order to receive payment, the DME must meet the following criteria:

- The allowable charge must exceed $100.
- It must be medically necessary for the treatment of a covered illness or injury.
- It must improve the function of a malformed, diseased, or injured body part or prevent further deterioration of the patient's physical condition.
- It must be patient-specific.
- It must be primarily and customarily used to serve a medical purpose. The equipment is not covered if used primarily for transportation, comfort, or convenience.
- It must withstand repeated use.
- It is not for a patient in a facility that provides or can provide the equipment.
- It is not available from a local uniformed service medical facility.
- It cannot be a luxury or deluxe model of the needed equipment.

Durable medical equipment must be prescribed by a physician or an authorized health care professional. TRICARE also shares the cost of repairing a DME already owned by the patient as long as the equipment continues to be medically necessary. The patient's attending physician must provide a signed and dated statement with the claim for DME repair. The statement must include the patient's diagnosis, the nature of the required repair, and the estimated length of time the equipment will be needed. In addition, the cost must be less than the rental or lease/purchase of a new item, and the need for repair must not be due to willful or malicious conduct on the part of the patient.

REINFORCEMENT EXERCISES 14–2

Fill in the blank.

1. _____ providers agree to accept the TRICARE allowable charge as payment in full.

2. Wheelchairs and prostheses are examples of _____.

3. _____ providers are subject to the limited charge for a given service or procedure.

4. Participating providers may charge the patient for _____ services.

Provide a short answer for each item.

1. List three conditions under which TRICARE Standard covers cosmetic surgery.

_____

_____

_____

2. Define "durable medical equipment."

_____

_____

_____

3. Identify five items that do *not* qualify as durable medical equipment.

_____

_____

_____

4. List three items that qualify as durable medical equipment.

_____

_____

_____

TRICARE BILLING

Participating providers are required to file insurance claims for TRICARE beneficiaries. Nonparticipating providers may or may not file the insurance claim. If the nonparticipating provider does not file the claim, the payment is sent to the beneficiary. TRICARE claims must be filed within one year from the date a service is provided or within one year from a patient's discharge from an inpatient facility. Claims received by the TRICARE contractor after the filing deadline are denied,

TABLE 14–5

Exceptions to TRICARE Filing Deadlines	
Exception	**Description/Documentation**
Retroactive eligibility	The uniformed service makes this determination, and the provider submits a copy of the decision with the claim.
Administrative error	The TRICARE contractor delays the claim. A copy of the letter, report, or statement explaining the error must accompany the provider's claim.
Mental incompetency	The patient is or was mentally incompetent and does not have a legal representative. A physician's statement attesting to the mental incompetency must accompany the claim.
Adequate access to care	The patient's access to care, based on procedure code and locality, delayed claims processing.
Primary payer delay	Payment from the primary payer delays the timely submission of the TRICARE claim. The EOB from the primary payer must accompany the provider's TRICARE claim. The TRICARE claim must be submitted within 90 days of the primary payer's final action on the claim.

unless there is sufficient evidence to grant an exception. Examples of exceptions to the deadline are listed in Table 14–5.

The billing specialist submits claims to the **TRICARE contractor** in the designated TRICARE region. The TRICARE contractor is similar to an insurance carrier. TRICARE contractors are responsible for enrollment, care authorization, and processing claims in one of four regions. Three regions are in the U.S. and the fourth region covers overseas beneficiaries. The U.S. TRICARE contractors at the time this text was published are listed in Table 14–6.

Deductibles, Cost Sharing, and Allowable Charges

Provider reimbursement under TRICARE Standard depends on the patient's deductible, the cost-share amount, and the TRICARE **allowable charge**. The TRICARE allowable charge is the payment to providers that is the lower amount of the provider's fee or the **maximum allowable charge**. The maximum allowable charge, also called the CHAMPUS **maximum allowable charge** (CMAC), is the most TRICARE Standard will allow for a procedure or service. Examples A and B illustrate the determination of the TRICARE allowable charge.

EXAMPLE A
Dr. Johnson's fee for diabetic testing is $50. The CMAC for diabetic testing is $40. In this case, the TRICARE Standard allowable charge for diabetic testing is $40, which is the lower amount of the provider's fee and the maximum allowable charge.

EXAMPLE B
Dr. McMiller's fee for diabetic testing is $30. The CMAC for diabetic testing is $40. In this case, the TRICARE Standard allowable charge is $30 because the provider's fee is the lower amount.

TABLE 14–6

TRICARE Contractors, Regions, and States		
TRICARE Contractor	**Region**	**States**
Health Net Federal Services (Health Net) www.healthnetfederalservices.com Cordova, California	North	Connecticut, Deleware, District of Columbia, Illinois, Indiana, Kentucky, Massachusetts, Maryland, Maine, Michigan, New Hampshire, New Jersey, New York, North Carolina, Ohio, Pennsylvania, Rhode Island, Virginia, Vermont, West Virginia, Wisconsin and sections of Iowa, Missouri, and Tennessee
Humana Military Health Care Services (Humana Military) www.humana-military.com Louisville, KY	South	Alabama, Arkansas, Florida, Georgia, Louisiana, Mississippi, Oklahoma, South Carolina, Tennessee, and sections of Texas
TriWest Healthcare Alliance (TriWest) www.triwest.com Phoenix, Arizona	West	Alaska, Arizona, California, Colorado, Hawaii, Idaho, Iowa, Kansas, Minnesota, Missouri, Montana, Nebraska, Nevada, North Dakota, Oregon, South Dakota, Texas, Utah, Washington, and Wyoming

The billing specialist can find the maximum allowable charge for provider services by using the CHAMPUS Maximum Allowable Charge (CMAC) System. Carefully read the following example, which is a step-by-step procedure for the CMAC System. If you have access to the Internet, go to www.tricare.mil/CMAC/home.aspx and then follow the instructions in the example.

EXAMPLE

1. First Screen: Copyright statement for ASC Public Use and CPT codes. Click Accept.
2. Second Screen: Click CMAC Procedure Pricing.
3. Third Screen: CMAC Procedure Pricing and effective dates. Dialog box with five choices: Locality code; State; Catchment Area; Zip Code; Foreign Country. Only one choice is used to search for a procedure price. Enter 49855 in the Zip Code box. Click Search. (Note: In this example, 49855 is a Michigan ZIP code.)
4. Fourth Screen: Displays the state and a list of **locality codes** on the far left. A locality code is a three-digit number that represents a group of ZIP codes. If there is more than one locality code, select one for your area. (Note: In this example, there is only one locality code.) Enter the CPT code 30110 in the textbox. Click Show pricing.

Dr. Rhinehard removed nasal polyps from Ms. Wellington, a TRICARE beneficiary. Dr. Rhinehard is a participating physician and his fee is $200.
The CMAC for excision of nasal polyps, simple (CPT code 30110) is $160.

Estimated TRICARE Payment Calculation

TRICARE allowable charge (Lower amount of physician charge and CMAC)	$160.00
Minus patient cost-share amount (20% of TRICARE allowable charge)	$ 32.00
Estimated TRICARE Payment	$128.00

The patient pays the $32 cost-share.
The billing specialist submits a claim for $128.
The payment is sent to the provider.

The difference between the physician's fee and the TRICARE allowable charge ($40) cannot be billed to the patient.

Delmar/Cengage Learning

FIGURE 14–1 Estimated TRICARE Payment

5. Fifth Screen: Displays CMAC Search Results. CMAC Detail Screen for Procedure Code 30110. Pricing is listed in four different categories. Category 1: Facility Physician applies to a physician provider in a hospital setting, inpatient, outpatient, and ambulatory surgery center. Category 2: Non-Facility Physician applies to a physician provider in a nonfacility setting such as the provider's office or the patient's home. Category 3: Facility Non-Physician applies to a health care professional in a facility setting who is not a physician. Category 4: Non-Facility Non-Physician applies to a health care professional in a nonfacility setting who is not a physician. Each category has a different fee or reimbursement level.

Estimating TRICARE Payment

By using the information from the CMAC System and computing the cost-sharing percentage, the billing specialist can estimate the TRICARE payment for provider services. Figure 14–1 is an example of estimating the TRICARE payment for a participating physician. The procedure code is 30110, simple excision of nasal polyps.

Figure 14–2 is an example of estimated TRICARE payments for nonparticipating providers. Item B is the estimated payment when the patient has not met the annual deductible.

The billing specialist requests payment for the cost-share amount and the 15 percent adjustment. Unless the billing specialist can verify the status of the patient's deductible, the deductible cannot be collected until the TRICARE payment is received. If the provider submits the insurance claim, payment is sent to the provider. Otherwise, payment is sent to the beneficiary, and the provider must bill the patient.

REINFORCEMENT EXERCISE 14–3

Fill in the blank.

1. The billing specialist submits TRICARE claims to the _____.

2. The _____ is the most TRICARE Standard will pay for a procedure or service.

3. The TRICARE _____ is the lower of the provider's fee and the maximum allowable charge.

4. A TRICARE _____ code is a three-digit number that represents a group of ZIP codes.

5. _____ may or may not submit insurance claims for TRICARE beneficiaries.

Procedure: Excision, nasal polyps, simple   CPT: 30110

CMAC: $160   Nonparticipating Provider Fee: $200

A. Estimated TRICARE Payment Calculation: Nonparticipating provider

TRICARE allowable charge, nonparticipating provider (CMAC + 15% of CMAC; $160 + $24 = $184)	$184.00
Minus patient cost-share amount (20% of TRICARE CMAC)	$ 32.00
Minus 15% paid by patient (Patient pays the $24)	$ 24.00
Estimated TRICARE Payment	$128.00

B. Estimated TRICARE Payment Calculation with Deductible (Nonparticipating Provider)

TRICARE allowable charge, nonparticipating provider (CMAC + 15% of CMAC; $160 + $24 = $184)	$184.00
Minus patient cost-share amount (20% of TRICARE CMAC)	$ 32.00
Minus 15% paid by patient (Patient pays the $24)	$ 24.00
Minus patient deductible (Patient pays the deductible)	$ 50.00
Estimated TRICARE Payment	$ 78.00

FIGURE 14–2 Estimated TRICARE Payment, Nonparticipating provider

CMS-1500 Completion for TRICARE

TRICARE claims are submitted via the CMS-1500 form. General instructions for completing the claim form are given here. A specific TRICARE contractor may have some unique variations to the general instructions. The TRICARE contractor provides specific CMS-1500 completion guidelines. When the instructions refer to the "insured," they are referring to the military sponsor. The military sponsor is the active-duty, retired, or deceased service member.

Block 1	Enter an X in TRICARE/CHAMPUS.
Block 1a	Enter the sponsor's Social Security number.
Block 2	Enter the patient's name as directed on the form.
Block 3	Enter the patient's eight-digit birth date (MM/DD/YYYY). Enter an X in the appropriate gender box.
Block 4	If the sponsor is *not* the patient, enter the sponsor's name. If the sponsor is the patient, leave this blank.
Block 5	Enter the patient's address, including the ZIP code. Do not enter a P.O. box number.
Block 6	Enter an X in the box that best describes the patient's relationship to the sponsor.
Block 7	Enter the sponsor's address, including the ZIP code.
Block 8	Enter an X in the box that applies to the patient's marital, employment, or student status.
Note: Blocks 9–9d are required when the patient has another health insurance plan, as indicated by an X in block 11d.	
Block 9	Must be completed if block 11d is checked Yes. Enter the name of the person with other health insurance (OHI) that covers the patient.
Block 9a	Enter the policy number or group number of the other insured's policy.
Block 9b	Enter the other insured's birth date and sex.
Block 9c	Enter the name of the other insured's employer or school.
Block 9d	Enter the name of the insurance plan or program name of the other health insurance.
Blocks 10–10c	Enter an X in *Yes* or *No* as applicable. If treatment is related to an automobile accident (10b), enter the two-character abbreviation for the state where the accident occurred.
Block 10d	Leave this blank.
Note: Block 11 through Block 11c pertain to the **sponsor**, named in block 4.	

continued on the next page

continued from the previous page

Block 11	Enter the policy group or FECA number, if applicable. If TRICARE is the only insurance, enter NONE.
Block 11a	Enter the sponsor's date of birth and an X in the gender box if different from block 3.
Block 11b	Enter the sponsor's branch of service.
Block 11c	Enter TRICARE.
Block 11d	Enter an X in Yes if there is another health insurance plan that is primary to TRICARE. If Yes, complete blocks 9a–d. If TRICARE is the only insurance, enter an X in No.
Block 12	Enter SIGNATURE ON FILE if the signature is updated annually.
Block 13	Enter SIGNATURE ON FILE.
Block 14	Enter the date of current illness, injury, or last menstrual period (LMP), for pregnancy.
Block 15	Leave this blank.
Block 16	Enter the date, if applicable.
Block 17	Enter the name and credential of the referring physician or provider.
Block 17a	Enter the referring physician/provider's non-NPI number with qualifier, if applicable. Use the same codes as for Medicare.
Block 17b	Enter the referring physician/provider's NPI number.
Block 18	Enter the hospitalization dates, if applicable.
Block 19	Enter the referral number for services that require a referral from the primary care manager (PCM).
Block 20	Enter an X in No if lab work was performed in the provider's lab. Enter an X in Yes if lab work was performed outside of the provider's office. When Yes is checked, enter the total amount charged by the outside lab for the services reported on the claim form.
Block 21	Enter up to four ICD-9-CM diagnosis codes. Enter the first-listed diagnosis in 1. Codes must be entered to the highest level of specificity.
Block 22	Leave this blank.
Block 23	Enter additional prior authorization number(s), if applicable.
Block 24A	Enter the month, day, and year for each procedure/ service or supply. If From and To dates are shown here for a series of identical services, enter the number of services in block 24G.
Block 24B	Enter the place of service code. Use the same codes as Medicare.
Block 24C	Enter a Y for yes if the service provided was an emergency. Enter an N for no if the service was not an emergency.

continued on the next page

continued from the previous page

Block 24D	Enter CPT/HCPCS, code for each service. Enter modifiers, if applicable.
Block 24E	Enter the diagnosis pointer (1–4) for the diagnosis that best justifies the medical necessity for the service.
Block 24F	Enter the charge for each listed service.
Block 24G	Enter the days, units, or number of services for each line item.
Block 24H	Enter an X, if applicable. Otherwise, leave this blank.
Block 24I	In the shaded portion, enter the qualifier that identifies the non-NPI number entered in the shaded portion of block 24J. When only the NPI is reported, leave this blank.
Block 24J	Enter the NPI number (unshaded portion of 24J) of the provider rendering the service in each line. Note that NPI is preprinted in the unshaded portion of Block 24I.
Block 25	Enter the provider's federal tax ID number (EIN). Enter an X in the EIN box.
Block 26	Enter the patient's account number, if one is assigned by the provider.
Block 27	Enter an X in Yes if the provider accepts TRICARE assignment under TRICARE. Enter an X in No if the provider does not.
Block 28	Enter total charges for the services being reported on the claim.
Block 29	Enter the amount paid by the patient or other health insurance.
Block 30	Enter balance due by subtracting the amount in block 29 from the amount in block 28.
Block 31	Provider signature and date. SIGNATURE ON FILE acceptable for electronic claims.
Block 32	Enter the name, address, city, state, and zip code of the physical location where services were provided.
Block 32a	Enter the NPI of the facility identified in block 32.
Block 32b	Enter the qualifier and non-NPI number of the facility identified in block 32, if applicable.
Block 33	Enter the name, complete address, and telephone number of the billing provider.
Block 33a	Enter the NPI of the billing provider identified in block 33. For solo-practice physicians, enter the physician's NPI. For group-practice physicians/providers, enter the group practice NPI.
Block 33b	Enter the qualifier and non-NPI number of the billing provider identified in block 33, if applicable.

Figure 14–3 illustrates a completed CMS-1500 when TRICARE is the only payer.

HEALTH INSURANCE CLAIM FORM

(1500)

APPROVED BY NATIONAL UNIFORM CLAIM COMMITTEE 08/05

PICA / PICA

1. MEDICARE	MEDICAID	TRICARE CHAMPUS	CHAMPVA	GROUP HEALTH PLAN	FECA BLK LUNG	OTHER	1a. INSURED'S I.D. NUMBER (For Program in Item 1)
(Medicare #)	(Medicaid #)	[X] (Sponsor's SSN)	(Member ID #)	(SSN or ID)	(SSN)	(ID)	698785432

2. PATIENT'S NAME (Last Name, First Name, Middle Initial)
COLONEL, SARA, M

3. PATIENT'S BIRTH DATE
MM 09 | DD 05 | YY 2005   SEX M [ ] F [X]

4. INSURED'S NAME (Last Name, First Name, Middle Initial)
COLONEL, ROY, P

5. PATIENT'S ADDRESS (No., Street)
89 CIRCLE DRIVE

6. PATIENT RELATIONSHIP TO INSURED
Self [ ] Spouse [ ] Child [X] Other [ ]

7. INSURED'S ADDRESS (No., Street)
89 CIRCLE DRIVE

CITY BLUEBERRY   STATE ME

8. PATIENT STATUS
Single [X] Married [ ] Other [ ]

CITY BLUEBERRY   STATE ME

ZIP CODE 49855   TELEPHONE (Include Area Code) (906) 228 2612

Employed [ ] Full-Time Student [ ] Part-Time Student [ ]

ZIP CODE 49855   TELEPHONE (Include Area Code) (906) 228 2612

9. OTHER INSURED'S NAME (Last Name, First Name, Middle Initial)

10. IS PATIENT'S CONDITION RELATED TO:

11. INSURED'S POLICY GROUP OR FECA NUMBER
NONE

a. OTHER INSURED'S POLICY OR GROUP NUMBER

a. EMPLOYMENT? (Current or Previous) [ ] YES [X] NO

a. INSURED'S DATE OF BIRTH
MM 08 | DD 11 | YY 1970   SEX M [X] F [ ]

b. OTHER INSURED'S DATE OF BIRTH
MM | DD | YY   SEX M [ ] F [ ]

b. AUTO ACCIDENT? PLACE (State) [ ] YES [X] NO

b. EMPLOYER'S NAME OR SCHOOL NAME
USAF

c. EMPLOYER'S NAME OR SCHOOL NAME

c. OTHER ACCIDENT? [ ] YES [X] NO

c. INSURANCE PLAN NAME OR PROGRAM NAME
TRICARE

d. INSURANCE PLAN NAME OR PROGRAM NAME

10d. RESERVED FOR LOCAL USE

d. IS THERE ANOTHER HEALTH BENEFIT PLAN?
[ ] YES [X] NO If yes, return to and complete item 9 a-d.

READ BACK OF FORM BEFORE COMPLETING & SIGNING THIS FORM.
12. PATIENT'S OR AUTHORIZED PERSON'S SIGNATURE I authorize the release of any medical or other information necessary to process this claim. I also request payment of government benefits either to myself or to the party who accepts assignment below.

SIGNED SIGNATURE ON FILE   DATE

13. INSURED'S OR AUTHORIZED PERSON'S SIGNATURE I authorize payment of medical benefits to the undersigned physician or supplier for services described below.

SIGNED SIGNATURE ON FILE

14. DATE OF CURRENT: ILLNESS (First symptom) OR INJURY (Accident) OR PREGNANCY (LMP)
MM 03 | DD 02 | YY 20YY

15. IF PATIENT HAS HAD SAME OR SIMILAR ILLNESS. GIVE FIRST DATE MM | DD | YY

16. DATES PATIENT UNABLE TO WORK IN CURRENT OCCUPATION
FROM MM | DD | YY   TO MM | DD | YY

17. NAME OF REFERRING PROVIDER OR OTHER SOURCE
MARY SMITH MD

17a.
17b. NPI 8901234567

18. HOSPITALIZATION DATES RELATED TO CURRENT SERVICES
FROM MM | DD | YY   TO MM | DD | YY

19. RESERVED FOR LOCAL USE

20. OUTSIDE LAB? [ ] YES [X] NO $ CHARGES

21. DIAGNOSIS OR NATURE OF ILLNESS OR INJURY (Relate Items 1, 2, 3, or 4 to Item 24E by Line)
1. 599 . 0
2. ___ . ___
3. ___ . ___
4. ___ . ___

22. MEDICAID RESUBMISSION CODE   ORIGINAL REF. NO.

23. PRIOR AUTHORIZATION NUMBER

24. A. DATE(S) OF SERVICE From MM DD YY	To MM DD YY	B. PLACE OF SERVICE	C. EMG	D. PROCEDURES, SERVICES, OR SUPPLIES (Explain Unusual Circumstances) CPT/HCPCS	MODIFIER	E. DIAGNOSIS POINTER	F. $ CHARGES	G. DAYS OR UNITS	H. EPSDT Family Plan	I. ID. QUAL.	J. RENDERING PROVIDER ID. #
1	03 02 YY	03 02 YY	11	N	99212		1	45 00	1		NPI	4567890123
2	03 02 YY	03 02 YY	11	N	81000		1	25 00	1		NPI	4567890123
3											NPI	
4											NPI	
5											NPI	
6											NPI	

25. FEDERAL TAX I.D. NUMBER SSN [ ] EIN [X]
22498765

26. PATIENT'S ACCOUNT NO.
45678

27. ACCEPT ASSIGNMENT? (For govt. claims, see back) [X] YES [ ] NO

28. TOTAL CHARGE $ 70 00

29. AMOUNT PAID $ 14 00

30. BALANCE DUE $ 56 00

31. SIGNATURE OF PHYSICIAN OR SUPPLIER INCLUDING DEGREES OR CREDENTIALS
(I certify that the statements on the reverse apply to this bill and are made a part thereof.)
SIGNATURE ON FILE
SIGNED   DATE

32. SERVICE FACILITY LOCATION INFORMATION
MEDICAL CARE SOUTH
809 CIRCLE DRIVE
BLUEBERRY ME 49855
a. 8901234567 b.

33. BILLING PROVIDER INFO & PH # (906) 336 4020
MEDICAL CARE SOUTH
809 CIRCLE DRIVE
BLUEBERRY ME 49855
a. 8901234567 b.

NUCC Instruction Manual available at: www.nucc.org

APPROVED OMB-0938-0999 FORM CMS-1500 (08-05)

FIGURE 14–3 TRICARE CMS-1500 (For instructional use only. Courtesy of the Centers for Medicare and Medicaid Services, www.cms.hhs.gov)

TRICARE as Secondary Payer

With the exception of Medicaid and supplemental insurance plans, TRICARE is the secondary payer when the patient is covered by another insurance plan or is eligible for Medicare. The billing specialist first submits a claim to the other insurance company and after receiving payment sends a claim to the TRICARE contractor. When billing TRICARE as the secondary payer, complete blocks 9–9d of the CMS-1500. You may be required to furnish additional information from the other health insurance program, such as an explanation of benefits (EOB). Remember to include the other health insurance payment in block 29 of the CMS-1500. The insurance billing specialist should contact the TRICARE contractor if there are any questions about TRICARE primary or secondary payer status.

FRAUD AND ABUSE

The **TRICARE Management Agency (TMA)** is the agency that administers the TRICARE program. The TMA's **Program Integrity Office** manages TRICARE's fraud and abuse program. Fraud is defined as the "intent to deceive or misrepresent to secure unlawful gain." The TRICARE Program Integrity Office maintains a website that lists all providers who have been sanctioned for fraud. Sanctions include monetary penalties, criminal convictions, and exclusion from all federally funded health programs. As with Medicare fraud and abuse, the purpose of this program is to reduce or eliminate unnecessary medical costs. Table 14–7 lists examples of fraud.

In addition to fraud, the Program Integrity Office reviews cases of potential abuse, which is defined as practices inconsistent with sound fiscal, business, or medical procedures and as services not considered reasonable and necessary. Abusive activities often result in inappropriate claims for TRICARE payment. Table 14–8 lists examples of abuse.

TABLE 14–7

Examples of Fraud
Fraudulent Billing Practices   • Billing for services, supplies, or equipment not furnished to the patient   • Billing for noncovered services that are disguised as covered services   • Billing more than once for the same service—known as duplicate billing   • Billing for services provided by another provider—known as reciprocal billing   • Billing the beneficiary for amounts that exceed the TRICARE Standard allowable charge or cost
Other Fraudulent Practices   • Misrepresentations of dates, frequency, duration, or description of services rendered   • Practicing with an expired or revoked license   • Assigning medical codes that reflect a higher level of service than that which was provided—known as upcoding   • Assigning medical codes at a lower level so as to avoid billing oversight—known as downcoding

TABLE 14–8

Examples of Abuse
• A pattern of waiving beneficiary cost-share or deductible
• A pattern of submitting claims for services that are not medically necessary or, if necessary, not to the extent rendered
• Charging TRICARE beneficiaries higher rates than those charged to other patients or insurance programs
• Providing inferior care
• Failure to maintain adequate clinical or financial records
• Unauthorized use of the term TRICARE

Fraudulent actions can result in criminal or civil penalties. Fraudulent or abusive activities may result in administrative sanctions, such as suspension or exclusion as an authorized provider.

REINFORCEMENT EXERCISES 14–4

Provide a short answer for each question.

1. When is TRICARE the primary payer?

2. When is TRICARE the secondary payer?

3. What is the purpose of TRICARE's Program Integrity Office?

4. What is upcoding?

continued on the next page

continued from the previous page

5. What is downcoding?

_____

_____

6. Describe the difference between fraud and abuse.

_____

_____

CHAMPVA

CHAMPVA is a health care benefits program for the spouse or widow(er) and children of a veteran who meets one of the following criteria:

1. Permanently and totally disabled due to a service-connected disability, as determined by a Veterans Administration (VA) regional office
2. Permanently and totally disabled due to a service-connected condition at the time of death
3. Died from a service-connected disability
4. Died while on active duty

To qualify for CHAMPVA, the dependents *cannot* be eligible for Department of Defense (DoD) TRICARE benefits.

CHAMPVA is administered through the **Health Administration Center (HAC)** in Denver, Colorado. Table 14–9 provides a list of terms and definitions related to CHAMPVA eligibility.

Except for stepchildren, the divorce or remarriage of the spouse or surviving spouse does not affect the CHAMPVA eligibility of children.

Covered and Noncovered Services

In general, CHAMPVA covers most health care services and supplies that are medically and psychologically necessary. There are preauthorization requirements for the following covered services:

TABLE 14–9

CHAMPVA Eligibility Definitions	
Term	**Definition**
Sponsor	The veteran; CHAMPVA eligibility is based on an individual's relationship to the veteran.
Service-connected disability/condition	VA determination that a veteran's illness or injury was incurred or aggravated while on active duty in military service and resulted in some degree of disability
Dependent	Child, spouse, or widow(er) of a qualifying sponsor

- Organ and bone marrow transplants
- Hospice services
- Most mental health/substance abuse services
- Dental care
- Durable medical equipment worth more than $2,000
- Failure to obtain preauthorization for applicable services results in the denial of the claim.

General exclusions from CHAMPVA payment include the following:

- Services determined by the VA to be medically unnecessary
- Care as part of a grant, study, or research program
- Care considered experimental or investigational
- Care for persons eligible for benefits under other government agency programs, except Medicaid and State Victims of Crime Compensation programs
- Care that is provided free of charge, such as services obtained at a health fair
- Care provided outside the scope of the provider's license or certification
- Custodial, domiciliary, or rest cures
- Dental care, except treatment related to certain covered medical conditions
- Medications that do not require a prescription, except insulin
- Personal comfort and convenience items
- Services rendered by providers who are suspended or sanctioned by other federal entities

Only the VA's Health Administration Center in Denver, Colorado, can authorize benefits and process claims. Therefore, it is strongly recommended that all inquiries for CHAMPVA-related matters are made directly to the Center. The address is VA Health Administration Center, CHAMPVA, P.O. Box 469064, Denver, CO 80246-9064. The phone number is 1-800-733-8387.

Providers, Deductibles, and Cost Sharing

Except for certain mental health categories and freestanding ambulatory surgical centers, the Health Administration Center does not establish contracts with health care providers or maintain provider listings. Beneficiaries are free to select any provider who is appropriately licensed or certified to perform the services offered.

By law, all health care providers are prohibited from balance-billing beneficiaries for amounts that exceed the CHAMPVA-allowed amount. Once the deductible is met and the cost-share amount is paid, providers must accept the CHAMPVA-allowed amount as payment in full.

With the exception of inpatient services, ambulatory surgery facility services, partial psychiatric day programs, and all hospice services, the annual deductible must be met before CHAMPVA pays its share. At the time of publication, the calendar year deductible was $50 per beneficiary or a maximum of $100 per CHAMPVA-eligible family, whichever is satisfied first.

For most CHAMPVA-covered services, the beneficiary's cost-share is 25 percent of the allowable charge, and CHAMPVA pays 75 percent. Remember, balance-billing is not an option for CHAMPVA-covered services. The billing specialist can estimate the CHAMPVA-allowed charge by using TRICARE's CMAC procedure pricing information. Figure 14–4 is an example of beneficiary and CHAMPVA payment amounts for CPT code 30110, Excision, nasal polyps, simple. The patient has met the annual deductible.

CPT CODE: 30110   DESCRIPTION: Excision, nasal polyp(s), simple

PROVIDER FEE: $200   ALLOWABLE CHARGE: $160

Physician Fee	$200.00
Allowable Charge	$160.00
Minus Beneficiary Cost-share Amount (25% of the allowable charge)	$ 40.00
Estimated CHAMPVA Payment	$120.00

The provider collects the $40 cost-share from the patient.

The $40 difference between the Physician Fee and the Allowable Charge cannot be billed to the patient.

Delmar/Cengage Learning

FIGURE 14–4 CHAMPVA Estimated Payment

CHAMPVA BILLING

The billing specialist can verify the eligibility status of CHAMPVA beneficiaries by calling a toll-free number (1-800-733-8387), following the voice-activated instructions, and entering the beneficiary's Social Security number and the provider's federal tax ID number.

Except for Medicaid, insurance policies that supplement CHAMPVA benefits, and State Victims of Crime Compensation programs, CHAMPVA is always the secondary payer. The beneficiary has the option of filing the CHAMPVA claim and receiving the payment. The beneficiary completes the CHAMPVA claim form and attaches a copy of the provider's itemized bill and a copy of any other health insurance program's explanation of benefits. When the beneficiary files the insurance claim, the provider must bill the beneficiary for services rendered.

When the provider files the insurance claim, the beneficiary may be asked to pay the cost-share amount at the time of service. The billing specialist submits the claim to CHAMPVA. If a deductible amount is subtracted from the provider's payment, the provider must bill the beneficiary for the deductible amount.

CMS-1500 GUIDELINES FOR CHAMPVA

Hospitals and ambulatory service centers complete a UB-04. Other providers use the CMS-1500. Each CHAMPVA beneficiary receives his or her own ID card. Under CHAMPVA, when the beneficiary is the patient, the patient is always the insured.

Block 1	Enter an X in CHAMPVA.
Block 1a	Enter the beneficiary's CHAMPVA Authorization Card ID number. (This may be the beneficiary's Social Security number.)
Block 2	Enter the patient's name as directed on the form.
Block 3	Enter the patient's eight-digit birth date (MMDDYYYY). Enter an X in the appropriate gender box.
Block 4	Leave this blank.
Block 5	Enter the patient's address, ZIP code, and telephone number.
Block 6	Enter an X in Self. (Note: Because each beneficiary has an individual ID card, the patient is the insured.)
Block 7	Leave this blank.
Block 8	Enter an X in the box that applies to the patient's marital, employment, and student status.
Blocks 9–9d are completed when the beneficiary is covered by other health insurance (OHI) and YES is answered in block 11d.	
Block 9	Enter the name of the insured with another insurance plan that covers the beneficiary.
Block 9a	Enter the policy or group number of the other insurance plan.
Block 9b	Enter the other insured's eight-digit birth date (MMDDYYYY). Enter an X in the appropriate gender box.
Block 9c	Enter the name of the other insured's employer or school.
Block 9d	Enter the name of the insurance plan or program name of the other health insurance.
Blocks 10–10c	Enter an X in Yes or No, as applicable. If treatment is related to an automobile accident (10b), enter the two-character abbreviation for the state where the accident occurred.
Block 10d	Leave this blank.
Blocks 11–11c	Leave this blank.
Block 11d	Enter an X in Yes if the patient is covered under another health insurance plan. Complete blocks 9–9d. Enter an X in No if the patient's only health insurance is CHAMPVA.

continued on the next page

continued from the previous page

Blocks 12 and 13	Enter SIGNATURE ON FILE.
Block 14	Enter the date of current illness, injury, or last menstrual period (LMP), for pregnancy.
Block 15	Leave this blank.
Block 16	Enter the date, if applicable.
Block 17	Enter the name and credential of the referring physician or provider.
Block 17a	Enter the referring physician/provider's non-NPI number with qualifier. Use the same codes as for Medicare.
Block 17b	Enter the referring physician/provider's NPI number.
Block 18	Enter the hospitalization dates, if applicable.
Block 19	Leave this blank.
Block 20	Enter an X in No if lab work was performed in the provider's lab. Enter an X in Yes if lab work was performed outside of the provider's office. When Yes is checked, enter the total amount charged by the outside lab for the services reported on the claim form.
Block 21	Enter up to four ICD-9-CM diagnostic codes in priority order. The first-listed diagnosis is entered in item 1. Codes must be entered to the highest level of specificity.
Block 22	Leave this blank.
Block 23	Enter the authorization number, if applicable.
Block 24A	Enter the month, day, and year for each procedure/ service or supply. If From and To dates are shown here for a series of identical services, enter the number of services in block 24G.
Block 24B	Enter the place of service code. Use the same codes as Medicare.
Block 24C	Enter a Y for Yes if the service provided was an emergency. Enter an N for No if the service was not an emergency.
Block 24D	Enter CPT/HCPCS code for each service.
Block 24E	Enter the diagnosis pointer (1–4) for the diagnosis that best justifies the medical necessity for the service.
Block 24F	Enter the charge for each listed service.

continued on the next page

continued from the previous page

Block 24G	Enter the days, units, or number of services for each line item.
Block 24H	Enter an X, if applicable. Otherwise, leave this blank.
Block 24I	In the shaded portion, enter the qualifier that identifies the non-NPI number entered in the shaded portion of block 24J. When only the NPI is reported, leave this blank.
Block 24J	Enter the NPI number (unshaded portion of 24J) of the provider rendering the service in each line. Note that NPI is preprinted in the unshaded portion of block 24I.
Block 25	Enter the provider's federal tax ID number (EIN). Enter an X in the FIN box.
Block 26	Enter the patient's account number if one is assigned by the provider.
Block 27	Enter an X in Yes.
Block 28	Enter total charges for the services being reported on the claim.
Block 29	Enter the amount paid by the patient or other health insurance.
Block 30	Enter balance due by subtracting the amount in block 29 from the amount in block 28.
Block 31	Provider signature and date or SIGNATURE ON FILE
Block 32	Enter the name, address, city, state, and ZIP code of the physical location where services were provided.
Block 32a	Enter the NPI of the facility identified in block 32.
Block 32b	Enter the qualifier and non-NPI number of the facility identified in block 32, if applicable.
Block 33	Enter the name, complete address, and telephone number of the billing provider.
Block 33a	Enter the NPI of the billing provider identified in block 33. For solo-practice physicians, enter the physician's NPI. For group-practice physicians/providers, enter the group practice NPI.
Block 33b	Enter the qualifier and non-NPI number of the billing provider identified in block 33, if applicable.

Figure 14–5 illustrates a completed CMS-1500 when CHAMPVA is the only payer.

The provider receives an EOB with the payment. This detailed form explains how reimbursement was determined. Figure 14–6 is a sample CHAMPVA explanation of benefits.

(1500)

HEALTH INSURANCE CLAIM FORM

APPROVED BY NATIONAL UNIFORM CLAIM COMMITTEE 08/05

PICA							PICA

1. MEDICARE	MEDICAID	TRICARE CHAMPUS	CHAMPVA	GROUP HEALTH PLAN	FECA BLK LUNG	OTHER	1a. INSURED'S I.D. NUMBER (For Program in Item 1)
(Medicare #)	(Medicaid #)	(Sponsor's SSN)	[X] (Member ID #)	(SSN or ID)	(SSN)	(ID)	481508649

2. PATIENT'S NAME (Last Name, First Name, Middle Initial)	3. PATIENT'S BIRTH DATE MM DD YY SEX	4. INSURED'S NAME (Last Name, First Name, Middle Initial)
COLLINS, MARTHA, V	12 14 1948 M☐ F[X]	

5. PATIENT'S ADDRESS (No., Street)	6. PATIENT RELATIONSHIP TO INSURED	7. INSURED'S ADDRESS (No., Street)
723 MARQUETTE PLACE	Self [X] Spouse ☐ Child ☐ Other ☐	

CITY	STATE	8. PATIENT STATUS	CITY	STATE
BLUEBERRY	ME	Single ☐ Married [X] Other ☐		

ZIP CODE	TELEPHONE (Include Area Code)		ZIP CODE	TELEPHONE (Include Area Code)
49855	(906) 555 3417	Employed ☐ Full-Time Student ☐ Part-Time Student ☐		( )

9. OTHER INSURED'S NAME (Last Name, First Name, Middle Initial)	10. IS PATIENT'S CONDITION RELATED TO:	11. INSURED'S POLICY GROUP OR FECA NUMBER
a. OTHER INSURED'S POLICY OR GROUP NUMBER	a. EMPLOYMENT? (Current or Previous) ☐ YES [X] NO	a. INSURED'S DATE OF BIRTH MM DD YY SEX M☐ F☐
b. OTHER INSURED'S DATE OF BIRTH MM DD YY SEX M☐ F☐	b. AUTO ACCIDENT? PLACE (State) ☐ YES [X] NO	b. EMPLOYER'S NAME OR SCHOOL NAME
c. EMPLOYER'S NAME OR SCHOOL NAME	c. OTHER ACCIDENT? ☐ YES [X] NO	c. INSURANCE PLAN NAME OR PROGRAM NAME
d. INSURANCE PLAN NAME OR PROGRAM NAME	10d. RESERVED FOR LOCAL USE	d. IS THERE ANOTHER HEALTH BENEFIT PLAN? ☐ YES [X] NO **If yes,** return to and complete item 9 a-d.

READ BACK OF FORM BEFORE COMPLETING & SIGNING THIS FORM.

12. PATIENT'S OR AUTHORIZED PERSON'S SIGNATURE I authorize the release of any medical or other information necessary to process this claim. I also request payment of government benefits either to myself or to the party who accepts assignment below.

SIGNED SIGNATURE ON FILE   DATE _____

13. INSURED'S OR AUTHORIZED PERSON'S SIGNATURE I authorize payment of medical benefits to the undersigned physician or supplier for services described below.

SIGNED SIGNATURE ON FILE

14. DATE OF CURRENT: MM DD YY 04 04 20YY ILLNESS (First symptom) OR INJURY (Accident) OR PREGNANCY (LMP)	15. IF PATIENT HAS HAD SAME OR SIMILAR ILLNESS, GIVE FIRST DATE MM DD YY	16. DATES PATIENT UNABLE TO WORK IN CURRENT OCCUPATION MM DD YY MM DD YY FROM TO
17. NAME OF REFERRING PROVIDER OR OTHER SOURCE	17a. / 17b. NPI	18. HOSPITALIZATION DATES RELATED TO CURRENT SERVICES MM DD YY MM DD YY FROM TO
19. RESERVED FOR LOCAL USE		20. OUTSIDE LAB? ☐ YES [X] NO $ CHARGES

21. DIAGNOSIS OR NATURE OF ILLNESS OR INJURY (Relate Items 1, 2, 3, or 4 to Item 24E by Line)	22. MEDICAID RESUBMISSION CODE ORIGINAL REF. NO.
1. 250 00 3. ___ . ___	
2. 562 10 4. ___ . ___	23. PRIOR AUTHORIZATION NUMBER

24. A. DATE(S) OF SERVICE From / To MM DD YY MM DD YY	B. PLACE OF SERVICE	C. EMG	D. PROCEDURES, SERVICES, OR SUPPLIES (Explain Unusual Circumstances) CPT/HCPCS MODIFIER	E. DIAGNOSIS POINTER	F. $ CHARGES	G. DAYS OR UNITS	H. EPSDT Family Plan	I. ID. QUAL.	J. RENDERING PROVIDER ID. #
1	04 04 YY 04 04 YY	11	N	99213	1	60 00	1		NPI	2311287891
2	04 04 YY 04 04 YY	11	N	83036	1	40 00	1		NPI	2311287891
3									NPI	
4									NPI	
5									NPI	
6									NPI	

25. FEDERAL TAX I.D. NUMBER SSN EIN	26. PATIENT'S ACCOUNT NO.	27. ACCEPT ASSIGNMENT? (For govt. claims, see back)	28. TOTAL CHARGE	29. AMOUNT PAID	30. BALANCE DUE
23508765 ☐ [X]	51260	[X] YES ☐ NO	$ 100 00	$ 25 00	$ 75 00

31. SIGNATURE OF PHYSICIAN OR SUPPLIER INCLUDING DEGREES OR CREDENTIALS (I certify that the statements on the reverse apply to this bill and are made a part thereof.) SIGNATURE ON FILE SIGNED DATE	32. SERVICE FACILITY LOCATION INFORMATION SUPERIORLAND CLINIC 714 HENNEPIN AVENUE BLUEBERRY ME 49855 a. 4567890123 b.	33. BILLING PROVIDER INFO & PH # (906) 336 4020 SUPERIORLAND CLINIC 714 HENNEPIN AVENUE BLUEBERRY ME 49855 a. 4567890123 b.

NUCC Instruction Manual available at: www.nucc.org

APPROVED OMB-0938-0999 FORM CMS-1500 (08-05)

FIGURE 14–5 CHAMPVA CMS-1500 (For instructional use only. Courtesy of the Centers for Medicare and Medicaid Services, www.cms.hhs.gov)

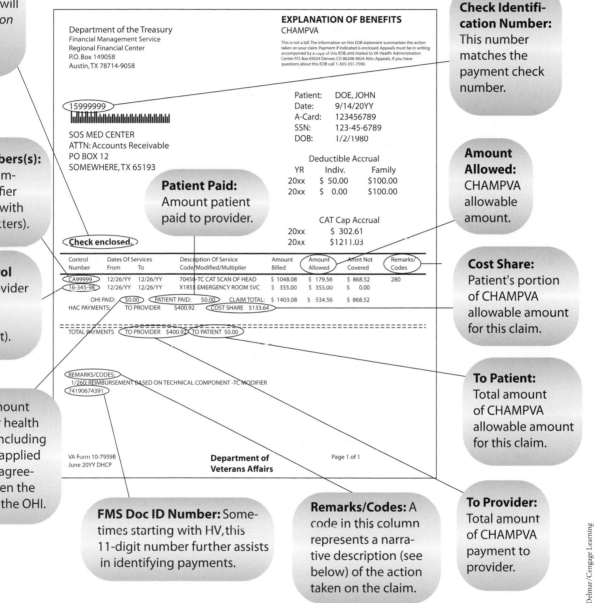

Check Enclosed: Indicates that a U.S. Treasury check is enclosed. When there is no payment, this will read *Information only, no check enclosed.*

Control Numbers(s): CHAMPVA claim-specific identifier (always starts with 2 alpha characters).

Patient Control Numbers: Provider claim-specific identifier (not always present).

OHI Paid: Amount paid by other health insurance—including adjustments applied as a result of agreements between the provider and the OHI.

FMS Doc ID Number: Sometimes starting with HV, this 11-digit number further assists in identifying payments.

Patient Paid: Amount patient paid to provider.

Remarks/Codes: A code in this column represents a narrative description (see below) of the action taken on the claim.

Check Identification Number: This number matches the payment check number.

Amount Allowed: CHAMPVA allowable amount.

Cost Share: Patient's portion of CHAMPVA allowable amount for this claim.

To Patient: Total amount of CHAMPVA allowable amount for this claim.

To Provider: Total amount of CHAMPVA payment to provider.

EXPLANATION OF BENEFITS
CHAMPVA

This is not a bill. The information on this EOB statement summarizes the action taken on your claim. Payment if indicated is enclosed. Appeals must be in writing accompanied by a copy of this EOB, and mailed to VA Health Administration Center P.O. Box 65024 Denver, CO 80206-9024 Attn. Appeals. If you have questions about this EOB call 1-303-331-7599.

Department of the Treasury
Financial Management Service
Regional Financial Center
P.O. Box 149058
Austin, TX 78714-9058

15999999

SOS MED CENTER
ATTN: Accounts Receivable
PO BOX 12
SOMEWHERE, TX 65193

Patient:	DOE, JOHN
Date:	9/14/20YY
A-Card:	123456789
SSN:	123-45-6789
DOB:	1/2/1980

Deductible Accrual

YR	Indiv.	Family
20xx	$ 50.00	$100.00
20xx	$ 0.00	$100.00

CAT Cap Accrual

| 20xx | $ 302.61 |
| 20xx | $1211.03 |

Check enclosed.

Control Number	Dates Of Services From	To	Description Of Service Code/Modified/Multiplier	Amount Billed	Amount Allowed	Amnt Not Covered	Remarks/ Codes
CA99999	12/26/YY	12/26/YY	70450-TC CAT SCAN OF HEAD	$ 1048.08	$ 179.56	$ 868.52	280
16-345-98	12/26/YY	12/26/YY	X185$ EMERGENCY ROOM SVC	$ 355.00	$ 355.00	$ 0.00	

OHI PAID: $0.00   PATIENT PAID: $0.00   CLAIM TOTAL: $ 1403.08 $ 534.56 $ 868.52
HAC PAYMENTS: TO PROVIDER $400.92   COST SHARE $133.64

TOTAL PAYMENTS   TO PROVIDER $400.92   TO PATIENT $0.00

REMARKS/CODES:
1/260: REIMBURSEMENT BASED ON TECHNICAL COMPONENT -TC MODIFIER
74190674391

VA Form 10-7959B
June 20YY DHCP

Department of Veterans Affairs

Page 1 of 1

FIGURE 14–6 Sample CHAMPVA EOB

ABBREVIATIONS

Table 14–10 lists the abbreviations and meanings in this chapter.

TABLE 14–10

Abbreviations and Meanings	
Abbreviation	Meaning
CHAMPUS	Civilian Health and Medical Program of the Uniformed Services
CHAMPVA	Civilian Health and Medical Program of the Veterans Administration
CMAC	(CHAMPUS) Maximum Allowable Charge
DEERS	Defense Enrollment Eligibility and Reporting System
DME	durable medical equipment
DoD	Department of Defense
MTF	medical treatment facility
NATO	North Atlantic Treaty Organization
NOAA	National Oceanic and Atmospheric Administration
PCM	primary care manager
TFL	TRICARE for Live
TMA	TRICARE Management Agency

SUMMARY

TRICARE and CHAMPVA are military services medical benefit programs that serve very different populations. TRICARE is available to active-duty and retired members of the uniformed services, their spouses, and their dependents. CHAMPVA has a much narrower scope and is available to the dependents and survivors of totally and permanently disabled veterans and veterans who died in the line of duty, respectively. Cost sharing and deductibles are features of both programs.

TRICARE options include Prime, Extra, and Standard. TRICARE Standard is often referred to as the old CHAMPUS program. TRICARE beneficiaries receive services from military treatment facilities, preferred provider networks, and civilian providers of choice. Beneficiary out-of-pocket expenses are highest under TRICARE Standard.

Billing specialists must verify TRICARE and CHAMPVA eligibility. Checking the dates on program ID cards is the most common way to verify eligibility. Under TRICARE, participating providers are paid directly and cannot balance-bill the difference between the TRICARE-allowable charge and the provider's fee. Balance-billing is also prohibited under CHAMPVA regulations.

REVIEW EXERCISES

CASE STUDY

Read the case study information and complete a CMS-1500 for TRICARE Standard. Your instructor will tell you how to obtain the form.

PATIENT NAME: Rebecca Wadsworth
DOB: 03/05/1954
SSN: 503-72-1941
ADDRESS: 92 Specker Drive; Blueberry, ME 49855
PHONE: (H) (906) 336-1313
EMPLOYER: T-Mart, 43 Mall Drive, Blueberry, ME 49855
INSURANCE: TRICARE Standard
SPOUSE: Lt. Colonel John R. Wadsworth (retired, USAF)
DOB: 06/15/1952
SSN: 381-60-2997
PROGRESS NOTE:
DATE: 02/05/20YY

Mrs. Wadsworth is seen today for a follow-up visit related to her diabetes. She has been successful in maintaining her blood sugar within normal limits, but she complains that she "is really hungry all the time." We reviewed her diabetic diet and increased the caloric intake to 1,800 calories per day. Her insulin regimen will remain the same. Fasting blood sugar today reveals a blood glucose of 115. Remainder of exam is normal. Mrs. Wadsworth was advised to return in one month unless further problems develop.

SIGNED: Henry Romero, MD
DIAGNOSIS AND TREATMENT CODES: Office visit 99213; insulin-dependent diabetes mellitus, type II 250.00; blood glucose test 82947; venipuncture 36415
SUPERIORLAND CLINIC
714 HENNEPIN AVE.
Blueberry, ME 49855
PHONE (906) 366-4020
TAX ID#: 49-4134726
CLINIC NPI: 4567890123
CHARGES: Office visit $60; blood glucose test $20; venipuncture $6.
Dr. Romero accepts assignment.
Dr. Romero NPI: 2311287891

Fill in the Blank

1. Dependents who are eligible for TRICARE or CHAMPVA are called _____.

2. A(n) _____ is defined as an individual who has served in the armed forces and is honorably discharged.

3. _____ is the term for the active-duty service member.

4. A(n) _____ is a hospital, an institution, or a provider who meets the licensing and certification requirements of TRICARE.

5. Insurance carriers for TRICARE are called _____.

6. The _____ assists beneficiaries and providers with preauthorizations for specific procedures.

7. The _____ allows the billing specialist to retrieve TRICARE pricing information.

8. CHAMPVA is administered through the _____.

9. CHAMPVA is usually the _____ payer for health care services.

10. CHAMPVA requires preauthorization for _____ worth more than $2,000.

Multiple Choice

Circle the correct answer from the choices provided.

1. Under TRICARE Prime, most health services are provided by

   a. a military treatment facility.

   b. the nearest health care provider.

   c. preferred provider organizations.

   d. health maintenance organizations.

2. Individuals enrolled in TRICARE Prime are assigned a

   a. military ID number.

   b. sponsor.

   c. designated health care provider.

   d. primary care manager.

3. TRICARE Extra is

   a. available to all active-duty personnel.

   b. an option available to TRICARE Standard beneficiaries.

   c. a health maintenance organization.

   d. administered by the Office of Veterans Affairs.

4. The DEERS program is

   a. a conservation program managed by the armed services.

   b. a database used to verify TRICARE eligibility.

   c. available to active-duty personnel only.

   d. available to persons who provide services to TRICARE beneficiaries.

5. Cost sharing under TRICARE programs is the same as

   a. deductibles.

   b. coordination of benefits.

   c. Co-payment and co-insurance.

   d. out-of-pocket expenses.

6. Nonparticipating TRICARE providers

   a. are limited in the amount they are allowed to charge.

   b. usually balance-bill the patient.

   c. receive the allowable charge as payment in full.

   d. do not submit insurance claims for TRICARE patients.

7. TRICARE guidelines define "durable medical equipment" by all but one of the following statements:

   a. It improves function.

   b. It retards further deterioration.

   c. It enhances vision and hearing.

   d. It provides a medical function.

8. TRICARE requires preauthorization for all but one of the following procedures:

   a. tonsillectomy

   b. hernia repair

   c. magnetic resonance imaging

   d. chest x-ray

9. Select the condition that is *not* an exception to TRICARE claims submission deadlines.

   a. adequate access to care

   b. provider's statement was lost

   c. retroactive eligibility

   d. primary payer delay

10. TRICARE is secondary to all other insurance plans except

   a. Medicaid.

   b. BC/BS.

   c. Medicare.

   d. Medicare Supplemental Insurance.

True or False

Write True or False on the line following each statement.

1. CHAMPVA is available to active-duty military forces. _____

2. CHAMPVA does not identify participating providers. _____

3. Under TRICARE and CHAMPVA, the beneficiary pays the cost-sharing amount.

   _____

4. Providers who treat TRICARE beneficiaries are obligated by law to accept assignment.

   _____

5. CHAMPVA is available to dependents of permanently disabled veterans. _____

6. Military dependents are covered by TRICARE and CHAMPVA. _____

7. High-cost procedures may require CHAMPVA preauthorization. _____

8. The billing specialist collects the cost-share amount only after receiving TRICARE payment. _____

9. Nonparticipating providers can request payment in full prior to receiving TRICARE payment. _____

10. The beneficiary or the provider is allowed to file CHAMPVA insurance claims.

    _____

CHALLENGE ACTIVITIES

1. Search the Internet for the TRICARE regional office that covers your state. Find the name of the TRICARE contractor for your region. Request a copy of claims filing guidelines from the contractor.

2. Interview a billing specialist at a local physician's office. Ask about the unique problems, if any, associated with TRICARE claims. How does the allowable charge compare with other insurance programs' reimbursement rates?

WEBSITES

CHAMPUS Maximum Allowable Charge (CMAC): www.tricare.mil/CMAC
CHAMPVA: www4.va.gov/hac
Defense Enrollment Eligibility Reporting System: www.tricare.mil
Health Net Federal Services: www.healthnetfederalservices.net
Humana Military Health Care Services: www.humana-military.com
TriWest Healthcare Alliance: www.triwest.com

CHAPTER 15

Workers' Compensation

LEARNING OBJECTIVES

Upon successfully completing this chapter, the reader should have the knowledge to:

1. Define all key terms and abbreviations.
2. Describe four federal workers' compensation programs.
3. Discuss the function and purpose of the Occupational Safety and Health Administration.
4. Compare the four categories of state workers' compensation programs.
5. List the eligibility requirements for workers' compensation benefits.
6. Describe three classifications of work-related injuries.
7. Explain the workers' compensation documentation requirements.
8. Complete the CMS-1500 insurance claim form for workers' compensation.

KEY TERMS

Black Lung Program
Combination program
Commercial workers'
 compensation program
Employer self-insured
 program
Federal Coal Mine Health
 and Safety Act
Federal Employees'
 Compensation Act
 (FECA)
First report of injury

Longshoremen and Harbor
 Workers' Compensation
 Act (LHWCA)
Material safety data sheet
 (MSDS)
Medical claim with no
 disability
Occupational Safety and
 Health Administration
 (OSHA)
Partial disability
Permanent disability

Radionuclides
State compensation board/
 commission
State compensation fund
Temporary disability
Total disability
Vocational rehabilitation
Workers' Compensation
 Law of the District of
 Columbia

OVERVIEW

Workers' compensation laws are designed to ensure that employees who are injured or disabled on the job are provided with wage replacement and medical and rehabilitation benefits. Prior to 1912, a worker who was injured on the job had to sue his or her employer for compensation. In 1912, as a result of a federal government mandate, most states adopted a Workmen's Compensation Act. Over time and with the advent of women entering the workforce, many states changed the name to Workers' Compensation.

The intent of most workers' compensation acts is to establish a system under which a worker no longer has to prove negligence on the part of the employer. Employers covered by workers' compensation acts are required to compensate a worker for any injury suffered on the job, regardless of fault. State compensation acts do not cover all employees or employers. Some states exclude employers with only three to five employees. Temporary employees, babysitters, domestic help, and volunteers may also be excluded.

FEDERAL WORKERS' COMPENSATION PROGRAMS

Until 1908, workers injured on the job simply lost their jobs. Employees bore the full responsibility for on-the-job safety, and employers expressed little if any concern for the health or well-being of their workforce.

In 1908, the federal government instituted the **Federal Employees' Compensation Act (FECA)**, which is still in force today. FECA provides benefits for work-related injuries to all federal employees. Other federal workers' compensation programs include the following:

- **Longshoremen and Harbor Workers' Compensation Act (LHWCA)**, which became effective in 1927 and provides benefits for private or public employees engaged in maritime work nationwide.
- **Workers' Compensation Law of the District of Columbia**, which became effective in 1928 and provides benefits for individuals working in Washington, D.C.
- **Federal Coal Mine Health and Safety Act**, often referred to as the **Black Lung Program**, which became effective in 1941 and provides benefits to coal miners.

Although it is not a workers' compensation act per se, the federal **Occupational Safety and Health Administration (OSHA) Act** of 1970 was enacted to protect employees from injuries resulting from occupational hazards. The act established the federal Occupational Safety and Health Administration and also allowed the states to create an OSHA plan. Once the federal government approves the plan, the state assumes responsibility for carrying out OSHA policies.

OSHA regulations have been updated many times since 1970. The Bloodborne Pathogens Act, passed in the early 1990s, has special significance for health care employees. Any employee who comes into contact with human blood or infectious materials must have specific training in handling such materials and must be offered a hepatitis B vaccination. The employer must maintain comprehensive records of all vaccinations and training program attendance. Figure 15–1 illustrates a training session.

Another amendment that addresses chemicals and hazardous substances also affects the health care industry. OSHA's hazardous-chemical policy mandates that employers must provide employees with the manufacturers' **material safety data sheets (MSDSs)**. An MSDS identifies the risks associated with exposure to specific chemicals or hazardous substances. Physicians and

Donna Mirco

Delmar/Cengage Learning

FIGURE 15-1 Training Session

other health care employers are required to obtain material safety data sheets for each hazardous substance used by the office or health care facility. Examples of hazardous substances include oncology drugs or medications, radiation, and **radionuclides**. Radionuclides are radioactive substances that are used for nuclear imaging or scanning and for treating tumors and cancer.

Compliance with OSHA regulations and guidelines reduces the number of work-related injuries and illnesses.

REINFORCEMENT EXERCISES 15-1

Spell out each abbreviation.

1. FECA

_____

2. LHWCA

_____

3. OSHA

_____

4. MSDS

_____

STATE-SPONSORED WORKERS' COMPENSATION PROGRAMS

Each state has established some type of workers' compensation program. The state, employer, or private insurance companies may assume responsibility for providing benefits to injured workers. State programs usually fall into one of the following categories:

- **State compensation fund:** The state identifies a specific agency to function as the insuring body to cover workers' compensation claims. Employers pay premiums to the state fund.
- **Employer self-insured programs:** Some employers have enough capital and other resources to fund their own workers' compensation program. The employer is obligated by state regulation to set aside a specific percentage of the company's funds to cover medical expenses and wage compensation for work-related injuries.
- **Commercial workers' compensation programs:** Employers purchase insurance policies that provide benefits for injured employees. Commercial workers' compensation programs must meet state regulations and guidelines related to workers' compensation.
- **Combination programs:** Some states allow employers to select a combination of state, employer self-insured, and commercial workers' compensation programs.

In addition to workers' compensation programs and regulations, each state has a **state compensation board** or **commission**. This government agency is responsible for administering state compensation laws and handling appeals related to workers' compensation claims. Both employer and employee have appeal rights if and when either believes the compensation case was not fairly resolved.

WORKERS' COMPENSATION BASICS

Basic workers' compensation information includes eligibility, classification of work-related injuries, disabilities, and documentation requirements.

Eligibility

To qualify for workers' compensation benefits, the employee must:

- Be injured while working within the scope of the employment agreement or job description
- Be injured while performing a service required by the employer
- Develop a disorder that can be directly linked to employment (e.g., asbestosis, mercury poisoning, or black lung disease)

In some states, work-related stress may also be covered by workers' compensation.

A work-related injury does not have to happen at the primary place of employment. Employees injured while traveling on company business, with the exception of sightseeing activities, are eligible for workers' compensation.

Classification of Work-Related Injuries

According to federal regulations, on-the-job or work-related injuries are classified as follows:

- Medical claims with no disability, temporary disability, or permanent disability
- Vocational rehabilitation claims
- Death

Medical Claims With No Disability

Medical claims with no disability are minor injuries that, once treated, permit the employee to continue working or return to work within a few days. Workers' compensation insurance pays for medical treatment and related follow-up. The employee may use sick time for any days off work or the employer may authorize time off with pay.

Temporary Disability

Temporary disability is a disability that can be overcome by medical treatment or retraining. When an employee becomes temporarily disabled because of a work-related injury, workers' compensation covers medical expenses and lost income. Temporary disability ends when the individual is able to return to gainful employment. Compensation for lost income may be as much as two-thirds of the worker's salary.

Permanent Disability

Permanent disability, as applied to workers' compensation, is not the same as medical disability. In fact, many individuals with a medical disability, such as mobility limitations, are valuable and productive employees. Under workers' compensation regulations, permanent disability refers to the individual's ability to return to the position held before the injury or to the workforce in general.

In order to meet the legal or workers' compensation definition of permanent disability, the physician or other health care providers must document that the injury is stabilized and the employee is permanently impaired and unable to return to his or her previous position.

Compensation for permanent disability depends on the following:

- Severity of the injury
- Amount of permanent loss of function
- Age of the employee
- Occupation before the injury
- Rehabilitation potential

Based on an assessment of these factors, permanent disability is divided into two groups:

- **Partial disability**, expressed as a percentage of loss of function
- **Total disability**, defined as 100 percent loss of function

Partial disability is exemplified by the loss of a portion or all of a body part (an arm, a leg, or a hand) or the presence of a neurological disorder that prevents full use of the affected body area. Partial disability is described as a percentage of loss—for example 20 percent loss of the use of a limb or 60 percent loss of memory capacity. When the loss reaches 100 percent, the individual is unable to return to work in any capacity.

Workers' compensation insurance carriers and state compensation commissions have developed specific descriptions related to an employee's diminished capacity. Documentation related to an employee's condition should incorporate these accepted descriptions. Tables 15–1 through 15–3 list the definitions and descriptions associated with the employee's disability.

Vocational Rehabilitation

Vocational rehabilitation claims cover the cost of retraining employees who have suffered some type of on-the-job injury that results in permanent or temporary disability. Retraining allows the employee to return to the workforce but not necessarily to the same occupation or position held before the injury.

TABLE 15–1

Pulmonary Disease, Heart Disease, Abdominal Weakness, or Spinal Disabilities
Disability resulting in limitation to light work: The individual is capable of working in a standing or walking position that demands minimum effort.
Disability precluding heavy work: The individual has lost approximately 50 percent capacity to perform bending, stooping, lifting, pushing, pulling, and climbing activities.
Disability precluding heavy lifting, repeated bending, and stooping: The individual has lost 50 percent capacity to perform the activities listed in the statement.
Disability precluding heavy lifting: The individual has lost 50 percent capacity for lifting.
Disability precluding very heavy work: The individual has lost 25 percent capacity for bending, pulling, climbing, or other comparable activities.
Disability precluding very heavy lifting: The individual has lost 25 percent of lifting capacity.

TABLE 15–2

Disabilities Related to Extremities
Disability resulting in limitation to sedentary work: The individual can work while sitting with minimal demands for physical effort and may do some standing and walking.
Disability resulting in limitation to semi-sedentary work: The individual can work in a position that allows for sitting half the time and standing half the time or walking with minimal demands for physical effort while standing, walking, or sitting.

TABLE 15–3

Disability Related to Pain
Minimal pain: The pain is an annoyance but will not handicap the performance of the individual's work.
Slight pain: The pain is tolerable, but there may be some limitations in performance of assigned duties.
Moderate pain: The pain is tolerable, but there may be marked handicapping of performance.
Severe pain: The individual is excluded from performing any activity that precipitates pain.

Work-Related Death

Work-related deaths are taken very seriously and usually result in an OSHA investigation. Employee death may also result in civil or criminal litigation and substantial financial settlements to the employee's survivors or dependents.

If the work-related death occurs while the employee is traveling for the employer, other insurance programs may contribute to or bear the full burden of settling financial claims for survivors or dependents. Motor vehicle accidents involving a company car, the employee's vehicle while engaging in work-related activities, and another driver may result in all three automobile insurance programs becoming involved in the claim.

Motor vehicle accidents often include assignment of blame. Police officers are called to the scene and assess contributing factors, such as right-of-way, speed, and condition of the driver. If alcohol or substance abuse impaired the employee's driving ability, the employer may contest any financial settlement.

Common carrier or public transportation accidents (e.g., accidents involving airplane, bus, or train travel) that result in employee death while engaged in work-related travel may involve the common carrier's insurance company. Factors such as the health of the pilot or driver, mechanical failure, pilot or driver negligence or reckless behavior, and acts of war or terrorism may limit the employer's insurance liability.

When a work-related death occurs on company property, there is a state or federal OSHA investigation. The purpose of the investigation is to determine all the facts related to the employee's death and to identify ways to prevent similar occurrences in the future.

REINFORCEMENT EXERCISES 15–2

Provide a brief definition for each term.

1. State compensation fund

_____

_____

_____

2. Employer self-insured program

_____

_____

_____

3. Private or commercial workers' compensation programs

_____

_____

_____

4. Combination program

_____

_____

_____

continued on the next page

continued from the previous page

5. State compensation board/commission

_____

_____

_____

Fill in the blank.

1. _____ refers to the individual's ability to return to the job held before the injury.

2. Loss of all or part of a body part is an example of _____.

3. _____ ends when the individual is able to return to gainful employment.

4. Pain that excludes the individual from performing any task that precipitates pain is called _____.

5. _____ pain does not interfere with the individual's work performance.

Workers' Compensation Documentation Requirements

Physicians and providers who treat patients covered by workers' compensation insurance are required to complete and file a **first report of injury** form. A first report of injury form is just what its name says it is: a written report of the initial contact with the patient. The report is distributed as follows:

- The original in the employee's medical record or workers' compensation file
- A copy to the state workers' compensation board or commission
- A copy to the employer-designated workers' compensation insurance carrier
- A copy to the employer

Figure 15–2 is an example of a workers' compensation first report of injury form, which can also be used for progress reports and the final report.

Note that the patient is not required to sign the first report of injury form or to authorize release of work-related injury information to the state board or insurance carrier.

The patient supplies most of the information with particular attention to the following:

- Name and address of the employer
- Name of immediate supervisor
- Date and time of the accident, injury, or onset of disease
- Site or location where the accident or injury occurred
- Patient's description of the circumstances surrounding the work-related problem

The employer must furnish the following information:

- Name and address of the employer's workers' compensation insurance carrier
- Confirmation of the work-related injury

INSTRUCTIONS

1. Type answers to All questions and file original with the Workers' Compensation Commission within 72 hours after first treatment.
2. DO NOT FAIL to forward to the Workers' Compensation Commission PROGRESS REPORTS and FINAL REPORT upon discharge of patient.

DO NOT WRITE IN THIS SPACE

WORKERS' COMPENSATION COMMISSION
6 NORTH LIBERTY STREET, BALTIMORE, MD. 21201-3785
SURGEON'S REPORT

WCC CLAIM #

EMPLOYER'S REPORT Yes ☐ No ☐

This is First Report ☒   **Progress Report** ☐   **Final Report** ☐

1. Name of Injured Person: Maureen A. Santega	Soc. Sec. No. 610-98-7432	D.O.B. 7/19/69	Sex M ☐ F ☑

2. Address: (No. and Street) 905 Raymond Lane	(City or Town) Atlanta	(State) GA	(Zip Code) 30385-8893

3. Name and Address of Employer:
Majors Concrete Company, 238 Leaf Lane, Atlanta GA 30342-3329

4. Date of Accident or Onset of Disease: 4/9/YY	Hour: A.M. ☑ P.M. ☐	5. Date Disability Began: 4/9/YY

6. Patient's Description of Accident or Cause of Disease:
Concrete truck struck and backed over patient's foot while she was pouring concrete at the job site

7. Medical description of Injury or Disease:

massive bruising to left foot, no broken bones, great deal of pain associated with bruises

8. Will Injury result in:
(a) Permanent defect?   Yes ☐   No ☑   If so, what?   (b) Disfigurement   Yes ☐   No ☑

9. Causes, other than injury, contributing to patients condition:
None

10. Is patient suffering from any disease of the heart, lungs, brain, kidneys, blood, vascular system or any other disabling condition not due to this accident?
Give particulars: No

11. Is there any history or evidence present of previous accident or disease? Give particulars:
No

12. Has normal recovery been delayed for any reason? Give particulars:
No

13. Date of first treatment: 4/10/YY	Who engaged your services? Patient

14. Describe treatment given by you:
Darvon, 100 mg q4h prn for pain

15. Were X-Rays taken: Yes ☑ No ☐	By whom? — (Name and Address) Edwin Gordon, M.D. 802 Manor Lane, Atlanta, GA 30303	Date 4/10/—

16. X-Ray Diagnosis:
No broken bones

17. Was patient treated by anyone else? Yes ☐ No ☑	By whom? — (Name and Address)	Date

18. Was patient hospitalized? Yes ☐ No ☑	Name and Address of Hospital	Date of Admission: Date of Discharge:

19. Is further treatment needed? Yes ☐ No ☑	For how long?	20. Patient was ☑ will be ☐ able to resume regular work on: 4/14 Patient was ☐ will be ☐ able to resume light work on:

21. If death ensued give date:	22. Remarks: (Give any information of value not included above)

23. I am a qualified specialist in: orthopedics	I am a duly licensed Physician in the State of: Maryland	I was graduated from Medical School (Name) Johns Hopkins	Year 1967

Date of this report: 6/21/YY   (Signed) *John N. Sparks, M.D.*

8504 Capricorn Drive Atlanta, GA 30312   (This report must be signed PERSONALLY by Physician)
Address: Phone: (404) 544-0078

EVERY QUESTION MUST BE ANSWERED AND FORM SIGNED

FIGURE 15–2 First Report of Injury

Under all circumstances, whether the employer agrees that the problem is work-related or not, the provider should file the first report of injury.

The provider's staff must be aware that, by law, the state workers' compensation board or commission and the designated insurance carrier are entitled only to information about the patient's work-related injury. Any other patient information must not be released, even inadvertently, to either of these two entities.

Progress Reports

The physician must file progress reports during the course of treating the patient. Progress reports include enough detail to clearly describe the patient's progress and any significant change in medical or disability status. The first report of injury form may be used for progress reports or the physician may provide the information in narrative form.

The progress report must include the following information:

- Patient's name and workers' compensation file or case number
- Treatment and progress report
- Work status at the time of the report
- Statement of continued need for treatment and the type of treatment
- Estimate of patient status regarding return to work, disability, or loss of function
- Copies of x-ray, laboratory, or consultation reports related to treatment and progress

The physician signs the report and all copies. The original report is maintained in the patient's record, and a copy is sent to the insurance carrier.

Reimbursement and CMS-1500 Completion

The physician or provider must accept the workers' compensation allowable fee as payment in full for covered services. There is no deductible or co-payment for workers' compensation cases. Workers' compensation claims are submitted via the CMS-1500 form. Completion instructions for the CMS-1500 are presented in two sections: blocks 1–13 and blocks 14–33. Refer to Figure 15–3 for blocks 1–13 and Figure 15–4 for blocks 14–33.

Block 1	Enter an X in the FECA box for all work-related injury claims.
Block 1a	First claim: Enter the patient's Social Security number. Subsequent claims: Enter the insurance carrier's assigned claim number or the patient's Social Security number.
Block 2	Enter the patient's name as directed.
Block 3	Enter the patient's eight-digit birth date (MM/DD/YYYY), and check the appropriate box for gender.
Block 4	Enter the name of the employer at the time of injury. Note: This block may be left blank.
Block 5	Enter the patient's home address and phone number.
Block 6	Enter an X in Other.

continued on the next page

continued from the previous page

Block 7	Enter the employer's address and phone number, if known.
Block 8	Leave the patient's marital status blank. Enter an X in Employed.
Blocks 9–9d	Leave this blank.
Blocks 10–10c	Enter an X in Yes for block 10a. Enter an X in Yes or No in box 10b and 10c, as appropriate.
Block 10d	Leave this blank.
Block 11	Enter the workers' compensation insurance carrier's claim number, if known. Otherwise, leave this blank.
Block 11a	Leave this blank.
Block 11b	Enter the employer's name.
Block 11c	Enter the workers' compensation insurance carrier.
Block 11d	Leave this blank.
Block 12	Leave this blank. The patient's signature is not required for workers' compensation claims.
Block 13	Leave this blank.

Review Figure 15–3 for completed blocks 1–13.

FIGURE 15–3 CMS-1500, Blocks 1–13 (For instructional use only. Courtesy of the Centers for Medicare and Medicaid Services, www.cms.hhs.gov)

Block 14	Enter the date the symptoms started or the injury occurred.
Block 15	Enter the date the provider first rendered services for this injury, if available or applicable.
Block 16	Enter the dates as directed.
Block 17	Enter the name and title of any referring health care provider, if applicable.
Block 17a	Leave this blank.
Block 17b	Enter the NPI of the provider named in block 17.
Block 18	Enter the hospitalization dates, if applicable.
Block 19	Leave this blank.
Block 20	Enter an X in Yes or No. Enter the total charges, if applicable.
Block 21	Enter up to four ICD-9-CM diagnostic codes in order of priority.
Block 22	Leave this blank.
Block 23	Enter any assigned managed care preauthorization number.
Block 24A	Enter the month, day, and year (MM/DD/YYYY) in the From column. Do not enter the To date unless the insurance carrier requests it.
Block 24B	Enter the place of service code.
Block 24C	Leave this blank.
Block 24D	Enter CPT codes or HCPCS codes and modifiers, as applicable.
Block 24E	Enter the diagnosis reference code from block 21 that best proves the medical necessity for each service listed in block 24D.
Block 24F	Enter the charge for the service identified in each line.
Block 24G	Enter the days or units for each line item. Enter 1 if only one service is provided. This block should be used for multiple visits for identical services, the number of miles, the units of supplies, or the oxygen volume.
Block 24H	Leave this blank.
Block 24I	Shaded area: Leave this blank.
Block 24J	Enter the NPI of the physician who provided the service.
Block 25	Enter the provider's employer federal tax ID number (EIN). If there is not one, enter the provider's Social Security number. Enter an X in the appropriate box.
Block 26	Enter the patient's account number, if one is assigned by the provider.
Block 27	Leave this blank.

continued on the next page

continued from the previous page

Block 28	Enter the total charges.
Blocks 29–30	Leave this blank.
Block 31	Provider's signature or SIGNATURE ON FILE and date
Block 32	Enter the name, address, city, state, and ZIP code of the place services were provided.
Block 32a	Enter the NPI for the entity named in block 32.
Block 33	Enter the name, complete address, and telephone number of the billing entity.
Block 33a	Enter the NPI of the entity named in block 33. For a solo practitioner, enter the physician's NPI. For a group-practice practitioner, enter the NPI of the group practice.
Block 33b	Leave blank.

Review Figure 15–4 for completed blocks 14–33.

FIGURE 15–4 CMS-1500, Blocks 14–33 (For instructional use only. Courtesy of the Centers for Medicare and Medicaid Services, www.cms.hhs.gov)

ABBREVIATIONS

Table 15–4 lists the abbreviations in this chapter.

TABLE 15–4

Abbreviations and Meanings	
Abbreviation	Meaning
FECA	Federal Employees' Compensation Act
LHWCA	Longshoremen and Harbor Workers' Compensation Act
MSDS	material safety data sheet
OSHA	Occupational Safety and Health Administration

SUMMARY

Workers' compensation insurance is intended to ensure that employees who are injured or disabled on the job are provided with wage replacement and medical and rehabilitation benefits. A federal mandate issued in 1912 directed each state to establish a Workers' Compensation Act that established a system for providing these benefits. There are several federal workers' compensation programs that cover employees who work in the maritime industry, in Washington, D.C., or in the coal mining industry. State-sponsored workers' compensation programs may be managed by the state, the employer, private insurance companies, or a combination of these groups.

Workers' compensation programs identify various levels of disability, ranging from temporary to permanent. Permanent disability is further categorized as partial or total disability. Vocational rehabilitation is an important part of workers' compensation.

REVIEW EXERCISES

Case Study

Read the following case study and then complete a CMS-1500 by using the workers' compensation guidelines in this chapter. Your instructor will tell you how to obtain the form.
PATIENT NAME: Dennis Wood
DOB: 11/11/1960
SSN: 492-61-0830
ADDRESS: 80 Visitor Drive; Blueberry, ME 49855
PHONE: (H) (906) 302-9090
EMPLOYER: Painting Place, 40 Industrial Drive, Blueberry, ME 49855
INSURANCE: Workers' Compensation, State Insurance Fund, 300 Capital Ave., Capital ME 42212.
FECA NUMBER: WCF555000

continued on the next page

continued from the previous page

PROGRESS NOTE
DATE: 01/05/20YY
Mr. Wood is seen today for injuries sustained as a result of a fall from a ladder while painting the window trim on a building. He sustained a closed fracture of the left radius and multiple abrasions on the arms and face. X-rays revealed a Colles's fracture of the left radius that was reduced and a plaster cast applied. He will be unable to work for six weeks. No permanent disability is anticipated. Mr. Wood will return tomorrow for a cast check. A first report of injury was completed.
SIGNED: Denzel Hamilton, MD
Superiorland Clinic
714 Hennepin Ave.
Blueberry, ME 49855
PHONE: (906) 336-4020
Superiorland Clinic NPI: 4567890123
Denzel Hamilton NPI: 5567890123
DIAGNOSIS AND TREATMENT CODES: Colles's fracture 813.41; abrasion, arms 913.0; abrasion, face 910.0; office visit 99214; forearm x-ray 73090; closed reduction of Colles's fracture 25600; application of plaster cast 29085.
CHARGES: Office visit $75; closed reduction of fracture $200; application of plaster cast $50; x-ray forearm $60.

Fill in the Blank

1. The _____ provides benefits for employees engaged in maritime work.

2. The Black Lung Program is another name for the _____.

3. _____ work is defined as work while sitting with minimal demands for physical effort.

4. _____ work is defined as work in a position that allows for sitting half the time and standing or walking half the time.

Multiple Choice

Circle the correct answer from the choices provided.

1. Which act is *not* a workers' compensation program?

    a. FECA

    b. LHWCA

    c. Black Lung Program

    d. OSHA

2. An employer self-insured workers' compensation program

   a. sets aside a percentage of the company's financial resources to cover the medical expenses of injured employees.

   b. combines state and federal money for injured employees.

   c. identifies a specific agency to function as an insuring body.

   d. purchases insurance policies from private companies.

3. To qualify for workers' compensation benefits, the employee must

   a. file for benefits within 30 days of the injury.

   b. be injured while working within the scope of the employment agreement.

   c. document the reason the injury occurred.

   d. file a first report of injury form.

4. Under workers' compensation guidelines, permanent disability

   a. is the same as a medical disability.

   b. means the employee will never return to work.

   c. is dependent on the age of the employee.

   d. must be reevaluated on an annual basis.

5. A first report of injury form is completed by the

   a. employer.

   b. employee.

   c. physician.

   d. billing specialist.

6. Compensation for permanent disability depends on all but one of the following:

   a. Assessment by an independent physician

   b. Age of the employee

   c. Amount of loss of function

   d. Occupation before the injury occurred

7. Eligibility for workers' compensation depends primarily on the

   a. occupation of the employee.

   b. location of the injury.

   c. age of the employee.

   d. relationship of the injury to the job.

8. Black lung disease is an example of a

    a. hazard associated with coal mining.

    b. disorder that is directly linked to employment.

    c. temporary disability.

    d. permanent disability.

CHALLENGE ACTIVITIES

1. Search the Internet for your state's workers' compensation information. Print the guidelines for eligibility.
2. Interview a billing specialist at a local physician's office. Ask about the unique problems, if any, associated with workers' compensation claims.

WEBSITES

Federal Employees' Compensation Act (FECA): www.dol.gov
Occupational Safety and Health Administration (OSHA): www.osha.gov
Workers' Compensation: www.workerscompensation.com

Superiorland Clinic Practice Manual

INTRODUCTION

This practice simulation is intended to provide you with insurance billing application exercises. In order to complete the exercises, you need the following references:

- The *Superiorland Clinic Practice Manual* that is included in this appendix
- Instructions for completing the CMS-1500 and the UB-04, which are included in the textbook
- ICD-9-CM and CPT coding references
- SimClaim student practice software, free with this textbook

Review the *Superiorland Clinic Practice Manual* before you attempt the exercises.

SUPERIORLAND CLINIC PRACTICE MANUAL

Welcome to Superiorland Clinic! You have recently been hired as an insurance billing specialist. The clinic sees a variety of patients and accepts commercial, private, and government insurance programs. Superiorland prides itself on providing excellent patient care while adhering to all insurance billing regulations.

This is an exciting time to begin your career! We recently upgraded our electronic billing software, so all of us are learning something new. More than 90% of all our insurance claims are filed electronically. Of course, there are challenges associated with electronic billing that may cause frustration. Keep in mind that no system is perfect, and if you are having problems with the software, ask your supervisor for help.

Superiorland Clinic Insurance Information

All physicians who practice at Superiorland Clinic are participating providers for Medicare, Medicaid, TRICARE, and Blue Cross/Blue Shield. Essential insurance billing information is given here.

Billing name:	Superiorland Clinic
Address:	714 Hennepin Ave.
	Blueberry, ME 49855
Phone:	(906) 336-4600
Fax:	(906) 336-4020
EIN/Tax ID:	49-4134726
NPI (National Provider Identification)	4567890123

Clinic Physicians

There are six physicians in group practice at Superiorland Clinic. In addition, four family practice physicians refer patients to the general surgeons and internists.

Superiorland Clinic Physicians

CHARLES FRENCH, M.D.		ROBERT HOWARD, M.D.	
Internal Medicine		Family Practice	
SSN	123 45 6789	SSN	234 56 7890
NPI	2345678901	NPI	3456789012

DENZEL HAMILTON, M.D.		ROBERTA PHARYNGEAL, M.D.	
General Surgery		Family Practice	
SSN	345 67 8901	SSN	456 78 9012
NPI	5567890123	NPI	5678901234

HENRY ROMERO, M.D.		ELIZABETH FOY, M.D.	
General Surgery		Internal Medicine	
SSN	567 89 0123	SSN	678 90 1234
NPI	2311287891	NPI	7890123456

Referring Physicians

MARK BECKWITH, M.D.		RACHEL SHASKI, M.D.	
EIN	22-234596	EIN	33-345607
NPI	1357913579	NPI	2468024680

JESSICA YOHA, M.D.		WADE MORRISON, M.D.	
EIN	44-4567718	EIN	55-567829
NPI	1245780134	NPI	1215194805

Blueberry Community Hospital Information

Superiorland Clinic physicians admit patients to Blueberry Community Hospital.

Name:	Blueberry Community Hospital
Address:	418 Treatment Drive
	Blueberry, ME 49855
Phone:	(906) 312-9446
Fax:	(906) 312-8557
NPI:	0520194812

Place of Service Codes

Place of Service Codes for Superiorland Clinic are listed in Table A–1. Use these codes, as required, for CMS-1500 and UB-04 completion.

TABLE A–1: Place of Service Codes

Place of Service Codes			
Location	Code	Location	Code
Provider's office	11	Patient's home	12
Inpatient hospital	21	Outpatient hospital	22
Emergency room hospital	23	Ambulatory surgery center	24
Birthing center	25	Military treatment facility	26
Skilled nursing facility	31	Nursing home	32

Insurance Companies with PAYER ID and COBA ID Numbers

Insurance company PAYER ID and COBA ID Numbers are listed in Table A–2. COBA ID numbers consist of five digits and begin with the number 5.

TABLE A–2: Insurance carriers with PAYER ID and COBA ID Numbers

Insurance Carriers with PAYER ID and COBA ID Number			
Company	Number	Company	Number
Aetna	226543712	Medicaid	112345671
Aetna Medigap	50505	Metropolitan	312346782
American Life	772345003	Metropolitan Medigap	52727
Blue Cross/Blue Shield	4456712	Prudential	512556782
Blue Cross/Blue Shield Medigap	51616	Teacher's Health	001133232
Government Employee Plan	782345112	Union Health	991123452
LEXCO Homeowner Insurance	893456223	County Compensation (Workers' comp)	512556782

Evaluation and Management Fee Schedule

Superiorland Clinic's CPT codes and fee schedule for evaluation and management services are listed in Table A–3.

TABLE A–3: Evaluation and Management CPT Codes and Fees.

Evaluation/Management Codes and Fees			
Office Visit—New Patient		**Office Visit—Established Patient**	
99201	40.00	99211	30.00
99202	50.00	99212	40.00
99203	60.00	99213	50.00
99204	70.00	99214	60.00
99205	90.00	99215	80.00
Office Consultation Service		**Hospital Inpatient Services**	
99241	40.00	99223	70.00
99242	50.00	99231	40.00

TABLE A–3 Continued

99243	60.00	**Emergency Department Services**	
99244	70.00	99281	60.00
99245	80.00	99282	70.00
		99283	80.00
		99284	90.00
		99285	100.00

Diagnostic Test, Treatment, and Procedure Fees

Diagnostic tests, treatments, and procedure fees are listed in Table A–4.

TABLE A–4: Diagnostic Test, Treatment, and Procedure Fees

Diagnostic Test, Treatment, and Procedure Fees			
Diagnostic Test	**Fee**	**Treatment**	**Fee**
A/P/chest x-ray	45.00	Flu shot	25.00
DXA scan	145.00	Pneumovax	30.00
EKG int. & report	65.00	**Procedure**	**Fee**
Rhythm EKG	45.00	Appendectomy	1,000.00
Holter 24 Hr	170.00	Cholangiogram	270.00
Sigmoidoscopy	195.00	Cholecystectomy, laproscopic	1,300.00
Stress test	170.00	Fistulectomy, fistula repair	345.00
		Hemorrhoidectomy	395.00

Laboratory Test Fees

Laboratory test fees are listed in Table A–5.

TABLE A–5: Laboratory Test Fees

Laboratory Test Fees			
Laboratory Test	**Fee**	**Laboratory Test**	**Fee**
AST (cardiac enzyme)	25.00	Hepatitis panel	45.00
Albumin	20.00	Lipid panel	45.00
Alk phos	20.00	Metabolic panel	25.00
BUN	25.00	Obstetric panel	25.00
Blood culture	40.00	Occult blood, fecal	35.00
CBC	30.00	PAP (prostate)	45.00
CBC/diff	35.00	PAP smear	45.00
CK/CPK (cardiac)	25.00	PPD skin test	20.00
Drug screen	40.00	PSA	35.00
Electrolyte panel	35.00	Rapid strep screen	25.00

Laboratory Test	Fee	Laboratory Test	Fee
Epstein-Barr titer	54.00	Sed rate	25.00
Glucose	25.00	TSH	35.00
GTT	50.00	Urine culture	40.00
HgbA1C	40.00	Urinalysis	15.00
HIV screen	50.00	Wet mount	40.00

CMS-1500 QUICK REFERENCE GUIDELINES

The Quick Reference Guidelines provided by our clearinghouse for electronic claims submission has the information you need to complete the CMS-1500 for the cases assigned to you.

BC/BS CMS-1500 Guidelines (Chapter 11)

Block 1	Enter X in Other.
Block 1a	Subscriber's ID number
Block 2	Patient's name
Block 3	Eight-digit birth date; M or F
Block 4	Name of the insured
Block 5	Enter the patient's mailing address and telephone number
Block 6	Enter X in Self, Spouse, Child. Unmarried domestic partner, use Other
Block 7	Enter the insured's (subscriber's/enrollee's) address and phone number
Block 8	Enter an X to indicate the patient's marital status. Unmarried domestic partner, use Other
Blocks 9–9d	Leave this blank or complete these blocks when there is a secondary payer
Blocks 10a–10c	Yes or No. For 10b (auto accident), enter the two-character abbreviation for the state where the accident occurred
Block 10d	Leave this blank.
Block 11	Enter the insurance group number.
Block 11a	Enter the subscriber's eight-digit date of birth. Enter an X in M or F.
Block 11b	Leave this blank.
Block 11c	Enter the name of the insurance plan and the state (i.e., BCBS MI).
Block 11d	Enter an X in YES if there is another health insurance plan. If YES, complete blocks 9 through 9d. Enter an X in NO if there is only one insurance.
Block 12	Enter SIGNATURE ON FILE and MM DD YY.
Block 13	Enter SIGNATURE ON FILE.
Block 14	Eight-digit date of service
Block 15	Enter an eight-digit date, if applicable. Otherwise, leave this blank.
Block 16	Enter an eight-digit date, if applicable.
Block 17	First name, last name, middle initial, and credential of referring physician/provider
Block 17a	Leave this blank.
Block 17b	Referring physician's NPI
Block 18	Eight-digit hospital admission and discharge dates, if applicable
Block 19	Leave this blank.
Block 20	Enter an X in the NO box if all laboratory services reported on the claim were performed in the provider's office. Enter an X in the YES box if laboratory services were performed by an outside laboratory. Enter the total amount charged by the outside laboratory.

Block 21, 1–4	Enter ICD-9-CM diagnosis codes. First-listed diagnosis entered in 1.
Block 22	Leave this block blank for these claims.
Block 23	Enter Prior Authorization Number. If none, leave blank.
Block 24A	Eight-digit date(s). Enter the date in the FROM column. If the service was performed on consecutive days during a range of dates, enter an eight-digit date in the TO column.
Block 24B	Two-digit place-of-service code
Block 24C	Enter Y for YES if the service was an emergency; otherwise, leave this blank.
Block 24D	CPT/HCPCS code; modifier(s) if necessary
Block 24E	Enter reference number from block 21, 1–4, for the diagnosis code that best justifies the services identified in 24D.
Block 24F	Total charges for services in each line
Block 24G	Number of services provided in each line
Block 24H	Leave this blank. *Applies to Medicaid EPSDT claims only.*
Block 24I	Leave the shaded area blank. The unshaded area has NPI preprinted.
Block 24J	Leave the shaded area blank. Enter the physician's 10-digit NPI number in the unshaded area.
Block 25	Superiorland Clinic's EIN number: 494134726
Block 26	Patient's account number or leave blank
Block 27	Yes
Block 28	Total charges of all services in lines 1 through 6
Block 29	Amount paid by patient
Block 30	Difference between block 28 and block 29
Block 31	Provider's name and credential (i.e., LETITIA JOHNSON MD); date the claim was filed/completed
Block 32	Enter the facility name and address where procedures or services were provided.
Block 32a	NPI of agency named in block 32
Block 32b	Leave this blank.
Block 33	Superiorland Clinic's name, address, and phone number
Block 33a	Superiorland Clinic's NPI: 4567890123
Block 33b	Leave this blank.

Commercial Claims Guidelines (Chapter 8)

Commercial claims include all insurance companies *except* BC/BS, Medicare, Medicaid, TRICARE, and Workers' Compensation.

Block 1	Enter X in Other.
Block 1a	Insured's ID number
Block 2	Patient's name
Block 3	Eight-digit birth date; M, F, or leave blank
Block 4	Name of the insured
Block 5	Patient's address and phone number
Block 6	Enter X in Self, Spouse, or Child. Use Other if the patient is the unmarried domestic partner of the insured.
Block 7	Even if the insured's address is the same as the patient's, reenter the address in block 7 for these claims. SimClaim will not accept 'SAME' or 'SAME AS.'
Block 8	Enter X in appropriate box(es). Use Other if the patient is the unmarried domestic partner of the insured.
Blocks 9–9d	Leave this blank or complete this when there is another insurance company.
Block 9	Other insured's name

Block 9a	Other insured's ID number
Block 9b	Eight-digit birth date; M or F
Block 9c	Employer's name; or name of school
Block 9d	Insurance company name (e.g., AETNA) and group number
Blocks 10a–10c	Yes or No. If Yes is the answer for 10B (auto accident), enter the two-character abbreviation of the state where the accident occurred.
Block 10d	Leave this blank.
Block 11	Enter insurance group number of the insured (named in block 4).
Block 11a	Insured's eight-digit birth date; M or F
Block 11b	Employer/school name
Block 11c	Insurance company/carrier name (e.g., AETNA)
Block 11d	YES, if there is another insurance company; otherwise, NO. (If YES, complete blocks 9-9d.)
Block 12	SIGNATURE ON FILE
Block 13	SIGNATURE ON FILE
Block 14	Eight-digit date of service
Block 15	Eight-digit date, if applicable. Otherwise, leave this blank.
Block 16	Eight-digit date, if applicable. Otherwise, leave this blank.
Block 17	First name, last name, middle initial (if known), and credential of the referring physician/provider
Block 17a	Leave this blank.
Block 17b	NPI of the individual named in block 17
Block 18	Eight-digit hospital admission and discharge dates
Block 19	Leave this blank.
Block 20	Enter an X in NO if all lab work was done in the provider's office. Enter an X in YES if lab work was sent to an outside agency. (Outside lab is identified in block 32.)
Block 21, 1–4	ICD-9-CM diagnosis codes. First-listed diagnosis entered in 1.
Block 22	Leave this blank.
Block 23	Prior authorization number or leave blank
Block 24A	Eight-digit date(s). Same-day services, enter the date in From
Block 24B	Two-digit place-of-service code
Block 24C	Enter Y for Yes if the treatment was an emergency. Otherwise, leave this blank.
Block 24D	CPT/HCPCS code; modifier(s) if necessary
Block 24E	Enter reference number from block 21, 1–4, for the diagnosis code that best justifies the services identified in 24d.
Block 24F	Total charges for services in each line
Block 24G	Number of services provided in each line
Block 24H	Leave blank for these claims.
Block 24I	Leave the shaded area blank. NPI is preprinted in the unshaded area.
Block 24J	Leave the shaded area blank. In the unshaded area, enter the physician's NPI.
Block 25	Superiorland Clinic's Tax ID No.: 494134726. Enter an X in EIN.
Block 26	Enter the patient's account number or leave this blank.
Block 27	Yes
Block 28	Total charges of all services in lines 1 through 6
Block 29	Enter the amount paid by the patient or another insurance plan. Otherwise, leave this blank.
Block 30	Enter the difference between block 28 and block 29.
Block 31	SIGNATURE ON FILE
Block 32	Enter the facility name and address where procedures or services were provided.

Block 32a	NPI of facility named in block 32
Block 32b	Leave this blank.
Block 33	Superiorland Clinic's name, address, and phone number
Block 33a	Superiorland Clinic's NPI (4567890123)
Block 33b	Leave this blank.

Medicare Guidelines (Chapter 12)

Note that the guidelines for Medicare claims include requirements for Medicare as the primary payer, Medicare as the secondary payer, Medicare with Medigap, and Medicare-Medicaid crossover claims.

When Medicare is the secondary payer, a claim is first submitted to the primary insurance carrier. After payment is received, submit a claim to the Medicare administrative contractor (MAC).

Because Superiorland physicians are participating providers, Medigap claims are electronically transmitted from the MAC to the Medigap insurance carrier.

When a patient qualifies for both Medicare and Medicaid, the claim is submitted to the MAC. The MAC electronically transmits insurance claim information to the Medicaid insurance carrier.

Medicare as Primary Payer

Block 1	Enter X in Medicare.
Block 1a	Enter the patient's Medicare health insurance claim number (HICN).
Block 2	Enter the patient's last name, first name, and middle initial.
Block 3	Eight-digit birth date; M or F
Block 4	Leave this blank.
Block 5	Patient's address, phone number, and ZIP code
Block 6	Enter 'X' if patient's relationship to insured is self, spouse, child. Otherwise, use 'Other.'
Block 7	Even if the insured's address is the same as the patient's, reenter the address in block 7 for these claims. SimClaim will not accept 'SAME' or 'SAME AS.'
Block 8	Married, if married; Single, if single, divorced, or widowed; Employed, if employed; student status, if applicable
Blocks 9–9d	Complete these blocks if there is a secondary payer; otherwise, leave blank.
Blocks 10a–10c	Enter No. When the illness or injury is the result of an accident, the insurance company that applies to the accident must be billed first.
Block 10d	Leave this blank.
Block 11	Leave this blank.
Blocks 11a–11d	Leave this blank.
Block 12	Enter SIGNATURE ON FILE and MM DD YY.
Block 13	Enter SIGNATURE ON FILE.
Block 14	Eight-digit date of service
Block 15	Leave this blank.
Block 16	Eight-digit dates for time patient is unable to work, if applicable
Block 17	Enter the last name, first name, middle initial of referring physician/provider.
Block 17a	Leave this blank.
Block 17b	Enter NPI of referring/ordering physician listed in block 17.
Block 18	Eight-digit hospital admission and discharge dates, if applicable
Block 19	Leave this blank.
Block 20	Enter NO.
Block 21, 1–4	Enter ICD-9-CM diagnosis codes. Primary or first-listed diagnosis entered in 1.

Block 22	Leave this blank.
Block 23	Leave this blank.
Block 24A	Enter eight-digit date(s) in From and To.
Block 24B	Two-digit place-of-service code
Block 24C	Leave this blank.
Block 24D	Enter CPT/HCPCS code; modifier(s) if necessary.
Block 24E	Enter reference number from block 21, 1–4, for the diagnosis code that best justifies the services identified in 24D.
Block 24F	Enter the total charges for services in each line. Do not use dollar signs or decimal points.
Block 24G	Enter the number of services provided in each line.
Block 24H	Leave this blank.
Block 24I	Enter 1C in shaded portion.
Block 24J	Enter NPI of physician who performed the service in unshaded area. Leave shaded area blank.
Block 25	Enter Superiorland Clinic's Tax ID No.: 49-4134726 (include the hyphen); check EIN.
Block 26	Enter patient account number, if applicable. Otherwise, leave this blank.
Block 27	Yes
Block 28	Enter the total charges of all services in lines 1 through 6.
Block 29	Enter the total amount the patient paid (i.e., co-payment or deductible).
Block 30	Leave this blank.
Block 31	Enter Provider name and credentials if applicable, otherwise SIGNATURE ON FILE, MM DD YY.
Block 32	Enter the name and address for the place where services were provided (either Superiorland Clinic or Blueberry Hospital).
Block 32a	Enter NPI of location in block 32.
Block 32b	Leave this blank.
Block 33	Enter Superiorland Clinic's name, address, area code and phone number.
Block 33a	Enter Superiorland Clinic's NPI number: 4567890123.
Block 33b	Leave this blank.

Medicare Primary Payer with Medigap Insurance

Blocks 1–8	No change from Medicare as primary payer
Block 9	Enter SAME if the patient is the Medigap insured. Enter last name, first name, and middle initial of the Medigap insured if the name is different from the name in block 2.
Block 9a	Enter MEDIGAP followed by the policy number. Enter group number if there is a group number.
Block 9b	Enter the Medigap insured's eight-digit birth date. Enter an X in M or F.
Block 9c	Leave this blank.
Block 9d	Enter the COBRA Medigap ID number (a five-digit number beginning with a 5).
Blocks 10–12	No change from Medicare as primary payer
Block 13	SIGNATURE ON FILE
Blocks 14–33	No change from Medicare as primary payer

Medicare-Medicaid Crossover Claims

Block 1	Enter an X in one box for the primary carrier being filed.
Blocks 1a–10c	No change from Medicare as primary payer
Block 10d	Enter MCD and the patient's Medicaid ID number.

Blocks 11–26	No change from Medicare as primary payer
Block 27	Enter an X in YES.
Blocks 28–33b	No change from Medicare as primary payer

Medicaid Guidelines (Chapter 13)

Note that the guidelines for Medicaid claims include requirements for Medicaid as the primary or secondary payer. Medicaid is billed as the secondary payer only when the primary payer denies payment, reimbursement from the primary payer is less than the Medicaid payment, or Medicaid covers services not covered by the primary payer.

Block 1	Enter X for Medicaid.
Block 1a	Enter the patient's Medicaid identification number.
Block 2	Enter the patient's name as directed.
Block 3	Eight-digit birth date; M or F
Block 4	If Medicaid is the only payer, leave this blank.
	If Medicaid is the secondary payer: Enter the name of the person who has the primary insurance policy (last name, first name, middle initial). Do NOT use 'SAME'.
Block 5	Patient's address, phone number, and ZIP code
Block 6	If Medicaid is the only payer, leave this blank. When block 4 is completed, enter an X in the box that describes the patient's relationship to the individual named in block 4.
Block 7	Leave this blank.
Block 8	Enter an X in the box that describes the patient's marital status and whether the patient is employed or a student.
Blocks 9a–9d	Leave this blank.
Blocks 10a–10c	Enter No. When the illness or injury is the result of an accident, the insurance company that applies to the accident must be billed first.
Block 10d	Leave this blank.
Blocks 11–11d	If Medicaid is the only payer, leave this blank.
	When Medicaid is the secondary payer, complete 11–11d.
Block 11	Enter the insured's policy or group number or Medicare Health Insurance (HIC) number.
Block 11a	When the insured is not the patient, enter the insured's eight-digit birth date and an X appropriate gender. When the insured is the patient, leave this blank.
Block 11b	Enter the employer's name or school name, if applicable.
Block 11c	Enter the complete insurance plan or program name.
Block 11d	Enter an X in NO.
Block 12	Enter SIGNATURE ON FILE, MM DD YY.
Block 13	Enter SIGNATURE ON FILE.
Block 14	Enter the eight-digit date, as appropriate.
Blocks 15, 16	Leave this blank.
Block 17	Enter the first name, last name, middle initial, and professional credentials (e.g., MD) of the referring physician/provider.
Block 17a	Leave this blank.
Block 17b	Enter the NPI of the individual named in block 17.
Block 18	Eight-digit hospital admission and discharge dates, if services were provided in a hospital and referenced on the claim.
Block 19	Leave this blank.
Block 20	Leave this blank.

Block 21, 1–4	Enter ICD-9-CM diagnosis codes. Primary or first-listed diagnosis code is entered in 1.
Block 22	Leave this blank. If the claim is a Medicaid resubmission, enter the resubmission code.
Block 23	Leave this blank. If prior authorization is required, enter the authorization number.
Block 24A	Enter the eight-digit date(s) of service in the From and To column.
Block 24B	Two-digit place-of-service code
Block 24C	Enter Y for emergency services. Enter N for nonemergency services.
Block 24D	Enter CPT/HCPCS codes, with modifier(s) if necessary.
Block 24E	Enter reference number from block 21, 1–4, for the diagnosis that best justifies the services identified in 24D.
Block 24F	Enter the total charges for services listed on each line.
Block 24G	Enter the number of services provided. If only one service is provided, enter 1.
Block 24H	Leave this blank.
Block 24I	Shaded area: Leave this blank. The unshaded area is preprinted NPI.
Block 24J	Shaded area: Leave this blank.
	Unshaded area: Enter the physician's NPI.
Block 25	Enter Superiorland Clinic's Tax ID No.: 494134726; enter an X in EIN.
Block 26	Enter the patient's account number or leave this blank.
Block 27	Enter an X in Yes.
Block 28	Enter the total charges of all services in lines 1 through 6.
Block 29	Leave this blank.
Block 30	Enter the difference between block 28 and block 29.
Block 31	Enter provider name and credential, or SIGNATURE ON FILE and MM DD YY.
Block 32	Enter the name and address of the location where services and procedures were performed.
Block 32a	NPI for the location where services and procedures were performed.
Block 32b	Leave this blank.
Block 33	Superiorland Clinic's name, address, area code, and phone number
Block 33a	NPI for Superiorland Clinic: 4567890123.
Block 33b	Leave this blank.

TRICARE and CHAMPVA Guidelines (Chapter 14)

Note that the guidelines include requirements for TRICARE as the primary or secondary payer. Except for TRICARE supplemental insurance and Medicaid, TRICARE is always the secondary payer when another insurance policy is in effect. Remember that for TRICARE, the sponsor is the insured.

Block 1	Enter an X in TRICARE/CHAMPUS.
Block 1a	Enter the sponsor's Social Security number.
Block 2	Enter the patient's name.
Block 3	Enter the patient's eight-digit birth date; M or F.
Block 4	If the sponsor is not the patient, enter the sponsor's name. If the sponsor is the patient, leave this blank.
Block 5	Enter the patient's address and phone number.
Block 6	Enter X in the box that describes the patient/sponsor relationship.
Block 7	Enter the sponsor's address, including the ZIP code.
Block 8	Enter X in all boxes that apply to the patient.
Blocks 9–9d	TRICARE as primary: Leave this blank.

Block 9	TRICARE as secondary: Enter the name of the individual with other health insurance (OHI) that covers the patient.
Block 9a	TRICARE as secondary: Enter the policy number or group number of the other's insurance policy.
Block 9b	TRICARE as secondary: Enter the other insured's birth date; M or F.
Block 9c	TRICARE as secondary: Enter the name of the other insured's employer or school, if applicable.
Block 9d	TRICARE as secondary: Enter the name of the other health insurance policy or plan.
Blocks 10a–10c	Enter an X in Yes or No as applicable. If 10b is YES, enter the two-character abbreviation for the state where the accident occurred.
Block 10d	Leave this blank.
Block 11	TRICARE as primary: Enter NONE.
Block 11	TRICARE as secondary: Enter the policy or group number of the primary insurance plan.
Block 11a	Enter the sponsor's birth date and sex. If the sponsor is the patient, leave this blank.
Block 11b	Enter the sponsor's branch of service.
Block 11c	Enter TRICARE.
Block 11d	TRICARE as primary: Enter an X in NO.
	TRICARE as secondary: Enter an X in YES. Complete blocks 9a–9d.
Block 12	SIGNATURE ON FILE and MM DD YY
Block 13	SIGNATURE ON FILE
Block 14	Enter the eight-digit date of service.
Block 15	Leave this blank.
Block 16	Enter the eight-digit date, if applicable.
Block 17	Enter the name and credential of the referring physician/ provider, if applicable.
Block 17a	Leave this blank.
Block 17b	Enter the NPI number of the physician/provider named in block 17.
Block 18	Enter the hospital admission and discharge dates, if applicable.
Block 19	Enter the referral number for services that require a referral from the primary care manager, if applicable. Otherwise, leave this blank.
Block 20	Enter an X in NO.
Block 21	Enter ICD-9-CM diagnosis code(s); enter the primary or first-listed diagnosis code in 1.
Block 22	Leave this blank.
Block 23	Enter prior authorization code, if applicable.
Block 24A	Enter eight-digit date in the From and To columns.
Block 24B	Two-digit place-of-service code Enter Y (yes) if services were provided as an
Block 24C	emergency. Enter N (no) if services were not provided as an emergency.
Block 24D	Enter CPT/HCPCS code for each service, with modifier(s) as necessary.
Block 24E	Enter reference number from block 21, 1–4, for the diagnosis that best justifies the services identified in 24D.
Block 24F	Enter total charges for services in each line.
Block 24G	Enter the days, units, or number of services for each line items.
Block 24H	Enter an X, if applicable. Otherwise, leave this blank.
Block 24I	Leave the shaded area blank.
Block 24J	Enter the physician/provider's NPI in the unshaded area. Leave the shaded area blank.
Block 25	Enter Superiorland clinic's Tax ID No.: 49-4134726 (include the hyphen); check EIN.

Block 26	Enter the patient's account number, if applicable.
Block 27	Enter an X in YES.
Block 28	Enter total charges of all services in lines 1 through 6.
Block 29	Enter the amount paid by the patient or other health insurance, if applicable.
Block 30	Enter the balance due.
Block 31	Enter Provider Name and credential and MM DD YY or SIGNATURE ON FILE and MM DD YY.
Block 32	Enter the name, address, city, state, and ZIP code for the physical location where services were rendered.
Block 32a	Enter the NPI of the facility identified in block 32 (either Superiorland Clinic or Blueberry Community Hospital).
Block 32b	Leave this blank.
Block 33	Enter the Superiorland clinic's name, address, ZIP code, and phone number.
Block 33a	Enter Superiorland clinic's NPI number.
Block 33b	Leave this blank.

CHAMPVA Guidelines

Block 1	Enter an X in CHAMPVA.
Block 1a	Enter the patient's CHAMPVA ID number.
Block 2	Enter the patient's name.
Block 3	Enter the patient's eight-digit birth date; M or F.
Block 4	Leave this blank.
Block 5	Enter the patients address, ZIP code, and telephone number.
Block 6	Enter an X in Self.
Block 7	Leave this blank.
Block 8	Enter an X in the box that applies to the patient's marital, employment, and student status.
Blocks 9–9d	CHAMPVA as primary: Leave this blank.
Block 9	CHAMPVA as secondary: Enter the name of the insured with the other health insurance plan that covers the beneficiary.
Block 9A	CHAMPVA as secondary: Enter the policy or group number of the other insurance plan.
Block 9B	CHAMPVA as secondary: Enter the other insured's eight-digit birth date; M or F.
Block 9C	Enter the name of the other insured's employer or school.
Block 9D	Enter the name of the insurance plan of the other health insurance.
Blocks 10–10c	Enter an X in Yes or No, as applicable. If 10b is Yes, enter the two-character abbreviation for the state where the accident occurred.
Block 10d	Leave this blank.
Blocks 11–11c	Leave this blank.
Block 11d	CHAMPVA as primary: Enter an X in No. CHAMPVA as secondary: Enter an X in Yes if the patient is covered under another health insurance plan and then complete blocks 9–9d.
Blocks 12, 13	SIGNATURE ON FILE.
Blocks 14	Enter the eight-digit date.
Block 15	Leave this blank.
Block 16	Enter the date, if applicable.
Block 17	Enter the name and credential of the referring physician or provider.
Block 17a	Leave this blank.
Block 17b	Enter the NPI number of the physician/provider named in 17.
Block 18	Enter the hospitalization dates, if applicable.
Block 19	Leave this blank.

Block 20	Enter an X in No.
Block 21	Enter up to four ICD-9-CM codes. The primary or first-listed diagnosis is entered in item 1.
Block 22	Leave this blank.
Block 23	Enter the authorization number, if applicable.
Block 24A	Enter eight-digit dates in the From and To fields.
Block 24B	Enter the place of service code. Use the same codes as Medicare.
Block 24C	Enter a Y for Yes if the service provided was an emergency. Enter an N for No if the service was not an emergency.
Block 24D	Enter CPT/HCPCS code for each service, with modifiers as applicable.
Block 24E	Enter the diagnosis pointer (1–4) for the diagnosis that best justifies the medical necessity for the service.
Block 24F	Enter the charge for each listed service.
Block 24G	Enter the days, units, or number of services for each line item.
Block 24H	Enter an X, if applicable. Otherwise, leave this blank.
Block 24I	Leave this blank.
Block 24J	Enter the NPI number (unshaded portion of 24J) of the provider rendering the service in each line. Leave the shaded area blank.
Block 25	Enter the provider's federal tax ID number (EIN).
Block 26	Enter the patient's account number, if one is applicable.
Block 27	Enter an X in Yes.
Block 28	Enter total charges for the services being reported on the claim.
Block 29	Enter the amount paid by the patient or other health insurance.
Block 30	Enter the balance due.
Block 31	Enter Provider name and credential and MM DD YY, or SIGNATURE ON FILE and MM DD YY.
Block 32	Enter the name, address, city, state, and ZIP code of the physical location where services were provided.
Block 32a	Enter the NPI of the facility identified in block 32 (either Superiorland Clinic or Blueberry Community Hospital).
Block 32b	Leave this blank.
Block 33	Enter Superiorland Clinic's complete address and telephone number.
Block 33a	Enter Superiorland Clinic's NPI number.
Block 33b	Leave this blank.

Workers' Compensation Guidelines (Chapter 15)

There are no co-payments or deductibles for workers' compensation, and the provider must accept the compensation program's allowable fee as payment in full.

Block 1	Enter X in FECA if *Federal* workers' comp claim. Otherwise use 'Other.'
Block 1a	First claim: Enter the patient's Social Security number. All other claims: Enter the assigned workers' compensation claim number, which may be the patient's Social Security number.
Block 2	Patient's name.
Block 3	Eight-digit birth date; M or F.
Block 4	Enter the name of the employer at the time of injury.
Block 5	Enter the patient's home address.
Block 6	Enter X in Other.
Block 7	Enter the employer's address and phone number.
Block 8	Enter X in Employed; leave other boxes blank.
Block 9–9d	Leave this blank.

Block 10–10c	Enter X in 10a. Complete 10b and 10c, as necessary.
Block 10d	Leave this blank.
Block 11	Enter the workers' compensation insurance carrier's claim number, if known. Otherwise, leave this blank.
Block 11a	Leave this blank.
Block 11b	Enter employer's name.
Block 11c	Enter the name of the workers' compensation insurance carrier.
Block 11d	Leave this blank.
Blocks 12, 13	SIGNATURE ON FILE
Block 14	Enter the eight-digit date that the injury occurred or the eight-digit date that symptoms first appeared.
Block 15	Enter the date the provider first rendered services for this injury, if available; otherwise, leave this blank.
Block 16	Enter eight-digit dates as directed.
Block 17	Enter the referring physician/provider's first name, last name, and professional credentials, if applicable.
Block 17a	Leave this blank.
Block 17b	Enter the NPI of the provider named in block 17.
Block 18	Enter eight-digit hospital admission and discharge dates, if applicable.
Block 19	Leave this blank.
Block 20	Enter X in Yes or No. If Yes, enter the total charges for services provided by outside lab.
Block 21, 1–4	Enter ICD-9-CM code(s) in priority order.
Block 22	Leave this blank.
Block 23	Enter prior authorization code, if applicable.
Block 24A	Eight-digit date of service in the From column. Leave To column blank.
Block 24B	Enter the place of service code.
Block 24C	Leave this blank.
Block 24D	Enter CPT codes or HCPCS codes, as applicable. Enter modifiers in the spaces provided.
Block 24E	Enter reference number from block 21, 1–4, for the diagnosis that best justifies the services identified in 24D.
Block 24F	Enter total charges for service(s) identified in each line.
Block 24G	Enter the number of service(s) identified in each line.
Block 24H	Leave this blank.
Block 24I	Shaded area: Leave this blank.
Block 24J	Enter the NPI of the physician who provided the service.
Block 25	Enter Superiorland Clinic's Tax ID No.: 49-4134726 (include the hyphen). Enter an X in EIN.
Block 26	Enter the patient's account number if one is assigned by the provider.
Block 27	Leave this blank.
Block 28	Enter the total charges for all services.
Blocks 29, 30	Leave this blank.
Block 31	Enter Provider name and credential and MM DD YY or SIGNATURE ON FILE and MM DD YY.
Block 32	Enter the name, address, city, state, and ZIP code of the place services were provided.
Block 32a	Enter the NPI for the entity named in block 32.
Block 32b	Leave this blank.
Block 33	Enter Superiorland Clinic's complete address and telephone number.
Block 33a	Enter Superiorland Clinic's NPI.
Block 33b	Leave this blank.

ASSIGNMENTS: CASE STUDIES 1-1 THROUGH 1-10

As a newly hired insurance billing specialist, your first assignments require you to complete a CMS-1500 form for a total of 10 patients who were seen on January 3, 20YY, and January 4, 20YY. Your supervisor has provided you with the registration information and encounter forms for each patient. Using the information on these forms, complete a CMS-1500 for submission to the patient's insurance carrier.

The registration information is provided on the Case Study, and Encounter Forms are also included for each case. You may fill out the CMS-1500 form for each case electronically by using the SimClaim student practice software in Study, Test, or Blank Form modes.

Special notes for using SimClaim and for individual Case Studies 1-1 through 1-10 are given here. It is important that you refer to these notes *before* you attempt to complete the related case studies.

General Instructions and Hints for Using the SimClaim Student Practice Software

Please read the following general instructions before working with the software:

- **Turn on Caps Lock:** All data entered into SimClaim must be in ALL CAPS.
- **Do not abbreviate:** Spell out words like street, drive, avenue, Signature on File, Blue Cross/Blue Shield, etc. No abbreviations (other than state abbreviations) will be accepted by the program.
- **Do not use "Same As" or "None" in any block:** Even if patient information is the same as insured information, enter that information again on the claim.
- **More than one Diagnosis Pointer in block 24E:** For the SimClaim case studies, there may be more than one diagnosis pointer required in block 24E.
- **No Amount Paid indicated:** If there is no amount paid indicated on the case study, enter "0 00" in block 29.
- **Secondary Insurance Claims:** If a Case Study indicates that a patient's primary insurance carrier has paid an amount, fill out a second claim form for the secondary insurance that reflects the amount reimbursed by primary insurance.
- **More than one CMS form:** Remember, if the place of service or the provider changes, another claim form is needed.
- **Fill out block 32:** Always fill out service facility location information in SimClaim block 32.
- **Enter all dates as given in case study:** For dates that are not given (e.g., signature dates in blocks 12 and 31), use "MM DD YY."
- For additional help using SimClaim, refer to the Block Help within SimClaim.

SPECIAL NOTES FOR CASE STUDIES 1-1 THROUGH 1-10

To ensure proper grading when using SimClaim, enter diagnosis and procedure codes onto the CMS form in the order that they appear on the Encounter Form (from left to right, up and down).

Case Study 1-1: Jessica Y. Gervais

Jessica Gervais was seen by Dr. Elizabeth Foy on January 3, 20YY. Prepare a CMS-1500 by using the information from Jessica's registration form (Case Study) and her Encounter Form. Follow the guidelines for Commercial Claims.

Case Study 1-2: Roger S. Mattson

Roger Mattson was seen by Dr. Charles French on January 3, 20YY. Prepare a CMS-1500 by using the information from Roger's registration form (Case Study) and his Encounter Form. Follow the guidelines for Blue Cross/Blue Shield, primary payer.

Case Study 1-3: Grace N. Morrison

Grace Morrison was seen by Dr. Roberta Pharyngeal on January 3, 20YY. Prepare a CMS-1500 by using the information from Grace's registration form (Case Study) and her Encounter Form. Grace's insurance, Blue Cross/Blue Shield, is the primary payer.

Case Study 1-4: Connor T. Stulz

Connor Stulz was seen by Dr. Robert Howard on January 3, 20YY. Prepare a CMS-1500 by using the information from Connor's registration form (Case Study) and his Encounter Form. Follow the guidelines for Commercial Claims.

Case Study 1-5: Victoria H. Shaski

Victoria was seen by Dr. Elizabeth Foy on January 3, 20YY. Prepare a CMS-1500 by using the information from Victoria's registration form (Case Study) and her Encounter Form. Follow the guidelines for Medicare, primary payer.

Case Study 1-6: Emily M. Erickson

Emily Erickson was seen by Dr. Roberta Pharyngeal on January 4, 20YY. Prepare a CMS-1500 by using the information from Emily's registration form (Case Study) and her Encounter Form. Follow the guidelines for Medicare with Medigap.

Case Study 1-7: Nick L. Loynes

Nick Loynes was seen by Dr. Robert Howard on January 4, 20YY. Prepare a CMS-1500 by using the information from Nick's registration form (Case Study) and his Encounter Form. Follow the guidelines for Medicaid.

Case Study 1-8: Andrea S. Flachs

Andrea Flachs was seen by Dr. Charles French on January 4, 20YY. Prepare a CMS-1500 by using the information from Andrea's registration form (Case Study) and her Encounter Form. Follow the guidelines for workers' compensation.

Case Study 1-9: Scotti C. Ostwald

Scotti Ostwald was seen by Dr. Elizabeth Foy on January 4, 20YY. Prepare a CMS-1500 by using the information from Scotti's registration form (Case Study) and her Encounter Form. Use the guidelines for TRICARE, primary payer.

Case Study 1-10: Ben R. Whitman

Ben Whitman was seen by Dr. Robert Howard on January 4, 20YY. Prepare a CMS-1500 by using the information from Ben's registration form (Case Study) and his Encounter Form. Use the guidelines for Commercial Claims.

SUPERIORLAND CLINIC
714 HENNEPIN AVENUE
BLUEBERRY ME 49855
906   3364600

Patient Number: 1-1

EIN: 494134726   **NPI:**   4567890123

PATIENT INFORMATION:
Name: GERVAIS, JESSICA, Y
Address: 61 LAKESHORE DRIVE
City: BLUEBERRY
State: ME
Zip/4: 49855
Telephone: 906 3127098

Gender: M   F X
Status: Single   Married X   Other
Date of Birth: 08   07   1951
Employer:
Student: FT   PT   School:

Work Related?   Y   N X
Employment Related?   Y   N X
Other Accident: Y   N X
Date of Accident:

Referring Physician:
Address:
Telephone:
NPI #:

INSURANCE INFORMATION:
Primary Insurance
    Primary Insurance Name: AETNA
    Address: PO BOX 45
    City: STILLWATER
    State: PA
    Zip/4: 12345-0045

    Plan ID#: BRG38314210
    Group #: NPW8200
    Primary Policyholder: GERVAIS, BRAD, R
    Address: 61 LAKESHORE DRIVE
    City: BLUEBERRY
    State: ME
    Zip/4: 49855
    Policyholder Date of Birth: 04   09   1951
    Pt Relationship to Insured: Self   Spouse X **Child   Other**
    Employer/School Name: BOARD OF POWER & LIGHT

Secondary Insurance
    Secondary Insurance Name:
    Address:
    City:
    State:
    Zip/4:

    Plan ID#:
    Group #:
    Primary Policyholder:
    Address:
    City:
    State:
    Zip/4:
    Policyholder Date of Birth:
    Pt Relationship to Insured: Self   Spouse   Child   Other
    Employer/School Name:

ENCOUNTER INFORMATION:
Place of Service: 11

DIAGNOSIS INFORMATION

	Code	Diagnosis		Code	Diagnosis
1.	.		5.	.	
2.	.		6.	.	
3.	.		7.	.	
4.	.		8.	.	

PROCEDURE INFORMATION

	Description of Procedure/Service	Dates	Code	Mod	Dx Order	Unit Charge	Days/ Units
1.		–					
2.		–					
3.		–					
4.		–					
5.		–					
6.		–					

Special Notes: SEE ENCOUNTER FORM

FIGURE A–1 Case Study 1-1 Gervais

Elizabeth Foy, MD
Charles French, MD
Robert Howard, MD
Denzel Hamilton, MD
Roberta Pharyngeal, MD
Henry Romero, MD

Superiorland Clinic
714 Hennepin Avenue
Blueberry, ME 49855
Phone: (906) 336-4600   Fax: (906) 336-4020

NEW PATIENT	X	CODE	FEE	LAB TESTS	X	CODE	FEE	LAB TESTS	X	CODE	FEE
Level I		99201		AST		84450		LDH		83615	
Level II		99202		Albumin		82040		Lipid Panel		80061	
Level III		99203		Alk Phos		84075		Metabolic Panel		80053	
Level IV		99204		BUN		84520		Obstetric Panel		80055	
Level V		99205		CBC		85027		Occult Blood		82270	
ESTABLISHED PATIENT				CBC/diff		85025		PAP smear		88150	
Level I		99211		CK/CPK		82550		PPD Skin Test		86580	
Level II	X	99212	40.00	Drug Screen		80100		Prothrombin Time		85610	
Level III		99213		Electrolyte Panel		80051		PSA		84152	
Level IV		99214		Estrogen		82671		Rapid Strep Screen		87880	
Level V		99215		Glucose/blood		82947		Sed Rate		85651	
OFFICE CONSULTATION				GTT		82951		TSH		84443	
Level I		99241		HgbA1C		83036		Urinalysis		81000	
Level II		99242		Hepatitis Panel		80074					
Level III		99243		HIV Screen		86703					
Level IV		99244									
Level V		99245		**OTHER TESTS**				**OTHER TESTS**			
HOSPITAL INPATIENT				A/P Chest X-ray				Holter/24 hr			
Initial/Complex		99223		DXA Scan		77080		Sigmoidoscopy		45330	
Subsequent		99231		EKG Int/Report		93000		Stress Test		93015	
EMERGENCY DEPARTMENT SERV.				Rhythm EKG		93040					
Level I		99281									
Level II		99282									
Level III		99283		**TREATMENTS**	X	CODE	FEE	**TREATMENTS**	X	CODE	FEE
Level IV		99284		Flu Shot		90658					
Level V		99285									

DIAGNOSIS

Abdominal Pain	789.00	Gastritis	535.50	OTHER DIAGNOSIS	CODE
Angina Pectoris, Unspec.	413.9	Hemorrhoids, NOS	455.6		
Asthma, Unspecified	493.90	Hiatal hernia	553.3		
Bronchitis, Acute	466.0	Hyperlipidemia, NOS	272.4		
Bursitis	727.3	Hypertension, Unspec.	401.9		
CHF	428.0	Hyperthyroidism	242.90	REFERRAL/COMMENTS	
Colon polyp	211.3	Hypothyroidism	244.9		
Conjunctivitis, Unspec.	372.00	Osteoarthritis, Unspec	715.90		
Diabetes Mellitus, Type I	250.01	Osteoporosis, postmen.	733.01		
Diabetes Mellitus, Type II	250.00	Pleurisy	511.0		
Diverticulosis, colon	562.10	Serious Otitis Media, Acute	381.01		
Emphysema	492.8	UTI	599.0		

DATE 01/03/20YY	PATIENT NAME GERVAIS JESSICA	DOB 08/07/1951	CHARGES 40.00	PAYMENT 0	BALANCE 40.00

I authorize my insurance benefits to be paid directly to the above named physician. I understand that I am obligated to pay deductibles, copayments, and charges for non-covered services. I authorize release of my medical information for billing purposes.

PATIENT SIGNATURE: *Jessica Gervais*   **DATE:** 01/03/20YY

FIGURE A–2 Gervais

SUPERIORLAND CLINIC
714 HENNEPIN AVENUE
BLUEBERRY ME 49855
906   3364600

Patient Number: 1-2

EIN: 494134726   **NPI:** 4567890123

PATIENT INFORMATION:
Name: MATTSON, ROGER, S
Address: 1312 WEST EASTERDAY
City: BLUEBERRY
State: ME
Zip/4: 49855
Telephone: 906 3121987

Gender: M X   F
Status: Single   Married X   Other
Date of Birth: 09   30   1945
Employer:
Student: FT   PT   School:

Work Related? Y   N X
Employment Related? Y   N X
Other Accident: Y   N X
Date of Accident:

Referring Physician: CHARLES FRENCH MD
Address:
Telephone:
NPI #: 2345678901

INSURANCE INFORMATION:
Primary Insurance
  Primary Insurance Name: BLUE CROSS BLUE SHIELD
  Address: PO BOX 1121
  City: MEDICAL
  State: PA
  Zip/4: 12357-1121

  Plan ID#: XWY312987982
  Group #: 92992
  Primary Policyholder: MATTSON, ROGER, S
  Address: 1312 WEST EASTERDAY
  City: BLUEBERRY
  State: ME
  Zip/4: 49855
  Policyholder Date of Birth: 09   30   1945
  Pt Relationship to Insured: Self X Spouse   Child   Other
  Employer/School Name: BEEBAH GREETING CARDS

Secondary Insurance
  Secondary Insurance Name:
  Address:
  City:
  State:
  Zip/4:

  Plan ID#:
  Group #:
  Primary Policyholder:
  Address:
  City:
  State:
  Zip/4:
  Policyholder Date of Birth:
  Pt Relationship to Insured: Self   Spouse   Child   Other
  Employer/School Name:

ENCOUNTER INFORMATION:
Place of Service: 11

DIAGNOSIS INFORMATION

	Code	Diagnosis		Code	Diagnosis
1.	.		5.	.	
2.	.		6.	.	
3.	.		7.	.	
4.	.		8.	.	

PROCEDURE INFORMATION

	Description of Procedure/Service	Dates	Code	Mod	Dx Order	Unit Charge	Days/ Units
1.		–					
2.		–					
3.		–					
4.		–					
5.		–					
6.		–					

Special Notes: SEE ENCOUNTER FORM

FIGURE A–3 Case Study 1-2 Mattson

Elizabeth Foy, MD
Charles French, MD
Robert Howard, MD
Denzel Hamilton, MD
Roberta Pharyngeal, MD
Henry Romero, MD

Superiorland Clinic
714 Hennepin Avenue
Blueberry, ME 49855
Phone: (906) 336-4600   Fax: (906) 336-4020

NEW PATIENT		CODE	FEE	LAB TESTS	X	CODE	FEE	LAB TESTS	X	CODE	FEE
Level I		99201		AST		84450		LDH		83615	
Level II		99202		Albumin		82040		Lipid Panel	X	80061	45.00
Level III		99203		Alk Phos		84075		Metabolic Panel		80053	
Level IV		99204		BUN		84520		Obstetric Panel		80055	
Level V		99205		CBC	X	85027	30.00	Occult Blood		82270	
ESTABLISHED PATIENT				CBC/diff		85025		PAP smear		88150	
Level I		99211		CK/CPK		82550		PPD Skin Test		86580	
Level II		99212		Drug Screen		80100		Prothrombin Time		85610	
Level III		99213		Electrolyte Panel		80051		PSA		84152	
Level IV	X	99214	60.00	Estrogen		82671		Rapid Strep Screen		87880	
Level V		99215		Glucose/blood		82947		Sed Rate		85651	
OFFICE CONSULTATION				GTT		82951		TSH		84443	
Level I		99241		HgbA1C		83036		Urinalysis		81000	
Level II		99242		Hepatitis Panel		80074					
Level III		99243		HIV Screen		86703					
Level IV		99244									
Level V		99245		**OTHER TESTS**				**OTHER TESTS**			
HOSPITAL INPATIENT				A/P Chest X-ray				Holter/24 hr			
Initial/Complex		99223		DXA Scan		77080		Sigmoidoscopy	X	45330	175.00
Subsequent		99231		EKG Int/Report		93000		Stress Test		93015	
EMERGENCY DEPARTMENT SERV.				Rhythm EKG		93040					
Level I		99281									
Level II		99282									
Level III		99283		**TREATMENTS**	X	CODE	FEE	**TREATMENTS**	X	CODE	FEE
Level IV		99284		Flu Shot		90658					
Level V		99285									

DIAGNOSIS						
Abdominal Pain	789.00	Gastritis	535.50	OTHER DIAGNOSIS		CODE
Angina Pectoris, Unspec.	413.9	Hemorrhoids, NOS	455.6			
Asthma, Unspecified	493.90	Hiatal hernia	553.3			
Bronchitis, Acute	466.0	Hyperlipidemia, NOS	272.4			
Bursitis	727.3	Hypertension, Unspcc.	401.9			
CHF	428.0	Hyperthyroidism	242.90	REFERRAL/COMMENTS		
Colon polyp	211.3	Hypothyroidism	244.9			
Conjunctivitis, Unspec.	372.00	Osteoarthritis, Unspec	715.90			
Diabetes Mellitus, Type I	250.01	Osteoporosis, postmen.	733.01			
Diabetes Mellitus, Type II	250.00	Pleurisy	511.0			
Diverticulosis, colon	562.10	Serious Otitis Media, Acute	381.01			
Emphysema	492.8	UTI	599.0			

DATE	PATIENT NAME	DOB	CHARGES	PAYMENT	BALANCE
01/03/20YY	MATTSON ROGER	09/30/1945	310.00	0	310.00

I authorize my insurance benefits to be paid directly to the above named physician. I understand that I am obligated to pay deductibles, copayments, and charges for non-covered services. I authorize release of my medical information for billing purposes.

PATIENT SIGNATURE: *Roger Mattson*   **DATE:** 01/03/20YY

FIGURE A–4 Mattson

SUPERIORLAND CLINIC
714 HENNEPIN AVENUE
BLUEBERRY ME 49855
906 3364600

Patient Number: 1-3

EIN: 494134726   **NPI:** 4567890123

PATIENT INFORMATION:
Name: MORRISON, GRACE, N
Address: 609 OSBORNE
City: BLUEBERRY
State: ME
Zip/4: 49855
Telephone: 906 3123336

Gender: M   F X
Status: Single   Married X   Other
Date of Birth: 08 05 1954
Employer: BURGER WORLD
Student: FT   PT   School:

Work Related?   Y   N X
Employment Related?   Y   N X
Other Accident: Y   N X
Date of Accident:

Referring Physician: ROBERTA PHARYNGEAL MD
Address:
Telephone:
NPI #: 5678901234

INSURANCE INFORMATION:
Primary Insurance
     Primary Insurance Name: BLUE CROSS BLUE SHIELD
     Address: PO BOX 1121
     City: MEDICAL
     State: PA
     Zip/4: 12357-1121

     Plan ID#: ZJW319549729
     Group #: 00310
     Primary Policyholder: MORRISON, GRACE, N
     Address: 609 OSBORNE
     City: BLUEBERRY
     State: ME
     Zip/4: 49855
     Policyholder Date of Birth: 08 05 1954
     Pt Relationship to Insured: Self X Spouse   Child   Other
     Employer/School Name:

Secondary Insurance
     Secondary Insurance Name: METROPOLITAN
     Address:
     City:
     State:
     Zip/4:

     Plan ID#: 481600830
     Group #: Y679
     Primary Policyholder: MORRISON, MICHAEL
     Address: 609 OSBORNE
     City: BLUEBERRY
     State: ME
     Zip/4: 49855
     Policyholder Date of Birth: 12 10 1952
     Pt Relationship to Insured: Self   Spouse X Child   Other
     Employer/School Name: AUTOWORLD

ENCOUNTER INFORMATION:
Place of Service: 11

DIAGNOSIS INFORMATION

	Code	Diagnosis		Code	Diagnosis
1.	.		5.	.	
2.	.		6.	.	
3.	.		7.	.	
4.	.		8.	.	

PROCEDURE INFORMATION

	Description of Procedure/Service	Dates	Code	Mod	Dx Order	Unit Charge	Days/ Units
1.		-					
2.		-					
3.		-					
4.		-					
5.		-					
6.		-					

Special Notes: SEE ENCOUNTER FORM

FIGURE A–5 Case Study 1-3 Morrison

Elizabeth Foy, MD
Charles French, MD
Robert Howard, MD
Denzel Hamilton, MD
(Roberta Pharyngeal, MD)
Henry Romero, MD

Superiorland Clinic
714 Hennepin Avenue
Blueberry, ME 49855
Phone: (906) 336-4600   Fax: (906) 336-4020

NEW PATIENT	X	CODE	FEE	LAB TESTS	X	CODE	FEE	LAB TESTS	X	CODE	FEE
Level I		99201		AST		84450		LDH		83615	
Level II		99202		Albumin		82040		Lipid Panel		80061	
Level III		99203		Alk Phos		84075		Metabolic Panel		80053	
Level IV		99204		BUN		84520		Obstetric Panel		80055	
Level V		99205		CBC	X	(85027)	30.00	Occult Blood		82270	
ESTABLISHED PATIENT				CBC/diff		85025		PAP smear		88150	
Level I		99211		CK/CPK		82550		PPD Skin Test		86580	
Level II	X	(99212)	40.00	Drug Screen		80100		Prothrombin Time		85610	
Level III		99213		Electrolyte Panel		80051		PSA		84152	
Level IV		99214		Estrogen		82671		Rapid Strep Screen		87880	
Level V		99215		Glucose/blood		82947		Sed Rate		85651	
OFFICE CONSULTATION				GTT		82951		TSH		84443	
Level I		99241		HgbA1C		83036		Urinalysis		81000	
Level II		99242		Hepatitis Panel		80074					
Level III		99243		HIV Screen		86703					
Level IV		99244									
Level V		99245		**OTHER TESTS**				**OTHER TESTS**			
HOSPITAL INPATIENT				A/P Chest X-ray				Holter/24 hr			
Initial/Complex		99223		DXA Scan		77080		Sigmoidoscopy		45330	
Subsequent		99231		EKG Int/Report		93000		Stress Test		93015	
EMERGENCY DEPARTMENT SERV.				Rhythm EKG		93040					
Level I		99281									
Level II		99282									
Level III		99283		**TREATMENTS**	X	CODE	FEE	**TREATMENTS**	X	CODE	FEE
Level IV		99284		Flu Shot		90658					
Level V		99285									

DIAGNOSIS						
Abdominal Pain	789.00	Gastritis	535.50	OTHER DIAGNOSIS		CODE
Angina Pectoris, Unspec.	413.9	Hemorrhoids, NOS	455.6			
Asthma, Unspecified	493.90	Hiatal hernia	553.3			
Bronchitis, Acute	(466.0)	Hyperlipidemia, NOS	272.4			
Bursitis	727.3	Hypertension, Unspec.	401.9			
CHF	428.0	Hyperthyroidism	242.90	REFERRAL/COMMENTS		
Colon polyp	211.3	Hypothyroidism	244.9			
Conjunctivitis, Unspec.	372.00	Osteoarthritis, Unspec	715.90			
Diabetes Mellitus, Type I	250.01	Osteoporosis, postmen.	733.01			
Diabetes Mellitus, Type II	250.00	Pleurisy	511.0			
Diverticulosis, colon	562.10	Serious Otitis Media, Acute	381.01			
Emphysema	492.8	UTI	599.0			

DATE	PATIENT NAME	DOB	CHARGES	PAYMENT	BALANCE
01/03/20YY	MORRISON GRACE	08/05/1954	70.00	0	70.00

I authorize my insurance benefits to be paid directly to the above named physician. I understand that I am obligated to pay deductibles, copayments, and charges for non-covered services. I authorize release of my medical information for billing purposes.

PATIENT SIGNATURE: *Grace Morrison*   **DATE:** 01/03/20YY

FIGURE A–6 Morrison

SUPERIORLAND CLINIC
714 HENNEPIN AVENUE
BLUEBERRY ME 49855
906 3364600

Patient Number: 1-4

EIN: 494134726   **NPI:** 4567890123

PATIENT INFORMATION:
Name: STULZ, CONNOR, T
Address: 103 LAKESHORE ROAD
City: BLUEBERRY
State: ME
Zip/4: 49855
Telephone: 906 3129676

Gender: **M**   F X
Status: Single X   **Married**   **Other**
Date of Birth: 02   03   1997
Employer:
Student: FT   PT   School:

Work Related?   Y   N X
Employment Related?   Y   N X
Other Accident: Y   N X
Date of Accident:

Referring Physician:
Address:
Telephone:
NPI #:

INSURANCE INFORMATION:
Primary Insurance
 Primary Insurance Name: UNION HEALTH
 Address: PO BOX 1976
 City: LOBSTERTOWN
 State: ME
 Zip/4: 44437-1976

 Plan ID#: XWV779448354
 Group #:
 Primary Policyholder: STULZ, WILLIAM
 Address: 103 LAKESHORE ROAD
 City: BLUEBERRY
 State: ME
 Zip/4: 49855
 Policyholder Date of Birth: 01   01   1970
 Pt Relationship to Insured: Self   Spouse   Child X Other
 Employer/School Name: MARATHON MANUFACTURING

Secondary Insurance
 Secondary Insurance Name:
 Address:
 City:
 State:
 Zip/4:

 Plan ID#:
 Group #:
 Primary Policyholder:
 Address:
 City:
 State:
 Zip/4:
 Policyholder Date of Birth:
 Pt Relationship to Insured: Self   Spouse   Child   Other
 Employer/School Name:

ENCOUNTER INFORMATION:
Place of Service: 11

DIAGNOSIS INFORMATION

	Code	Diagnosis		Code	Diagnosis
1.	.		5.	.	
2.	.		6.	.	
3.	.		7.	.	
4.	.		8.	.	

PROCEDURE INFORMATION

	Description of Procedure/Service	Dates	Code	Mod	Dx Order	Unit Charge	Days/ Units
1.		–					
2.		–					
3.		–					
4.		–					
5.		–					
6.		–					

Special Notes: SEE ENCOUNTER FORM

FIGURE A–7 Case Study 1-4 Stulz

Elizabeth Foy, MD
Charles French, MD
(Robert Howard, MD)
Denzel Hamilton, MD
Roberta Pharyngeal, MD
Henry Romero, MD

Superiorland Clinic
714 Hennepin Avenue
Blueberry, ME 49855
Phone: (906) 336-4600   Fax: (906) 336-4020

NEW PATIENT	X	CODE	FEE	LAB TESTS	X	CODE	FEE	LAB TESTS	X	CODE	FEE
Level I		99201		AST		84450		LDH		83615	
Level II	X	(99202)	50.00	Albumin		82040		Lipid Panel		80061	
Level III		99203		Alk Phos		84075		Metabolic Panel		80053	
Level IV		99204		BUN		84520		Obstetric Panel		80055	
Level V		99205		CBC		85027		Occult Blood		82270	
ESTABLISHED PATIENT				CBC/diff		85025		PAP smear		88150	
Level I		99211		CK/CPK		82550		PPD Skin Test		86580	
Level II		99212		Drug Screen		80100		Prothrombin Time		85610	
Level III		99213		Electrolyte Panel		80051		PSA		84152	
Level IV		99214		Estrogen		82671		Rapid Strep Screen		87880	
Level V		99215		Glucose/blood		82947		Sed Rate		85651	
OFFICE CONSULTATION				GTT		82951		TSH		84443	
Level I		99241		HgbA1C		83036		Urinalysis		81000	
Level II		99242		Hepatitis Panel		80074					
Level III		99243		HIV Screen		86703					
Level IV		99244									
Level V		99245		**OTHER TESTS**				**OTHER TESTS**			
HOSPITAL INPATIENT				A/P Chest X-ray				Holter/24 hr			
Initial/Complex		99223		DXA Scan		77080		Sigmoidoscopy		45330	
Subsequent		99231		EKG Int/Report		93000		Stress Test		93015	
EMERGENCY DEPARTMENT SERV.				Rhythm EKG		93040					
Level I		99281									
Level II		99282									
Level III		99283		**TREATMENTS**		CODE	FEE	**TREATMENTS**		CODE	FEE
Level IV		99284		Flu Shot		90658					
Level V		99285									

DIAGNOSIS						
Abdominal Pain	789.00	Gastritis	535.50	OTHER DIAGNOSIS		CODE
Angina Pectoris, Unspec.	413.9	Hemorrhoids, NOS	455.6			
Asthma, Unspecified	493.90	Hiatal hernia	553.3			
Bronchitis, Acute	466.0	Hyperlipidemia, NOS	272.4			
Bursitis	727.3	Hypertension, Unspec.	401.9			
CHF	428.0	Hyperthyroidism	242.90	REFERRAL/COMMENTS		
Colon polyp	211.3	Hypothyroidism	244.9			
Conjunctivitis, Unspec.	372.00	Osteoarthritis, Unspec	715.90			
Diabetes Mellitus, Type I	250.01	Osteoporosis, postmen.	733.01			
Diabetes Mellitus, Type II	250.00	Pleurisy	511.0			
Diverticulosis, colon	562.10	Serious Otitis Media, Acute	(381.01)			
Emphysema	492.8	UTI	599.0			

DATE	PATIENT NAME	DOB	CHARGES	PAYMENT	BALANCE
01/03/20YY	STULZ CONNOR	02/03/1997	50.00	0	50.00

I authorize my insurance benefits to be paid directly to the above named physician. I understand that I am obligated to pay deductibles, copayments, and charges for non-covered services. I authorize release of my medical information for billing purposes.

PATIENT SIGNATURE: *Connor Stulz*   **DATE:** 01/03/20YY

FIGURE A–8 Stulz

SUPERIORLAND CLINIC
714 HENNEPIN AVENUE
BLUEBERRY ME 49855
906 3364600

Patient Number: 1-5

EIN: 494134726   **NPI:**   4567890123

PATIENT INFORMATION:
Name: SHASKI, VICTORIA, H
Address: 1514 WEST FIFTH AVENUE
City: BLUEBERRY
State: ME
Zip/4: 49855
Telephone: 906 3129817

Gender: M   F X
Status: Single X   Married   Other
Date of Birth: 01   04   1932
Employer:
Student: FT   PT   School:

Work Related?   Y   N X
Employment Related?   Y   N X
Other Accident: Y   N X
Date of Accident:

Referring Physician: ELIZABETH FOY MD
Address:
Telephone:
NPI #:   7890123456

INSURANCE INFORMATION:
Primary Insurance
  Primary Insurance Name: MEDICARE
  Address: PO BOX 9929
  City: BOXBURY
  State: MD
  Zip/4: 45678-9929

  Plan ID#: 312981729A
  Group #:
  Primary Policyholder: SHASKI, VICTORIA, H
  Address: 1514 WEST FIFTH AVENUE
  City: BLUEBERRY
  State: ME
  Zip/4: 49855
  Policyholder Date of Birth: 01   04   1932
  Pt Relationship to Insured: Self X Spouse   Child   Other
  Employer/School Name:

Secondary Insurance
  Secondary Insurance Name:
  Address:
  City:
  State:
  Zip/4:

  Plan ID#:
  Group #:
  Primary Policyholder:
  Address:
  City:
  State:
  Zip/4:
  Policyholder Date of Birth:
  Pt Relationship to Insured: Self   Spouse   Child   Other
  Employer/School Name:

ENCOUNTER INFORMATION:
Place of Service: 11

DIAGNOSIS INFORMATION

	Code	Diagnosis			Code	Diagnosis
1.	.			5.	.	
2.	.			6.	.	
3.	.			7.	.	
4.	.			8.	.	

PROCEDURE INFORMATION

	Description of Procedure/Service	Dates	Code	Mod	Dx Order	Unit Charge	Days/ Units
1.		-					
2.		-					
3.		-					
4.		-					
5.		-					
6.		-					

Special Notes: SEE ENCOUNTER FORM

FIGURE A–9 Case Study 1-5 Shaski

Elizabeth Foy, MD
Charles French, MD
Robert Howard, MD
Denzel Hamilton, MD
Roberta Pharyngeal, MD
Henry Romero, MD

Superiorland Clinic
714 Hennepin Avenue
Blueberry, ME 49855
Phone: (906) 336-4600   Fax: (906) 336-4020

NEW PATIENT	X	CODE	FEE	LAB TESTS	X	CODE	FEE	LAB TESTS	X	CODE	FEE
Level I		99201		AST		84450		LDH		83615	
Level II		99202		Albumin		82040		Lipid Panel	X	80061	45.00
Level III		99203		Alk Phos		84075		Metabolic Panel		80053	
Level IV		99204		BUN		84520		Obstetric Panel		80055	
Level V		99205		CBC	X	85027	30.00	Occult Blood		82270	
ESTABLISHED PATIENT				CBC/diff		85025		PAP smear		88150	
Level I		99211		CK/CPK		82550		PPD Skin Test		86580	
Level II	X	99212	40.00	Drug Screen		80100		Prothrombin Time		85610	
Level III		99213		Electrolyte Panel		80051		PSA		84152	
Level IV		99214		Estrogen		82671		Rapid Strep Screen		87880	
Level V		99215		Glucose/blood	X	82947	25.00	Sed Rate		85651	
OFFICE CONSULTATION				GTT		82951		TSH		84443	
Level I		99241		HgbA1C		83036		Urinalysis		81000	
Level II		99242		Hepatitis Panel		80074					
Level III		99243		HIV Screen		86703					
Level IV		99244									
Level V		99245		OTHER TESTS				OTHER TESTS			
HOSPITAL INPATIENT				A/P Chest X-ray				Holter/24 hr			
Initial/Complex		99223		DXA Scan		77080		Sigmoidoscopy		45330	
Subsequent		99231		EKG Int/Report		93000		Stress Test		93015	
EMERGENCY DEPARTMENT SERV.				Rhythm EKG		93040					
Level I		99281									
Level II		99282									
Level III		99283		TREATMENTS	X	CODE	FEE	TREATMENTS	X	CODE	FEE
Level IV		99284		Flu Shot		90658					
Level V		99285									

DIAGNOSIS

Abdominal Pain	789.00	Gastritis	535.50	OTHER DIAGNOSIS	CODE
Angina Pectoris, Unspec.	413.9	Hemorrhoids, NOS	455.6		
Asthma, Unspecified	493.90	Hiatal hernia	553.3		
Bronchitis, Acute	466.0	Hyperlipidemia, NOS	272.4		
Bursitis	727.3	Hypertension, Unspec.	401.9		
CHF	428.0	Hyperthyroidism	242.90	REFERRAL/COMMENTS	
Colon polyp	211.3	Hypothyroidism	244.9		
Conjunctivitis, Unspec.	372.00	Osteoarthritis, Unspec	715.90		
Diabetes Mellitus, Type I	250.01	Osteoporosis, postmen.	733.01		
Diabetes Mellitus, Type II	250.00	Pleurisy	511.0		
Diverticulosis, colon	562.10	Serious Otitis Media, Acute	381.01		
Emphysema	492.8	UTI	599.0		

DATE	PATIENT NAME	DOB	CHARGES	PAYMENT	BALANCE
01/03/20YY	SHASKI VICTORIA	01/04/1932	140.00	0	140.00

I authorize my insurance benefits to be paid directly to the above named physician. I understand that I am obligated to pay deductibles, copayments, and charges for non-covered services. I authorize release of my medical information for billing purposes.

PATIENT SIGNATURE: *Victoria Shaski*   **DATE:** 01/03/20YY

FIGURE A–10 Shaski

SUPERIORLAND CLINIC
714 HENNEPIN AVENUE
BLUEBERRY ME 49855
906 3364600

Patient Number: 1-6

EIN: 49413726   **NPI:** 4567890123

PATIENT INFORMATION:
Name: ERICKSON, EMILY, M
Address: 1500 DIVISION STREET
City: BLUEBERRY
State: ME
Zip/4: 49855
Telephone: 906 3121098

Gender: M   F X
Status: Single X   Married   Other
Date of Birth: 10 02 1932
Employer:
Student: FT   PT   School:

Work Related? Y   N X
Employment Related? Y   N X
Other Accident: Y   N X
Date of Accident:

Referring Physician: ROBERTA PHARYNGEAL MD
Address:
Telephone:
NPI #: 5678901234

INSURANCE INFORMATION:
Primary Insurance
    Primary Insurance Name: MEDICARE
    Address: PO BOX 9929
    City: BOXBURY
    State: MD
    Zip/4: 45678-9929

    Plan ID#: 382609845A
    Group #:
    Primary Policyholder: ERICKSON, EMILY, M
    Address: 1500 DIVISION STREET
    City: BLUEBERRY
    State: ME
    Zip/4: 49855
    Policyholder Date of Birth: 10 02 1932
    Pt Relationship to Insured: Self X Spouse   Child   Other
    Employer/School Name:

Secondary Insurance
    Secondary Insurance Name: BCBS MEDIGAP
    Address:
    City:
    State:
    Zip/4:

    Plan ID#: XWY609845
    Group #: BC7109
    Primary Policyholder: ERICKSON, EMILY, M
    Address: 1500 DIVISION STREET
    City: BLUEBERRY
    State: ME
    Zip/4: 49855
    Policyholder Date of Birth: 10 02 1932
    Pt Relationship to Insured: Self   X Spouse   Child   Other
    Employer/School Name:

ENCOUNTER INFORMATION:
Place of Service: 11

DIAGNOSIS INFORMATION

	Code	Diagnosis		Code	Diagnosis
1.	.		5.	.	
2.	.		6.	.	
3.	.		7.	.	
4.	.		8.	.	

PROCEDURE INFORMATION

	Description of Procedure/Service	Dates	Code	Mod	Dx Order	Unit Charge	Days/ Units
1.		–					
2.		–					
3.		–					
4.		–					
5.		–					
6.		–					

Special Notes: SEE ENCOUNTER FORM

FIGURE A–11 Case Study 1-6 Erickson

Elizabeth Foy, MD
Charles French, MD
Robert Howard, MD
Denzel Hamilton, MD
(Roberta Pharyngeal, MD)
Henry Romero, MD

Superiorland Clinic
714 Hennepin Avenue
Blueberry, ME 49855
Phone: (906) 336-4600   Fax: (906) 336-4020

NEW PATIENT	X	CODE	FEE	LAB TESTS	X	CODE	FEE	LAB TEST	X	CODE	FEE
Level I		99201		AST		84450		LDH		83615	
Level II		99202		Albumin		82040		Lipid Panel		80061	
Level III		99203		Alk Phos		84075		Metabolic Panel		80053	
Level IV		99204		BUN		84520		Obstetric Panel		80055	
Level V		99205		CBC	X	(85027)	30.00	Occult Blood		82270	
ESTABLISHED PATIENT				CBC/diff		85025		PAP smear		88150	
Level I		99211		CK/CPK		82550		PPD Skin Test		86580	
Level II		99212		Drug Screen		80100		Prothrombin Time		85610	
Level III	X	(99213)	50.00	Electrolyte Panel		80051		PSA		84152	
Level IV		99214		Estrogen		82671		Rapid Strep Screen		87880	
Level V		99215		Glucose/blood	X	(82947)	25.00	Sed Rate		85651	
OFFICE CONSULTATION				GTT		82951		TSH		84443	
Level I		99241		HgbA1C		83036		Urinalysis		81000	
Level II		99242		Hepatitis Panel		80074					
Level III		99243		HIV Screen		86703					
Level IV		99244									
Level V		99245		**OTHER TESTS**				**OTHER TESTS**			
HOSPITAL INPATIENT				A/P Chest X-ray				Holter/24 hr			
Initial/Complex		99223		DXA Scan	X	(77080)	125.00	Sigmoidoscopy		45330	
Subsequent		99231		EKG Int/Report		93000		Stress Test		93015	
EMERGENCY DEPARTMENT SERV.				Rhythm EKG		93040					
Level I		99281									
Level II		99282									
Level III		99283		**TREATMENTS**	X	**CODE**	**FEE**	**TREATMENTS**	X	**CODE**	**FEE**
Level IV		99284		Flu Shot		90658					
Level V		99285									

DIAGNOSIS							
Abdominal Pain	789.00	Gastritis	535.50	OTHER DIAGNOSIS			CODE
Angina Pectoris, Unspec.	413.9	Hemorrhoids, NOS	455.6				
Asthma, Unspecified	493.90	Hiatal hernia	553.3				
Bronchitis, Acute	466.0	Hyperlipidemia, NOS	272.4				
Bursitis	727.3	Hypertension, Unspec.	401.9				
CHF	428.0	Hyperthyroidism	242.90	REFERRAL/COMMENTS			
Colon polyp	211.3	Hypothyroidism	244.9				
Conjunctivitis, Unspec.	372.00	Osteoarthritis, Unspec	(715.90)				
Diabetes Mellitus, Type I	250.01	Osteoporosis, postmen.	(733.01)				
Diabetes Mellitus, Type II	250.00	Pleurisy	511.0				
Diverticulosis, colon	562.10	Serious Otitis Media, Acute	381.01				
Emphysema	492.8	UTI	599.0				

DATE	PATIENT NAME		DOB	CHARGES	PAYMENT	BALANCE
01/04/20YY	ERICKSON EMILY		10/02/1932	230.00	0	230.00

I authorize my insurance benefits to be paid directly to the above named physician. I understand that I am obligated to pay deductibles, copayments, and charges for non-covered services. I authorize release of my medical information for billing purposes.

PATIENT SIGNATURE: Emily Erickson   **DATE:** 01/04/20YY

FIGURE A–12 Erickson

SUPERIORLAND CLINIC
714 HENNEPIN AVENUE
BLUEBERRY ME 49855
906 3364600

Patient Number: 1-7

EIN: 494134726   **NPI:** 4567890123

PATIENT INFORMATION:
Name: LOYNES, NICHOLAS, L
Address: 812 BRULE
City: BLUEBERRY
State: ME
Zip/4: 49855
Telephone: 906 3126590

Gender: M X   F
Status: Single   Married X   Other
Date of Birth: 12 12 1974
Employer:
Student: FT   PT   School:

Work Related?   Y   N X
Employment Related?   Y   N X
Other Accident: Y   N X
Date of Accident:

Referring Physician: ROBERT HOWARD MD
Address:
Telephone:
NPI #: 3456789012

INSURANCE INFORMATION:
Primary Insurance
    Primary Insurance Name: MEDICAID
    Address: PO BOX 300
    City: SPRINGFIELD
    State: ME
    Zip/4: 44437-0300

    Plan ID#: ST3817097
    Group #:
    Primary Policyholder: LOYNES, NICHOLAS, L
    Address: 812 BRULE
    City: BLUEBERRY
    State: ME
    Zip/4: 49855
    Policyholder Date of Birth: 12 12 1974
    Pt Relationship to Insured: Self X Spouse Child Other
    Employer/School Name:

Secondary Insurance
    Secondary Insurance Name:
    Address:
    City:
    State:
    Zip/4:

    Plan ID#:
    Group #:
    Primary Policyholder:
    Address:
    City:
    State:
    Zip/4:
    Policyholder Date of Birth:
    Pt Relationship to Insured: Self Spouse Child Other
    Employer/School Name:

ENCOUNTER INFORMATION:
Place of Service: 11

DIAGNOSIS INFORMATION

	Code	Diagnosis		Code	Diagnosis
1.	.		5.	.	
2.	.		6.	.	
3.	.		7.	.	
4.	.		8.	.	

PROCEDURE INFORMATION

	Description of Procedure/Service	Dates	Code	Mod	Dx Order	Unit Charge	Days/ Units
1.		-					
2.		-					
3.		-					
4.		-					
5.		-					
6.		-					

Special Notes: SEE ENCOUNTER FORM

FIGURE A–13 Case Study 1-7 Loynes

Elizabeth Foy, MD
Charles French, MD
Robert Howard, MD
Denzel Hamilton, MD
Roberta Pharyngeal, MD
Henry Romero, MD

Superiorland Clinic
714 Hennepin Avenue
Blueberry, ME 49855
Phone: (906) 336-4600   Fax: (906) 336-4020

NEW PATIENT	X	CODE	FEE	LAB TESTS	X	CODE	FEE	LAB TESTS	X	CODE	FEE
Level I		99201		AST		84450		LDH		83615	
Level II		99202		Albumin		82040		Lipid Panel		80061	
Level III		99203		Alk Phos		84075		Metabolic Panel		80053	
Level IV		99204		BUN		84520		Obstetric Panel		80055	
Level V		99205		CBC	X	85027	30.00	Occult Blood		82270	
ESTABLISHED PATIENT				CBC/diff		85025		PAP smear		88150	
Level I		99211		CK/CPK		82550		PPD Skin Test		86580	
Level II	X	99212	40.00	Drug Screen		80100		Prothrombin Time		85610	
Level III		99213		Electrolyte Panel		80051		PSA		84152	
Level IV		99214		Estrogen		82671		Rapid Strep Screen		87880	
Level V		99215		Glucose/blood		82947		Sed Rate		85651	
OFFICE CONSULTATION				GTT		82951		TSH		84443	
Level I		99241		HgbA1C		83036		Urinalysis		81000	
Level II		99242		Hepatitis Panel		80074					
Level III		99243		HIV Screen		86703					
Level IV		99244									
Level V		99245		OTHER TESTS				OTHER TESTS			
HOSPITAL INPATIENT				A/P Chest X-ray				Holter/24 hr			
Initial/Complex		99223		DXA Scan		77080		Sigmoidoscopy		45330	
Subsequent		99231		EKG Int/Report		93000		Stress Test		93015	
EMERGENCY DEPARTMENT SERV.				Rhythm EKG		93040					
Level I		99281									
Level II		99282									
Level III		99283		TREATMENTS	X	CODE	FEE	TREATMENTS	X	CODE	FEE
Level IV		99284		Flu Shot		90658					
Level V		99285									

DIAGNOSIS						
Abdominal Pain	789.00	Gastritis	535.50	OTHER DIAGNOSIS		CODE
Angina Pectoris, Unspec.	413.9	Hemorrhoids, NOS	455.6			
Asthma, Unspecified	493.90	Hiatal hernia	553.3			
Bronchitis, Acute	466.0	Hyperlipidemia, NOS	272.4			
Bursitis	727.3	Hypertension, Unspec.	401.9			
CHF	428.0	Hyperthyroidism	242.90	REFERRAL/COMMENTS		
Colon polyp	211.3	Hypothyroidism	244.9			
Conjunctivitis, Unspec.	372.00	Osteoarthritis, Unspec	715.90			
Diabetes Mellitus, Type I	250.01	Osteoporosis, postmen.	733.01			
Diabetes Mellitus, Type II	250.00	Pleurisy	511.0			
Diverticulosis, colon	562.10	Serious Otitis Media, Acute	381.01			
Emphysema	492.8	UTI	599.0			

DATE	PATIENT NAME	DOB	CHARGES	PAYMENT	BALANCE
01/04/20YY	LOYNES NICK	11/12/1974	70.00	0	70.00

I authorize my insurance benefits to be paid directly to the above named physician. I understand that I am obligated to pay deductibles, copayments, and charges for non-covered services. I authorize release of my medical information for billing purposes.

PATIENT SIGNATURE: Nick Loynes   **DATE:** 01/04/20YY

FIGURE A–14 Loynes

SUPERIORLAND CLINIC
714 HENNEPIN AVENUE
BLUEBERRY ME 49855
906   3364600

Patient Number: 1-8

EIN: 494134726   **NPI:**   4567890123

PATIENT INFORMATION:
Name: FLACHS, ANDREA, S
Address: 812 LASALLE STREET
City: BLUEBERRY
State: ME
Zip/4: 49855
Telephone: 906 3129667

Gender: M   F X
Status: Single X   Married   Other
Date of Birth: 12   12   1976
Employer: MEDICAL CARE FACILITY
Student: FT   PT   School:

Work Related?   Y X N
Employment Related?   Y   N X
Other Accident: Y   N X
Date of Accident:

Referring Physician:
Address:
Telephone:
NPI #:

INSURANCE INFORMATION:
Primary Insurance
   Primary Insurance Name: COUNTY COMPENSATION
   Address: PO BOX 227
   City: SPRINGFIELD
   State: ME
   Zip/4: 47743-0227

   Plan ID#: WC38117097
   Group #:
   Primary Policyholder: MEDICAL CARE FACILITY
   Address: 104 MEDICAL STREET
   City: BLUEBERRY
   State: ME
   Zip/4: 49855
   Policyholder Date of Birth:
   Pt Relationship to Insured: Self   Spouse   Child   Other X
   Employer/School Name:

Secondary Insurance
   Secondary Insurance Name:
   Address:
   City:
   State:
   Zip/4:

   Plan ID#:
   Group #:
   Primary Policyholder:
   Address:
   City:
   State:
   Zip/4:
   Policyholder Date of Birth:
   Pt Relationship to Insured: Self   Spouse   Child   Other
   Employer/School Name:

ENCOUNTER INFORMATION:
Place of Service: 11

DIAGNOSIS INFORMATION

	Code	Diagnosis		Code	Diagnosis
1.	.		5.	.	
2.	.		6.	.	
3.	.		7.	.	
4.	.		8.	.	

PROCEDURE INFORMATION

	Description of Procedure/Service	Dates	Code	Mod	Dx Order	Unit Charge	Days/ Units
1.		-					
2.		-					
3.		-					
4.		-					
5.		-					
6.		-					

Special Notes: SEE ENCOUNTER FORM

FIGURE A–15 Case Study 1-8 Flachs

Elizabeth Foy, MD
Charles French, MD
Robert Howard, MD
Denzel Hamilton, MD
Roberta Pharyngeal, MD
Henry Romero, MD

Superiorland Clinic
714 Hennepin Avenue
Blueberry, ME 49855
Phone: (906) 336-4600   Fax: (906) 336-4020

NEW PATIENT	X	CODE	FEE	LAB TESTS	X	CODE	FEE	LAB TESTS	X	CODE	FEE
Level I		99201		AST		84450		LDH		83615	
Level II		99202		Albumin		82040		Lipid Panel		80061	
Level III		99203		Alk Phos		84075		Metabolic Panel		80053	
Level IV		99204		BUN		84520		Obstetric Panel		80055	
Level V		99205		CBC		85027		Occult Blood		82270	
ESTABLISHED PATIENT				CBC/diff		85025		PAP smear		88150	
Level I		99211		CK/CPK		82550		PPD Skin Test		86580	
Level II	X	99212	40.00	Drug Screen		80100		Prothrombin Time		85610	
Level III		99213		Electrolyte Panel		80051		PSA		84152	
Level IV		99214		Estrogen		82671		Rapid Strep Screen		87880	
Level V		99215		Glucose/blood		82947		Sed Rate		85651	
OFFICE CONSULTATION				GTT		82951		TSH		84443	
Level I		99241		HgbA1C		83036		Urinalysis		81000	
Level II		99242		Hepatitis Panel		80074					
Level III		99243		HIV Screen		86703					
Level IV		99244									
Level V		99245		**OTHER TESTS**				**OTHER TESTS**			
HOSPITAL INPATIENT				A/P Chest X-ray				Holter/24 hr			
Initial/Complex		99223		DXA Scan		77080		Sigmoidoscopy		45330	
Subsequent		99231		EKG Int/Report		93000		Stress Test		93015	
EMERGENCY DEPARTMENT SERV.				Rhythm EKG		93040					
Level I		99281									
Level II		99282									
Level III		99283		**TREATMENTS**	X	CODE	FEE	**TREATMENTS**	X	CODE	FEE
Level IV		99284		Flu Shot		90658					
Level V		99285									

DIAGNOSIS

Abdominal Pain	789.00	Gastritis	535.50	OTHER DIAGNOSIS	CODE
Angina Pectoris, Unspec.	413.9	Hemorrhoids, NOS	455.6	Lumbosacral sprain	846.0
Asthma, Unspecified	493.90	Hiatal hernia	553.3		
Bronchitis, Acute	466.0	Hyperlipidemia, NOS	272.4		
Bursitis	727.3	Hypertension, Unspec.	401.9		
CHF	428.0	Hyperthyroidism	242.90	REFERRAL/COMMENTS	
Colon polyp	211.3	Hypothyroidism	244.9		
Conjunctivitis, Unspec.	372.00	Osteoarthritis, Unspec	715.90		
Diabetes Mellitus, Type I	250.01	Osteoporosis, postmen.	733.01		
Diabetes Mellitus, Type II	250.00	Pleurisy	511.0		
Diverticulosis, colon	562.10	Serious Otitis Media, Acute	381.01		
Emphysema	492.8	UTI	599.0		

DATE	PATIENT NAME	DOB	CHARGES	PAYMENT	BALANCE
01/04/20YY	FLACHS ANDREA	11/12/1976	40.00	0	40.00

I authorize my insurance benefits to be paid directly to the above named physician. I understand that I am obligated to pay deductibles, copayments, and charges for non-covered services. I authorize release of my medical information for billing purposes.

PATIENT SIGNATURE: *Andrea Flachs*   DATE: 01/04/20YY

FIGURE A–16 Flachs

SUPERIORLAND CLINIC
714 HENNEPIN AVENUE
BLUEBERRY ME 49855
906   3364600

Patient Number: 1-9

EIN: 494134726   **NPI:**   4567890123

PATIENT INFORMATION:
Name: OSTWALD, SCOTTI, C
Address: 418 WEST RIDGE
City: BLUEBERRY
State: ME
Zip/4: 49855
Telephone: 906 3125949

Gender: M X   F
Status: Single   Married X   Other
Date of Birth: 09   04   1958
Employer: UNITED STATES NAVY
Student: FT   PT   School:

Work Related?   Y   N X
Employment Related?   Y   N X
Other Accident: Y   N X
Date of Accident:

Referring Physician: ELIZABETH FOY MD
Address:
Telephone:
NPI #:   7890123456

INSURANCE INFORMATION:
Primary Insurance
    Primary Insurance Name: TRICARE
    Address: PO BOX 555
    City: TRICITY
    State: SC
    Zip/4: 76654-0555

    Plan ID#: 373914589
    Group #:
    Primary Policyholder: OSTWALD, SCOTTI, C
    Address: 418 WEST RIDGE
    City: BLUEBERRY
    State: ME
    Zip/4: 49855
    Policyholder Date of Birth: 09   04   1958
    Pt Relationship to Insured: Self X Spouse   Child   Other
    Employer/School Name: UNITED STATES NAVY

Secondary Insurance
    Secondary Insurance Name:
    Address:
    City:
    State:
    Zip/4:

    Plan ID#:
    Group #:
    Primary Policyholder:
    Address:
    City:
    State:
    Zip/4:
    Policyholder Date of Birth:
    Pt Relationship to Insured: Self   Spouse   Child   Other
    Employer/School Name:

ENCOUNTER INFORMATION:
Place of Service: 11

DIAGNOSIS INFORMATION

	Code	Diagnosis		Code	Diagnosis
1.	.		5.	.	
2.	.		6.	.	
3.	.		7.	.	
4.	.		8.	.	

PROCEDURE INFORMATION

	Description of Procedure/Service	Dates	Code	Mod	Dx Order	Unit Charge	Days/ Units
1.		–					
2.		–					
3.		–					
4.		–					
5.		–					
6.		–					

Special Notes: SEE ENCOUNTER FORM

FIGURE A–17 Case Study 1-9 Ostwald

Elizabeth Foy, MD
Charles French, MD
Robert Howard, MD
Denzel Hamilton, MD
Roberta Pharyngeal, MD
Henry Romero, MD

Superiorland Clinic
714 Hennepin Avenue
Blueberry, ME 49855
Phone: (906) 336-4600   Fax: (906) 336-4020

NEW PATIENT	X	CODE	FEE	LAB TESTS	X	CODE	FEE	LAB TESTS	X	CODE	FEE
Level I		99201		AST		84450		LDH		83615	
Level II		99202		Albumin		82040		Lipid Panel		80061	
Level III		99203		Alk Phos		84075		Metabolic Panel		80053	
Level IV		99204		BUN		84520		Obstetric Panel		80055	
Level V		99205		CBC		85027		Occult Blood		82270	
ESTABLISHED PATIENT				CBC/diff	X	85025	35.00	PAP smear		88150	
Level I		99211		CK/CPK		82550		PPD Skin Test		86580	
Level II		99212		Drug Screen		80100		Prothrombin Time		85610	
Level III	X	99213	50.00	Electrolyte Panel		80051		PSA		84152	
Level IV		99214		Estrogen		82671		Rapid Strep Screen		87880	
Level V		99215		Glucose/blood		82947		Sed Rate		85651	
OFFICE CONSULTATION				GTT		82951		TSH		84443	
Level I		99241		HgbA1C		83036		Urinalysis	X	81000	15.00
Level II		99242		Hepatitis Panel		80074					
Level III		99243		HIV Screen		86703					
Level IV		99244									
Level V		99245		**OTHER TESTS**				**OTHER TESTS**			
HOSPITAL INPATIENT				A/P Chest X-ray				Holter/24 hr			
Initial/Complex		99223		DXA Scan		77080		Sigmoidoscopy		45330	
Subsequent		99231		EKG Int/Report		93000		Stress Test		93015	
EMERGENCY DEPARTMENT SERV.				Rhythm EKG		93040					
Level I		99281									
Level II		99282									
Level III		99283		**TREATMENTS**	X	CODE	FEE	**TREATMENTS**	X	CODE	FEE
Level IV		99284		Flu Shot		90658					
Level V		99285									

DIAGNOSIS						
Abdominal Pain	789.00	Gastritis	535.50	OTHER DIAGNOSIS		CODE
Angina Pectoris, Unspec.	413.9	Hemorrhoids, NOS	455.6			
Asthma, Unspecified	493.90	Hiatal hernia	553.3			
Bronchitis, Acute	466.0	Hyperlipidemia, NOS	272.4			
Bursitis	727.3	Hypertension, Unspec.	401.9			
CHF	428.0	Hyperthyroidism	242.90	REFERRAL/COMMENTS		
Colon polyp	211.3	Hypothyroidism	244.9			
Conjunctivitis, Unspec.	372.00	Osteoarthritis, Unspec	715.90			
Diabetes Mellitus, Type I	250.01	Osteoporosis, postmen.	733.01			
Diabetes Mellitus, Type II	250.00	Pleurisy	511.0			
Diverticulosis, colon	562.10	Serious Otitis Media, Acute	381.01			
Emphysema	492.8	UTI	599.0			

DATE	PATIENT NAME	DOB	CHARGES	PAYMENT	BALANCE
01/04/20YY	OSTWALD SCOTTI	09/04/1958	100.00	0	100.00

I authorize my insurance benefits to be paid directly to the above named physician. I understand that I am obligated to pay deductibles, copayments, and charges for non-covered services. I authorize release of my medical information for billing purposes.

PATIENT SIGNATURE: Scotti Ostwald   **DATE:** 01/04/20YY

FIGURE A–18 Ostwald

SUPERIORLAND CLINIC
714 HENNEPIN AVENUE
BLUEBERRY ME 49855
906 3364600

Patient Number: 1-10

EIN: 494134726   **NPI:** 4567890123

PATIENT INFORMATION:
Name: WHITMAN, BEN, R
Address: 1414 WEST FAIR
City: BLUEBERRY
State: ME
Zip/4: 49855
Telephone: 906 3122900

Gender: M X   F
Status: Single   Married X   Other
Date of Birth: 08 05 1967
Employer: LAKE STATE UNIVERSITY
Student: FT   PT   School:

Work Related?   Y   N X
Employment Related?   Y   N X
Other Accident: Y   N X
Date of Accident:

Referring Physician: ROBERT HOWARD MD
Address:
Telephone:
NPI #: 3456789012

INSURANCE INFORMATION:
Primary Insurance
   Primary Insurance Name: PRUDENTIAL
   Address: PO BOX 99
   City: SALT LAKE CITY
   State: UT
   Zip/4: 89000-0099

   Plan ID#: PAR273403729
   Group #: LSU
   Primary Policyholder: WHITMAN, BEN, R
   Address: 1414 WEST FAIR
   City: BLUEBERRY
   State: ME
   Zip/4: 49855
   Policyholder Date of Birth: 08 05 1967
   Pt Relationship to Insured: Self X Spouse   Child   Other
   Employer/School Name: LAKE STATE UNIVERSITY

Secondary Insurance
   Secondary Insurance Name:
   Address:
   City:
   State:
   Zip/4:

   Plan ID#:
   Group #:
   Primary Policyholder:
   Address:
   City:
   State:
   Zip/4:
   Policyholder Date of Birth:
   Pt Relationship to Insured: Self   Spouse   Child   Other
   Employer/School Name:

ENCOUNTER INFORMATION:
Place of Service: 11

DIAGNOSIS INFORMATION

	Code	Diagnosis		Code	Diagnosis
1.	.		5.	.	
2.	.		6.	.	
3.	.		7.	.	
4.	.		8.	.	

PROCEDURE INFORMATION

	Description of Procedure/Service	Dates	Code	Mod	Dx Order	Unit Charge	Days/ Units
1.		-					
2.		-					
3.		-					
4.		-					
5.		-					
6.		-					

Special Notes: SEE ENCOUNTER FORM

FIGURE A–19 Case Study 1-10 Whitman

Elizabeth Foy, MD
Charles French, MD
(Robert Howard, MD)
Denzel Hamilton, MD
Roberta Pharyngeal, MD
Henry Romero, MD

Superiorland Clinic
714 Hennepin Avenue
Blueberry, ME 49855
Phone: (906) 336-4600   Fax: (906) 336-4020

NEW PATIENT	X	CODE	FEE	LAB TESTS	X	CODE	FEE	LAB TESTS	X	CODE	FEE
Level I		99201		AST		84450		LDH		83615	
Level II		99202		Albumin		82040		Lipid Panel	X	(80061)	45.00
Level III		99203		Alk Phos		84075		Metabolic Panel		80053	
Level IV	X	(99204)	70.00	BUN		84520		Obstetric Panel		80055	
Level V		99205		CBC	X	(85027)	30.00	Occult Blood		82270	
ESTABLISHED PATIENT				CBC/diff		85025		PAP smear		88150	
Level I		99211		CK/CPK		82550		PPD Skin Test		86580	
Level II		99212		Drug Screen		80100		Prothrombin Time		85610	
Level III		99213		Electrolyte Panel		80051		PSA		84152	
Level IV		99214		Estrogen		82671		Rapid Strep Screen		87880	
Level V		99215		Glucose/blood	X	(82947)	25.00	Sed Rate		85651	
OFFICE CONSULTATION				GTT		82951		TSH		84443	
Level I		99241		HgbA1C	X	(83036)	40.00	Urinalysis	X	(81000)	15.00
Level II		99242		Hepatitis Panel		80074					
Level III		99243		HIV Screen		86703					
Level IV		99244									
Level V		99245		OTHER TESTS				OTHER TESTS			
HOSPITAL INPATIENT				A/P Chest X-ray				Holter/24 hr			
Initial/Complex		99223		DXA Scan		77080		Sigmoidoscopy		45330	
Subsequent		99231		EKG Int/Report		93000		Stress Test		93015	
EMERGENCY DEPARTMENT SERV.				Rhythm EKG		93040					
Level I		99281									
Level II		99282									
Level III		99283		TREATMENTS	X	CODE	FEE	TREATMENTS	X	CODE	FEE
Level IV		99284		Flu Shot		90658					
Level V		99285									

DIAGNOSIS

Abdominal Pain	789.00	Gastritis	535.50	OTHER DIAGNOSIS	CODE
Angina Pectoris, Unspec.	413.9	Hemorrhoids, NOS	(455.6)		
Asthma, Unspecified	(493.90)	Hiatal hernia	553.3		
Bronchitis, Acute	466.0	Hyperlipidemia, NOS	272.4		
Bursitis	727.3	Hypertension, Unspec.	401.9		
CHF	428.0	Hyperthyroidism	242.90	REFERRAL/COMMENTS	
Colon polyp	211.3	Hypothyroidism	244.9		
Conjunctivitis, Unspec.	372.00	Osteoarthritis, Unspec	(715.90)		
Diabetes Mellitus, Type I	250.01	Osteoporosis, postmen.	733.01		
Diabetes Mellitus, Type II	(250.00)	Pleurisy	511.0		
Diverticulosis, colon	562.10	Serious Otitis Media, Acute	381.01		
Emphysema	492.8	UTI	599.0		

DATE	PATIENT NAME	DOB	CHARGES	PAYMENT	BALANCE
01/04/20YY	WHITMAN BEN	08/05/1967	225.00	0	225.00

I authorize my insurance benefits to be paid directly to the above named physician. I understand that I am obligated to pay deductibles, copayments, and charges for non-covered services. I authorize release of my medical information for billing purposes.

PATIENT SIGNATURE: Ben Whitman   **DATE:** 01/04/20YY

FIGURE A–20 Whitman

ASSIGNMENTS: CASE STUDIES 2-1 THROUGH 2-10

Congratulations! You have successfully completed Superiorland Clinic's probationary period for insurance billing specialists. You will now be completing claims for an independent billing company, for both Superiorland Clinic and for Blueberry Hospital. These cases include assigning ICD-9-CM and CPT medical codes, completing patient encounter forms, and completing CMS-1500s, as well as UB-04s for hospital services. Depending on your supervisor's instructions, you can complete these cases by using the SimClaim software that accompanies the textbook. Good luck!

Review all the patient information for each case. The blank encounter form has some of the frequently used diagnosis codes at Superiorland Clinic. When the patient's diagnosis, treatment, and related codes are not on the encounter form, you must assign the code and enter the information on the encounter form. If you do not have ICD-9-CM and/or CPT coding references, ask your supervisor for the correct codes.

The quick reference CMS-1500 guidelines have all the information you need to complete that form. For UB-04 claim forms, you must use the guidelines in Chapter 9 of the text. If the patient source documents do not have information for some of the UB-04 blocks, leave those blocks blank. **Please Note:** the UB-04 form available in SimClaim will allow you to complete, save, and print a UB-04 form, but there is no auto-grading or feedback with any claims you complete on the UB-04 form. You will need to print out any required UB-04s and submit to your supervisor for grading.

You may want to review the hints for using SimClaim that was given before Case Studies 1-1 through 1-10 *before* you attempt to complete the related case studies.

Special notes for using SimClaim and for individual Case Studies 2-1 through 2-10 are given here. Refer to these notes *before* you attempt to complete the related case studies.

General Instructions and Hints for Using The SimClaim Student Practice Software

Please read the following general instructions before working with the software:

- **Turn on Caps Lock:** All data entered into SimClaim must be in ALL CAPS.
- **Do not abbreviate:** Spell out words like street, drive, avenue, Signature on File, Blue Cross Blue Shield, etc. No abbreviations (other than state abbreviations) will be accepted by the program.
- **Do not use "Same As" or "None" in any block:** Even if patient information is the same as insured information, enter that information again on the claim.
- **More than one Diagnosis Pointer in Block 24E:** For the SimClaim case studies, there may be more than one diagnosis pointer required in block 24E.
- **No Amount Paid indicated:** If there is no amount paid indicated on the case study, enter "0 00" in block 29.
- **Secondary Insurance Claims:** If a Case Study indicates that a patient's primary insurance carrier has paid an amount, fill out a second claim form for the secondary insurance that reflects the amount reimbursed by primary insurance.
- **More than one CMS form:** Remember, if the place of service or the provider changes, another claim form is needed.
- **Fill out Block 32:** Always fill out service facility location information in SimClaim block 32.

- **Enter all dates as given in case study:** For dates that are not given (e.g., signature dates), use "MM DD YY." "YY" or "YYYY" is always used in place of an actual year, except for birthdates.
- For additional help using SimClaim, refer to the Block Help within SimClaim.

SPECIAL NOTES FOR CASE STUDIES 2-1 THROUGH 2-10

Case Study 2-1: Lucy C. Aguardo

Lucy Aguardo was seen by Dr. French on August 1, 20YY. Review the Case Study and Office Notes for this case, and complete the Encounter Form and a CMS-1500. Follow the guidelines for Commercial Claims.

Case Study 2-2: Charles Lightfoot

Charles Lightfoot is a new patient seen by Dr. Foy on August 1, 20YY. Review the Case Study and Office Notes for this case, and complete the Encounter Form and a CMS-1500. Follow the guidelines for Commercial Claims.

Case Study 2-3: Jenny Chen

Jenny Chen was seen by Dr. Pharyngeal on August 1, 20YY. Review the Case Study and Office Notes for this case, and complete the Encounter Form and a CMS-1500. Follow the guidelines for Blue Cross/Blue Shield, primary payer.

Case Study 2-4: Ronald G. Lawrence

Ronald Lawrence was seen by Dr. French on August 1, 20YY. Review the Case Study and Office Notes for this case, and complete the Encounter Form and a CMS-1500. Follow the guidelines for Commercial Claims, with Ronald's insurance as the primary payer.

Case Study 2-5: Michael R. Wood

1. Michael R. Wood was seen by Dr. Howard on August 1, 20YY. Review the Case Study and Office Notes for this case, and complete the Encounter Form and a CMS-1500, following the guidelines for Medicaid.
2. Complete a UB-04 for the services provided by Blueberry Hospital. Follow the guidelines in Chapter 9. Remember to save and print the UB-04 to PDF in order to submit the form to your supervisor for grading.

Case Study 2-6: Joline Z. Pelletier

Joline Pelletier was seen by Dr. Denzel Hamilton on July 20, 20YY; had surgery on July 23, 20YY; and was seen for a routine postoperative follow-up on August 2, 20YY. Review the Case Study and the Office and Hospital Notes for this case. The office visit of July 20, 20YY, is not part of the global surgery package because it was the encounter that resulted in the decision for surgery. An insurance claim was submitted for the July 20, 20YY, office visit. Complete an Encounter Form for the diagnoses, procedures, related codes, and charges for the surgery. The hospital visits following surgery are part of Medicare's "global surgery" package. Follow the guidelines for Medicare, primary payer.

Case Study 2-7: Jacob Niemi

Jacob Niemi was seen by Dr. Pharyngeal on August 2, 20YY. Review the Case Study and Office Notes for this case, and complete the Encounter Form and a CMS-1500. Follow the guidelines for Medicare/Medicaid Crossover. *Hint:* only one CMS claim is needed.

Case Study 2-8: Henrietta P. Wadsworth

1. Henrietta Wadsworth was seen by Dr. Romero on August 2, 20YY, for a routine postoperative office visit following laparoscopic cholecystectomy and cholangiography on July 16, 20YY. Review the Case Study, the Office and Hospital Notes, and complete an Encounter Form and CMS-1500 claim that includes services and charges for July 16, 20YY. Use the guidelines for Commercial Claims.
2. Complete a UB-04 for Henrietta's outpatient/ambulatory procedure provided by Blueberry Hospital. Remember to save and print the UB-04 to PDF in order to submit the form to your supervisor for grading.

Case Study 2-9: Takeesha A. Samuelson

1. Takeesha Samuelson was seen by Dr. Denzel Hamilton on August 2, 20YY, for a routine postoperative office visit following an emergency appendectomy on July 27, 20YY. Review the Case Study and Office and Hospital Notes for this case. Complete an Encounter Form that includes services and charges for July 27, 20YY. Complete a CMS-1500 for Medicare as primary payer. Follow the guidelines for Medicare, primary payer.
2. The UB-04 includes information related to hospital services. For Takeesha's inpatient hospital episode care, complete a UB-04 for services provided. Remember to save and print the UB-04 to PDF in order to submit the form to your supervisor for grading.

Case Study 2-10: Peter K. Fraun

Peter Fraun is a new patient seen by Dr. Foy on August 2, 20YY. Review Peter's physical examination report, and complete the encounter form and a CMS-1500. Use the guidelines for Commercial Claims.

SUPERIORLAND CLINIC
714 HENNEPIN AVENUE
BLUEBERRY ME 49855
906   3364600

Patient Number: 2-1

EIN: 494134726   **NPI:**   4567890123

PATIENT INFORMATION:
Name: AGUARDO, LUCY, C
Address: 1920 DIVISION
City: BLUEBERRY
State: ME
Zip/4: 49855
Telephone: 906 3122560

Gender: M   F X
Status: Single   Married X   Other
Date of Birth: 06   17   1970
Employer: BLUEBERRY REDIMIX
Student: FT   PT   School:

Work Related?   Y   N X
Employment Related?   Y   N X
Other Accident: Y X   N
Date of Accident:

Referring Physician: CHARLES FRENCH MD
Address:
Telephone:
NPI #:   2345678901

INSURANCE INFORMATION:
Primary Insurance
       Primary Insurance Name: LEXCO HOMEOWNERS INSURANCE
       Address: PO BOX 4123
       City: SPRINGFIELD
       State: ME
       Zip/4: 44437-4123

       Plan ID#: PP0537491
       Group #:
       Primary Policyholder: AGUARDO, LUCY, C
       Address: 1920 DIVISION
       City: BLUEBERRY
       State: ME
       Zip/4: 49855
       Policyholder Date of Birth: 06   17   1970
       Pt Relationship to Insured: Self X Spouse   Child   Other
       Employer/School Name: BLUEBERRY REDIMIX

Secondary Insurance
       Secondary Insurance Name:
       Address:
       City:
       State:
       Zip/4:

       Plan ID#:
       Group #:
       Primary Policyholder:
       Address:
       City:
       State:
       Zip/4:
       Policyholder Date of Birth:
       Pt Relationship to Insured: Self   Spouse   Child   Other
       Employer/School Name:

ENCOUNTER INFORMATION:
Place of Service: 11

DIAGNOSIS INFORMATION

	Code	Diagnosis		Code	Diagnosis
1.	.		5.	.	
2.	.		6.	.	
3.	.		7.	.	
4.	.		8.	.	

PROCEDURE INFORMATION

	Description of Procedure/Service	Dates	Code	Mod	Dx Order	Unit Charge	Days/ Units
1.		-					
2.		-					
3.		-					
4.		-					
5.		-					
6.		-					

Special Notes: SEE ENCOUNTER FORM AND OFFICE NOTES

FIGURE A–21 Aguardo

Elizabeth Foy, MD
Charles French, MD
Robert Howard, MD
Denzel Hamilton, MD
Roberta Pharyngeal, MD
Henry Romero, MD

Superiorland Clinic
714 Hennepin Avenue
Blueberry, ME 49855
Phone: (906) 336-4600   Fax: (906) 336-4020

NEW PATIENT	X	CODE	FEE	LAB TESTS	X	CODE	FEE	LAB TESTS	X	CODE	FEE
Level I		99201		AST		84450		LDH		83615	
Level II		99202		Albumin		82040		Lipid Panel		80061	
Level III		99203		Alk Phos		84075		Metabolic Panel		80053	
Level IV		99204		BUN		84520		Obstetric Panel		80055	
Level V		99205		CBC		85027		Occult Blood		82270	
ESTABLISHED PATIENT				CBC/diff		85025		PAP smear		88150	
Level I		99211		CK/CPK		82550		PPD Skin Test		86580	
Level II		99212		Drug Screen		80100		Prothrombin Time		85610	
Level III	X	99213		Electrolyte Panel		80051		PSA		84152	
Level IV		99214		Estrogen		82671		Rapid Strep Screen		87880	
Level V		99215		Glucose/blood		82947		Sed Rate		85651	
OFFICE CONSULTATION				GTT		82951		TSH		84443	
Level I		99241		HgbA1C		83036		Urinalysis		81000	
Level II		99242		Hepatitis Panel		80074					
Level III		99243		HIV Screen		86703					
Level IV		99244									
Level V		99245		OTHER TESTS				OTHER TESTS			
HOSPITAL INPATIENT				A/P Chest X-ray				Holter/24 hr			
Initial/Complex		99223		DXA Scan		77080		Sigmoidoscopy		45330	
Subsequent		99231		EKG Int/Report		93000		Stress Test		93015	
EMERGENCY DEPARTMENT SERV.				Rhythm EKG		93040					
Level I		99281									
Level II		99282									
Level III		99283		TREATMENTS	X	CODE	FEE	TREATMENTS	X	CODE	FEE
Level IV		99284		Flu Shot		90658					
Level V		99285									

DIAGNOSIS

Abdominal Pain	789.00	Gastritis	535.50	OTHER DIAGNOSIS			CODE
Angina Pectoris, Unspec.	413.9	Hemorrhoids, NOS	455.6				
Asthma, Unspecified	493.90	Hiatal hernia	553.3				
Bronchitis, Acute	466.0	Hyperlipidemia, NOS	272.4				
Bursitis	727.3	Hypertension, Unspec.	401.9				
CHF	428.0	Hyperthyroidism	242.90	REFERRAL/COMMENTS			
Colon polyp	211.3	Hypothyroidism	244.9				
Conjunctivitis, Unspec.	372.00	Osteoarthritis, Unspec	715.90				
Diabetes Mellitus, Type I	250.01	Osteoporosis, postmen.	733.01				
Diabetes Mellitus, Type II	250.00	Pleurisy	511.0				
Diverticulosis, colon	562.10	Serious Otitis Media, Acute	381.01				
Emphysema	492.8	UTI	599.0				

DATE	PATIENT NAME		DOB	CHARGES	PAYMENT	BALANCE

I authorize my insurance benefits to be paid directly to the above named physician. I understand that I am obligated to pay deductibles, copayments, and charges for non-covered services. I authorize release of my medical information for billing purposes.

PATIENT SIGNATURE: DATE:

FIGURE A–22 Aguardo

OFFICE NOTE: Lucy Aguardo

DATE: August 1, 20xx

SUBJECTIVE: Mrs. Aguardo slipped and fell at home, landing on her left wrist on July 30, 20xx. She was seen in the Blueberry Community Hospital Emergency Department, and x-rays taken at that time were negative for fracture. A volar splint was placed in the position of function, and she was instructed to follow-up with her family physician, Dr. Charles French. Today, Mrs. Aguardo states she has minimal pain.

OBJECTIVE: A review of the x-rays taken in the emergency department confirms no fractures are present. I removed the splint and examined the wrist. No swelling was noted. A small bruise was noted on the volar aspect of the wrist. No tenderness in the anatomical snuffbox, the scaphoid tubercle, or ulnar style was noted. Full range of motion of the elbow was present. The wrist had decreased range of flexion and extension secondary to slight pain. There was good supination and pronation.

ASSESSMENT: Contusion of right wrist.

PLAN: Discontinue splint. Mrs. Aguardo was advised to resume normal activities as tolerated.

SIGNED: Charles French, MD

FIGURE A–23 Case Study 2-1 Aguardo

SUPERIORLAND CLINIC
714 HENNEPIN AVENUE
BLUEBERRY ME 49855
906 3364600

Patient Number: 2-2

EIN: 494134726   **NPI:** 4567890123

PATIENT INFORMATION:
Name: LIGHTFOOT, CHARLES
Address: 610 LASALLE STREET
City: BLUEBERRY
State: ME
Zip/4: 49855
Telephone: 906 3123671

Gender: M X   F
Status: Single   Married X   Other
Date of Birth: 10   03   1965
Employer: BLUEBERRY REDIMIX
Student: FT   PT   School:

Work Related? Y   N X
Employment Related? Y   N X
Other Accident: Y   N X
Date of Accident:

Referring Physician: ELIZABETH FOY MD
Address:
Telephone:
NPI #: 7890123456

INSURANCE INFORMATION:
Primary Insurance
  Primary Insurance Name: AETNA
  Address: PO BOX 45
  City: STILLWATER
  State: PA
  Zip/4: 12345-0045

  Plan ID#: VXY648502
  Group #: 6659
  Primary Policyholder: LIGHTFOOT, CHARLES
  Address: 610 LASALLE STREET
  City: BLUEBERRY
  State: ME
  Zip/4: 49855
  Policyholder Date of Birth: 10   03   1965
  Pt Relationship to Insured: Self X Spouse   Child   Other
  Employer/School Name: BLUEBERRY REDIMIX

Secondary Insurance
  Secondary Insurance Name:
  Address:
  City:
  State:
  Zip/4:

  Plan ID#:
  Group #:
  Primary Policyholder:
  Address:
  City:
  State:
  Zip/4:
  Policyholder Date of Birth:
  Pt Relationship to Insured: Self   Spouse   Child   Other
  Employer/School Name:

ENCOUNTER INFORMATION:
Place of Service: 11

DIAGNOSIS INFORMATION

	Code	Diagnosis		Code	Diagnosis
1.	.		5.	.	
2.	.		6.	.	
3.	.		7.	.	
4.	.		8.	.	

PROCEDURE INFORMATION

	Description of Procedure/Service	Dates	Code	Mod	Dx Order	Unit Charge	Days/ Units
1.		-					
2.		-					
3.		-					
4.		-					
5.		-					
6.		-					

Special Notes: SEE ENCOUNTER FORM AND OFFICE NOTES

FIGURE A–24 Lightfoot

Elizabeth Foy, MD	Superiorland Clinic
Charles French, MD Robert Howard, MD Denzel Hamilton, MD Roberta Pharyngeal, MD Henry Romero, MD	**Superiorland Clinic** 714 Hennepin Avenue Blueberry, ME 49855 Phone: (906) 336-4600 Fax: (906) 336-4020

NEW PATIENT	X	CODE	FEE	LAB TESTS	X	CODE	FEE	LAB TESTS	X	CODE	FEE
Level I		99201		AST		84450		LDH		83615	
Level II		99202		Albumin		82040		Lipid Panel		80061	
Level III		99203		Alk Phos		84075		Metabolic Panel		80053	
Level IV		99204		BUN		84520		Obstetric Panel		80055	
Level V		99205		CBC		85027		Occult Blood		82270	
ESTABLISHED PATIENT				CBC/diff		85025		PAP smear		88150	
Level I		99211		CK/CPK		82550		PPD Skin Test		86580	
Level II		99212		Drug Screen		80100		Prothrombin Time		85610	
Level III		99213		Electrolyte Panel		80051		PSA		84152	
Level IV		99214		Estrogen		82671		Rapid Strep Screen		87880	
Level V		99215		Glucose/blood		82947		Sed Rate		85651	
OFFICE CONSULTATION				GTT		82951		TSH		84443	
Level I		99241		HgbA1C		83036		Urinalysis		81000	
Level II		99242		Hepatitis Panel		80074					
Level III		99243		HIV Screen		86703					
Level IV		99244									
Level V		99245		**OTHER TESTS**				**OTHER TESTS**			
HOSPITAL INPATIENT				A/P Chest X-ray				Holter/24 hr			
Initial/Complex		99223		DXA Scan		77080		Sigmoidoscopy		45330	
Subsequent		99231		EKG Int/Report		93000		Stress Test		93015	
EMERGENCY DEPARTMENT SERV.				Rhythm EKG		93040					
Level I		99281									
Level II		99282									
Level III		99283		**TREATMENTS**	X	CODE	FEE	**TREATMENTS**	X	CODE	FEE
Level IV		99284		Flu Shot		90658					
Level V		99285									

			DIAGNOSIS				
Abdominal Pain	789.00	Gastritis	535.50	OTHER DIAGNOSIS			CODE
Angina Pectoris, Unspec.	413.9	Hemorrhoids, NOS	455.6	*Strep throat*			*034.0*
Asthma, Unspecified	493.90	Hiatal hernia	553.3				
Bronchitis, Acute	466.0	Hyperlipidemia, NOS	272.4				
Bursitis	727.3	Hypertension, Unspec.	401.9				
CHF	428.0	Hyperthyroidism	242.90	REFERRAL/COMMENTS			
Colon polyp	211.3	Hypothyroidism	244.9				
Conjunctivitis, Unspec.	372.00	Osteoarthritis, Unspec	715.90				
Diabetes Mellitus, Type I	250.01	Osteoporosis, postmen.	733.01				
Diabetes Mellitus, Type II	250.00	Pleurisy	511.0				
Diverticulosis, colon	562.10	Serious Otitis Media, Acute	381.01				
Emphysema	492.8	UTI	599.0				

DATE	PATIENT NAME	DOB	CHARGES	PAYMENT	BALANCE

I authorize my insurance benefits to be paid directly to the above named physician. I understand that I am obligated to pay deductibles, copayments, and charges for non-covered services. I authorize release of my medical information for billing purposes.

PATIENT SIGNATURE: **DATE:**

FIGURE A–25 Lightfoot

NEW PATIENT OFFICE VISIT: Charles Lightfoot

DATE: August 1, 20xx

HISTORY OF PRESENT ILLNESS: Mr. Lightfoot is seen today as a new patient and complains of difficulty breathing, a low-grade fever for the past three days, and a sore throat.

PAST MEDICAL HISTORY: Mr. Lightfoot states that he has been in relatively good health. Recent illnesses include bronchopneumonia in 1999, salmonella poisoning in 1994, and an episode of depression following the death of his father in 1990. He has had the usual childhood diseases.

FAMILY HISTORY: Mr. Lightfoot states that his father died of a massive stroke and his mother is a diabetic. She is insulin-dependent. He has three siblings—one brother and two sisters—who are in good health as far as he knows. He was not aware of any history of heart, kidney, or liver disease in his immediate family. One uncle died of prostate cancer at age 89.

SOCIAL HISTORY: Mr. Lightfoot has been married for 15 years and has two children: a son age 12 and a daughter age 9. He states that he and his wife are happy, and the children are well-adjusted. He denies any tobacco, alcohol, or other substance use. He drinks 2–3 cups of coffee a day and exercises regularly by taking a daily 30-minute walk with his wife.

PHYSICAL EXAMINATION: The patient is a well-nourished, well-developed Native American male who expresses no other distress other than the reason he is here today. Weight: 210 lb. Height: 6'. Blood Pressure: 162/82. Pulse: 80. Respirations: 16. Temperature: 100.6° F.

Patient states he has NO ALLERGIES.

HEENT: Head, eyes, ears, and nose are unremarkable. Throat is beefy red with tonsillar exudatepresent.

NECK: Normal jugular venous pressure. Normal carotid pulses. No bruits present. Thyroid is not enlarged. No nodes palpable.

LUNGS: On auscultation, scattered high- and low-pitched rhonchi are heard. There are occasional crackling and moist-sounding rales at the lung bases. Wheezing is noted on expiration.

CARDIAC: Regular rhythm with normal S1 and S2. There is no murmur, rub, click, or gallop. Cardiac apex is not palpable. No heaves or thrills are detected.

ABDOMEN: Soft and nontender, with normal bowel sounds and no bruits. No organomegaly or masses noted. Liver edges are discernible.

EXTREMITIES: No evidence of edema. Peripheral pulses are adequate.

NEUROLOGIC: Grossly within normal limits.

LABORATORY FINDINGS: Rapid strep throat culture revealed the presence of group A beta-hemolytic streptococcus. A/P chest x-ray was negative.

DIAGNOSES: Acute bronchitis. Strep throat.

PLAN: Mr. Lightfoot was started on penicillin G 250 mg orally q 6 h for 10 days. He is to call if his symptoms worsen or if he notices any type of rash. He is to return in 10 days for a recheck.

SIGNED: Elizabeth Foy, MD

REFERRED BY: Wade Morrison, MD

FIGURE A–26 Case Study 2-2 Lightfoot

SUPERIORLAND CLINIC
714 HENNEPIN AVENUE
BLUEBERRY ME 49855
906 3364600

Patient Number: 2-3

EIN: 494134726   **NPI:**   4567890123

PATIENT INFORMATION:
Name: CHEN, JENNY
Address: 1815 EAST TRUMAN
City: BLUEBERRY
State: ME
Zip/4: 49855
Telephone: 906 3129643

Gender: M   F X
Status: Single   Married X   Other
Date of Birth: 03   15   1959
Employer: FIRST NATIONAL BANK
Student: FT   PT   School:

Work Related?   Y   N X
Employment Related?   Y   N X
Other Accident: Y   N X
Date of Accident:

Referring Physician: ROBERTA PHARYNGEAL MD
Address:
Telephone:
NPI #:   5678901234

INSURANCE INFORMATION:
Primary Insurance
    Primary Insurance Name: BLUE CROSS BLUE SHIELD
    Address: PO BOX 1121
    City: MEDICAL
    State: PA
    Zip/4: 12357-1121

    Plan ID#: WXY497808167
    Group #: 219
    Primary Policyholder: CHEN, JENNY
    Address: 1815 EAST TRUMAN
    City: BLUEBERRY
    State: ME
    Zip/4: 49855
    Policyholder Date of Birth: 03   15   59
    Pt Relationship to Insured: Self X Spouse   Child   Other
    Employer/School Name: FIRST NATIONAL BANK

Secondary Insurance
    Secondary Insurance Name:
    Address:
    City:
    State:
    Zip/4:

    Plan ID#:
    Group #:
    Primary Policyholder:
    Address:
    City:
    State:
    Zip/4:
    Policyholder Date of Birth:
    Pt Relationship to Insured: Self   Spouse   Child   Other
    Employer/School Name:

ENCOUNTER INFORMATION:
Place of Service: 11

DIAGNOSIS INFORMATION

	Code	Diagnosis		Code	Diagnosis
1.	.		5.	.	
2.	.		6.	.	
3.	.		7.	.	
4.	.		8.	.	

PROCEDURE INFORMATION

	Description of Procedure/Service	Dates	Code	Mod	Dx Order	Unit Charge	Days/ Units
1.		-					
2.		-					
3.		-					
4.		-					
5.		-					
6.		-					

Special Notes: SEE ENCOUNTER FORM AND OFFICE NOTES

FIGURE A–27 Chen

Elizabeth Foy, MD
Charles French, MD
Robert Howard, MD
Denzel Hamilton, MD
Roberta Pharyngeal, MD
Henry Romero, MD

Superiorland Clinic
714 Hennepin Avenue
Blueberry, ME 49855
Phone: (906) 336-4600 Fax: (906) 336-4020

NEW PATIENT	X	CODE	FEE	LAB TESTS	X	CODE	FEE	LAB TESTS	X	CODE	FEE
Level I		99201		AST		84450		LDH		83615	
Level II		99202		Albumin		82040		Lipid Panel		80061	
Level III		99203		Alk Phos		84075		Metabolic Panel		80053	
Level IV		99204		BUN		84520		Obstetric Panel		80055	
Level V		99205		CBC		85027		Occult Blood		82270	
ESTABLISHED PATIENT				CBC/diff		85025		PAP smear		88150	
Level I		99211		CK/CPK		82550		PPD Skin Test		86580	
Level II		99212		Drug Screen		80100		Prothrombin Time		85610	
Level III		99213		Electrolyte Panel		80051		PSA		84152	
Level IV		99214		Estrogen		82671		Rapid Strep Screen		87880	
Level V		99215		Glucose/blood		82947		Sed Rate		85651	
OFFICE CONSULTATION				GTT		82951		TSH		84443	
Level I		99241		HgbA1C		83036		Urinalysis		81000	
Level II		99242		Hepatitis Panel		80074					
Level III		99243		HIV Screen		86703					
Level IV		99244									
Level V		99245		**OTHER TESTS**				**OTHER TESTS**			
HOSPITAL INPATIENT				A/P Chest X-ray				Holter/24 hr			
Initial/Complex		99223		DXA Scan		77080		Sigmoidoscopy		45330	
Subsequent		99231		EKG Int/Report		93000		Stress Test		93015	
EMERGENCY DEPARTMENT SERV.				Rhythm EKG		93040					
Level I		99281									
Level II		99282									
Level III		99283		**TREATMENTS**	X	CODE	FEE	**TREATMENTS**	X	CODE	FEE
Level IV		99284		Flu Shot		90658					
Level V		99285									

DIAGNOSIS

Abdominal Pain	789.00	Gastritis	535.50	OTHER DIAGNOSIS	CODE
Angina Pectoris, Unspec.	413.9	Hemorrhoids, NOS	455.6		
Asthma, Unspecified	493.90	Hiatal hernia	553.3		
Bronchitis, Acute	466.0	Hyperlipidemia, NOS	272.4		
Bursitis	727.3	Hypertension, Unspec.	401.9		
CHF	428.0	Hyperthyroidism	242.90	REFERRAL/COMMENTS	
Colon polyp	211.3	Hypothyroidism	244.9		
Conjunctivitis, Unspec.	372.00	Osteoarthritis, Unspec	715.90		
Diabetes Mellitus, Type I	250.01	Osteoporosis, postmen.	733.01		
Diabetes Mellitus, Type II	250.00	Pleurisy	511.0		
Diverticulosis, colon	562.10	Serious Otitis Media, Acute	381.01		
Emphysema	492.8	UTI	599.0		

DATE	PATIENT NAME	DOB	CHARGES	PAYMENT	BALANCE

I authorize my insurance benefits to be paid directly to the above named physician. I understand that I am obligated to pay deductibles, copayments, and charges for non-covered services. I authorize release of my medical information for billing purposes.

PATIENT SIGNATURE: **DATE:**

FIGURE A–28 Chen

OFFICE NOTE: Jenny Chen

DATE: August 1, 20xx

CHIEF COMPLAINT: Return office visit and PAP smear.

SUBJECTIVE: Ms. Chen presents today for a return office visit for fatigue, dermatitis, and a PAP smear. She is currently on Tegretol 200 mg q day. She complains of being chronically tired and falls asleep at inopportune times. She has noticed a whitish discharge and irritation of her vagina. She states her dermatitis has recurred on both elbows and knees and believes this is related to stress.

PHYSICAL EXAM: Examination today reveals a healthy-appearing female who is alert and in no acute distress. Blood pressure: 118/72. Weight: 165 lb. Pulse: 84. Denies any allergies.

HEENT: Pupils are equal and react to light and accommodation. Extraocular movements are within normal limits. Conjunctivae are normal. The fundi and anterior chambers are unremarkable. Tympanic membranes were pearly gray. Throat is unremarkable.

NECK: Supple. No adenopathy or thyromegaly.

LUNGS: Bilateral inspiratory wheezes are heard.

HEART: Regular sinus rhythm. No murmurs, gallops, or clicks.

BREASTS: Unremarkable. No masses, tenderness, discharge, or dimpling.

ABDOMEN: Soft, flat, and nontender. No hepatosplenomegaly.

PELVIC: Bartholin's, urethral, and Skene's glands are normal. The vulva is edematous. The vaginal vault has diffuse reddening, and there is a thick white discharge. The cervix is nulliparous. The uterus is midline, mobile, anterior, and nontender. There are no adnexal masses palpable. The vagina appears to be stimulated and irritated by the discharge.

EXTREMITIES: Nonremarkable.

SKIN: Knees and elbows exhibit patchy areas of maculopapular dermatitis.

LABORATORY DATA: Wet mount of vaginal discharge positive for yeast. Negative for pus cells or trichomonas.

ASSESSMENT: Monilial vaginitis. Atopic dermatitis. Fatigue.

PLAN: 1. Terazol 7 vaginal cream; one application q hs times seven days. 2. Atarax 25 mg tid as needed for pruritus and anxiety. 3. Hepatic panel, Epstein-Barr titer, and CBC today. 4. PAP smear is deferred until the yeast infection clears. 5. Return in two weeks for recheck and PAP smear.

SIGNED: Roberta Pharyngeal, MD

FIGURE A–29 Case Study 2-3 Chen

SUPERIORLAND CLINIC
714 HENNEPIN AVENUE
BLUEBERRY ME 49855
906 3364600

Patient Number: 2-4

EIN: 494134726   **NPI:** 4567890123

PATIENT INFORMATION:
Name: LAWRENCE, RONALD, G
Address: 360 SOUTH 35TH STREET
City: BLUEBERRY
State: ME
Zip/4: 49855
Telephone: 906 3126558

Gender: M X   F
Status: Single   Married X   Other
Date of Birth: 01   04   1946
Employer: COUNTY ROAD COMMISSION
Student: FT   PT   School:

Work Related?   Y   N X
Employment Related?   Y   N X
Other Accident: Y   N X
Date of Accident:

Referring Physician:
Address:
Telephone:
NPI #:

INSURANCE INFORMATION:
Primary Insurance
  Primary Insurance Name: GOVERNMENT EMPLOYEE PLAN
  Address: PO BOX 7998
  City: SPRINGFIELD
  State: ME
  Zip/4: 44437-7998

  Plan ID#: PP581039
  Group #: 303
  Primary Policyholder: LAWRENCE, RONALD, G
  Address: 360 SOUTH 35TH STREET
  City: BLUEBERRY
  State: ME
  Zip/4: 49855
  Policyholder Date of Birth: 01   04   1946
  Pt Relationship to Insured: Self X Spouse   Child   Other
  Employer/School Name: COUNTY ROAD COMMISSION

Secondary Insurance
  Secondary Insurance Name: PRUDENTIAL
  Address:
  City:
  State:
  Zip/4:

  Plan ID#: PP04158
  Group #:
  Primary Policyholder: LAWRENCE, JUDITH
  Address: 360 SOUTH 35TH STREET
  City: BLUEBERRY
  State: ME
  Zip/4: 49855
  Policyholder Date of Birth: 09   29   1945
  Pt Relationship to Insured: Self   Spouse X Child   Other
  Employer/School Name: GRANDMAS GARDEN

ENCOUNTER INFORMATION:
Place of Service: 11

DIAGNOSIS INFORMATION

	Code	Diagnosis		Code	Diagnosis
1.	.		5.	.	
2.	.		6.	.	
3.	.		7.	.	
4.	.		8.	.	

PROCEDURE INFORMATION

	Description of Procedure/Service	Dates	Code	Mod	Dx Order	Unit Charge	Days/ Units
1.		-					
2.		-					
3.		-					
4.		-					
5.		-					
6.		-					

Special Notes: SEE ENCOUNTER FORM AND OFFICE NOTES

FIGURE A–30 Lawrence

Elizabeth Foy, MD
Charles French, MD
Robert Howard, MD
Denzel Hamilton, MD
Roberta Pharyngeal, MD
Henry Romero, MD

Superiorland Clinic
714 Hennepin Avenue
Blueberry, ME 49855
Phone: (906) 336-4600   Fax: (906) 336-4020

NEW PATIENT	X	CODE	FEE	LAB TESTS	X	CODE	FEE	LAB TESTS	X	CODE	FEE
Level I		99201		AST		84450		LDH		83615	
Level II		99202		Albumin		82040		Lipid Panel		80061	
Level III		99203		Alk Phos		84075		Metabolic Panel		80053	
Level IV		99204		BUN		84520		Obstetric Panel		80055	
Level V		99205		CBC		85027		Occult Blood		82270	
ESTABLISHED PATIENT				CBC/diff		85025		PAP smear		88150	
Level I		99211		CK/CPK		82550		PPD Skin Test		86580	
Level II		99212		Drug Screen		80100		Prothrombin Time		85610	
Level III		99213		Electrolyte Panel		80051		PSA		84152	
Level IV		99214		Estrogen		82671		Rapid Strep Screen		87880	
Level V		99215		Glucose/blood		82947		Sed Rate		85651	
OFFICE CONSULTATION				GTT		82951		TSH		84443	
Level I		99241		HgbA1C		83036		Urinalysis		81000	
Level II		99242		Hepatitis Panel		80074					
Level III		99243		HIV Screen		86703					
Level IV		99244									
Level V		99245		**OTHER TESTS**				**OTHER TESTS**			
HOSPITAL INPATIENT				A/P Chest X-ray				Holter/24 hr			
Initial/Complex		99223		DXA Scan		77080		Sigmoidoscopy		45330	
Subsequent		99231		EKG Int/Report		93000		Stress Test		93015	
EMERGENCY DEPARTMENT SERV.				Rhythm EKG		93040					
Level I		99281									
Level II		99282									
Level III		99283		**TREATMENTS**	X	CODE	FEE	**TREATMENTS**	X	CODE	FEE
Level IV		99284		Flu Shot		90658					
Level V		99285									

DIAGNOSIS

Abdominal Pain	789.00	Gastritis	535.50	OTHER DIAGNOSIS	CODE
Angina Pectoris, Unspec.	413.9	Hemorrhoids, NOS	455.6		
Asthma, Unspecified	493.90	Hiatal hernia	553.3		
Bronchitis, Acute	466.0	Hyperlipidemia, NOS	272.4		
Bursitis	727.3	Hypertension, Unspec.	401.9		
CHF	428.0	Hyperthyroidism	242.90	REFERRAL/COMMENTS	
Colon polyp	211.3	Hypothyroidism	244.9		
Conjunctivitis, Unspec.	372.00	Osteoarthritis, Unspec	715.90		
Diabetes Mellitus, Type I	250.01	Osteoporosis, postmen.	733.01		
Diabetes Mellitus, Type II	250.00	Pleurisy	511.0		
Diverticulosis, colon	562.10	Serious Otitis Media, Acute	381.01		
Emphysema	492.8	UTI	599.0		

DATE	PATIENT NAME	DOB	CHARGES	PAYMENT	BALANCE

I authorize my insurance benefits to be paid directly to the above named physician. I understand that I am obligated to pay deductibles, copayments, and charges for non-covered services. I authorize release of my medical information for billing purposes.

PATIENT SIGNATURE: **DATE:**

FIGURE A–31 Lawrence

OFFICE NOTE: Ronald Lawrence

DATE: August 1, 20xx

CHIEF COMPLAINT: Rash on feet and trunk.

SUBJECTIVE: Mr. Lawrence is seen today for several problems, including a dry cough, which has been present for about one month. He has a rash on his feet and left lateral trunk that blisters and bleeds when he scratches it. The rash has been present for two or three days. He denies fever and chills.

PHYSICAL EXAM: Examination today reveals a healthy-appearing male who is alert and in no acute distress, other than the rash and itching. Blood pressure: 148/82. Weight: 185 lb. Pulse: 80. Denies any allergies.

HEENT: Within normal limits and without inflammation.

NECK: Supple.

CHEST: Clear.

SKIN: The left lateral abdomen reveals an erythematous and raised patch, with overlying clear vesicles, that is very tender to the touch. No cellulitis is appreciated. The feet reveal peeling tinea pedis, with no secondary infection. The hands are clear.

ASSESSMENT: Acute herpes simplex, left lateral trunk. Tinea pedis. Cough, possible bronchospasm.

PLAN: 1. Zovirax 200 mg tid. 2. Micatin 2% powder to feet morning and evening. 3. Macrodantin 50 mg qid with meals and at bedtime. 4. Trial of Ventolin inhaler. Return in two weeks, or sooner if necessary, depending on course of herpes simplex, tinea pedis, and reaction to Ventolin.

SIGNED: Charles French, MD

FIGURE A–32 Case Study 2-4 Lawrence

SUPERIORLAND CLINIC
714 HENNEPIN AVENUE
BLUEBERRY ME 49855
906   3364600

Patient Number: 2-5

EIN: 494134726   **NPI:**   4567890123

PATIENT INFORMATION:
Name: WOOD, MICHAEL, R
Address: 1501 JOLIET STREET
City: BLUEBERRY
State: ME
Zip/4: 49855
Telephone: 9063127669

Gender: M X   F
Status: Single X   Married   Other
Date of Birth: 05   20   1950
Employer:
Student: FT   PT   School:

Work Related? Y   N X
Employment Related? Y   N X
Other Accident: Y   N X
Date of Accident:

Referring Physician: ROBERT HOWARD MD
Address:
Telephone:
NPI #: 3456789012

INSURANCE INFORMATION:
Primary Insurance
  Primary Insurance Name: MEDICAID
  Address: PO BOX 300
  City: SPRINGFIELD
  State: ME
  Zip/4: 44437-0300

  Plan ID#: ME500389
  Group #:
  Primary Policyholder: WOOD, MICHAEL, R
  Address: 1501 JOLIET STREET
  City: BLUEBERRY
  State: ME
  Zip/4: 49855
  Policyholder Date of Birth: 05   20   1950
  Pt Relationship to Insured: Self X Spouse   Child   Other
  Employer/School Name:

Secondary Insurance
  Secondary Insurance Name:
  Address:
  City:
  State:
  Zip/4:

  Plan ID#:
  Group #:
  Primary Policyholder:
  Address:
  City:
  State:
  Zip/4:
  Policyholder Date of Birth:
  Pt Relationship to Insured: Self   Spouse   Child   Other
  Employer/School Name:

ENCOUNTER INFORMATION:
Place of Service: 11

DIAGNOSIS INFORMATION

	Code	Diagnosis		Code	Diagnosis
1.	.		5.	.	
2.	.		6.	.	
3.	.		7.	.	
4.	.		8.	.	

PROCEDURE INFORMATION

	Description of Procedure/Service	Dates	Code	Mod	Dx Order	Unit Charge	Days/ Units
1.		-					
2.		-					
3.		-					
4.		-					
5.		-					
6.		-					

Special Notes: SEE ENCOUNTER FORM AND OFFICE NOTES

FIGURE A–33 Wood

Elizabeth Foy, MD
Charles French, MD
Robert Howard, MD
Denzel Hamilton, MD
Roberta Pharyngeal, MD
Henry Romero, MD

Superiorland Clinic
714 Hennepin Avenue
Blueberry, ME 49855
Phone: (906) 336-4600   Fax: (906) 336-4020

NEW PATIENT	X	CODE	FEE	LAB TESTS	X	CODE	FEE	LAB TESTS	X	CODE	FEE
Level I		99201		AST		84450		LDH		83615	
Level II		99202		Albumin		82040		Lipid Panel		80061	
Level III		99203		Alk Phos		84075		Metabolic Panel		80053	
Level IV		99204		BUN		84520		Obstetric Panel		80055	
Level V		99205		CBC		85027		Occult Blood		82270	
ESTABLISHED PATIENT				CBC/diff		85025		PAP smear		88150	
Level I		99211		CK/CPK		82550		PPD Skin Test		86580	
Level II		99212		Drug Screen		80100		Prothrombin Time		85610	
Level III		99213		Electrolyte Panel		80051		PSA		84152	
Level IV		99214		Estrogen		82671		Rapid Strep Screen		87880	
Level V		99215		Glucose/blood		82947		Sed Rate		85651	
OFFICE CONSULTATION				GTT		82951		TSH		84443	
Level I		99241		HgbA1C		83036		Urinalysis		81000	
Level II		99242		Hepatitis Panel		80074					
Level III		99243		HIV Screen		86703					
Level IV		99244									
Level V		99245		**OTHER TESTS**				**OTHER TESTS**			
HOSPITAL INPATIENT				A/P Chest X-ray				Holter/24 hr			
Initial/Complex		99223		DXA Scan		77080		Sigmoidoscopy		45330	
Subsequent		99231		EKG Int/Report		93000		Stress Test		93015	
EMERGENCY DEPARTMENT SERV.				Rhythm EKG		93040					
Level I		99281									
Level II		99282									
Level III		99283		**TREATMENTS**	X	CODE	FEE	**TREATMENTS**	X	CODE	FEE
Level IV		99284		Flu Shot		90658					
Level V		99285									

DIAGNOSIS							
Abdominal Pain	789.00	Gastritis	535.50	OTHER DIAGNOSIS			CODE
Angina Pectoris, Unspec.	413.9	Hemorrhoids, NOS	455.6				
Asthma, Unspecified	493.90	Hiatal hernia	553.3				
Bronchitis, Acute	466.0	Hyperlipidemia, NOS	272.4				
Bursitis	727.3	Hypertension, Unspec.	401.9				
CHF	428.0	Hyperthyroidism	242.90	REFERRAL/COMMENTS			
Colon polyp	211.3	Hypothyroidism	244.9				
Conjunctivitis, Unspec.	372.00	Osteoarthritis, Unspec	715.90				
Diabetes Mellitus, Type I	250.01	Osteoporosis, postmen.	733.01				
Diabetes Mellitus, Type II	250.00	Pleurisy	511.0				
Diverticulosis, colon	562.10	Serious Otitis Media, Acute	381.01				
Emphysema	492.8	UTI	599.0				

DATE	PATIENT NAME	DOB	CHARGES	PAYMENT	BALANCE

I authorize my insurance benefits to be paid directly to the above named physician. I understand that I am obligated to pay deductibles, copayments, and charges for non-covered services. I authorize release of my medical information for billing purposes.

PATIENT SIGNATURE: **DATE:**

FIGURE A–34 Wood

OFFICE NOTE: Michael R. Wood
DATE: August 1, 20xx
CHIEF COMPLAINT: Angina pectoris.
SUBJECTIVE: Mr. Wood presents with angina pectoris. He is status post-angioplasty approximately two months ago. He has been experiencing increasing angina pains. The patient states that he had an episode of jaw-squeezing pain when he was mowing the lawn this past weekend. Nitro-Bid relieved the pain. Mr. Wood is quite upset about these episodes. He feels his heart disease is still present.
PHYSICAL EXAM: Examination today reveals a 51-year-old male with angina pectoris, who is in some distress. Blood pressure: 130/85. Weight: 192 lbs. Pulse: 60. **Denies any allergies.**
HEART: There was a regular rate and rhythm. EKG done today was essentially normal.
CHEST: Clear to percussion and auscultation.
EXTREMITIES: Without edema.
ASSESSMENT: Angina pectoris, worsening. Status post-angioplasty.
PLAN: 1. CBC, AST, CK/CPK, Lipid panel today. 2. Refer to his cardiologist for further assessment and treatment. 3. Continue the Procardia XL 60 mg daily, atenolol 50 mg daily, and Isordil 10 mg q 8h. Return in 10 days, unless symptoms persist or exacerbate. 4. Patient was instructed to seek emergency treatment if pain is not relieved with Nitro-Bid.
SIGNED: Robert Howard, MD

HOSPITAL DISCHARGE INFORMATION PATIENT: Michael R. Wood
PATIENT CONTROL NO.: 568358223
MEDICAL RECORD NO.: 11659
ADMISSION/HOUR/TYPE/SOURCE: June 10, 20xx; 10 A.M.; urgent; physician referral
DISCHARGE/STATUS: June 15, 20xx; 1 P.M.; home.
ADMITTING DIAGNOSIS: Unstable angina pectoris; 411.1
FINAL DIAGNOSIS: Coronary atherosclerosis; 414.01
PRINCIPAL PROCEDURE/DATE: Percutaneous transluminal coronary angioplasty, native artery, single vessel; 36.01. June 12, 20xx
OTHER PROCEDURE/DATE: Angiocardiography, 88.5. June 11, 20xx.
ATTENDING PHYSICIAN: Rachel Shaski, MD; NPI 2468024680
ASSISTANT SURGEON: Tyler Frank, MD; NPI 3579135791
INSURANCE: See Registration Form; Figure A-35.
MEDICAID PAYER ID NO.: 112345671
RESPONSIBLE PARTY: Not applicable for Medicaid.
HOSPITAL: Blueberry Community Hospital; Federal Tax ID No. 50-3721941; NPI 0520194812.
TYPE OF BILL: 111
ROOM RATES: ICU, $600/day; Semiprivate, general, $350/day.
CHARGES: ICU, 2 days; General medical, 3 days; pharmacy, $750; IV solutions, $15; Lab/chemistry, $400; OR services, $2,000; Angiocardiography, $200.

FIGURE A–35 Case Study 2-5 Wood

SUPERIORLAND CLINIC
714 HENNEPIN AVENUE
BLUEBERRY ME 49855
906   3364600

Patient Number: 2-6

EIN: 494133726   **NPI:**   4567890123

PATIENT INFORMATION:
Name: PELLETIER, JOLINE, Z
Address: 410 EAST ARCH
City: BLUEBERRY
State: ME
Zip/4: 49855
Telephone: 906 3128742

Gender: M   F X
Status: Single X   **Married   Other**
Date of Birth: 10   03   1939
Employer:
Student: FT   PT   School:

Work Related?   **Y   N** X
Employment Related?   Y   N X
Other Accident: Y   N X
Date of Accident:

Referring Physician:
Address:
Telephone:
NPI #:

INSURANCE INFORMATION:
Primary Insurance
    Primary Insurance Name: MEDICARE
    Address: PO BOX 9929
    City: BOXBURY
    State: MD
    Zip/4: 45678-9929

    Plan ID#: 386607056A
    Group #:
    Primary Policyholder: PELLETIER, JOLINE, Z
    Address: 410 EAST ARCH
    City: BLUEBERRY
    State: ME
    Zip/4: 49855
    Policyholder Date of Birth: 10   03   1939
    Pt Relationship to Insured: Self X **Spouse   Child   Other**
    Employer/School Name:

Secondary Insurance
    Secondary Insurance Name:
    Address:
    City:
    State:
    Zip/4:

    Plan ID#:
    Group #:
    Primary Policyholder:
    Address:
    City:
    State:
    Zip/4:
    Policyholder Date of Birth:
    Pt Relationship to Insured: Self   Spouse   Child   Other
    Employer/School Name:

ENCOUNTER INFORMATION:
Place of Service: 11

DIAGNOSIS INFORMATION

	Code	Diagnosis		Code	Diagnosis
1.	.		5.	.	
2.	.		6.	.	
3.	.		7.	.	
4.	.		8.	.	

PROCEDURE INFORMATION

	Description of Procedure/Service	Dates	Code	Mod	Dx Order	Unit Charge	Days/ Units
1.		-					
2.		-					
3.		-					
4.		-					
5.		-					
6.		-					

Special Notes: SEE ENCOUNTER FORM AND OFFICE NOTES

FIGURE A–36 Pelletier

Elizabeth Foy, MD
Charles French, MD
Robert Howard, MD
(Denzel Hamilton, MD)
Roberta Pharyngeal, MD
Henry Romero, MD

Superiorland Clinic
714 Hennepin Avenue
Blueberry, ME 49855
Phone: (906) 336-4600   Fax: (906) 336-4020

NEW PATIENT	X	CODE	FEE	LAB TESTS	X	CODE	FEE	LAB TESTS	X	CODE	FEE
Level I		99201		AST		84450		LDH		83615	
Level II		99202		Albumin		82040		Lipid Panel		80061	
Level III		99203		Alk Phos		84075		Metabolic Panel		80053	
Level IV		99204		BUN		84520		Obstetric Panel		80055	
Level V		99205		CBC		85027		Occult Blood		82270	
ESTABLISHED PATIENT				CBC/diff		85025		PAP smear		88150	
Level I		99211		CK/CPK		82550		PPD Skin Test		86580	
Level II		99212		Drug Screen		80100		Prothrombin Time		85610	
Level III		99213		Electrolyte Panel		80051		PSA		84152	
Level IV		99214		Estrogen		82671		Rapid Strep Screen		87880	
Level V		99215		Glucose/blood		82947		Sed Rate		85651	
OFFICE CONSULTATION				GTT		82951		TSH		84443	
Level I		99241		HgbA1C		83036		Urinalysis		81000	
Level II		99242		Hepatitis Panel		80074					
Level III		99243		HIV Screen		86703					
Level IV		99244									
Level V		99245		OTHER TESTS				OTHER TESTS			
HOSPITAL INPATIENT				A/P Chest X-ray				Holter/24 hr			
Initial/Complex		99223		DXA Scan		77080		Sigmoidoscopy		45330	
Subsequent		99231		EKG Int/Report		93000		Stress Test		93015	
EMERGENCY DEPARTMENT SERV.				Rhythm EKG		93040					
Level I		99281									
Level II		99282									
Level III		99283		TREATMENTS	X	CODE	FEE	TREATMENTS	X	CODE	FEE
Level IV		99284		Flu Shot		90658					
Level V		99285									

DIAGNOSIS

Abdominal Pain	789.00	Gastritis	535.50	OTHER DIAGNOSIS		CODE
Angina Pectoris, Unspec.	413.9	Hemorrhoids, NOS	455.6			
Asthma, Unspecified	493.90	Hiatal hernia	553.3			
Bronchitis, Acute	466.0	Hyperlipidemia, NOS	272.4			
Bursitis	727.3	Hypertension, Unspec.	401.9			
CHF	428.0	Hyperthyroidism	242.90	REFERRAL/COMMENTS		
Colon polyp	211.3	Hypothyroidism	244.9	Post-Op Visit,		
Conjunctivitis, Unspec.	372.00	Osteoarthritis, Unspec	715.90	simple hemorroidectomy		
Diabetes Mellitus, Type I	250.01	Osteoporosis, postmen.	733.01	w/fistulectomy 7/23/20YY		
Diabetes Mellitus, Type II	250.00	Pleurisy	511.0			
Diverticulosis, colon	562.10	Serious Otitis Media, Acute	381.01			
Emphysema	492.8	UTI	599.0			

DATE	PATIENT NAME		DOB	CHARGES	PAYMENT	BALANCE

I authorize my insurance benefits to be paid directly to the above named physician. I understand that I am obligated to pay deductibles, copayments, and charges for non-covered services. I authorize release of my medical information for billing purposes.

PATIENT SIGNATURE: DATE:

FIGURE A–37 Pelletier

OFFICE NOTE: Joline Pelletier
DATE: August 2, 20xx
PROGESS NOTE: Mrs. Pelletier is seen today for postoperative follow-up for a hemorrhoidectomy with fistulectomy done 10 days ago. Operative site is well-healed. No complaints of pain. She was instructed to resume all normal activities and to call if problems develop. See operative report dated July 23, 20xx.
SIGNED: Denzel Hamilton, MD

HOSPITAL NOTES: Joline Pelletier
DATE: July 25, 20xx
DISCHARGE NOTE: Mrs. Pelletier was discharged today. She is scheduled for postoperative follow-up in one week.
SIGNED: Denzel Hamilton, MD

DATE: July 24, 20xx
PROGRESS NOTE: Hospital visit, brief. Mrs. Pelletier stated she was in slight pain but feels comfortable enough to be discharged tomorrow.
SIGNED: Denzel Hamilton, MD

DATE: July 23, 20xx
ADMISSION NOTE: Admitted to Blueberry Community Hospital. Underwent hemorrhoidectomy with fistulectomy with no complications. See copies of admission history and physical exam.
SIGNED: Denzel Hamilton, MD

OFFICE NOTE: Joline Pelletier
DATE: July 20, 20xx
CHIEF COMPLAINT: Constipation and some rectal bleeding.
HISTORY OF PRESENT ILLNESS: Mrs. Pelletier is seen today for constipation and rectal bleeding, which she noticed two days ago.
PHYSICAL EXAMINATION: The patient is well-nourished, well-developed, and in no acute distress. Weight: 160 lb. Height: 5'4''. Blood Pressure: 136/82. Pulse: 74. Respirations: 15. She is afebrile.

NO KNOWN ALLERGIES.
Rectal exam reveals internal and external hemorrhoids; some bleeding from the hemorrhoids; anal fistula. CBC and differential are normal.
DIAGNOSIS: Internal and external hemorrhoids. Anal fistula.
PLAN: Hemorrhoidectomy with repair of fistula. Patient agrees. Surgery scheduled for July 23,20xx.
SIGNED: Denzel Hamilton, MD
REFERRED BY: Jessica Yoha, MD

FIGURE A–38 Case Study 2-6 Pelletier

SUPERIORLAND CLINIC
714 HENNEPIN AVENUE
BLUEBERRY ME 49855
906 3364600

Patient Number: 2-7

EIN: 494134726   **NPI:** 4567890123

PATIENT INFORMATION:
Name: NIEMI, JACOB, E
Address: 708 WEST NICOLE
City: BLUEBERRY
State: ME
Zip/4: 49855
Telephone: 906 3125434

Gender: M X   F
Status: Single   Married X   Other
Date of Birth: 06 20 1935
Employer:
Student: FT   PT   School:

Work Related?   Y   N X
Employment Related?   Y   N X
Other Accident: Y   N X
Date of Accident:

Referring Physician: ROBERTA PHARYNGEAL MD
Address:
Telephone:
NPI #: 5678901234

INSURANCE INFORMATION:
Primary Insurance
    Primary Insurance Name: MEDICARE
    Address: PO BOX 9929
    City: BOXBURY
    State: MD
    Zip/4: 45678-9929

    Plan ID#: 372612869A
    Group #:
    Primary Policyholder: NIEMI, JACOB, E
    Address: 708 WEST NICOLE
    City: BLUEBERRY
    State: ME
    Zip/4: 49855
    Policyholder Date of Birth: 06 20 1935
    Pt Relationship to Insured: Self X Spouse   Child   Other
    Employer/School Name:

Secondary Insurance
    Secondary Insurance Name: MEDICAID
    Address:
    City:
    State:
    Zip/4:

    Plan ID#: JEN12869
    Group #:
    Primary Policyholder: NIEMI, JACOB, E
    Address:
    City:
    State:
    Zip/4:
    Policyholder Date of Birth: 06 20 1935
    Pt Relationship to Insured: Self X Spouse   Child   Other
    Employer/School Name:

ENCOUNTER INFORMATION:
Place of Service: 11

DIAGNOSIS INFORMATION

	Code	Diagnosis		Code	Diagnosis
1.	.		5.	.	
2.	.		6.	.	
3.	.		7.	.	
4.	.		8.	.	

PROCEDURE INFORMATION

	Description of Procedure/Service	Dates	Code	Mod	Dx Order	Unit Charge	Days/ Units
1.		-					
2.		-					
3.		-					
4.		-					
5.		-					
6.		-					

Special Notes: SEE ENCOUNTER FORM AND OFFICE NOTES

FIGURE A–39 Niemi

Elizabeth Foy, MD
Charles French, MD
Robert Howard, MD
Denzel Hamilton, MD
Roberta Pharyngeal, MD
Henry Romero, MD

Superiorland Clinic
714 Hennepin Avenue
Blueberry, ME 49855
Phone: (906) 336-4600   Fax: (906) 336-4020

NEW PATIENT	X	CODE	FEE	LAB TESTS	X	CODE	FEE	LAB TESTS	X	CODE	FEE
Level I		99201		AST		84450		LDH		83615	
Level II		99202		Albumin		82040		Lipid Panel		80061	
Level III		99203		Alk Phos		84075		Metabolic Panel		80053	
Level IV		99204		BUN		84520		Obstetric Panel		80055	
Level V		99205		CBC		85027		Occult Blood		82270	
ESTABLISHED PATIENT				CBC/diff		85025		PAP smear		88150	
Level I		99211		CK/CPK		82550		PPD Skin Test		86580	
Level II		99212		Drug Screen		80100		Prothrombin Time		85610	
Level III		99213		Electrolyte Panel		80051		PSA		84152	
Level IV		99214		Estrogen		82671		Rapid Strep Screen		87880	
Level V		99215		Glucose/blood		82947		Sed Rate		85651	
OFFICE CONSULTATION				GTT		82951		TSH		84443	
Level I		99241		HgbA1C		83036		Urinalysis		81000	
Level II		99242		Hepatitis Panel		80074					
Level III		99243		HIV Screen		86703					
Level IV		99244									
Level V		99245		OTHER TESTS				OTHER TESTS			
HOSPITAL INPATIENT				A/P Chest X-ray				Holter/24 hr			
Initial/Complex		99223		DXA Scan		77080		Sigmoidoscopy		45330	
Subsequent		99231		EKG Int/Report		93000		Stress Test		93015	
EMERGENCY DEPARTMENT SERV.				Rhythm EKG		93040					
Level I		99281									
Level II		99282									
Level III		99283		TREATMENTS	X	CODE	FEE	TREATMENTS	X	CODE	FEE
Level IV		99284		Flu Shot		90658					
Level V		99285									

DIAGNOSIS						
Abdominal Pain	789.00	Gastritis	535.50	OTHER DIAGNOSIS		CODE
Angina Pectoris, Unspec.	413.9	Hemorrhoids, NOS	455.6			
Asthma, Unspecified	493.90	Hiatal hernia	553.3			
Bronchitis, Acute	466.0	Hyperlipidemia, NOS	272.4			
Bursitis	727.3	Hypertension, Unspec.	401.9			
CHF	428.0	Hyperthyroidism	242.90	REFERRAL/COMMENTS		
Colon polyp	211.3	Hypothyroidism	244.9			
Conjunctivitis, Unspec.	372.00	Osteoarthritis, Unspec	715.90			
Diabetes Mellitus, Type I	250.01	Osteoporosis, postmen.	733.01			
Diabetes Mellitus, Type II	250.00	Pleurisy	511.0			
Diverticulosis, colon	562.10	Serious Otitis Media, Acute	381.01			
Emphysema	492.8	UTI	599.0			

DATE	PATIENT NAME	DOB	CHARGES	PAYMENT	BALANCE

I authorize my insurance benefits to be paid directly to the above named physician. I understand that I am obligated to pay deductibles, copayments, and charges for non-covered services. I authorize release of my medical information for billing purposes.

PATIENT SIGNATURE: DATE:

FIGURE A–40 Niemi

OFFICE NOTE: Jacob Niemi
DATE: August 2, 20xx
CHIEF COMPLAINT: Hypercholesterolemia and peptic ulcer disease.
SUBJECTIVE: Mr. Niemi is a retired dishwasher with peptic ulcer disease. He also has asymptomatic hiatal hernia and a history of coronary artery disease. He states he has generally felt well, except for a chronic cough. He uses several pillows at night in order to breathe. He denies any swelling in the lower extremities.
PHYSICAL EXAM: Examination today reveals a well-developed, well-nourished man who is in no acute distress. Blood pressure: 150/90, both arms while sitting. Weight: 220 lb. Pulse: 80. Respirations: 18. **Allergic to shellfish and strawberries. Denies allergy to any medication.**
HEART: Heart rate is regular. Carotid pulses normal. S1 is single. S2 splits physiologically, with A2 louder than P2. No murmurs or gallops are noted.
CHEST: Clear to percussion and auscultation.
ABDOMEN: Reveals a large ventral hernia in the epigastric region. This is approximately 10 centimeters in diameter and is easily reducible. Bowel sounds are present over the hernia and the abdomen in general. There are no masses noted.
EXTREMITIES: Without edema. Deep tendon reflexes are normal.
ASSESSMENT: Hypercholesterolemia, per lipid panel results, today. Peptic ulcer disease, treated with Zantac. Hiatal hernia, symptomatic.
PLAN: 1. Hepatic panel to follow liver function per Mevacor therapy. 2. Try Lasix 20 mg q d with potassium supplement. 3. Continue the Mevacor as currently taken and Zantac 150 mg hs for reflux. 4. Return in six weeks, but the patient is to call in 4 or 5 days to tell me how he is feeling.
SIGNED: Roberta Pharyngeal, MD

FIGURE A–41 Case Study 2-7 Niemi

SUPERIORLAND CLINIC
714 HENNEPIN AVENUE
BLUEBERRY ME 49855
906 3364600

Patient Number: 2-8

EIN: 494134726   **NPI:** 4567890123

PATIENT INFORMATION:
Name: WADSWORTH, HENRIETTA, P
Address: 3608 LAKEWOOD LANE
City: BLUEBERRY
State: ME
Zip/4: 49855
Telephone: 906 3122987

Gender: **M**   F X
Status: Single   Married X   Other
Date of Birth: 02   14   1953
Employer: BLUEBERRY HIGH SCHOOL
Student: FT   PT   School:

Work Related?   Y   N X
Employment Related?   Y   N X
Other Accident: Y   N X
Date of Accident:

Referring Physician:
Address:
Telephone:
NPI #:

INSURANCE INFORMATION:
Primary Insurance
      Primary Insurance Name: TEACHERS HEALTH
      Address: PO BOX 123A
      City: ALBANY
      State: ME
      Zip/4: 44437-123A

      Plan ID#: PP0391403726
      Group #: BSHS
      Primary Policyholder: WADSWORTH, HENRIETTA, P
      Address: 3608 LAKEWOOD LANE
      City: BLUEBERRY
      State: ME
      Zip/4: 49855
      Policyholder Date of Birth: 02   14   1953
      Pt Relationship to Insured: Self X Spouse   Child   Other
      Employer/School Name: BLUEBERRY HIGH SCHOOL

Secondary Insurance
      Secondary Insurance Name:
      Address:
      City:
      State:
      Zip/4:

      Plan ID#:
      Group #:
      Primary Policyholder:
      Address:
      City:
      State:
      Zip/4:
      Policyholder Date of Birth:
      Pt Relationship to Insured: Self   Spouse   Child   Other
      Employer/School Name:

ENCOUNTER INFORMATION:
Place of Service: 22

DIAGNOSIS INFORMATION

	Code	Diagnosis		Code	Diagnosis
1.	.		5.	.	
2.	.		6.	.	
3.	.		7.	.	
4.	.		8.	.	

PROCEDURE INFORMATION

	Description of Procedure/Service	Dates	Code	Mod	Dx Order	Unit Charge	Days/ Units
1.		−					
2.		−					
3.		−					
4.		−					
5.		−					
6.		−					

Special Notes: SEE ENCOUNTER FORM AND OFFICE NOTES

FIGURE A–42 Wadsworth

Elizabeth Foy, MD
Charles French, MD
Robert Howard, MD
Denzel Hamilton, MD
Roberta Pharyngeal, MD
Henry Romero, MD

Superiorland Clinic
714 Hennepin Avenue
Blueberry, ME 49855
Phone: (906) 336-4600   Fax: (906) 336-4020

NEW PATIENT	X	CODE	FEE	LAB TESTS	X	CODE	FEE	LAB TESTS	X	CODE	FEE
Level I		99201		AST		84450		LDH		83615	
Level II		99202		Albumin		82040		Lipid Panel		80061	
Level III		99203		Alk Phos		84075		Metabolic Panel		80053	
Level IV		99204		BUN		84520		Obstetric Panel		80055	
Level V		99205		CBC		85027		Occult Blood		82270	
ESTABLISHED PATIENT				CBC/diff		85025		PAP smear		88150	
Level I		99211		CK/CPK		82550		PPD Skin Test		86580	
Level II		99212		Drug Screen		80100		Prothrombin Time		85610	
Level III		99213		Electrolyte Panel		80051		PSA		84152	
Level IV		99214		Estrogen		82671		Rapid Strep Screen		87880	
Level V		99215		Glucose/blood		82947		Sed Rate		85651	
OFFICE CONSULTATION				GTT		82951		TSH		84443	
Level I		99241		HgbA1C		83036		Urinalysis		81000	
Level II		99242		Hepatitis Panel		80074					
Level III		99243		HIV Screen		86703					
Level IV		99244									
Level V		99245		OTHER TESTS				OTHER TESTS			
HOSPITAL INPATIENT				A/P Chest X-ray				Holter/24 hr			
Initial/Complex		99223		DXA Scan		77080		Sigmoidoscopy		45330	
Subsequent		99231		EKG Int/Report		93000		Stress Test		93015	
EMERGENCY DEPARTMENT SERV.				Rhythm EKG		93040					
Level I		99281									
Level II		99282									
Level III		99283		TREATMENTS	X	CODE	FEE	TREATMENTS	X	CODE	FEE
Level IV		99284		Flu Shot		90658					
Level V		99285									

DIAGNOSIS					
Abdominal Pain	789.00	Gastritis	535.50	OTHER DIAGNOSIS	CODE
Angina Pectoris, Unspec.	413.9	Hemorrhoids, NOS	455.6		
Asthma, Unspecified	493.90	Hiatal hernia	553.3		
Bronchitis, Acute	466.0	Hyperlipidemia, NOS	272.4		
Bursitis	727.3	Hypertension, Unspec.	401.9		
CHF	428.0	Hyperthyroidism	242.90	REFERRAL/COMMENTS	
Colon polyp	211.3	Hypothyroidism	244.9		
Conjunctivitis, Unspec.	372.00	Osteoarthritis, Unspec	715.90	*Lap cholecystectomy and*	
Diabetes Mellitus, Type I	250.01	Osteoporosis, postmen.	733.01	*Cholangiograms—outpt.*	
Diabetes Mellitus, Type II	250.00	Pleurisy	511.0		
Diverticulosis, colon	562.10	Serious Otitis Media, Acute	381.01		
Emphysema	492.8	UTI	599.0		

DATE	PATIENT NAME	DOB	CHARGES	PAYMENT	BALANCE

I authorize my insurance benefits to be paid directly to the above named physician. I understand that I am obligated to pay deductibles, copayments, and charges for non-covered services. I authorize release of my medical information for billing purposes.

PATIENT SIGNATURE: **DATE:**

FIGURE A–43 Wadsworth

OFFICE NOTE: Henrietta Wadsworth

DATE: August 2, 20xx

CHIEF COMPLAINT: Postoperative office visit. Status post laparoscopic cholecystecomy and cholangiograms for cholelithiasis and cholecystitis.

PROGRESS NOTE: Mrs. Wadsworth is seen today for her postoperative follow-up care. She states that she feels fine. She is alert and in no acute distress. Blood pressure: 140/80. Pulse: 78. Respirations: 18. She is afebrile. The operative site is well-healed with no indurations, swelling, or redness. She was advised to return to all normal activities and call if she experiences any problems. See discharge summary and operative report for details of the procedure.

SIGNED: Henry Romero, MD

HOSPITAL DISCHARGE INFORMATION

PATIENT: Henrietta Wadsworth

PATIENT CONTROL NO.: 679469334

MEDICAL RECORD NO.: 222760

ADMISSION DATE/HOUR/TYPE/SOURCE: July 16, 20xx; 8 A.M.; elective; physician referral

DISCHARGE DATE/STATUS: July 16, 20xx; 6 P.M.; home.

ADMITTING DIAGNOSIS: Cholelithiasis and cholecystitis, 574 10.

FINAL DIAGNOSIS: Cholelithiasis and cholecystitis, 574 10.

PRINCIPAL PROCEDURE/DATE: July 16, 20xx. Laparoscopic cholecystectomy with cholangiography, CPT code 47563. Laparoscopic cholecystectomy, ICD-9-CM code 51.23.

OTHER PROCEDURE/DATE: July 16, 20xx. Cholangiograms (cholangiography), ICD-9-CM code 51.11.

ATTENDING PHYSICIAN: Henry Romero, MD.

INSURANCE: See Registration Form; Figure A-44.

TEACHER'S HEALTH PAYER ID.: 001133232

RESPONSIBLE PARTY: Henrietta Wadsworth

HOSPITAL: Blueberry Community Hospital; Federal Tax ID No. 50-3721941; NPI 0520194812

TYPE OF BILL: 121; hospital outpatient surgery from admission to discharge.

SERVICES/CHARGES/CODES: Ambulatory surgery, CPT code 47563, $600. Recovery room, $200. General anesthesia, CPT code 00740, $200. Diagnostic nuclear medicine, CPT code 74300, $200.

FIGURE A–44 Case Study 2-8 Wadsworth

SUPERIORLAND CLINIC
714 HENNEPIN AVENUE
BLUEBERRY ME 49855
906   3364600

Patient Number: 2-9

EIN: 494134726   **NPI:**   4567890123

PATIENT INFORMATION:
Name: SAMUELSON, TAKEESHA
Address: 29 SHOWSHOE HEIGHTS
City: BLUEBERRY
State: ME
Zip/4: 49855
Telephone: 906 3122845

Gender: M   F X
Status: Single   Married X   **Other**
Date of Birth: 05   05   1936
Employer: RETIRED
Student: FT   PT   School:

Work Related?   Y   N X
Employment Related?   Y   N X
Other Accident: Y   N X
Date of Accident:

Referring Physician: DENZEL HAMILTON MD
Address:
Telephone:
NPI #:   5567890123

INSURANCE INFORMATION:
Primary Insurance
    Primary Insurance Name: MEDICARE
    Address: PO BOX 9929
    City: BOXBURY
    State: MD
    Zip/4: 45678-9929

    Plan ID#: 267504567A
    Group #:
    Primary Policyholder: SAMUELSON, TAKEESHA
    Address: 29 SNOWSHOE HEIGHTS
    City: BLUEBERRY
    State: ME
    Zip/4: 49855
    Policyholder Date of Birth: 05   05   1936
    Pt Relationship to Insured: Self X **Spouse   Child   Other**
    Employer/School Name: RETIRED

Secondary Insurance
    Secondary Insurance Name: UNION HEALTH
    Address: 29 SNOWSHOE HEIGHTS
    City: BLUEBERRY
    State: ME
    Zip/4: 49855

    Plan ID#:
    Group #: NT380
    Primary Policyholder: SAMUELSON, TAKEESHA
    Address:
    City:
    State:
    Zip/4:
    Policyholder Date of Birth: 05   05   1936
    Pt Relationship to Insured: Self X **Spouse   Child   Other**
    Employer/School Name: NORTHWEST TELECOMMUNICATION!

ENCOUNTER INFORMATION:
Place of Service: 22

DIAGNOSIS INFORMATION

	Code	Diagnosis		Code	Diagnosis
1.	.		5.	.	
2.	.		6.	.	
3.	.		7.	.	
4.	.		8.	.	

PROCEDURE INFORMATION

	Description of Procedure/Service	Dates	Code	Mod	Dx Order	Unit Charge	Days/ Units
1.		-					
2.		-					
3.		-					
4.		-					
5.		-					
6.		-					

Special Notes: SEE ENCOUNTER FORM AND OFFICE NOTES

FIGURE A–45 Samuelson

Elizabeth Foy, MD
Charles French, MD
Robert Howard, MD
Denzel Hamilton, MD
Roberta Pharyngeal, MD
Henry Romero, MD

Superiorland Clinic
714 Hennepin Avenue
Blueberry, ME 49855
Phone: (906) 336-4600   Fax: (906) 336-4020

NEW PATIENT	X	CODE	FEE	LAB TESTS	X	CODE	FEE	LAB TESTS	X	CODE	FEE
Level I		99201		AST		84450		LDH		83615	
Level II		99202		Albumin		82040		Lipid Panel		80061	
Level III		99203		Alk Phos		84075		Metabolic Panel		80053	
Level IV		99204		BUN		84520		Obstetric Panel		80055	
Level V		99205		CBC		85027		Occult Blood		82270	
ESTABLISHED PATIENT				CBC/diff		85025		PAP smear		88150	
Level I		99211		CK/CPK		82550		PPD Skin Test		86580	
Level II		99212		Drug Screen		80100		Prothrombin Time		85610	
Level III		99213		Electrolyte Panel		80051		PSA		84152	
Level IV		99214		Estrogen		82671		Rapid Strep Screen		87880	
Level V		99215		Glucose/blood		82947		Sed Rate		85651	
OFFICE CONSULTATION				GTT		82951		TSH		84443	
Level I		99241		HgbA1C		83036		Urinalysis		81000	
Level II		99242		Hepatitis Panel		80074					
Level III		99243		HIV Screen		86703					
Level IV		99244									
Level V		99245		OTHER TESTS				OTHER TESTS			
HOSPITAL INPATIENT				A/P Chest X-ray				Holter/24 hr			
Initial/Complex		99223		DXA Scan		77080		Sigmoidoscopy		45330	
Subsequent		99231		EKG Int/Report		93000		Stress Test		93015	
EMERGENCY DEPARTMENT SERV.				Rhythm EKG		93040					
Level I		99281									
Level II		99282									
Level III		99283		TREATMENTS	X	CODE	FEE	TREATMENTS	X	CODE	FEE
Level IV		99284		Flu Shot		90658					
Level V		99285									

DIAGNOSIS

Abdominal Pain	789.00	Gastritis	535.50	OTHER DIAGNOSIS		CODE
Angina Pectoris, Unspec.	413.9	Hemorrhoids, NOS	455.6			
Asthma, Unspecified	493.90	Hiatal hernia	553.3			
Bronchitis, Acute	466.0	Hyperlipidemia, NOS	272.4			
Bursitis	727.3	Hypertension, Unspec.	401.9			
CHF	428.0	Hyperthyroidism	242.90	REFERRAL/COMMENTS		
Colon polyp	211.3	Hypothyroidism	244.9			
Conjunctivitis, Unspec.	372.00	Osteoarthritis, Unspec	715.90	Appendectomy on 7/27/20YY		
Diabetes Mellitus, Type I	250.01	Osteoporosis, postmen.	733.01	Post-op office visit 8/02/20YY		
Diabetes Mellitus, Type II	250.00	Pleurisy	511.0	(no charge)		
Diverticulosis, colon	562.10	Serious Otitis Media, Acute	381.01			
Emphysema	492.8	UTI	599.0			

DATE	PATIENT NAME		DOB	CHARGES	PAYMENT	BALANCE

I authorize my insurance benefits to be paid directly to the above named physician. I understand that I am obligated to pay deductibles, copayments, and charges for non-covered services. I authorize release of my medical information for billing purposes.

PATIENT SIGNATURE: DATE:

FIGURE A–46 Samuelson

OFFICE NOTE: TaKeesha Samuelson
DATE: August 2, 20xx
POSTOPERATIVE FOLLOW-UP: Mrs. Samuelson is seen today for a routine postoperative follow-up for an appendectomy performed on July 27, 20xx, at Blueberry Community Hospital. Surgical site is well-healed. She has no complaints and has remained afebrile. Her appetite is good, and she states she "eats whatever" she wants. Mrs. Samuelson may increase her activity level as tolerated. She was instructed to call me if any problems surface.
SIGNED: Denzel Hamilton, MD

HOSPITAL NOTES: TaKeesha Samuelson
DATE: July 28, 20xx
DISCHARGE NOTE: Mrs. Samuelson is doing well. She has been afebrile since yesterday. She is tolerating a surgical soft diet and has been ambulating with minimal assistance. She states she has "good help" at home and is eager to return there. Given her current condition and eagerness to go home, I see no reason to keep her here. The nursing staff will provide discharge instructions. A follow-up office visit will be scheduled for August 2, 20xx. I instructed the patient to return immediately to the ER if she experiences fever, pain, or oozing in the operative site.
SIGNED: Denzel Hamilton, MD

DATE: July 27, 20xx
OPERATIVE REPORT
PREOPERATIVE DIAGNOSIS: Acute appendicitis.
POSTOPERATIVE DIAGNOSIS: Acute appendicitis.
OPERATION: Laparoscopic exploration with appendectomy.
ANESTHESIA: General anesthesia via endotracheal tube.
PROCEDURE: After obtaining her consent, the patient was anesthetized with general anesthesia via endotracheal tube. The abdomen was prepped and draped in the usual manner and the patient placed in the Trendelenburg position. An indwelling Foley catheter was in place. The abdomen was palpated, and no masses were felt. An incision was made below the umbilicus, and the Verres needle inserted toward the pelvis. This was tested with normal saline, and the abdomen was then insufflated with 5 liters of CO_2. A 1/2 cm camera was introduced through this opening, and the area of the appendix was visualized. Some exudate and free fluid were noted in the area. Under direct visualization, a 1/2 cm trocar was passed through the right edge of the rectus sheath in the mid-abdomen. Using blunt and sharp dissection, the appendix and cecum were mobilized. The mesoappendix was serially ligated with hemoclips and then divided and the appendix freed to its base. The base was identified and two #1 PDS endolopps were placed at the base. A single 0 chromic suture was placed approximately 1 cm distally and then the appendix was divided between and through the 11 mm trocar. The abdomen was irrigated with normal saline and the contents aspirated. The skin was closed with 4-0 Vicryl and Benzoin steri-strips applied. Estimated blood loss was 10 cc. Sponge and needle counts were correct. 2. The patient tolerated the procedure well and returned to the recovery room in stable condition.
SIGNED: Denzel Hamilton, MD

FIGURE A–47 Case Study 2-9 Samuelson

continues

DATE: July 27, 20xx
PREOPERATIVE NOTE: Mrs. Samuelson presented at Blueberry Community Hospital emergency department with cardinal signs of acute appendicitis. I performed a complete physical and determined that surgery was necessary. See the chart for the admission history and labs.
SIGNED: Denzel Hamilton, MD
REFERRED BY: Mark Beckwith, MD

HOSPITAL DISCHARGE INFORMATION
PATIENT: TaKeesha Samuelson
PATIENT CONTROL NO.: 780570445
MEDICAL RECORD NO.: 333871
ADMISSION DATE/HOUR/TYPE/SOURCE: July 27, 20xx; 4:00 P.M.; emergency
DISCHARGE DATE/STATUS: July 28, 20xx; 5:00 P.M.; home
ADMITTING DIAGNOSIS: Acute appendicitis, 540.9.
FINAL DIAGNOSIS: Acute appendicitis, 540.9.
PRINCIPAL PROCEDURE/DATE: July 27, 20xx. Laparoscopic appendectomy, CPT code 44970. Laparoscopic appendectomy, ICD-9-CM: 47.01.
ATTENDING PHYSICIAN: Denzel Hamilton, MD
INSURANCE: See Registration Form; Figure A-47.
UNION HEALTH PAYER ID: 991123452
RESPONSIBLE PARTY: TaKeesha Samuelson
HOSPITAL: Blueberry Community Hospital; Federal Tax ID No. 50-3721941; NPI 0520194812
TYPE OF BILL: 111; hospital inpatient from admission to discharge
SERVICES/CHARGES: General Medical, semiprivate (R/B semi), $350/day, 1 day; OR services, $900; Recovery room, $150; Anesthesia, general $200; Lab/chemistry, $150; Lab/pathological, histology (LAB/PATH/HIST), $70; Pharmacy, general, $50.

FIGURE A–47 *continued*

SUPERIORLAND CLINIC
714 HENNEPIN AVENUE
BLUEBERRY ME 49855
906 3364600

Patient Number: 2-10

EIN: 494134726   **NPI:**   4567890123

PATIENT INFORMATION:
Name: FRAUN, PETER, K
Address: 1007 DIVISION STREET
City: BLUEBERRY
State: ME
Zip/4: 49855
Telephone: 906 3127397

Gender: M X   **F**
Status: Single   Married X   **Other**
Date of Birth: 09   05   1948
Employer: BRADY PHARMACEUTICAL
Student: FT   PT   School:

Work Related?   **Y   N** X
Employment Related?   Y   N X
Other Accident: Y   N X
Date of Accident:

Referring Physician: ELIZABETH FOY MD
Address:
Telephone:
NPI #:   7890123456

INSURANCE INFORMATION:
Primary Insurance
    Primary Insurance Name: AETNA
    Address: PO BOX 45
    City: STILLWATER
    State: PA
    Zip/4: 12345-0045

    Plan ID#: ZPY604892
    Group #: BP1776
    Primary Policyholder: FRAUN, PETER, K
    Address: 1007 DIVISION STREET
    City: BLUEBERRY
    State: ME
    Zip/4: 49855
    Policyholder Date of Birth: 09   05   1948
    Pt Relationship to Insured: Self X **Spouse   Child   Other**
    Employer/School Name: BRADY PHARMACEUTICAL

Secondary Insurance
    Secondary Insurance Name:
    Address:
    City:
    State:
    Zip/4:

    Plan ID#:
    Group #:
    Primary Policyholder:
    Address:
    City:
    State:
    Zip/4:
    Policyholder Date of Birth:
    Pt Relationship to Insured: Self   Spouse   Child   Other
    Employer/School Name:

ENCOUNTER INFORMATION:
Place of Service: 11

DIAGNOSIS INFORMATION

	Code	Diagnosis		Code	Diagnosis
1.	.		5.	.	
2.	.		6.	.	
3.	.		7.	.	
4.	.		8.	.	

PROCEDURE INFORMATION

	Description of Procedure/Service	Dates	Code	Mod	Dx Order	Unit Charge	Days/ Units
1.		–					
2.		–					
3.		–					
4.		–					
5.		–					
6.		–					

Special Notes: SEE ENCOUNTER FORM AND OFFICE NOTES

FIGURE A–48 Fraun

Elizabeth Foy, MD
Charles French, MD
Robert Howard, MD
Denzel Hamilton, MD
Roberta Pharyngeal, MD
Henry Romero, MD

Superiorland Clinic
714 Hennepin Avenue
Blueberry, ME 49855
Phone: (906) 336-4600   Fax: (906) 336-4020

NEW PATIENT	X	CODE	FEE	LAB TESTS	X	CODE	FEE	LAB TESTS	X	CODE	FEE
Level I		99201		AST		84450		LDH		83615	
Level II		99202		Albumin		82040		Lipid Panel		80061	
Level III		99203		Alk Phos		84075		Metabolic Panel		80053	
Level IV		99204		BUN		84520		Obstetric Panel		80055	
Level V		99205		CBC		85027		Occult Blood		82270	
ESTABLISHED PATIENT				CBC/diff		85025		PAP smear		88150	
Level I		99211		CK/CPK		82550		PPD Skin Test		86580	
Level II		99212		Drug Screen		80100		Prothrombin Time		85610	
Level III		99213		Electrolyte Panel		80051		PSA		84152	
Level IV		99214		Estrogen		82671		Rapid Strep Screen		87880	
Level V		99215		Glucose/blood		82947		Sed Rate		85651	
OFFICE CONSULTATION				GTT		82951		TSH		84443	
Level I		99241		HgbA1C		83036		Urinalysis		81000	
Level II		99242		Hepatitis Panel		80074					
Level III		99243		HIV Screen		86703					
Level IV		99244									
Level V		99245		**OTHER TESTS**				**OTHER TESTS**			
HOSPITAL INPATIENT				A/P Chest X-ray				Holter/24 hr			
Initial/Complex		99223		DXA Scan		77080		Sigmoidoscopy		45330	
Subsequent		99231		EKG Int/Report		93000		Stress Test		93015	
EMERGENCY DEPARTMENT SERV.				Rhythm EKG		93040					
Level I		99281									
Level II		99282									
Level III		99283		**TREATMENTS**	X	CODE	FEE	**TREATMENTS**	X	CODE	FEE
Level IV		99284		Flu Shot		90658					
Level V		99285									

DIAGNOSIS							
Abdominal Pain	789.00	Gastritis	535.50	OTHER DIAGNOSIS			CODE
Angina Pectoris, Unspec.	413.9	Hemorrhoids, NOS	455.6				
Asthma, Unspecified	493.90	Hiatal hernia	553.3				
Bronchitis, Acute	466.0	Hyperlipidemia, NOS	272.4				
Bursitis	727.3	Hypertension, Unspec.	401.9				
CHF	428.0	Hyperthyroidism	242.90	REFERRAL/COMMENTS			
Colon polyp	211.3	Hypothyroidism	244.9				
Conjunctivitis, Unspec.	372.00	Osteoarthritis, Unspec	715.90	Family history DMII V18.0			
Diabetes Mellitus, Type I	250.01	Osteoporosis, postmen.	733.01				
Diabetes Mellitus, Type II	250.00	Pleurisy	511.0				
Diverticulosis, colon	562.10	Serious Otitis Media, Acute	381.01				
Emphysema	492.8	UTI	599.0				

DATE	PATIENT NAME	DOB	CHARGES	PAYMENT	BALANCE

I authorize my insurance benefits to be paid directly to the above named physician. I understand that I am obligated to pay deductibles, copayments, and charges for non-covered services. I authorize release of my medical information for billing purposes.

PATIENT SIGNATURE: **DATE:**

FIGURE A–49 Fraun

NEW PATIENT: Peter Fraun
DATE: August 2, 20xx
CHIEF COMPLAINT: Fever and chills for the past four days.
HISTORY OF PRESENT ILLNESS: Mr. Fraun is a new patient and is seen today with complaints of fever and chills over the past four days. He has had a fever of 103 degrees for one day and dysuria for two days. He has not traveled or consumed any unusual foods. He denies nausea, vomiting, diarrhea, chest pain, cough, sore throat, or abdominal pain.
PAST MEDICAL HISTORY: Mr. Fraun has a history of hypertension, controlled with medication, hypercholesterolemia, and urinary retention.
PAST SURGICAL HISTORY: He has had a transurethral resection of the prostate and repair of a right leg fracture. Both procedures were done within the past five years.
FAMILY HISTORY: Both parents lived well into their 80s with few health problems. He has a sister with Type II diabetes, a brother with hypertension and BPH, and a maternal uncle who was an alcoholic.
SOCIAL HISTORY: Mr. Fraun is a research chemist. He and his wife recently moved to Blueberry. She is a housewife and volunteers with several organizations. They have two children: a son aged 22 and a daughter aged 24. According to Mr. Fraun, both children enjoy good health and are pursuing their careers. He denies tobacco use, drinks about 4 cups of coffee per day, and has an occasional drink.
REVIEW OF SYSTEMS:
Head and Neck: No change in vision but frequent watering of the eyes. He does have an ophthalmologist in the area. No complaints of headaches or hearing problems. **Pulmonary:** No complaint of cough or dyspnea. No history of TB or pneumonia. **Cardiovascular:** No complaint of chest pain, palpitations, or history of heart murmur or rheumatic fever. EKG done today revealed normal sinus rhythm with no apparent abnormalities. **Gastrointestinal:** No history of ulcers or hepatitis. His appetite has diminished in the last two days because of his recent illness. Denies diarrhea. **Genitourinary:** Mr. Fraun reports dysuria for the last two days. **Endocrine:** No history of diabetes, thyroid disease, or anemia. He has a longstanding history of hypertension and hypercholesterolemia.
PHYSICAL EXAMINATION: Examination today reveals a well-developed, well-nourished male patient who is in some distress due to fever and chills X four days. Blood pressure: 170/90. Pulse: 90 and regular. Respirations: 20 and unlabored. Temperature today is 101.8 degrees. Height: 5'11''. Weight: 220 lb. **Patient denies any allergies.**
HEENT: Pupils are equal, round, and reactive to light and accommodation. There are small bilateral cataracts with mild arteriolar narrowing. The tympanic membranes and nares are clear. The pharynx is clear, and the mucous membranes are dry.
NECK: Supple. No adenopathy or thyromegaly.
CHEST: Clear, without rales or rhonchi.
HEART: Regular rate and rhythm. No clicks, murmur, or gallop. Pulses are 2+ and equal. There are nocarotid bruits, and there is no edema.
ABDOMEN: The abdomen is obese. There are active bowel sounds. The abdomen is soft, without masses, tenderness, or organomegaly.
GENITALIA: The testes are descended bilaterally and soft. The patient is an uncircumcised male with some phimosis. No discharge is noted.
RECTAL: Sphincter tone is normal. Prostate is minimally enlarged but smooth and symmetric. The stool is brown and guiac negative.
EXTREMITIES: No lesions are noted. He does have decreased range of motion and some stiffness in the right knee.
IMPRESSION: Possible sepsis. Hypercholesterolemia. Hypertension, controlled.
PLAN: Obtain following labs today: CBC with differential, lipid panel, blood glucose, and urinalysis. In addition, blood and urine cultures are needed. Antibiotic therapy to be determined based on lab results. The patient was advised to take analgesics to relieve symptoms until results confirm or rule out sepsis and causative agent. He is to call tomorrow to let me know how he feels and seek immediate treatment if his fever reaches 103.5 degrees.
SIGNED: Elizabeth Foy, MD

FIGURE A–50 Case Study 2-10 Fraun

Appendix B

REFERENCES

The information in this text is the result of many hours of research. Books, periodicals, and the Internet were invaluable resources that provided the most current data available at the time of publication. Because medical coding and insurance billing guidelines and regulations are frequently revised and updated, the listed references provide students with the opportunity to access professional and governmental organizations that mandate these revisions. Internet sites are also listed in chapters throughout the book.

BOOKS

Basic CPT/HCPCS Coding, Gail I. Smith, MA, RHIA, CCS-P, American Health Information Management Association, Chicago, 2009.

Basic ICD-9-CM Coding, Lou Ann Schraffenberger, MBA, RHIA, CCS, CCS-P, American Health Information Management Association, Chicago, 2009.

ICD-9-CM, published by the U.S. Department of Health and Human Services, Washington, D.C., 2009.

ICD-10-CM, ICD-10-PCS Preview, Anita C. Hazelwood, MLS, RHIA, FAHIMA; Carol A. Venable, MPH, RHIA, American Health Information Management Association, Chicago, 2009.

PERIODICALS

Coding Clinic for ICD-9-CM, Central Office on ICD-9-CM, American Hospital Association, Chicago, IL.

For the Record, Great Valley Publishing Company, Inc., Valley Forge, PA.

Journal of the American Health Information Management Association, American Health Information Management Association, Chicago, IL.

NEWSLETTERS

Briefings on APCs, Opus Communications, Inc., Marblehead, MA.

Coding and Reimbursement for Physicians, St. Anthony's Publishing, Reston, VA.

Physician Practice Compliance Report, Medical Group Management Association, Englewood, CO, and Opus Communications, Marblehead, MA.

WEB SITES

Web Site	Internet Address
American Academy of Professional Coders	http://www.aapc.com
American Health Information Association	http://www.ahima.org

American Medical Billing Association   http://www.ambanet.net

Centers for Medicare and Medicaid Services   http://www.cms.hhs.gov

Department of Health and Human Services,
Office of Civil Rights   http://www.dhs.gov/ocr/hipaa

Medical Association of Billers   http://physicianswebsites.com

National Uniform Billing Committee   http://www.nubc.org

TRICARE   http://www.tricare.com

ICD-9-CM Official Guidelines for
Coding and Reporting   www.cdc.gov/nchs/icd9.htm

ICD-10-CM National Center for Health Statistics   www.cdc.gov/nchs/icd10cm.htm

ICD-10-PCS (CMS)   www.cms.gov//ICD10PCS.asp

TRICARE   www.tricare.osd.mil

Glossary

A

7th character extension The seventh character of an ICD-10-CM diagnosis code that provides additional information about the patient's condition.

18/19 A combination of Medicare and Medicaid programs available to individuals who are Medicare-eligible and whose incomes fall below the federal poverty level; also called Medi/Medi or Care/Caid.

Abuse Actions that are inconsistent with accepted, sound medical, business, or fiscal practices and that directly or indirectly result in unnecessary costs to the Medicare program through improper payments.

Accepts assignment Physicians and providers who accept the benefit paid by the insurance company for a specific service as payment in full for that service; the patient does not have to pay any difference.

Accommodation code A two-character code that identifies the type of hospital bed the patient occupies.

Add-on codes CPT codes that must be used with a related procedure code.

Admitting diagnosis The condition that caused the patient to seek treatment.

Admitting physician The physician who arranges for a patient's admission to the hospital.

Adult primary policy The insurance policy that lists the patient as the subscriber or policyholder.

Adult secondary policy The insurance policy that lists the patient as a dependent on a second insurance policy.

Aid to Families with Dependent Children (AFDC) A program that provides financial assistance to children and families who meet specific income level requirements and to pregnant women who meet the income requirements.

Allowable charge/allowable fee The payment to a provider that is the lower amount of the provider's fee and the allowed fee; also called the maximum allowable charge.

Allowed charge The maximum amount the insurance company pays for the service.

Ambulatory Payment Classification (APC) A payment calculation method based on grouping procedures that have similar clinical characteristics and similar costs by CPT/HCPCS codes.

Ambulatory surgery center (ASC) Freestanding facility that specializes in same-day surgery.

American Health Information Management Association (AHIMA) One of the Cooperating Parties that provides training and certification for coding professionals.

American Hospital Association (AHA) One of the Cooperating Parties that maintains the Central Office on ICD-9-CM, answers questions about coding, and produces the *Coding Clinic for ICD-9-CM*.

American Medical Association (AMA) The governing body responsible for the development of the procedure codes found in the *Current Procedural Terminology* (CPT).

Ancillary (services) code A two-character code that identifies services not included in the room and board charges related to an inpatient episode of care.

Approach The technique or method used to reach a given procedure site; a component of ICD-10-PCS procedure codes.

Assignment of benefits Identifies who actually receives the insurance payment.

Attending physician The physician responsible for the patient's care while in the hospital.

Authorized provider A hospital, an institution, a physician, or another professional who meets the licensing and certification requirements of TRICARE and is practicing within the scope of that license.

B

Balance-billing Billing the patient for the amount not covered by insurance.

Beneficiaries Dependents eligible for TRICARE or CHAMPVA; individuals eligible for Medicare.

Benefit period Period of time that begins when an individual is admitted to a hospital or skilled nursing facility and ends 60 days after discharge; used to determine deductibles and co-payments for Medicare Part A.

Birthday rule Determines the primary payer when the patient is a child living with both parents and each carries health insurance.

Black Lung Program Act that provides benefits to coal miners; also known as the Federal Coal Mine Health and Safety Act.

BlueCard Program A plan that covers expenses for treatment (including non-emergencies) that occur anywhere in the United States.

BlueChoice Point of Service A group coverage health insurance plan that requires members to choose a personal care physician.

Blue Cross and Blue Shield Association (BCB-SA) The combined board of directors from the Blue Cross program and the Blue Shield program.

Blue Cross/Blue Shield (BC/BS) A nationwide federation of nonprofit health insurance companies.

Blue Cross Traditional A health insurance plan available to individuals and groups that covers hospital, surgical, and medical care.

Blue Preferred PPO A health insurance plan that encourages subscribers to seek care from providers who have contracted with the insurance company to provide services for a reduced fee.

Body system The general physiological system or anatomic region involved in a given procedure; a component of ICD-10-PCS procedure codes.

Brackets ([ ]) Symbol used to enclose synonyms, alternate wording, and explanatory phrases.

Bullet (•) Symbol used to identify a new addition or new code in the CPT codebook.

C

California Physicians' Service The first plan to achieve physician cooperation in prepaid health plans.

Capitation A reimbursement method that depends on the number of individuals covered by the health insurance contract.

Care/Caid A combination of Medicare and Medicaid programs available to individuals who are Medicare-eligible and whose income falls below the federal poverty level; also called Medi/Medi and 18/19.

Carrier-direct A claims submission method that allows the provider to submit claims directly to the insurance carrier.

Carryover line Format used when a complete entry does not fit on one line.

Catchment area A geographic location associated with CMAC procedure pricing.

Categories/subsection Divisions within the CPT codebook sections.

Category A three-digit code that represents a single disease or a group of closely related conditions.

Centers for Medicare and Medicaid Services A division of the Department of Health and Human Services responsible for managing Medicare and Medicaid health insurance programs; one of the Cooperating Parties that maintains and updates ICD-9-CM procedure codes.

Certification The process that involves successful completion of a professionally recognized exam.

Certified coding associate (CCA) An entry-level medical coding credential offered by the American Health Information Management Association.

Certified coding specialist (CCS) The title given to an individual upon successful completion of the national coding exam of the American Health Information Management Association.

Certified coding specialist–physician-based (CCS-P) A credential offered by the American Health Information Management Association that is appropriate for experienced coders in physician-based settings.

Certified healthcare reimbursement specialist (CHRS) A credential offered by the National Electronic Billers Alliance for individuals with experience in all areas of medical billing.

Certified medical billing specialist (CMBS) An entry-level credential offered by the Medical Association of Billers.

Certified medical billing specialist-hospital (CMBS-H) An intermediate-level credential offered by the Medical Association of Billers that is appropriate for individuals working in a hospital.

Certified professional coder (CPC) The title given to an individual upon successful completion of the national coding exam of the American Academy of Professional Coders.

Certified professional coder–hospital (CPC-H) A credential offered by the American Academy of Professional Coders that is appropriate for experienced coders in hospital outpatient and ambulatory facility settings.

Certified professional coder-payer (CPC-P) A credential offered by the American Academy of Professional Coders that is appropriate for individuals in insurance-related settings.

CHAMPUS maximum allowable charge (CMAC) The highest amount TRICARE will pay for a service.

CHAMPVA Authorization Card (A-card) The identification card issued to individuals who qualify for CHAMPVA.

CHAMPVA claim form The paperwork required to request payment from CHAMPVA.

Chargemaster A computer program or database that contains the charges and medical codes for services and supplies provided to patients.

Charge slip A source document for financial, diagnostic, and treatment information; also called an encounter form, a routing form, or a superbill.

Circle (○) Annotation placed before a CPT code to indicate that the code has been reinstated or recycled.

Circled bullet (⊙) Annotation placed before a CPT code to indicate that the service or procedure includes the use of moderate sedation.

Civilian Health and Medical Program of the Uniformed Services (CHAMPUS) A federally funded comprehensive health benefits program for dependents of personnel serving in the uniformed services; now known as TRICARE.

Civilian Health and Medical Program of the Veterans Administration (CHAMPVA) A program to cover medical expenses of dependent spouses and children of veterans with total, permanent service-connected disabilities.

Claims assistance professional (CAP) An individual who assists patients in the completion of paperwork necessary to obtain insurance payment.

Clean claim Claim paid on the first submission.

Clearinghouse A service that distributes claims to the correct insurance carrier.

CMS-1450 Alternate name for the UB-04, a universal claims submission form.

CMS-1500 A universal insurance claims submission form; formerly called the HCFA-1500.

Code first Phrase used to identify the need for two codes.

Code first [the] underlying condition Phrase used to signify that the condition is the result of another underlying disease.

Coding conventions The rules of the ICD-9-CM that include instructional notes, abbreviations, cross-reference notes, punctuation marks, and specific usage of the words "and," "with," and "due to."

Co-insurance A specific percentage of the charge the patient must pay the provider for each encounter; also called co-insurance payment.

Co-insurance days Covered days of care that require the patient to pay part of the charges for services rendered.

Co-insurance payment A specific percentage of the charge the patient must pay the provider for each encounter; also called co-insurance.

Colon/comma (:) (,) Punctuation used to identify essential modifiers related to ICD-9-CM and CPT code assignment.

Combination code A single code that is used to classify two diagnoses.

Combination program A combination of state, employer self-insured, and commercial workers' compensation programs.

Commercial workers' compensation program Program in which employers purchase insurance policies that provide benefits to injured employees.

Compliance monitoring Identifying provider and insurance carrier responsibilities related to coding accuracy and verification of services provided.

Complication/co-morbidity (CC) A condition that substantially increases the use of hospital resources.

Concurrent condition A problem that exists along with a primary diagnosis and complicates the treatment of the primary diagnosis.

Conditional primary payer status A situation in which Medicare is billed as the primary payer for a temporary period of time.

Condition code A two-character code that relates to the patient's insurance eligibility and primary and secondary payer status; part of the UB-04.

Confidential information Information that is not open to public inspection.

Confidentiality The principle that certain information is not to be shared with others.

Congenital A condition that is present at or since the time of birth.

Connecting words Terms that indicate a relationship between the main term and the associated conditions or causes of disease.

Consultation Service Provided by a physician whose opinion or advice regarding evaluation or management of a specific problem is requested by another physician or other appropriate source.

Contract number A unique identifier that identifies a specific health insurance plan.

Cooperating Parties Organizations responsible for maintaining and updating the ICD-9-CM; consist of two professional parties—the American Hospital Association (AHA) and the American Health Information Management Association (AHIMA)—as well as two governmental agencies: the Centers for Medicare and Medicaid Services (CMS) and the National Center for Health Statistics (NCHS).

Coordination of benefits (COB) Statement of how benefits are paid when the patient is covered by more than one insurance policy so the total amount of the bill is not exceeded.

Co-pay A specific dollar amount the patient must pay the provider for each encounter; also called co-payment.

Co-payment A specific dollar amount the patient must pay the provider for each encounter; also called co-pay.

Cost sharing Co-payment and co-insurance.

Coverage Statement of the medical conditions that may or may not be paid by the insurance policy.

Coverage code Identifies any unique benefits.

Covered days The number of hospital days eligible for reimbursement by a health insurance plan.

Covered entities Health plans, health care clearinghouses, and any health care provider who transmits health information in electronic form.

Covered services Services identified as covered by the health insurance plan.

Current Procedural Terminology **(CPT)** The coding system used to report physician and ambulatory services and procedures.

Custodial parent The divorced parent the child lives with; the parent responsible for medical bills, unless the divorce decree states otherwise.

Customary fee The fee that other providers in the same geographic area or with similar training charge for a given service.

D

Daily accounts receivable journal A chronological summary of all transactions posted to patient ledgers on a given day; also called a day sheet.

Day sheet A chronological summary of all transactions posted to patients' ledgers on a given day; also called a daily accounts receivable journal.

Defense Enrollment Eligibility and Reporting System (DEERS) A database used to verify TRICARE beneficiary eligibility.

Delinquent claim Claim for which payment is overdue; also called pending claim.

Department of Defense (DoD) Governmental department that manages the TRICARE program.

Department of Health and Human Services (HHS) Governmental body that plays an active role in investigating health insurance fraud and abuse.

Department of Justice (DOJ) Governmental body that plays an active role in investigating health insurance fraud and abuse.

Department of Veterans Affairs Governmental department that manages programs for veterans of the armed services; formerly known as the Veterans Administration.

Dependent Individual who is covered by the insured's health insurance policy.

Diagnosis-related category A three-digit numeric code that represents diagnoses that consume like amounts of provider resources.

Diagnosis-related groups fees (DRG) A payment method that pays a fixed amount based on the patient's diagnosis rather than on services provided.

Direct pay The patient pays the physician or health care practitioner for services provided.

Dirty claim Claim that has been denied or rejected.

Downcoding Selecting codes at a lower level than the service requires.

Durable medical equipment (DME) Devices that improve function or retard any further deterioration of a physical condition; nondisposable medical devices.

Durable medical equipment Medicare administrative contractor (DME MAC) An organization that processes Medicare claims related to durable medical equipment.

Durable power of attorney Voluntary transfer of decision-making authority from one competent individual to another competent individual that continues after the granting individual's death or loss of ability to make decisions.

E

E codes A supplementary classification of the ICD-9-CM: "Classification of External Causes of Injury and Poisoning."

Early and Periodic Screening, Diagnostic, and Treatment Services (EPSDT) A congressional law mandating that states provide routine pediatric checkups to all children enrolled in Medicaid and provide treatment for any problems identified during these checkups.

Elective surgery A surgical procedure that is not an emergency, that is scheduled in advance, and for which failure to undergo the surgery is not life-threatening.

Electronic claim An insurance claim that is submitted to the insurance carrier by computer, tape, diskette, modem, fax, or personal computer upload or download.

Electronic claims processor (ECP) An individual with experience or training related to electronic claims submission.

Electronic claims submission (ECS) Submission of a claim via computer, tape, diskette, modem, fax, or personal computer upload or download.

Electronic data interchange (EDI) A process that sends information back and forth between two or more individuals by computer linkages.

Electronic protected health information (EPHI) Protected health information that is maintained or transmitted in electronic form.

Emancipated minor An individual who has not reached the age of majority as established by state law but who lives independently, is self-supporting, and has decision-making rights.

Embezzlement Stealing money that an individual has access to but does not have any legal claim to take, keep, or spend.

Emergency (EMG) Category of patient service that preserves the patient's life or prevents the loss of a limb or sensory functioning.

Employer identification number (EIN) A number that identifies a physician who provides services to patients.

Employer liability The employer is responsible for the actions of employees that are within the context of employment.

Employer self-insured program Program in which the employer sets aside a specific percentage of the company's funds to cover medical expenses and wage compensation for work-related injuries.

Employer-sponsored health insurance plan A health insurance plan in which the employer pays all or part of the fee necessary to purchase health insurance for employees and their dependents.

Encoder A computer-assisted medical coding software program.

Encounter form A source document for financial, diagnostic, and treatment information; also called a charge slip, a routing form, or a superbill.

Enrollee An individual enrolled in Medicaid programs; an individual enrolled in a health insurance plan; also known as a subscriber.

Enrollment code A number on an insurance card that identifies the type of plan the subscriber is enrolled in.

Episode-of-care reimbursement Charging a single fee for all services associated with a particular problem, illness, or procedure.

Error-edit feature A feature built into the electronic claims system that edits claims for errors.

Essential modifiers Subterms that are indented under the main term and affect accurate code assignment.

Etiology Cause of disease.

"Evaluation and Management" section (E/M) Section of the CPT coding system that captures information about medical services for office visits, hospital visits, and consultations.

Examination The physical examination of the patient.

Excludes 1 An ICD-10-CM notation that indicates the excluded code cannot be coded to a given category.

Excludes 2 An ICD-10-CM notation that indicates the excluded condition is not a part of the condition represented by a given code or that more than one code is needed to accurately describe the patient's condition.

Exclusion Statement of the conditions not covered by the health insurance policy.

Exclusion note A note that identifies when a medical code cannot be used.

Exclusive provider organization (EPO) A managed care organization that contracts with health care providers to obtain services for members; members are restricted to using the participating providers.

Explanation of benefits (EOB) A document that explains how the reimbursement is determined.

F

Facing triangles (▶ ◀) Symbol used to set off new or revised information in the CPT codebook.

Family coverage A term related to the Federal Employee Health Benefit Program that means the subscriber's spouse and dependents are covered by the insurance plan.

Federal Bureau of Investigation (FBI) Governmental body that plays an active role in investigating health insurance fraud and abuse related to federal or private health insurance programs.

Federal Coal Mine Health and Safety Act Act that provides benefits to coal miners; also known as the Black Lung Program.

Federal Employee Health Benefit Plan (FEHB) A health insurance program that serves federal government employees.

Federal Employee Program (FEP) Another name for the Federal Employee Health Benefit Program (FEHB).

Federal Employees' Compensation Act (FECA) Governmental act that provides benefits for work-related injuries to all federal employees.

Fee-for-service A price or fee is charged for each individual service.

First listed code The condition that describes the main reason for providing care in health care settings other than hospitals; an ICD-10-CM sequencing guideline.

First report of injury A written statement of the initial contact of the physician with the patient in a workers' compensation claim.

Fiscal agent A health insurance company that handles payments for Medicare Part B and Medicaid; also called insurance carrier.

Fiscal intermediaries Insurance carriers.

Five- and six-character subclassification A letter and two digits followed by a period/decimal point and up to three numbers that provides more information on the description of a condition; applies to ICD-10.

Flash symbol An annotation placed before CPT codes that classify products pending FDA approval.

Florida Shared System (FSS) A Medicare database that includes the number of covered days remaining for each Medicare beneficiary.

Form locator (FL) UB-04 data field that captures information needed for insurance reimbursement.

Four-character subcategory A letter with two digits followed by a period/decimal point and one number that provides more information on the description of a condition; applies to ICD-10.

Fraud An intentional deception or misrepresentation that an individual knows to be false or does not believe to be true and makes, knowing that deception could result in some unauthorized benefit to himself or herself or some other person.

G

General note A note printed in italics or bold in the ICD-9-CM that serves to clarify unique coding situations.

Geographic adjustment factor (GAF) A factor that allows fees to be adjusted to accommodate variations in regional costs.

Global surgery concept Medicare term used to describe the range of services that are included in a surgical intervention.

Government-sponsored health care program A health insurance plan in which the government pays all or part of the fees related to health care services; for example, Medicare, Medicaid, TRICARE.

Group model A type of health maintenance organization in which the HMO contracts with physicians who are organized as a partnership, professional corporation, or other association.

Group number Identifies the name of the employer or other group that provides health insurance for the enrollee.

Guardian An individual who is legally designated to act on behalf of a minor or an incompetent adult.

Guardianship The legal authority to act as an individual's guardian.

Guardianship of the estate Responsibility for the financial resources of a minor or an incompetent adult.

Guardianship of the person Responsibility for the nonfinancial decisions related to medical care and other services for a minor or an incompetent adult.

H

HCPCS Level II codes Codes used to report items such as drugs, chiropractic services, dental procedures, durable medical equipment, and other procedures; also known as National Codes.

Headings Subdivisions of CPT sections that identify a group of CPT codes.

Health Administration Center (HAC) Agency that administers CHAMPVA.

Healthcare Common Procedure Coding System (HCPCS) System used to code the procedures or treatments a patient receives at a physician or provider's office, at an ambulatory surgery center, or as a hospital outpatient.

Health care finder A health care specialist who assists TRICARE beneficiaries and providers with preauthorizations.

Health care fraud Knowingly and willfully executing or attempting to execute a scheme or artifice (1) to defraud any health care benefit program or (2) to obtain—by false or fraudulent pretenses—representations or promises any of the money or property owned by or under the custody or control of a health care benefit program.

Health care provider The generic term for anyone who provides health or medical services to persons who need such services.

Health insurance A contract that provides money to cover all or a portion of the cost of medically necessary care.

Health insurance claim number (HICN) A unique identifier assigned to Medicare beneficiaries.

Health Insurance Portability and Accountability Act of 1996 (HIPAA) A federal regulation that provides extensive protection for the confidentiality and security of an individual's health information; also makes health insurance billing fraud a federal offense.

Health maintenance organization (HMO) A prepaid group practice that can be sponsored and operated by the government, insurance companies, consumer groups, employers, labor unions, physicians, or hospitals.

HIPAA Privacy Rule Federal regulation that gives individuals a federally protected right to control the use and release of their health information.

HIPAA Security Rule Standards set forth by HIPAA that ensure the security of electronic protected health information.

Histological Tissue-related.

History Information about the patient's previous health care encounters, family health, and lifestyle.

Hypertension/Hypertensive Table A table from the *Alphabetic Index* of the ICD-9-CM that provides an arrangement of codes for hypertension.

I

ICD-10-CM *International Classification of Diseases, Tenth Revision, Clinical Modification;* the classification system that will replace the ICD-9-CM.

Inclusion note A note that identifies lists of conditions that are similar enough to be coded or classified by the same medical code.

Indemnity insurance plan A fee-for-service plan.

Independent practice association (IPA) A type of health maintenance organization in which the HMO contracts directly with physicians, who continue in their existing practices.

Indirect payer The fee for services provided is paid by the insurance company and not by the patient; also known as third-party payer.

Individual policy A health insurance policy purchased by an individual or a family.

Inpatient prospective payment system (IPPS) Prospective payment system that applies to inpatient hospital services.

Instructional note Provides the billing specialist with details about code selection; appears at the beginning of a heading, in parentheses before or after a code, or in parentheses as part of the code's description.

Insurance billing specialist An individual who processes health insurance claims in accordance with legal, professional, and insurance company guidelines and regulations.

Insurance carrier A health insurance company that handles payments for Medicare Part B; also called fiscal agent.

Insurance collection specialist An individual who works with insurance companies to resolve billing and payment problems.

Insurance counselor An individual who helps the patient identify the amount that health insurance pays for a given service and how much the patient is responsible for paying; also known as a patient account representative.

Insurance policy A legal contract between an individual or organization and the company that provides the insurance.

Integrated delivery system (IDS) A managed care organization that brings together physicians, physician groups, hospitals, HMOs, PPOs, insurance companies, management services, and employers to integrate all aspects of patient care into one comprehensive system.

Interactive communication and transactions The ability to share information online.

International Classification of Diseases, Ninth Revision, Clinical Modification (ICD-9-CM) The coding system for medical diagnoses.

International Statistical Classification of Diseases and Related Health Problems, Tenth Revision (ICD-10) The coding and classification system for medical diagnoses that will replace the ICD-9.

International Classification of Diseases, Tenth Revision, Procedure Coding System (ICD-10-PCS) The coding and classification system developed to replace *Volume 3 ICD-9-CM* procedure codes that will be used to code and report inpatient surgical and diagnostic procedures.

L

Last menstrual period (LMP) The date of the patient's last menstruation.

Late effect The residual condition that remains after the acute phase of an illness or injury has been resolved.

Ledger card Summarizes the financial transactions for each patient.

Length of stay The number of hospital inpatient days from admission to discharge.

Lifetime reserve days Specific number of days covered by Medicare Part A when a beneficiary is hospitalized for more than 90 days during a benefit period.

Limited charge One hundred fifteen percent of the allowable charge billed by nonparticipating providers.

Limiting fee charge A fee set at a maximum of 15% above the NonPAR Medicare-approved rate.

Locality A specific geographic area.

Locality code A three-digit number that represents a group of zip codes.

Longshoremen and Harbor Workers' Compensation Act (LHWCA) Act that provides benefits for private and public employees engaged in maritime work nationwide.

M

Main term Identifies diseases, conditions, or injuries.

Main terms The organizational framework for the CPT Alphabetic Index; always printed in bold.

Major complication/co-morbidity (MCC) A more severe complication/co-morbidity.

Malfeasance A category of malpractice in which the wrong action was taken.

Malpractice Any professional behavior by one individual that results in damages to another individual.

Managed care Any method of organizing health care providers that provides access to high-quality, cost-effective health care.

Managed care organization (MCO) A type of pre-paid health plan.

Material safety data sheet (MSDS) A document that identifies the risks associated with exposure to specific chemicals or hazardous substances.

Maximum allowable fee An amount established by a PPO that a physician may charge for a service.

Medi/Medi A combination of Medicare and Medicaid programs available to individuals who are Medicare-eligible and whose income falls below the federal poverty level; also called Care/Caid and 18/19.

Medicaid A federal/state medical assistance program to provide health insurance for specific populations.

Medicaid expansion program Any federal or state health insurance program that is funded by Medicaid legislation with the intent to provide additional services to Medicaid recipients.

Medical claims with no disability Minor injuries that are treated once and after which the individual is able to return to work within a few days.

Medical coder An individual who assigns numeric codes to diagnostic, procedure, and treatment information.

Medical coding The process of assigning numeric codes to medical information.

Medical decision making The complexity associated with establishing a diagnosis or selecting a management or treatment option.

Medical terminology The language of the health care industry.

Medicare A federal health insurance program created in 1965 as Title 18 of the Social Security Act.

Medicare Administrative Contractor (MAC) An organization responsible for processing Medicare claims.

Medicare advantage (MA) Medicare health insurance plans offered by private insurance companies.

Medicare advantage prescription drug plan (MA-PDP) Prescription drug plans that are part of a Medicare advantage plan.

Medicare fee schedule (MFS) A list of Medicare-approved fees for physician/provider services.

Medicare Part A The portion of the Medicare program that pays for care received in hospitals and skilled nursing facilities, home health care, and hospice care.

Medicare Part B The portion of the Medicare program that pays for physician services, outpatient hospital care, and other medical services.

Medicare Part C Medicare health insurance plans offered by private insurance companies.

Medicare Part D A Medicare program that covers some of the costs associated with prescription medications.

Medicare special needs plan (SNP) A Medicare Advantage Plan that usually limits membership to individuals with specific diseases or conditions.

Medicare-severity diagnosis related groups (MS-DRG) Prospective payment system for hospital inpatient care that replaced the original diagnosis related groups.

Medicare Summary Notice (MSN) An explanation of benefits or remittance advice.

Medicare supplemental plan (MSP) A health insurance plan that supplements the Medicare plan to cover deductibles and co-insurance costs.

Medicare-Medicaid Crossover Program (MCD) A combination of Medicare and Medicaid programs available to individuals who are Medicare-eligible and whose income falls below the federal poverty level; also called Medi/Medi, Care/Caid, and 18/19.

Medigap A supplemental insurance plan that provides coverage for services, deductibles, and co-insurance not covered by Medicare.

Medigap Compare A website developed by the Centers for Medicare and Medicaid Services that helps Medicare beneficiaries locate insurance companies that sell Medigap plans and to compare coverage costs.

Military treatment facility (MTF) Facility where health care services are administered to members of the armed forces.

Minimum necessary Provision of the HIPAA Privacy Rule that limits the release of protected health information only to that needed to accomplish the intended use, disclosure, or request.

Misfeasance A category of malpractice in which the correct action was done incorrectly.

Moderate sedation Sedation with or without analgesia.

Modifier A two-digit code that may be added to a five-digit CPT code to further explain the service provided; may also be reported as a five-digit code.

Modifier-51 Identifies multiple procedures performed by the same provider during a single encounter.

More specific subterm Provides more-specific information about a subterm.

N

National Center for Health Statistics (NCHS) The governmental body responsible for developing the ICD-10-CM.

National conversion factor (CF) A figure that is multiplied by the relative value unit (RVU) to convert the RVU into a payment amount.

National Electronic Billers Alliance An association that offers a medical billing credential.

National Electronic Information Corporation (NEIC) A corporation formed by 11 insurance companies to provide physician practices with a national computer network that electronically transmits insurance claims to various insurers.

National Oceanic and Atmospheric Administration (NOAA) A branch of the uniformed services whose members are eligible for TRICARE benefits.

National provider identification (NPI) A unique identification number assigned to providers who submit claims to government-sponsored health insurance programs.

National Uniform Billing Committee (NUBC) A committee of health care professionals responsible for revising the UB-04.

NEC Not elsewhere classified.

Negligence The failure to exercise the standard of care that a reasonable person would exercise in similar circumstances.

Network model A type of health maintenance organization in which the HMO contracts with more than one physician group and may contract with single-specialty and multi-specialty groups.

New patient A person who is being seen by a physician for the first time or who has not received services within the past three years.

Noncustodial parent The divorced parent who does not have legal custody of the child.

Nonessential modifiers Terms that do not affect code selection.

Nonfeasance A category of malpractice in which no action was taken.

Nonparticipating provider (NonPAR) A physician who does not contract with Medicare and therefore does not agree to accept the Medicare-approved payment rate for services rendered for all Medicare patients.

North Atlantic Treaty Organization (NATO) A branch of the uniformed services whose members are eligible for TRICARE benefits.

NOS Not otherwise specified.

Not elsewhere classified (NEC) Indicates that a diagnosis or condition does not have a separate code.

Not otherwise specified (NOS) Indicates an unspecified diagnosis.

Null zero (ø) Symbol used to identify CPT codes that may or may not be used with modifier-51; also known as the universal no code.

O

Occupational Safety and Health Administration Act (OSHA) Act to protect employees from injuries due to occupational hazards.

Occurrence code A two-character code for a specific event that affects the payment of an insurance claim.

Office of Civil Rights Federal agency responsible for implementing and enforcing the HIPAA Privacy and Security Rules.

Office of the Inspector General (OIG) A division of the Department of Health and Human Services that plays an active role in investigating insurance fraud and abuse in cases related to Medicare, Medicaid, workers' compensation, and other federal health care insurance programs.

Out-of-pocket expenses The amount of money the patient must pay for a service.

Outpatient Prospective Payment System (OPPS) An outpatient/ambulatory services payment system that establishes a preset reimbursement rate for related procedures and services.

P

Paper claim Claim that is not submitted electronically.

Parentheses Symbol used to enclose nonessential modifiers.

Partial disability A type of permanent disability in which loss of function is expressed as a percentage.

Participant An individual enrolled in Medicaid programs.

Participating provider (PAR) Physicians who contract with Medicare and agree to accept the Medicare-approved payment rate for services rendered to all Medicare patients.

Patient account ledger A permanent record of financial transactions between the patient and the agency.

Patient account representative An individual who helps the patient identify the amount that health insurance pays for a given service and how much the patient is responsible for paying; also known as an insurance counselor.

PCS Abbreviation noting prescription medication coverage.

Pending claim Claim for which payment is overdue; also called delinquent claim.

Per capita Per person.

Perinatal period The period of time that begins before birth and lasts through the 28th day of life.

Permanent disability Designation indicating that the injury has permanently impaired the worker and that the worker is not able to return to his or her previous position.

Personal care physician (PCP) A physician responsible for the overall management of an individual's medical care; also known as a primary care physician.

Personal qualifications Behaviors that define the character or personality of an individual.

Physical status modifiers Additional coding that addresses the overall health status of the patient.

Placeholder x A character used in ICD-10-CM diagnoses codes to create a six-character code when a code with fewer than six characters requires a 7th character extension; also called the dummy x.

Plus sign (+) Symbol used to identify CPT add-on codes.

Point dash (.–) ICD-10-CM symbol used to indicate that the code is incomplete and an additional digit (or more than one) is needed.

Policyholder The purchaser of a health insurance policy.

Power of attorney Voluntary transfer of decision-making authority from one competent individual to another competent individual.

Preauthorization Determines the medical necessity of the treatment.

Precertification Determines if a treatment is covered by the insurance policy.

Predetermination An estimated insurance payment for a given treatment.

Pre-existing condition Statement of the conditions the individual had prior to implementation of the insurance policy.

Preferred provider organization (PPO) A managed care organization that contracts with a group of providers, who are called preferred providers, to offer services to the managed care organization's members.

Premium The cost of the insurance contract; the fee paid by the policyholder at regular intervals.

Prepaid health plan Contract between a specific group of people and local hospitals and physicians, in which each member of the group pays a premium in order to be included in the contract.

Primary care manager (PCM) An individual who provides or coordinates the member's care, maintains health records, and makes referrals to specialists.

Primary diagnosis The patient's major health problem or the reason for the medical encounter.

Primary payer The insurance company that is billed first.

Principal diagnosis The diagnosis determined after study to be the reason for the patient's admission to a hospital.

Principal procedure The procedure that is closely related to the principal diagnosis and is performed for definitive treatment rather than for diagnostic purposes.

Privacy officer An individual employed by a covered entity and responsible for monitoring compliance with HIPAA Privacy and Security Rules.

Private fee for service (PFFS) A Medicare Advantage plan administered by private health insurance companies.

Procedures/services Identification of specific procedures or services rendered by a physician.

Professional Component Services provided by a radiologist that include interpreting and writing a report for diagnostic imaging.

Program Integrity Office A branch of the TRICARE Management Agency that analyzes and reviews cases of potential fraud.

Prospective Payment System (PPS) A hospital reimbursement system based on the diagnosis, procedure, and treatments provided to a patient.

Protected health information (PHI) Individually identifiable health information that relates to a person's past, present, or future physical or mental health condition; the health care provided to the person; and the past, present or future payment for the health care provided to the person.

Puerperium The period of time that begins at the end of the third stage of labor and continues for six weeks.

Q

Qualified Medicare Beneficiary Program (QMB) Program that pays the premiums, deductibles, and patient co-payments for Medicare-eligible persons with incomes below federal poverty guidelines.

Qualifier The seventh character of an ICD-10-PCS procedure code that defines an additional attribute of the procedure.

Qualifying Individual (QI) A Medicare assistance program for beneficiaries with incomes slightly above the federal poverty level.

R

Radionuclides Radioactive substances that are used for nuclear imaging or scanning and treating tumors and cancer.

Reasonable fee A fee that is higher than the usual or customary fee that can be justified by the patient's condition.

Receipt form Document indicating patient payments.

Recipient An individual enrolled in Medicaid programs.

Reciprocity health insurance plan A plan that covers expenses for treatment (including non-emergencies) that occur anywhere in the United States.

Referral The transfer of the management of patient care from one physician to another.

Relative value scale fees (RVS) A payment method that establishes fees for services based on the provider's time, skill, and overhead costs associated with providing a service.

Relative value unit (RVU) A numeric unit designating physician work, practice expenses, and malpractice costs.

Release of information (ROI) The written authorization or consent of an individual to release confidential information.

Remittance advice (RA) A detailed explanation of claim denial or approval; also known as the explanation of benefits (EOB).

Remittance notice A document that recaps, by patient, the services rendered, the amount billed, the amount allowed, co-insurance, and the amount the provider was paid.

Residual A temporary or permanent medical problem or condition that results from a treated illness or injury.

Resource-based relative value scale (RBRVS) A calculation of approved fees based on relative value unit, geographic adjustment factor, and national conversion factor.

Respondeat superior Literally, let the master answer; the legal description of employer responsibility.

Root operation A term that identifies the objective of a procedure; a component of ICD-10-PCS procedure codes.

Routing form A source document for financial, diagnostic, and treatment information; also called a charge slip, an encounter form, or a superbill.

S

Secondary condition A condition that co-exists with the primary diagnosis but does not directly affect the outcome or treatment of the primary diagnosis.

Section A group of three-digit categories that represent a single disease or a group of closely related conditions; one of six main parts of the CPT codebook that are preceded by coding conventions.

Section guidelines Provide the billing specialist with information that increases coding accuracy; precede each of the six main CPT sections.

See An ICD-9-CM cross-reference that is a mandatory direction to look elsewhere for the correct code.

See also An ICD-9-CM cross-reference that is a suggestion to look elsewhere if the selected code does not adequately describe the disease or condition.

See category An ICD-9-CM cross-reference that is a mandatory direction and provides a three-digit category code from the *Tabular List*.

See condition An ICD-9-CM cross-reference that identifies when an adjective has been referenced rather than a main term or condition.

See/see also References that direct the coder to look at other sections or CPT codes.

Semicolon (;) The symbol used to identify the common part or main entry for indented modifying terms or descriptions in the CPT codebook.

Sequencing Placing diagnostic codes in the correct order.

Service provider The generic term for anyone providing care.

Signature on file (SOF) Statement or abbreviation used to indicate that an individual's signature is maintained by the health care agency

Single coverage A term related to the Federal Employee Health Benefit Program that means only the employee/retiree is covered by the plan.

Skilled nursing facility (SNF) A facility that meets specific regulatory certification requirements and primarily provides inpatient skilled nursing care and related services to patients who require medical, nursing, or rehabilitative services but does not provide the level of care or treatment available in a hospital.

Social Security number (SSN) A personal identification number assigned by the Social Security Administration .

Specified Low-Income Medicare Beneficiary (SLMB) A Medicare program for beneficiaries with incomes slightly above the federal poverty level.

Sponsor An active-duty service member.

Square brackets ([ ]) Punctuation that encloses synonyms, alternate wordings, and explanatory phrases associated with a given code.

Staff model A type of health maintenance organization in which the HMO operates and staffs the facility or facilities where members receive treatments.

State Children's Health Insurance Program (SCHIP) An amendment to the Social Security Act that allows states to create health insurance programs for children of low-income working families; also known as Title 21.

State Compensation Board/Commission A government agency responsible for administering state compensation laws and handling appeals related to workers' compensation claims.

State compensation fund Type of workers' compensation in which the state identifies a specific agency to function as the insuring body to cover workers' compensation claims.

Statute of limitations The period of time in which an agency, business, or individual is vulnerable to civil or criminal proceedings.

Subcategories Divisions within the CPT codebook categories.

Subcategory Four digits that provide more information about the disease, such as site, cause, or other characteristics.

Subclassification A fifth digit that allows even more-specific information about a disease.

Subpoena A legal document, signed by a judge or an attorney that requires an individual to appear in court as a witness.

Subpoena duces tecum A legal document, signed by a judge or an attorney that requires an individual to appear in court and bring records.

Subscribers Individuals enrolled in a health insurance plan; also known as enrollees.

Subterm Identifies site, type, or etiology for diseases, conditions, or injuries.

Superbill A source document for financial, diagnostic, and treatment information; also called a charge slip, a routing form, or an encounter form.

Supplemental Security Income (SSI) A federal income assistance program that provides cash payments to blind, disabled, and aged individuals.

Surgical package The range of services included in a surgical intervention.

T

Taxonomy code A code assigned to a hospital that identifies services provided by the hospital; associated with the UB-04.

Technical component Services provided by a radiology technician.

Technical qualifications Measurable abilities and skills that can be learned through education and experience.

Temporary disability A disability that can be overcome by medical treatment or retraining.

Third-party administrator (TPA) A processing center for insurance claims; also known as a clearinghouse.

Third-party payer The fee for services provided is paid by the insurance company and not by the patient; also known as indirect payer.

Third-party reimbursement Receiving payment from someone other than the patient.

Three-character category A letter with two digits that represents a single disease or a group of closely related conditions associated with ICD-10.

Title 19 An amendment to the Social Security Act that established a federal medical assistance program called Medicaid.

Title 21 An amendment to the Social Security Act that allows states to create health insurance programs for children of low-income working families; also known as State Children's Health Insurance Program (SCHIP).

Total disability A type of permanent disability in which loss of function is 100%.

Triangle (▲) Symbol used to identify a revision in the narrative description of a code in the CPT codebook.

TRICARE A federally funded comprehensive health benefits program for dependents of personnel serving in the uniformed services; formerly known as CHAMPUS.

TRICARE contractor An individual who processes claims and sends the provider an explanation of benefits; similar to an insurance carrier.

TRICARE Extra A network of health care providers that dependents can use without required enrollment.

TRICARE for Life (TFL) A health benefit program available to TRICARE beneficiaries who are eligible for Medicare.

TRICARE Management Agency (TMA) The agency that administers the TRICARE program.

TRICARE Plus A primary care enrollment option for Military Health System beneficiaries who are not enrolled in TRICARE Prime, a civilian HMO, or a Medicare HMO.

TRICARE Prime A managed care program affiliated with a full-service health maintenance organization.

TRICARE Standard Provides all the benefits of the original CHAMPUS, which allows more choice of health care providers but with higher out-of-pocket expenses.

Turnaround time The length of time from claims submission to claims payment.

Type of bill (TOB) A three-digit number that identifies the type of facility where an individual received services; a UB-04 field locator.

U

UB-04 A universal hospital claims submission form; also known as the CMS-1450.

Unbundling Billing separately for procedures that are delivered as a package.

Uniformed services Term for organizations such as the army, navy, air force, marines, coast guard, Public Health Service, National Oceanic and Atmospheric Administration, and North Atlantic Treaty Organization.

Universal no code (ø) Symbol used to identify CPT codes that may or may not be used with modifier -51; also known as the null zero.

Upcoding Selecting codes at a higher level than the service requires.

Use additional code, if desired Signifies that it may be necessary to use more than one code to provide the complete picture of the patient's problem.

Usual, customary, and reasonable (UCR) fee (1) The fee the provider usually charges for a given service; (2) the fee that other providers in the same geographic area or with similar training charge for the same service; (3) a fee that is higher than the usual fee and can be justified by the patient's condition.

Usual fee The fee the provider usually charges for a given service; sometimes known as the provider's full fee.

V

V codes A supplementary classification of the ICD-9-CM: "Classification of Factors Influencing Health Status and Contact with Health Services."

Veteran An individual who has served in the U.S. armed forces, is no longer in service, and has an honorable discharge.

Vocational rehabilitation The retraining of employees to perform another job duty when they are unable to return to their previous duties because of permanent or temporary disability.

W

Waiver An addendum to the health insurance policy that excludes certain conditions from coverage; also known as a rider.

Workers' Compensation Law of the District of Columbia Act that provides benefits to individuals working in Washington, D.C.

Workforce members Employees, volunteers, trainees, and other persons under direct control of the covered entity.

Write-off The difference between a full fee and an allowed fee.

Index